Two Hundred Years of American Communes

Two Hundred Years of American Communes

Yaacov Oved

Transaction Books
New Brunswick (U.S.A.) and Oxford (U.K.)

Library of Congress Catalog Number: 87-5988
ISBN: 0-88738-113-8 (cloth)
Printed in the United States of America

Library of Congress Cataloging in Publication Data

Oved, Yaácov.
Two hundred years of American communes.

Includes index.
1. Collective settlements—United States—History—Case studies. 2. Religious communities—United States—History—Case studies. I. Title.
HX653.084 1987 335′.973 87-5988
ISBN 0-88738-113-8

Contents

Preface

This book ensued from the questions and deliberations that originated in my way of life as a kibbutz member. The more I was involved with the subject the more my curiosity grew, urging me to study remote and secluded cases of communal life. Gathering information, I felt compelled to share it with others, and when the Department for Communal Studies was established at the Yad Tabenkin Institute (the research center of the United Kibbutz movement), I was given the opportunity to realize my aspiration. The institute provided the means to acquire books and publications, and thus an extensive library was at the disposal of students in academic institutions as well as those involved in various courses arranged by the kibbutz movement.

After a period of teaching and the positive feedback from my students I was prompted to arrange the material in a methodical manner in order to meet the challenge of presenting it to the general public. The deeper I delved into the material, the stronger was the urge, to the point of inspiring me with a missionary zeal, to undertake the task. This feeling was reinforced when I realized how meagre the information about the communes was, mostly in the form of generalizations and stereotypes. I deemed it of vital importance that a historian should save the communitarian experience from oblivion. He would thus contribute to the understanding of the processes the communes experienced and provide background material for an in-depth study in the various disciplines of social sciences, sociology, social anthropology, social psychology, education, and economics. Prompted by these considerations I set out on my study.

Until I began writing I never realized the many obstacles and pitfalls ahead, especially as I had set myself a number of targets: to provide the general public with information, to write a textbook for students of the communal experience, and to include cases that would serve as a basis for study and debate. I pondered upon the scope of the historical reviews dealing with the various communes. My intent was to focus on the general aspect rather than limit myself to a reduced number of cases or classify them according to criteria such as religious, socialist, stable, and long-lived communes, big or small ones. My aim was to present an optimal number of cases in order to demonstrate the variety and scope of the communes. I therefore abstained from adhering to any single criterion in choosing the subjects, and even included some communities characterized by a blending of communal and cooperative elements, because of the importance I ascribed to discerning quasi-communitarian tendencies which were in vogue during certain periods, and especially among socialist, secular communities.

From among the 277 communes which I traced, approximately 70 are presented here in 16 narrative chapters. As the writing progressed, the scope widened and expanded. I soon realized that I would have to add a chapter of generalizations, to avoid reducing my work to a mere collection of historical episodes, thus missing the target that I had set out to achieve. My starting point had, after all, been to locate parallel communal experiences with the Israeli kibbutz. Only later did I face the challenge of searching for the phenomenology of communal life at large, which brought me to the American communes. However, the deeper I delved into their history, the more I became aware of their uniqueness and difference from the kibbutz. The historical review, even though detailed and extensive, did not add up to the significance I was looking for.

At the same time, whenever I depicted the way of life and the existential problems of the various communes, my mind was filled with associations and comparisons that bridged the uniqueness and the distance between them, raising relevant questions. In each commune I located common areas of problematics, and the best way to face the challenge of finding a communal phenomenology was through the method of comparative history in its broadest perspective. As soon as I adopted this method, significant characteristics began to emerge, adding up to a generalized profile.

Yet, not only parallels emerged. Many unique aspects stressed the esoteric elements existent in most communes, but as soon as I had isolated these elements I was able to draw a portrait and point out the problematics and dynamics of communitarian life, thus advancing toward a communal phenomenology.

I chose to do that only after having completed the historical review of each commune, hence making it feasible to understand the process of their development throughout their existence. Thus, only after learning the entire case histories could I juxtapose them and draw conclusions without the danger of making generalizations divorced from historical reality. I adopted two different methods in order to ensure a meaningful result. Had I used only the historical review, there would have been the danger of presenting merely a set of episodes, while a comparative examination of selected problems, without a proper background of historical processes, might have led to an ahistorical theoretical hypothesis. A combination of both methods seemed best for examining the universal significance of the subject. Consequently, the book is divided into two parts, the first dealing with the historical sequence, and the second with a profile of the communitarian society, through a comparative study of selected issues.

During this study I had extensive communication with colleagues and friends who not only ''fertilized''my writing, but also granted me a feeling of togetherness inherent in the communal experience I was dealing with. The stamp of the commune is not only in the subject of the book, but also in the process of its being written. Yad Tabenkin, the research institute of the United Kibbutz movement, to which I belong, provided me with essentials such as the means, a place of work, literature, and most important, time. For this I am profoundly grateful; furthermore I appreciate the spirit of collaboration in thought deliberations, and the aid and understanding I encountered throughout.

I wish to express gratitude to all those who furthered my study. The list is long and it would be impossible to mention them all, but they are all in my thoughts. However, there are those whose contribution was particularly significant. First and foremost, Joseph Rabinowitz, my colleague at the Yad Tabenkin Institute and a member of kibbutz Na'an, who was the mentor of this study from the early stages and until its completion. His help and advice were always a source of inspiration.

Nancy Farchi, of kibbutz Revivim, was of special assistance in arranging the scientific apparatus and bibliography with great diligence and responsibility.

Funds contributed by Tel Aviv University and Yad Tabenkin made my visits to the United States feasible. This enabled me to collect the documentation and the bibliographic material, in which I was assisted by my colleagues at The Project for Kibbutz Studies at Harvard University during my stay there as a visiting scholar. In editing the Hebrew version, I am grateful to Zvi Dror of kibbutz Lochamei Ha'getaot, whose friendship and diligence contributed to the book's form. Special thanks are due to Hannah Lash (kibbutz Sdot-Yam), who undertook the challenge of the translation with admirable dedication, and to Norman and Judy Fridgut for their contribution in the translation of the final chapters.

Last, but not least, my profoundest thanks are due to my wife, Tehilla (Titi), who followed my work during all its stages, showing understanding and sympathy, help and advice. Throughout, she devoted herself to copying the manuscript in her spare time, providing me with a continuous feedback on the style and contents. Without exaggeration I can state that her mark is on every line of the book. She and my entire family deserve my deepest gratitude for accepting with understanding my preoccupation and absences due to my research commitments.

To repeat, the book which deals with communitarianism was conceived, written, and published in a communitarian spirit.

My deepest gratitude to all.

Introduction: My Encounter with American Communes

My first encounter with an American commune was in September 1978 when I arrived at Deer Spring,[1] a small community in a valley of the wooded Berkshire Mountains. It was a bright, sunny autumn day. The magic of the pastoral setting with its colored maple trees was bewitching, and from the minute I arrived at the settlement I sensed the idyllic mood that surrounded me. At first glancc I had the feeling that I was on an Israeli kibbutz, transplanted to the United States. It was noon and my host took me straight to the dining hall, where I met all the members of the commune who had been expecting me. After I had taken a seat I was greeted with an Israeli song, which was a surprising and touching gesture, and a suitable introduction to the whole experience of this first encounter. For the two days of my visit I was made to feel at home. Soon partitions disappeared and I startcd to feel a special relationship develop between me, the Israeli kibbutz member, and the Christian pacifist members of the commune, the latter about whom I had until then only read.

In the evening there was a meeting with commune members who wanted to hear about my kibbutz. Spontaneously I greeted them as "distant brothers," not attaching any special meaning to the phrase. At the end of the meeting one of the old-timers, a tall, white-haired, solemn-faced man came over to me and said, "You were right in defining our relationship; we are indeed brothers and though the geographical and spiritual distance is vast . . ., let us keep in touch."

And, indeed, since that day I have kept in touch. The impact of this first meeting still affects me, and whenever I think about that encounter, the words *distant brothers* comc to mind. When, in time, I began my research on the history of the communes, I often wondered about the impulse that had motivated my choice of words. It was not curiosity per se. I believe that the search for the "distant brothers" who live in communes has all along been of profound concern to me.

My visit to Deer Spring was not the first step in my search. This had started as far back as 1949, when I was among a group of young people who laid the cornerstone of a new kibbutz, Palmachim, on the sand dunes of the Mediterranean. Since those early days as a kibbutz member I have wondered about the universal meaning of my chosen path. Even then I was curious to find out whether the courage to establish and live a communal life in a world in which private property was the norm was unique to the generation of the Zionist renaissance, whether it was the result of the special circumstances in which the pioneers found themselves in Palestine of those days, or whether, perhaps, there was a similar phenomenon in other nations and in different historical circumstances. My curiosity led me on to obscure episodes in the past, far away from the mainstream of history. Thus, I became acquainted with the wonderful and sometimes odd worlds of distant peoples, other nations, or cultures who had attempted to establish communal societies. Whenever I could get away from my work on the kibbutz I travelled on the byroads of history in search of communes.

I encountered many fascinating historical phenomena. That is how I came across the Essens, the people of the Dead Sea scrolls, who established collective communities on the shores of the Dead Sea; the early Christians in Jerusalem, disciples of Jesus, whose communal way of life after his death is depicted in the New Testament. Continuing on my journey of discovery I encountered the first monastic communities, the founders of Coenobite monasticism as well as the first Eastern monasteries that led a collective life. I met Benedictus of Nursia who founded the monastery at Monte Cassino, Italy, and paved the way in Western monasticism to a productive communal structure. From there, through a time tunnel, I reached the communal Jesuit settlements in the wilderness of the Paraguayan jungle, in the seventeenth and eighteenth centuries.

My wanderings led me down the byroads of Christianity to the heretic sects which, according to the surviving evidences, seem to have led a communal life. Thus I "encountered" the Catharists and the Bogomiles, the Waldenses, Albigenses, Beghards, and Lollards as well as the Taborites during the Hussite wars in Bohemia and Moravia, and the Anabaptists during the religious wars of the Reformation and after them. Later I "encountered" the vast variety of Protestant sects that flourished in sixteenth- and seventeenth-century western and central Europe. Some of these adopted communal ways of life in the tradition of Apostolic Christianity in order to have a chance of survival against the persecution of both the Catholic and the Lutheran Church.

Following the routes of the persecuted Protestant sects that had to flee Europe, I reached the New World of North America. Until that time I had a vague image of communal failures related to this continent. Now, on a systematic journey, I rediscovered the American continent. For this I am indebted to Shalom Worm from kibbutz Ramat Yochanan, who in the 1950s wrote a series of articles published in *Niv Ha'Kevutza*, in which he describes the communes in the United States.[2] Perusing his articles, I began to see the full picture which had intrigued me since my days in the youth movement. Until then I had not been aware of the wide range of American communal history. New horizons opened when I discovered a surprisingly extensive literature on the subject, the richness of which caused me to neglect any further urge to search for communes elsewhere in the world and to stay instead on the "American station." I had the feeling that I had arrived at my destination.

A Survey of the Extent of Communes and Their Distribution

At an early stage of my study I planned an extensive and general survey of the communal phenomenon in the United States in order to set the whole picture. I limited myself to the basic categories: (1) the number of communes and the chronological appearance; (2) the length of their existence; (3) their religious and/or ideological classification; and (4) their places of settlement.

The extent of this survey soon convinced me to limit myself to a certain period in history in which most communal phenomena could be depicted. I therefore decided to open my study with a description of the communes from the early days of the English colonies in North America until the 1930s, when there was a lull which ended in the 1960s. Since then modern communes have appeared, established by children of the affluent society. In spite of the great interest I had as a kibbutz member in contemporary communal experiments, I decided in the present study to abstain from chapters that lack a historical perspective which is essential for a study of this kind.

The results of this survey are expressed in the appendix, which includes a list of 277 communes in chronological order.

I soon realized an important fact, namely that after the sporadic appearances of the first communes in the English colonies of North America at the end of the seventeenth century, there was an ongoing process of establishing communes that started in the eighteenth century and has continued until the present. From 1732, when Ephrata was founded, there was not a single year in the history of the United States without the existence of at least one commune. In the nineteenth century there existed several simultaneously. In the 1840s there were about sixty of them. This was repeated at the end of the nineteenth century. Furthermore, if we look at the list of communes according to the year of their establishment and the states, we will realize that there was not a single decade in the history of the United States in which no new commune had been founded. They were distributed throughout about forty states and their disintegration could not affect the establishing of new ones in a variety of other geographical and demographic areas.

The historical survey showed that the extent and continuity of the communal phenomenon had no equal outside the United States. This was reinforced by a comparative survey of voluntary communes in the Western world. It became clear that in modern times the United States is the only place where voluntary communes have existed continuously for 250 years. Is this a coincidence or were there historical circumstances which fostered communes over such a long period? The extent and continuity of the phenomenon make me believe in neither coincidence nor chance but rather in the uniqueness of the American experience. Time and again I was faced with this question and I therefore decided to study American history in order to understand the background which maintained the commune phenomenon in spite of an alien social environment.

From the viewpoint of my communal studies, I discovered the vast and comprehensive picture of American history. It enabled me to pinpoint those specific historical processes which were at the root of this country's uniqueness and have made it a hotbed for communes in the modern world.

Characteristics and Meanings of This Study

Studying the communes in the context of American history reinforced my conviction that the varied historical experience inherent in the communes makes them a worthy subject even though the phenomenon is incidental and peripheral. The great effort to establish alternative social units which are completely different from their surroundings made it imperative for them to strive for solutions to the basic problems of a new way of life. Members of the commune had to clear their own way. They had to forge a new mode suitable to their special vision and establish an economic system without the incentive of wages and personal profits. They had to create social units without any enforcement, live a family life within a collective community, and find an educational system which would socialize people who had grown up in a competitive society. They had to establish a relationship with a hostile, often antagonistic environment while guarding their uniqueness and their inner strength in order to survive in an alien world.

The experience accumulated by hundreds of communes in the United States is of great importance to each and every commune throughout the world, including the Israeli kibbutz. In spite of significant differences between American communes and those in other parts of the world, and between those and the kibbutz in Israel, one may look for a common denominator typical of a voluntary communal way of life. In each experience one may find elements worthy of being studied. In the rich and variegated American experience there are many interesting instances, whether those of long-lasting communes or those which existed for only a short while. A lot may be learned from these experiments in collective living and also from the reasons for their disintegration.

Equipped with this material I set out to tell the story of the communes and soon realized that there was a difference in studying them and in writing about them. Having read everything available about each and every commune, I could not write about them all in a book meant for a wide readership. Had I chosen to tell the detailed story of just one type of commune, I would have missed the purpose of what I had set out to do. My aim was to depict the variety of the American communes, thus discovering the typical trends of the phenomenon. I overcame this dilemma by compromising, knowing well the disadvantages of my choice. I therefore divided the book into two parts, Part I is a historical narrative which represents currents, types, and prevailing characteristics of the U.S. communes. Based on this data, Part II is devoted to a comprehensive profile of the communes as a religious, social, and ideological phenomenon.

Even after I reduced the number of communes dealt with, I must confess that at certain stages of the writing, I had some regrets about the restraint I had put upon myself. More than once I felt that I was overcome by the episodes of the community I was describing, by their fascinating characters, their way of life, and their pathetic struggles to survive in a hostile world. I felt that I could have presented the reader with unique life stories but I adhered to my purpose and never stopped for any length of time at a single station. I continued toward the mountaintop from which the whole panorama of American communes would lie spread out beneath me for inspection. I doubt whether this decision will please everybody. I assume that some readers may not be interested in all the communes. My suggestion is that they skip the narrative chapters and proceed straight on to the comprehensive ones which draw a collective profile of the American communes. This part, too, is based on the historical narrative and the reader may, from time to time, go back to the story of those communes which are of interest to him.

Notes

1. Deer Spring, or the Utterian Society of Brothers, is a Christian pacifist commune called *Bruderhof*. This commune has two sister communes in the United States and one in England. They are modern offsprings of the ancient Hutterian sect which in 1530 established its first commune (see chapter on the Hutterians in this book). In the 1920s a group of young people in Germany founded a Christian youth movement led by the theologist Ebcrhardt Arnold. They were pacifist idealists who searched for a harmonious and collective way of life as the ultimate Christian way and established a rural commune to realize it. When Hitler rose to power they were persecuted and had to flee from Germany. After years of hardship and wandering in exile they found a haven in the United States in 1954. Uniting with American Christian pacifists, they founded three communes, Rifton in New York state, New Meadow Run in Pennsylvania, and Deer Spring in Connecticut. There are about 1,200 inhabitants in these three communes and they earn

their living making wooden toys for children in three modern plants, owned collectively by the three communes.

2. Shalom Worm's articles appear in *Niv Ha'Kevutza* from no. 10 March 1954 through no. 32 December 1959. He later published them in a book entitled *Communes and Their Way of Life* (Tel Aviv: Ayanot, 1968).

Part I
THE HISTORICAL SEQUENCE

1

Communes in the History of the United States

Since 1735 there has been a continuous and unbroken existence of communes in the United States. There is no equivalent in any of the other countries in the modern world. A history of the communes would not be complete unless this phenomena were thoroughly examined. The task is not an easy one, mainly because American historians have, on the whole, ignored them. It seems that it would be impossible to give a monistic explanation to the continuity of the communal phenomenon. But there are elements in American history which might explain the background in which communes took root. The following is an attempt to throw light on the phenomenon by means of two sets of causes: (1) background factors of a lasting effect which, during the formative years of the communes and of the American society as a whole, enabled them to take root; (2) changing historical factors which throughout history aided and abetted the growing process of the communes after they had taken root on American soil.

The Wide Open Frontier Settlement

From the days of the English colonies on the coast of North America and throughout its history, land was always available for the new settlers. The opening up of the West with its wide open spaces attracted settlers from among the separatist religious sects and utopian reformers who were looking for distant places to establish their unique world of independent and separate social communities. This was ideal for the various communes that required space for their isolated existence.[1] However, though this was an important condition of the communal phenomenon, it was not the only one. In South and Central America, in Asia as well as in Africa and Australia there were abundant lands for settlement, but only in the United States did communes flourish continuously for centuries. Conditions other than the physically wide open spaces must be prevalent for the formation of communes. I believe that these conditions may be found in the special circumstances surrounding the formation of the new lifestyles of the early settlement days.

A Tradition of Independent Communities

One of the characteristics of the early settlements which laid the foundation for the United States was the independent organization of communities. Historical circumstances had caused the English Puritan settlers in New England to establish independent communities, thus influencing later settlers. The first wave of Puritans, a separatist English sect, arrived in 1630 as a unique group of settlers with a mission. They kept their independence and uniqueness in the New World when they received a legal charter as The Massachusetts Bay Company.

This enabled them to manage their settlement ventures according to their principles. During the first stages they established settlements of heterogeneous groups which had come from various parts in England and were of different social classes. They succeeded in establishing a cohesion mainly because of their deep religious belief and their sense of missionary zeal.[2]

The typical Puritan community in the early stages of settlement was one where independent settlers lived their lives according to a religious covenant. This strong inner cohesion sufficed to establish a functional social framework even before there were any official authorities and institutions in New England. In these independent communities there were many elements of mutual aid and of social as well as economic security. This was typified by the common land in the center of every township in New England. The community tradition of the New England Puritans would be irradiated into space and time. At a later date it enabled the oldtimers to understand the motives of additional independent settlers who came to the United States in order to establish their own unique religious or ethnic communities. Among them were the groups who would establish communes.

There were, however, limitations to this influence because of the religious isolation of the "God chosen" communities of the Puritans.[3] In spite of this, the tradition of these communities did not disappear from the American scene. It took root in other parts of the country and under different circumstances—in the settlements of independent religious groups in Pennsylvania, Maryland, Delaware, and Rhode Island in the East. It was also rooted in the western territories in spite of the strong individualistic motivation of those settlers.[4]

Aspiring to an Ideal Society

From the early days of settlement in North America the communities aspired to establish an ideal society. It was the time of utopian thought and, inspired by the possibilities of the New World, the utopians in Europe hoped that there they might realize their dream of a new society.[5] It was no surprise that when a new colonization of independent groups started in the New World, the inspiration to establish a new and reformed society took root among them.

Not all kinds of colonization were suited to communitarian settlement. The imperialistic colonization enterprises that were influenced by mercantilistic theories were diametrically opposed to such a trend. Communitarian living needed a group of idealistically motivated people with a capacity to realize their dreams. The Puritans were such a group and their leader, John Winthrop, who later became governor of Massachusetts, gave expression to this vision. In a speech on board the *Arbela* on the eve of their departure to the American continent, he called on his group to unite and form ties of brotherhood and friendship. He urged them to form a covenant with each other and with God, in order to be worthy of the mission they had undertaken to establish an ideal society, to be, in the gospel of Matthew, "a light unto the world, a city upon a hill."[6]

The expectations with which the Puritans set out did not last in the reality of the New World. Their settlements were soon institutionalized and segregated because of their puritanical characteristics and could become neither object nor subject of utopianism. Furthermore, those few who dared to think for themselves and strove toward religious freedom soon had to leave in order to found new communities. Yet the aspiration for a better society in the United States, one that would convey a message to mankind and serve as an example for all, reappeared again and again in religious and secular circles.[7]

The War of Independence against colonial English rule which brought about the establishment of the American Republic and the crystallization of its constitution, reinforced the belief in the country's mission to set an example of a perfect society. Thomas Jefferson, one of the founding fathers of the American nation, gave it expression in his well-formulated sociopolitical theories. According to him, the United States, being independent of the old system, would carry the message of a social experiment for all of humanity. It would be the place where those social and political ideals, which European thinkers had cogitated but which could not be carried out there, might materialize.

Jefferson's ideal society would be based on small craftsmen or artisans as well as on independent farmers who would be a strong and steady foundation for a democratic system of equality. He was open to wide-ranging social experiments. Late in his life Jefferson came across some of the utopian plans for communal settlements and regarded them as positive and meaningful social experiments in small communities.[8]

After the 1820s, the trend to establish a model society expanded and branched out. The sources of these activities were internal and external. Thinkers who were sensitive to society's ills began to realize the evils of the existing policy of developing an industrial society. Right from the start there was a vast gap between the ideals of the founding fathers and reality. The hardships caused reactions that turned into reform movements in various areas. During the 1840s this trend of social reforms and experiments was also reinforced from the outside.

The image of the New World as a place in which utopia could be realized attracted many European utopians, among them Robert Owen, Victor Considerant, Wilhelm Weitling, and Etienne Cabet. Some of them were social reformers, others—religious sectarian radicals. They arrived full of ideas and aspirations and were accompanied by people intent on social and religious reforms. Together with the local reformers they extended their activities during the second half of the nineteenth century.[9]

A new wave of utopian thought and experiments started in the 1880s. It was unique in that it was purely American. Utopian theories were formulated by Henry George, William Dean Howells, L. Gronlund, and Edward Bellamy. They tried to find utopian solutions to problems that were the outcome of the American reality. Experiments in realizing utopian dreams, including communal ones, were undertaken mostly by native Americans rather than by immigrants, as was the case previously. The tendency of utopian thought continues well into the twentieth century.[10] The uniqueness of these aspirations was in their being linked to actions. In the Old World this had not been the case. In addition to the opportunity provided by the wide open frontier, the American society was open to experimentation in various fields which included social utopian reform.[11]

Liberty and Religious Tolerance

Freedom of religion was one of the founding principles of the American Constitution. It had started with the religious life experience of the settlers in some areas of colonial America. The large variety of religions of the first settlers had motivated them to achieve religious tolerance as a matter of principle after achieving independence and to aspire to a clear separation between church and state.[12] This became the law of the land when the federal government turned the principle into the First Amendment of the U.S. Constitution. Gradually, during the nineteenth century, this amendment was adopted by all the states, and religious liberty became one of the cornerstones of American society and its government. The separation between church and state as a matter of principle gave legitimation to all churches, religions, and sects. There was no official religion and the various sects could claim equal rights with the established churches. Membership in a religious sect was a norm accepted by the law. Furthermore, there being no preferred religion, many of the sects flourished without assistance or backing of external or political agents.

Immigration and an Immigrant Society

Immigration was the mainspring of American society. It took many forms, and each new wave had different characteristics. Usually, mass immigration was caused by economic pressures in the native country. The immigrants were attracted by the supposedly unlimited material opportunities that the New World could offer. This kind of immigration had little if any impact on the communal phenomena.

Alongside this type of immigration, there was a thin stream of organized waves of immigrants whose motivation was religious and ideological. They were fertile soil for the communal idea. The first waves consisted of religious sects that were attracted by the wide open frontiers in which they would establish a society to their liking. They hoped that the religious tolerance and the willingness to absorb new immigrants would further their dream. From within these sects the first communes were established in North America at the end of the seventeenth and beginning of the eighteenth century.[13] The formation of communes started in the very process of emigration and during the period of transition and settlement in the New World.

These communes were founded during a period of social mobility which characterized a society that absorbs immigration. Some of those who founded communes in the United States adopted this way of life out of necessity. Having been attracted to the wide open frontier and the religious tolerance, they realized that they would have to defend themselves against these very factors that threatened their integration. The open frontiers and religious tolerance enabled their members to spread out and assimilate into the new society. Under these circumstances the communal, separatist way of life served to guard against external influences, especially as it also conformed to their religious values.

So far we have enumerated the factors involved in the establishment of communes. Yet each of these and all of them together were not the reasons for communes in America. The communes had been created within radical dissenting groups of central and eastern European Protestants (from an area that extended from Moravia in the east, through Germany and the Rhine valley to the Netherlands and England). These groups had reached America in the eighteenth century and established an isolated independent existence. They could have disappeared without leaving a trace and without having had any influence. The history of the commune in the United States would not have been as rich had there not been special conditions which brought about the establishment and development of the native American communes.

In the first years after the American War of Independence, New York and New England, the scene of many battles, were a meeting place for two groups whose origins were remote. The first was a small isolated group of English

Quakers known as Shakers. They lived collectively and did missionary work, spreading their unique gospel. There appeared at the same time an American movement for religious revival which had mass appeal. Their agitation against the existing religious structures caused the disintegration of many established churches and denominations. Hundreds of believers set out in search of a more significant religious way of life and ultimately adopted the Shakers' collective way of life.

What was the secret of the Shakers' success? They lived an exemplary life. The small group of Shakers in upstate New York seemed to the revivalists to live the saintly life they were searching for. The Shakers themselves, having realized that their way of life influenced people, turned it into an important element of their missionary campaigns in the revival area in New England. Wherever they went they persuaded their followers to adopt a similar way of life. These groups were the hotbed from which a dozen communes sprang until the end of the eighteenth century. Those who joined the Shaker settlements came from a background spanning all ethnic, social, professional, political and religious strata. Evidently, they were not a marginal phenomenon in their times, but attracted many of the inhabitants of those hilly backwood territories of New England who had been swept up by the Revolution.[14]

For seventy years the Shakers' communes were socially and economically viable and impressed everyone who had any contact with them. The Shakers appeared in the early history of the independent United States at a time when political, social, and economic institutions were still being formed. Their communal settlements flourished financially; they were well organized and impressive in their setting. These were pivotal factors that would later attract the sympathy, understanding, and tolerance of the outside world toward other communes.

It was an extraordinary combination of historical factors which contributed to the stability of the first American communes. These would have a far-reaching effect on the future of the American communes. Many propounders of the commune, even those who were spiritually averse to the Shakers, admired them for proving, for the first time in modern history, that communal life was feasible.

The Shaker communes did not remain alone. At the beginning of the nineteenth century German separatists established Harmony (1805), which proved to be an economic success. Soon after, Zoar, Amana, and Bishop Hill colonies were established. Their backgrounds were similar to the Shakers, and they gained outside appreciation as had the Shaker communes. In the 1820s many intellectuals, authors, poets, philosophers, economists, and politicians visited the communes and published their impressions.[15]

The early nineteenth century was an age of great spiritual, social, and political upheavals in Europe and the United States. The religious communes were considered to exemplify the possibilities inherent in communal life as an alternative to the system of private property. These communes inspired European thinkers, reformers, and utopians. As had occurred earlier, the Old World thinkers sought the realization of their dreams in the New World. The United States absorbed these utopian theories which influenced the nation's society and spiritual world, thus enabling experimentation. From the 1820s until the end of the 1840s, American society underwent an ideological and cultural upheaval. An abundance and a variety of reform movements, in which the communal ideas played an important part, swept the country. The evident success of the intensive settlement endeavors in the first decades of American independence inspired wide circles of utopians with a belief in man and his ability to better himself as well as his social condition. They believed that society could change and establish its institutions according to similar ideals. The characteristic openness to experimentation was reinforced in these circumstances, ideas were advanced to change the government without undermining the old system. America was yet again regarded as ''A City upon a Hill.'' The wide open frontiers left abundant room for experimentation within the existing social framework.[16]

In the 1820s, Robert Owen's utopian ideas started to infiltrate America by means of periodicals and literature from England. In the United States circles were formed to reexamine the social system which was supposedly unaffected by the evils of the European governments. The first crises, though minimal, of a growing industrial society during the seasonal recession after the Napoleonic Wars, caused tension between workers and employers. The feeling of harmony was disrupted with the first sign of social unrest.[17] Some thinkers and intellectuals who were sensitive to social problems realized, even at this early stage, that more violent controversies were in the making and suggested social reforms. One was the establishment of communes in which social harmony would combine with agriculture and industry and provide economic security.

Robert Owen's arrival in the United States, where he stayed from 1825 to 1827 in order to experiment with his utopian ideas, proved a turning point for the dissemination of the communal ideas as a means of solving social problems.

Three main factors which promoted the communal idea in the 1820s were:

- the experience gained by the religious communes;
- social stress which prompted a search for solutions;
- Owenist theories which infiltrated American society.

The 1840s were years of reform movements in a variety of fields. A universal attitude toward reform prompted the reexamination of almost everything among intellectual circles. Emerson gave expression to this feeling in a letter to his friend Carlyle, saying: ''We are all a little wild here with numberless projects of social reform. Not a reading man but has a draft of a new community in his waistcoat pocket.''[18] Indeed, the belief in progress and in man's ability to better himself and reach perfection was applied to the major areas of life—education, church, state, and family, as well as social life. The communes were considered to be a realistic and immediate cure for social ills. The reformation flood was influenced by the economic crisis of 1837, which caused a bad recession in the urban areas of the eastern United States. The phenomenon of communal life drew attention to the social ills that seemed to accompany industrial development.[19]

This was the background for the utopian ideas of Fourier in the vision of Albert Brisbane. Fourierism was a comprehensive plan of social reconstruction based on cooperation and harmony. It quickly took root in American circles, mainly among those who had suffered during the recession and intellectuals who were overtaken by the spiritual unrest of their generation. Fourierist centers were based in New York, Philadelphia, Cincinnati, and Rochester in upstate New York.[20]

But not only in the eastern cities were the Fourierists active; they quickly spread to the Midwest. Their propaganda was disseminated by newspapers and pamphlets, and intellectuals followed their ideas with interest. Many joined Fourierist circles. Some even decided to participate in the experiment and formed associations. The apex of Fourierist activities in the United States was between 1843 and 1846. Scores of organizations sprang up, encompassing tens of thousands of people who established about forty Fourierist settlements throughout the eastern states and the Midwest. This overwhelming response was caused by the economic hardships, the search for new ideas, new attitudes, and by the impressive success of the communal movement in the past, but most of all by the attraction of Fourierist theories which portrayed individual development through harmony without the use of force. There was no element of atheism involved, but rather the pluralistic religious vision.[21]

The ideological upheaval affected wide circles of the middle classes and the lower classes as well. It was a continuation of the Owenist doctrine that had prevailed in the 1820s, and rekindled the embers of Owenism. Fourierism reached the apex of massive influence that no communal theory in the United States had achieved. It started to recede when the main causes that had prompted it disappeared. Externally, the economic situation had improved. On the internal level most of the Fourierist settlements had failed socially and economically. The massive support abated.

A freeze which would last for about thirty years halted the establishment of American socialist communes. Some, however, would be established by socialist immigrants from Europe. The most outstanding of these was the Icaria movement founded in France by Etienne Cabét, who personally led his followers in 1848 to establish communes in Texas and Illinois. In 1856 this movement split. Cabét, with a minority, left to establish a short-lived commune in St. Louis, Missouri. The majority turned West to found the successful and stable commune in Corning, Iowa. The movement underwent a further crisis in 1878 when two new communes were established on the land of the Iowa settlement, the New Icaria community and Jeune Icaria. In the 1880s the latter would establish a California commune together with San Francisco socialists. Even though the Icaria colonies were established in the United States and existed there for many years, they maintained their distinct French character. French and Belgian socialists participated in one of the last French communal experiments in the 1850s. Victor Considerant, the French Fourierist leader, initiated the establishment of a mixed French-American colony in 1855 in Texas: Reunion, which never attracted settlers, was rejected by the local population and disintegrated within four years.

During the 1870s and 1880s individual socialists and groups from Europe attempted unsuccessfully to establish collective settlements. In that period the new Odessa community was established in Oregon on the West Coast by Russian Jewish immigrants. They belonged to the Am Olam (eternal people) movement and had socialist utopian ideals.

The spiritual-religious upheaval of the 1830s and the 1840s is the background in which Oneida commune flourished. This was an American religious commune whose members had come from among the well-established settlers in New England and upstate New York. Their spiritual leader was J.H. Noyes, who had established the perfectionists' colony in Putney, Vermont. They favored the abolishment of the monogamous family and introduced group marriage. Persecuted by the local inhabitants of Vermont, Oneida colony moved to upstate New York in 1848 and, in cooperation with local perfectionists, established a flourishing, socially and economically successful community. They were well organized and culturally active, thus influencing other communities. Their way of life was extraordinary in that they abolished the monogamous family. They also adopted a system of "mutual criticism" as a means of socialization. In the 1860s they attempted to regulate the birth rate (stirpiculture). Oneida was a landmark in the history of the American communes, being native American in its origin and its population.

In the second half of the nineteenth century, the newly established communities had more original American elements both as to their spiritual motivation and their members who were mostly American born. These communities were inspired by spiritualism, religious mystics, doomsday prophets, adventists, propounders of an esoteric cosmology, theosophists, various Mormon groups, vegetarians, religious women, followers of "free love," and anarchists.

A late additional wave of immigrants, the Hutterites, arrived in the United States in 1874. The Hutterians were an Anabaptist sect which had started out as a communal sect in 1530 in Moravia. They had experienced severe persecutions and were on the move continuously in order to maintain their creed and communal way of life. In the second half of the nineteenth century, when they were being persecuted in Russia, to where they had fled from Moravia, they decided to emigrate to the United States. In 1874 the first Hutterite commune, Bon-Homme, was established in the New World, in the prairies of Dakota. They adapted easily to the harsh conditions and their vitality helped them in the economic development of their commune and prompted their demographic growth.

After World War I they numbered nineteen communities. They flourished during the twentieth century. After World War I they even expanded into central Canada. In the 1980s the Hutterite communes in the United States and Canada numbered about 300, with about 30,000 members. From the 1880s until the beginning of the twentieth century, there was a revival in the activity of groups which strove toward communalism. Even though fewer new communes were established, their overall number exceeded that of the 1840s. The most significant phenomenon of that period was indigenous communalism. It was influenced by American thinkers and intellectuals who were affected by the development of United States society and its economy. This renewed communal activity was set against the background of the economic and social struggles of an industrialized nation in the 1880s and 1890s. The strife between capitalism and labor was intensified when the latter began to organize in unions. Economic recessions hit a wide section of the population and prompted them to reassess their social framework.[22] It was a period of a flourishing utopian literature to such an extent as the United States had not experienced before.[23]

Between 1880 and 1900 scores of utopian works appeared. Most of them never had any impact, but a few serious ones did, and they influenced political thought and actions. Gronlund, Bellamy and William Dean Howells all formulated communal solutions to social problems. Bellamy's *Looking Backwards* (1888) had the strongest impact. Generally, these utopians had an impetus toward communitarianism, even though their main concern was with an overall social reform rather than with the establishment of individual communes. They were doubtlessly inspired by the tradition of American religious and socialist communes which had been in existence for decades, thus proving that this way of life was a viable alternative to the ills of society.[24]

Disappointed with the political struggle after the failure of populism in 1896, socialist circles turned toward utopian answers via communitarianism. There appeared a historical opportunity for socialist communes resulting from the combination of causes which could have promoted the search for alternatives: disappointment in the political struggle, utopian ideologies which extol communal life, and the opportunity to take advantage of the wide open spaces available for colonization in the American west. The 1890s were a time of grace for the utopian movement. Socialist circles in different parts of the country, influenced by periodicals and newspapers, formed groups in order to set up communes. Members came mainly from the eastern states and the communes were established in the southern ones (Georgia and Tennessee) and in the West (Washington and Oregon). Most active was the Brotherhood of Cooperative Commonwealths, which organized in 1895 in Maine with the intention of helping to solve the unemployment problem by establishing colonies in the western states. They also hoped that the commune would serve as a base for their political struggle. Their ideals attracted a strong following from among some small socialist groups and they organized to establish the American Socialist Democratic party which included the B.C.C. (Brotherhood of Cooperative Commonwealth).

At the first party convention in 1897 the settlement program of B.C.C. was adopted, which was popular among socialists. Nevertheless, a year later, when the decision was to be formalized, a large number of the party functionaries objected to the communal way because they regarded it as nonessential to the political struggle. This caused a schism in the socialist party; those who were loyal to the settlement cause did not survive as a political party and at the end of the century vanished. While on the political level it disappeared rapidly, on the settlement level it lasted longer. At the time when the party strove to formulate their program a colonization project began on Puget Sound in Washington State.[25] The settlers came from heterogeneous backgrounds and did not have any social or agricultural preparation. They had been strangers to each other and their mutual commitment was not strong enough for the community to survive. After about five years the Washington communes disintegrated, leaving no impact. The American socialist movement had missed its chance to develop a communal settlement movement, inter alia because its leaders and theorists did not believe in the communitarian alternative.

Morris Hillquit, one of the socialist leaders in those years, expressed the prevailing attitude when he published *The History of Socialism in the United States* (1903). He devoted the first part to the history of religious and socialist communes. He concluded by criticizing the founders of the commune for the illusion they created when they claimed that separatist social units were viable. ''The times for Robinson Crusoe's individual or social life-style have passed,'' he stated, and went on to explain the intricate system which connects parts of modern society:

> And no man or group can separate himself or themselves from it without relapsing into Barbarism. This indivisibility of the social organism was the rock

> on which all communistic experiments foundered. The communists could not create a society all sufficient in itself. . . . Modern socialists have long discarded the idea of mending the present capitalist system by isolated patches of communism.[26]

Realizing that society is a whole organism, leading socialists understood that the socialist struggle for the betterment of everyone had to be on a political and professional level. Utopian settlements were regarded as harmful and therefore were to be deleted from the party's platform, though not from socialist ideology. In the first half of the twentieth century there were no social, religious or political upheavals which prompted communal experiment. Although some continued to exist, most of them were in the process of deterioration (the Shakers, Amana). Only the Hutterian communes continued to flourish, their vitality not impaired. In fact their secluded life in the midwestern prairies of the American continent enabled them to increase and prosper.

Several new communes were established but none had any substantial influence in the outside world. Llano was a socialist commune formed in California and later established in Louisiana. Many joined, passed through, supported, or heard about it, yet Llano never became a focus of influence, nor did Sunrise, the anarchist commune in Michigan, founded during the Depression years.

The study of the history of communes in the United States and their affinity to American origins observes three main periods:

1. The period between the seventeenth century and the appearance of the Shakers (1787), in which the communal idea and its founders arrived from Europe. They existed then in complete isolation in the New World.
2. A period of coexistence which lasted for one hundred years, between the 1780s and the 1880s. Ideas and people continued to arrive from Europe but American communes were being established as well.
3. The period in which the communes were formed by groups of native Americans inspired by the utopian ideas that emerged in the United States and influenced local events. This period of indigenous communes which began in the 1880s has continued until the present.

Although there is an obvious tendency to Americanize when communes are established here, it should be stressed that this tendency did not necessarily promote their status in the society. Indeed, when studying American history, we realize that the communes were not actively involved in any historical processes, nor did they influence historical development. The commune never became an integral part of the forces that formed the nation. They existed on the byroads of history. Social, political, as well as spiritual and intellectual struggles took place far from the boundaries of communal settlements. Even when they flourished, the commune and its revolutionary lifestyle never endangered the trend of American society. Communes remained a marginal factor, and this, in addition to their characteristic integral pluralism, is perhaps the reason that there was no attempt to undermine or to uproot them. There does not seem to be an active affinity in the relation between communes and the course of American history. If anything, historical events had an impact on the establishment of communes. There was a very limited number of periods in which the communal alternative was paramount, but it gained significance when seen together with the frequent appearance of communes and the sequence of their existence throughout American history. Thus it could be treated as a thread interwoven in the American social fabric, as well as a substantial chapter of experimentations in alternative lifestyles. It should be emphasized that the inherent pluralism of American values, though far removed from the communal world, did not check their existence. For scores of believers, those communes remain as rays of hope for the Kingdom of Heaven, and as nuclei for an alternative society.

Notes

1. Frederick Jackson Turner, *The Frontier in American History* (New York: Holt, 1950), pp. 261-63.
2. Merle Curti, *The Growth of American Thought* (New York: Harper, 1951), p. 264.
   Samuel Eliot Morison, *Builders of the Bay Colony* (New York: Houghton Mifflin, 1930), pp. 70-74. Arthur Bestor, *Backwoods Utopias: The Sectarian Origins and the Owenite Phase of Communitarian Socialism in America, 1663-1829*, 2d ed. (Philadelphia: University of Pennsylvania Press, 1978), pp. 16-19.
3. Oscar Handlin, *America: A History* (New York: Holt, Rinehart & Winston, 1968), pp. 36, 38-39.
4. Robert V. Hine points out the important role of the community in frontier life. Describing a number of cases from the history of the West, he notes the cooperation and mutual aid which characterized the covered wagon caravans, mining town communities, and those of various ethnic groups. He mentions the many aspects of mutual aid among midwestern farmers, farming cooperatives, and religious and socialist communes. Their communitarian vision did not, in the end, materialize because strong adverse tendencies were at play. However, the great number of cases Hine mentions show that the community played a vital role in the settlement of the frontier and was the background for the establishment of communal settlements. Hine is not alone in his theory. Modern American historians hold similar attitudes. Among them is Daniel Boorstin, who claims that during the settlement of the West there existed a strong tendency to establish communities and that this characterized the frontier era in which communities were established wherever settlers arrived. Robert V. Hine, *Community on the American Frontier: Separate but Not Alone* (Norman: University of Oklahoma Press, 1980), pp. 49-199; David Russo, *Families and Communities; A New View of American History* (Nashville, Tenn.: The American Association for State and Local History, 1977), pp. 25-38, 42-51, 297; Page Smith, *As a City upon a Hill: The Town in American History* (Cambridge, Mass.: MIT Press, 1973), pp. 20-54.

5. Vernon Louis Parrington, Jr., *American Dreams* (New York: Russel & Russel, 1964), pp. 3-5; Harold V. Rhodes, *Utopia in American Political Thought*, in *Political Theory Studies*, No. 1 (University of Arizona Press, 1967), p. 18; Edwin Erle Sparks, *The Expansion of the American People, Social and Territorial* (Chicago: Scott, Foresman, 1900), p. 376.
6. Morison, pp. 73-74.
7. Kenneth M. Roemer, *The Obsolete Necessity: America in Utopian Writings, 1888-1900* (Kent: Kent State University Press, 1976), pp. 15-41, 153-61; Michael Fellman, *The Unbounded Frame* (Westport, Conn.: Greenwood Press, 1973), introduction; Sparks, pp. 376-401; Charles L. Sanford, *The Quest for Paradise: Europe and the American Moral Imagination* (Urbana: University of Illinois Press, 1961), pp. 97-101, 107-13, 176-78.
8. Mathew, 5/14 ''The Sermon on the Mount.'' See Handlin, pp. 267-68; Bestor, *Backwoods*, p. 99.
9. Handlin, p. 358.
10. Parrington, pp. 57, 72-76, 97, 166-70, 177-84.
11. Handlin, p. 420; Bestor, *Backwoods*, pp. 1-3, 18-19.
12. Charles A. Beard et al., *New Basic History of the United States* (New York: Doubleday, 1960), pp. 29-37.
13. Oscar Handlin, *Immigration as a Factor in American History* (Englewood Cliffs, N.J.: Prentice-Hall, 1959), pp. 24-26; Marcus Lee Hansen, *The Immigrant In American History* (Boston: Harvard University Press, 1940), pp. 97-128; Maldwyn Allen Jones, *American Immigration* (Chicago: University of Chicago Press, 1960), pp. 6-38.
14. Donald Egbert and Stow Persons, eds., *Socialism and American Life*, 2 vols. (Princeton: Princeton University Press, 1952), pp. 130, 134-35; Stephen A. Marini, *Radical Sects of Revolutionary New England* (Cambridge: Harvard University Press, 1982), pp. 78-80, 88-101.
15. Edward Everett, ''The Shakers,'' *The North American Review* 16 (1823): 76-102; Jane Louise Mesik, *The English Traveler in America, 1785-1835* (New York: Columbia University Press, 1922), p. 267.
16. J.S. Buckingham, *The Eastern and Western States of America*, vol. 2 (London, 1842), pp. 234-36; Harriet Martineau, *Society in America*, vol. 2 (London: Saunders & Otley, 1834), pp. 55-65; Handlin, *America*, pp. 419-20.
17. J.R. Commons, *History of Labor in the United States*, vol. I (New York: Macmillan, 1921), pp. 116-17; Arthur E. Bestor, ed., *Education and Reform at New Harmony*, correspondence of William Maclure and Marie Duclos Fretageot, 1820-1833 (Indiana Historical Society Publications, vol. 15, no. 3, 1948), p. 304.
18. Ivan Doig, *Utopian America Dreams and Realities* (Rochelle Park, N.J.: Hayden, 1976), p. 11.
19. Alice Felt Tyler, *Freedom's Ferment* (New York: Harper & Row, 1962), p. 46; Egbert and Persons, pp. 174-75; Henry Steele Commanger, *The Era of Reform, 1830-1860* (New York: Van Nostrand, 1960), p. 7.
20. Whitney Cross, *The Burned-Over District: The Social and Intellectual History of Enthusiastic Religion in Western New York, 1800-1850* (New York: Harper & Row, 1965), pp. 328-32.
21. Redelia Brisbane, *Albert Brisbane: A Mental Biography, with a Character Study* (Arena Publishing Co., 1893; New York: Franklin, 1969), pp. 196-212; Robert Allerton Parker, *A Yankee Saint: John Humphrey Noyes and the Oneida Community* (New York: Putnam, 1935), pp. 145-52; Commons, vol. 1, pp. 496-502.

22. Robert S. Fogarty, ''American Communes, 1865-1914,'' *Journal of American Studies* 9 (Summer 1975): 145-62.
23. Commons, vol. 2, chap. 9; Parrington, pp. 51-52; Roemer, pp. 4-5; Handlin, pp. 542-46, 579-91, 615-16.
24. Parrington, pp. 72-97, 177-78.
25. Charles Pierre Le Warne, *Utopias on Puget Sound, 1885-1915* (Seattle: University of Washington Press, 1975), pp. 5-13; Howard Quint, *The Forging of American Socialism: Origins of the Modern Movement* (South Carolina, 1953), pp. 282-318; Ira Kipnis, *The American Socialist Movement* (New York: Columbia University Press, 1952), pp. 43-61, 230-35.
26. Morris Hillquit, *History of Socialism in the United States*, 5th ed. (New York: Dover, 1971), pp. 127-28.

2

Ephrata and the First Communes in North America

In the fertile and densely populated county of Lancaster, Pennsylvania, about 60 miles west of Philadelphia, in pastoral scenery and rolling green hills, lies Ephrata. In the center of this township is the historical site of the Ephrata Cloister. It was reconstructed in the twentieth century to save the remains of the old commune Ephrata, established in the 1730s, from decay. Amid well-tended lawns and massive trees, there is a cluster of small cottages and two wooden, three-story houses. They are prominent because of their quaint architecture and adjoining wings which form a right angle. Narrow windows are set in the walls, under a steep gabled roof. At the low, narrow gates long-robed guides await the visitor. Their white, Capuchine monk's costume used to be the habit of commune members in the past. Visitors are taken along somewhat gloomy, narrow corridors and told the story of Ephrata. Artifacts of the period in living rooms, assembly halls, and places of work make history come alive. Everything is meticulously reconstructed to bring back the special atmosphere of the past. Most impressive are the solidly built wooden houses which were constructed without any iron tools or nails. These houses have stood since 1740 and are as good as new. They are the oldest remaining concrete evidence of the American communes. Among their walls the first stable commune lived its life for over a generation, leaving an impact on the society of their period in the United States as well as in Europe.[1]

Ephrata was the first in a line of many communes established in the New World. There had been several prior attempts in the English colonies of North America to establish independent collective communities, even communes. However, they were all short-lived and nothing remained of them.[2] The first of these were established at the end of the seventeenth century, when a wave of persecuted Protestant refugees from northwestern Europe immigrated. They brought with them a tradition of communal values which had originated in their homelands. These ideas found fertile soil in the broad expanses of America and in the atmosphere of religious tolerance that characterized Pennsylvania and the adjacent areas.[3]

Bohemia Manor

The first communal settlement which managed to survive and to leave its mark on the development of Ephrata was Bohemia Manor, a commune established in 1683 by the Labadists, a sect whose members came from Holland and other northwestern European countries.[4]

From its inception this Labadist settlement was a commune. Every newcomer had to hand over his property and to accept the collective way of life in production as well as consumption. The Labadists' commune was not based on a clear-cut doctrine but emanated from their affinity with early Christianity and the apostolic way of life. However, their predominant urge was to live isolated from the alien world of sinners, independent of any external economic system.

The Labadists believed in an ''inward illumination of the spirit'' which would lead them to be reborn in the kingdom of heaven. They believed in the coming of the millennium even though they were not dealing with escatological calculations. This was the reason for their isolation and urge to be purified. Members were housed in cells in communal dwelling; men and women lived separately. According to their creed, celibacy was an asset but marriage was not forbidden. ''Perfect'' members were celibate, and those who married had to do so within the sect. They advocated a Spartan way of life of nonindulgence. The rigors of everyday life called for tasteless meals, uncomfortable living quarters, and no heating even during the coldest winter. Most of the daylight hours were devoted to back-breaking labor in the fields. Housework and agricultural jobs were equally shared between men and women.

About 100 men, women, and children lived in Bohemia Manor, which at its peak reached 125. Then, sixteen years after its establishment, it began to disintegrate; private farms existed side by side with the commune. Members could choose either way, and some, together with their spiritual leader, (Bishop) Peter Sluyter, began to produce tobacco on their estates and even became slave owners. This went on for thirty years,[5] so that in the 1720s there were still people who lived a communal life there. Bohemia Manor was in fact the first commune on American soil and suffered from all the trials of being a unique and isolated experiment in a world of completely alien values. In addition, they had to endure their voluntary celibacy, mortification, and harsh discipline combined with the autocratic leadership of Peter Sluyter. Under those circumstances it seems a miracle that Bohemia Manor survived for almost forty-four years.[6]

The Woman in the Wilderness

In 1694, while Bohemia Manor was still practicing a communal way of life, a group of 40 pietists arrived in America from Germany. They hoped to greet the Kingdom of Heaven, which according to them, was expected that year. The group landed on the northern shore of Chesapeake Bay, near Bohemia Manor. Most of them were students and university graduates who had gathered from among German pietists. Influenced by Jacob Zimmerman—the founder of their sect—and driven by persecution, they decided to emigrate to America.[7] A short time before sailing, Zimmerman died of an illness. His place was taken by Johann Kelpius, a 20-year-old pietist, who, like Zimmerman, was a graduate of Altdorf University in mathematics. He too was a mystic and millenarian. As soon as they had landed, the pietist group turned toward Germantown, Pennsylvania (within Philadelphia today).[8] They bought a tract of 175 acres and on a hill constructed a "tabernacle" which was to serve as the community's dwelling place. Forty was their symbolic number, hence their house measured 40 square feet.[9] It had an assembly hall, study rooms, and 40 cells for the brethren. On the roof there was an observation tower, from which they could follow the movement of the heavenly bodies that would announce the millennium.

A vegetable and herb garden surrounded the house. The commune chose the name *Woman in the Wilderness* because of their isolation while expecting the kingdom of heaven. It was adopted from the Revelation to John (chap. 12/G) (i.e. the apocalypse about the woman who was about to bear a male child "who is to rule all the nations with a rod of iron . . . but her child was caught up to God and to his throne and the woman fled into the wilderness where she had a place prepared by God, in which to be nourished for 1,260 days"). It was ironical that the group did not include a single woman and that they settled not in the wilderness but on a wooded hill close to a populated area. From inception they organized communal production and consumption. Like former pietist communes, the concept of early Christianity merged with the practical necessity of mutual help and cooperation in an antagonistic world. To fund their emigration they decided to pool their resources. They began their communal life when they moved to their new dwellings. Being used to self-discipline and having given up any individual aspirations, they encountered no difficulty in their communal way of life. Expecting the Kingdom of Heaven and salvation, they practiced mortification, and several recluses even preferred a solitary life away from the house. Their life was centered around millenarian expectations which, according to Jacob Zimmerman, was expected in 1694, namely, a short while after their arrival in Pennsylvania. They therefore stood watch, night after night, in their tower on the roof searching the heavens for signs of the coming of the Messiah. When 1694 had passed without any sign of salvation, they did not despair and kept their nightly watch while Johann Kelpius repeatedly postponed the millennium. When Kelpius died in 1708, the group began to disintegrate. The first to leave were from among the intellectuals who were easily absorbed in the surrounding society. The community tried to remain 40 brethren—their holy number—and absorbed new members. These came from among pietists in Germany, where the reputation of Woman of the Wilderness was as high as ever.[10] In 1720 there were still members of the commune who lived in the tabernacle. Several stayed until 1741, when the estate and all on it were sold and the community was finally dissolved.

Ephrata

In 1720 a small group of pietists arrived at the Woman of the Wilderness. They were young mystics who had left Germany hoping to join an idealistic community in the New World and purify themselves in expectation of the kingdom of heaven. On arriving at the tabernacle they were extremely disappointed to find thc place neglected and only a handful of people, whose existence had deteriorated spiritually as well as physically. Disillusioned, most of them abandoned their dream and went to live in nearby Germantown. Among those few who were determined to adhere to their aspirations of a life of purity in the New World was Johann Conrad Beissel, who in time would found the new commune of Ephrata.[11]

Johann Conrad Beissel was born in 1690 in the small town of Eberbach, in the palatinate, Germany. His father was a baker and died before Johann's birth. The orphan received a Lutheran education and was apprenticed to a baker. From an early age he was a nonconformist and attracted to pietist circles within the Lutheran Church. In 1710 he set out as a journeyman to wander on foot from town to town in order to be accepted by the guild as a "master baker." He was introduced into inspirationist and pietist circles, and when he arrived in Heidelberg he met Rosicrucians and their secret brotherhood. When in 1716 he openly attacked the leaders of the bakers' guild, he was expelled and departed from the city. Wandering from one place to another during the years 1716 to 1720, he searched for a haven of religious tolerance and met further dissident sects, the Baptists, Mennonites, and inspirationalists. Hearing about The Woman of the Wilderness, he realized that the New World could offer him a place where he could live in spiritual purity and according to his convictions. He found someone who lent him enough money to gather a group of young people who would set out to the wilds of the New World, hoping to realize their dream of a holy life.[12]

After the disappointing visit to The Woman of the Wilderness and a short stay at Germantown, Johann Conrad Beissel turned west to the woods of

Conestoga County. This is where he and his friends built log cabins and lived as recluses on mutual aid. A new period began for Beissel which lasted fifteen years. In the dense woods of Conestoga, in the isolation of his log cabin, he formulated his religious ideas that led him to found Ephrata. However, he was not completely cut off from the spiritual-religious upheavals of the German communities in the nearby areas. In the first year, while he was still intent on joining a collective community, he visited a friend in Bohemia Manor, at that time the only commune in America. It appealed to him more than the Woman of the Wilderness and was of a greater ideological influence,[13] but he felt no urge to join this disintegrating commune and returned to the secluded life in his log cabin.

The German Sabbatarian Baptists

In the first years in Conestoga Forest Johann Conrad Beissel formulated the idea of observing the Sabbath, which would prove to be an important decision.[14] Other Sabbatarians in the area regarded him as their spiritual leader, and gradually a following was formed. Other religious doctrines influenced him at the time. In southern Pennsylvania between 1722 and 1724 there was a religious revival among the Baptists. Preachers who roamed the country discovered Beissel and his followers and convinced him to be baptized as a sign of acceptance of their creed and thus join their revival movement. Within a short time he was accepted as their leader because of his personality and ability to preach during revivals. In 1724 the German Baptist community was established in Conestoga County. They were Sabbatarians, and in addition to observing the Sabbath some of them had adopted other Jewish customs such as eating special food and circumcision. There was considerable tension and objection expressed by the Baptists in Germantown, and Beissel rejected the excessive adoption of Jewish habits, even though he himself observed the Sabbath and never ate any pork.[15]

Between 1725 and 1732 Beissel continued to live in his cabin in Conestoga Forest but was simultaneously the spiritual leader of a growing community of Baptists. In 1728 he published his first theological book in German, the *Mysterion Anomias*. A third of it was devoted to the sacredness of the Sabbath according to the Old Testament. His disciples' convictions were reinforced, but at the same time the schism with German Baptists in Germantown widened. At the convention of German Baptists in Pennsylvania in 1728, they realized that there was no way to bridge the discord, and Johann Conrad Beissel and his followers seceded and established their own sect—The Seventh-Day German Baptists—with their center in Conestoga.[16]

Naturally the Baptist Church and the local authorities were displeased. Even the tolerant Quakers in Pennsylvania could not accept the schism. They feared that public order would be disrupted because of the differing Sabbath days.

The authorities began to persecute the Sabbatarians and force them to keep the Sunday as their Sabbath. Unless they did so they were arrested and fined. Landowners in the county exploited the situation and tried to evict Beissel's followers from their land. This was the background of the suggestion to transfer them to another secluded spot where they could practice their beliefs without interference, on a farm of their own. However, under the prevailing conditions it was impossible to transform the whole sect. They were too numerous and too heterogeneous. Beissel therefore decided to return to his hermit's existence. In 1732 he found a secluded corner north of Conestoga which even the Indians avoided, because of a legend that the place was infested with snakes. This proved to be a myth and the charming spot, at the foot of a wooded hill, where springs formed into a stream, was later to be known as Ephrata. Beissel built a cabin near the river intending to live in seclusion. This was soon disrupted when his followers came to live nearby. The women were the first to arrive, causing some gossip in the area. Later several men joined them to form the foundation of an independent sect of The Seventh-Day German Baptists. It developed as a community of hermits in the tradition of the Eastern Monasticism founded by Pachomius.[17]

The Establishment of Ephrata as a Celibate Community

The area was populated gradually. During 1732 to 1735 many of Beissel's followers arrived with their families, establishing private farms close to the hermit's colony near the river. The community of "brothers" and "sisters" grew as well but at a slower pace. Only a few could adopt their monastic ascetism, but a relationship of mutual aid was formed and Beissel was regarded as the spiritual leader of both communities. At this stage there was little cooperation among the hermits. The first collective venture was a wheat silo and a bakery which handed out flour and bread to the needy. In 1735, following a revival, a group of intellectuals joined the community, among them Peter Miller, who would inherit Beissel's leadership after his death. The growing number of hermits required lodgings as well as an assembly place. The first communal house was constructed in 1735 with the combined efforts of the whole community. It was a three-story wooden house called *Kedar*. It had living quarters as well as assembly and dining halls.

That "brothers" and "sisters" lived in the same house caused again some gossip in the neighborhood and one of the sect's followers donated enough money to build an additional house for the brothers. It was finished within the year and was the largest building in the whole county. As a result, life in Ephrata began to take an orderly course. At this stage it began to function as a commune. The dining-room, supervised by the sisters, served all, but a partition divided the sexes.[18]

Between 1735 and 1740 the commune's collective effort was devoted to building living quarters, a prayer house, a dining hall, and places of work. Lacking an overall plan, the buildings were scattered some distance from each other and had to be dismantled after a few years. Yet they were well-planned structures and constructed according to the sect's concept with tiny, uncomfortable living quarters, low doors and narrow corridors. There were partitions everywhere to divide men from women. Even the assembly's prayer meetings, and *agape* (love feasts) were conducted separately. One of the important principles which guided the builders was their adherence to the biblical tradition of not using any iron for the temple (Kings 1/7; Exodus 25/20; Deuteronomy 27/5). They were careful to use neither iron tools nor any nails to fasten the beams. It proved to be an efficient method which withstood cold as well as heat, and the climate inside was very mild. Some of the houses survived scores of years.[19]

In 1740 another large building, Bethania, was constructed to serve as the sisters' house. Beside it stood the prayer house, Zion Hall of Peniel, which has survived and still stands in the center of the historic site. At that time the name *Ephrata* was chosen for the community as a whole.[20]

An Ascetic Communal Way of Life

In 1735 the celibate groups of brothers and sisters crystallized into a commune. The sisters were the first to adopt the communal way of life when they moved into a house which they named "Kedar." The brothers followed suit. They all had lived a communal life before, but it took them three more years to abolish private property completely. From 1740 every member, on joining Ephrata, had to hand over his entire property. Owning private property was regarded as "Anannias' sin."[21] At the time of its establishment on 130 acres, the settlement numbered 40 brothers and sisters. During the formative years they reached 70 members. The first years were a time of hardship, as their main effort was devoted to building the settlement. This was in tune with the ascetic preference and practice of the members, who regarded this way of life as a virtue and the means of salvation.[22]

Each cell contained a mattressless bunk with a wooden headrest. Austere communal meals were served once a day only. Ritual "love feasts" were celebrated from time to time. Members of the sect were fully occupied by work, prayer, and meditation. Only a few hours were allowed for sleep. Their garments were of a simple, unbleached cotton or wool with a Capuchine or White Friar's robe and cowl intended to abolish individuality. Whenever weather permitted, they went barefoot. They repressed any materialist instincts in order to devote themselves to "entering the Gates to the Kingdom of Heaven." Their ascetic way of life befitted the "chosen" and therefore they meticulously examined any new candidate. New candidates had to pass severe physical and spiritual tests for over a year.[23]

Celibacy was practiced from the day of Ephrata's inception until its dissolution. This principle was of religious significance, and was influenced by its founder, Johann Conrad Beissel, who had practiced celibacy throughout his life in Germany and in Pennsylvania.[24] Not all of Beissel's followers agreed to a life of ascetism and celibacy. Many of the German Baptist Sabbatarians were married and owners of private property. Even among those who did join the commune, some got married. In that case they had to leave the commune and live close by. In time this caused a clear division between the "perfect" brothers and sisters who lived on the commune and the secular ones who lived nearby and participated in religious rituals and in economic activities as well. At a certain stage houses were constructed for the secular members as well and all faithfully accepted Beissel's authoritative leadership.[25]

Their ascetism and celibacy could not have lasted on the strength of Beissel's leadership alone. Members needed a strong inner conviction and had to make a continuous effort to withstand temptation. They therefore introduced individual confessions, in which each member wrote his or her own confession every Friday night. Several were collected and published. Those confessions were a part of a general process to abolish the ego and experience the rebirth which every member undertook on joining. It was expressed by taking on a new identity and a new name. Most of these were adopted from the Bible (e.g. Amaziah, Amos, Elimelich, Gideon, Haggar, Joel, Lamech, Manoah, Abigail, Amalia, Esther, Ketura, Miriam).

Just as Judaism had influenced the sect and contributed to its separate existence, so the tradition of the Old Testament had a strong impact on the way of life at Ephrata. One of the most significant of those was the adoption of the Jewish day, which begins at 6 P.M. The Sabbath could thus be observed according to the Jewish hours. The long beards of the brothers and their abstaining from eating meat may have their roots in the Jewish tradition as well. Most buildings in Ephrata had biblical names such as Kedar, Bethania, Peniel. The sisters' order was called Sharon, the brothers'—Zion Saal, Zionitic Brotherhood. But most important, the Star of David was their adopted sacred symbol with the words "Lord of Hosts" enhancing it with magic significance. Chapters from the Old Testament, mainly from the Prophets, were read out at community meetings, more frequently than chapters from the New Testament.[26]

Ephrata, as other communes before it, adhered to the belief in the millennium, and its members lived in expectation of the Kingdom of Heaven, for which they prepared themselves. But they avoided millenial calculations and thus were saved from frustration and crises. From start they were zealous missionaries and organized missions far and wide, establishing Baptist Sabbatarian communities in eastern Pennsylvania and in New Jersey. The religious revival caused by the missionaries brought new candidates to Ephrata. Some were men of letters, others were from religious circles; most of them were of German origin, but some of the new members were English, Swedish, Swiss, and even native Americans.

The missionary zeal molded the commune into a spiritual-religious center. In 1739 the foundation was laid for a systematic educational activity. Under Ludwig Hocker (Bro Obed) a school was established, intending at first to serve only the adjacent secular community, but soon it expanded and accepted children from nearby and far away communities. The curriculum included penmenship, the Old and New Testaments (mainly learning by rote) as well as arithmetic and other secular subjects. It soon developed into The Academy of Classical Studies, its reputation reaching even the large urban centers of Philadelphia and Baltimore. One of the most important innovations was the founding of a Sabbath School, intended to teach religion to the neighborhood children, most of whom could not attend school regularly because of their having to work on their parents' farms.[27]

Musical Activities

The outstanding feature of Ephrata's educational system was its musical activity, which was inspired by the importance of music in the community's life. Moreover, it soon became one of the unique characteristics of Ephrata. Johann Conrad Beissel, a budding musician in his youth, became deeply involved in musical activity soon after the establishment of Ephrata. Even though he had no formal education, he invented an original musical theory, claiming to have been inspired by God. Beissel composed hundreds of hymns and their lyrics and urged other members to do likewise. In time this caused talented musicians to join the commune, among them Ludwig Blum. The culture of singing enriched the community, and the whole population would join the choir. Many hours were devoted to the daily rehearsals under Beissel's baton. It was the focal point of all other activities. Beissel declared that food as well as morals influenced singing. A special diet was therefore introduced for various voices. All choir members had to "cleanse their hearts" perpetually in order to maintain the quality of their voices. Music added grace to the commune's routine and served as sublimation to the rigors and repressions of their life. It gave scope to artistic temperament and talent and many members participated in the composition of hymns. The choir developed a unique sound that impressed audiences who called it "heavenly song." It soon acquired fame and many came on a pilgrimage to Ephrata just to hear it and to learn the unique method. Beissel published several books on music, explaining the method of the Ephrata's musical harmony.[28]

Hymn books as well as others were printed locally, and the press soon became one of the main branches of Ephrata. The first printing press in Pennsylvania had Gothic and English lettering. It was one of the first German presses in America. They also had a big advantage in that the members of the commune themselves provided the paper and the printer's ink. They had their own carpenters and metal workers for repair and maintenance. There were also members who had a talent for illuminating the books artistically with stylized Gothic letters. The commune also had its own fine binding shop. Most of the printing work during the first years were provided by Beissel and other members who wrote religious tracts. Later they accepted outside work, mainly religious literature in German. Their largest project was the ''Martyrs Book of the Mennonites.'' It was a big volume and printed in thousands of copies in order to be distributed in America. From 1748, fifteen members worked at it continuously for fifteen years. Another large hymn book published was the *Zionitic Incense Hill.*[29]

The Zionitic Brethren were an extraordinary group of followers who joined Ephrata in 1739. They had a different set of principles and customs as well as secret rituals similar to those of the Free Masons. Every new candidate had to undergo forty days of trials. He had to endure physically and be ''brainwashed'' until he lost his identity in order to be reborn. After passing the trials he was accepted; as proof he received a scroll with the Shield of David, whose center was inscribed with the words ''Lord of the Hosts: The Eckerlings Yews.''

Relations between Beissel's old followers and the Zionitic Brethren were problematic. They were led by the three Eckerling brothers, who were talented leaders and soon became involved in the economic development of Ephrata. The new incentive under their leadership changed the ways of the commune.[30] In the early days of Ephrata there was little interest in economics. The brothers and sisters did the housework, some printing jobs, and a primitive cultivation of their land. They would even pull the ploughs and carts themselves, because they objected to the use of tools and farm animals. Work provided them with their elementary necessities and was not done for profit or material gain. The brothers grew wheat and corn, most of it for their own use, the rest was given to the needy. They also gave away surplus bread. Beissel and his friend Wohlfahrt (Bro Agunius), who was in charge of the daily management, objected to a materialistically affluent way of life. When William Penn, governor of Pennsylvania, offered them a tract of 5,000 acres, they refused the gift. However, they did not object to the aid given them by several of their secular members. This situation changed radically when Wohlfahrt died in 1740 and Israel Eckerling, of the Zionitic Brotherhood, took over his job. It was a matter of principle for him to achieve a stable, independent economy without any help from the secular members.[31]

As soon as Israel Eckerling took the reins of economic management into his hands he introduced a new spirit and revolutionized work methods. He bought farm horses for the ploughs and carts, planted fruit trees, and introduced various agricultural produce. He bought an old, neglected water mill in the neighborhood, which after being repaired became a focal point of industries. A sawmill was constructed as well as a paper-mill and a bookbinding shop, all auxilliaries to the printing press. In addition he established a flax weaving factory, a leather shop, a shoemaker's shop, and a pottery shop. The commune began to quarry stones for building houses, fences, and bridges. Some of the workshops were planned for the sisters such as embroidery, lace coupling, basket weaving, match production, all of which also attracted members of the secular community. Agents in the larger cities marketed their produce. Eckerling did not despise commercial activities. His agents would buy up agricultural produce cheaply at harvest time, only to store it in the same granary which had been constructed in order to distribute the surplus to the needy. Ironically, it was now sold at a high price in times of scarcity. A visitor described Ephrata at that time as a place of diligence and activity. The Eckerling brothers' initiative between 1740 and 1745 had brought prosperity, and the commune's economic growth was the highest in the whole province. However, Johann Conrad Beissel was troubled by what he called the "worship of Mammon;" the greed and avarice of commune members was about to extinguish their religious fervor, he believed, and even more the spiritual uniqueness of the community. He also had personal reasons for feeling slighted—a rivalry had sprung up between him and the Eckerling brothers. Five years after they had joined Ephrata, Beissel found himself relegated into the background.

In the summer of 1745, Beissel expressed his displeasure with the high-handed leadership of Israel Eckerling and his extravagance. Exploiting a moment of opposition against Eckerling, he managed to demote him and soon after the four brothers were manipulated into leaving Ephrata. They wandered in the direction of the southern frontier. Determined to break any internal opposition, Beissel disbanded the Zionitic Brotherhood as a separate order. At the same time he took over the management of the economy, which he had never done before. This immediately caused a drastic halt in the economic development. All the innovations of the Eckerling brothers were abolished, the workshops stopped producing, contracts and orders were disregarded. Even the fruit trees were uprooted. An economic standstill set in, and Ephrata returned to austerity.[32]

In contrast with the economic recession, Ephrata's society prospered when new immigrants from the palatinate joined the commune some time later. It was Beissel's direct influence which brought them over. He had corresponded with pietist circles for years, keeping them informed of Ephrata and his doctrines. His family and others kept in touch, and when the persecution in the palatinate worsened, he encouraged them to emigrate.

In 1748 money was sent from Ephrata to help them on their journey and a year later the first of the persecuted pietists arrived. They were all family people and that is perhaps the reason why most of them joined the secular community rather than the commune. Their coming filled the gap left by the Eckerlings, but they had a hard time adjusting to the new way of life and especially to Beissel's autocratic leadership. There were additional and personal reasons for tension, and in order to avoid a further schism Beissel encouraged those who were a potential opposition to set out and establish a new community in the West. These attempts did not prosper, but a schism was avoided.[33]

Johann Conrad Beissel's Autocratic Leadership

The Eckerling affair made Beissel more aware of any potential opposition and strengthened his zeal as the spiritual leader of his followers in the commune and outside it. A good example can be found in the first contract between the Moravian Brothers who had arrived in Pennsylvania in 1736, instilled with similar ideals as those of the pietists' who had established the first communes. They visited Ephrata, which was in its first years, and even though there was an immediate rapport nothing came of it. The Moravians set out northward and established their first communities, Bethlehem and Nazareth, based on semicommunal elements.

In 1741, Count Zinzendorf, whose estate in Germany served as a base for the Moravians and who was regarded as their spiritual leader, arrived in America. He intended to promote their settlements and hoped to unite the many German Protestant sectarians who had gathered in Pennsylvania. With that in mind, he organized a convention in Germantown in 1741 in which members of Ephrata participated. There were severe disagreements between them and most of the others and Count Zinzendorf, hoping to bridge the gap, initiated a meeting with Beissel. He went to Ephrata and was invited to stay at Zion Hall of the Zionitic Brotherhood; but even though Beissel was at the time staying at home—a short distance away—they never met. Each of them was convinced that the other had to make the effort and walk over to meet him. Sheer pride on both sides prevented the meeting which might have been cardinal to the two sects which had both undertaken missionary and settlement work in Pennsylvania at the time.[34]

In the 1750s Ephrata reached the apex of its development. It numbered 100 members, and prided itself on a well-balanced economy. Some bad years in agriculture were followed by good ones, and the industrial activity continued although on a smaller scale. A detailed description of life at Ephrata during that period came down to us through the Reverend Israel Acrelius, provost of the Swedish Lutheran Church, who visited the place in 1753. We get the impression that it was a period of harmony between the members' beliefs and way of life. Those who talked to the visitor were proud that although their number was limited and their life austere, they had some influence on their neighbors. Many of the prominent men in Pennsylvania visited them and found their life and doctrine of great interest. Israel Acrelius gave a first-hand description of their work on the field, their narrow living quarters, their collective but meagre meals. He described their unique customs, many of them being of "Jewish origin."[35]

Only a decade later, a slow deterioration set in. Beissel was in his seventies, and although he maintained his autocratic leadership, his spiritual influence diminished. In a private diary of one of the brothers—which was found by chance many years after the commune had disintegrated—there was harsh criticism and accusations against Beissel's leadership.[36] He accused him of intrigues and thirst for power and drunkenness, even though this evidence could not be substantiated. Perhaps there was some personal rancor involved, but most students of Ephrata's history agree that Beissel's impact weakened, his spiritual influence diminished, and he suffered from tuberculosis in his final years.

Beissel was 76 when he died in 1768. It was the end of a charismatic personality, the son of a poor baker from the palatinate who had never had any formal education yet rose within the spiritual hierarchy of the dissenting sects to found his own sect and become its leader. He led his congregation during a generation of communal life.

Peter Miller's Leadership: Years of Disintegration

The natural heir of Ephrata's leader was Peter Miller, Brother Agrippa, one of the elders. He had been Beissel's right hand during the latter's final years and had always been one of the active members. He was completely different from Beissel, a well-educated man who had graduated cum laude from Heidelberg University, in theology and law. A pastor of the Lutheran Reform Church, he emigrated to America and joined Ephrata in 1735 where he soon became a devoted follower of Beissel. He took charge of the printing press but somehow managed to continue his studies in several areas even in applied sciences. He experimented with new methods of agriculture and in 1768 was elected member of the American Society of Science in Philadelphia. His reputation as theologian, scientist, and linguist attracted many visitors to Ephrata. They included the social elite of America such as William Penn, Benjamin Franklin, and even George Washington.

Peter Miller took up the leadership of Ephrata at a time when the settlement had already passed its apex and a slow deterioration set in. Most of the brothers and sisters were elderly, and no new young members were absorbed. Those few who did join the commune came from the German Baptist Sabbatarians who had left the frontier settlement in the West and returned to the mother community in Pennsylvania. Production suffered; only the printing shop and its auxiliary workshops remained. The whole area was now being intensely settled and the church institutions stabilized. Ephrata found itself isolated and the source of possible growth had disappeared. During the years of the American War of Independence, Ephrata encountered difficulties in its relations with the outside world. Their way of life and doctrines prevented its members from taking sides in the political unrest in Pennsylvania. On the other hand, their close connections with Pennsylvania's social elite, who were all actively involved in the uprising against Britain, caused Ephrata to lend assistance to George Washington's army.[37]

Ephrata's geographical position complicated matters further and undermined its stability, when after the battle at nearby Brandywine, the wounded of George Washington's army were hospitalized at Ephrata. The historian Sachse believes that it was Washington himself who advised the move, knowing that Ephrata's members would never refuse this humanitarian aid.[38] Thus, a few days after the battle hundreds of wounded filled the houses on Mt. Zion. The houses Kedar and Zion were evacuated and turned into crowded wards. The life of the community was paralyzed when brothers and sisters tended the wounded with devotion. Because of the lack of doctors, a typhoid epidemic broke out which felled many of the patients and members of Ephrata as well. It was a magnificent chapter of self-sacrifice, but it took a heavy toll. One-third of Ephrata's members perished in the epidemic; all the houses that had served as hospital wards were incinerated. Zion Hill of the Zionitic Brotherhood was deserted and turned into a graveyard. The survivors settled at the foot of the hill near the creek.

In the aftermath of the war, Ephrata did not recover. The 1780s were years of disintegration. The final stage was set when in 1786, private ownership of personal belongings was allowed, though land and buildings were still communal property. Ironically, the first edition of *Chronicon Ephratense: A History of the Community of the Seventh-Day Baptists at Ephrata* was published in the same year. It was begun by Brother Lamech, who had kept a journal since the early days of the commune. The book was completed and edited by Brother Agrippa (Peter Miller) in 1777.[39]

In the 1790s only a handful of old timers were left in Ephrata. Nevertheless, when Peter Miller died in 1796 he still believed in the future of the commune. He might have found consolation in the new commune Snowhill (Schneeberg), which he had initiated and which was then just taking its first steps.

Communities Modeled on Ephrata

A sect of German Sabbatarian Baptists had existed in southern Pennsylvania, across the Susquehanna in Franklin County, since the 1750s. It was founded by Ephrata missionaries in Johann Conrad Beissel's time and remained active even after his death. Peter Miller, who thought highly of this group, kept in touch. When in 1788 it was clear that Ephrata was fast disintegrating, he sent Peter Lehman, one of the sects' mainstays in Franklin County, to organize a collective community modeled on Ephrata. Peter Lehman accepted the mission and, supported by the Schneeberger family, who donated the land, even joined the commune. Snowhill was established in the early 1790s. Communal life was crystallized there in the early nineteenth century. A well-organized community of about 40 members, it flourished between 1820 and 1840. Its way of life was modeled on Ephrata. Being closely interwoven with Ephrata, Snowhill created a continuity of communal history of the German Sabbatarian Baptists which lasted until the end of the nineteenth century. It disintegrated gradually, and in 1895 the last of its members died.

Ephrata was privileged to be the first commune that existed longer than one generation and its heritage passed on to other communes. Of special importance may be the fact that it was the first of a line of communes that formed their historical continuity in the United States. In addition to the direct influence Ephrata had on Snowhill, it also had an indirect impact on the inception and way of life of the other communes of its period. Among them was Harmony, established in the early nineteenth century by German immigrants from Wittenberg. The other—New Jerusalem—was established in the 1790s under the leadership of Jemima Wilkinson, descendant of a Quaker family from Rhode Island, third-generation Americans. It was a small commune with little influence, but its importance lies in the fact that it was founded by an American-born religious leader whose doctrine grew on American soil and whose members were all native Americans.[40] At the same time and in the same county, the foundation of the largest and most stable American communal movement was laid by the Shakers, whose founders were immigrants from England.

Notes

1. Proof of Ephrata's fame in the eighteenth century is that Voltaire included it in his *Dictionnaire Philosophique*. See Voltaire, *Dictionnaire Philosophique* (Amsterdam: 1789), vol. 4, p. 81; quoted in John E. Jacoby, *Two Mystic Communities in America* (Paris: Les Presses Universitaires de France, 1931; New York: Hyperion, 1975), p. 51.
2. The first signs of communitarianism in North America appeared right from the beginning of British colonization. In Jamestown, Virginia (1607), and in Ply-

mouth, Massachusetts (1620), the early settlers were asked to sign a contract with the colonization company according to which they undertook to live, work, consume, and own their means of production communally. This led to a form of communal living that was enforced by the colonizers, who regarded it the most efficient way to keep the settlers at their new domain and also gain high profits and achievements in the early stages. As far as is known, the settlers themselves were not ideologically or morally motivated, and as soon as their contract expired the community was dissolved, leaving no future foundation for a commune. Ernest Sutherland Bates, *American Faith: Its Religious, Political and Economic Foundations* (New York: W.W. Norton, 1940), pp. 104-14; William Franklin Atwood, *The Pilgrim Story* 12th ed. (Plymouth, Mass.: MPG Communications, 1980), pp. 25-26; William Alfred Hinds, *American Communities and Cooperative Colonies* (1878. Reprinted and enl. Philadelphia: Porcupine, 1975), pp. 13-14; Sigmund Diamond, ''From Organization to Society: Virginia in the Seventeenth Century,'' *The American Journal of Sociology* 53, no. 5 (March 1968); Mark Holloway, *Heavens on Earth: Utopian Communities in America, 1680-1880* (New York: Dover, 1966), pp. 31-32.

3. The first of these communes was established in 1663 by Dutch Mennonites under Peter Cornelius Plockhoy, in Delaware, which at the time was under Dutch rule. A year later, in 1664, the region was conquered by the British and the settlement looted and destroyed. After the conquest the British rulers refused to let the Dutch reestablish their commune. It was a short-lived experiment, and there are hardly any documents or memoirs to tell about their way of life and experiences. Arthur Bestor, *Backwoods Utopias*, 2d ed. (Philadelphia: University of Pennsylvania Press, 1978), p. 27.
4. The founder of the settlement, Jean de Labadie (1610-1674), was born in Bordeaux, France. In his youth he was Jesuit, but he soon rejected the Catholic dogma. His nonconformist attitude resulted in his adopting Protestantism, but not for long. Once again his nonconformism caused him to be expelled. Forming his own sect, he became its spiritual leader. When the sect adopted the purity of early Christianity, they were persecuted. They chose a secluded communitarian way of life, at first in Amsterdam and later in an independent settlement in Frieseland, North Holland. In 1674 Labadie died, but his followers continued to develop as a separate sect, searching for ways to expand while adhering to their faith undisturbed. The governor of Surinam (a Dutch colony) who was close to some of the members in the sect, offered them a place in the New World. Although nothing came of it the idea took root, and in 1679 two emissaries, Peter Sleuter and Dankerst, set out to tour the English colonies in North America in search for a place to settle and spread their gospel. They soon attracted a small group of local followers who helped them acquire 3,750 acres on an estate that belonged to the father of one of them. It was located on the border intersection of Maryland, Pennsylvania, and Delaware and was called Bohemia Manor. Returning to Europe, the emissaries organized a group of settlers and in 1683 established a Labadist colony in America; they were a branch of the Labadist community in Europe and adopted their way of life. V.F. Calverton, *Where Angels Dared to Tread* (New York: Bobbs-Merrill, 1941), pp. 18-26; Bestor, *Backwoods*, p. 28.
5. Members of the commune abstained from luxury, worked hard and diligently, were disciplined, and achieved an outstanding economic success. They grew wheat, corn, tobacco, flax and marketed their produce. As a result they gave up their isolation from the ''world of sin'' and the sect which had established their communal way of life, motivated by their wish for seclusion, was open to alien

ideological influences due to their economic success and integration. Delburn Carpenter, *The Radical Pietists: Celibate Communal Societies Established in the United States before 1820* (New York: AMS Press, 1975), pp. 20, 28, 31, 34; Bartlett B. James, *The Labadist Colony in Maryland*, Series 17, no. 6 of *Johns Hopkins University Studies* (Baltimore: Johns Hopkins University Press, 1899), pp. 16-17, 25, 39-40; Calverton, pp. 34-37; Holloway, pp. 32-36.

6. Julius Friedrich Sachse, *The German Sectarians of Pennsylvania, 1742-1880: A Critical and Legendary History of the Ephrata Cloister and the Dunkers*, vol. 1 (1899. Reprint. New York: AMS Press, 1971), pp. 57-59, 63-65; James, pp. 40-41.
7. Jacob Zimmerman was born in Wurtemberg, Germany. He studied mathematics and graduated from Tübingen University, later becoming a lecturer at Heidelberg. He was influenced by Jacob Böhme's mysticism and adopted the millenarian creed. He thought that the millennium would start in 1694, and sent out a call to be prepared. In his writings he preached against the Lutheran Church's formalism. Persecuted, he approached the Pietists and the secret Rosicrucians sect and had to abdicate from his position at Heidelberg University. Wandering across Germany, he reached Ehrfurth in 1690 and attracted a following. Holloway, pp. 37-38; Carpenter, pp. 38-42.
8. In this settlement there was the largest community of German immigrants in Pennsylvania who had originated in the dissident sects of their European homelands. When Johan Kelpius's group arrived in Germantown, they were amazed at the poor religious activities and started a "revival campaign" to prepare for the future "kingdom of heaven." Some time later they decided to isolate themselves and establish a separate community near Germantown in a forested hilly area along the Wissahikon River. (Today it is in the northern part of Fairmont Park in Philadelphia.) Carpenter, pp. 32, 43-44, 49, 55; Holloway, pp. 39, 41; Calverton, p. 46.
9. Carpenter, pp. 58-59.
10. Their intensive religious life, while expecting the Kingdom of Heaven and the various traditions (from sources such as the Anabaptists, the Theosophists, Rosicrucians, pietists, and even from the Jewish Kabbala), crystallized into a unique doctrine. Attempting to disseminate their belief via missionaries, they started in the nearby areas but reached the West and even Indian Country. In addition to their missionary work they were also involved in educational and cultural activities in their neighborhood. They developed their own culture of music which contributed much to their ascetic way of life. Johan Kelpius was the living spirit behind these activities. He composed hundreds of hymns and trained his community to perform them to the accompaniment of various instruments. With this in mind he imported from Europe an organ and a cenbalo (the first ever on the American continent). Carpenter, p. 58; Calverton, pp. 48-50; Holloway, p. 42.
11. Lamech and Agrippa, *Chronicon Ephratense: A History of the Community of Seventh Day Baptists and Ephrata*, trans. J. Max Hark (Lancaster, Pa.: S.H. Zahn, 1889. Reprint. B. Franklin, 1972), p. 13-15; Sachse, pp. 42-44; Walter C. Klein, *Johann Conrad Beissel: Mystic and Martinet, 1690-1768* (Philadelphia: Porcupine, 1972), p. 41.
12. Lamech and Agrippa, pp. 1-12; Klein, pp. 26-35; Sachse, pp. 34-42; Jacoby, pp. 5-6.
13. Sachse, pp. 57-59; Klein, pp. 43, 46; Lamech and Agrippa, p. 16.
14. The background is complicated. The historian Julius Friedrich Sachse, who in the nineteenth century studied the German pietist sects in Pennsylvania, dealt with the

subject and claimed that the turning point was a meeting of Johann Conrad Beissel with the Sabbatarians who lived in the vicinity. He began to ask himself which day was considered holy by God. Examining the Scriptures he concluded that the Sabbath was indeed the holy day and found nothing to refute his claim. Walter C. Klein, who wrote Beissel's biography, pointed to a theological change of direction which had preceded this, namely the adoption of Jacob Böhme's mystical doctrines, which he encountered while still in Heidelberg. Böhme promoted the holiness of the Sabbath and filled it with mysticism. He did not propose to alter the holy day but rather to adopt the Sabbath in addition to the customary Sunday. Beissel regarded this as a compromise and ignored it, adopting the holy Sabbath as a mandatory principle. Sachse raised another interesting point. Close to Conrad Beissel's settlement there were Jewish influences brought into the area by Jewish traders who reached the Appalachian frontier in southern Pennsylvania early in the eighteenth century. They usually arrived alone from New York or Philadelphia to trade with the Indians. Many married local girls and some of the Jewish traditions were maintained in these mixed marriages for generations. His study also pointed to the many families in Lancaster, Lebanon, and Burk counties who in the nineteenth century were careful not to mix milk and meat dishes. In time, the Jewish population expanded, community institutions such as synagogues and graveyards appeared in Heidelberg and Shephardstown in Adams and Cumberland counties. Some of these Jews may have been converts who thus continued the German and Lutheran traditions of their homeland. These small groups of converts and assimilated Jews disseminated beliefs of Jewish origin in these frontier areas where they grew on fertile soil among settlers who had come from one religious background or another. These traditions were adopted mainly by German settlers and were reinforced by a group of British Sabbatarians who found a haven in Lancaster County after having been persecuted by their neighbors in nearby Chester County. It was, therefore, a fitting background for Conrad Beissel's theory of the holy Sabbath and a good place to realize it. Sachse, p. 72, 115-19, 121; Klein, pp. 67-68, 188; Lamech and Agrippa, pp. 16, 44.

15. Klein, pp. 58-59; Sachse, pp. 101-4, 111-15.
16. Eugene E. Doll, *The Ephrata Cloister: An Introduction* (Ephrata, Pa.: Ephrata Cloister Associates, 1978), p. 9; Klein, pp. 60-65; Lamech and Agrippa, p. 44; Sachse, pp. 134-35.
17. Pachomius—a Coptic monk. He lived in the fourth century and founded the first *coenumbion* (community of monks). He composed the first *regula* (rule) for the monk's communal life. Its main principles were: renunciation of private property, subsisting on manual labor, communal meals, obedience to the abbot, celibacy, and asceticism. Sachse, pp. 179-181, 189-90.
18. Ibid., pp. 228-47; Lamech and Agrippa, pp. 76, 79, 81.
19. Hinds, pp. 19-20; Sachse, pp. 401-3; S.G. Zerfass, *Souvenir Book of the Ephrata Cloister* (Lititz, Pa.: Zook, 1921; New York: AMS Press, 1975), p. 12.
20. It is known that Beissel used this name in 1735. The name that the members of the sect chose for their community also is evidence of their faithfulness to the church. Ephrata is another name for Bethlehem, where Jesus was born. (Genesis 35:16, 35:19, also Micha 5:1: "But thou, Bethlehem Ephrathah, which art little to be among the thousands of Judah, out of thee shall one come forth unto me that is to be ruler in Israel"). Doll, *The Ephrata Cloister*, p. 6; Carpenter, p. 77; Sachse, pp. 258-59.
21. Lamech and Agrippa, pp. 121, 138.
22. Eugene E. Doll, "Social and Economic Organization in Two Pennsylvania Ger-

man Religious Communities," *The American Journal of Sociology* 57 (September 1951): 169; Doll, *The Ephrata Cloister*, p. 7; Robert S. Fogarty, *American Utopianism* (Itasca, Ill.: Peacock, 1972), p. 2.

23. Sachse, vol. 2, pp. 193-202; Lamech and Agrippa, p. 88.
24. After the establishment of Ephrata, he developed his theories of abstention and marriage further, and formulated his theological doctrine in three books which he published. He connected his thoughts about marriage and abstention with man's condition after the Fall and his chances for salvation. His theory did not differ from the Pauline doctrine, adopted by most churches and sects and according to which although abstention is preferable, marriage is permitted (see Corinthians 7: 25-38).
25. Carpenter, pp. 81-89; Sachse, vol. 1, pp. 468-74; Lamech and Agrippa, p. 5; Klein, pp. 110-11.
26. Klein, pp. 112-16; Sachse, vol. 1, pp. 261, 307-11, 359; Sachse, vol. 2, pp. 171, 184-85, 328; Fogarty, p. 7.
27. Carpenter, p. 98; Sachse, vol. 2, pp. 261-65, 297-308; Hinds, pp. 22-23.
28. Lamech and Agrippa, p. 4; Sachse, vol. 2, pp. 128-60, Klein, pp. 144-48; Russell P. Getz, "Music in the Ephrata Cloister," *Communal Societies* 2 (Journal of the National Historic Communal Societies Assoc.) (Autumn 1982): 30-38.
29. Doll, *The Ephrata Cloister*, p. 11.
30. Sachse, vol. 1, pp. 352-64.
31. Doll, "Social and Economic Organization," pp. 174-75; Sachse, vol. 2, pp. 114-15, 410; Holloway, p. 47; Hinds, p. 17; Carpenter, pp. 99-100.
32. Sachse, vol. 2, pp. 115-18, 214-21; Carpenter, pp. 100-110; Klein, pp. 154-56, 165-66.
33. Sachse, vol. 2, pp. 268-71; Klein, p. 171.
34. Jacob John Sessler, *Communal Pietism among Early American Moravians* (New York: Holt, 1933; New York: AMS Press, 1971), p. 42; Sachse, vol. 1, pp. 290-94, 427-48.
35. Fogarty, pp. 3-6; Sachse, vol. 2, pp. 312-30; Doll, *The Ephrata Cloister*, pp. 7-8.
36. Klein, pp. 180-81; Carpenter, p. 111.
37. Sachse, vol. 2, pp. 386-87; 401-3; 408-9; 426-32; 435-36; Zerfass, p. 46.
38. Sachse, vol. 2, pp. 419-32.
39. Sachse, vol. 1, p. 472, vol. 2, pp. 432-26; Carpenter, pp. 104, 105, 111.
40. Herbert Wishbey, *Pioneer Prophetess: Jemima Wilkinson, the Public Universal Friend* (Ithaca, N.Y.: Cornell University Press, 1964); Hinds, pp. 27-28; Holloway, pp. 59, 60-63; Everet Webber, *Escape to Utopia: The Communal Movement in America* (New York: Hastings House, 1959), pp. 77-78; J.F.C. Harrison, *Robert Owen and the Owenites in Britain and America: The Quest for the New Moral World* (London: Routledge & Kegan Paul, 1969), p. 98; Carpenter, pp. 103-13, 119-25, 145-58; Sachse, vol. 2, pp. 360-71.

3

The Shakers: American Religious Communes

On the eve of the American Revolution, the followers of a small group of Shakers reached the western frontier of New York State. They had acquired the name *Shakers* because of the religious frenzy which shook them during their rituals. The period was one of religious fervor and revivals, and the Shakers soon had a large following. Hundreds of believers from different ways of life joined them. A few years later they would be the nucleus of a large communal movement, the most extensive and stable of all the American communes (with the exception of the Hutterites, whose communes have existed for over 450 years, but most of them outside of America). They would play a vital part in the crystallization of the communal tradition in the United States during the last century.

First Steps: Ann Lee's Manifestation

The Shakers first set foot in America in 1774 as a small group of nine immigrants from Manchester, England, with their spiritual leader Ann Lee. They belonged to a small esoteric set of Quakers of French Protestant origin. They had appeared in the second half of the seventeenth century in the Cevennes Mountains in southern France. The sect, known as the Camisards or the French Prophets, expected the millennium and Christ's Second Coming while believing that the prophecy was given to both men and women and that the Messiah would appear as a woman. At the end of the seventeenth century, when Protestants were persecuted in France, they fled across the English Channel and found a haven among the English Quakers and Methodists. Their message found favor mainly with the lower classes of artisans and workers. Only a few of the upper middle classes joined them.[1]

In the 1740s the French influence waned and only one group in Manchester, led by James and Jane Wardley, remained true to their doctrine. This couple, ex-Quakers and tailors by profession, added their own English brand of Methodist and Quaker tradition. One of the most outstanding characteristics of the group was their religious ecstasy, which would manifest itself in violent trembling and agitation of body and limbs during their rituals. They thus acquired the name of the *Shaking Quakers.*[2] In 1758, the family of John Lee, a poor blacksmith from Manchester, joined them. Their daughter, Ann Lee, took to the sect's beliefs with ardor. Participating in the sect's rituals, she became obsessed with religion very early in life.

As the daughter of a family of very limited means Ann Lee had to add to the scanty income of her father. Lacking even the most elementary education she worked from childhood in cotton factories. She found solace in the spiritual world of the sect, its visions, revelations, and "tribulations of the soul." She soon stood out because of her religious fanaticism and her abstention from anything she regarded as sin. It led her on to reject all carnal vanities.[3] A few years after joining Wardley's sect, she was compelled by her family to marry Abraham Stanley, a village blacksmith. In time four children were born to them but all died in their infancy. Perhaps it was this traumatic experience, which Ann Lee regarded as heavenly retribution for her carnal relations with her husband, that made her transfer all her powers to the religious activity in Wardley's group.

Though remaining Stanley's legal wife, she no longer cohabitated with him. Her intensive religious experience, her frequent revelations, and her speaking out against sin, soon made her the central figure in the sect which under her influence became even more hostile to the church establishment. The sect was regarded as a public menace and was persecuted by the authorities. Ann Lee was arrested in 1772, and during her imprisonment she experienced a divine revelation in which Christ instilled her with his powers and with the authority to preach celibacy and purity and to found a church which would fight Satan's temptations and open the Gates of Heaven to its followers.[4]

Her imprisonment and the many instances of her "miraculous deliverance" from danger and death caused the members of her sect to regard her as a saint and martyr. After reporting the divine revelation she was accepted as the Shakers' spiritual leader; they considered this as the actual Second Coming of Christ through a woman. Under her leadership the Shakers' missionary zeal increased and their members were called upon to fight sin, to live ascetically, and to practice strict purity and start their new life by confessing to their sins.

This change in the sect caused some internal soul searching. Among those who could not accept the new zeal and left were the Wardleys. The members who remained loyal to Ann Lee continued their ecstatic rituals in closed meetings, avoiding public preaching in order not to invite persecution. These limitations and their enforced isolation brought about a drastic decrease in their membership and caused them to opt for emigration. Ann Lee was the living spirit behind this move but she had accomplices among other members who experienced revelations promising them a bright future in the New World.

Thus, in an atmosphere of exaltation, a group of nine members led by Ann Lee embarked in May 1774 on their way to America.[5] With the departure of this little band, the Shakers soon ceased to exist in England. When they arrived in New York the Shakers scattered in order to find a living. However they kept in touch. Ann Lee found a job as laundress and a maid. Some time later her husband deserted her, not wishing to continue what he considered unnatural bonds.[6]

During their first year in New York, the Shakers established a permanent framework. Being isolated from the surrounding society because of their way of life and their doctrines, they felt the need to find a secluded place where they could practice their beliefs unmolested. They found it in Niskeyuna, on the Hudson River, Upstate New York, and the land was bought by John Hocknell, one of the brothers who had come with Ann Lee from England and who was a wealthy man. This was to be the sect's settlement for the next three years. They lived in a log cabin completely isolated in the middle of a dense forest and this was where Ann Lee joined them in 1776, after having separated from her husband.

It was the turbulent period of the American Revolution. The English-born Shakers, who practiced pacifism and lived completely isolated in their forest, were often suspected of being spies and set upon by hostile crowds. They kept to themselves, and their doctrine slowly crystallized. Guided by Ann Lee they established a daily routine, expecting prospective converts and the fulfillment of Ann Lee's revelation.[7] During the War of Independence certain circumstances brought about the bridging of the gap between the Shakers and their neighbors. Within a short period many joined the sect. It was the period of the Revivals which had invaded the frontier states since the 1740s.[8] It swept across the land and brought thousands of people to open air conventions and prayer meetings. Those were usually held in the open and would last several days. An atmosphere of religious ecstasy and excitement prevailed, and many of the participants experienced revelations. They expected immediate salvation and, searching for new ways and new beliefs, they left their established churches in order to found The New Light sects.

In 1779, the area adjacent to the Shaker community hosted revival meetings that lasted throughout the summer. It was initiated by a dissident sect of New Light Baptists, but many others joined—Methodists, Presbyterians, and Old Light Baptists among them. When the summer was over and with it the revival meetings, many of the New Light Baptists were frustrated. A group was formed to find a way to continue their religious fervor in their daily life. Their leader was Joseph Meacham, born in Connecticut and a graduate of Yale University. While searching for a framework to establish their group relations, they came across the nearby Shaker community by chance.[9]

During the winter and spring of 1780, Meacham's followers often visited the Shakers. They were joined by others who were motivated by curiosity about the recluses' way of life. The Shakers practiced hospitality, systematically preaching their doctrine. The small group regarded their visitors as the realization of Ann Lee's vision on mass conversion in the New World. Many testimonies have survived in Shakers' writings and in others' about the discussions and disputes during those visits.

The Shakers attempted to elaborate on their new doctrinal insight without presuming any systematic theology. Ann Lee was the prime speaker. For the first time in America, their tenets were publicly presented. They rejected the dogma of the Holy Trinity and instead proclaimed that "Christ was manifested in male and female form" and that the Second Coming would be in the shape of a woman. Resurrection, salvation, and the kingdom of heaven were evident by revival of "proper spiritual sensations," and the kingdom of heaven would arrive as a result of individual purification—confessing sins, overcoming carnality, and living a moral, abstinent life. They believed that the Second Coming was already evident in their settlements which had been cleansed of all sin. The combination of their communal way of life and their special doctrine attracted many of the revivalists. As soon as the Shakers realized this they adopted the collective way as a predominant element in their spreading the gospel. Concentrating mainly on the schismatic sects in their area, they would invite them to visit their collective community in Niskeyuna. The visitors would stay for several days and the time would mainly be devoted to discussions of religion and to a first-hand acquaintance with the detailed practice of their faith. Some of the guests testified that they were most impressed by the Shakers' communal way of life, their modesty, celibacy, and rejection of materialism. But most were impressed by their hospitality. They regarded the Shakers as a holy community and "the people of God." It was clear that they lived according to what they preached.[10]

It may be questioned what had greater impact on the sects of the New Light—the theological discussions, the Shakers' mode of life, or Ann Lee's charismatic personality, but it is clear that the meetings between the Shakers and the schismatic-Baptist sects of the New Light in that log cabin in the forest of Niskeyuna during the winter of 1780 was a turning point for the Shakers in the United States. The joining of Joseph Meacham, the Baptist preacher, and his group, was the beginning of the Shakers' Americanization and the end of their isolation. They started on their missionary work in the nearby areas. There was some danger involved in leaving their backwoods home, because in 1780 the War of Independence was still going on and the Shakers, like other Englishmen, and especially being pacifists on principle, would often get caught up in confrontations with the American militia. Furthermore, they boycotted all government and legal authorities and were regarded by those as law breakers. Their leaders were eventually accused of spying for the British forces and arrested. Rather than harming their reputation, this enhanced it and they became famous. The confrontation with American legal authorities was a further step in their adjusting to American society.

A few years later the Shaker movement expanded, mainly on the East Coast.[11] Between 1781 and 1783 three pairs of Shaker missionaries set out to proselytize in various communities in New York State and in other parts of northeast New England. With the help of a core of believers from among those who had visited Niskeyuna in the winter of 1780, they set up a number of Shaker communities. It was Ann Lee's finest hour. She was now called "Mother Ann" by her followers, and even though the war was not yet over and the Shakers often persecuted, suffering from every kind of deprivation, she continued on foot, disregarding all physical hardships.[12]

Ann Lee died in 1784, about a year after returning from her travels. She was also depressed by the death of her brother, William Lee, in July of that year. He had been a pillar of strength of the English group and the loss of her principal supporter deeply affected her. Within a few weeks apart the Shakers were bereft of their founder and her chief companion. It was a hard blow, and even though Ann Lee had never spoken of immortality, her followers, who regarded her as a Messiah, were deeply disappointed by her death, and a few even left the sects.[13] Nevertheless, the group itself soon took heart and organized itself to consolidate Ann Lee's gospel and charismatic heritage.

James Whittaker became their recognized leader if for a short time only, until his death in 1787. He was born in England and had come all the way with Ann Lee. During his leadership the Shakers were transformed from an esoteric group of foreigners to an organized religious sect calling themselves "The United Society of Believers in Christ's Second Appearing." After his death the leadership passed on to two indigenous Americans, a man and a woman, and the English hegemony was over. Joseph Meacham, born in Connecticut, established the dual leadership and chose Lucy Wright, who was born in Pittsfield, Massachusetts, to share it with him. Soon the native Americans outnumbered the English founders of the sect. It was the first time in the history of the U.S. communes that an immigrant sect became an American one. Simultaneously with the Americanization process, the sect began to get organized on a communal basis and to crystallize their way of life.[14] That was part of the transition toward church structure, which developed after Ann Lee's death in order to defend the sect from alien pressure and persecution, and also as a way of preaching the gospel.

Collective consumption among the Shakers preceded the establishment of their communal settlements. It started in Niskeyuna in 1775, when they felt the need for expressing their unity of motivation, beliefs, and interests through sharing: "We who are many are one body, for we all partake of the one bread" (1 Corinthians 10/17). The process of evolving a full communal property, even though it had spiritual roots in their beliefs, was formed under the special circumstances they encountered during their missionary work. This entailed a solid material base from which they could set out on their sermons and preaching crusades. In the gradual process of leaving their private homesteads the Shakers incorporated them into collective units. Those of the Shakers who had no possessions and who had been living in the homes of the more affluent ones now moved into the new settlements, which had been constructed a priori as communes. In September 1787 the first Shaker commune was established in Mount Lebanon, when 100 settlers moved there.

Mount Lebanon

The land for the settlers was purchased by some of the new affluent members, and the buildings were planned for communal living quarters from the start. It was the first of eight other Shaker settlements in New York State, New England, Connecticut, Massachusetts, Maine, and New Hampshire. They were established one after the other between 1787 and 1794, at the time of James Meacham and Lucy Wright's leadership.[15]

The Shakers' way of life on the communes, their economy, and organization developed gradually through the needs and experience of the first years. They had no theory to begin with; like all other religious communes, they were inspired by the Scriptures and the tradition of early Christianity. The two leaders'—Meacham and Wright's—contribution to the form and the set of rules of the communes was decisive. They initiated the move to Mount Lebanon and lived there, leading the experiment of spiritual, social, and economic communal life. Within two years the mode of communal life in Mount Lebanon crystallized, and it became the model for all other Shaker communes. Most lands were contributed by wealthy farmers who earlier had given shelter to the homeless nomadic believers of the sect. Their property—whether capital, working tools, far-stock, etc.—was consolidated into one communal holding.

Every Shaker "family" included between 80 to 100 men and women and was managed on a basis of communal production and consumption. There were usually several "families" in each commune and they practiced economic cooperation and mutual aid. At first there was no formal covenant to govern property relationships, just verbal agreements. Gradually, a communal covenant evolved and was formalized seven years after the establishment of Mount Lebanon, based on the social and organizational experience of that model commune.[16] This covenant established the spiritual hierarchy within the sect and the organization of formal worship which would include the first set of "gospel orders" to be obeyed by all who belonged to the "United Society of Believers in Christ's Second Appearance."

In the late 1780s the Shakers were no longer a small, isolated community who were all equally committed to the cause. There was a growing periphery of believers who, although attracted to the Shaker way of life and doctrines, did not join their communal venture. There arose a need to find a compromise between the perfectionist attitude and the peripheral groups. To facilitate this, three gradual stages of membership were established:

1. The first stage, the Novitiate Order, was made up of the peripheral members who accepted the main tenets of faith but preferred to continue in their former mode of private property and family life. Being members of the United Society, they accepted the spiritual authority of the elders and were called upon to contribute from time to time to the sect's activities.
2. The second stage, the Junior Order, was made up of those who had joined a Shaker commune, sharing in its production and consumption, but were allowed to keep their property yet not to use it. They adhered to the accepted rules and daily routine and had the same privileges as full members. Their only limitation was that they could not be elected to any of the spiritual or economic positions in the community.
3. The third stage, the Senior Order or Church Order, was the final stage of full membership. It included those who had handed over their entire property to the commune, denounced all external family ties, and accepted complete communal commitment. They were regarded as "perfect" members and in Shaker theology were living in a spiritual kingdom of heaven.

Attaining the third stage was controlled. Minors could only serve as disciples and adults had to give up all their property and sever external family ties. An additional condition was that they pay all their debts before being accepted as full members. Whenever one of them left the commune he would get only a severance grant. This stage of full membership encompassed most of the Shakers; the peripheral circles were always a minority and in time completely disappeared.[17]

From the early days of Shakers' communal life it had no elements of democracy. It started with the establishment of a spiritual hierarchy. Their leaders' authority was a divine gift. After the death of the first spiritual leaders, the "ministry of four," two men and two women, was established. Mount Lebanon was the seat of the ministry which had absolute authority over the church, the communities, and all families. In addition there were the trustees, who were in charge of property, economics, and trade with the external world.

The trustees had to report to the ministry, who had granted them their authority. Supervision was efficient and functional, without any democratic aspects on the local or church level. The ministry appointed the spiritual leaders on the communes. These were the "elders," who were in charge of managing the communes. They in turn appointed work managers, the "deacons," who were responsible for the economic, financial, and representative matters of the commune. The elders' authority was absolute, and they appointed those who would take over the authority from them.[18]

According to the principle of celibacy, there was a strict separation between men and women. Although they lived in the same communal quarters, a separate corridor and staircase divided the men's wing from the women's. There were strict rules for arranging all social and economic relations between the brothers and sisters of the Shaker family. They were intended to minimize contact between the sexes and absolutely prevent any intimate relations. In spite of these similarities, the communes should not be considered monasteries, the men and women who lived under one roof were members of a "family." Their social relations were well defined and included communal cultural activities and religious rituals such as thc famous Shaker dances. The family functioned on the same basis as in a typical monogamous family—men did the physical jobs in the fields and workshops, while the women were in charge of the housework; cleaning, cooking, washing, and mending. Only during seasonal work would women lend a hand in the field.[19] Having abolished the biological monogamous family, there was the question of what to do about children in the Shaker society: how to absorb and educate them, and what standing in the rigid social hierarchy they would have. A set of rules was established from the first years. Children lived in a separate wing or house, supervised by elders.[20] Since there was no natural increase, most children were absorbed together with their parents or were charity cases and orphans who were integrated into the local Shaker community's school.

Expansion

James Meacham was the Shakers' spiritual leader until he died in 1796, when Lucy Wright, his coleader, took over. During their period of leadership the first settlements were consolidated and the Shakers' missionary activity led to the founding of three additional communes until the end of the eighteenth century. In the beginning of the nineteenth century there existed eleven settlements which numbered about 1,600 members. Within three decades the Shakers had branched out from a small immigrant group of nine members to become an extensive movement.

The Shakers' influence was enhanced mainly by the reputation of their settlements, which though remote, they were not isolated. In the beginning their neighbors were suspicious, even hostile. Yet, this soon made way for genuine admiration. The attractive settlements, the orderly, clean, and well-tended farms, and the collective way of life, but especially the Shaker dance at their rituals, all attracted many visitors and generated curiosity. Among those were people of high standing. Explorers of the frontier described in their travelogues what they had seen in the Shaker settlements and these, in turn, brought more tourists. There are scores of book chapters as well as articles in American and European newspapers that give a detailed description of the Shakers.[21]

Timothy Dwight, president of Yale University, one of the outstanding intellectuals of his time, visited the Shakers in 1799. He returned on several occasions and noted down his impressions in a travel book published in 1822. He marvelled at the solid buildings and the economic prosperity of Mount Lebanon. He admired the Shakers' diligence and many innovations at work and production. Nevertheless, he criticized their odd religion and theological eccentricity. A similar impression is given in the travel book of Benjamin Silliman, a renowned Yale professor of chemistry and natural sciences. Silliman described the prosperous settlements but derided their religious practices. However, he praised their collective way of life and their contribution to society when they gave shelter to the underprivileged, the lonely, and the destitute.[22]

In 1805 a new period opened for the Shakers. They expanded, new members joined them, new settlements were established, and they branched out in new directions. This development also was connected with a religious revival that encompassed the southwestern frontier states of those days: Ohio, Kentucky, and Indiana. It was the third wave of revivalism since the early nineteenth century and was also the result of a massive migration of settlers who had left the infertile hilly areas of New England for the fertile plains of the West. Former loyalties to sect and church were undermined, and the revival movement encompassed even more tempestuous open air meetings in the forests which were to become famous throughout the United States. Here, as well, sectional seceders searched for new meaning and found the Shakers, who by that time were already established in a dozen stable communes. They sent missionaries among the revivalists to spread the Shaker gospel.[23]

On January 1, 1805, three Shaker missionaries set out on foot, with one horse that carried their possessions, to visit the massive revival meetings and spread the gospel. In three months they crossed over 1,200 miles and reached Ohio on the Kentucky border. Their mission became a success when some of the local revival preachers joined the Shaker movement. The most outstanding was the Reverend McNemar, a Presbyterian preacher from Ohio, who in 1803 had led his congregation to join the New Light Baptists and later, discovering the Shakers, joined them with his entire congregation. After this success, the emissaries returned to Mount Lebanon in order to raise funds for new settlements for their followers and also to get additional members to spread the gospel. Their movement expanded and many joined in Ohio as well as in Kentucky, Indiana, and Tennessee.[24]

By 1810 five new communes were established in those areas—Watervliet and Union Village in Ohio, Pleasant Hill and South Union in Kentucky, and Busro in Indiana. It was not to be a simple venture; the neighbors were suspicious of the strangers and their odd religion and customs. Most hostile were the seceders of the New Light sect, who first approached the Shakers but then could not identify with them. They started a vicious and slanderous attack on them, thus causing the Shakers to be persecuted and even to be set on by a southern lynch mob. Those first years in the Southwest were similar to what had happened to the Shakers in Massachusetts in the 1780s. However, they succeeded in overcoming the persecutions and pogroms and earned their neighbors' admiration, with their quiet and solid ways.[25]

New waves of revivalism in those areas between 1817 and 1827 expanded the Shakers' movement, and two new settlements were established, one in Ohio, the other, which was to be the last one, in New York, in 1826. (Two further settlements were established in the 1880s in Georgia and Florida, but they existed for a short while only and should not be counted among the Shaker communities.)

In the 1830s and 1840s another religious upheaval swept the East Coast. The millenial calculations of William Miller fixed 1843 as the year of the Second Coming of Christ. Many followed his call and readied themselves for the cosmic change. However, their disappointment was followed by a massive secession and about 300 of them found their way to the Shaker communes, which had managed to institutionalize their millenial expectations through their way of life that prepared them for salvation and the kingdom of heaven; most of them were small farmers from the agricultural areas of New England, New York, and the Midwest.[26] It may be assumed that most of the new members were young men and women. If they arrived with their families, they would have to separate within the different framework of the commune. The Shakers knew no racial discrimination. Ex-slaves could join, but only a few opted for a communal life. South Union had one Black family, and located in a southern state, the community suffered because of this.[27]

Formulation of the Shakers' Tenets

Crystallization of Theology

At the beginning of the nineteenth century, after the Shakers had expanded westward, they realized that they would have to formulate their principles systematically. Until then their lives had been regulated by the oral dogma of their spiritual leaders—Lee, Whittaker, Meacham and Wright. Now the missionaries encountered followers as well as opposition, and in the heated debates they felt the need for an authorized doctrine. The rapid growth of the Shakers added many members who had never known the sect's founders and their spiritual leaders. A group of Ohio elders under S. Youngs undertook to formulate the tenets of the Shaker sect.

In 1808 they published their book *The Testimony of Christ's Second Appearing*, which was to be the authorized text of the Shakers' religious principles. The treatise included a theological and some historiosophical chapters and was compiled with an encyclopaedic knowledge which testified to its author's background. Between 1808 and 1823 several editions were published, and it was distributed in thousands of copies throughout the country, even in secular circles. President Thomas Jefferson wrote in an acknowledgement that he had read the book with interest and deep appreciation of its authors' erudition.

The Shaker theology, as expressed in *The Testimony*, included several radical elements. It rejected the doctrine of the Holy Trinity, of predestination, of salvation through Jesus Christ, and of bodily resurrection. The deity in their theology was manifest in male and female form like all other beings in nature. With all their respect for the Scriptures, those were not regarded as a source of the absolute truth. Just like the universalists and perfectionists of their generation, the Shakers claimed that man was too good to be condemned to eternal damnation because of the Fall. They believed that man could attain salvation through the means of grace, confession, celibacy, pain and suffering, and spiritual purity. According to them, the Pentecostal Church in Jerusalem, which lived a harmonious communal life, was closest to total sublimity. Therefore, those in search of salvation had to reject the sins of the world and, imitating the early Christians, establish a communal society.[28]

Communal Principles

A comprehensive formulation of the communal principles of the Shakers was first published in 1818. Ten years after *The Testimony*, John Donlevy, a Shaker scholar from Pleasant Hill, Kentucky, published *The Manifesto*. He stressed the Shakers' principle that "doctrine is not enough, belief in the brotherhood of man is of no significance unless it is accompanied by a way of life in which daily actions are in accordance with this belief." True followers of Christ differ from "worldly" people not only because of their doctrinal insights and the rejection of carnality but because of spiritual and material communalism. Their "communal holding," with its religious elements and collective property, is the materialization of equality and brotherly love combined with total selflessness. *The Manifesto* gave a detailed formulation of the Shaker way of communal life as it had crystallized after forty years of experience, and it became their constitution.[29]

Rituals

Parallel to the formulation of Shaker theology and communal principles, the religious rituals were formalized. The spontaneous eruptions, violent trembling, and mighty agitation of body and limbs which had characterized the ritualists' early years gave way to more controlled modes of worship. The "leaps" were incorporated in rhythmic dances in which the whole community would participate, though the sexes were strictly separate, dancing side by side without touching. The dances were accompanied by religious singing, and both became the focal point of the Shaker ritual. That had been the tendency at the time of Lucy Wright's leadership in the early nineteenth century. This Shaker "dance and song" drew visitors from far and wide; they were welcome to join. In the 1820s this tourist attraction was turned into a theatrical show.[30] The music and dances of the Shakers underwent change. From the ecstatic individualistic song it became a melodic rhythmic lyric to be sung by the choir as an integral part of the religious ritual. Shaker songs were unique in that they drew inspiration from the local American folksongs, maintaining their simple lyric motives without transcribing them into vocalized poliphonic compositions. The Shakers avoided using instruments until the nineteenth century. Inspired by their moral aesthetic approach their songs remained simple, following the notion of "simple is beautiful." They were collectors of folksongs and airs. Their repertoire was astonishing, and musicologues have laid their hands on not less than 10,000 lyrics. No other sect has surpassed them, and the reason is twofold: (1) the fostering of ecstatic, spontaneous singing; (2) the adaption of tunes and songs to the commune's various functions. Many members composed during a moment's inspiration and ecstasy, without any formal musical education. In the nineteenth century Isack Newton Youngs was the only one among them with a reputation as a composer. The Shakers had their own special method of notes in which they wrote their hymns. At a later stage they adopted the usual notation. An important stage in their music was the adaptation of singing to the dance steps during their religious rituals. Among their hymns there were ballads which had been adapted in order to transmit the Shakers' religious and communal ideology. Their rhythmic melodies were easy to memorize and were one of the ways of enhancing the individual's communal commitment through a shared experience.[31]

The Shakers' Prosperous Farms

From the establishment of their first communes, the Shakers excelled in their economic activities. Their farms stood out from among their neighbors' in their size, their solidly constructed buildings, the order and cleanliness of their farmyards, their well-tended fields, vegetable gardens and orchards, and their large and functional farmhouses. This impressive prosperity was the result of Shaker diligence, hard labor and professionalism. Their moralistic-religious attitude toward work and industry contributed more than anything to their economic success.

Many members were practical Yankees, farmers and artisans who had contributed their property as well as their experience to the collective. On the commune they found fertile soil for their expertise and were soon encouraged to acquire new skills. One could often notice men and women rotating at several jobs, all of them executed with a high degree of professionalism. Their creative dexterity was much appreciated, not only for economic reasons, which weighed heavily since poverty and asceticism were unacceptable, but mainly because their doctrine abhorred sloth and idleness. Work was of vital, even sacred importance, in the Shakers' spiritual and religious world. They devoted heart and soul to their labors. This was their most profound commitment to the commune—"Put your hands to work and your heart to God"—Mother Ann preached, and it had become one of their main imperatives. The sanctity of work was not meant to weigh one down but to inspire with values and beliefs; it should provide the daily economic and social necessities. In Sister Margot Frost's words, "Many mistakenly believe that the Shakers are a group of people who have made work their religion. However, bearing one another's burden entails the active participation of each and every Shaker with a will and the utmost dexterity."

The Shakers aspired to achieve harmony between physical and intellectual work. There was no status symbol attached to managerial or spiritual-religious positions. The elders, even though they were at the top of the sect's hierarchy, would work as artisans or farmers simultaneous to their spiritual occupation. They all industriously aspired to do the most efficient job. They searched for ways to make work easier and more pleasant, while increasing production and improving its quality.[32]

Their work-day was long, but this did not prevent the Shakers from setting aside time for reading, writing, and religious rituals. They tried very hard to avoid unnecessary tedium at work. Achieving higher economic standards than most of the neighboring farms may have been the result of a high work morale, better methods of production, and the communal set up. The Shakers excelled in the use of working implements and improved their workshops in order to provide their members with a pleasant place of work.

Joseph Meacham claimed: "We have the right to improve man's inventions in order to exploit their full potential but not for vain glory." This approach evolved into a rich tradition of improvements and inventions, and all those who study the Shaker's economy are impressed with the enormous number of machines and tools they fashioned. A round saw was invented in Watervliet by a Shaker woman, a washing machine in Canterbury, a flat reed broom in Mount Lebanon, later produced on a commercial basis in most Shaker settlements. There were many inventions on a smaller scale such as a nail-cutting machine, a lathe to produce broomsticks, an automatic spring, and a propeller for a water turbine. The Shakers also were creative in other fields; their gardens produced a variety of medical herbs and seeds of specially developed plants. In their carpentry shops they produced furniture still renowned today.

This is only a short list of Shaker inventions. E.D. Andrews devoted most of his life to the study of the Shakers and documentation of their movement. In his books *The People Called Shakers* and *The Community Industries of the Shakers*, he lists all their inventions. Their variety and extent are amazing, especially when we take into account that it was a small group of people with no materialistic incentive who managed to do it all.[33]

The Shakers regarded their settlements as places where the kingdom of heaven had been realized and therefore paid special attention to their order and cleanliness. Ann Lee used to say that, "Order is a cardinal heavenly law and it protects souls." And, "Work is sacred so are order and cleanliness." The result was evident in every corner of the Shaker communes, whether in living quarters or public places. One of the Shaker rules of daily life used to be "Clean your room properly, after all good souls don't dwell in filth, there is none in heaven."[34] This rule also applied to the workshops, fields, and orchards.

There were several reasons for the Shakers' economy to be based on agriculture. As a result of their wish to retreat from densely populated areas they established an autarchic system; also, many farmers had contributed their lands to the commune upon joining the Shakers. Compelled by their urge to turn the wilderness into a fertile garden, a heavenly place on earth, the Shakers developed a deep affinity to the land and their fields, and orchards were lovingly tended. Order and cleanliness prevailed everywhere, making a great impression on all visitors. The author W.H. Dixon mentions after having visited Mount Lebanon, that for the Shakers, their barn is like the Temple for the Jews.[35] Their architecture was solidly constructed without any frill. After seeing all the Shakers' material and spiritual creations, their adage "simple is beautiful" may be paraphrased "beauty is in simplicity."[36]

The development of agriculture was followed by workshops that in time absorbed many of the artisans who joined the Shaker communes. After supplying their own needs they began to market their surplus, mainly household goods such as furniture, brooms, clothing, etc., utilizing the available raw material. They produced conserves from their agricultural surplus, but they were best known for their medicinal herbs and vegetable seedlings. They never produced more than they could comfortably do in their small workshops, and they never compromised as to quality. Their produce was also simply and aesthetically designed.[37]

The Shakers' System of Education

Until 1808 no special attention was paid to the sect's educational activities. The children who joined the commune with their parents were separated from them and absorbed into the Shaker family. Boys and girls lived apart. They were in charge of "adoptive brothers" who prepared them for integration into the "family" and its various labors. After 1808 special thought was invested in establishing educational principles and institutions. The emphasis was put on character forming, moral values, and the development of self-discipline. Only elementary subjects were taught and the practical arts were fostered. Higher education and the classics were considered to be impractical, "filling the brain with sawdust."

The Shakers did not intend their children to become scholars, as that would foster doubt and undermine their belief. The aim was to integrate the children into the productive life of their community. Yet they did not ignore individual talent, which was considered to be a gift from heaven, and gifted children were fostered though not in excess to the usual activities.

The organization of their educational system continued from 1813 to 1817. The first to be opened were evening classes which gradually extended to afternoons as well. Day schools were opened in 1817. They were based on the Lancaster method, in which one teacher with the help of young assistants was in charge of a large number of pupils. These day schools functioned during the four winter months for boys and during spring and summer for girls. This enabled the children to continue their framework as needed.[38]

In 1821 Seth Wells was put in charge of supervising all the Shakers' schools. He had been an experienced teacher before joining the sect and contributed much to improve the educational system. In 1823 he initiated the publication of a book, *The Summary View of the Millenial Church*, which deals with the children's behavior, the Shakers' educational doctrine, and the values which should guide educators.

The principles of his educational doctrine were the fostering of honesty, punctuality, diligence, cleanliness, order, and discipline, but also tolerance, politeness, respect, and the love of God and man. Wells added mathematics, geography, astronomy, agricultural chemistry, and music to the curriculum without undermining the vocational foundation of the schools. He also opened the schools to outside pupils. This put the Shakers' schools under the supervision of the state's educational inspectors, who spread the reputation of their high level. Some of the neighborhood children who were absorbed in the Shakers' schools would later join as members, but their numbers were never substantial and in time even decreased. The Shakers considered their schools to be a bridge to the world and staffed them with professional teachers who were all meticulously chosen for their educational qualities. It was not by chance that their schools had a good reputation and attracted many children of families from the general society, among them also children from charity institutions and orphanages.[39]

Contemporaries' Impressions

The Shaker phenomenon and their communal settlements drew the attention of many a reporter and other people who were sensitive to social change, even though theirs was not the only movement of its kind. In the beginning of the nineteenth century separatist German communes were established in the United States—the first was Harmony. In the 1820s visitors were greatly impressed by the social aspect of the communities and stressed the inherent advantage of the communal economy. The number of intellectuals, writers, poets, philosophers, economists, and politicians who visited Shaker settlements and wrote about their impressions increased. Charles Dickens was the only one who found nothing commendable in them and stressed the dreariness and the drabness of the Shakers with whom he met. He even claimed that they managed to oppress everything beautiful and left no hope in life.

In the 1830s and 1840s, years of religious and social upheavals, intellectuals were on the lookout for an alternative society. It was only natural that they should single out the Shakers and Harmony when describing the American society. One of the outstanding books published in 1834 was Harriet Martineau's comprehensive work, in which a long chapter was devoted to the Shakers and Rappists. This English woman was extremely impressed with the economic success of their collective settlements. Another comprehensive description was published in 1841 by James Buckingham, who after a visit to the United States wrote *America, Historical Statistic and Descriptive*, and *The Eastern and Western States of the America.* Buckingham visited communes of several religious sects comparing them with each other. He reached the conclusion that the communal way of life had a great potential and could pave the way to overcome the evils of private property. He regarded them as a model for an alternative way of life and remarked that the Shaker and Rappist communes might have been much larger had they not adhered to their esoteric beliefs and celibate way of life.[40]

In 1845 Friedrich Engels cited the American communes as a concrete example for the viability of a collective society in which private property had been abolished. He lectured on this in public and later published his ideas in the *Deutsches Burgerbuch* (1845). He disputed with those who claimed that communism was not feasible by citing the example of the Shaker communes, their peaceful and moral way of life, and their economic superiority.[41] For a social writer such as Robert Owen, the Shakers' collective way of life served as a model for his utopian ideal. He hoped that his experiments would succeed much as the Shakers' had. Later, when all his ventures had failed, some of his followers joined the Shakers' settlements. In the 1840s scores of Fourierist utopian settlements were established. They soon disintegrated and some of their frustrated members turned toward Shaker communes, even though Fourierist leaders in the United States were extremely critical of their ways and ideology. For the Shakers this was a passing episode; their human reservoir, then as before, were the recurring waves of revivals on the East Coast. Even though no new settlements were established, the number of members grew significantly to about 4,000 members in 18 settlements between 1840 and 1850.[42]

Spiritualism

In the 1830s a change occurred among the Shakers. Though the organizational and economic structure of the commune had remained constant since Joseph Meacham's days, other significant changes in their spiritual life caused the Shakers to purge their communes of embittered and disloyal elements. This strengthened the internal, spiritual commitment and was the beginning of a new period of revivals as intense as the preceding ones. It all began with a kind of spiritualism in 1837, in Watervliet, New York. When children were overcome by the ague-like trance of leaping and dancing while uttering mumbo-jumbo in all tongues,[43] it was considered by the elders as a spiritualist visitation—the children seen as mediums in contact with spirits from the hereafter. Soon adults too got carried away, and the phenomenon spread like wildfire, and the leadership did nothing to control it. Furthermore, spiritualism was presented as the spiritual manifestation and reappearance of Ann Lee, who had returned to her congregation in order to put things right. Several of the mediums through whose voice Ann Lee spoke, criticized the laxity concerning the laws of celibacy and the lack of frugality of some of the younger members. However, there was also outspoken criticism on general matters such as the neglect of equipment, lack of cleanliness, and indifference to the communal property. In 1840 there was a direct "intervention" of Ann Lee through a medium concerning economic matters. She gave instructions to curtail the industrial activity which entailed extensive contact with the external world and to concentrate on agriculture. In the same year the eating of meat was forbidden and many of the new modes of behavior. There was a tendency to promote equality between the elders and regular members. Life on the communes was immediately affected by these messages from the netherworld, the spiritual one, in which Shakers ruled supreme. Historical figures such as George Washington, William Penn, Neron (who had repented), Alexander the Great (who had turned modest), and Napoleon, apparently all belonged to the Shaker hegemony.

Of great interest is the relationship between Shakers and Indians at the spiritualist level. They would discuss matters of modern civilization with their guests from a nether world. The fate of the Indians had worried the Shakers for a long time since they had expanded their missionary activity among tribes in the West. The Shakers were very critical of the extermination policy of the U.S. government and its institutions.[44] The apex of spiritualism was the appearance of "holy Mother Wisdom," who was believed to be the female incarnation of God and Ann Lee's successor. The addiction to this creed caused the almost complete isolation of the sect from the outside world. Even those few contacts which had been open before were now curtailed. Sunday rituals were closed hermetically to outsiders because the Shakers believed that they would prevent the spirits from seeking contact. The seclusion lasted as long as spiritualism prevailed. The involvement with spiritualism came to an end when there was fear of false inspiration misleading the Shakers and causing anarchy. The spiritualist movement took a different direction, advancing into New York and New England with the visitation of the experienced Fox sisters in 1848. Shaker spiritualism was thus the beginning of a social phenomenon throughout the United States.[45]

In the late 1840s the social, spiritual, and economic upheavals ebbed. Economic stability mainly in the rural areas, less revivals, and less new joiners brought about a long period of stagnation. This period may be called "post revivals" and was characterized by a process of internalization. The missionary zeal was lost together with the belief in the imminence of the kingdom of heaven. Shaker communes would now have to continue for a further period in an alien and hostile environment.[46] Their expanding industry and economic activity forced even the recluses to seek external contacts. One of the most problematic of external relations was with the state and the political establishment.[47] As mentioned above, the Shakers' religious principles prevented them from acknowledging any secular authorities. They abstained from all political activities, even from elections, but they were forced to find some sort of modus vivendi in order to exist. They compromised by paying taxes under specific conditions, paying compensation and exemption money for not serving in the army or in the local militia. This was a matter of principle which caused a lot of tension between the Shakers and their neighbors, especially when in 1812 the war against England broke out. The Shakers refused to take sides and until a compromise was reached, had to pay dearly. The problem, though on a different scale, recurred during the Civil War.[48]

The 1860s were a period of hardships. The Civil War posed difficult problems when on the one hand the Shakers refused on principle to serve in the army and on the other hand they ardently supported the North and the abolishment of slavery. Seventy young members had to enlist, and only a petition to President Lincoln, formulated by Frederic Evans, one of the Shaker elders, and in which he proposed to pay a high ransom, brought about the postponement of their serving in the army. Nevertheless, they remained enlisted until the end of the fighting. The situation in the Southwest was even worse. Kentucky, Ohio, and Indiana were near the battlefields and the Shakers opposed the Federals and the proslavery attitude. In 1863 these southern states were freed from the Federals but this caused the same enlistment problems that had occurred in the North. Again a petition like the one Evans had written was formulated by Harry Eads with the same result. E.M. Stanton, secretary of war, gave an express order to release the Shakers from army service. He not only understood their way, but admired them for their conviction and even visited Mount Lebanon in October 1867, praising the members of the sect.[49]

Frederic Evan's Leadership

The years following the Civil War opened up a new period in the economic, social, and cultural history of the United States. For the Shakers it was a period of decline. Many left the communes and among those who remained there was an increase in undisciplined behavior.[50] From the 1850s and until his death in 1893, Frederic Evans served as elder. He had great influence even in distant circles. Evans was born in England in 1808 and emigrated to the United States with this elder brother when he was eighteen. Both brothers were active in a number of social reforms such as the curtailing of land ownership, the abolishment of monopolies, and women's emancipation. This was the background for Evan's discovering the utopian movement of Owen, and in 1828 he joined an Owenist settlement in Ohio. Although this community disintegrated a few months later, he did not despair and with a group of others established a collective settlement in 1830. At that time he chanced to visit the Shaker settlement at Mount Lebanon, and soon adopted their ways and faith. He believed that the sect was in fact realizing the principles of socialism.[51]

Evans quickly rose in the Shaker hierarchy and in 1843 became one of the elders of Mount Lebanon and their outstanding representative. He fulfilled a role of foreign representative until his death, weaving an intricate network of connections. Evans' spiritual influence in the Shaker movement was due to his great prestige and his accomplished penmanship. He was influential in publishing the Shaker periodical *The Shaker and the Shakeress* (1871-1899), and contributed to the molding of its form, even serving as its editor between 1873 and 1875. Under Evans the periodical strove to establish contact with other, secular reform movements. This was contrary to the prevailing religious seclusion of the sect, and conservatives among the Shakers opposed Evans' initiative. He, however, continued to strive for contact with liberal and socialist circles. He claimed that there should be a dividing line between religious beliefs and ways of life which are personal matters, and between the involvement in public and social struggles. These should be held in collaboration with other circles even if they had different social or religious convictions. Evans was convinced that the sect should wield its economic and spiritual powers in order to influence others. He believed that the Shaker's communal way of life should serve as a model for social reformers, whether religious or secular. Frederic Evans called upon the Shakers to abandon their isolationism and to become involved in social struggles while guarding their religious and communal uniqueness.[52] In this he was consistently opposed by Harvey Eads, one of the leading elders who was active simultaneously with Evans and died a year before him, in 1892. Both personalities represent the two opposites of the Shakers' spiritual dogma in the nineteenth century.

Harvey Eads personified the traditional conservative attitude that refused to adapt to the change of time. He was hostile to Frederic Evan's liberalism and adhered to Shaker theology, claiming that theirs was the one and only true Christianity. He did not try to fit into modern ways of life and kept to their eschatological concept, which was difficult for modern man to swallow. The prevalent social change in the United States during the second half of the nineteenth century prompted him to preach isolationism further, and he called on the Shakers to adhere to their principles of purity and ways of life. The controversy between Harvey Eads and Frederic Evans was exposed in the periodicals. Evans addressed the external world and tried to present the Shakers as pioneers of reform. Eads ignored the world and, addressing the Shakers, preached conservatism, isolation, and purification. Their argument receded after the Civil War. But even though Evans found ways of adapting to the new era, he could not prevent the rapid shrinking of Shaker membership.[53]

Efforts of Expansion

In the early 1870s Evans attempted unsuccessfully to organize missionary activities in the eastern cities, where social unrest was rife. The urban population was alien to the Shakers' spiritual world and ignored their message. At the same time the Shakers tried to expand their settlements and attract new members from Europe. In 1869 their emissaries left for Sweden and returned with scores of new settlers, but most of them soon returned to their homeland.[54] In 1871 Evans himself set out to his native England. His mission was a success as to the impact he left in liberal and intellectual circles; yet the results were poor, and he failed to enlist new members for the Shaker community.

A unique experiment for the Shakers was tried when in 1874 some American newspapers carried advertisements calling on people to join their settlements and promising them a comfortable, tranquil, and economically secure life.[55] This, like other attempts to revive the aging and petrified Shaker movement failed. There would be no more such attempts. The conservative elements were reinforced in their knowledge that there was no hope from the outside world, and they retired into their eschatological beliefs to await better days. The handful that were left in the various settlements devoted themselves to keep the place clean and orderly. In 1874 the Shakers celebrated their centenary in America. It called for a large measure of optimism to believe that the movement would ever thrive again.

Decline

In the period following the Civil War, Shaker settlements were as a whole economically stable. Their shrinking membership did not immediately affect economic activities. Nevertheless, the industrial revolution left the Shaker communes far behind, and they lost their advantage of a large communitarian settlement which combined agriculture and industry. The Shakers' economic leadership nonetheless found ways and means to adapt to the changing economic reality. Those industries which were not viable were closed down and the few that remained, e.g. the furniture workshops, were modernized and efficiently managed in order to compete. In agriculture, the big farms proved to have a definite advantage, but the lack of manpower was felt as many of the remaining Shakers were women and old people who could not work in the fields. To overcome this problem, agricultural workers were employed. Charles Nordhof, who visited the American communes in 1874, reported that 380 hired laborers worked in the Shakers' 18 settlements at the time.[56]

Relying on agriculture, the Shakers began to acquire more land and even established new settlements in Florida (1894) and Georgia (1898), the first since the beginning of the century. The small number of their members caused them to abandon these settlements soon after. Even some of the old communes were dissolved—first the Kentucky and Ohio settlements and later those in the Northeast, Connecticut, Massachusetts, and New York. The remaining Shakers at the beginning of the twentieth century were concentrated in 14 viable settlements, two of which were in the final stages of dissolution. Nevertheless, the settlements were economically stable and their members maintained their belief in a better future.[57]

In the second half of the nineteenth century, the Shakers were no longer persecuted. In 1887, a century after their first settlement was established in New York, the *New York World* published an article praising the positive aspects of the Shaker movement, and the successful attempt to establish communism. Throughout the nineteenth century they were a model for those who wanted to establish communes. Even if those people disagreed with their doctrine and ways of life, they admired the Shakers and were encouraged by their success. Outstanding among the Europeans who shared interest in the Shakers' communities was Lev N. Tolstoi, who corresponded with Frederic Evans.[58] In 1904 two Shaker sisters, Anna White and Leila S. Taylor, published a book on Shaker history, *Shakerism: Its Meaning and Message*. The final chapters cite the elders' optimistic belief in the future of their message. Nevertheless, they could not ignore the facts of deterioration. At the beginning of the twentieth century there were only about 1,300 members, the same number as a century ago. The graph of the ascents and descents of the Shakers' numbers is almost symmetrical, for the two low points are at the beginning and the end of the century and the apex is in the 1850s, when Shaker membership reached about 3,500.[59]

There is no definite explanation as to the drastic decrease of Shaker population at the end of the nineteenth century. We can only speculate. Andrews points out the lowering of the rentability of the settlement; generally expenses exceeded the income. The policy of territorial expansion that had formerly characterized the Shakers and brought about an enormous prosperity, later became an economic liability when not enough manpower was available. The hiring of farm workers harmed the members morally and socially. Moreover, many of the farms were mismanaged.[60] Still, all agree that the most important factor was the negative impact which the developing U.S. industrial society had on Shaker economy. As long as the national economy was based on agriculture, Shaker communes prospered. The farms had the advantage of good work management, joint exploitation of resources, and excellent produce. The industrialized society crowded Shaker produce off the market and left them only with the option of manufacturing specific things such as furniture, clothing, baskets, decorative boxes, and herbs. In addition, this society promoted values—i.e. private initiative, daring, and expansion—which were diametrically opposed to the Shakers' spiritual basis. The Shakers' advantage of security, communal and solid communities, were frowned upon by American society at the second half of the nineteenth century and considered liabilities. Their tendency for celibacy did not endear them to the young people, few of whom could accept it. Margaret Melcher adds the intellectual and spiritual deterioration of the Shakers at that time. They were no longer a people who could inspire others with a strong belief, or influence them with their zeal. Most of them had isolationist tendencies that did not attract others. The gap between them and the external world widened.

Involvement in World Struggles

In spite of the Shaker movement's significant deterioration during the later part of the nineteenth century, there were circles, mainly the followers of Frederic Evans, who were not yet ready to give up and retreat. They regarded the present situation as just another phase of cosmic change and kept up their hopes for a revival of the Shaker mission. They rejected isolationism and seclusion and searched for ways of involvement in social reform movements.

Their reduced numbers did not deter them. They regarded their movement as the "gulfstream in the wide ocean" which carries warmth to "the shores of humanity." Therefore their mission was to be involved in world struggles while guarding their uniqueness: "Living within the world but not belonging to it."[61]

Under Frederic Evans the Shakers joined the U.S. chapter of the World Peace Movement from its inception. Mount Lebanon was their center of activity in New York State. One of the Shaker leaders, the eldress Anna, cooperated with the Union of Women for Peace, whose center was in Paris. She was active in formulating the petition for world disarmament and in gratitude for her activities was nominated the vice-president of the Union of Peace in New York. In 1905 a convention was held at Mount Lebanon in which activists from all over the world participated. Some of the proposals asked for the limitation of arms sales, others proposed a ban on war and the establishment of taxation for war purposes.[62] The Shakers were also active in various philanthropical and humanitarian movements. Their settlements volunteered to assist the underprivileged classes, a long standing tradition of the Shakers who had also been active in the movement for the emancipation of slaves, in the struggle against agrarian monopolies, in fighting alcoholism and in the suffragette movement. In spite of the reduced numbers, the Shakers were still a model for their neighbors, striving to achieve humanitarian reforms. Yet nothing could disguise the fact that in the early twentieth century the Shakers were only a handful. Although a few followers joined them, they could not fill the gap. A movement which had abolished the biological family and which believed in celibacy could not hope to maintain its numbers. The source of absorbing external pupils from orphanages and broken families had dried up as well; only about 20 percent of all those who had been educated in Shaker settlements joined them.[63]

An Aptitude for Survival

Even though they were facing a growing social pressure, their settlements apparently seemed to be economically stable. Cleanliness and orderliness, peace and solidity were maintained as before. In reality the economic situation was deteriorating. The settlements, whose membership was steadily dropping, tried to adhere to their way of life while adapting to new circumstances. Since the middle of the nineteenth century Shaker dancing was no longer part of their religious ritual, only their songs and hymns remained. Their clothing too was still unique. Even though modern innovations were gradually accepted, the settlements could not remain autocratic. Reality forced them to expand their contacts with the outside world. In the twentieth century Shakers agreed to leave their settlements in order to receive medical treatment or even enjoy a visit to the circus or a sports event.[64] Shakers had never objected to technical innovations, therefore they adopted many of the twentieth-century's inventions that were not totally averse to their way of life. In the 1920s they introduced cars on their farms, in some cases even earlier than their neighbors. Later they were connected to the national telephone and electric grids. They used modern machinery on their farms, modern kitchen utensils, electric washing machines instead of those that had been invented by their own people and were now relegated to a museum. However, their ability to adopt modern ways did not save them from a further deterioration of their settlements in the early twentieth century. Slowly, the large established settlements in the East were eroded as well. In 1930, Mount Lebanon, the eldest and most famous of Shaker communes, decided to sell 40 buildings and 300 acres to an outside educational institution. The remaining members stayed on until 1947, when the settlement was abandoned and its assets sold to private developers who established a summer camp for New York youngsters there. The last members of Mount Lebanon joined Hancock, Massachusetts, a commune which would survive a few years longer.[65]

The Twentieth Century

In the 1920s, while the movement was on the decline, an increasing interest in the Shaker movement took place in the American public. Researchers and collectors specializing in early American culture began to save the Shaker heritage from extinction. They collected documents and literature, and remnants of Shaker villages were reconstructed. In 1920, the first Shaker museum was established at Harvardtown, Massachusetts, on the estate of Clara Endicot Sears, the daughter of a Fourierist activist whose lands were adjacent to the Shaker communes Harvard and Shirley. In 1923 a young researcher, Edward D. Andrews, visited the Shaker commune of Hancock, wishing to buy some of the famous Shaker bread. He was impressed by the beauty of the unique Shaker furniture, and the visit greatly affected him and his wife. He devoted the rest of his life to publishing studies on the Shakers' spiritual and economic heritage, culminating with the publication of *The People Called Shakers*, in 1953. During the 1930s several museums, in states where Shaker communities had existed, exhibited Shaker furniture, clothing, handicraft, tools, and instruments. Artists, painters, choreographers, and musicians began to use Shaker themes in their art.

The first comprehensive history of the Shakers was published in 1940 by Margaret Melcher, who was not of the sect. Shaker literature grew between 1940 and 1970, and a bibliography published in 1977 includes 4,000 entries compared to 500 in 1905. In the 1960s, four Shaker settlements were reconstructed and became popular historical sites.[66] In the 1970s, the time of the

U.S. bicentennial, a public movement proposed to celebrate 200 years of Shaker settlements (1774-1974). They discovered that the sect was not just a memory of the past but that in the North, in Maine and New Hampshire, some Shakers were still living in two of the old settlements. In Canterbury, New Hampshire, and in Sabbathday Lake, Maine, communal life had continued throughout the twentieth century. They too had encountered the difficulties of other Shaker settlements and their numbers had steadily diminished. In the 1960s there were eleven women left in Canterbury, the last male member having died in 1939.[67] In Sabbathday Lake, there were fourteen members left, one of them 98 years old, but two sisters in their thirties. There was a difference between these two settlements; while the sisters in Canterbury refused to accept new candidates and the settlement stagnated, the members of Sabbathday Lake tried to adapt to the new circumstances and were ready to accept new candidates. They altered their dresses, introduced radios, and expanded their relations with the outside world. The new members enabled the commune to remain economically viable even though they had to hire seasonal agricultural workers.

In 1975, the circle of Shaker friends organized as a society with the intention of giving the Shakers public backing and economic aid. But there was schism within the Shakers. The tension between the two remaining communes was because the three old sisters in Canterbury questioned the motives of new members, suspecting them to be after the Shaker possessions, which were estimated at about $3 million. The Maine Shakers on the other hand believed that the sect's duty was to keep the door open to all those who believed in its message, and they trusted their new members. It was a schism which caused the two settlements to celebrate their bicentennial separately.[68]

In January 1981, on a cold winter day, my wife and I visited Sabbathday Lake in northern Maine. This short visit to the last existing Shaker commune of ten brothers and sisters, was for us a profound experience. Time there seemed to have stood still. A number of white wooden houses surrounded a three-story brick building. They seemed to have been petrified in a nineteenth-century painting, and the snow added to the peace and harmony of the frozen silence. Inside the house it was warm and cozy. A young Shaker bade us welcome and he even shook hands with my wife. This would have been unthinkable in the past. We were further astonished to find a transistor radio on the table of the typically furnished Shaker room in which we sat down for a conversation. Down the hall that divided the sisters' living quarters from the brothers', we halted in front of a notice board which advertised the films shown in the nearby town. The two Shaker women who smilingly passed us on the way were dressed in the modern fashion of the outside world. Indeed, a spirit of adaptation prevailed.

On our short tour in the Shakers' home we encountered a strange mixture of traditional Shaker elements of the structure of the building—its furniture, assembly room, and dining hall—together with modern fixtures in the kitchen and a washing machine. Wherever we went we noticed an openness to the external world. We visited the workshop in which wooden boxes were manufactured, coats sewn, and herbs packaged. We were taken to the sheep pen and the garage in which an old Ford pickup was stationed.

Talking to the young Massachusetts-born guide, we learned that he had joined the community a few years earlier, choosing this life from conviction and belief in the Shaker message. Before departing we could not refrain from asking him whether they did not feel isolated and frustrated because of their diminished numbers. He answered in the traditional Shaker way: "Nay, Ann Lee had ever claimed that deeds were better than words and that there was an advantage to a model way of life. As long as there is a Shaker settlement and a group of Shakers, even though small, Ann Lee's light will enlighten the world and there is hope for her message to encompass all."

Notes

1. Henri Desroche, *The American Shakers: From Neo-Christianity to Presocialism*, trans. John K. Savacool (Boston: University of Massachusetts Press, 1971), pp. 16-27; William Alfred Hinds, *American Communities and Cooperation Colonies* (1878. Reprinted and enl. Philadelphia: Porcupine, 1975), pp. 35-36.
2. Edward D. Andrews, *The People Called Shakers: A Search for the Perfect Society* (New York: Dover, 1963), pp. 4-6; Desroche, p. 27; Flo Morse, *The Shakers and the World's People* (New York: Dodd Mead, 1980), p. 9-10; Charles Edson Robinson, *The Shakers and Their Homes* (Canterbury [Shaker village], N.H.: New Hampshire Publishing Co., 1976), p. 12-13.
3. M. Fellows Melcher, *The Shaker Adventure* (New York: The Shaker Museum, 1975), pp. 8-9.
4. Calvin Green and Seth Y. Wells, *A Summary View of the Millenial Church, or United Society of Believers, Commonly Called Shakers* (Albany: Hoffman and White, 1848; New York: AMS Press, 1973), pp. 12-19; Andrews, *The People*, pp. 7-11.
5. Andrews, *The People*, pp. 1-13; Robinson, pp. 15-16; Hinds, pp. 35-36.
6. Andrews, *The People*, pp. 13-16.
7. Hinds, *American Communities*, pp. 37-38; Clara E. Sears, ed., *Gleanings from Old Shaker Journals* (Boston: Houghton Mifflin, 1916; New York: Hyperion, 1975), pp. 20-24.
8. The Revival movement was a phenomenon rooted in European Christianity, mainly in Protestantism. In the New World it was part of the routine religious experience and at certain times an important factor in religious circles. The rebirth of the Revival movement in North America was directly associated with the drive westward to the frontier. The colonizers who got out to the new areas established communities with people of various sects. Conditions prevented regular relations with their mother church. Being scattered all over a district, they had difficulties in establishing parishes and their former rituals were almost impossible to maintain. As a result church loyalties were undermined and their religious way of life

was disrupted. Yet they still had religious needs and even more so due to their loneliness in face of danger and the unknown. On the lookout for the road they should take, they were open to new doctrines that might fulfill their spiritual needs. This, then, was the reality in certain areas of New York and New England during and following the years of the Revolution. Following the waves of revival meetings, controversies erupted between the followers of the established denomination called the *Old Light* and the seceders who opposed them and were named the *New Light*. In those circles the emphasis was on the inner light which would lead them to salvation. They fostered millenary expectations and hoped for change in the world. Those who attended the frontier revival meetings began to believe in the advent of the kingdom of God and in man's remorse and purification while expecting the glories of salvation. They broke with all conventions and the message of deliverance from all evil for those who had "seen the light" and repented, attracted multitudes from among the frontier men, who were almost completely isolated from both state and church authorities. New sects were being formed which seceded from the established churches and were characterized by being originally American rather than the result of European influence. Those who joined these sects were believers who had experienced revival meetings; not finding peace after that excitement, they could not face their former routine and return to their earlier religious practices. Believing that man's salvation was in his own hands through revelation and a holy way of life, they were unable to return to the established church. Their millenary doctrine led them on to search for ways to enter the kingdom of heaven via purification and seclusion. In the late eighteenth century this spiritual upheaval overcame thousands of people and was of paramount importance in the religious life of New England. Oscar Handlin, *America: A History* (Holt, Rinehart & Winston, 1968), pp. 132-33; Donald Egbert and Stow Persons, eds., *Socialism and American Life*, 2 vols. (Princeton: Princeton University Press, 1952), pp. 128-30; Stephen A. Marini, *Radical Sects of Revolutionary New England* (Boston: Harvard University Press, 1982), pp. 4-6, 12-13, 27-39, 52-53, 55-57; A. Leland Jamison, "Religion in Christian Perimeter," in *Religion in American Life*, vol. 1, ed. J.W. Smith (Princeton: Princeton University Press, 1961).

9. Marini, pp. 52-53, 78.
10. Green and Wells, pp. 24-27; Marini, pp. 88-90.
11. Andrews, *The People*, pp. 17-34.
12. Ibid, pp. 35-44; Anna White and Leila S. Taylor, *Shakerism: Its Meaning and Message* (Columbus, Oh.: Heer, 1904; New York: AMS Press, 1971), chap. 3.
13. Andrews, *The People*, pp. 49-50; Morse, *The Shakers*, pp. 35-55, Sears, ed., *Gleanings*, pp. 167-75.
14. Andrews, *The People*, pp. 50-53; Desroche, pp. 51-52, 92; Robinson, pp. 24-26; Sears, *Gleanings*, pp. 159-66.
15. Three years after the establishment of Mount Lebanon, in 1790, Hancock, Massachusetts, was established, followed by Enfield, Connecticut. Two years later, Canterbury, in New Hampshire, Harvard and Shirley in Massachusetts, Enfield, in New Hampshire, and Alfred, in Maine, were established. In 1794 the most northern Shaker commune was established in Maine, at first called "New Gloucester" and later "Sabbath Day Lake." Hinds, *American Communities*, pp. 39-42; Andrews, *The People*, pp. 56-61; Desroche, pp. 92-94; Robinson, pp. 48-58.
16. Edward R. Horgan, *The Shaker Holy Land: A Community Portrait* (Harvard: The Harvard Common Press, 1982), pp. 47-56; Charles Nordhoff, *The Communistic*

Societies of the United States (1875. Reprint. New York: Shocken, 1965), p. 136; Hinds, *American Communities*, pp. 42-44; Desroche, pp. 196-202.

17. Hinds, *American Communities*, pp. 42-45; Desroche, pp. 188-92.
18. Louis J. Kern, *An Ordered Love: Sex Roles and Sexuality in Victorian Utopias—The Shakers, the Mormons, and the Oneida Community* (Chapel-Hill: University of North Carolina Press, 1981), p. 570; Nordhoff, pp. 137-40; Desroche, pp. 210-18.
19. Hinds, *American Communities*, p. 45; Kern, chap. 5, pp. 91-103.
20. Harvey Elkins, *Fifteen Years in the Senior Order of the Shakers: A Narration of Facts Concerning That Singular People* (Hanover: Dartmouth Press, 1853; New York: AMS Press, 1973), pp. 40-45.
21. Mesick, Jane Louise. *The English Traveler in America (1785-1835)*. (Columbia University Press, 1922.) p. 267.
22. Timothy Dwight, *Travels in New England and New York*, vol. 3 (1822. Reprint. Boston: Harvard University Press, 1969), pp. 101-16; Benjamin Silliman, *Remarks Made on a Short Tour between Hartford and Quebec in the Autumn of 1819*, 2d ed. (New Haven, Conn.: 1824), pp. 40-44; Edward Everett, "The Shakers," *The North American Review*, 16 (1823): 86-102.
23. John Patterson MacLean, *Shakers of Ohio* (1907. Reprint. Philadelphia: Porcupine, 1974), pp. 1-26; Melcher, pp. 59-66; Andrews, p. 71. Julia Neal, *By Their Fruits: The Story of Shakerism in South Union, Kentucky* (North Carolina University Press, 1947); Philadelphia: Porcupine, 1975), chap. 2; William Warren Sweet, *Revivalism in America* (New York, Scribner's, 1944), pp. 113-23; Egbert and Persons, p. 138.
24. Richard McNemar, *The Kentucky Revival* (New York: Jenkins, 1846; New York: AMS Press, 1974); Melcher, pp. 67, 70; Neal, *By Their Fruits*, pp. 32-36; MacLean, 38-40; Hinds, pp. 53-54.
25. Melcher, pp. 76-78; Hinds, pp. 51-52; Herbert A. Wisbey, *The Sodus Shaker Community* (Lyons, N.Y.: Wayne County Historical Society, 1982), pp. 5-24.
26. Whitney Cross, *The Burned-Over District* (New York: Harper & Row, 1965), pp. 297, 310; MacLean, pp. 97-89, 250.
27. *The American Socialist*, vol. 1, no. 30(October 19, 1876); White and Taylor, p. 123; Julia Neal, "The American Shakers," *Communities: Journal of Cooperation* 68 (Winter 1985): 16, 17.
28. Melcher, pp. 103, 105-6, 114; Andrews, *The People*, pp. 95-99.
29. An extensive formulation of the Shakers' religious principles and their way of life was accomplished in 1830 and adapted for both internal use and external propaganda. It was published in book form in 1834. See Green and Wells, *A Summary View of the Millenial Church*.
30. Morse, *The Shakers*, pp. 152-71; Andrews, *The People*, pp. 136-51; Hinds, *American Communities*, pp. 62-67.
31. Daniel W. Patterson, *The Shaker Spiritual* (Princeton: Princeton University Press, 1979); Daniel W. Patterson, "Shaker Music," *Communal Societies* 2 (Autumn 1982): 54-63; Andrews, *The People*, pp. 138-40; Desroche, p. 118; Harriet Martineau, *Society in America*, vol. 2 (New York: AMS Press, 1966 originally published London: Saunders & Otley, 1834), p. 55.
32. Martineau, pp. 66, 104, 108-13; Morse, *The Shakers*, p. 133; Rosemary D. Gooden, "A Preliminary Examination of the Shaker Attitude toward Work," *Communal Societies* 3 (Fall 1983): 3-14; *The American Socialist* 2, no. 46 (November 1877): 365.
33. Andrews, *The People*, pp. 113-22, 135; Edward D. Andrews, *The Community*

Industries of the Shakers (Philadelphia: Porcupine, 1972), pp. 39-44; Benson T. Lossing, "Visiting the Shakers," *Harper's New Monthly Magazine* 86 (July 1857): 164-77; Melcher, pp. 120-35.

34. Morse, *The Shakers*, p. 123.
35. William Hepworth Dixon, *A New America*, vol. 2 (London: Hurst & Blackett, 1867), pp. 322-23.
36. Andrews, *The People*, p. 120.
37. Andrews, *The Industries*, pp. 60-66; Sears, *Gleanings*, pp. 222-56; Horgan, pp. 98-102.
38. Elkins, pp. 23-31, 37, 40-44, 76-84.
39. Neal, "American Shakers," p. 18; Andrews, *The People*, pp. 180-84; Horgan, pp. 68-70.
40. Everett, pp. 86-102; Ralph Waldo Emerson, *Letters*, vol. 1, ed. R.L. Rusk (New York: 1939), pp. 225-26; Nathaniel Hawthorne, *Blithedale Romance* (New York: W.W. Norton, 1958), pp. 153-66; James Fenimore Cooper, *Nations of the Americans*, vol. 2 (1833. Reprint. New York: F. Unger, 1963), pp. 247-50; Charles Dickens, *American Notes for General Circulation* (London: Everyman's Library, 1907), pp. 109-10; Martineau, pp. 55-65; Mary Hennel, *An Outline of the Various Systems and Communities Which Have Been Founded on the Principle of Cooperation* (London, 1841), pp. 39-45; J.S. Buckingham, *The Eastern and Western States of America*, vol. 2 (London, 1842), pp. 234-35.
41. Lewis S. Feuer, "The Influence of the American Communist Colonies on Engels and Marx," *The Western Political Quarterly* 19 (1966):456-65; Andrews, *The People*, pp. 129-35; Desroche, pp. 293-96; Morse, *The Shakers*, pp. 90-92.
42. White and Taylor, pp. 156-60; Desroche, pp. 126-38, 268-76, Nordhoff, p. 256; William A. Hinds, "Pleasant Hill Shakers," *American Socialist* 1, no. 32 (October 1876).
43. Kern, p. 106; Neal, *By Their Fruits*, chap. 2; MacLean, pp. 388-415.
44. MacLean, pp. 349-62.
45. Alice Felt Tyler, *Freedom's Ferment* (New York: Harper & Row, 1962) pp. 72-86; Cross, pp. 341-52, Morse, *The Shakers*, pp. 171-84; Andrews, *The People*, pp. 152-74.
46. Hinds, *American Communities*, p. 49.
47. Andrews, *The People*, pp. 113-16, 204-12; Desroche, pp. 84-87; Morse, *The Shakers*, pp. 124-32.
48. MacLean, pp. 362-87; Hinds, *American Communities*, pp. 51-53.
49. Neal, *By Their Fruits*, pp. 177-214; White and Taylor, pp. 196-99; Morse, *The Shakers*, pp. 204, 211-15; Andrews, *The People*, pp. 224-32.
50. Kern, p. 103; "Decay of Shaker Institutions," *American Socialist* 1 (1876):75; "South Union Shakers," *American Socialist* 1 (1876): p. 127.
51. Frederick William Evans, *Autobiography of a Shaker and Revelation of the Apocalypse* (1888. Reprint. New York: AMS Press, 1973), pp. 1-25; John McKelvie Whitworth, *God's Blueprints: A Sociological Study of Three Utopian Sects* (London: Routledge & Kegan, 1975), p. 56.
52. Robinson, pp. 124-29; Andrews, *The People*, pp. 232-36; Whitworth, p. 75; Morse, *The Shakers*, pp. 215-27; Melcher, p. 177.
53. Robinson, pp. 67-74; Melcher, pp. 274-80; Whitworth, p. 76; Nordhoff, p. 256.
54. Neal, *By Their Fruits*, p. 234; William Alfred Hinds, "The Pleasant Hill Shakers," *American Socialist* 1, no. 31 (November 1876):245; *American Socialist* 3, no. 27 (July 1878): 213.
55. Whitworth, p. 75; *American Socialist* 3, no. 23 (June 1878):181.

56. William Alfred Hinds, "Enfield Shakers," *American Socialist* 1, no. 11 (June 1876):85; "A Shaker Village," (extracts from W.D. Howell, *Atlantic Monthly*) *American Socialist* 1, no. 8 (May 1876):58; Melcher, pp. 227-41; MacLean, pp. 100-11; Neal, *By Their Fruits*, pp. 216-37; Kern, p. 97; Nordhoff, p. 256.
57. White and Taylor, pp. 212-14; Wisbey, *Sodus Shakers*, p. 27; Melcher, pp. 234, 256-58.
58. Morse, *The Shakers*, pp. 231-36; Andrews, *The People*, pp. 221, 233.
59. For an up-to-date report on the Shaker population in the nineteenth century see William Sims Bainbridge: "The Decline of the Shakers," *Communal Societies* 4 (Fall 1984); Melcher, p. 284; Evans, p. 259; White and Taylor, chap. 23; Alexander Kent, "Cooperative Communities in the United States," *Bulletin of the Department of Labor*, no. 35 (July 1901):578. "Shaker Depletion," *American Socialist* 4, no. 5 (1879):35.
60. Hinds, *American Communities*, pp. 33-34; William Alfred Hinds, "The Shakers at Union Village," *American Socialist* 1, no. 32 (November 1879):253.
61. Desroche, pp. 112-15; Melcher, pp. 234-55; Andrews, *The People*, pp. 224-32.
62. White and Taylor, pp. 215-17; Morse, *The Shakers*, pp. 243-45.
63. Hinds, *American Communities*, p. 59; Morse, *The Shakers*, pp. 245-47.
64. Neal, "American Shakers," p. 18; Neal, *By Their Fruits*, pp. 256-57.
65. Horgan, pp. 138, 146-53; Melcher, pp. 262-65; Neal, *By Their Fruits*, pp. 254-67; Morse, *The Shakers*, pp. 278-83.
66. Ibid., pp. 264-77, 291-98.
67. Donald Walsh, "Canterbury: New Challenges," *The Shaker Messenger* 3, no. 1 (Fall 1880).
68. Morse, *The Shakers*, pp. 316-46; Horgan, pp. 179-85.

4

Religious Immigrant Communes

In the early nineteenth century, a few years after the advent of the Shakers, further waves of religious immigrant sects from Europe reached the shores of the United States to establish communal settlements there. Most of them came from various German states, from Wurtemberg, Hessen, and Alsace-Lorraine as well as from the Netherlands and Sweden. These sects, which were persecuted in their native countries, had begun to practice mutual aid and cooperation while still in Europe. During their immigration to the United States those ties were reinforced and their settlements established as communes. In the first half of the nineteenth century, they established 17 flourishing and prosperous communes in the Northeast and in the Midwest, which at that time was frontier land.

Harmony Society

The first to arrive were the separatists, in 1804, under George Rapp's leadership. They chose Pennsylvania as the place for establishing their independent settlements. They were Lutherans in origin, and had lived around Stuttgart, and formed their sect in 1786 under the influence of George Rapp.

George Rapp was born in 1757 in the town of Iptingen Wurtemberg, the son of a peasant. He learned the trade of weaving and from early on was deeply interested in religion. A member of the established Lutheran Church, he was soon dissatisfied with its doctrine and became acquainted with mystics and pietists whose teachings made a deep impression on him. When he began to preach against Lutheran rituals[1] he got into confrontation with the church establishment and called on his followers to establish a separate sect. His strong personality and charisma attracted peasants, landowners, laborers, and artisans from the area. As his congregation increased steadily, the Wurtemberg government asked them to draw up their principles in order to acknowledge them as a separate sect.

Their principles included: (1) rejection of the Lutheran Church's rituals; (2) baptism of adults by choice and through conviction; (3) agape as an expression of their spiritual brotherhood and cooperation; (4) a separate education for their children; (5) recognition of the government's institutions and their vital functions, but refusal to take an oath in court as Jesus had forbidden it; and (6) objection to army service because it was averse to Christian morality.

Immigration to the United States and the Formation of Communes

At the beginning of the nineteenth century secular and religious authorities began to persecute the sect and they searched for ways and means to emigrate from Wurtemberg. Their motives and ecstatic enthusiasm for emigration were considered among the sectarians as part and parcel of millennial expectancies for a cosmic renewal. They regarded the Napoleonic Wars as a sign from God, a kind of war between Gog and Magog which was to precede the kingdom of heaven. Emigration seemed to be an inner religious urge equivalent to a revelation. Moreover, many regarded themselves as loyal to Zion and on their way to the promised land.[2]

The impetus to emigrate was widespread among the peasants of Wurtemberg and was also prompted by the economic conditions. Their soil had deteriorated, and their small lots did not suffice to provide their needs. Some turned east toward Russia and Hungary, others toward the New World. George Rapp and his followers opted for the United States, and in 1803 he left with a small pioneer group to prepare the land for those of his sect who were to follow. He bought a parcel of 5,000 acres in Butler County, west Pennsylvania, and called his followers to set out on their way. The first group of about 500 arrived in America in 1804 and within a year organized the Harmony Society, founded on February 15, 1805. The drawing-up of a contract legalized the society, and it may be regarded as their founding charter.[3] According to this document, members of the society agreed to all of the sect's principles, transferred their entire property to the society, and were committed to the Christian way of life of the sect. The document was formulated as a contract between the new candidate and George Rapp and his society. Immediately following the signing of the contract, the separatists began to establish their independent settlement as a commune. Members set out to clear the land and plant vines (many of them had been expert viniculturalists in their homeland). They also constructed their first buildings, houses for accommodation and workshops, a flour- and a sawmill, etc. In 1806 the commune started to weave woollen cloth. New members who kept arriving from Wurtemberg steadily increased the commune's membership, which in 1810 reached a population of 800; this process was halted in 1819.

Harmony and New Harmony

During their first years in Pennsylvania the Harmony group underwent a religio-spiritual upheaval. Inspired by this they adopted the celibate way of life, in accordance with George Rapp's preaching and the theological Christian principles reinforced by the sect's millennial expectations. Although families continued to exist, sexual relations and hence also childbirth were forbidden. This caused consternation among members of the sect in Germany and as a result the number of immigrants decreased.[4]

The rapid economic development, the large number of members, the new branches for marketing, and the prospectives of the sect called for a new place where there would be better chances for development and expansion. An additional impetus to search for a new site were the strained relations between the people of Harmony and their neighbors. The areas around Pittsburg were relatively densely populated. Some, mainly those of an English background, were hostile toward the German settlers with their odd ways. Tension was also caused by the sect's desire to live a life of seclusion in order to maintain their creed without any external interference.[5] To ensure this they turned west in 1814 and acquired a tract of 30,000 prime, government-owned lands on the Wabash River. Later this territory would become the state of Indiana. The new region promised wide options for development: fertile but cheap land in a state that was just forming. However, the area was infested with malaria and in the first years the settlers suffered cruelly. Within a short period the whole population of Harmony was transferred from Pennsylvania to Indiana and the settlement was named *New Harmony*. In spite of difficulties and diseases they developed rapidly and became the focal point of settlement activity in the new state.[6]

New Harmony was one of the largest communities in Indiana; the state was in the process of forming its political institutions, and many of the politicians courted the commune. Frederick Rapp, George Rapp's adopted son, represented New Harmony to the outside world. He invested a lot of effort in maintaining the religious and social-political principles of the sect. He thus voted against slavery, was active in the economic and financial institutions, and proposed a law to protect local industry from competition. He also initiated the founding of a local bank and in 1820 was a member of the committee that planned the capital Indianapolis.[7]

The rapid economic development of New Harmony was widely admired. Visitors arrived from far away to gain impressions of the "great wonder" of the settlements in the West. New Harmony's reputation reached others who were involved in the communal experiment—Robert Owen in England and the Shakers in the United States. George Rapp did not exploit this reputation for missionary activities; on the other hand, he did not limit contact with the neighboring communities and even encouraged involvement in local politics and philanthropy among needy immigrants and other religious sects.[8]

Back to Pennsylvania: Economy

Ten years after having settled in Indiana the sect was compelled to abandon the place for several reasons. One was the difficulties they had encountered with their neighbors, who felt alienated from the group in spite of New Harmony's efforts to assist them. Members of the sect wished to return to Pennsylvania, where they would find a more congenial environment with German background. Another factor was Indiana's climate which the settlers from Wurtemberg found very hard to get used to. The economic motive was the soil being unfit for vineyards—their main agricultural occupation. The settlers also discovered that there were no outlets for their produce in the West, while in Pennsylvania the population clamored for their woven cloth.[9] In 1824 Frederick Rapp asked the English traveler and colonizer Richard Flower to assist in selling the lands of New Harmony. Through his mediation, a deal was made with the English reformer Robert Owen. In 1825 the entire settlement of New Harmony, its buildings, equipment, and its agricultural and industrial inventory were acquired by Robert Owen, who hoped to realize his utopian dream there.

The new settlement in Pennsylvania was called *Economy*, signifying the economic-industrial activity of the community. The settlers devoted themselves to the development of those industrial branches in which they had become proficient. They had therefore chosen their new site with an eye on easy transport routes east and west. Their experience in manufacturing and marketing helped them expand throughout the Ohio and Mississippi basin, and their reputation reached even New Orleans. Within a short period they were economically viable. When in 1826 the German economist Frederick List visited the settlement, he was impressed with the well-organized economic unit.[10] In the 1830s Frederick Rapp, the commune's economic driving force, reported that they had added silk weaving, hat making, the production of wines and the distilling of whisky as well as flour mills to their industries. Their marketing increased and their agents were active in all the big cities. The economic activity of the commune was overextended and outgrew its membership; they therefore had to employ hired labor.

In 1831 Economy numbered about 700, of which 440 were adults. They employed 135 workers (60 women, 60 men, and 15 children). Their economic success was the envy of their competitors mainly in Pittsburgh, where the commune's goods achieved a hegemony on the market. In 1829 a local paper published a series of articles accusing Economy of having a monopoly with which private industrialists and traders could not hope to compete. (This so-called monopoly was because of their owning the sheep that provided the raw material for their wool industry.)

Economy was also accused on a political level. Since they had participated in the local and national election campaigns, they had adopted a collective system of voting, and in 1828 they all voted for Andrew Jackson;[11] this was denounced as monopolistic as well. In the late 1820s the commune's life was disrupted by a number of secessions and the consequent claims on the society. During a court litigation the rights of collective property were established, and an agreement was reached in which all claims of seceders were relinquished and they could take with them only their personal belongings. These attacks from various directions, incited by their economic success, had the adverse effect of strengthening the commune whose members closed ranks in spite of all their trials.[12]

The Schism and Its Effect

The worst crisis in the Harmony Society history occurred in 1831, when few hundred of its members seceded under a religious leader who called himself Count de Leon. The background of the affair was the sect's millenary doctrine, according to which 1829 was the year of divine manifestation (later this was postponed to 1836). While being under the spell of millenarian expectation, a letter arrived from Germany proclaiming the "Annointed of the Lord," the Lion of Judah who would reveal himself in order to prepare the constitution of his divine kingdom. The letter echoed the beliefs prevailing in the sect and evoked the trust of its leaders. Count de Leon was in reality Bernhart Mueller, who had collected a number of followers and proceeded to the United States in order to join Harmony. George Rapp regarded this as a sign of the forthcoming redemption and accepted the count's statement without question, inviting him to come to Economy. The guest arrived in 1831 with fifty of his followers and was greeted with great formality by George Rapp himself. The latter soon realized that the count was an imposter and not the bearer of a message, but it was too late. The guests had been settled in a hotel and in some houses that had been put at their disposal, and since it was winter, they were not dislodged.

Meanwhile, the count became the focus of attraction for the discontented and frustrated members of Economy. He claimed to be one of their own sect, but, adverse to their customs, he permitted marriage, thus undermining George Rapp's leadership. During the winter about 250 members joined Count de Leon, and when in spring the time came for him to leave, a struggle broke out over the hegemony in Economy. Finally, in March 1832 an agreement was reached, and Count de Leon left the settlement with 176 members of Economy who decided to join him. About 250 adults remained loyal to George Rapp. The seceders attempted to establish a communal settlement in nearby Phillipsburg, but this was abandoned after Count de Leon's leadership was undermined. He left for Louisiana, where he died two years later.

A small group of his followers tried to return to Economy but were not accepted.[13] Others joined the Mormons and the Shakers, and a large group joined Dr. Keil to establish the commune Beth El. The schism in Economy was traumatic and left its members with a profound suspicion of every newcomer. They were especially suspicious when attempts were made by larger groups to form a union. For example, in the middle of the nineteenth century, religious and cultural relations with the Shakers were initiated, but Economy's members severed those because they thought that the Shakers were scheming to merge with them. Even connections with Zoar who were of the same origin, were very restricted. Merger was never mentioned.[14] Economy soon overcame the schism and life returned to normal even though some of the central members had left. George Rapp's leadership was reinforced. Belatedly he regarded the schism as a "purification of his community" and strove to establish a number of institutions that would watch over the commune's homogeneity. A council was elected of twelve elders who were granted wide social and economic authority; but as long as George Rapp and Frederick Rapp were alive these were theoretical only. Nevertheless, the council was to be the core from which future leaders would emerge after both leaders' deaths.[15]

Music in Economy

From its inception music played a vital role in the spiritual-cultural life of Harmony. This was the result of the sectarian tradition in Germany, where liturgical music was part of all religious meetings, combined with the collective values of the sect. In music they found a collective means of expression. The spiritual experience of music enhanced the ties of brotherhood and harmony among the members. Emphasis was laid on the collective execution of vocal or instrumental music, the choir, and the orchestra rather than on virtuoso-solo performance. Musical compositions were kept anonymous. Saturdays and festivals were celebrated with music; singing accompanied their work and daily activities as well. The importance of music in their daily life may be inferred from the spiritual leaders' activity. Frederick Rapp, a talented composer, used to compose hymns for special occasions. Together with George Rapp he composed the Harmony hymn. Gertrude Rapp, George Rapp's granddaughter, received a musical education from childhood and became a skillful musician.

One of the outstanding musicians of Harmony was Dr. Johann Christoff

Muller, the third in Harmony's hierarchy and the community's physician. He founded the orchestra and composed most of the music it performed.[16] In 1827 he hired as his assistant a young English musician, William Peters, who lived in nearby Pittsburgh. Peters elevated the orchestra to a high performance level and expanded its repertoire to include, besides religious and light music, classical compositions such as operas, overtures, symphonies, and large choral compositions. In 1831 Peters dedicated a symphony he composed to the local orchestra. It was probably the earliest composition west of the Alleghenies.[17] The years 1817 through 1832 were the most intensive and fruitful years for the orchestra. But the ideological schism curtailed its activities for a while because Dr. Muller was one of the seceders. Being of cardinal importance to the community's life, musical activities were soon revived. An English tourist, G.S. Buckingham, who had visited Harmony in 1840 wrote in his travelogue about the joys of music and the tranquility he had experienced.[18]

Frederick Rapp died in 1834 after a prolonged illness, at the age of sixty. After Frederick's death, all the reins of leadership passed into the hands of George Rapp, including economic activities and relations with the outside world, which had been his son's responsibility. George Rapp nominated Romelius Baker and Jacob Henrici to be his aides. After the schism, the absorption of new members became a tortuous process that only a handful managed to pass. As a result the commune gradually declined.[19] When in 1847 George Rapp died at the age of ninety, there were only 288 adults and children left.

Economic Prosperity and Social Decline

After George Rapp's death, the rules of the leadership by the Council of Elders were altered. The new rules specified a council of nine elders and two trustees who were practically in charge. Another change occurred in the commune's economy. Until 1868, when trustee Baker died, the economy had been stable, with most activities located on the commune itself. However, the diminishing number of members and various other difficulties caused a growing curtailment of the economic activity in the settlement. In 1852 the prosperous silk factory was closed and in 1858 the cotton factories. High tax on whisky caused the closure of the distillery in 1862. The sale of these brought in much capital, which was invested in land acquisitions and in industries and bonds outside the commune. Most of the work on the commune was now done by hired labor. The land was leased and clothing bought in Amana—which may be evidence of the Harmonists' continued affinity with the communal idea.[20]

Harmony Society became a capitalist enterprise, its enormous capital invested in a variety of economic activities whose extent is as astonishing as its business acumen. Economy was now one of the many capitalist and financial success stories of the industrial revolution in the United States. The driving force behind the investment policy was Jacob Henrici who had succeeded Romelius R.L. Baker as senior trustee and spiritual leader of the society. His way of joining the commune was special in that he was not a member of the founding sect from Wurtemberg. Henrici was born in Bavaria in 1804 and emigrated to the United States with his Lutheran parents when he was twenty years old. While still in Germany he had heard about Harmony and was inspired by the communal idea. After having helped his parents to settle down he asked to be accepted as a member of Economy. George Rapp, who interviewed him, was very impressed by his personality and integrity. He not only accepted him but took him under his wing. He was a trained teacher who also had a talent for economics, and when Frederick Rapp died, George Rapp proposed Henrici as manager of the commune's economic affairs. After George Rapp died Henrici was elected as one of the trustees.[21] It was Henrici who proposed the investment of the society's capital in railway stock when the lines were expanded into Pennsylvania. This move turned Economy into one of the biggest investors and the society participated in the management of some of the lines.

At the same time the society purchased some coal mines in an area that turned out to be one of the richest in the East. In 1859 Economy was one of the biggest investors and promoters of coal mining. However, the most important enterprise was the drilling of oil, and the society was among the pioneers of oil refinement. That happened when the society acquired a large tract of timber land in Warren County, Pennsylvania. Some time later oil drilling was started in the area and in 1857 a few wells were dug on Economy's property. Three years later a rich source of oil was found. In 1862 they began to refine it and the wise and enterprising management of one of Economy's members advanced the society's sale to 100,000 barrels in 1868. Between 1868 and 1873 the society drilled 73 wells, the most abundant of which produced 250 barrels a day. Economy Oil Company soon acquired a reputation for excellence and reliability as "an oasis of civilization" in the jungle of violent competition during the oil rush in the area.[22] The oil wells continued to produce until 1892, when Economy had to sell a large part of its possessions to overcome financial difficulties.

Wilhelm Weitling's Warning

At a time when the financial enterprises of the society were expanding, life on the commune stagnated and its membership diminished because of death and secession. There were only a few new candidates, most of them relatives of former members.

The settlements continued to attract tourists and visitors, especially from Germany. Among them was the tailor Wilhelm Weitling, one of Germany's first communists who later established his own commune in the United States. In 1851 he visited Economy and his impressions were those of an objective observer—critical and farsighted but with a positive attitude. He opened his description with the wonder he experienced at the beauty, order, and cleanliness of the settlement. The utopian in him naively exclaimed: "Ah, if our union had such a settlement, all the workers of Pittsburgh would within half a year join us, and all the workers of the U.S. would follow within a year."[23] He continued to relate at length all the conversations he had with commune members who freely informed him about their collective consumption, their kitchen and communal dining rooms and stores, and all the other aspects of communal life. Weitling criticized their celibate way of life which meant the absence of a second generation. In this connection he raised his fears about the communal property once all members had died and left no heirs. This would cause the commune's assets, accumulated through the labor of hundreds of members during scores of years, to fall into avaricious hands. (Weitling wrote this in 1851 without suspecting that his prophecy would be fulfilled fifty years later.)

Weitling was shocked by the indifference of the commune members to these matters and proposed they donate their property to charity as was befitting their religious convictions. There was no reaction to this proposal for which he blamed the society's materialistic spirit. This attitude was also at the root of commune members' criticism of the diminishing rentability of agriculture and industry. They claimed that it paid to invest their capital in marketable shares. In spite of his reservations Weitling summed up his visit on a positive note, saying that in such a settlement people "lived in Paradise."[24]

Economy—Benefactor of Other Communes

The turbulence of the Civil War which strongly affected most of the communes was not apparent in Economy. Only five men were enlisted because of the advanced age of most members. Harmony Society developed an ambivalent attitude toward the state and its institutions. They ignored authority, since they were "God's chosen people," and the core of the kingdom of heaven. Still, being pragmatic they made the best of the state's help, admitted its usefulness in keeping law and order, and even took a political stand. During the war they openly supported the North.

When in 1868 Romelius Baker, one of the two trustees, died, the administrative management of Economy passed on to Jacob Henrici.[25] He controlled a financial empire of millions of dollars without any kind of bookkeeping. All his transactions were undertaken according to his conscience and memorized, and he regarded himself the keeper of the sacred trust of Economy and their success as God's blessing. He was convinced that the vast capital was not meant to enrich individuals and should not be divided or donated. He therefore objected to any talk of dividing the heritage as long as any member of the commune survived (when the last of the sect died this resulted in a calamity). Intestate, many claimants fought over the property. In spite of his attitude Henrici was very generous when it came to helping other Christian communes. Economy lent assistance to Amana, Zoar, and the Shakers but particularly to the Hutterites, with whom they established a special relationship.

From the beginning of the Bon-Homme settlement in South Dakota in 1784, the members of Economy sent generous donations to finance various Hutterite activities. They also helped them market their produce. The Hutterites were family men who objected to celibacy, yet despite differences in their ways of life, Economy's members felt an affinity with them, and for a time they even considered bequeathing them their lands. There was an unsuccessful attempt to transfer a group of Hutterites to settlements in Pennsylvania with the intention of their joining Harmony Society.

Economy had connections with other communes, mainly religious ones. The members of Zoar were closest to their doctrine, but relations were barely correct (a few mutual visits and some legal aid) when seceders demanded property compensation from their commune. There seems to have been no economic or administrative connections, and when Zoar reinstituted the family, the gap widened. There were better relations with Amana, mostly through trade when Economy bought all their cloth from them, having closed down their own weaving mills.

The Shakers too showed interest in Economy. They even attempted to convince them of the Shaker doctrine, but the members of Harmony Society were unwilling to depart from their profound Lutheran convictions to embrace the Shakers' nebulous millennial doctrine. A unique relationship developed between Economy and the socialist colony Icaria. When in 1854 members of Icaria asked for help to develop their commune in Illinois, Henrici tactfully rejected their plea. He wrote them with esteem of their communal experiment but expressed his doubts about their optimistic socialist belief in human nature: Henrici believed in the fall and had no hope that secular (unreligious) man could adapt to the ideals of communal life. He could not trust the socialist doctrine of Icaria and hoped they would not be offended by his refusal to help; a decision based on bitter experience in the past.[26] Large donations were given to the Templers, the so-called Zionitic Christians, who had begun to settle in the Holy Land in 1870. Remembering George Rapp's belief that salvation would come from Jerusalem, the people of Economy regarded their help to the Templers as imperative and sent them $10,000 through 1890.[27]

Economy Under Henrici

During Henrici's leadership the number of members in Economy continued to drop. Those who remained were some of the founding fathers and their sons who had been born before celibacy was introduced. According to Charles Nordhoff's book on the American communes in 1874, there were 110 adults over forty and about 30 adopted children in Economy at the time, compared with Weitling's testimony of seventeen years earlier, when there were 280 members, 2 of them children. (And in 1868 there were 146 people, in 1889 only 25 survived.) Nordhoff mentions about 100 hired workers and their families who did most of the chores. Hired labor was not frowned upon. They were employed not only on the farm and in the local workshops but in other factories in their possession. Outstanding among them was the cutlery factory in the neighboring town which employed 200 Chinese. This was the background for a tense relationship with the local unions, who resented the competition of cheap Chinese labor. In 1873 this flared up and during the negotiations the Harmony Society tried to compromise in order to avoid the closure of the factory. They compensated the workers generously. This incident reflects the ambivalence of Economy in being a capitalist enterprise striving to make money and at the same time contributing to society. In order to appease their conscience the society donated generously to charity and turned their hotel, which had formerly been a business enterprise, into a doss-house where vagrants could find food and bed.[28]

The end of Economy as a communal settlement was approaching. There were still new applications for membership, but most of them were turned down because of the suspicion that the new candidates were eager for the commune's inheritance. During 1890-91 only 20 new candidates were accepted, most of them relatives of members. Their motives were usually not religious, and most of them were indeed motivated by avarice. One of them was 20-year-old John S. Duss, born in Cincinnati, Ohio, whose father had been killed in the Civil War. His mother had been accepted into Economy as a war widow, and young John was first educated in the commune, then transferred to an orphanage until 1876, when he returned for two years to the commune. He left for the West (1879-1890), where he married and had a variety of jobs, only to return to Economy in 1890 as a member. Within a year he was elected elder side by side with the aging Henrici, who died in 1892, when John Duss took over the leadership.[29]

How the Commune's Assets Were Wasted

In the 1890s a new period set in. Economy was no longer a functioning commune. A rapid process of disintegration began with a fight over the inheritance. The number of members dropped drastically when most of them died, others were expelled, and some, having received compensation, left willingly. Among the few left were John Duss and his wife, who had joined the commune shortly after her husband. During the first years of his trusteeship, Duss devoted himself to saving the commune—which had been prosperous and extremely affluent—from the financial disaster that threatened it in 1892 because of mismanagement. Duss hired the best lawyers and accountants and within a short period succeeded in saving the society from bankruptcy. However, he was unable to relax; a number of lawsuits followed, most of them with seceders who sued for their share of the commune's property.[30]

John Duss succeeded in winning the litigation but not in order to save the commune. He now put the vast riches of the society at his and his wife's disposal. As fate would have it, the 1902 verdict declared that the estate was the sole property of the commune and not dividable. Duss could therefore continue to use the commune's capital in order to further his own musical ambitions.[31]

Duss had received his musical education while studying on the commune, and his self-esteem prompted him to look for a way to resume this activity. So he reformed the orchestra, mainly by hiring musicians from the outside. He became its conductor and later combined the Economy and Pittsburgh orchestras to tour the East.[32] Duss spent a fortune on advertising the concert tour and presented himself as ''a musical wonder.'' He was invited to perform in New York in the summer of 1902. In the winter of 1902-3 Economy sold some of its land to a large steel company, which established a huge bridge-constructing firm on the site. The eight members of the society, of whom only John Duss and his wife were young, became extremely rich. In the election of that year Duss and a senile, 75-year-old member were elected elders. In this capacity Duss could use sums of up to $20,000 without authorization from other members. He left for New York a millionaire musician. His being a member of the small religious commune added to his attraction, and when the Metropolitan Opera got into financial difficulties Duss could save the day. Indeed in the summer of 1903 he was made guest conductor of the Metropolitan Opera orchestra with a ghost conductor assisting him in the job. After the summer season the orchestra went on a coast to coast tour, all expenses paid by the commune.[33] That same year John Duss left the commune. After he left his wife filled in the vacancy of trustee and with her fellow trustee's agreement, granted Duss $50,000 in compensation. Thus the pessimistic prediction of Weitling in 1851 became a reality. Those members who had not established any rules for utilizing their property for communal or religious purposes had caused their property to fall into the unscrupulous hands of one who spent it on aims far removed from those of Rapp and his followers.

A Sad Epilogue

Susie Duss was trustee until 1905 together with the aged Benjamin Gillman, who served as a sort of rubber stamp and agreed to the dissolution of the commune and handed over the entire property to Susie Duss. After John Duss had fulfilled his musical aspirations he returned to the commune. But now the Dusses encountered unexpected opposition to their wish of acquiring Economy's property. The state of Pennsylvania claimed that Economy was regarded as a religious society for the purpose of charity and the state was meant to be its sole heir. The lawsuit went on for several years because the Dusses prevented the state lawyers to make use of the commune's archives with its relevant documents. In 1916 a compromise was reached and the property was split between the two sides.[34] The capital received by the state of Pennsylvania was invested in a fund intended to preserve the tradition and the past of Harmony Society on Economy lands. The remaining buildings were turned into a historical site which is well maintained until this very day.

It was the state of Pennsylvania that erected a monument for Harmony, not its members or their descendants.

Zoar

A short while after the Rappists abandoned their first settlement—Harmony—in Pennsylvania and moved to Indiana, another immigrant group arrived from Germany in 1817 and established an independent settlement called *Zoar*. They had been influenced by the same mystic doctrines as the followers of George Rapp; they also left the Lutheran Church to establish a pietist-separatist sect. They kept in strict isolation from secular authorities and refused to honor rulers and potentates. Tradition will have it that one of the sect's elders even accused Napoleon of his responsibility for the mass murder his wars had caused, adding that he would stand before a higher court one day. This ostentatious civil rebellion caused them to be persecuted by the authorities, and they were driven to seek refuge in a place where they could practice their religion freely. Therefore in 1817 a group of 300, most of them farmers from Wurtemberg, Baden, and Bayern (Bavaria) decided to emigrate.[35] Their spiritual leader was Joseph Baumler (later Bimeler), a farmer's son who became a weaver and later a teacher. He was outstanding in his skillful and charismatic leadership even though he was a cripple and a hunchback. Most of the sect were too poor to afford their own fare, and it was paid for by the kind contributions of English Quakers who had heard about their persecutions. They acquired their first land with a loan from the American Quakers of Philadelphia and an additional one from their English friends. The tract of 5000 acres in the northeastern part of Ohio was near Harmony.

In the spring of 1818 the group began to build their first log huts, but most of the settlers were so poor they had to hire out with richer farmers in order to repay the loan on their land.[36] Until then they had not even considered collective farming. They soon realized that the dispersion of members in search of work would cause the disintegration of the sect. Bimeler and some central members therefore suggested the establishment of a commune. The idea was not unfamiliar, because they had already shared their property during the period of persecution in Germany. In a meeting of all members, 225 men, women, and children who remained in the settlement, decided to abolish all private accounts and to introduce a community of goods. Fifty-three men and 104 women signed the charter to establish a commune on April 19 1819.[37]

The name Zoar was given after the biblical town to which Lot fled (Genesis 19/22), and it expressed their millennial expectations of cosmic change.[38] They lived in an oasis of purity amidst a desert of sin and violence. In time these expectations were turned inward in the hope of improving their own morality. During the first years the sect practiced celibacy, which was initiated as a way to salvation by the rank and file, similar to their separatist brothers from Harmony. Bimeler was passive and ambivalent; he was married and realized that marriage was part of the earthly life. However, he believed that in the kingdom of heaven there was no place for this institution and when the pressure to establish celibacy increased, he accepted it. Ten years later Bimeler was among those who proposed a return to family life. It is agreed that he did so because he intended to marry a young and pretty member of the commune who was in charge of his housekeeping. He did marry her in 1830, and this was the signal to abolish celibacy, which Zoar had never taken seriously. Most members resumed a monogamous married life.[39]

Families began to take an active part in social life. Meals were cooked centrally but eaten in the family home. Supplies and kitchen utensils were accorded to each family from a central store, but clothing was allocated according to a fixed budget and chosen individually.[40] Each family had its house and garden. The children stayed with their mothers up to kindergarden age, after which they were collectively educated; until 1845 they slept in children's houses, but because of parents' discontent with the collective housing, they were returned to their parents' houses.[41]

From its inception, the people of Zoar arranged their lives in an orderly manner. Those who had been renegades in Wurtemberg now tried to adapt to the law of the country, and in 1824 their founding covenant became their constitution, signed by 60 men and 100 women. Six years later Zoar was legally recognized by the state of Ohio. This legalized their property and business practices, their members' standing and rights and the commune became known as The Separatist Society of Zoar. Throughout its history, women were in the majority. They had equal rights, took part in the general meetings, voted, and were elected to responsible positions. Zoar's constitution was democratic, and the commune was managed by a committee that was elected every three years. The highest executive authority was often the board of trustees, among whom Bimeler had a special place. He was the "general agent" who represented the commune in all external dealing but had to report to the trustees.[42]

Years of Prosperity

Zoar's communal organization proved to be very efficient. Economically Zoar stood out among all the surrounding farms in its economic prosperity. It profited when the Ohio-Erie Canal was being dug between 1825 and 1833. The commune had undertaken to provide labor for the construction work near the settlement. They also agreed to supply the work camps in the area with fresh farm produce. The profits were invested in the purchase of additional land in the area. They now owned 12,000 acres, and during this period of prosperity, 170 new members of the sect arrived from Germany,[43] their population now reaching 500 (all except one, who had been a Shaker, were immigrants).

The additional members and the prosperous years during the 1840s brought economic expansion and diversification of the farm branches. In addition to the cultivated farm lands they now had a herd of about 1,000 sheep, two large saw mills, a wool-weaving factory and looms for weaving linen as well as a dying house and tannery, a foundry that produced iron stores, a distillery, and a cider mill. Zoar's property was estimated at $2 million. Until 1838 only commune members did all the jobs, but when an epidemic of cholera struck and many died, they began to hire outside labor. This was to be the state of affairs from then on.

In spite of their prosperity, Zoarites never attempted to embellish their environment. There were about 40 unattractive living quarters and farm buildings. The only aspect which elevated the general air of neglect and shabbiness were the flower gardens around the houses.[44] The single house of distinction was the "palace" built for Bimeler. The initiative came from commune members and was accompanied by lengthy discussions of whether such a building would fit the communal way of life. Bimeler himself took care to be equal among equals, although his spiritual leadership had established him as a central figure in Zoar. His sermons and preachings were the only spiritual food for thought of commune members. He was musically active and cultivated choral singing and instrumental playing. There also was an excellent orchestra conducted by a member of the commune, which often performed in the neighborhood.[45]

Bimeler died in 1853, and this was the beginning of Zoar's deterioration. After his death there was no one who could carry on his spiritual leadership. Missing his sermons, the members decided to publish them. Bimeler had never written down or edited any of his sermons. He used to say: "When I arrive, I am an empty vessel. . . . I never know what I am going to say . . . but then inspiration comes, leading me on to preach, and as soon as I begin to speak an endless flood of ideas appears and all I have to do is to navigate my way and choose to say that which seems imperative." Yet some members had taken notes, which though inaccurate, they were published in three volumes between 1856 and 1861, and give us a good idea of Bimeler's characteristic teachings. Bimeler was a severe critic of the church establishment, calling it bigoted, enslaved by the state, and subject to avarice. He called on his sect to maintain their inner morality because "true Christianity must be a thing of the heart. Man must divest himself of his bad qualities and of his passion and deny his own vicious will and subordinate it to God in order that old Adam die in him and Christ may arise anew."[46] The reading of Bimeler's sermons on Sundays became a noninspiring ritual. The first trustee to follow Bimeler as spiritual leader was Jacob Sylman. He had no talent for rhetoric. The next was Christian Weebel, who took over in 1862 but was unpopular with most members of the commune. In 1871 he was followed by Jacob Ackermann, who continued his trusteeship for many years but was not blessed with any intellectual ability. He could not stand up to the young members who criticized the ideological ways of the commune.[47]

In the 1860s Zoar was still a stable and affluent commune. Its strength helped members at a time when there was not charismatic leadership. However, forces from within and without began to undermine the commune and in the 1880s they burst out openly when seceders demanded a proportional compensation. Since the 1850s a number of law suits were won by the commune, which had had the foresight to establish its constitution legally. In a precedental verdict given in *Gosele v. Zoar* Justice McLean stated that according to Zoar's constitution the claimant had agreed to give up all private property and to work in cooperation with others for the general good; his right of ownership became immersed in the general right of the association; he had no individual right and could transmit none to his heirs. It was clear therefore that individuals had no claim on the property except using it, and even that according to limitations established in the constitution.[48]

The Decline

During the 1860s many of the young members left the commune. They had been discontent with the separatist way of life, far from the mainstream of the developing country. When the Civil War broke out twenty members enlisted for the North, in spite of the commune's pacifist attitude. None of them returned to the commune—some were killed, others were no longer attracted to communal life.[49] Henceforth the commune began to lag behind its neighbors' economic development. Technical innovations and industrial growth of the U.S. economy left the commune with none of the advantages it had had. Some of their most prosperous branches—the dye house, the weaving plant, and the iron stove factory closed down. Production and marketing went down while the expense did not, and when Charles Nordhoff visited the settlement in 1874 he found about 50 hired workers in a community of 300 men, women, and children.[50]

In the 1880s deterioration became evident. Zoar was an aging settlement, culturally and spiritually petrified, while Ohio at large was prospering, and most of the young people of Zoar were attracted by the dynamic reality of their surroundings. Those who were born after Bimeler had died were no longer inspired by the communal theories. Many were alien to his preachings which were read in church, and most of the young people stayed away altogether from religious meetings. In the 1890s it became clear that the commune could no longer count on the loyalty of its members: there were instances of refusing to work, others openly sold commune property, and greed and materialism became evident. It is ironical that Levi Bimeler, the grandson of Zoar's founder and leader, was the driving force of the opposition that brought about the final dissolution. Educated at a government teachers' college, he began a campaign to change Zoar's constitution in order to pay compensation to seceders.

In his monthly bulletin *Nugitna* Levi Bimeler violently attacked the tradition of Zoar, focusing his attack on "communism" which, according to him, had not been planned by the founders but had been forced on them by the weak and destitute who constituted the majority in the first years of the commune. In the fourth issue of *Nugitna*, which never appeared, he concluded his attack thus: "Communism may be a good thing in the interior of Africa, but in the center of the highly civilized state of Ohio it is an outrage." The editorial went on to count all the drawbacks of communism which enslaves man to work and behavior imposed by an elite: "Only fools and religious bigots or self-conceited ones are so blind to believe there is no difference in rank and fortune." He ridiculed the "hypocrisy of equality."[51] *Nugitna* was stopped after three issues. The commune's leadership curtailed the activities of the internal opposition that was undermining the very existence of Zoar. But it was too late; Levi Bimeler had found willing partners, because economic hardships had visited the commune and its income had dwindled drastically. The opposition blamed the unwillingness of members to exert themselves for the common good. Under the circumstances of economic deterioration and the loss of the commune's confidence in its way of life, a proposal was put forward to dissolve the commune and to divide its property. This was accepted in January 1898, and in December 1898 the property was divided among the remaining members.

Professor E. Randall, who wrote the first comprehensive book on Zoar, visited the settlement in the summer of 1898. The prevailing atmosphere was one of disintegration, and the local doctor, a resident of many years, told him that the old people did not want to leave, but the young were eager to dissolve the commune because they had tasted life outside and realized the variety of opportunities there compared with the quiet, remote commune. On returning they were not absorbed. The local barber, who had lived in Zoar for many years without being a member, said that Zoar was no place for the young. Indeed, when Randall visited members' homes he got the impression that most had at least one son living away from the commune. Most of the oldtimers talked lovingly of the past and were worried about the dangers of dissolving the commune. One of them, the local shepherd, claimed that "communism was and is a success" and objected to any change. The man in charge of the steam engine in the cider factory said that his life on Zoar had been one of security and peace, but he did not believe that there was any way of maintaining the communal way of life any longer.

Many were critical of the present state of affairs. They complained about the injustice of not getting paid for special efforts. The blacksmith said that he would earn much more if he had worked independently. The man who got up early to milk the cows added that others who worked less had had the same rights and benefits. However, Randall got the impression that even the most ardent critics did not blame individuals or the authorities. Most attacks were aimed at the system which "rewarded the lazy." Everyone he talked to told Randall that the present situation could not continue. Even those who supported the commune realized that there were too many loopholes in the commune's way of life. For instance, many of the young people were riding bicycles they bought with their "private money." Randall heard of many such instances where members earned an extra penny selling eggs and chickens which they had grown privately, to guests in the local hotel. Women would serve the guests, launder, mend and press their clothes for a fee. The young went fishing and sold their catch in the market; they went on errands for privately owned factories near the commune. It was a sad picture of deterioration, and Randall realized that the days of the commune were numbered.[52]

During the division of the property many problems arose. One of them was the question of how to divide the different kinds of land. There were 220 members. Everyone received $250 in cash, a piece of land, and a share in the rest of the property. The farm was divided into 135 units, thus every member received property valued at $2,500. Most of the young members sold their share and left but those who stayed formed a noncommunal municipality.

W. Hinds and E. Randall, who had known Zoar during its final years, each returned a few years later. They both reported that there was a tendency to adapt to modern ways: a public telephone had been put up at the hotel. Nearby automats rendered sweets and chewing gum. On the other side of the street an ice cream parlor was installed. The house fronts had been renovated, the streets given new names, and new families had constructed their homes. With the establishment of the family units, divorce materialized for the first time. In conversations with the local people, the visitors got the impression that people had mixed feelings about Zoar's past. Oldtimers who had no profession met with difficulties in adjusting to the new conditions; others seemed happy. The blacksmith and cowmen who had complained about the lack of equality admitted that they were working harder but getting paid much more. Most of the people seemed to be proud of their new acquisition. At the end of a long conversation Hinds, who revisited Zoar in 1900, asked an old acquaintance of his whether he and his friends regarded their lives as a failure. The answer was: "In a way I do. Communism is the only true way of life. In heaven, everything is communal and the community is a way to prepare people for the next world."[53]

Amana

The last wave of German separatist immigration, the inspirationalists, began to arrive in the United States in 1842. They hoped to establish independent communal settlements in which to practice their beliefs. This was the largest and best organized of the German sects and had experienced communal life for a short period in their homeland. The origins of this sect were in the early seventeenth century within pietist circles in Wurtemberg and Hessen. Most of the sectarians came from among peasants and the lower middle classes. From among them the sect of the Community of True Inspiration emerged. They were conspicuous in their belief that prophecies still existed as in the days of the Bible, and God would speak through certain chosen individuals who were called *Werkzeuge* (instruments). During the early 1700s the sect was led by two *Werkzeuge*—Eberhard Ludwig Gruber, a Lutheran minister, and Johann Frederick Rock, a harness maker, son of a Lutheran minister.

The center of the sect was the principality of Wurtemberg, but they branched out to other areas in Alsace-Lorraine and some Swiss cantons. This expansion caused the secular authorities and the Lutheran Church to start persecuting them, and many sectarians moved to Hessen, the most tolerant of the German states. This period ended when the "instruments" died and no new "prophets" followed.[54] A period of decline began for the Society of true Inspiration which lasted until the appearance of new trustworthy *Werkzeuge* in 1817. The first was Michael Krausert who was soon followed by Christian

Metz, a carpenter, and Barbara Heineman, an uneducated factory worker who, when inspired, quickly mastered the Scriptures as well as secular studies. Under their leadership the inspirationalists renewed their activities. This, in turn, prompted further persecutions, and only Hessen remained a haven for the sect. Many of them arrived destitute and depended on the help of the more affluent members. It was Metz's idea to lease some estates in the area of Marienburg and an old monastery in Engenthal in which the sect could settle down to a communal life.

There were two reasons for this step: the first was necessity, the other the Christian apostolic tradition of Jesus' disciples as related in the New Testament.[55] At first all sectarians handed over their possessions to a common fund. This sharing later branched out to include education, work organization, and cooperative agriculture and industry. The community prospered for a decade, then came a series of setbacks. The first was caused by the tense relations with envious neighbors, then came a few years of drought. But the worst setback occurred when the political and religious tolerance of Hessen ceased. The demand to emigrate to the United States grew,[56] but no moves could be made unless they were legitimized from above through the *Werkzeuge*. Since 1826 a series of prophecies had called them to emigrate across the sea to the New World.

In a convention in Engenthal in the summer of 1842, prompted by the prophecies, the sect decided to send a number of elders to examine the possibility of settlement in the United States.[57] A year later Christian Metz sailed with a group of elders, and arrived in New York in October 1843. During the cold winter months they searched for land in northwest New York. Finally, they bought 5,000 acres in an area which had been an Indian reserve of the Seneca, some distance from Buffalo (which at the time was a small frontier town). Now the first group could organize from among the sect in Hessen. Not all were eager to emigrate to a remote place in the west, but the first group of 320 arrived at the beginning of 1844, and in May the first settlement was established. Some time later 4,000 additional acres were purchased, and the area became the center of the sect.

The first settlement was named *Ebenezer* (taken from 1 Sam. 7:12). New settlers kept arriving and in the summer of 1845 the population was about 800.[58] Most of them were peasants and artisans, some had property, others were penniless. A Dutch Mennonite family was accepted and contributed land from across the Canadian border. During these first years four Ebenezer villages were established, in this order: Middle, followed by Upper, Lower, and New Ebenezer. There was as yet no definition of the communal characteristics of the settlement. A provisional constitution stipulated that all property be collectively owned, but each member maintained the rights of property and the income thereof. This soon caused a widening of the gap between members, and some pressure was brought to permit private property although this was to be restricted according to the commune's traditions of mutual aid during the interim period. However, the leadership realized the danger of disintegration that threatened the community. They insisted on sharing their property in order to enable the rest of the sect, most of whom were destitute, to emigrate. They had to be helped with traveling expenses, housing, and a plot of land. In addition, some were old or sick and some had no farming experience.

The communal way of life seemed ideal under these circumstances; it had after all, been the tradition of most sectarians before their emigration. At this stage again the *Werkzeuge* were inspired by the Holy Spirit to prophesy and openly preach the communal idea. Thus reinforced, a provisional constitution was adopted in 1843 and after several amendments it was legalized by the state in 1845 as the Ebenezer Society.[59]

The inspirationalists had from the beginning insisted on a legal set of rules. This later served them well in their dealings with the authorities and also enabled them to take a stand against oppositional currents which were against communitarian policy and aspired to enhance the realm of private property. The commune's leadership dealt with this opposition through religious sanctions and claimed that they undermined the instructions of the Holy Spirit. The height of the opposition was overcome in 1854, when the *Werkzeuge* were visited by a vision which bade them strengthen the commune and reject the doubters.[60]

The crystallization of the sect as a federation of communes proved to be an economic success. Within a few years all four Ebenezer settlements were prospering. Nevertheless, ten years later, unforeseen difficulties arose when the remaining Seneca Indians refused to leave the land. The inspirationalists discovered that they had been misled by the real estate agents who had claimed the Indian land was for sale. The settlers now found themselves involved in a growing tension with the Indians. This went against their principles and they were forced to ask the authorities for help in settling the disagreement through mediation.[61] There was also tension with envious neighbors in the area that began to be densely settled after the opening of the Erie Canal. The price of land rose stiffly, and there was no way to acquire additional plots for the inspirationalist settlers who kept arriving from Germany. Doubts as to the future of the settlement in the area grew when Buffalo expanded, reaching the boundaries of Ebenezer and putting temptations in their way. All this combined to urge the inspirationalists to settle further west. This intention was reinforced when in August 1854 Christian Metz was ordered by the Holy Spirit to look west and search for the sect's future there.[62]

Once again emissaries set out to tour new places for settlement. They first went to Kansas, but after weeks of searching found no suitable place that would accommodate their whole prosperous community. Turning north they arrived in Iowa and discovered fertile and cheap land in abundance. They bought 20,000 acres in a wide forested valley through which a river flowed, about 20 miles from Iowa City. It was ideal for their purpose to establish a farming commune.

In the summer of 1855 the first settlement was established in Iowa. Its biblical name Amana was symbolical. Geographically, the hills overlooking the wide valley reminded them of the lines in chapter 4 of Song of Solomon: "Come with me from Lebanon, my bride. . . . Depart from the peak of Amana, from the peak of Senir and Hermon, from the dens of lions . . ."; the name also expressed the stability and profound beliefs and loyalties characteristic of the sect. During the resettlement process in Iowa the practical approach and organizational talent of the collective was fully exploited. The transfer took ten years to be completed; it was accomplished gradually, in a controlled manner, and in those years the sect's orderly life was maintained in both areas and in spite of the disturbance. Christian Metz was instrumental in keeping the sect intact while wandering from one center to the other. They even managed to sell the property in New York State without a considerable financial loss.

Seven new settlements sprang up in Iowa—Amana, East Amana, Middle Amana, West Amana, South Amana, High Amana, and Homestead. More land was added, and they now owned 20,000 acres. In 1865 the transfer was completed and the sect numbered 1,200 members, including new immigrants from Germany.[63] In 1859 they were recognized by the Iowa authorities as a religious and benevolent society. The most important aspect of this was that the communal idea was recognized as a principle of the society, enabling it to fulfill its Christian duty.[64]

Economic Stability

The Civil War broke out during the last stages of transfer to Iowa. Like other communes, the members of Amana had ambivalent feelings toward it. On the one hand they supported abolition, on the other they objected to active participation in the fighting. They compromised by donating $20,000 to the war effort of the North. A large amount was contributed by members from their personal property, clothing, household goods, and blankets. This involvement in the war effort expressed the awareness of some members of the political events, but the leadership halted any tendency to be fully integrated and to participate in the elections. Eventually the sect stayed away from politics.[65]

Two years after the completion of the resettlement in Iowa, Christian Metz died after having been the sect's leader and *Werkzeuge* for fifty years. Every decision, big or small, had been inspired by him. Through him the Holy Spirit had prophesied 3,654 times.[66] A few years later, in 1883, Barbara Heineman died and with her the last of the *Werkzeuge*, and prophesy ceased to occur. This in no way harmed the development of Amana which continued to prosper socially and economically and was a model for other communal experiments.

In 1874 the journalist Charles Nordhoff visited Amana on his tour of communes in the United States. In his book he described the economic and social developments and prosperity of the Iowa communes. From his statistics we learn that the population in the seven communities was 1,480. The largest of them, Amana, had 450 souls. All had a variety of agricultural branches, cereals, vegetables, orchards, a herd of 3,000 sheep, 1,300 cows, 2,500 pigs and horses. Side by side with agriculture they developed industry and craftsmanship. In each settlement there were workshops for local needs such as a shoemaker, tailor, and blacksmith. In some communes there were wool-weaving factories, saw mills, flour mills, and a print shop.

Economic expansion replaced the population growth. The arrival of new immigrant groups had ceased. Those who came were mostly individuals who had applied while still in Germany. Most of them had religious convictions similar to the sect's, but some Catholics and even Jews were also accepted after a period of two years candidacy. At the time of Nordhoff's visit there were about 200 agricultural hands, a considerable number of them hired workers. He stresses the good conditions these workers received in the communal settlement.[67]

Nordhoff's impressions of Amana were very positive. He described the orderly arrangements of the commune, its collective consumption in kitchens and communal dining rooms, and its well-organized social life and work schedule. According to the structure established in 1843 the sect's affairs were managed by a board of trustees elected from among the elders. This board had to report annually to the general assembly on financial and economic affairs. Nordhoff emphasized that the principle of cooperation was valid not just within each single commune, but also on the federative level of all three Amana settlements.[68] Most impressive was that hardly any of the young left the commune, and those who did usually returned after a while. The period 1880-1890 passed peacefully in Amana, which continued to prosper. It owed its steady growth to natural increase, the absorption of single immigrants from Germany, and Americans who had opted for communal life. Among them were former members of Zoar and Harmony, which were then in a process of disintegration. Some of the new candidates were motivated not by religion but by socialist ideology.[69]

There were secessions here as well. In 1905 a suit was brought against Amana in which one of the disgruntled ex-members demanded a share in the commune's property. As before, the commune won and the collective property was legally recognized.

In the early twentieth century several books and articles on communes in the United States appeared. In all of them Amana is extensively described. Hinds gives exact information on the population of Amana which at the time numbered 1,770 (604 men, 663 women, 503 children).[70] Hinds's descriptions of the communal way of life at Amana were similar to those of Nordhoff's. He too was impressed by their stability, mixed farming, and use of technology in both agriculture and industry, distinguishing the commune from the surrounding farms. He also was impressed by the efficiency and diligence of the members which contributed to their prosperity. During the agricultural season they had to employ 170 hired laborers in order to overcome the shortage of hands. In the industrial branches, e.g. wool weaving, there were only 18 hired hands who worked side by side with 125 members. The picture that emerges is one of tranquility in the field and factory. There were some critical descriptions as well that pinpointed the external aspects of the village. Although there were gardens by the houses there was little awareness of the general state of neglect and no interest in culture. The local schools taught secular and religious subjects but did not become centers of cultural inspiration. In contrast to its economic prosperity Amana seems to have been a cultural desert. One point agreed on by all the books published in 1908 is that the young people of Amana showed an outstanding attachment to their settlement and most stayed on.[71]

Amana in the Twentieth Century

There was no significant change during the first two decades of the twentieth century. The Amanas were socially stable, and even if some members left and their number was down to 1,500 there was no danger that this might affect their existence. There continued to be a healthy proportion of young and old on each commune.

The first signs that not all was well were external, but they were harbingers of change. The somber traditional German garb, which had distinguished Amana members, was disappearing and being replaced by typical midwestern farmers' attire. Only on holidays could the habitual headwear of women and men still be seen. German, which had been the sacred and the profane language of all, made way for English. Contact with the outside world became extensive; American civilization had reached the outposts of the West, and the enclosure in which the founding fathers of Amana had established their settlement was made accessible. Bertha Shambaugh defines the change in her book *Amana That Was and Amana That Is*, claiming that Amana was no longer inaccessible: "The forefathers had drawn a circle around the community, designed to keep the world out; but the world made a larger circle and drew the community within its orb."[72] Roads and railways which now ran from shore to shore passed through the plains of Iowa, crossing Amana's lands. As the number of cars steadily grew, thousands of tourists stopped to visit the "religious reservation" of Amana. Convenient roads facilitated this invasion of visitors who brought with them cars, radios, bicycles, cameras, and other luxury items which, once discovered, became the object of craving to the younger generation.[73]

This vast change could not by itself have undermined the commune's foundations had there not been also an internal process of disintegration of the religious doctrines.[74] After Metz's death in 1867 and Barbara Heineman's in 1883, it became ever more difficult to maintain the religious dogma. There were no *Werkzeuge* who could instill their prophetic inspirations in the people. The new leaders lacked the spiritual authority to combat secular and religious threats.[75] The second and third generation, who had not been spiritually inspired by the *Werkzeuge*, could not withstand the many temptations that the world offered them. The elders' authority was too feeble to check external influences.[76]

First to be undermined were the communal principles. The commune had been established as a result of the sect's immediate needs and had not been anchored in social philosophy other than a normative adherence to apostolic Christianity.[77] When the urge for seclusion waned, the younger generation began to doubt the restrictions and limitations that prevented them from enjoying the luxuries they craved. The desire for money grew, and the norms of three generations foundered. The accumulation of private property, which had been secretly going on for some time, now became general practice. Roads that had been opened to the neighboring states gave access to private occupations and income. Parallel to their avid desire for private property, work discipline was deteriorating and members no longer aspired to social responsibility. Additional workers were hired for the factories and the commune's profits went down.[78]

World War I brought tensions and conflicts with the American society and its authorities. Amana's German tradition and pacifism gave rise to suspicion and hostility. In 1918 all the young men of Amana were conscripted. After intensive lobbying they were transferred to nonbeligerent units. To overcome the continued suspicion and hostility after the war, the elders were prompted to curtail the isolationist tradition of Amana. They adopted English, which soon replaced German, as their everyday language. This was just one step in the direction of radical reforms in Amana's way of life.

Since the 1920s the call for revision was openly heard but to no effect. The authoritarian rule of the elders withstood the change, but not for long. When the Depression hit the United States in 1929 Amana economists realized that the settlement was on the verge of bankruptcy. Their debts grew to $0.5 million. In 1930 there was a real danger of total collapse, and the leaders called all adult members over twenty-one to attend emergency meetings in their respective communes. After hearing a detailed report of the grave economic situation they were asked to reexamine the economic foundation of their settlement. A committee of "47" was democratically and proportionally elected. The younger generation was represented for the first time, somewhat of a revolution after the autocratic rule of the elders.[79] The council met in April 1931 to formulate proposals for a referendum. On June 10, 1931, members had to choose between two options: (1) to return to their forefathers' lifestyle, to reinforce the communal way and principle, and to uproot all deviance which had infested their society ruthlessly and return to an austerity until better times arrived; or (2) to reorganize the building up of Amana and its enterprises and to establish a holding company, providing work for its shareholders and paying their salaries, i.e., to abolish the commune as an economic entity while maintaining its unity as a religious sect. We must remember that the referendum was held at a time of a serious recession and that everyone felt the need for a different approach in order to achieve relief. Seventy-five percent voted for the reorganization. In six out of seven communes, a majority supported the change. As a result, committees were set up to prepare a comprehensive plan, helped by experts, on aspects of formality.

The plan that crystallized between July 1931 and May 1932 was a masterpiece of compromising between the individualistic and the collective tendencies of Amana. All the real estate and factories remained the property of the community and were operated on a collective basis. They were estimated to be worth $2 million and included land, orchards, livestock, and factories. Everything was divided into stock. Of the $50 shares, 1,200 were voting shares which the adult members received. They were non-negotiable, and on leaving the settlement their owners lost their voting right. The other shares were divided according to different criteria and the majority (32,400) were alloted according to seniority and were the foundation of members' property, providing them with the means to acquire homes and cattle.

The plan was accepted by 90 percent of the members and went into effect in May 1932.[80] That summer Amana began to function according to the new policy. Members worked for pay, the work roster was reorganized, new jobs were created and most hired workers were discharged, because one of the foremost priorities was to supply work for everyone. The act that most symbolized the change was the abolishment of the communal kitchens and dining rooms. On May 31, 1932, members ate their last collective meal. It was a sad moment—the dining room, which had been the focal point of communal life, was now deserted. A different reality had begun. Yet the transition was gradual and there was no feeling of a radical change, rather that of an adaptation to new circumstances.[81] Amana had dissolved the commune but not the community and its religious framework. The seven settlements continued to maintain close contact on an economic, social, and religious basis. The uniqueness of their religion was kept and was now called "The Amana Church Society" (instead of "The Sect of True Inspiration").

Economic cooperation has prospered. The stockholders have not been tempted by the options of private enterprise. Their factories have remained corporations until this very day and are owned and operated jointly. The lines of production have changed and have become modern and efficient. Besides agriculture and woolen mills, *Amana* now means refrigeration, air-conditioning, and microwave ovens. Their far-reaching economic success has not turned the people away from their communal heritage. They are proud to hold on to cooperation in the form of mutual help and the responsibility of the community for every individual. The inhabitants of Amana show their respect to the past in many ways. A local museum has been reconstructed, and many of the documents that survived after ninety years of communal life in the United States are kept there. Accessibility to a main road enables thousands of tourists to visit each year and get an impression of this chapter in the history of the commune in the United States.

Beth El and Aurora

Beth El

Parallel to the establishment of the German immigrant communes, a group of Germans who had been living in the United States for some time established a commune in 1843. Most of them were too poor to buy their own plots. Not having put down roots anywhere, they wandered all over Pennsylvania until, influenced by the revival meetings of the early 1840s, they began to seek salvation. The man who changed these nomads into a closely knit community and established a commune in Missouri was Dr. Wilhelm Keil.[82]

Keil had immigrated from Germany and was wandering all over Pennsylvania at the time of the revival meetings of the 1840s. Abandoning his Methodist creed he began to preach independently, calling on his listeners to live modestly and be reborn. He was a gifted rhetorician, and his apocalyptic sermons drew many followers from among the German immigrants who were adrift in Ohio and West Virginia, Kentucky, and Indiana. His first group of followers came from the Philipsburg Rappists who had seceded from Economy under Count de Leon. Searching for a leader, they found Dr. Wilhelm Keil. Their communal way of life was in tune with Keil's religious preachings of millenial expectations and a moral way of life.[83] After he had established his influence over the small group of Rappists, Keil set out on a tour in Pennsylvania, Ohio, and Kentucky, calling on his followers to join the communitarian experiment. Many did, and, selling their property, they joined the Pennsylvania group which had adopted the name of Beth El. They had no definite tenets, since Keil refused to formulate any theories. He regarded the Bible as their theoretic foundation and maintained that their communal practices should grow spontaneously. This characterized Beth El as one of the few communes that never defined any regulations and was thus never legalized by state authorities. They remained a "voluntary association" to the end.[84]

By the spring of 1844 the organizational stage had ended, and emissaries set out to the newly opened areas in the West. They managed to buy 4,000 acres of government land in northeast Missouri. In the autumn of that year Wilhelm Keil, his family, and several others laid the foundation for a new settlement, which was planned as a commune from the start. In early 1845 additional groups of Keil's followers arrived from Pennsylvania. They all put their money into a common chest; affluent members contributed $1,000 while others gave nothing. Each member received clothing, accommodation, and food according to need, regardless of how much they had contributed. Within the first year the commune owned a capital of $30,802. Keil's leadership was absolute as there were no binding regulations.[85] Among the early members were some adventurers with no religious motivation. When they were faced by the harsh conditions and the malaria-infested area, they abandoned the community. The commune was sued for compensation by those who had left, but these law suits did not undermine the spirit of the community. Within several years it prospered mainly because of the diligence of its members, many of whom were accomplished artisans.

After the first few years, in which they were chiefly engaged in farming, Beth El developed various industries and handicrafts, a sawmill, a flour mill, a grist mill, and a tannery, some weaving looms, and a large sewing shop, a cabinet-makers' and a wagon makers' who provided the many pioneers that passed on their way West with their covered wagons. They were also expert leather workers marketing their shoes and gloves in the neighborhood. (These got a first prize for design in the 1858 New York Trade Fair.) In 1855, ten years after settling in Missouri, Beth El was economically prosperous compared with their neighbors; their property was estimated at $200,000, and they attracted many new candidates, reaching a population of 650.[86] More land was purchased, daughter communes sprang up and were also given biblical names: Elim, Hebron, Nineveh.

Property relations were rather hazy. There was no accounting on the commune, and later it transpired that some members had kept part of their property instead of handing it over to the commune. They could, however, make little use of their private funds, because, except for some special items, nothing was bought with money on the commune; members took what they needed from the store without bothering to note it down. An additional source of private income was the sale of fruit from private gardens. Some researchers therefore regard Beth El as an economically "mixed" settlement in which everyone received according to his needs but led an individualistic life with no interference in his private affairs or property.

Beth El members regarded themselves as a Christian community even though they belonged to no specific denomination. One of the first public buildings was an impressive church, in which Wilhelm Keil, their spiritual shepherd, preached. Every Sunday people from the area would gather to listen to his sermons. People would also come from far away to participate in festivals organized on days not usually celebrated by the other Christian sects. Later this caused a controversy and was stopped for fear of heresy, but it did not affect the good relations with their Missouri neighbors which were also based on cultural activities such as concerts given by the Beth El orchestra in other settlements in the area. The children went to the local elementary school. Wilhelm Keil objected to a higher education, although many of Beth El's members were intellectuals and university graduates.

Westward to Oregon: Aurora

In the early 1850s Beth El found itself on the route of massive migration westward over the Rockies to the newly developed West Coast. The commune was also affected by it. Many members wanted to get away from the crowds and establish an isolated settlement for their unique way of life, without the danger of interference from the outside world. In 1854 the decision was taken and in 1855 the first group of 250 men, women, and children set out on their long trek westward,[87] through unknown territories and Indian country. It was to become a legendary tale. Besides the usual elements of the "covered wagons" here was a collective religious community that set a stamp of uniqueness on the venture. It started tragically when Wilhelm Keil's son, who was eager to go west, died on the eve of the departure. He had entreated his father to be buried on the new site of the commune. Keil, who headed the caravan, took the embalmed body of his son on the 2,000 mile trek in a covered wagon. They had to face hostile Indians among other dangers, but their continuous religious singing made a great impression on the tribes and the caravan crossed peacefully. Toward the end of 1855 they tried to settle on a site near the Pacific Ocean. It was found to be unsuitable and the caravan continued inland to an area that would become a part of the state of Oregon. They settled near Portland, calling their new commune *Aurora*, the name of Wilhelm Keil's daughter.[88]

During the following years additional members arrived overland or by sea and soon the commune had a population of 400. They owned 18,000 acres of timber and agricultural land. Their diligence and former communal experience in Missouri soon brought prosperity. The commune started some workshops, a sawmill, a carpentry shop, a flour mill, and a blacksmith, but most successful were the orchards they planted all around the settlement.

Relations with other settlements in the area were good. Keil was a popular doctor and for a time he even lived in Portland, where he had a large practice. Aurora became the center of the whole area. A general store provided the members' needs and also sold merchandise to their neighbors. In time a hotel, post office, and a bank were opened for the area's population.[89] Work was done by members and some hired workers. Every new candidate could choose to work as a hired laborer during his candidacy. In 1863 the last caravan arrived from Beth El. It was headed by one of the most outstanding leaders of Beth El, Dr. Wolf, whose influence was almost equal to Dr. Keil's. He was a graduate of Göttingen University, where he had received a secular education and was a socialist in his outlook.[90] He was actively involved in formulating the commune's ideology and frequently disputed with Keil matters of principle, dealing with a deepening of their communal way of life.

Many young people from Beth El arrived at Aurora because Keil wanted to help them get away from the battle fields of the Civil War. Like other religious communes, Beth El and Aurora were ambivalent in their attitude toward war. They tried to remain neutral, avoid enlistment or any other war-related activity. However, they openly supported the North and most of the members, whether in Missouri or in Oregon, were Republicans. When Missouri, which was part of the Confederacy, was conquered by the North, the commune meticulously kept its neutrality, and both sides accepted this.[91] After 1863 Aurora expanded rapidly, and its population reached about 1,000 in the early 1870s. It soon became a religious center and renowned in its many-sidedness. It grew at the expense of the mother commune Beth El, which was deteriorating after its charismatic leaders had gone west.

Aurora was managed by a council of four, under Wilhelm Keil's guidance. Until the 1870s it had no written constitution, and its property was registered in Wilhelm Keil's name. In 1872, under pressure from seceders and an internal opposition that threatened to dissolve the commune, a compromise was reached. The entire property was divided and a title-deed given to each head of a family, thus ensuring the collective for, as it happened, as long as Keil lived. Keil's influence was such that even after the property had formally been divided, the communal way of life went on as before. When Charles Nordhoff visited Aurora in 1873 he was impressed by its achievements and especially by its young remaining on despite the opportunities of the rapidly developing society of Oregon. A similar attitude is expressed by Hinds.[92]

Dissolution

It was Wilhelm Keil's personality that ensured stability. Three years after his death in 1876 Beth El was dissolved, and a year later Aurora ceased to exist as a commune. Beth El had steadily deteriorated and in the 1850s there were only 250 people left. Essential work was done by a growing number of hired workers.[93] The absence of their leaders caused irregularity in communal practices, and a coexistence between the communal economy and private property developed. Public places were neglected; on his visit in 1873 Charles Nordhoff was little impressed by the exterior appearance of the settlement. Yet he found the economy prospering and the workshops—the sawmill, flour mill, distillery, carpentry, and general store—all actively involved in serving the area's population. Nordhoff also noticed the looseness of communal relations. Its 175 members continued to live as a community. The former president of Beth El, Jacob Miller, wrote to Hinds in 1900 that a large number of former members regret the dissolution of Beth El and Aurora and regard their period on the commune as the best years of their lives.[94] According to his letter most of the members had originally come from Germany but had lived in Pennsylvania, Ohio, Iowa, and Indiana before joining the commune, and only a few had arrived as immigrants directly from Germany. In this respect the commune was slightly different from the other religious communes that were composed of immigrants.

The Swedish Commune of Bishop Hill

In 1846, a few years after the Society of True Inspiration had immigrated from Germany, another persecuted European sect immigrated to the United States. They were Swedish farmers and artisans from Norland who hoped they would be allowed to practice their religion without interference and lead a communal life in the New World. Their leader at that time was Eric Jansen,[95] who had been driven from his native land in the summer of 1846 by the Lutheran Church, which persecuted those who belonged to the pietist separatist sect and its millennial expectations. On his arrival in the United States he found several groups of Swedes, some of whom had settled in Illinois; looking for a suitable site, Jansen chose west Illinois. He had left some of his trustees in charge of organizing the immigrants as soon as he would find a place for them in the United States. He now sent out a call to his followers to emigrate and establish a New Jerusalem in the United States. Their commune would be the kernel of the Church of All Saints which would greet the Messiah on his Second Coming. An additional reason to opt for the communal way was the variegated background of the Swedish sectarians. Some of them were affluent farmers and artisans, others were workers and miners who could not afford to pay their fare. The communal property arrangement ensured the emigration of the entire sect and was also a moral principle tenet of the Apostolic Church.

When the call to emigrate was first heard, 1,100 Jansonists declared their wish to leave the "vale of tears" in Sweden and go to the New World to join the heavenly Jerusalem there. Difficulties of transportation forced the immigrants to travel in small groups. Within two years 800 had settled on the small tract of 200 acres in west Illinois; this was all they could afford to purchase with their limited means. They called their settlement *Bishop Hill* after Jansen's birthplace. It was virgin land which had been opened to settlement a decade earlier. They met with extreme hardships, most of them living in caves dug in the hills.[96]

Jansen's followers in New Jerusalem fared no better. In addition to their extreme poverty and economic hardships, they were overcome by disease and many died. Their misfortunes deterred many from joining the commune and instead they settled in nearby Illinois, where other Swedes had immigrated to earlier. A relatively large and stable core remained, and inspired by Eric Jansen's fiery sermons, they overcame the hard pioneering stage and built an economic foundation for the developing settlement.

The year 1849 was a turning point. Collectively they managed to construct large and solidly built living quarters. These brick houses accommodated the families in separate units. Singles shared quarters and had attached kitchens and dining rooms. They paid special attention to the sanitary conditions. One of the first buildings to be constructed was the church, around which their intensive religious activity was centered. The economic development of Bishop Hill was begun at the same time. Most of their land was cleared and cultivated. Their diversified economy included the growing of flax which served as raw material in their weaving shop. Their inexperience was made up by enthusiasm, and soon the commune increased to 1,000 inhabitants by attracting many newcomers.[97]

In 1850 tragedy struck when Eric Jansen was murdered in a dispute with one of the newcomers, an American adventurer. This man had married a local girl and promised to live on the commune. When eventually he decided to leave he forced his wife to go with him. The commune's members came to her assistance, and the husband sued Jansen for kidnapping his wife. While in court, the husband shot and killed Jansen. The death of this popular leader did not spell out the end of the commune. In spite of his authoritarian position the commune had healthy foundations. At first his wife was elected as their leader together with some other members of her family. But some members led by Jonas Olsen, an elder of the sect, refused to recognize Jansen's leadership and took it over.[98] This revolt did not harm the commune; on the contrary, Olsen was blessed with an economic flair which Eric Jansen, who was a fanatic though charismatic leader, had lacked. At the time of the murder, Jonas Olsen was away in California, where he had been sent by Jansen in search of gold. After hearing the news he returned immediately to take over the leadership. One of his first steps was to write a constitution and to legalize the commune in the state of Illinois in 1853. According to this constitution, seven trustees were elected for life on condition that their leadership was good, or else they could be demoted. The leaders had to report annually to the general meeting of the members. In spite of the democratic procedure the trustees were empowered with considerable authority. Even though they were efficient and the commune's economy prospered, the trustees' unlimited power caused tension and corruption which finally led to the commune's disintegration in 1860.

The years 1850 through 1860 were years of prosperity. Land was purchased and cultivated. Livestock was added and housing conditions on the commune improved. With its well-tended gardens the settlement attracted many visitors. These were the first years of statehood in Illinois, and Bishop Hill stood out as one of the best-organized settlements in the area. In 1853 a chance visitor wrote of his impressions in one of the local papers; he was much impressed by the beauty and size of the commune. He describes the broad expansion of the fields cultivated by groups of commune members, the large cattle holds, well-organized workshops, but most of all their efficient and orderly management. In 1856 Bishop Hill owned 8,500 acres of which 3,250 were cultivated and 500 forestry land. They had 300 milk cows, 150 horses, and controlled several industries in the area. In short they were rich.[99]

Under Olsen's leadership the commune participated in large economic projects such as the construction of the Quincy Railway. The township Galfa, a station on the Chicago-Burlington line, became the center of their economic and financial transactions. One of the members, Olaf Johansen, represented the commune's interests in Galfa and established an automatic financial enterprise there, with the result that the trustees soon lost control. There was talk of corruption, and strife and tension mounted.

While all this dynamic activity was going on outside the commune, life continued placidly at home. The founding principles were maintained, work was well organized and large groups cultivated the fields and attended the workshops. Communal consumption was improved, new kitchens and dining rooms were built, and the food and service were pleasant. Material conditions prospered, but not so the spiritual life of the sect. Their fundamentalist Christian attitude prevented any widening of cultural horizons. Religious books only were read, and hardly any secular literature reached the commune. Only the school, which had been established in the first year of the settlement in 1846, was a cultural oasis. The teaching language was English, and a wide education was given by local teachers and others. The gap between the narrow religious attitude and the broad horizons of the school soon caused tension.

Families lived in separate apartments, and consumption and education were collective. In the 1850s close relations developed with the Shaker communes, which at the time were considered to be the most established religious communes in the United States. Through their influence one of the elders of Bishop Hill was convinced of the many benefits that celibacy would have on the religious and communal life of their settlement and succeeded in convincing Jonas Olsen as well. Olsen, who had absolute authority, used this in order to force the whole commune to adopt celibacy. In 1854 a decision froze any new marriages and forbade carnal relations. This was not a unanimous decision, and those who objected were forced to leave the commune. Others waited silently for the opportunity to reap the seeds of discord.[100]

In 1857 a recession hit agriculture and industry. The financial expansion under Olaf Johansen had tied the commune to enterprises which now went bankrupt. Discontent, which had been dormant during times of prosperity, now raised its head. The young members, who had learned the spiritual and ideological openness of the outside world, now rebelled against the spiritual stagnation of the trustees, whose authority was further undermined by financial irregularities. In 1859 their revolt came to a head with the demand to dissolve the commune.

A year later the general meeting decided to do so, but for two years discussions continued on the ways and means of how to divide the property. Finally in 1862 every member, male or female, received 20 acres or their equivalent in value. The commune's religious unity, which had characterized Bishop Hill, had suffered as well during the dissolution, and many members sold their property. They dispersed all over the Midwest, taking advantage of the economic opportunities that had followed the Civil War. A population of about 300 remained in Bishop Hill. They too were not inclined to keep the traditions of the past.[101]

Notes

1. Aaron Williams, *The Harmony Society at Economy* (1866. Reprint. New York: AMS Press, 1971), pp. 35-39. Harmony was founded by George Rapp. John Archibald Bole, *The Harmony Society: A Chapter in German-American Culture-History* (Philadelphia: Americana Germanica Press, 1904. New York: AMS Press, 1973), pp. 65-66; Hilda Adam Kring, *The Harmonists: A Folk-Culture Approach*, ATLA Monograph Series, no. 3 (Metuchen, N.J.: Scarecrow Press and American Theological Library Association, 1973), pp. 1-15.
2. Karl J.R. Arndt, *George Rapp's Harmony Society, 1785-1847*, rev. ed. (New York: Associated University Presses, 1972), pp. 35-40, 43-54, 58; Bole, p. 53.
3. Williams, pp. 48-53; Bole, pp. 6-9, 29-37; Kring, pp. 11, 24-27; Arndt, *Harmony Society*, pp. 72-82; Donald E. Pitzer and Josephine M. Elliott, "New Harmony's First Utopians," special ed. Reprint. from *Indiana Magazine of History* 75, no. 3 (September 1979): 228, 230.
4. Williams, pp. 56-59; Bole, p. 52; Kring, p. 12; Hinds, William A. *American Communities and Cooperative Colonies* (Philadelphia: Porcupine Press, 1975; 1st ed. 1878), p. 91; Arndt, *Harmony Society*, pp. 91-200. About George Rapp's son and his marriage see Daniel B. Reibel, ed., *The Harmonic Herald, 1966-1979*,

selected reprints (Old Economy Village, Ambridge, Pa.: Harmonie Associates, 1980), pp. 21-22; Pitzer and Elliott, pp. 231-32, 251.

5. For documents concerning the period of moving to the Wabash see John C. Andressohn, trans. and ed., "The Arrival of the Rappites at New Harmony," *Indiana Magazine of History* 42 (1948): 83-89. Karl J.R. Arndt, ed., *A Documentary History of the Indiana Decade of the Harmony Society, 1814-1824*, vol. 1, 1814-1819; vol. 2, 1820-1824 (Indianapolis: Indiana Historical Society, 1978), vol. 1, p. 60.
6. Pitzer and Elliott, p. 227; Reibel, pp. 2-3; Andressohn, pp. 395-409; Arndt, *Harmony Society*, 250-51; Arndt, *Documentary History*, vol. 1, pp. 43, 68-72, 75-85, 228.
7. Arndt, *Documentary History*, vol. 1, pp. 226-29; Bole, pp. 79-85; Arndt, *Harmony Society*, pp. 164-80; Arndt, *Documentary History*, vol. 2, pp. 159-67; Pitzer and Elliott, pp. 233, 235-36, 237-38, 241-42, 254.
8. Arndt, *Documentary History*, vol. 2, pp. 30-32, 247-49, 388-89, 842-51; Arndt, *Harmony Society*, pp. 201-10, 226-42, 250-55; Bole, p. 89.
9. Arndt, *Harmony Society*, pp. 292-95; Harlow Lindley, ed., *Indiana Historical Commission.* "Indiana as Seen by Early Travelers" (Indianapolis: Indiana Historical Commission, 1916), pp. 328-38; Bole, pp. 286-95; Delburn Carpenter, *The Radical Pietists* (New York: AMS Press, 1975), p. 163; Karl J.R. Arndt, "George Rapp's Harmony Society," *Communities: Journal of Cooperation,* no. 68 (Winter 1985): 25; Pitzer and Elliott, pp. 252-53, 255. See also Arndt, *Documentary History*, vol. 2, pp. 89-90, 270-71, 856-58, 865-66, 915-16; Hinds, pp. 73-75; Reibel, pp. 4-8.
10. Arndt, "George Rapp's Harmony Society," p. 23: "Although the colony was begun only a year ago, all the people are already living in very clean and comfortable homes. . . . All the people bid me a hearty welcome. . . . The faces reflected satisfaction, cheerfulness, purity and consideration toward each other. . . . Whoever needs clothes, shoes, goes to the office, where he obtains what he needs. . . . Flour was distributed according to need. . . . Vegetables at the time were available on demand." Frederick List (1789-1846) was one of the leading German economists in the first half of the nineteenth century. He was in favor of using taxes to protect national industry. In 1825 he was exiled from Wurtemberg because of his liberal outlook; emigrating to the United States he soon became active in commercial and industrial circles as well as in politics. In the 1830s he returned to Germany as the American consul in Leipzig. Arndt, *Harmony Society*, pp. 321-23; Bole, pp. 97-103; Reibel, pp. 55-57; John S. Duss, *The Harmonists: A Personal History* (Philadelphia: Porcupine, 1972), p. 64.
11. Arndt, *Harmony Society*, p. 405. On collective voting, see Arndt, *Harmony Society*, pp. 379-415; Duss, pp. 72-73.
12. Williams, pp. 82-89; Duss, chap. 3; Arndt, *Harmony Society*, pp. 353-77; Hinds, pp. 85-88. For the story about the Schriber family which made a lawsuit against the community, see Reibel, pp. 28-30.
13. Arndt, *Harmony Society*, pp. 468-95, 520-44; Bole, pp. 124-26; Carpenter, pp. 188-90; Hinds, pp. 92-95; Williams, pp. 72-82; Reibel, pp. 14-20.
14. Bole, pp. 126-27; Arndt, *Harmony Society*, pp. 565-77; Carpenter, p. 190.
15. Williams, pp. 45-47.
16. Pitzer and Elliott, pp. 238-40; Kring, pp. 56, 59, 95-132. Stephen A. Marini, "Hymnody in the Religious Communal Societies of Early America," *Communal Studies* 2 (Autumn 1982):12-23; Reibel, pp. 22-24; Duss, pp. 365-72.

17. Richard D. Wetzel, "Harmonist Music between 1827 and 1832: A Reappraisal," *Communal Studies* 2 (Autumn 1982):65.
18. Pitzer and Elliott, pp. 290-91; J.S. Buckingham, *The Eastern and Western States of America*, vol. 2 (London, 1842), p. 230.
19. Arndt, *Harmony Society*, pp. 567-77; Carpenter, p. 190.
20. Arndt, *Successors and Material Heirs, 1847-1916*, pp. 63-65.
21. Hinds, pp. 70-71.
22. Arndt, "George Rapp's Harmony Society," p. 21; Williams, pp. 90-96; Bole, pp. 132-35; Arndt, *Successors*, pp. 62-80; Reibel, pp. 96-100.
23. Arndt, *Successors*, pp. 34-40.
24. Ibid., p. 58.
25. Bole, pp. 132-42.
26. For Icaria's call for help, see Arndt, *Successors*, pp. 40-41, 129-40.
27. Bole, pp. 139-40; Arndt, *Successors*, pp. 125-29.
28. Nordhoff, pp. 63-68; Arndt, *Successors*, pp. 112-14; Hinds, pp. 69-70; Reibel, pp. 31-47.
29. Hinds, pp. 81-84; Duss, chaps. 9, 10.
30. Arndt, *Successors*, pp. 254-66; Duss, chaps. 11, 12.
31. Arndt, *Successors*, pp. 320-21; Duss, chap. 13.
32. Arndt, *Successors*, pp. 270-88; Duss, pp. 372-86.
33. Arndt, *Successors*, pp. 289-317.
34. Ibid., pp. 320-53.
35. Hinds, pp. 99-100; Hilda Dischinger Morhart, *The Zoar Story* (Dover, Oh.: Seibert, 1967), pp. 13, 91-93; "Zoar: An Ohio Experiment in Communalism (Columbus, Oh.: The Ohio Historical Society, 1972), pp. 11, 14; Kent, p. 587.
36. Kathleen Fernandez, "The Separatist Society of Zoar," *Communities: Journal of Cooperation*, no. 68 (Winter 1985): 27; Emilius O. Randall, "History of the Zoar Society," *Ohio Archaeological and Historical Quarterly* 8 (July 1899): 5, 59, 63, 97; "Zoar," pp. 15-17; Morhart, pp. 93-95; Kent, pp. 587-88.
37. For various theories on the way to the commune see Randall, pp. 7, 97-98; Morhart, p. 17-128; "Zoar," pp. 18-20; Kent, p. 589.
38. Morhart, p. 16.
39. Randall, p. 20; Kent, p. 591.
40. Randall, pp. 34-35.
41. On the cancelation of communal education see Randall, pp. 44-46; "Zoar," pp. 42-43; Hinds, p. 46.
42. Fernandez, p. 29; Nordhoff, p. 102; Randall, pp. 8-12.
43. Hinds, pp. 104-10; Carpenter, p. 199; Morhart, p. 23.
44. Fernandez, p. 30; "Zoar," pp. 27-39; Randall, p. 98.
45. "Zoar," pp. 27-39, 51-61; Morhart, pp. 19, 23, 99-101.
46. Randall, 16-29; "Zoar," pp. 54-56.
47. Fernandez, p. 30; Hinds, pp. 107-29.
48. Carol Weisbrod, *The Boundaries of Utopia* (New York: Pantheon, 1980), pp. 138-44; Randall, pp. 23-31; Morhart, p. 117.
49. Fernandez, p. 30; Carpenter, p. 208.
50. Hinds, p. 104; Randall, pp. 36, 53; Nordhoff, pp. 102-3; Herbert A. Wisbey, "Research Note: Rufus Rockwell Wilson's Tour of Five Utopian Communities in 1888," *Communal Societies* 3 (1983).

51. Randall, pp. 38-51, 53-68; Kent, p. 593.
52. Randall, pp. 69-72; Kent, pp. 593-94; "Zoar," pp. 64-73; Hinds, pp. 119-21, 129-31.
53. Ibid., pp. 119-21; Randall, pp. 73-77.
54. Hinds, pp. 302-3; Charles F. Noe, "A Brief History of the Amana Society, 1714-1900," *Iowa Journal of History and Politics* 2 (April 1904): 162-65.
55. Bertha M. Shambaugh, *Amana That Was and Amana That Is* (Iowa City: State Historical Society of Iowa, 1932), pp. 31-35, 349.
56. Diane L. Barthel, *Amana, from Pietist Sect to American Community* (Lincoln: University of Nebraska Press, 1984), pp. 8-16; Noe, pp. 165-73.
57. W.R. Perkins and B.L. Wick, *History of the Amana Society*, Historical Monograph, no. 1 (Iowa City: State University of Iowa Publications, 1891), pp. 24-49; Noe, pp. 173-76; Kent, pp. 579-80.
58. Jonathan Andelson, "Living the Mean: The Ethos, Practice and Genius of Amana," *Communities: Journal of Cooperation*, no. 68 (Winter 1985), pp. 32, 34, 35; Noe, pp. 176-77.
59. Perkins, p. 52.
60. Shambaugh, pp. 57-62; Worm, pp. 322-20; Noe, p. 178.
61. Shambaugh, p. 63; Perkins, pp. 50-53.
62. Barthel, pp. 29-32; Shambaugh, p. 66; Noe, pp. 178-84.
63. Shambaugh, pp. 75-76.
64. Perkins, pp. 56-61; Noe, pp. 180-82.
65. About pacifism in Amana see Barnett Richling, "The Amana Society: A History of Change," *The Palimpsest*, 58, no. 2 (March-April 1977): 42. Charles Nordhoff, *The Communist Societies of the United States* (1875. Reprint. New York: Shocken, 1965), pp. 38-39, 43; Shambaugh, pp. 146-47.
66. Shambaugh, pp. 73-74.
67. Nordhoff, pp. 39-40.
68. Andelson, "Living the Mean," p. 36; Richling, p. 39.
69. Shambaugh, pp. 109-10.
70. Hinds, pp. 315-25; Frederick A. Bushee, "Communistic Societies in the United States," *Political Science Quarterly* 20 (1905):643-44; Kent, pp. 580-81, 644; Shambaugh, 85-192.
71. Shambaugh, p. 158; Barbara S. Yambura, *A Change and a Parting: My Story of Amana* (Iowa City: Iowa State University Press, 1974), pp. 127-42, 163-68, 185-211; Kent, pp. 584-86; Bertha M. Horak, "Amana Colony," *Midland Monthly* 6 (1896): 27-36; Barthinius L. Wick, "Christian Communism in the Mississippi Valley," *Midland Monthly* 6 (1896): 340-41.
72. Shambaugh, p. 362.
73. Barthel, pp. 88-92; Shambaugh, pp. 340-45; Yambura, pp. 241-45.
74. Jonathan G. Andelson, "The Double Bind and Social Change in Communal Amana," *Human Relations* 34 (1981):116-24.
75. Richling, pp. 37-39, 46-47.
76. Ruth Shonle Cavan, "The Future of a Commune: Amana," in *Communes: Historical and Contemporary*, Ruth S. Cavan and Man S. Das, eds. (New Delhi: Vikas Publishing House, 1979), p. 261; Andelson, pp. 121-24.
77. Shambaugh, p. 352.
78. Andelson, "Living the Mean," p. 38; Richling, p. 41.
79. Richling, pp. 45-47; Shambaugh, p. 346; Yambura, pp. 229, 275-79.

80. Shambaugh, pp. 372-78; Yambura, pp. 280-81, 287-300; Shambaugh, p. 339.
81. About life in Amana after the commune no longer existed see Barthel, pp. 121-46.
82. Wilhelm Keil, born in Ehrfurth, Prussia, in 1812, emigrated to the United States in 1836 and on arriving in New York earned his living as a tailor. However, he soon found another rewarding business—medicine. Keil had no medical education and was not officially registered as a doctor. He practiced medicine because he was enhanced with personal traits of a suggestive character which enabled him to persuade people to believe in their health. Keil somewhat broadened his knowledge of chemistry and of witch doctors craft and learned how to prepare several medicines. The combination of these and his intuitive understanding of the human spirit helped him cure his patients and he was called "Doc" by everybody. F.V. Calverton, *Where Angels Dared to Tread* (New York: Bobbs-Merrill, 1941), pp. 87-90; H. Roger Grant, "Missouri's Utopian Communities," *Missouri Historical Review* 65 (October 1971): 23-24.
83. Hinds, p. 328; Grant, p. 24; William G. Beck, "A German Communistic Society in Missouri," *Missouri Historical Review* (October 1908-January 1909): 58-61.
84. Beck, p. 64.
85. Robert J. Hendricks, *Bethel and Aurora: An Experiment in Communism as Practical Christianity* (New York: Press of Pioneers, 1933), pp. 4-5, 13-17.
86. *Oregon Historical Quarterly* (Fall 1978):233-69; Nordhoff, p. 327; Grant, pp. 25-28.
87. Calverton, p. 91.
88. Hendricks, pp. 51-107; Grant, p. 29.
89. Hendricks, *Oregon Historical Quarterly* (Fall 1978):109-10, 233-69.
90. Calverton, pp. 94-95.
91. Hendricks, p. 117; Beck, p. 103.
92. Nordhoff, pp. 319-23; Hinds, pp. 330-34; Grant, pp. 29-31.
93. Nordhoff, p. 328.
94. Hinds, pp. 333, 337-39.
95. The beginning of the sect was in the 1820s, at a time when the pietists were on the rise in the Swedish Lutheran Church. In 1842 these circles underwent a spiritual upheaval influenced by Erik Janssen's preachings. He was a farmer's son from a nearby area who had gone through a deep religious experience and became a fundamentalist-pietist preacher. His sermons fell on fertile ground among those pietists who had participated in the revival meetings and as a result had challenged the Lutheran Church authorities and its rituals, literature, and festivals. Thousands joined Janssen's community of believers, the majority were the pietist followers of Jonas Olsen. When the fundamentalist-pietist spiritual upheaval grew stronger, the Lutheran Church authorities denounced them as heretics. When in 1844 members of the sect burned Lutheran theological books, keeping on the Old and New Testaments, matters deteriorated further and they were persecuted. Erik Jansen was arrested and tried, and only royal intervention saved him and he was released. (The royal family was sympathetic to the spiritual upheavals.) The zealots, however, continued burning books and the schism between Janssen's followers and the Lutheran Church widened. Persecution followed and Janssen himself was threatened with a

heavy punishment. Under these circumstances his followers decided to smuggle him into Norway and on to Denmark, from where he boarded a ship to the United States in the summer of 1846. M.A. Mikkelsen, *The Bishop Hill Colony: A Religious Communistic Settlement in Henry County, Illinois* (Baltimore: Johns Hopkins University Press, 1892), pp. 1-26; Hinds, pp. 340-42; Nordhoff, pp. 342-43.

96. Calverton, pp. 118-20; Mark Holloway, *Heaven on Earth: Communities in America, 1680-1880* (New York: Dover, 1966), p. 164.
97. Mikkelsen, pp. 33-37; Hinds, p. 350; Nordhoff, p. 345.
98. Mikkelsen, pp. 43-44; Holloway, pp. 166-67.
99. Hinds, pp. 353-54.
100. Calverton, p. 126.
101. Hinds, pp. 355-60; Mikkelsen, pp. 63-71; *American Socialist* 1, no. 23 (August 1876):181-82.

5

Robert Owen and the First Socialist Communes

The first communes whose inceptors were motivated by secular socialism rather than religious sectarianism began to appear in the United States in the 1820s as a result of European ideas and socialist doctrines that reached the New World at the time. Among them, Robert Owen's socialist theory was cardinal to those who aspired to a better world. A milestone was the publication of some chapters from Owen's book *A New Outlook on Society* in the Jeffersonian periodical, *Aurora* in Philadelphia in 1817. At the same time and without any apparent connection, a Quaker pharmacist, Cornelius Blatchley, published his own theory in the United States. There were many similarities and parallels in their outlook concerning the advantages of collectivism; the main difference was in the importance Cornelius Blatchley ascribed to the experience and contribution of the religious communes of the Shakers, Harmony, and The Moravian Brotherhood.

In 1820 Cornelius Blatchley founded the Society for Promoting Communities in New York. In 1822 this society published a booklet, *Essay on Commonwealths*, that included Blatchley's original essay, other articles on the Harmony commune, and chapters from Robert Owen's book. The booklet was sent to Thomas Jefferson who, being sympathetic but noncommittal, replied that although he admired communitarianism, which under certain circumstances brought much content, it was feasible only for small numbers of people and not for mankind as a whole. However he wished them well and supported the society's philanthropic motives.[1]

Through the New York Society, Owenist ideas reached Cincinnati, Ohio. The area was experiencing a religious revival, and following the Shakers example, many began to organize in communitarian groups based on a secular rationalistic ideology. Among those stood out James Dorsey's group. He was the principal of Oxford College in Butler County, and in 1816 developed his first communitarian project called "The Rational Brethern of Oxford," whose members came from liberal circles. The society was dissolved a year later, but one of its members, William Ludlow, moved to Warren County where he attempted to revive the project. In 1823 a tract of 1,000 acres was purchased in Coal Creek, Indiana, and Ludlow informed President Jefferson of the establishment of a communitarian society. In his reply the president was encouraging but not overenthusiastic. The settlement resumed its organization, and through a coincidence they adopted their constitution in the very year of Robert Owen's arrival in the United States. It was thus that the communal idea had already taken root in Cincinnati before Robert Owen reached it on his first propaganda tour in 1825.

Another area in which secular communitarian ideas had already appeared prior to Robert Owen, were Philadelphia and Pittsburgh, in Pennsylvania, where the religious communes of Ephrata, the Rappists, and the Moravians provided the background for communitarian thought.

A small circle of Owenists crystallized in Philadelphia in 1823 intending to establish a community. Many of the activists were from among the scientific and academic elite in the city. William Maclure, the president of the Academy of National Sciences, was most interested in Owen's ideas and so were many of his fellow scientists and members of the upper-middle-classes. One of those was Benjamin Bakewell, owner of a flint-glass factory. In 1820 Owenists' circles got organized from among the English farmers who had settled in Illinois, near New Harmony, Indiana.[2]

Robert Owen in the United States: Success and Failure

After years of activity in England, where his ideas had been crystallized,[3] Robert Owen arrived in the United States, hoping to materialize his theories. He was greeted by a group of his followers who belonged to Blatchley's group, and among them he spent his first days in the land of his expectations. They introduced him to New York's high society, its businessmen, reformers, educators, scientists, and politicians.

After a few days of hospitality he left for a visit to the Shakers in Watervliet, Albany. The Shakers greeted him cordially, and he presented them with his plan for communal settlements, each of which would have a population of 2,000. On his arrival in the United States local newspapers began to publish his plans, promoting his social experiments of communal settlements. These articles received much attention and Owen was encouraged, hoping he could interest politicians in his project and convince them that it was a solution to social ills. After a short stay in New York he went on a tour of the East.

On his way to New Harmony, Indiana, he passed through Philadelphia and Pittsburgh, where he was enthusiastically received.[4] He met the Rappists in New Harmony and made formal arrangements to acquire the land. On January 3, 1825, he signed a contract to purchase the 20,000 acres and the 180 buildings of the commune. The equipment was intended for a community of 700.

Robert Owen then decided to proceed on a propaganda campaign throughout the country before settling in New Harmony. He therefore set out for a 100 days propaganda campaign, and his biographers estimate this to have been the most successful of his entire career. The highlight of the tour was his reception in Washington, D.C., by the outgoing president, James Monroe, and the presidential incumbent, John Quincy Adams. Washington was in a political turmoil as the indecisiveness of the presidential elections of 1824 became increasingly apparent, and the capital abounded with politicians from all over the country. When Owen talked to the Congress on Capitol Hill, it was filled to capacity, and he was given the opportunity to extend his speech to two sessions. His audience included the two presidents, the secretary of state, both cabinets, and many of the leaders of the country.[5]

If Owen had had any illusions that his lectures would convince the politicians to accept his social plans, he was disappointed. There was no change in their attitude, and many of the politicians were skeptical. Yet his speech was a propaganda boon. It was printed and distributed in thousands of copies by the official congressional journal, the *National Intelligencer*, and attracted widespread curiosity. This brought instant success, and hundreds set out to join the New Harmony project. On his return to the banks of the Wabash, Owen found that about 800 people had gathered there.[6]

New Harmony: The Temporary Society

Most of those who arrived during the first period had come from the adjacent areas in Indiana. They were farmers from the area as well as drifters and adventurers. Gradually people arrived from further away, mainly from Owenists strongholds in Cincinnati, Pittsburgh, and Philadelphia. Most of them were intellectuals and members of the middle classes who had been attracted by Owen's social ideology.[7]

The first step was to organize the settlement in order to absorb the newcomers. Buildings had to be adapted to the requirements of a secular commune. The task was undertaken by William Owen, Robert Owen's younger son and Captain Donald MacDonald, a Scotsman friend who had joined Robert Owen on his travels. They were left in charge as Robert Owen's deputies while the latter was away on his propaganda tour. They were faced with two problems: (1) the application of obligatory rules for private property rights, and (2) the criteria to be applied in the acceptance of new members. On these cardinal questions MacDonald and William Owen could take no definite stand. Most of the newcomers continued to hold on to their possessions.

Upon his arrival back at New Harmony Robert Owen gave a programmatic address to his followers on April 27, 1825 in which he presented a constitution for the Preliminary Society. He explained that it would not be feasible to move straight from the individualistic, competitive way of life they had been used to to a collective one. He declared that contrary to his own inclinations he would be "forced to admit for a time, a certain degree of financial inequality," and postpone his communal plans temporarily. During the Preliminary Society they would all live on a temporary basis in the existing buildings and in time plan their new settlement according to his vision.

Following the first meeting Robert Owen formulated a constitution for the transition period which he called the "halfway house," and it was confirmed by the second public meeting. Among other things it was approved by vote to leave Robert Owen in charge, with help from a committee of members. After three years New Harmony would be established as a communal settlement and Robert Owen's trusteeship would be terminated, since the settlement would then be economically and socially viable. During the "halfway house" members would continue to own property and furniture. Their daily labors would be evaluated and recorded, and they would be debited for goods they consumed. Each member would be credited with $80 per year on account of his future work. This would enable him to buy goods in the general store.

At the end of the year profits were shared proportionally: whoever invested more work got a larger share of the profits after expenses (production, consumption, and labor expenses) were deducted. Services, e.g. education, health, etc., were free and provided by the community, and every member could benefit according to his needs. The constitution did not refer to the kind of communitarianism they would establish in the future. Moreover, Robert Owen himself did not stay in New Harmony during the first period and could not implement their experience in future plans. Five weeks after the publication of the constitution he resumed his travels. This time he stayed away for a period of seven months in which he toured the eastern states. In July 1825 he returned to England on family matters and in order to transfer his family to the United States.[8]

Robert Owen's Propaganda Tour

Robert Owen left New Harmony at a time when the settlement was experiencing its first difficulties in order to impress public opinion and to inspire through his ideas a large settlement movement. The minimal results of his first tour encouraged him to believe that the United States, especially the area west of the Alleghenies, was suitable for his new social system. He believed that the large number of people who attended his lectures were all convinced by the communal argument and preferred it to the competitive individualistic society. He did not realize that except for a few intellectuals who supported him, and some positive articles, most newspapers were skeptical. His ideas were rejected mainly because of his antireligious doctrine, which was adverse to the general atmosphere in the country at the time. During his second tour most of the press rejected his ideas; Robert Owen ignored the signs and remained self-confident.

While he was back in England, an architect friend, Steadman Whitwell, built a model communal settlement according to Robert Owen's specifications. It was built to scale, and Owen brought it back to the United States in November 1825. He exhibited the model in the various halls where he lectured and even showed it at the White House, where he visited President John Quincy Adams. From there it went on exhibition on Capitol Hill, a thing unheard of in those days.[9]

Robert Owen did not hurry back to New Harmony and spent two more months on tour. The highlight of this propaganda campaign was the organization of an elite group of intellectuals in Philadelphia, who in January set out to join New Harmony. They were scientists, educators, members of the Academy of National Sciences, and therefore their ship was named *A Boatload of Knowledge*. Among them was William Maclure, president of the Philadelphia Academy of Sciences and the ''father'' of geology of North America, Marie D. Fretageot, and Thomas Say. Their wish to join the communal experiment was a feather in Robert Owen's cap and would turn New Harmony not only into a model settlement but also into an important center of education and sciences in the West.[10] Thus with confidence and full of grandiose ideas, Robert Owen returned to New Harmony on January 12, 1826, only to encounter a reality far removed from his pretentious expectations.

Birth Pangs

During the six months of Robert Owen's absence, New Harmony's social and economic life expanded. William Owen had been left in charge without any clear instructions on how to deal with the complicated issues of the Preliminary Society, especially as to the organization of manpower. The continuous stream of newcomers were all accepted without any selective criteria, and as a result New Harmony was in the summer of 1825 an extremely heterogeneous settlement. This was most evident in the area of work and production. From among a population of 800, only 140 were adept at working on the local industry, and only 36 were farmers. George Rapp, who had promised to leave some agricultural experts behind, did not keep his word. The existing agricultural branches deteriorated rapidly and could not even provide the commune's needs and some food had to be bought.

The situation was not better in industry, even though the potential was there. Many of the workshops stood neglected—the textile plant, distillery, soap and candle factory which had been constructed by Rapp's people, were not fully utilized, because nobody knew how. Only the soap, glue, and candle factory, and a small shoemaking plant were somewhat successful. The only prosperous venture was the local hotel, where the many tourists and the curious who came to see with their own eyes Robert Owen's famous social experiment were put up. Most of the craftsmen, shoemakers, bakers, tailors, carpenters, watchmakers, and blacksmiths were occupied in serving the commune. They had no income, and at the end of the year New Harmony was in debt. According to the constitution of the Preliminary Society, Robert Owen undertook to provide for his people; he covered all the losses from a special fund.[11]

At first there was some mismanagement at fault, but this was overcome with much enthusiasm and euphoria. In spite of the difficulties, the work morale was high. Many of the members had joined the commune with the idealistic belief that they were opening a new page not only in their own lives but in human history as well. The feeling of euphoria was evident in some of their letters. Thomas Pears, one of the intellectual elite of Pittsburgh, came to New Harmony with his wife and seven children. He wrote to his industrialist friend, the Owenist reformer Benjamin Bakewell:

> I am not yet a complete Harmonite, but I am beginning to think that I have caught some of Mr. Owen's spirit; for the more I see of the social system the more I wish it to succeed and the more I am convinced that it will succeed. But whatever may be the fate of this establishment, its principles will never be lost; and if not suddenly, they will gradually bring about the change in society so ardently desired by its founder. . . . New Harmony now presents to the world a novel and, I think, a sublime spectacle—an assemblage of people meeting together to try to do the utmost good for each other; and my hope is that we shall act as tho' the eyes of the world were upon us.[12]

William Pelham from Ohio, who joined New Harmony in September 1825, wrote in a similar way. He described the atmosphere on the settlement in his letter to his son, trying to induce him to join them and telling him that he himself intended to spend the rest of his life in that peaceful setting:

> In this abode of peace and quietness, I have experienced no disappointment. I did not expect to find everything regular, systematic, convenient—nor have I found them so. I did expect to find myself relieved from a most disagreeable state of life, and be able to mix with my fellow citizens without fear or imposition—without being subject to unjust censures and suspicions—and this expectation has been realized—I am at length free—my body's at length my own command, and I enjoy mental liberty, after having long been deprived of it.[13]

The *New Harmony Gazette*, which first appeared on October 1, 1826 tells about New Harmony's pleasant social atmosphere. Although most of the articles in the first issue of the *Gazette* dealt with the theoretical aspect of Robert Owen's theory and with the Owenist movement in England and the United

States, some of the letters to the editor written by members express the prevailing mood. These letters show that members had come from almost every state "except for two in the far south," and that in spite of this heterogeneity there were no disputes between people with different religious, ideological, or political convictions. In a letter to his friend in Boston one of the members wrote that there were no differences of opinion because there was no clash of interests. Memoirs published about that period depict the harmonious tolerance of the members. This religious and ideological pluralism was reflected in Pelham's letters; for instance, he mentioned the Shakers who joined New Harmony and the Methodist preachers who regularly preached on Sundays in the central hall which had earlier been the Rappists' church. The same congregation of members and guests would later listen to lectures of William Owen and Mr. Jennings on Owen's theories.[14]

Attending lectures of all sorts was a popular pasttime to which three evenings were devoted weekly. This was unusual in the frontier areas. Every Wednesday there were discussions on local problems or on the theoretical aspects concerning everyday problems. Lectures would also be given on science and culture. Every Tuesday there was a dance, and on Thursdays the local orchestra would perform. The *New Harmony Gazette* devoted an enthusiastic article in its October 1825 number to the advantages of the commune's cultural activities compared with those places that members had left. The article described the combination of culture, entertainment, education and creativity in the frontier settlements. This was in part due to the young age of the new members.[15]

The feeling of youthfulness was reinforced when the local school was organized at an early stage of the commune's life with the intention of undertaking the important task of communal education. The school in New Harmony was established according to the principles of Robert Owen's educational institution in New Lanark. Within the first few months 200 pupils had registered, all of them receiving in addition to their education also board and clothing paid for by the commune. This was indeed an innovation unheard of at the time.[16]

These advantages soon enhanced the commune's reputation, and as stated above, the number of intellectuals who joined New Harmony steadily grew. The only limitation to additional absorption of new members was the lack of housing. One of the few complaints in Pelham's usually optimistic letters concerned the harsh housing conditions from which he suffered; conditions got worse with the approach of winter.

From the Pears' letters we learn about social problems such as secessions, disputes between farmers and artisans, worries, inefficiency in production, but mainly about their hardships caused by a lack of funds for even the most elementary provisions. The first period of enthusiasm was followed by a feeling of disappointment. Thomas Pears wrote in a letter to Bakewell: "It seems that 'the promised land' is farther away than most of us had expected.'' There was later also direct criticism of the leadership which Pears called ''an aristocracy'' while his wife called it ''despotism.'' Under these circumstances everyone eagerly expected the return of Robert Owen, believing that he would find solutions to all their frustrating problems.[17]

In Search of a Proper Way

When in the beginning of 1826 Robert Owen returned to New Harmony he could still have improved the situation had he made immediate use of the objective financial-economic conditions. The Preliminary Society was well equipped to supervise all economic activities and to enforce its decisions. Social activities were lively, the school prospered, and Robert Owen was trusted by everybody. If he had taken his son William's advice to change the rules of the Preliminary Society gradually, things might have turned out differently and the situation in New Harmony could have improved. But Robert Owen returned full of confidence in his venture and decided that the time was ripe to establish a community based on full equality and communitarianism right away. Two weeks after his return to New Harmony a resolution was adopted to transform immediately the Preliminary Society into a full-fledged Community of Equality. The public meeting elected a special committee to prepare a draft of the new constitution; it was headed by Robert Owen and William Maclure. Robert Owen's sons, William and Robert Dale Owen were also elected, and within a short time they had drafted a proposal which was adopted on February 5. The new constitution pronounced all members equal as to their rights and level of consumption. There was to be no accounting for their work and its quality. The constitution did not clearly define the duties and rights of commune members or of those who might leave. It was also vague as to the legal aspect of the commune's property, perhaps because Robert Owen still regarded himself as its owner. It was clearly stated that the popular meeting was to be the highest authority and every adult over 21 had voting rights.[18]

Shortly after the constitution was adopted the Preliminary Society published its annual balance sheet. Only then did the picture of the vast deficit emerge. Those members who had been responsible for the economic and fiscal situation realized the implications and began to retreat from further responsibility. It was only two weeks since the new constitution had been adopted but already there were suggestions to reexamine those paragraphs that concerned the commune's management. In March Robert Owen was requested to conduct and supervise the concerns of the community for one year, with the assistance of a committee of his choice. He now held absolute power and the new constitution ''had become as a nothing'' before the voyage had begun.[19]

Robert Owen did not succeed in using his authority to remedy a single defect. The situation in industry and agriculture grew steadily worse. The belief in establishing a large and variegated community based on equality and communitarianism was undermined. In the days that followed members began to realize what they had done when they had welcomed everyone into the society without discrimination. The attempt to bring about equality and union at a single stroke had the paradoxical effect of opening wide fissures in the community. Some of the intellectuals and upper-class members were impatient with the backwoodsmen, the farmers, and the drifters. They found it difficult to be at ease with their fellow members from other backgrounds. Sara Pears gave voice to these sentiments when she wrote to Benjamin Bakewell:

> No one is to be favoured above the rest as we are all in a state of perfect equality. Oh, if you could see some of the rough, uncouth creatures here, I think you would find it rather hard to look upon them exactly in the light of brothers and sisters, I am sure! I cannot in sincerity look upon these as my equals, and if I must appear to do it, I cannot either act or speak the Truth.[20]

In addition to social, cultural, and personal differences the religious ones became acute. Two weeks after the new constitution had been adopted the first separate clique had evolved. They were a group of "native backwoodsmen strongly tinctured with Methodism" who could not accept the prevailing atmosphere of atheism. Robert Owen cooperated fully with their demand to form a separate community. He turned over to the group of 150 people 1,300 acres of uncleared land two miles away from New Harmony. This second community, which officially adopted the name *Macluria* (in tribute to William Maclure), did not survive long; it disintegrated late in 1826.

Disintegration

Soon after, a second separatist movement arose among a group of English farmers from Illinois who had difficulties integrating with the mostly American-born Owenists. They established the third commune on 700 acres of the best land of New Harmony and called it *Feiba Peveli*.[21]

Following the secession of the previous two groups an attempt was made to reorganize New Harmony. Yet in April 1826 the settlement was faced with another secession. They were the young intellectuals who regarded themselves as the active core of the commune and were led by Robert Dale Owen. They demanded to take over most of the buildings of New Harmony and to exclude all "summer soldiers" and "sunshine patriots." Most of the members regarded them as snobs and as a danger to the commune. Robert Owen saw the danger and avoided actual partitioning of New Harmony by offering the young enthusiasts a tract of virgin woodland in which they might "cut down trees and build log cabins as fast as they pleased,'' and the movement quickly collapsed.

The secession of the two groups did not harm the life of the group; it may have even had a stabilizing and healing effect. In the first months of 1826 it seemed as though the settlement was on its way to becoming a commune, and the leading members were optimistic as to the chances of the new social system. In the *New Harmony Gazette*, in Robert Owen's memories, and in travelogues of visitors, this optimism was reflected. However, those who were sharp eyed could discern signs of a widening schism beneath the surface.[22]

Visitors' Impressions

In April 1826 Karl Bernhard, Duke of Saxe-Weimar-Eisenach, visited New Harmony on his New World tour. In his travelogue he devoted a chapter to this social experiment, admitting to having been extremely prejudiced against Robert Owen and his theories. The visit presented him with the opportunity to observe the New Harmony experiment with his own eyes. He found Robert Owen a modest, easy-going, and unostentatious man who managed New Harmony with devotion and trust in the future of the community. The duke described the comfortable but simple life of the nearly 1,000 inhabitants. During the five days of his visit he wandered about freely, visiting the seceders, talking to many members, and observing them at work, in their homes, at public meetings, concerts, and dances. His vivid descriptions leave us with an impression of a dynamic social life and variegated economic enterprises. The duke nevertheless noticed that most of the jobs were joylessly executed. In his conversations with those members who had come from the upper classes and the intelligentsia he heard about disappointments with the attempt to integrate people from different backgrounds. In all the social functions he attended he noticed members sticking to their own former social classes. He saw upper-class girls refusing to dance with lower-class men and concluded that in spite of all the talk about equality these people would never mix with their ''inferiors.'' He even publicized that they would soon leave and that the community would cease to exist. When he broached the subject with Robert Owen he was amazed to realize that the latter completely ignored reality and was misled by his ardent desire to correct the whole world:

> It grieved me to see that Mr. Owen should allow himself to be so infatuated by his passion for universal improvement, as to believe and to say that he is about to reform the whole world; and yet that almost every member of his society that I have conversed with apart, acknowledged that he was deceived in his expectations; and expressed the opinion that Mr. Owen had commenced on too grand a scale and had admitted too many members without the requisite selection![23]

Deterioration

A different problem threatened New Harmony in the summer of 1826 when the heavy debt they owed George Rapp fell due. In order to help overcome the shortages, most members agreed to return to a system of bookkeeping which would supervise the amount of work everyone invested. This was supposed to put check to the parasitic element who had taken advantage of the full partnership. Although Robert Owen was still in charge he selected a committee of 24 who agreed to reorganize the community. They were the core of New Harmony but their good will did not serve them in finding ways of communicating with the social periphery of New Harmony. Bookkeeping had not increased work motivation and many found ways of misleading the accountants. William Maclure, who had noticed this as well as the deterioration, proposed in an article in the *New Harmony Gazette* of May 17, 1826 to divide the population into different communities, each consisting of the persons engaged in a particular occupation. According to him, individuals within each community would be laboring for their group reference, especially when they realized that each group would be autonomous and sell their services to the others, buying whatever they needed. The federated communities would exchange their services and products freely with one another. Robert Owen was convinced that this was a viable solution, and he put the proposal to the vote of the popular meeting on May 28, where it was adopted.

After some preliminary discussions three independent communities emerged—a School and Educational Society, an Agricultural and Pastoral Society, and a Mechanic and Manufacturing Society. They traded with one another with labor notes, the first mechanism of exchange Robert Owen had suggested. This new reorganization had made the task no easier. The community produced no more and consumed no less when divided into three. Furthermore, there was strife as to the funds to be put at their disposal. The only community which profited was the School Society, which in the summer of 1826 absorbed some excellent teachers, laboratory equipment, and a library donated by friends in Philadelphia. Maclure now had a free hand to order educational affairs in New Harmony. The 400 children on the commune received an excellent education. The exclusive financial support the School Society received magnified the mutual distrust that was reinforced by their demand of very high fees, and in the autumn of 1826 everyone agreed that the system did not work. The three societies were abolished, and New Harmony was now managed by William Owen.

In addition to the internal problems, the commune suffered from strong external attacks. These followed Robert Owen's Fourth of July speech titled "A Declaration of Mental Independence," in which he proclaimed his intention of freeing mankind from "a Trinity of the most monstrous evils that could combine to inflict mental and physical evil," namely, "Private or Individual Property—absurd and irrational Systems of Religion and Marriage founded on individual property combined with some of these irrational systems of religion." His speech was widely circulated and the reaction was one of suspicion and hostility, mainly because of his attack on the institution of marriage which offended the American puritanical society.

Rumors of sexual infidelity and of atheism in New Harmony began to circulate. These baseless accusations prompted Maclure, who was distrustful of Owen in some matters, to publish a letter defending the commune and to assert that "he never was in any place farther removed from every species of vice" or one "where the married are so faithful or the young so chaste."[24]

Internal Opposition

In the autumn of 1826 the breach between Robert Owen and William Maclure widened. In Maclure's opinion Owen was not only dissipating his resources by his extravagant subsidies but was actually corrupting the members, whose responsibility for their own existence was taken from them. A year and a half of Owen's paternalistic management "had produced nothing but waste and destruction of property and undermined the fitness of the inhabitants for cooperative society," he wrote.

Maclure decided to withdraw the School Society from the financial partnership with Owen, but this led to the deterioration of relations with the other societies that accepted Robert Owen's leadership. Finally the ideological conflict erupted into a land and property dispute which ended in the district court. The matter was settled by arbitration, and Maclure paid Robert Owen for an unrestricted deed of 490 acres of school property. In the end of 1827 New Harmony school became a separate educational institution.[25]

Robert Owen's position was further undermined by a radical group that aspired to establish full communal life in New Harmony. Its leader and spokesman was Paul Brown, who had joined New Harmony in April 1826; having been impressed by Robert Owen's communitarian doctrine, he left Massachusetts penniless but full of hope. He was deeply disappointed by what he found and quickly became a tireless opponent to Robert Owen's leadership. He sharply criticized the accountancy of work hours and individual budgeting and also the ways of communal consumption and the appearance of private property. He claimed that the prevailing system would never inspire the community with a communitarian spirit, the dependence on work notes only served to promote greed and mistrust, and that the members of New Harmony would never achieve "unity of hearts," a paramount condition for any communal life.

Paul Brown was extremely active in the community's public life and meetings and published his critical articles in the *New Harmony Gazette*. When this was stopped he still continued to put notices in public places; most were personal attacks on Robert Owen. He could not accept the latter's position as property owner and leader of the commune. Paul Brown regarded this as duplicity and bigotry which had a negative impact on the community. He accused Robert Owen of having manipulated the constitution so that his private property rights were maintained, rather than foster the society's independence; in the same spirit he criticized William Maclure and demanded that both completely give up their private property and join the commune as members with equal rights in order to cure New Harmony's ills.[26]

Paul Brown's radical opposition never gained momentum, and only a few came to the meetings he initiated. At the time private and group tensions were rife. His sharp criticism of the leadership and his attack on Robert Owen, whom he regarded as responsible for the failure of the communal spirit, ignited discontent and bitterness and contributed to the process of disintegration.[27]

Dissolution of the Commune

Any attempts of reorganization were by now useless. Between 1825 and 1827 seven constitutions had been composed, all of them variations on the first one. In 1827 the prevailing mood was one of estrangement and distrust. Robert Owen's leadership had been undermined by the secessions and strife. His ability and willingness to carry the financial load diminished. His own financial position was in a bad state and the only option was to lease some of the land to several groups. (Owen insisted that only cooperatives would do.) In April he advertised, and in May eight groups had undertaken to establish cooperatives on the land. Among them was a Mr. Tailor who promised to establish a commune but later turned out to be a swindler who instead opened an inn and a saloon. Not one of the eight groups fulfilled their promises, and Robert Owen was too tired to care.

On May 27, 1827 Owen decided to leave New Harmony and set out on a propaganda tour. Before leaving he bade farewell to the members of New Harmony and the other communities which had seceded. He reviewed the development of the settlement from the days of the Preliminary Society. Conceding that the frequent alterations he had introduced had been a mistake but that lacking prior experience, trial and error had been the only way to adapt to the change in the circumstances of communal life. He went on to say that there was a positive aspect to the trial because future communes in England and the United States would profit from the experience. He admitted that among the many who had joined New Harmony there were some who were unfit for communitarian life and should henceforth be rejected in order to save the commune. He estimated that the experimental period was now over, and that the social system was well established as was evident in the "ten socialist colonies of equality and common property" that surrounded New Harmony.[28]

Paul Brown, who was among the listeners to Robert Owen's departure speech, reacted with a merciless attack. He criticized Owen's disregard to reality when he had stated that the New Harmony communities were "colonies of equality and common property." Brown rightly claimed that those settlers who had opted to stay had leased their land on a private basis and that the socialist system was bankrupt.[29] Owen ignored him just as he had ignored reality. In those days he was bothered by problems which had sprung up between him and Maclure over some financial affairs. At the last moment a judiciary confrontation between them was avoided and the dispute was settled when 500 acres of New Harmony were transferred to the ownership of Maclure.

On May 14, while Owen was concluding the formalities to leave New Harmony, Maclure declared his educational institution open to orphans and external students. He was no longer dependent on the children of Owenist New Harmony, which was in the last stages of disintegration. A few months later he acquired the *New Harmony Gazette* and turned it into a platform for his educational theories.

Owenist Communities in the East

New Harmony as a social experiment came to an end in June 1827 with the departure of its founder. Robert Owen however would not admit that his movement had failed, mainly because he had been reenforced by the information about the Owenist communities that were being organized as communal societies in the cities with the intent of establishing independent settlements. Word had also reached him about the existence of communal groups struggling to overcome the problems of their first days in Pennsylvania, New York, and Ohio.[30]

These Owenist groups profited from the opening of the Erie Canal and the prosperity of 1825-26 that followed it. These settlers who went West could purchase or lease state-owned land cheaply. Conversely, this atmosphere of prosperity was not fertile ground for Owen's ideology. Only those whom the recession of 1819 was still affecting were receptive to his social reforms; through them they could protest against social evils and the take-over of local and federal government by the aristocracy and the moneyed oligarchy. The Owenist ideology never went very deep and as soon as other spiritual or religious ideas emerged in the 1830s the promised Owenist gospel petered out.[31]

In spite of the enthusiastic support of the hundreds who joined New Harmony, the Owenist following was limited to eastern United States. They came from a clearly defined geographical area of the seaboard cities of New York and Philadelphia and spread throughout the Ohio Valley from Pittsburgh and Cincinnati, to the mouth of the Wabash. Many were unable to make the long and hazardous journey to Indiana, and instead seven local projects were born, but they were short lived.

The first group organized in Philadelphia in 1825—The Friendly Association for Mutual Interests. In the spring of 1826 they set out to Valley Forge, but were immediately subjected to bitter attack by religious groups in the vicinity, and by September the settlement had broken up. Among the disappointed members, a small minority with ascetic inclinations found their way to the Shaker communes.[32]

New York, too, had been stirred by the ideas of Owen. One of the communities that organized to settle on a site of 120 acres near Haverstraw, on the Hudson, was the Franklin Community. They drew up their constitution in March 1826, led by George Houston, an Englishman who had immigrated after he had been imprisoned for publishing atheistic writings. Most of the members were intellectuals, journalists, lawyers, and other professionals of rationalist-atheistic convictions. The families who in May moved to the settlement and began to farm the land, soon crystallized into a group that could not accept the atheistic activities of those who had remained in New York. This group joined the settlement and began to put their atheistic ideas into practice by secularizing the schools and establishing a Church of Reason. The schism widened and weakened the young settlement, which broke up five months after it had been established.

In the Upper Hudson Valley near Coxsackie, a second Owenist experiment—the Forestville Community—was organized in December 1825. The local people were in communication with the Owenists in New York City. Although smaller in number than the Franklin commune, it lived longer. When the latter disbanded, a number of its members moved to the community at Coxsackie. In October 1827 they had to dissolve the settlement and sell their property, but half of the members remained loyal to the communal idea and decided to join the Kendall community in Ohio, in spite of the arduous winter journey this entailed.[33] Kendall was the most outstanding of the Owenist experiments in the area. Its founders were a group of men in the vicinity of Canton and Massilon in northeastern Ohio. They began to organize in January 1826 and by March had drafted a statement of principles in the Owenist spirit, but differentiated from other Owenist documents by the frequent allusions to the deity and the gospels. Some of the members were Quakers. In May they moved to their domain in Kendall. The relative success of the community may be attributed to their knowledge of the local conditions and their long acquaintance with each other. Most of the members were local farmers who had sold their farms and collectively bought the larger tract which they proposed to manage cooperatively. They introduced a period of one-year candidacy. Its members were diligent and carried on with modest success, absorbing some of New Harmony's seceders. The end of the Kendall community came early in 1829. More than two years of steady labor had not created the Owenist millennium and seemed unlikely ever to do so. In that period of prosperity individualism offered brighter prospects than communitarianism. The first to leave were the leading members and in January 1829 the community ceased to exist and the property was sold with a moderate loss to its founders.[34]

In southwestern Ohio, near Cincinnati, Owenist activity was prospering. The Shakers' impact was felt there and even before Robert Owen's arrival in the area The Rational Brethern of Oxford had developed a communal project. When Owen came to Cincinnati he found his books and pamphlets on sale and a large circle of supporters who were already in the process of organizing communal life at Yellow Springs up the Little Miami River.

In its social and economic practices the community endeavored to be a faithful copy of New Harmony and succeeded in being so in its dissensions as well. The belief in equality floundered on the different mentality of the members who soon formed factions. Problems of work, property, and communal living overtook the community which, unlike New Harmony, had no serious leading members. Disintegration followed a few months after its establishment and caused Owen a great disappointment. He attempted to reestablish the commune and was helped by Maclure and Paul Brown. Two active groups were formed to settle in Yellow Springs, each pulling in a different direction. Maclure gave financial aid in order to purchase the land, then established an educational institution according to the New Harmony model, while Paul Brown on the other hand encouraged his group to adopt radical communist attitudes. They regarded themselves as the "laboring class" who were entitled to full partnership in the enterprise to which they had contributed their labor. There was no way to bridge the gap. The community disappeared and in January 1827 the property was deeded back to its original owners.[35]

The impact of the New Harmony experiment was felt also in Indiana, a 100 miles to the northeast. Owen's ideas inspired a group of independent farmers to sell their farms in order to buy a tract of 80 acres in Blue Springs; they established a community there in the spring of 1826. The membership, like that of Kendall, was homogeneous and familiar with the area as well as used to farming. The community disintegrated a year later for the same reasons as Kendall when they realized that individually they could achieve more.[36]

Nashoba: A Daring Experiment in Racial Equality

Side by side with the short-lived Owenist communes, another communal experiment was created—the movement for emancipating the slaves, cross fertilized by Owenism, which produced Nashoba on a small farm in Tennessee. Frances Wright, a young Scotswoman, daughter of a prosperous merchant, had been involved since youth with various revolutionary circles and radical reform movements. She had visited the United States several times and in 1824 joined her friend and protector Lafayette on his visit to Washington which coincided with Robert Owens' visit there. She was greatly impressed by his utopian ideas and formulated a plan for combining his communal ideas with the gradual emancipation of slaves through settling them in small, independent communities in which they would be educated to become free people.

From Washington Wright continued to Illinois to visit the English immigrant communities whose leaders were George Flower and Morris Birkbeck. In Flower she found a soul mate who as early as 1819 had been turning over in his mind the idea of adapting the Harmony Plan to Negro emancipation. Wright wrote a detailed memorandum in the summer of 1825 in which she formulated her plan for the establishment of a communal Owenist settlement "in which 50 to 100 slaves could earn the money for their emancipation at the same time that they learned the skills and attitudes requisite for freedom."

In her preface Wright mentions not only the Owenist communes but also the religious ones in the United States. Her plan was submitted through Lafayette to many of the influential people in the country, but before there was any approval she proceeded to carry it out. With the help of her friend George Flower she bought 2,000 acres of Chickasaw land near Memphis, Tennessee, and the Chickasaw name *Nashoba* was bestowed upon the leased land.

During the winter of 1825-26 Miss Wright was joined by her sister, by George Flower and his family, and other friends and began preparation for the new settlement. There were additional conversations with Robert Owen and she decided to expand the doctrine on which her settlement was founded. In addition to slave emancipation she proposed freedom from religious bondage and a family unit in which sexual relations would not be confined. These ideas prompted her to open the commune to White settlers, thus abolishing the color discrimination prevalent in the South in those days. She wanted to begin racial integration in the school she was about to open at Nashoba, where Black and White children would learn together. After having thrown this daring and dangerous bombshell in the southern state of Tennessee, Miss Wright did not stay to see her ideas through. Leaving the management of Nashoba to her sister and other even less experienced people, she set out on a propaganda tour with Robert Dale Owen, who shared her ideas.

The Nashoba team which was left to take charge of the daring and complicated social experiment, to establish a mixed communal society with free love and racial equality, was unable to cope. When the facts about free love across race line became public knowledge, a storm broke out and the neighbors started to persecute the commune and its members.

Frances Wright returned in December 1827. She wrote a series of "Explanatory Notes Respecting the Nature and Objects of the Institution of Nashoba," in which she defined her convictions on questions of property, religion, and sexual liberty. These could not make any difference in the Tennessee of those days. The situation on the commune was discouraging too. There were not enough Negroes whose motivation and understanding justified the communal ideology. In early 1828 Wright took stock of Nashoba's practical affairs and admitted that the people were not ripe "to form a community of equality and common property." In its year of existence it had not consolidated a substantial group of slaves with the motivation to live on the commune. The Preliminary Social Community at Nashoba was stillborn. Wright sailed with the slaves to Haiti, where their emancipation concluded the Nashoba experiment.[37]

Failure but Not Defeat

Robert Owen returned to New Harmony in April 1828 to be confronted with the fact that his belief in the communal future of his socialist settlement had been unrealistic. On those settlements which had survived on New Harmony land, the individualistic method prevailed; none of them had any vestige of communitarianism. Owen now had to admit his failure; yet his belief remained intact, and he adhered to his vision to convince individual farmers and workers to cooperate.[38]

In the summer of 1829 Owen left the United States for England to renew his activities there. The wave of communitarianism, so promising when he arrived in the United States five years earlier, receded. New Harmony was dissolved as were all other Owenist settlements. The Owenist movement was in ruins. Most of its leaders joined other reform movements that had been influenced by Owen's theories. But of his communal experiment nothing remained.

In the long run, however, the sense of failure was unjustified. It soon transpired that even though the Owenist settlements had disintegrated, the Owenist doctrine of secular socialist communes had not. The communitarian idea, which until the advent of Owen had been limited to esoteric sects, had taken root in the public consciousness. From this period onwards it would be regarded as one of the reform options that could help the society of the United States to overcome its economic problems and social ills.

Notes

1. Arthur Bestor, *Backwoods Utopias*, 2d ed. (Philadelphia: University of Pennsylvania Press, 1978), pp. 94-99, 236; Donald Egbert and Stow Persons, eds., *Socialism and American Life*, 2 vols. (Princeton: Princeton University Press, 1952), pp. 161-62; Albert Fried, *Socialism in America from the Shakers to the Third International: A Documentary History* (Garden City, N.Y.: Doubleday, 1970), pp. 5-6, chap. 3; John Fletcher Clews Harrison, *Quest for the New Moral World: Robert Owen and the Owenites in Britain and America* (New York: Scribner's, 1969), pp. 100-102.
2. Bestor, *Backwoods*, pp. 207-14; Paul Brown, *Twelve Months in New Harmony* (Philadelphia: Porcupine, 1972), pp. 1-14; Harrison, pp. 101-8.
3. On Robert Owen's life see Gideon G. Freudenberg, *Robert Owen: Educator of the People* (Tel Aviv: Dvir, 1970), pp. 110-21 (Hebrew).
4. Donald Macdonald, *The Diaries of 1824-1826* (Clifton, N.J.: Kelley, 1973; 1st ed. 1942), pp. 188-90, 174-262; William Owen, *Diary of 1824-1825*, ed. Joel W. Hiatt (Clifton, N.J.: 1973; 1st ed. 1906), pp. 9-13, 28-36, 51; Bestor, *Backwoods*, pp. 94-108; Owen, pp. 71-78, 92.
5. George B. Lockwood, *The New Harmony Movement* (New York: Dover, 1971; 1st ed. 1905), pp. 72-99.
6. Ibid., pp. 69-72; Harrison, p. 106; Basset, p. 163; Macdonald, pp. 268-74, Everett Webber, *Escape to Utopia* (New York: Hastings House, 1959), p. 139; Fried, pp. 5-6. In the temporary by-laws of New Harmony that Owen himself composed it was written that people from all the nations of the world would have the right to join "except for the colored races."
7. Freudenberg, pp. 121-22; Lockwood, pp. 82-91.
8. Shalom Wurm, *Communal Societies and Their Way of Life* (Tel Aviv: Ayanot, 1968), pp. 117-18 (Hebrew); Bestor, *Backwoods*, pp. 113-22.
9. Macdonald, pp. 319-21.
10. F.V. Calverton, *Where Angels Dared to Tread* (New York: Bobbs-Merrill, 1941), p. 84; Lockwood, pp. 75-80; Arthur Bestor, ed., *Education and Reform at New Harmony* (Indiana Historical Society Publications, vol. 15, no. 3, 1948), pp. 304-16.
11. Bestor, *Backwoods*, pp. 164-65; P. Freudenberg, pp. 130-31.
12. Thomas and Sarah Pears, *New Harmony: An Adventure in Happiness*, ed. Thomas C. Pears, Jr. (Clifton, N.J.: Kelley, 1973), pp. 14-15. Letter, June 2, 1825.
13. William Pelham, "Letters of, Written in 1825-1826," *New Harmony as Seen by Participants and Travelers* (Philadelphia: Porcupine, 1975). Letter, September 8, 1825.
14. Ibid., November 27, 1825; September 19, 1825; October 10, 1825; October 3, 1825; *New Harmony Gazette*, November 29, 1825; November 30, 1825, quoted

in Lockwood, pp. 98-99. Robert Dale Owen, *Threading My Way: An Autobiography* (New York: Carlton, 1874; New York: Kelley, 1967), pp. 276, 282.
15. Lockwood, p. 99; Pelham Letters, November 7, 1825, October 29, 1825.
16. Donald E. Pitzer, "Education in Utopia: The New Harmony Experience," *Indiana Historical Society Lectures, 1976-1977*; Bestor, *Backwoods*, pp. 133-35, 168.
17. Pears, pp. 27, 40, 52; Pelham, Letter, January 6, 1826.
18. Lockwood, pp. 105-12; Owen, pp. 286-87.
19. Bestor, *Backwoods*, pp. 170-74; Lockwood, pp. 116 20; 123-25.
20. Pears, p. 60.
21. Lockwood, pp. 112-16; Webber, p. 147. The name was made up by the architect Whitwell. It is the literal meaning of the geographic spot of the settlement (longitude: west 81.53, latitude north 38.11).
22. Owen, pp. 282, 285-88; *New Harmony Gazette*, March 8, 1826; March 12, 1826; April 12, 1826, quoted in Lockwood, pp. 116-17, 137.
23. Duke of Saxe-Weimar-Eisenach, Karl Bernhard, "Account of a Visit to New Harmony," *New Harmony as Seen by Participants and Travelers*, vol. 2 (Philadelphia: Porcupine, 1975), pp. 105-24. The Duke of Saxe Weimar's observations were not shared by the active circle in New Harmony. Robert Dale Owen testifies that in those days "I was not haunted by doubts as to the success of the social experiment in which we were engaged. The inhabitants seemed to me friendly and well disposed." Owen, p. 281.
24. Bestor, *Backwoods*, pp. 222-23.
25. Ibid., pp. 190, 197-200.
26. Brown, *Twelve Months*, pp. 1-18, 67-70, 85-94.
27. Brown, *Twelve Months*, pp. 119-28; Egbert and Persons, pp. 170-72; Bestor, *Backwoods*, p. 199; Lockwood, p. 145; Robert S. Fogarty, *American Utopianism* (Itasca, Ill.: Peacock, 1972), pp. 43-49.
28. Lockwood, pp. 163-66.
29. Brown, *Twelve Months*, pp. 98-128.
30. Rosabeth Moss Kanter, *Communes, Creating and Managing the Collective Life* (New York: Harper & Row, 1973), pp. 450-55; John Humphrey Noyes, *History of American Socialism* (New York: Dover, 1966; 1st ed. 1870), p. 65.
31. Lockwood, pp. 174-86; Basset, pp. 167-68.
32. Bestor, *Backwoods*, pp. 202-3.
33. Ibid., pp. 203-4; Harrison, p. 167.
34. Bestor, *Backwoods*, p. 205; Harrison, p. 166.
35. Bestor, *Backwoods*, pp. 207-9; 210-13; Hinds, pp. 146-50; Harrison, p. 166; J.H. Noyes, *History of American Socialism* (1870). Reprinted as, *Strange Cults and Utopias of Nineteenth-Century America* (New York: Dover, 1966), pp. 59-65.
36. Richard Simons, "A Utopian Failure," *Indiana History Bulletin* 18 (February 1941):98-113; Harrison, pp. 165-66.
37. Richard Stiller, *Commune on the Frontier: The Story of Frances Wright* (New York: Crowell, 1972), pp. 107-54, 210-14; Bestor, *Backwoods*, pp. 218-25.
38. Bestor, *Backwoods*, p. 196; Webber, pp. 156-64; Freudenberg, p. 158.

6

Fourierist Communitarian Settlements

Fifteen years elapsed between the disintegration of the Owenist experiment and the appearance of a new wave of secular communes, influenced by Charles Fourier's utopian socialism. Most of Robert Owen's followers by then had ceased their reformist activities and only a few repeated their attempts to establish independent communes. Among those who had remained loyal to Owen's doctrines were his son Robert Dale Owen and Frances Wright, who had transferred their activities from Indiana to New York. There they founded the journal *The Free Enquirer*, which became a platform for the hundreds of local labor unions in the East between 1825 and 1837. These unions concentrated on their professional struggles and avoided political involvements, especially after the Jacksonian democracy that had left no room for such an involvement. The unions' activities increased when the economic prosperity enticed them to fight for a bigger share in the national income. Simultaneously, new spiritual trends appeared in the eastern states. Some took the form of religious revivals with millennial expectations, others of movements that aspired to reform the prevailing ways of life, to improve educational methods, abolish slavery, achieve women's rights, or to introduce prison reforms.

In 1837 a depression caused widespread unemployment in the industrial centers in the East. It was the biggest modern industrial crisis in the United States and its impact was felt in most social classes. After high expectations of the prosperity years, frustration followed among the workers and lower-middle-classes in the cities and in rural areas.[1] The economic and social depression caused the various reform movements to become more radical and to propose far-reaching solutions to society's ills. This was the social background for the religious fermentation, and revival meetings centered around Charles Finney (1792-1875), who preached in western New York State, and William Miller (1782-1849) in New England. In the electrifying atmosphere of economic depression, social frustration, spiritual upheavals, and millenary expectations there was spiritual readiness mainly among the intelligentsia to absorb new social ideas. In the late 1830s Albert Brisbane introduced his "new gospel," which he hoped would cure all social ills.[2] It was a revision of Fourier's ideas which he had learnt as the disciple of the socialist philosopher during his stay in Europe.

Albert Brisbane

Doctrine

The feeling of frustration that was prevalent in American society following the depression persuaded Albert Brisbane that the time was ripe to introduce the message he had brought from Europe. He began his propaganda campaign in 1837 and by 1839 had managed to acquire a strong following, mainly in the populated urban areas of New York and Philadelphia. When Brisbane's version of Fourier's ideas was published as a book, *The Social Destiny of Man*, in 1840, it soon became evident that this book fell on fertile ground and had an enormous impact on the period.

Brisbane had adapted Fourierism to American mentality. His book presented the complicated theory in a clear, precise manner, excluding those points that might have been unacceptable to the American reader. It was a popularization and Americanization of Fourier's plan of establishing settlements in the form of Associations. Brisbane had developed Fourierism into a dynamic plan of action, omitting all of Fourier's fantasies, his unacceptable ideas on women, marriage, and morals. On the practical side Brisbane established the Agricultural-Industrial Association, which was intended to solve the problem of capital versus labor. His Fourierism adopted the social principle of work leading to riches, and man's right to work for his share; he adopted the same attitude toward land.

The individualistic motivation behind the Fourierist Associations was presented as a manifestation of the theory of "attractive work." The combination of those elements was seen as immediately feasible. In his book Brisbane explained that Fourier had not intended to abolish private property but only the capitalist anarchy that led to the concentration of capital in the hands of a few while impoverishing the majority. The idea was close to the hearts of many Americans who had experienced the effects of the capitalist anarchy. In addition Brisbane denounced the destructive impact capitalism has on all areas of life, including the arts and literature. He described the deterioration of the working classes and the harsh conditions in the capitalistic factories, where health hazards and working conditions made the lot of a laborer worse than that of a slave. Not legislative reform, only association of work and capital according to Fourier, would bring the much longed for change.

First Steps

Brisbane's book was an immediate success. His ideas were absorbed by the many who had lost their social standing and sense of security and by intellectuals who were searching for solutions for the social ills.[3] One of them was Horace Greeley (1811-1872), the editor of the daily *New York Tribune*. His paper, which had been appearing since April 10, 1841, opened its pages to Fourier's ideas in March 1842, and gave Brisbane the opportunity "to lay these principles of Association before the public." Greeley later became active in the Fourier movement. In addition to the *Tribune* Brisbane published his ideas in the *Democratic Chronicle* and in the *Plebeian*, a radical periodical. As a result, Fourierism gained popularity mainly in New England, New York, Illinois, and Ohio and at a later stage in Wisconsin and Michigan.

Fourier's ideas, even though they had been amended by Brisbane, were adamantly opposed by conservative politicians and the church establishment who were appalled by the wide distribution of nonconformist ideas. This only served to promote Fourierist initiative and propaganda. In many places circles of followers established propaganda centers and organized meetings. Their former media did not suffice, and in 1842 Horace Greeley published in his paper information on all the Fourierist movement's activities, meetings, conventions, and the organization of the first settlement as well as ideological articles.

Many were attracted to Fourierism whether in the hope of bettering their individual lot or as a means of solving social ills throughout the world; some were careerists who hoped to further their personal ambitions of leadership. Affluent farmers invested their money in the association hoping to avoid conflict with migrant agricultural workers. The lower classes on the other hand, wished to improve their conditions as salaried workers by joining the local association which owned both the capital and the means of production. According to Fourierism they became partners through work shares, capital, or talent and could achieve social security. Brisbane's version was acceptable to a wide range of sectors in the American population because he promised cures for social ills and deliverance from the salaried bondage. He was not radical in his demand to abolish private property and altogether there seems to have been an apolitical combination which crossed traditional party lines and spread even faster than Brisbane had expected.[4]

Another reason for Brisbane's success was his practical approach to Fourier. From his first article in the *Tribune* he proposed plans about how to establish associations (which would be called "phalanx" after the first settlements were established). According to his proposal an association would need a founding capital of $400,000 to $500,000. This could be achieved either through private investment or by selling $1,000 shares to future members whose minimum number should be 400; otherwise the Fourier Association could not function. Brisbane left the option to the settlers themselves. He also agreed to having shareholders who were not actually settlers and remained external members.[5] In this he remained true to the unradical principles of Fourierism and widened the circle of followers to such an extent that in May 1843 the *Tribune* reported that no less than a dozen associations were in various stages of settling. Thousands attended Fourierist meetings intending to establish settlements in ten states—New York, Ohio, Pennsylvania, Massachusetts, New Jersey, Wisconsin, Michigan, Illinois, Indiana, and Connecticut.

This massive organization demanded an independent journal and in October 1843 the first issue of the *Phalanx* appeared. This periodical contributed much to Fourierist expansion and to a profounder ideological understanding among intellectuals and a wide periphery of followers. A glance at the list of writers whose articles appeared in the *Phalanx* points to the high standards of the journal. Side by side with Brisbane, Horace Greeley, William Channing, and E.P. Grant who were directly identified with Fourierism, we find Henry James[6] (1811-1882), the philosopher and theologian, father of William James and Henry James Jr. The *Phalanx* appeared in New York regularly and gave information on the movement's activities from 1843 to 1845. In those years Associations were organized into settlements near the main centers. In spite of their unexpected numbers, it soon became evident that not enough time and thought had been devoted to the preparations. Brisbane's rule of establishing associations of at least 400 members had not been followed. Nor had there been enough capital in any of the 30 settlements to buy the large tracts of land needed, and several of them had bought land cheaply in unsuitable areas and in unfavorable conditions of payment. A wide gap between their high expectations for a panacea for social ills and the bleak reality of the first days caused most associations to disintegrate. Only three or four survived.[7]

Fourierist Settlements in Pennsylvania, 1893-94

Sylvania

The Sylvania Association was the first phalanx to be established in May 1843 on a hilly region in northeastern Pennsylvania. The settlers, from New York and Albany, had organized under Brisbane's and Greeley's direct influence about a year earlier. Most of them were industrial workers and mechanics. A pamphlet issued by the executive committee in the early days of the settlement described the various stages of organization and pointed to the reason for taking this step as being "the present defective, vice engendering the ruinous system of society, with the wasteful complication of isolated households, its destructive competition and anarchy in industry, its constraint of millions to idleness and consequent dependence or famine for want of employment and its failure to secure education and development to the children growing up among us in ignorance and vice.'' They found that ''they were impelled to immediate and energetic action to resist this evil.'' Having earnestly studied Charles Fourier's social reform, they heartily adopted that system ''as a practical plan for melioration of the condition of man and his moral and intellectual elevation.''[8] After a period of activities such as organizing propaganda campaigns a group of 150, mainly family men, formed the Association in Sylvania. Greeley was their treasurer, and a group of 40 set out to prepare the site for the others. In August there were 137 inhabitants, including 51 children, in Sylvania. They all lived in crowded conditions in two buildings, and tension developed right from the start. The grand ideals soon turned into disappointments and frustrations. Most of the members had left their places of work and houses in the hope of bettering their individual lot as well as that of all mankind by showing a new way for society as a whole. The harsh conditions at Sylvania, which was located in an unsuitable area for agriculture, as well as their lack of experience, contributed to the poor crops. But their main difficulties were education and their social life. It became evident that the people had no aptitude for communal life. The community did not function as a disciplined and coordinated social or economic unit. The first controversy developed around methods of education. But in spite of the difficulties the founders insisted on establishing a collective community. They survived only until 1844, when Sylvania disintegrated and all the members returned to their original homes.[9]

The failure of the first Fourier settlement did not discourage others from repeating the experiment. In the same year six additional Fourier communities were established in Pennsylvania. One of them was established in Warren County in the summer of 1843 by a group of Germans with special Fourierist ideas who bought 10,000 acres of prime land there. Their founder was Andreas Bernhardus Smolnikar, an Austrian professor of biblical study and criticism, who had encountered Fourierist ideas in his native land and saw a connection between Fourier and the prophesies of the Bible. He believed that the time of universal peace was at hand and decided to immigrate to the United States to carry out its mission. Smolnikar was one of Brisbane's first followers. Nothing is known about the settlement in itself. Smolnikar remained true to the cause and, traveling all over Pennsylvania, he preached his ideas, influencing another group of German Fourierists.[10]

One Mentian Community

More details and relatively more stability may be found in the other Fourierist communities in Pennsylvania. One Mentian Community was established in a forest area in Monroe County, Pennsylvania, in 1843 by a group of 40 workers and mechanics, some of whom were influenced by the Owenist doctrine. They bought 800 acres and with hardly any preparations established their settlement, living in conditions of austerity. In spite of the hardships they were devoted to their work and achieved a good harvest. In 1844 they managed to repay their debts, but their success was incomplete and their standard of living remained low. They failed to attract more people to their settlements, and without a chance to grow they disintegrated within a year.[11]

Social Reform Unity

Another settlement, the Social Reform Unity, was established by workers and mechanics from Brooklyn who had been supporters of the Fourierist movement from its beginning. They were active in the education and propaganda union and printed a constitution for their future settlement which was never used. In 1843 they bought some cheap land in Pike County, Pennsylvania, and a group of 20 set out on their new venture, which did not last long.[12]

Fourierist Settlements in New York, 1843-1845

West New York was the region that responded most vigorously to the gospel of Fourierism proclaimed by Albert Brisbane. It was this area, known as the "burned-over district," which had experienced all the excitements of the last forty years, the revival meetings, and the preachers who had spread millennial expectations. Here the Mormons had been formed, and the Shakers and the Millerites had preached their gospel. Many reformers were combing the area with their messages of social and educational reform, the call for abstinence and for the abolishment of slavery.[13] The farmers who had been hit by the recession were a receptive audience of Fourier and his message of social reform. It left them the option of private property through the stock they retained on joining the association but offered security through the communal work and means of production. They were also convinced that the association would realize Christianity upon the earth, while people of various religious influences were accepted. The farmers who had gone through the revivals found an answer to their expectations in Fourierism. The Fourierist organizations in the city were mainly from among the more affluent walks of life while those who joined the settlements were mostly working-class people with only a sprinkling of professionals and middle-class members. Even so, these few were in most cases the leaders.[14]

Ontario Phalanx

At the beginning of 1843 Fourierist circles in western New York began to organize. They met in August 1843 at a massive convention at Rochester and discussed the constitution of the Fourierist association in the area—Ontario Phalanx. It was similar to the rules Brisbane had formulated shortly before and was characterized by its attempt to adapt the complicated theories to practical principles and financial norms; it was aimed at attracting people to join the Fourierist circles and settlements.

Ontario Phalanx did not survive the diversity of opinions and local loyalties, and the disagreements over choosing a site for the settlement. Added to this was the manipulation of speculators who were eager to exploit the Fourierist upheavals in order to advance their interests in the development of virgin lands. The disintegration of the Ontario Phalanx led to the establishment of four separate associations near Rochester; not one of them succeeded in attracting enough members and capital to establish a viable foundation for a Fourierist phalanx.[15]

Clarkson Phalanx

Clarkson Phalanx was the first and most important of the confederations of phalanxes around Rochester. Its members had organized in February 1844, according to Fourierist theories. They were tolerant with religious and political convictions. Voting rights were granted to members aged 18 and above. They were also tolerant about property matters and shared only the land and the means of production. New members were promised a "heaven and earth" and millennial prospects, and some joined for escapist reasons and with no ideological motivation whatsoever. The regulations stipulated direction by the trustees who were put in charge of the members' property on the basis of exact bookkeeping.

Members had contributed different amounts of money with which the trustees purchased a choice property of 2,000 acres on the shore of Lake Ontario for $95,000. In May 420 members settled in the few buildings they found there in addition to barns and a flour mill and sawmill. They started a vegetable garden and used the good pasture for their cattle. There was no common ownership but only common use thereof, and members earned according to the work they invested. However, housing, food, health services, and education were promised to everyone regardless of the amount of work. Soon their different religious backgrounds caused conflicts. A lack of Fourierist motivation prevented the formation of a strong core that would lead the phalanx through periods of crisis. A year after its inception Clarkson Phalanx was dissolved but without discord or litigations over the division of the property.[16]

Sodus Bay Phalanx

The Sodus Bay Phalanx was the second to be established in April 1844 on a Shaker commune that was dissolved a few years earlier. The Fourierists found on the site farm buildings, a flour mill and sawmill as well as orchards; it was a good foundation for a communal settlement. The settlers started to construct a dining-hall that was completed in September. The wooded area of Sodus Bay supplied the raw material for additional living quarters and farm buildings, but most of the work was devoted to agriculture, vegetables, orchards, and stock farming. A majority of the 300 settlers were farmers from different parts of northwestern New York and the good land, the comfortable climate, and lovely countryside contributed to their high hopes. However, they did not achieve that unity of purpose, without which the phalanx could not function.

Many persons were accepted without proper qualifications of character or diligence. Religious differences and lack of ideological motivation left their impact on the young society. The committees which were supposed to give the direction failed; for example, the housing committee did not stand up against the pressure for better accommodation. Even when the difficulties seemed to have been overcome Fourierism was not implemented. Work was not rotated as Fourier had proposed; not enough capital was available for economic development. But worst of all was the growing gap between ordinary members and the leadership who had come from among the Rochester Fourierists. Discord set in on practical issues as well as on matters of principle.

The first disharmony erupted over religious differences concerning the Sabbath. Soon educational problems and differences over the teaching staff of the local school were reasons for quarrels, and these were followed by ideological and cultural disharmony, resulting in the emergence of two parties. When in addition disease struck during the first summer, members left in a steadily increasing number. This raised the problem of the seceders' rights for compensation, and in the autumn of 1844 a Fourierist constitution was formulated—too late to save the phalanx. In the spring of 1845 there were only a few left, who valiantly struggled to survive. A year later they too gave up. Many who visited the settlement during its final year were impressed by the devotion of the few survivors and the harsh conditions, but predicted that unless new blood was added there would be no chance to renew the community.[17] In the spring of 1846 the last fifteen members left.

Other Settlements

Three other small settlements were established in the area in 1844. The first, Ontario Union was established on 150 acres in Hopewell, near Rochester; in the autumn of 1844 it had 150 persons. Nearby the Mixville Association was established, and its delegate participated in the confederated council in Rochester. The third was the Bloomfield Association, established in March 1844, which reached a membership of 150 but dissolved a few months later in August 1845. Another area in which Fourierism took roots was Jefferson County in northern New York. The local leader there was A.M. Watson, who promoted Fourierism in that section of the state.[18]

A short while after the establishment of the separate settlements in western New York they suggested a federation of phalanxes, and in 1844 The American Industrial Union was established. The foundations were laid in Rochester in March 1844 with the intention of exchanging and spreading information to further economic and financial coordination. This was to be the first of the Fourierist federations in the United States, and it influenced circles of followers in northwestern New York who rapidly increased to 20,000. But as soon as news of the difficulties of the Fourierist phalanxes reached them, their numbers decreased, especially since at the same time economic conditions in the state had improved. Fourier was denounced in local newspapers and the rapid disintegration of the settlements only added to the critical articles and cooled the enthusiasm of many of the followers.

Fourierist leaders and especially Albert Brisbane ignored the signs and blamed the failures on the lack of preparation of the phalanx members who had rushed to establish their settlements without a minimal foundation. They dissociated themselves from the struggling settlements, hoping to save the movement as a whole. This was a mistake that affected the few followers who remained loyal. When Fourierism began to organize as a national movement in the East Brook Farm, members were sent as emissaries to the area in 1847. A letter from John Orvis of Brook Farm reveals that he could assemble only a handful of listeners because the very name of *association* was an anathema to the people in the Rochester area. Those who had been unlucky enough to join the movement were now hiding the fact from their neighbors.[19]

Fourierism in Ohio

Fourierist ideas were widespread in Ohio. Between 1843 and 1845 seven settlements were established in an attempt to live up to Fourier's doctrine. There is some detailed evidence about several of these settlements. Even before Fourierism reached Ohio, social unrest had hit the area in 1841 and some socialist associations were established. The first gathering took place on the farm of the Brooke family, and the discussion turned to the evil and oppressive conditions of ordinary labor and commerce. The only remedy they saw was a return to the apostolic manner of living: "having all things in common." A family member, Dr. Brooke, took matters into his own hands and donated his farm to the members of the association who were ready to live a communal life. The Marlboro Community was thus established. The majority of its members were without property, and Dr. Brooke's farm was their only income. The nucleus was joined by several idealists but also by adventurers and escapists. When the community proved to be stable, more affluent members joined, and other farms were donated to the joint venture.

Life on Marlboro commune was modest; an atmosphere of rationalism prevailed in spite of the Christian apostolic motivation. When in 1843 the Fourierist message reached Ohio, a constitution in the Fourierist spirit was adopted. The community existed for four years, until 1845. Among the reasons for its disintegration were the disputes among its members about the intensity of their communitarianism. Dr. Brooke would not be convinced of anything less than true communism and objected to any kind of individualism. He left the community and tried an experiment of his own. Its members lived very modestly without the use of money and received according to their needs.[20]

In addition to the local social ferment, Ohio was influenced by Fourierist organization in the neighboring states. The Fourierist convention in 1843 in New York and Pennsylvania encouraged settlement in Ohio, and one of the first there was the Ohio Phalanx, also called the American Phalanx, whose founders came from Pittsburgh. Among them were E.P. Grant and Van Amringe, who would become renowned leaders of Fourierism on a national level.

The first announcement of the organization of the association is to be found in the December 1843 issue of the *Phalanx*. They acquired a tract of 20,000 acres in Belmont County on the Ohio River; beautiful and fertile, it was situated on one of the great thoroughfares, immediately accessible to several large markets and near the National Road leading through the heart of the West. They had great expectations and hoped to attract many members. The founders planned to build a phalanstery, the central building which in addition to members' accommodations was also to serve their cultural functions and as dining-hall. However they were soon frustrated when only 120 joined, most of them without any means. They lacked capital and found themselves in dire straights, leading a life of austerity which was disappointing to people who had expected a Fourierist paradise. The leaders tried to instill them with hope in their glorious enterprise, but lack of experience, too much enthusiasm, unproductive members, and lack of means transpired to be too much; a year later, in May 1845, after many had left, the local newspapers announced that the Ohio Phalanx had been dissolved.[21]

Another Fourier settlement which originated in Pittsburgh was the Trumbull Phalanx, established in the spring of 1844 in northeastern Ohio. It was one of the strongest settlements and existed for four years, until December 1847. Many items about Trumbull Phalanx are to be found in the *Phalanx* and *Harbinger*, and from them we can gather the history of its rise and decline. In August 1844 the number of persons belonging to the phalanx was about 200, most of them without means. They hoped to grow rapidly and everyone was accepted without selection; the only requirement was the purchase of a symbolic stock of $25. The founders had high Fourierist expectations and plans to build a magnificent phalanstery in order to accommodate the multitudes who would join the phalanx. Impatient to wait for the prescribed number (400 according to Albert Brisbane or 1,600 according to Fourier) they set out to organize work groups and series, and members got paid for their work as Brisbane had advocated. They aspired to achieve personal harmony and problems were discussed in the general meeting of the phalanx. Religious tolerance prevailed and members were instilled with the Fourier fervor. Delegates attended all Fourierist conventions in 1844-45.

We hear about the favorable impressions from letters in local papers. They report that in July 1845 there were 250 people in Trumbull Phalanx and tell of weekly arrivals of new members. They were well organized, combining industry and agriculture and providing their own necessities, clothing, and furniture. A flour mill and sawmill were economically viable and crops were abundant. The visitors were also impressed by the level of education. These impressions inspired others to join, including a group of affluent Fourierists from Pittsburgh. Yet it soon became evident that in spite of their early success the settlement did not thrive.

In the summer of 1847 a pessimistic note crept in. Their high Fourierist expectations had been exaggerated and the number of members did not increase fast enough to reach the optimal size of a phalanx. This disappointment drew attention to other drawbacks. The economic foundation was not stable. Only a few members were occupied in money-producing work. There was a lack of capital which had been covered in the first years by followers from Pittsburgh who kept on encouraging the phalanx to stand fast. In December of 1847, the association was dissolved.

Fourierist periodicals dealing with the reasons for the failure pointed out that "the Phalanx had admitted too indiscriminately so that the society was an asylum for the needy, the sick and disabled rather than a nucleus of efficient members." But worst of all was the discrepancy between their high expectations and reality. They had attempted to escape a life of penury, but this was their lot once again. For several years they suffered hardships, hoping, in vain, that a better time was soon to come. Their dissolution in 1847 in addition to the others boded no rosy future for Fourierism.[22]

Prairie Home Community was another Fourierist settlement inspired by the socialist convention in New York in 1843. On their way back to the West the delegates set out to inspire others and organized a group of 130 who settled in a beautiful location in Logan County, Ohio. Their domain consisted of 500 fertile acres of well-timbered hilly land. Most of the members were farmers, many had been Quakers. Some English and German socialists also joined them. Nearby, another small community of ten members named *Zensfield* was established. They led an anarchistic life without a constitution or any authority. Their land and property belonged to all who cared to join them, and they let members do as they pleased. A similar spirit prevailed in Prairie Home, which survived only for a year.

Fourierist activities established a phalanx near Cincinnati, Ohio, in May 1844. They bought 900 acres 30 miles away from the city, and a group of 80 members survived for two and one-half years in spite of many disputes and hardships. In May 1845 another Fourier settlement was established north of Cincinnati. It included three lawyers from the district attorney's office who were ideologically motivated. Six months later the settlement was abandoned and several of its members joined a Fourierist association in Illinois; others joined the Colombian Phalanx, a short-lived Fourierist settlement that was established in Ohio in 1845.[23]

Fourier Settlements in the Midwest

Ohio, which had been influenced by Fourierism from the East, now became a source of influence on Illinois. In October 1845 a group of Fourierists who had left the Integral Phalanx joined a group of Illinois Fourierists and purchased 500 acres in a wooded area, rich in brooks and rivers and near a major road. The situation looked promising, with the two groups merging gradually. The Ohio Fourierists were experienced, and having been disappointed before were in no hurry to establish the communal institutions. They decided on an interim period in which individualism would prevail. Housing was provided for family units in order to avoid crowding in large buildings. They planned to build a phalanstery only after having reached a membership of 400. The promising perspective was not realized. After 1846 there is no further news of the Integral Phalanx and we must assume that it was dissolved.[24]

In Indiana there was fertile ground for Fourierism after the Owenist settlement of New Harmony had failed. Nevertheless we know of only one phalanx which was established there in the autumn of 1843, La Grange. Most of its members were local farmers. In February 1844, 30 families had joined and 20 more were waiting for their accommodations. These were to be built according to Fourier's specifications within a two-story, 600-mile long phalanstery. The settlement, whose diligent farming members achieved good crops, prospered. Visitors' reports in the summer of 1846 were rosy. There is no information as to the reasons of its dissolution. But by the end of 1846 it no longer existed. In Michigan a large Fourierist settlement, Alphadelphia Phalanx, was established in the winter of 1844.

The February 1844 issue of the *Phalanx* published notice that a Fourierist industrial association, Alphadelphia Phalanx, had been formed in the area of Ann Arbor, Michigan, by a group of 56 people who assembled for three days and adopted a constitution. The article went on discussing why "it is extremely probable (judging from the information processed) that only half the applicants can be received into one Association because the number will be too great. . . . For such is the enthusiasm in the West that people will not suffer themselves to be disappointed." A domain of 2,800 acres was selected on the Kalamazoo River, and during 1844 about 200 members, most of them local farmers, gathered in Alphadelphia without any discrimination. Some industrial workers in textile and printing joined the Alphadelphia Phalanx, but in the winter of 1847 many began to leave; as far as we know the association dissolved after three and one-half years.[25]

The Wisconsin Phalanx

In the winter of 1843-44 there was much interest in Fourierism in Kenosha City on Lake Michigan. This movement began to advocate the association to establish one of the most stable of all phalanxes—the Wisconsin Phalanx, which would exist for seven years, until 1850. Its founder was Warren Chase, an ex-spiritualist who became an enthusiastic follower of Fourierism. He initiated several public meetings and was determined to make a practical experiment of a Fourier settlement. A few months later the Wisconsin Phalanx was formed by some of the outstanding citizens of the area. Most of the members were men of small means, a fact that turned out to be an advantage because they belonged to the working classes and were full of energy. The association drew up a constitution, raised $1,000, and bought a tract of land of 2,000 acres selected by their committee, in Fond du Lac, a county in central Wisconsin which was sparsely inhabited.

In May 1844 a group of eight pioneers set out a distance of 125 miles from their home to prepare the land and construct the first shelters. Their families joined them and in the fall they numbered 80, and according to a Fourierist scheme organized in two series—an agricultural and an industrial one. They built a kitchen and communal dining-hall. Most members were practical men and realists, ratifying reform movements. They organized according to state legislation, were recognized as a local council, and were active in local and municipal politics. Another characteristic of the Wisconsin Phalanx was their avoiding debt of any kind. It was Warren Chase's declared policy in order to remain independent. He was an ardent Fourierist, a practical though careful person who led his community to prosperity. Soon the economic success attracted others, and in August 1845 they numbered 180, half of them children. Not everybody was accepted. The phalanx had established harsh criteria of selection and those who had no productive professions or means to acquire stock were rejected.[26]

The settlement was tolerant and there were six different religious denominations. In elections votes were split between the parties. Their social life also was liberal. Families were the units of consumption. They could choose to cook their own meals or eat in the communal dining-hall and choose their living quarters as well. At first, separate housing were built for the families. Later there were those who advocated the building of a phalanstery according to Fourier. After lively discussions it was decided by a small majority to adopt the unitary plan. Whether this was the cause of failure or not, it induced many of the best members to leave. The dispute continued until the dissolution of the Wisconsin Phalanx. From 1845 to 1848 they prospered, having based their economy mainly on agriculture. However, their number slowly decreased, and in 1848 only 120 people were left, most of them westerners, farmers and farm workers whose intellectual horizons were limited. Even though a library had been established in which periodicals were available and many lectures on Fourierism and other subjects were given in the reading-room, this left no impact on the settlement.

The main factor that undermined the Wisconsin Phalanx was their disagreement on matters of principle. We have mentioned the dispute about housing and there were additional disagreements on communal consumption. Only some of the members used the communal dining-hall; the complicated system of labor and pay could never be satisfactorily arranged. Some found additional sources of income outside the phalanx. Their religious tolerance caused tension after a while. In spite of this they stood fast during the years when most of the other Fourier phalanxes were dissolved. In the winter of 1848-49 the founding nucleus gave up their Fourierist convictions and decided to return to the prevalent individualistic way of life. In order to avoid complete disintegration they prepared a plan to divide the property and share it among all members. In December 1849 a committee was elected that undertook to complete the dissolution themselves and without recourse to courts of law. In April 1850 the land was sold and the stockholders were compensated. It was the only one of the Fourier phalanxes that ended its life in profit for its members.[27]

Brook Farm

While the Fourierist associations and phalanxes were established, there existed in Massachusetts several communitarian settlements which had been established independently and which would adopt Fourierist theories only at a later stage. Brisbane reported on them in the first issue of the *Phalanx* in the summer of 1843.[28] He gave an account of the communities in Hopedale, in Northampton, and in Roxbury. The latter was Brook Farm, which was to be cardinal in the Fourierist revival in Massachusetts a year later. The incentive to establish a communal settlement came from intellectual circles in Boston in the 1830s in an atmosphere of philosophical-religious radicalism. Its center was the Unitarian Church, whose ministers Dr. Channing and George Ripley founded the Transcendentalist Club. Among its members were persons from the intellectual elite of Boston—Emerson, Thoreau, Hawthorne, Margaret Fuller, and others.[29]

The transcendentalists published the *Dial*, which was a platform for their ideology and deliberations. In the first four years (1836-1840) its editor was Margaret Fuller and some of the best minds in New England were among its contributors. Another outlet for the transcendentalists was at the philosophical symposia of Bronson Alcott in Concord, Cambridge, and Boston (1838). In 1840, after the transcendentalists had established their club, Dr. William Channing and George Ripley proposed a plan for a model farm on which members would live according to the principles of social justice in the spirit of transcendentalism. Shortly before Ripley abandoned his ministry, in order to realize personally the transcendentalist ideal, he suggested Brook Farm, nine miles from Boston, as the most suitable place in which to put their theories into practice. Aspiring to an independent life based on farming without any hired labor, but close enough to populated areas to be able to radiate ideas on society at large, they bought 200 acres with the funds obtained from members who had bought shares:[30] "The sum required cannot come from rich capitalists, their instinct would protest against such an application of their coins." Ripley wrote to his friend Emerson in the autumn of 1840, while he was making plans to purchase the farm. In his letter Ripley gave a detailed outline for raising funds and for organizing the people; he also explained his motives for choosing the farm which was so close to Boston. The letter was enthusiastic and full of ideals and expressed an intense belief in the importance of their mission. He concluded his letter saying: "I can imagine no plan which is suited to carry into effect so many divine ideas as this. If wisely executed it will be a light over this country and this age. If not the sunrise it will be the morning star."[31] In April 1841, shortly after the farm had been acquired, a group that included George Ripley, his wife, and a small circle of intellectual friends proceeded there, filled with enthusiasm but lacking any experience of farming.

At first they were only 20 members and devoted their time to laying the foundations for a settlement which would combine agriculture with spiritual activities. They established an educational institution which would accept boarders and teach them the love of work while giving them a broad education and instilling in them a moral responsibility to society. In September 1841 they formulated their constitution and legally established a holding company, The Institute for Agriculture and Education. Every stockholder of $500 became a member, and with the sum of $105,000 which they raised, the farm was bought in October 1841.

They decided on a "united household," in which every job would be done by members on a basis of a daily roster. Everyone would be paid an identical sum and at the end of the year receive a dividend. Basics such as food, clothing, housing, and health services were provided by the community regardless of the work they had invested. Those who were ill were paid salaries as if they had worked. There were no set rules about private property, and the approach was a pragmatic one of trial and error. Although they strove to achieve maximum equality they knew that it would have to be done gradually. They agreed to keep private property during the first years and pay dividends for their shares. However, right from the beginning they decided that the number of shares of each individual would not reflect on his or her social position. All were equal and so was consumption and work. Hard work and service jobs were done by all.[32]

It was not easy for the intellectual Brook Farmers to get used to the harsh conditions, and only their ideals helped them to carry out farm work. It was not so with Nathaniel Hawthorne, the young author who joined the pioneering group but gave it up after a short while. He described his experience in letters to his future wife Sophia Peabody, who had stayed in Boston, and to his mother. His letters reflected his changing moods as a result of hard physical work. At first he was exhilarated by the change in his life and the beauty of life in the countryside. He proudly described his work in the small cowshed, milking and clearing manure and raking hay with a pitchfork. He hinted at the "damages" his inexperience had caused, and tongue in cheek he boasted that he had almost become a "perfect farmer."[33] Soon, however, his mood changed, and his optimistic irony turned into bitter pessimism. In July he wrote: "I had never suspected that farming was so hard." He was no longer proud of his achievements but sneered at the waste of time and a month later decided to give up farming altogether. In a letter to his fiancée he wrote: "Labour is the curse of this world and nobody can meddle with it, without becoming proportionally brutified. Thank God my soul is not utterly buried under a dungheap, I shall yet rescue it, somewhat defiled."[34]

Hawthorne remained at Brook Farm for a short while and then left, but kept in close touch with the members despite his bitter personal experience. He would later use his impressions in the *Blithedale Romance*, a novel that deals with idealism, socialism, and the return of intellectuals to physical work. He claimed in it that intellectual activities could not coincide with physical activities.[35]

Hawthorne's reputation as a writer lent some importance to his attitude toward the ideal of Brook Farm, yet his experience was the exception to the rule. Most of the founders managed to combine spiritual and physical activities. When in time workers and mechanics joined the community there was no dividing partition between them and the intellectuals who combined physical work without giving up their spiritual world or their intellectual vocation. Those who had physical qualities found ways to contribute to their comrades. Their intellectual characteristics were especially important for the existence of the educational institution of Brook Farm but did not entitle them to special privileges. There was complete equality and George Ripley, the founder and spiritual leader, was granted no material or hierarchical benefit. He and his wife did all the jobs and were equal among equals. At the end of the first year the members of Brook Farm regarded themselves as a family of laborers, teachers, and students.[36]

The Educational Institution

Life on Brook Farm was centered around the local educational institution, which was the most important source of income and the focus of pride and local patriotism. Despite the limited number of students, it included elementary and high school classes as well as a prep school for those who wished to continue at Harvard University. The university authorities entrusted the teachers of Brook Farm to instill their potential university students with the necessary knowledge of the sciences, mathematics, classic and modern languages, music and theoretical agriculture. Brook Farm's reputation spread, and students began to arrive from distant areas and countries such as England, Cuba, and the Philippines. They were asked to pay only tuition and earned their board by working on the commune.

The teachers were conscious of their educational principles that guided them at all levels and provided the younger and older students with a liberal education. This included a regard for every kind of work and a special affinity for farming. It provided the young scientists of the future with a respect for agriculture and a practice thereof. At the same time it gave a theoretical background to those students who would not be scientists. The teachers themselves served as a model, doing stints of work on the farm and the services. The school accepted students without any strict policy of selection. Only those who could not adapt to the special spirit of Brook Farm—the attitude toward work and collective life—were expelled. There was an overt policy of recruiting pupils to join the commune after graduation. In January, 1844, the population of Brook Farm included 70 members only, among them four couples and 30 students at school.[37]

Friends and Visitors

From its inception Brook Farm maintained close contact with the outside world. Even though the founders had established a secluded community, they did not intend it to remain isolated but to serve as a model that would influence society in general. Having chosen a domain close to Boston, they maintained personal contact with those transcendentalists who had not joined the commune, for example Emerson. These ties spread out to other circles in the Boston area, including religious and scientific personalities. Relations were bilateral: Brook Farmers would come the short distance, usually on foot, take part in cultural activities, attend concerts and the theater as well as ideological or philosophical conventions. In the same manner there was a constant stream of visitors who came to Brook Farm in all seasons. Most of them were curious to get a glimpse of the idealists' way of life. Others stayed for longer periods in order to personally experience communal life. These included followers and sympathizers who contributed to the intensive cultural and artistic activities of the community; among them were Margaret Fuller, Ralph Waldo Emerson, Horace Greeley, William Channing and several other famous artists and musicians who enjoyed the sophisticated audience of Brook Farm.

Among the many visitors there were also some from other communities, e.g. some of the Shakers; Adin Ballow, the founder of Hopedale; Collins from Skaneateles Community; and Bronson Alcott, who was planning to establish Fruitlands Colony on individualistic principles. They all came in search of a union with Brook Farm, but George Ripley turned them down, insisting on the uniqueness of Brook Farm.[38] Yet in spite of this attitude, it was not a hermetically closed community; many new members were absorbed, some from among the transcendentalists, others from far and wide. Not everyone could join; there was usually a strict selection in order to avoid those elements that would undermine the Brook Farmers' moral way of life.

While the intellectual circles of Boston admired their idealism, the Brook Farm's neighbors in Roxbury were suspicious of their odd ways. They criticized their festivals and the fact that they ignored all religious rituals. Although they were invited to visit Brook Farm they kept their children away in order to guard them against heretic influence. There was also an element of jealousy, caused by the Brook Farmers' success in marketing their agricultural produce in the local market.[39] In spite of this achievement the first two years of Brook Farm were not prosperous. The crops were generally meager, the attempt to construct a carpentry shop failed, the work schedule was disorganized, mainly because of the members' constant coming and going between their place of work and the classrooms where they taught. Their only steady income was from the school and from members' stock and shares. The balance sheet of 1843 showed Brook Farm to be in debt of $2,000.[40]

The Attraction of Fourierism

After two years at Brook Farm its members still had no clear ideology. The economic and social difficulties they faced contributed to their receptivity to

Fourierist ideas. They had come across Fourierist publications and met Horace Greeley and Albert Brisbane, who often visited the farm, and had lectures and discussions on Fourierist principles. George Ripley adopted Fourierism, hoping to find in it the answer to all their problems.

Brook Farm's transcendentalist friends tried to check the Fourierist influence and to stop Ripley from joining Brisbane and Greeley. They claimed that the uniqueness of Brook Farm, its individualistic approach and acceptance of religious trends might be lost; they failed, and Fourierism took root rapidly. Brook Farm had several advantages over other Fourierist settlements in the East. It was a well-established, productive community with sufficient funds to keep it going, and they did not have to cope with the lack of capital and shoddy produce during the difficult first year. It also had the advantage of the well-organized educational institution which was apparent to all.[41]

Brisbane was eager to speed up the process of a union with Brook Farm, because he was aware of the criticism and hoped to prove that not all the Fourierist settlements were hastily established associations. He hoped to find optimal conditions for his social experiment at Brook Farm, and when William Channing joined the Fourierist movement, Brisbane was certain of success. Channing had just started to publish *The Present*, a New England periodical that served to spread Fourierist ideas and greatly influenced Brook Farmers.

In the winter of 1843-44 several conventions on Fourierism were held in Boston, and many of the Brook Farmers attended. Their numbers grew steadily, and Ripley, whose influence at Brook Farm was considerable, regarded Fourierism not only as a valuable social experiment but also as a chance to reorganize Brook Farm on a sounder basis. Fourierism was attractive, because it was close to their spiritual values of communitarianism while allowing them to maintain their individuality. It combined physical work with spiritual activities and strove to establish a farming community in which urban culture could flourish. At that time they only had few members, including some boys, and the option of accepting new members from among the working classes and farmers was very attractive.[42]

Brook Farm: A Fourierist Phalanx

In January 1844 Brook Farm decided to convert to Fourierism and a new constitution was adopted. In the preface to their constitution they offered themselves as a nucleus for a model phalanx. They were prepared to "assist in the forming of an extensive and complete association which would increase by natural and gradual aggregations. With a view to an ultimate expansion into a perfect Phalanx we desire to organize the three primary departments of labor, agriculture, domestic industry and the mechanic arts." For this purpose they published an appeal for additional capital and expressed their wish to increase their numbers mainly from among workers and mechanics who were asked to pay $100 each for their share; this was successful.[43]

The transformation to Fourierism was not without controversy. Some of the older transcendentalists felt that the new doctrine was formalistic and would severely curtail the spontaneity and spirituality of Brook Farm. Some of the transcendentalist farmers soon left the settlement, but many others applied for membership. This called for new criteria of selection which included a regard for the requirements of the developing community, the candidates' adaptability, and an acceptance of Fourierism.[44]

The final conversion to Fourierism occurred between January and April 1844, when the national convention of Fourierist activists took place in New York; delegates from Brook Farm were among the most active. George Ripley was honored to be chosen as president and Brook Farmers attempted to influence the debate with their transcendentalist ideology. There was quite a gap between their religious attitudes and those of the socialist Fourierists, whose background was secular. The movement now included a variety of doctrines and Brisbane's dominant influence was on the wane.[45] Brook Farm was ready to become the propaganda center of the Fourierist movement. They took over the publication of the Fourierist periodical, the *Phalanx*, which was then renamed the *Harbinger*. In addition the settlement undertook to send two or three of its members on regular lecture tours and propaganda missions throughout the country. The focus of Fourierism was now in Boston, where The National Union of Socialists[46] was established and was in charge of propaganda. They arranged tours to bring the idea of association to the American people and to raise funds. They organized circles of followers in several of the state capitals.

These activities caused Brook Farm to change its character. In 1845 it was renamed the *Phalanx of Brook Farm* and had completely accepted Fourierist principles. They now celebrated Fourier's and Brisbane's birthdays as well as other Fourierist anniversaries ostentatiously, in a manner alien to the founders who were descendants of puritan New Englanders.[47] Cultural activities were abundant. Debate sessions on Fourierism, a dramatic circle which provided entertainment and theater, and a variety of musical activities were part of the educational institute and filled the Brook Farmers' free time. The driving force was Charles Dwight, who would in time become one of America's renowned musicians.[48]

Meanwhile, economic reorganization took place in accordance with Brisbane's Fourierist series of agriculture, the services, industry, and education. A building had been constructed to house all the various workshops. New members, who had each purchased stock, contributed to the financial prosperity, and in 1844 Brook Farm's books were balanced. Brook Farm now had a capital of $10,000, and a feeling of optimism affected everyone. The integration of intellectuals and practical members seemed promising, and everyone expected Brook Farm to be the model phalanx.[49]

Trials

Not all was clear sailing. Most new members were practical farm workers and mechanics with materialistic attitudes. They strove for a higher work efficiency even if it would clash with other values. This, in turn, caused tension between them and the older members, mainly because they did not regard the school as important as the transcendentalists did. As long as the school was a substantial source of income it was accepted as such, but soon the situation changed. A new conflict emerged when the Fourierist transformation of Brook Farm increased their neighbors' alienation. Under these circumstances outside people were less inclined to send their children to study at the Brook Farm institution.[50] At the end of 1844 the population of Brook Farm was about 150. Only lack of housing prevented the absorption of new members who were urgently needed on the developing settlement. Accommodation was extremely crowded, and it was impossible to enrich the community's life as Fourier had envisioned it.

This situation caused everyone to join in the effort to construct a large unitary edifice, a phalanstery, as recommended by Fourier's social vision. The phalanstery was to be a 2-story wooden-building divided into fourteen distinct suites of apartments, ample accommodation for families as well as bachelors, and a spacious and convenient public hall and saloons. A portion of the second story had been set apart for a church or chapel. The construction of the phalanstery began in the spring of 1845 and attracted many visitors, among them many Fourierists who came on pilgrimage to marvel at the construction of a real phalanstery.[51]

In the winter of 1845-46 an epidemic of chicken pox, mostly among children, caused the school to be quarantined. This affected the considerable source of income from the educational institution and brought an immediate lowering of the quality of food and other supplies for members, which also lowered their morale. One of the Fourierist activists who visited Brook Farm early in 1846 was deeply disappointed to see the low morale of its members. A few weeks later a calamity which members considered to be fatal hit the settlement.[52]

The Fire at the Phalanstery and Its Effect

On March 3, 1846, the phalanstery, which was in its final building stage, went up in flames and was rapidly burned to the ground. It was caused by the negligence of workmen who had left a burning stove in one of the basement rooms in order to dry out the humidity. An enormous spiritual and financial effort had gone into the construction of the phalanstery. The $7,000 invested in it had not been insured, and the effect on the community was devastating. Nevertheless, there was an immediate attempt to return to normal life.[53]

As George Ripley wrote in the *Harbinger* a few days later: "The destruction of our edifice makes no essential change in our pursuits. It leaves no family destitute of a Home. . . . It puts us to no immediate inconvenience. . . . The morning after the disaster, if a stranger had not seen the smoking pile of ruins, he would not have suspected that anything extraordinary had taken place. Our schools were attended as usual, our industry in full operation and not a look of despondency could have been perceived."[54] However, the fire was a disaster from which Brook Farm never recovered. Depression and uncertainty set in after the first few days of "carrying on as usual."

The first one to voice his doubts of the future was Charles Dana, one of Brook Farm's outstanding members. But others continued to hope that new waves of Fourierism in New England would affect Brook Farm, and only in the fall of 1846, when no large Fourierist movement was evident, there was a note of despondency evident in many articles and in members' correspondence.[55] In Marianne Dwight's letter to her brother John S. Dwight on March 17, 1846, a few days after the fire, she expressed the hope that the settlement had sufficient means to repay the debts incurred by the fire. A few months later in a letter to her friend Ann Parsons, Dwight talked about the deliberations of the council in an attempt to overcome the financial crisis. She assured her friend that a "combination" would be found to repay the debt from costly assets and future incomes.[56] Yet, in July 1846 she wrote to her brother, Frank, about the atmosphere of despondency and the many secessions from Brook Farm:

> I must tell you with a deep feeling of disappointment, that I see little reason to hope for any success here. I think we might have it if the people were more persistent, but there is a general discouragement, a want of hope. . . . It seems to me that our secret control council, our leaders here, don't even care to have an industrial association. . . . Well—I don't know—my hope all along has been in the people; if the wise, the good and true think it their duty to quit, how or what shall I hope for Brook Farm?[57]

A Somber Farewell to High Hopes

In the first months after the fire, Brook Farmers received many encouraging letters. Fourierist followers offered help. Many visited and some even stayed to give a hand at work. Others raised funds and offered support. On the other hand, the two Fourierist leaders, Albert Brisbane and Horace Greeley, absented themselves conspicuously. Brisbane, who had given up his hope for Fourierism in the United States, abstained from visiting Brook Farm. When George Ripley went to Brisbane to find out the reasons for this change, he was soon convinced that Brisbane had completely despaired of Fourierism; he was planning to travel to Europe in search of new social trends, being attracted this time to Karl Marx.[58] Greeley was at the time involved in another Fourierist experiment, the North American Phalanx in New Jersey, and when Brook Farm appealed to him for help he suggested that they join the successful New Jersey Phalanx and give it support.

Ripley and his friends were unwilling to accept this ''friendly'' advice to abandon Brook Farm. They had invested too much of their sentiments and efforts, and for a time it seemed as though they might overcome the period of hardship and even get closer to each other in the process. But Ripley and his friends were alone in their optimism. One by one most of the new Fourierist members left, not being sufficiently involved with the settlement. By the end of 1846 only 60, half of the members at the time of the fire, remained. This affected also the founding members; in the autumn the first of them left and those who did not despair of Fourierism joined other phalanxes, mainly the North American Phalanx.

Among those who remained at Brook Farm three opinions prevailed. Ripley and a number of the founders believed that the phalanx stood a chance of being reestablished in the future on the Fourierist principles and that they only had to stand fast and maintain thc settlement as it was. Others claimed that they should stay on there but give up Fourierism. A third group was convinced that they had to carry on as usual as if nothing had changed. None of the three ways had a chance.[59] In the winter of 1847 Brook Farm lost most of its members. Only Ripley and some of his friends stayed on in order to sell the property and pay their debts in an orderly fashion. Ripley even sold his extensive library, which was a real sacrifice, and while he was packing the books he told his wife Sophie that ''he was feeling like a man who was attending his own funeral.''[60]

The final days of Brook Farm were a sad period of want. Work on the farm had ceased. Those few who were left tried to concentrate on the reestablishment of the school and on publishing the *Harbinger*. They failed because by then only a few students were sent to the school. There also was not enough manpower to continue the publication of the periodical, and it was now published by the editor of the *Tribune* in New York.

In August 1847, realizing that there was no chance for the commune, the last members left Brook Farm. Among them were George Ripley and his wife, who had invested six years and all their property in the commune. Penniless, they moved to New York, where Ripley was offered work on the *Tribune*. He and other founders of Brook Farm joined the world, deeply disappointed and hurting with disillusionment. A rich chapter in their life had ended, never to be repeated.[61]

Marianne Dwight, who was among the last to leave Brook Farm, expressed her feelings on March 3, 1847, in a moving letter to Anna Parsons:

> It is sad to see Brook Farm dwindling away, when it need not have been so. . . . Oh I love every tree and wood haunt, every nook and path, and hill and meadow. . . . I can hardly imagine that the sky will look down upon me in any spot, and where, where in the wide world shall I ever find warm hearts all around me again? No words can tell my thankfulness for having lived here, and for every experience here, whether joyful or painful. . . . Life could not possibly be so rich as it has been here.[62]

The last members who left Brook Farm were men of ability who soon were established in the spiritual and public life of the United States. Most of them would always keep a place in their heart for their idealistic period at Brook Farm. They would return to visit and remember it with nostalgia. Some wrote memoirs in which they felt urged to mention the significant role of Brook Farm in their lives. For many it was their North Star that guided them even when they wandered a great distance.[63] In 1849 the farm was to be auctioned off. When former members of Brook Farm heard about it they wanted to attend, but it was too much like a funeral of their vision; instead they gathered in a nearby wood to read chapters of literature as had been their custom during the good old days of Brook Farm. After the auction they paid their final visit to the place, to take with them a last impression of the disappearing settlement.[64]

The farm and its buildings went through many hands. Physical evidence of the community disappeared, and gradually the nearby town of Roxbury encroached. Nobody cared to preserve the uniqueness of the site. Most of the buildings were pulled down, and the documents of the settlement scattered among historical societies and museums in the United States.

Staying in Boston in 1981, I was curious to visit the site. Reaching the spot, I was greatly disappointed not to find even a sign to tell about or be evidence of the dream and the vision. The only place that carried the name was a small street in the suburb leading to the walls of a large cemetery. Oldtimers recalled that this had been the place in which Brook Farmers had intended to stay together in eternity. They dispersed and none of them was buried there. Katherine Burton ended her book *Paradise Planters*: *The Story of Brook Farm* (1973, 1939), saying: "Only their dreams were still buried on the soil of Brook Farm."

The North American Phalanx

The most stable and successful of all Fourier settlements was the North American Phalanx. It was organized from its inception according to the principles of the Fourier associations and outlasted all the others. This phalanx was established in 1843 during the first Fourierist wave, and its members came from among the circles that were first to respond to Albert Brisbane's gospel as it appeared in the *New York Tribune*. The initiative came from Fourierists from Albany and nearby, and their leader was Charles Sears, a wealthy corn merchant. They established an association to deal with the organization of a settlement. This association was in touch with the Fourier leaders Albert Brisbane and Horace Greeley and included them among its members; the latter even served as treasurer of the association.

Some of the members were middle-class people with a keen business instinct. Their practical approach left its mark on the association and they insisted on its being established on a sound financial foundation through fund raising. A special committee was elected to search for a proper domain, which was found in the summer of 1843 in Monmouth County, New Jersey. It was a 700-acre farm which had previously been worked with slave labor and cost $14,000, with $5,000 down payment. The land was fertile and situated near water sources, but it had deteriorated through exploitation. Its being close to the populated areas of New York and New Jersey was convenient for marketing their produce and so were the roads and other means of transportation.

In September 1843 the first settlers from Albany and Troy arrived and found accommodation in the existing buildings. They immediately started to build houses for the other families that planned to join them in the spring of 1844. During the winter and spring the phalanx steadily grew but reached a population of only 90, 40 of whom were children under 17.[65] The reason for this was the strict selection of members. Candidates were invited to stay as visitors for a whole month, and then they were accepted for a year's candidacy in which they had to work at a variety of jobs, to give members a chance to judge their characters. Only then could they apply for membership. Criteria for acceptance were professional dexterity and the ability to work and live in a community.

The North American Phalanx had learned from the experience of those Owenist and Fourierist communes that had failed because they had accepted unsuitable members. Horace Greeley, who regarded himself responsible for the commune's ideological education, summed up the wisdom he had gained from other socialist experiences, in the following invective:

> Along with many noble and lofty souls . . . there were throng scores of whom the world is quite worthy—the conceited, crotchety, the selfish, the headstrong, the pugnacious, the unappreciated, the played out, the idle and the good for nothing generally, who, finding themselves utterly out of place in the world as it is, rashly conclude that they are exactly fitted for the world as it ought to be. Destitute of means, of practical ability, of prudence, tact and commonsense they have such wealth of assurance that they clutch the responsible positions.[66]

In the long run this policy of selection had an adverse effect. The growing economic potential could have supported a population of 1,000, yet it never grew beyond 150. This entailed hiring agricultural laborers in spite of the lofty principles of the founders. On the other hand, the harshest selection could not prevent the infiltration of unsuitable members, some of whom were even adverse to Fourierist ideology. Many were disappointed when ten years later they still numbered 150. During its thirteen years of existence the North American Phalanx had numbered between 125 to 150 members, most of them from among the urban middle classes, professionals, some mechanics, and only a few experienced farmers.[67]

The first year was devoted to establishing the foundation of a communal settlement. They built large houses for a kitchen, a dining-room, a laundry, and several workshops, and a flour mill for local use which would later also serve the neighboring population. During that same year they also had to invest in the land and revitalize it, because the soil had been exploited during the years in which it had been cultivated by slaves. The first settlers were industrious and diligent but inexperienced and made many mistakes that resulted in a poor harvest. They were disappointed and frustrated, but after two years of hardships the economic situation gradually improved with the help of experienced farmers and mechanics who had joined the phalanx.

One of the factors that helped bring the North American Phalanx to economic prosperity was the combination of industry and agriculture. Their main income was from market gardening. They provided fruit and vegetables to New York City, and their produce—marketed in crates stamped NAP—had an excellent reputation. It was transported by sea from the Red Bank Port and reached the biggest markets in the area. In spite of its economic stability and prosperity, North American Phalanx existed in the shadow of Brook Farm until 1847. Only after the latter had disintegrated did the North American Phalanx turned into a Fourierist center. Its social stability and economic prosperity made it a model settlement and renewed the hope for additional waves of Fourierist settlements. The North American Phalanx's involvement with Horace Greeley also contributed to its becoming the new Fourierist capital.

Life at the North American Phalanx

Their new position as a Fourierist model and the prospect to expand considerably contributed to the North American Phalanx's ambition to improve its standard of living. They invested in housing, individual consumption, and culture. The construction of a phalanstery according to Fourierism was started that year. It was a 150-foot long, three-story wooden-building, and intended to accommodate about 100 people. On the ground floor there were offices, a reception hall, a library and reading room as well as a multipurpose central hall for meals, dances, and cultural activities such as concerts and theater. In one of its corners stood a large concert piano. Picture windows lit up the room and pictures decorated the walls. Two hundred people could comfortably eat at the tables. On the second floor were the family accommodations with 2-3 rooms each, and single rooms for bachelors. Heat was provided by steam that also served the kitchen and laundry.[68] The conditions were much improved.

The settlement attracted many visitors who were curious about life on a Fourierist phalanx. Located near New York, it attracted many people, among them social reformers. The aging Robert Owen visited it on his final tour in the United States; Frederika Bremer came from Sweden; and the commune researcher Macdonald visited the North American Phalanx three times and came away convinced of the viability of communitarianism. Often visitors included Fourierist activities such as George Ripley, Charles Dana, and William Channing as well as the American philosopher Henry James. Some French political exiles after the 1848 revolution tended a French garden on the phalanx that became one of the main attractions there. Most visitors' reports were positive, and all mentioned the pleasant cultural atmosphere.[69]

The dining-hall was much appreciated, as it combined communal practices with privacy when small tables enabled each family to eat separately. There were special tables for vegetarians and other diets. Food was well cooked and varied. At each table was a bill of fare and each individual called for whatever he chose and was pleasantly waited upon by young, well-dressed women. After the meal was over the waiters entered the sum upon the check which each person received in a book belonging to that person. The total was added up at the end of each month and the payment made. Macdonald, who visited the phalanx in 1852, estimated the weekly expenses on food, laundry, etc. as about $2 per person.

Women's Status

In 1849 the fashion of "bloomers" was adopted. It had been introduced a year earlier by a Mrs. Bloomers of New York and was a combination of Turkish trousers under "daringly" short skirts. This fashion was very popular among nonconformists and was adopted by several socialist communes because of its practicability. A detailed description of life on North American Phalanx was found in F. Bremer's travelogue. She visited the phalanx twice, in 1849 and in 1851, and being involved with the struggle for women's equality, she was impressed by the status of women on the phalanx. She found them to be intensively involved in community affairs, work, and social activities. They were also interested in general matters and took an active part in meetings. When she asked some young women whether they were happy with their work in the dining-hall they answered that they could not imagine better conditions and that their life was richer and more beautiful than before they had joined the phalanx.

Frederika Bremer found members to be tolerant of each other's convictions whether religious or political. She also was impressed by the way they had achieved individuality within the collective. Most members preferred the accommodations in small cabins rather than in the big phalanstery, in order to preserve their privacy. Everyone had to work ten hours daily; additional work earned special pay. Members could keep their possessions and private property and even invest in the phalanx's enterprises but they were not allowed to establish private industry on the domain. Frederika Bremer, who was not a socialist, regarded this combination of socialism and individualism as having the best chances for a model settlement. Nevertheless she was doubtful about individual development in such a small community, and in spite of her appreciation of this "noble and honorable" enterprise she doubted its viability after the founders' idealism had waned. Even if the experiment would not last long, the achievements which had already been gained in creating a life of social harmony pinpointed the potentials of communitarianism life.[70]

The Application of Fourierism

The North American Phalanx had adopted Fourierist principles in their first constitution of 1843. Five years later, after having experienced communal life, the need to amend it arose. In 1848 there were lively discussions that led to a new constitution based on Fourierist principles. One of the most significant changes was the preference given to phalanx inhabitants over absentee members. They also improved Fourier's work-system of "series," and came up with the following series:

1. *Agriculture*: groups for gardening, orchards, corn, and experimental farming.
2. *Animal husbandry.*
3. *Industry and handcrafts*: groups of millers, carpenters, and blacksmiths according to the various workshops.
4. *Domestic service*: cooking, dishwashing, laundry, and housecleaning jobs.
5. *Education*: children's schooling and adult education.
6. *Culture and entertainment*: in charge of all social events and activities, including dances and picnics.[71]

The heads of all the series formed the production council which steered the phalanx. Everybody, including children, chose their place of work. They were paid for their work, and the less attractive a certain job was the higher was the pay. After the accounts had been balanced, members were paid a dividend; men and women earned equal pay. Even though some of the shareholders were absentee members, the phalanx was managed by residents only. Committees were elected every two years, and some members rotated yearly. All activities were discussed democratically. One of the problems that came up in their first year was the question of authority: "One party contending for authority enforced with stringent rules and final appeal to the dictation of the chief officer, the other party standing out for organization and distribution of authority."[72] Finally, after a long and vigorous strife, the democratic attitude prevailed.

Education and Culture

At the end of the 1840s, when Fourierism was on the wane throughout the East, the North American Phalanx was steadily prospering. This was evident in the improved standard of living which attracted many new candidates, but the severe criteria for absorbing new members prevented the community from expanding. At the end of 1852 there were only 112 inhabitants (48 men, 37 women, and 27 children below 16). The assets of the phalanx were estimated at $80,000, namely, each of the members owned about $700, a considerable amount at the time.[73] Their life was a combination of organized work and intensive recreation. Members of the "series" who were in charge of culture were very active. They had to provide entertainment every evening. Usually all phalanx members would assemble every evening for communal singing or dancing. On summer evenings they would take a walk in the woods, go sailing on the lake, or play games on its shore. Children and adults participated in these activities.[74]

This integration of the whole phalanx population characterized the local school as well. It was located in a separate building one-half mile from the settlement, and its 20 pupils were taught according to a special method. The guiding principle was to link all theoretical studies to the practical experience of the child in the community. Subjects taught were connected with daily life, the various agricultural and industrial branches, bookkeeping, and household activities. The students were attached to the different series, and several hours daily were devoted to work, integrating it with their theoretical lessons. The toddlers were taken care of by kindergarten teachers, enabling mothers to do their own work. Young people who had finished school attended evening classes of math, music, and languages.

There were also lectures on general topics for the whole population given by lecturers from New York who enjoyed the alert and interested phalanx audience. Charles Dana, relating his observations on the North American Phalanx, said that its members benefited from all the intellectual pursuits of the city—lectures, concerts, daily newspapers, and an excellent library were all at their disposal.[75] There was also a drama circle that presented plays locally and from time to time even went on a tour. Just as at Brook Farm, Fourier's birthday on April 17 was also celebrated at North American Phalanx. On that date and on the Fourth of July they used to invite all their neighbors to join in their celebrations. Religiously they were very tolerant and laid no restriction on any rites or practices. Even so there was tension with the neighbors who did not accept them. The local papers published heresy and slander, accusing them of being atheists who practiced free love and of being economically "monopolistic."

Prosperity

In the early 1850s the North American Phalanx was at its apex. Visitors lauded the pleasant atmosphere and conditions they encountered. One of them wrote in the *New York Tribune* of July 29, 1852 that compared with the average farmers, the people of the phalanx had a definite advantage. The writer even wondered why their way of life was not widespread in the United States and advocated to propagate the association so that workers, mechanics, and farmers would be attracted. He used "American Farmer" for his signature, and explained that following this visit he became convinced of the advantages of Fourierism, which saved labor, lowered expenses, and raised the standard of living. At the same time he did not ignore its disadvantages and thought that the phalanx had not exploited all the inherent opportunities that an association offered, admitting, though, that the members were aware of their shortcomings and had tried to correct them. He went on to state: "If I had a boy to educate, who at 16 had acquired at home habits of continued persevering application of mind in study, and who was tolerably stocked with facts and formulas, I would a good deal prefer that he should spend the next four years of his life as a working member of the North American Phalanx than at Yale or Harvard." The article concluded with a prayer for the phalanx's well-deserved success.[76] A year later, in 1853, the process of disintegration set in.

Schism and Disintegration

The harmony that had been characteristic of the North American Phalanx started to dwindle. It began with a religious schism caused by the coming of missionary elements and got worse when a proposal to move the settlement closer to the sea raised a violent dispute. The intention was to exploit the large flour mill and to market the produce more efficiently. As a result, a small group left the phalanx to establish a settlement in nearby Perth Amboy, naming it the *Raritan Bay Union*. The seceders were mainly intellectuals who planned to establish an educational institution that would serve the surrounding population. They were soon joined by disgruntled members of the phalanx who had been at the bottom of the pay scale, but who also included some professionals whose secession left a gap in the production line of the phalanx.

Still, the community was about to overcome this crisis when in October 1854 calamity struck. A sudden fire burned the extensive flour mills and all the stored harvest to the ground. The flames also enveloped most of the adjoining workshops. As luck would have it, their insurance company went bankrupt, and the phalanx faced an impossible financial situation, with a debt of $30,000. Even though they were offered help by Fourierist friends such as Horace Greeley, who offered them a loan of $12,000, these were rejected by members of the phalanx. The fire coincided with the disputes over the new site near the sea; many of the leading members were unwilling to invest in the original location, and when, unable to agree on the future of the phalanx, they were also burdened by heavy debts and felt the loneliness of pioneers without any followers, they decided to sell the farm and dissolve the crippled phalanx.

In the winter of 1855-56 the property was sold. Evidence of the phalanx's prosperity may be found in the fact that all its debts were paid and shareholders were paid 60 percent of their stock value. As far as is known, most members continued as private farmers in the area.[77]

The cause of the rapid disintegration was the members' waning ideological commitment rather than economic reasons. The North American Phalanx had never had an outstanding ideological leadership, but most of its members were idealists. A spirit of harmony and a general wish to live according to the Fourierist doctrine, which had proved to be the way to a rich and beautiful life, had prevailed. However, as soon as this harmony was disrupted, the Fourierist ideal lost its splendor and the members no longer felt committed to their mission. Their unique way of life lost its significance, and when they compared their standard of living to that of their neighbors, they felt at a disadvantage. Under these circumstances many grasped at the opportunity to get out. Yet they were not embittered; in later years they would all fondly look back on their years at the Fourierist phalanx.

Most of the land was bought by John Bucklin, one of the settlement's former members. He turned it into a prosperous farm and kept the phalanstery intact for the future. It was still being lived in, even when the farm changed hands.[78] During the second half of the twentieth century it was neglected and began to disintegrate. In the 1970s the phalanstery was offered to a local historical society that intended to restore it as a historic monument. On November 15, 1972 it burned to the ground, and nothing remained to be restored.

A Glimpse at the Last Remnant

In the summer of 1978 I visited the United States to collect archive material on the American communes. During my search I arrived at the museum of the historical society of Monmouth County in Freehold, New Jersey, where I discovered a well-preserved collection of documents and papers including maps of the North American Phalanx. The old maps urged me to try and find the site which was near the town. When I compared the old maps with the current ones, I was surprised to find a main road called Phalanx Street, and it was not difficult to guess what lay ahead. Setting out, I arrived at the local college campus. None of the students I asked knew about the North American Phalanx. Continuing my search for it, I soon arrived at a place that without doubt was the site of the phalanx; it was not at all as I had imagined it: The lake had dried out, the stream was just a trickle, and on the hill where the phalanstery had stood was now a dense wood. I found a path that led to a large building-site nearby. There I discovered a pile of logs, doors, shutters, and other junk which seemed to have been part of the impressive phalanstery. Tracks of a bulldozer indicated that in a few days these too would disappear and a new condominium would spring up instead. In face of these sad relics of a glorious past I wondered whether to deplore, "sic transit gloria mundi," or to console myself with the addage, "Let the old make way for the new."

Notes

1. Donald Egbert and Stow Persons, eds., *Socialism and American Life*, 2 vols. (Princeton: Princeton University Press, 1952), pp. 173-75; Basset, p. 173; Alice Felt Tyler, *Freedom's Ferment* (New York: Harper & Row, 1962), pp. 214-16.
2. Albert Brisbane (1809-1890), born in Batavia, New York, of affluent American parents, received an excellent education and was receptive to modern spiritual trends. In his twenties he traveled to Europe, visiting centers of intellectual thought, and studied with the best thinkers of his time. In Paris he encountered the "old world" tradition and culture and got a glimpse of the deep class distinctions. He attended Hegel's lectures in Berlin and was attracted to the philosopher's circle of followers. However, the young man did not find satisfaction in the abstract Hegelian thought and after a year's study, left. His curiosity led him on to Eastern Europe and to the Ottoman Empire. Later he settled in Paris and was attracted to the circle of Saint Simon's followers. But the continuous strife in their midst put him off, and he roamed Europe once again, going from England to Ireland and Scotland then on to Holland and, once again, to Germany. While there, in 1832, he was given Charles' Fourier's book, *L'Association domestique agricole*, which, in his own words, caused in him an intellectual upheaval because he found a key to the problems that had troubled him. He became a follower of Fourier and while still in Germany started to preach his doctrine. The police got wind of this and he was deported back to France, where he ardently wished to approach Fourier. The latter, whose circle of followers was small because of his abrasive attitude toward people, nevertheless accepted the young American as his private pupil. Brisbane tried unsuccessfully to understand the obscure parts of Fourier's doctrine. This did not deter him from becoming an ardent admirer of Fourierism. He regarded it as a solution to basic problems and a way to open new horizons for society. In

1834 Brisbane returned to the United States instilled with Fourierist values and a vast amount of knowledge and impressions gained during his European travels. Prosperity was still prevalent in the United States and Brisbane retired to his native town in order to record Fourier's doctrine and adapt it to the U.S. social reality. At the same time he was actively involved in reform circles in his area. Redelia Brisbane (Bates), *Albert Brisbane: A Mental Biography with a Character Study* (1893. Reprint. New York: Burt Franklin, 1969), pp. 150-74, 198-203.

3. Brisbane, pp. 204-8; John Humphrey Noyes, *History of American Socialism* (1870). Reprinted as, *Strange Cults and Utopias of Nineteenth-Century America* (New York: Dover, 1966), pp. 229-30; William Alfred Hinds, *American Communities and Cooperative Colonies* (1878. Reprinted and enl. Philadelphia: Porcupine, 1975), pp. 247-51; Egberts and Persons, p. 175; J.R. Commons, *History of Labor in the United States*, vol. 1 (New York: Macmillan, 1921), pp. 403-7; Basset, pp. 176-77; Grace Adams and Edward Hutter, *The Mad Forties* (New York: Harper & Brothers,), p. 168.
4. Brisbane, pp. 211-12; "Owenism, Fourieris, Revivalism," *American Socialist* 1, no. 2 (April 1876).
5. Noyes, pp. 202-6.
6. Ibid., p. 212; Hinds, p. 248; "To subscribers," *Phalanx*, November 5, 1843.
7. Ralph Albertson, *A Survey of Mutualistic Communities in America* (1936. Reprint. New York: AMS Press, 1973), pp. 390-400; "The Socialists of 1843," *American Socialist* 1, no. 3 (April 1876); Hinds, p. 250; Mark Holloway, *Heavens on Earth: Utopian Communities in America 1680-1880* (New York: Dover, 1966), pp. 143-45; Arthur E. Bestor, "American Phalanxes: A Study of Fourierist Socialism in the United States" (Ph.D. dissertation, Yale University, 1938); Albert Fein, "Fourierism in Nineteenth-Century America: A Social and Environmental Perspective," *France and North American Utopias and Utopians*, ed. Mathe Allain (Proceedings of the 3d Symposium of French-American Studies, March 4-8, 1974), pp. 133-48; Carl Guarneri, "The Fourierist Movement in America," *Communities: Journal of Cooperation*, no. 68 (Winter 1985):51-52.
8. Noyes, pp. 235-36; "The Sylvania," *Phalanx*, p. 16.
9. Noyes, pp. 233-46; Basset, p. 180; "The Sylvania," *Phalanx* 16, p. 244.
10. Noyes, pp. 251-52.
11. Ibid., pp. 252-66.
12. Mary Chapin Warner White, *Annals of Lyons Hollow* (*Crawford County Pennsylvania*), (Indiana, Penn.: Heffelfinger's Office Services, 1962).
13. Whitney Cross, *The Burned-Over District* (New York: Harper & Row, 1965), pp. 328-32.
14. Arthur Bestor, who wrote his Ph.D. dissertation on Fourierism in the western part of New York State, established the names of 313 Fourierist activists in Rochester by searching for them in the newspapers, advertisements, and memoirs, and even in citizen registration books. He attempted to find out their professions and social standing. His detailed research reinforces the thesis that they were indeed from a varied background. Half of the Fourierist activists came from the working class—shoemakers, carpenters, tailors, printers, blacksmiths, etc. and the other half from the middle class—doctors, engineers, clerics, small industrialists, and merchants. Bestor, *American Phalanxes*, pp. 49-54.
15. Ibid., pp. 39-43, 76-79; Noyes, pp. 267-76; Cross, p. 331.
16. Noyes, pp. 278-83; "Clarkson," *Phalanx*, pp. 187, 222; Bestor, *American Phalanxes*, pp. 63-70.

17. Ibid., pp. 142-262; Noyes, pp. 286-92; Herbert A. Wisbey, *The Sodus Shaker Community* (Lyons, New York: Wayne County Historical Society, 1982), pp. 23-24.
18. The first information of this activity was published in the *Phalanx* in October 1843. It tells of the foundation of an association for settlement of local farmers who were influenced by Fourier and decided to unite their diverse farms; in addition to farming they also introduced workshops, industry, and construction. The early reports testify to a partial success. The settlement was popular in the area and the reaction of the local press was positive. Their representatives, who attended the convention of the Fourier Federation in Rochester on May 15, 1844, reported their economic success. A year later they realized that their lack of ideological motivation prevented unity. Strife among members was rife and they soon lost their economic initiative. A year after it was founded they dissolved the association. A unique Fourist settlement was established in May 1843 in the deserted, hilly region of the Adirondacks in upstate New York. A rich landowner attempted to exploit the Fourist enthusiasm in order to improve his land. He offered the "socialists" 10,000 acres on condition that they clear the land within three years. In May 1843 a man named Morehouse undertook the job together with a number of Fourist settlers and established their settlement on the Piseco River. They shared their meager belongings, worked together, and consumed communally. They had a varied background: there were Fourierist idealists as well as many adventurers. Conditions in the remote hilly area were harsh. Only the magic dream of establishing a settlement in the "promised land" maintained them for nine months. In March 1844 the group dissolved and the dream with it. Noyes, pp. 299-308.
19. Letter from John Orvis, August 31, 1847, quoted in Henry W. Sams, ed., *Autobiography of Brook Farm* (Englewood Cliffs, N.J.: Prentice-Hall, 1959), pp. 205-6.
20. Noyes, pp. 309-15.
21. "Ohio Phalanx," *Phalanx* 6, p. 83; Noyes, pp. 354-66.
22. "Trumbull, P.," *Phalanx* 16, p. 242; Noyes, pp. 328-53.
23. Noyes, pp. 316, 366, 377, 404-7; "Clermont, Ohio," *Phalanx* 21, p. 160.
24. "Western Convention," *Phalanx*, pp. 11-22; Noyes, pp. 382-87.
25. Noyes, pp. 388-403; "Alphadelphia," *Phalanx* 5, p. 70; "Alphadelphia," *Phalanx* 14, p. 212.
26. "Wisconsin," *Phalanx* 13, June 29, 1844; "Wisconsin," *Phalanx* 19, October 7, 1844; Joseph Schafer, "The Wisconsin Phalanx," *The Wisconsin Magazine of History* 9 (1936):466-70.
27. Schafer, pp. 470-72; Noyes, pp. 416-46; Hinds, pp. 285-86.
28. "The Spread of the Doctrine," *Phalanx* 1, p. 15.
29. Hinds, pp. 252-54; Katherine Burton, *Paradise Planters: The Story of Brook Farm* (New York: AMS Press, 1973; 1st ed. 1939), pp. 8-9; John Thomas Codman, *Brook Farm: Historic and Personal Memoirs* (1894. Reprint. New York: AMS Press, 1971), pp. 1-25.
30. Hinds, pp. 255-56; Burton, pp. 24-40.
31. Letter from George Ripley, November 9, 1940, quoted in Sams (see n. 19 above), pp. 5-7.
32. Articles of Association of Brook Farm, reprinted from O.B. Frothingham, *George Ripley* (Boston: Houghton Mifflin, 1882), pp. 112-17, quoted in Sams, pp. 45-48.
33. Letters from Nathaniel Hawthorne, April 13, 1841, quoted in Sams, p. 14; May 3, 1841, quoted in Sams, p. 18.

34. Letter from Nathaniel Hawthorne, August 12, 1841, quoted in Sams, p. 30.
35. Hawthorne, *Blithedale Romance* (New York: W.W. Norton, 1958), pp. 46, 47, 80-85.
36. Letter from George Ripley, reprinted from Frothingham (see n. 32 above), pp. 312-14, quoted in Sams, p. 61; Elizabeth P. Peabody, "Plan of the West Roxbury Community," *The Dial* 2 (January 1842):361-72, quoted in Sams, p. 65; Ralph Waldo Emerson, journal entry, May 7, 1843, reprinted from *Journals of Ralph Waldo Emerson*, E.W. Emerson and W.E. Forbes, eds. (Boston: Houghton Mifflin, 1911), vol. 6, pp. 391, 392, 393, quoted in Sams, p. 79.
37. John Van Der Zee Sears, *My Friends at Brook Farm* (New York: Desmond Fitzgerald, 1912), pp. 49-65; "Rev. George Ripley," *The Monthly Miscellany of Religion and Letters* (May 1841), pp. 293-95, quoted in Sams, p. 16; Peabody, pp. 361-72, quoted in Sams, pp. 66-68; Letter from Sophia Eastman, July 25, 1843, quoted in Sams, p. 85; Letter from George Ripley, November 24, 1843, quoted in Sams, p. 85; Arthur Sumner, "A Boy's Recollections of Brook Farm," *New England Magazine*, vol. 16, new series (March-August, 1894):309-13, quoted in Sams, pp. 241, 243; Georgiana Bruce Kirby, *Years of Experience* (1887. Reprint. New York: AMS Press, 1971), pp. 95-100, 148-51.
38. Kirby, pp. 101-2, 141-47; Burton, pp. 68-94. Peabody, quoted in Sams, p. 67; *Constitution of the Brook Farm Association, for Industry and Education, West Roxbury, Mass., with an Introductory Statement* (Boston: I.R. Butts, 1844), pp. 3-12, quoted in Sams, p. 94; Burton, pp. 104-5.
39. Peabody, quoted in Sams, pp. 69-70.
40. Burton, pp. 160-61, 246.
41. Kirby, pp. 176-82; *Constitution of the Brook Farm Assoc.*, quoted in Sams, p. 95.
42. Brisbane, pp. 216-17.
43. Noyes, pp. 512-26; Hinds, pp. 259-62; "Brook Farm," *Phalanx* 6, p. 80, *Phalanx* 20, p. 305; *Constitution of the Brook Farm Assoc.*, quoted in Sams, pp. 95-96, 97-100.
44. Burton, pp. 198-202; "Brook Farm," *Phalanx* 6, p. 80, *Phalanx* 20, p. 305; Michael Fellman, *The Unbounded Frame: Freedom and Community in Nineteenth-Century American Utopianism* (Westport, Conn.: Greenwood Press, 1973), pp. 92-93.
45. Albert Brisbane was not elected to any executive job in the movement. He was to be the contact man with the European Fourierism, an insignificant position. Perhaps this was also the result of his decision to take a vacation from his activities and go to France in order to collect additional material about Fourierism. Shortly after the convention, in June 1844, he left for Paris, where he stayed until December 1844. Although Brisbane returned to be active, armed with further knowledge of Fourier, his commitment and belief in the chances of the associations in America had deteriorated. His disappointment grew with every failing experiment. His prediction that social crisis would prompt people to search for solutions, was proven wrong. On his return to activity in 1846 he found an abundance of failed associations. Economic prosperity was another factor which reduced the number of those searching for the "new gospel" of Fourierism. At this stage he devoted his time to an in-depth study of Fourier's new books and to teaching his doctrine in Fourierist circles. Most suitable for that was Brook Farm, where he transferred the focus of ideological guidance in 1845. Noyes, pp. 213-28; "Boston," *Phalanx* 5, pp. 71-72; "Convention," *Phalanx* 20, p. 294; Boston," *Phalanx* 13, p. 181; "Letter from Brisbane," *Phalanx* 14 (July 13, 1844).

46. Noyes, pp. 530-33; Codman, pp. 101-5; Brisbane, pp. 243-46; ''Brook Farm,'' *Phalanx* 20, pp. 305-6; ''New England,'' *Phalanx* 21, p. 309.
47. Burton, pp. 248-50.
48. Marianne Dwight, *Letters from Brook Farm, 1844-1847* (Poughkeepsie, N.Y.: Vassar College, 1928; New York: AMS Press, 1974), pp. 50-52, 114-16.
49. ''Notice to the Second Edition of the Constitution of the Brook Farm Association,'' *Phalanx* 20, p. 305; *Phalanx* 15 (July 27, 1844).
50. Burton, pp. 253-44, 257.
51. Dwight, pp. 136-39; Codman, pp. 144-46.
52. Letter from E.P. Grant, January 28, 1846, printed from *Elijah P. Grant Papers*, box 1, letterbook 3, pp. 42-45, quoted in Sams, p. 162. Codman, pp. 123-25, 144-46; Dwight, pp. 130-32, 136-45.
53. Burton, pp. 278-82; Noyes, pp. 551-58.
54. George Ripley, ''Fire at Brook Farm,'' *The Harbinger* 2 (December 13, 1845-June 6, 1846):220-22, quoted in Sams, pp. 173-74.
55. Ibid., pp. 176, 178-80, 182, 185-91; Dwight, pp. 151-62.
56. Dwight, pp. 152-58.
57. Ibid., pp. 169-70.
58. Brisbane, pp. 252-67; Burton, pp. 284-87.
59. Burton, p. 291.
60. Ibid., p. 263.
61. ''Brook Farm,'' *American Socialist*, 4, no. 24 (June 1879):186.
62. Dwight, pp. 176-77.
63. Codman, pp. 237-38, 247-48, 254-55; ''Hopedale and Brook Farm Communities,'' *American Socialist* 1 (1876):101-2; Sumner, quoted in *Sams*, pp. 238-44.
64. Burton, pp. 326-27.
65. Noyes, pp. 449-53; ''North American Phalanx,'' *Phalanx* 19 and 20.
66. Norma Lippincott Swan, ''The North American Phalanx: Expose of the Condition and Progress of the North American Phalanx in Reply to the Enquiries of Horace Greeley (1853),'' *Monmouth County Historical Association Bulletin* 1 (May 1935. Reprint. Philadelphia: Porcupine Press, 1975), pp. 48-52; Harold F. Wilson, ''The North American Phalanx,'' *Proceedings of the New Jersey Historical Society* 70, no. 3 (July 1952):193. Noyes, p. 653.
67. Wilson, p. 194.
68. Swan, p. 55; Wilson, p. 197; Joseph M. Mokrzycki, ''Life and Times at the North American Phalanx,'' *The Monmouth Historian* (Spring 1974):21.
69. Noyes, pp. 468-86; Fredrika Bremer, ''Two Visits to the North American Phalanx,'' *The Homes of the New World*, trans. Mary Howitt, 2 vols. (New York: 1858), reprinted as *Expose of the Condition and Progress of the North American Phalanx: The American Utopian Adventure*, series 2 (Philadelphia: Porcupine, 1975).
70. Bremer.
71. Swan, p. 53; Wilson, p. 195; Mokrzycki, p. 25.
72. Noyes, pp. 454-55; Charles Sears, ''The North American Phalanx: Correspondence and Report, 1853,'' in *Expose of the Condition and Progress of the North American Phalanx: The American Utopian Adventure*, series 2 (Philadelphia: Porcupine, 1975).
73. Noyes, pp. 461-62.
74. Swan, p. 57; Wilson, pp. 200-201.

75. Wilson, pp. 199-200.
76. "The Phalanstery and the Phalansterians, by an Outsider," *New York Tribune*, July 29, 1852; Dalikst Wolski, "A Visit to the North American Phalanx," trans. Marion Moore Coleman, *Proceedings of the New Jersey Historical Society*, 83, no. 3 (July 1965).
77. Noyes, pp. 450-99; Hinds, pp. 267-69, 273-75.
78. Eric R. Schriber, "The End of an Experiment: The Decline and Final Dissolution of the Phalanx," *The Monmouth Historian* (Spring 1974):32-34.

7

Oneida: Commune with Complex Marriage

In February 1848, while the social upheavals which had spawned the Fourierist phalanxes were on the wane, the foundations for a new commune were laid. It was located in upstate New York in the "burned-over district" near Lake Oneida. The founders were a group of religiously motivated, well-established New Englanders and New Yorkers.

The establishment of this commune was the outcome of one of the final wavelets of religious revivals which had lapped the eastern U.S. in the last decades. In terms of its human components, it was a landmark in the history of the American communes. For the first time a commune was established by American-born believers and which was not rooted in European secterianism, and without any immigrants among its founders. It was unique in its radical, nonconformist, theological socio-sexual approach, combined with a conservative economic attitude toward industry and production.[1]

Its spiritual make up and activities were directly related to the personality of its founder and leader, John Humphrey Noyes. The various stages of its inception and its crystallization as a commune were involved with his personal biography, which therefore deserves to be related here.

John Humphrey Noyes was born on September 11, 1811, in Brattleboro, Vermont, of respectable New England parentage. His father's family had emigrated from England and his mother's from Scotland at the beginning of the seventeenth century. Both families had a tradition of involvement in politics; his father had sat in congress for Vermont, and his mother's nephew, Rutherford B. Hayes, would be elected the nineteenth president of the United States (1876-1880).

John Humphrey Noyes was educated in the usual mode of upperclass New Englanders and intended to read law, when his life suddenly took a different direction. It was during a 1831 revival meeting held in his home town, Putney. In that year a new wave of revivals, inspired by the preacher Charles Finney, swept the "burned-over district." In the wake of this wave tens of thousands of men and women returned to religion and joined the Free Churches, which sprang up like mushrooms after the rain. One of the preachers of this revival movement came to Putney and summoned open-air meetings, which sometimes lasted ten days.

John Humphrey Noyes related that he had been attracted to it out of curiosity, feeling alienated from the prevailing ecstatic atmosphere. Suddenly he was overcome by doubts about the significance of his whole life. It was an overwhelming experience, and as a result he decided to devote himself to God and to radically change his way of life.[2] He gave up his legal training and turned to the study of theology at the seminary in Andover. However, he was soon disappointed with its formalistic approach, and the seminary's professional attitude was not the answer to his troubled mind. A year later he transferred to the theological school at Yale, from which he graduated in 1833 as a licensed preacher.

Noyes became the spiritual shepherd of a small congregation of a Free Church in upstate New York, but only for a short period. While still at Yale and Andover he had been beset by questions on the Second Advent of the Messiah, man's achieving grace, and salvation in the kingdom of heaven. According to one of his teachers at Andover, whom he greatly admired, the Second Advent of Christ had already occurred at the time of the Apostles.

This exegesis was absorbed in his consciousness and never left him during the coming years, until he himself reached the same conclusions. He then developed a theory according to which the coming of the Messiah had already taken place in the year 70 A.D. (the destruction of the Temple), since then existing in the spiritual realm. According to his theory only through a deep and sincere belief could one be included in the kingdom of the Messiah in this world, and thus achieve a state of freedom from sin. Noyes believed himself to be the instrument that would lead them. His views included elements of heresy, and on the other hand he was close to the beliefs of the perfectionist current which was gaining in strength at the time.[3]

When he began to preach his convictions to the congregation of the Free Church, in which he served, announcing that he was perfect and free of sin, they were dumbfounded and believed him to be mad. His university professors renounced him and he was dismissed in February 1834, his licence to preach withdrawn.[4] The young preacher found himself completely isolated, without a church, without friends, and without a religion. He went through a period of spiritual depression and roamed the country, a homeless and rootless nomad. Reaching New York City he found himself in the "stronghold of Satan," in the neglected hangouts of prostitutes and criminals in Manhattan.

There, broken hearted and depressed, he attempted to preach to the underworld and "grapple with Satan." It was a descent into hell from which he had hoped to emerge cleansed and purified and strengthened in his belief. At this point his friends and family stepped in to save him from the entanglement in New York and brought him home to Putney for a period of spiritual rehabilitation. But soon he set out again on his missionary travels.[5] The years between 1834 and 1838 were the most trying of his life. He wandered aimlessly and lonely, tormented with doubts about his beliefs. He had severed all his ties with the perfectionists but could not form any other stable attachment, while seeking commitment to a new religious doctrine.

During that period Noyes formulated his early principles on the institution of marriage. According to his biographers, it was motivated by his bitter personal experience. He had fallen in love with Abigail Merwin, one of his first followers, but, beyond a deep spiritual affinity, did not achieve a lasting relationship with her. When she married somebody else, he wrote to his friend, David Harrison, on January 15, 1837. In his letter he expressed his opinions on the institution of marriage, which he considered presently to be in a period of transition and preparation for the promised kingdom of heaven:

> When the will of God is done on earth, as it is in heaven, *there will be no marriage*. The marriage supper of the Lamb is a feast at which *every dish is free to every guest*. Exclusiveness, jealousy, quarreling, have no place there. . . . In a *holy community*, there is no more reason why sexual intercourse should be restrained by law, than why eating and drinking should be, and there is little reason for shame in one case as in the other.

He made it clear that this did refer to the state of grace, and that "God has placed a wall of partition between the male and female during the apostasy." He concluded his letter with an admonition, saying: "But woe to him who abolishes the law of apostasy before he stands in the holiness of resurrection."[6]

David Harrison was astonished and overwhelmed by these ideas and did not keep them to himself. He showed the letter to some of his perfectionist friends, and it came into the hands of Theophilius T. Gates, editor of *The Battle Axe* who decided to publish it. A great storm broke out when the letter was made public. However, Noyes did not retract his ideas, explaining that they were valid only in a certain spiritual reality, namely, that of a pure and sanctified society. He was aware of the danger that his doctrine would be stamped promiscuous, as was the case with extreme groups among the perfectionists who were practicing "free love." He attempted to stop the slanders which were affecting some of his small body of followers, and therefore expanded his propaganda effort by preaching and writing.[7]

At this point one of his devoted followers, Harriet Holton, came to his aid and proposed marriage. She was aware of his radical ideas on family life but was willing to enter the state of matrimony based on a contract, according to which each of the partners agreed not to limit the other's "exclusive affairs of the heart,'' and to be involved in other relationships while honoring their partnership.[8]

Noyes accepted her proposal. He was aware that marriage would save him from the accusations of promiscuity, prompted by the publication of his letter. Marriage to Holton also benefited him materially, since she entered their partnership with a considerable property. This enabled him to lay the foundation for his propaganda effort. The first thing he did was to buy a printing press and publish his independent paper, the *Witness*. After the wedding the couple moved to Putney, where in the Noyes family circle a group of followers began to crystallize. They had been formed in the Putney Bible School in 1836, but now began to gradually branch out in other places in New England.[9]

Noyes's family members—brothers, sisters, and brothers-in-law—were his devoted followers. After a period of doubt, his mother too accepted her son's charismatic leadership and began to believe in his sacred mission.

Noyes maintained a strict authoritarian leadership among his followers. Right from the beginning he declared that he would not collaborate with a person or group unless they accepted his absolute spiritual leadership. Those who doubted him were rejected.

Noyes' dominant personality and the material and spiritual security, which life in the community ensured, provided his followers with their most substantial needs. After his bitter experience of trying to appeal to society as a whole, Noyes preferred to concentrate his efforts on a small, closely knit circle of followers rather than to continue on his Don Quixoitic crusade to conquer the whole society. At the same time he continued to publish his conviction in the *Witness*, the *Perfectionist*, and the *Spiritual Magazine*, whose readership were mostly from among the perfectionists—the natural periphery and source of followers in Vermont, Massachusetts, New York, and New Jersey.[10]

From 1838 through 1841 his Bible School followers maintained no stable social or economic framework. They shared some of their accommodations, work, and consumption, and their main social contact was realized in their daily Bible readings, interpreted by Noyes. When Noyes's father died in 1841 he left his property of land and houses in Putney, along with $20,000, to his sons and daughters who were all members of the Bible School circle. This capital was to be their common purse and the financial basis of a closely-knit community. In fact they soon legalized their group under the name of The Putney Research Community, and adopted a constitution.

Together with the property of other members they now owned $37,000, which enabled them to accept new, less affluent members. In 1834 they numbered 35—26 adults and 9 children—who lived in three communal houses close to their places of work, which were on the Noyes farm and at the general store in the center of town. Their life grew steadily more communal when they organized it in such a way as to enable every member to attend the daily

Bible lessons. In 1845 they decided to adopt the name of The Putney Community, and a year later they confirmed their communal constitution.[11]

A most significant development that did not find expression in the constitution was their system of "complex marriage"(group marriage), which Noyes formulated after twelve years of deliberations on the status of the family and relationships between the sexes. It had been one of the main subjects of the spiritual religious upheaval of the perfectionists and had caused a storm when some groups adopted promiscuity. Noyes was dismayed by the scandalous behavior of the perfectionists, but on the other hand he severely criticized the sexual mores of the society sanctioned by the church establishment.

There were also personal reasons behind Noyes's theory, but it presented mainly a social, spiritual, and religious problem for him; it had taken him years to formulate this theory, which he published in 1848 in a booklet, *The Bible Argument*. In it he expounded his theory on the family and sexual relations which he had adopted two years earlier in Putney. He abolished the monogamous family that gives the husband the "exclusive ownership of one woman," and hence is as harmful as any other form of private ownership. He refused to accept that "nature must take its course," and claimed that human experience had proven that sexual relations were not limited to couples, and that every individual had the secret longing to love more than one mate: "The more he loves, the greater his capacity for love." Noyes attacked the hypocrisy of marriage and morals and the harm caused to individuals and to the internal relationships within the community. He accused the monogamous set-up as being "egoism limited to two." His ideal was to exchange the concept of the *I* with that of *we*. His proposed relationships were more in the spirit of the conditions in the kingdom of heaven, where everyone was wedded to all the others in heart, body, and soul in a complex marriage. Fidelity to the community as a whole would take the place of fidelity to the monogamous family.[12]

The introduction of the complex marriage at Putney involved a unique method of sexual behavior which was also the brainchild of Noyes. It was called "male continence." At a time when no birth control methods were generally available, Noyes offered a unique way of his own to prevent pregnancy: He laid the responsibility of controlling intercourse on the man, who would have to contain himself at a certain moment. Noyes compared sexual relations to navigating a river with rapids on which only experienced sailors could avoid being carried along to a point of no return. He realized the importance of male continence for complex marriages, to avoid uncontrolled propagation. He was especially concerned with the fate of women who had to suffer many unwanted pregnancies.

Once again his general concern was the result of bitter personal experience. During their married life, Harriet Holton had suffered five miscarriages, and they were left with only one child, Theodore (who would fulfill an important role in the future of Oneida). His wife's heartbreak and his own frustration as a man and the spiritual leader of his community, prompted him to research for a way to prevent unwelcome consequences. He discovered and crystallized the method in which "the amative and propagative functions were distinct from each other," and which was introduced in 1846 in Putney and adopted throughout the history of Oneida.[13]

The effectiveness of this system can be measured by the fact that between 1848 and 1869 there were only 31 births in a community of about 200 adults. It took an outstanding amount of self-control and social criticism as well as the breaking of all conventions to maintain the unique complex marriage in Oneida. Noyes had always resented the free love or promiscuity of the perfectionists. He was aware of the danger of deterioration his method might encounter from within and its distortion by the external society. He therefore diligently attempted to clarify the differences between complex marriage and free love. Within Oneida he protected his method from malpractice by regulating sexual relations within a supervised framework. The core was a system of "mutual criticism," which he had learned while at the theological seminary in Andover. It was not by chance that he introduced mutual criticism together with complex marriage and male continence.

The transition to a new way of life was accompanied by severe social tensions, despite the profound trust all members had in Noyes. Mutual criticism enabled members to see themselves in the eyes of their peers. It allowed them to discuss personal problems openly, to get to know each other and help the individual to overcome his problems. When the first experiment of mutual criticism succeeded, it became a social catharsis that helped the whole community to overcome the trials of the transition period. It also gave the leadership an opportunity to keep an eye on the individual's behavior. In 1846 Noyes experimented with his three novel social methods, namely, the complex marriage, male continence, and mutual criticism, which were to pave the way to the establishment of a new society. The results encouraged his belief that the time had come to end the transition period. On July 1, 1847 he announced that the "Kingdom of Heaven has come," and that the members of his community in their way of life and their beliefs were worthy citizens thereof. In this Noyes saw the materialization of the Second Coming.

In his *Spiritual Magazine*, published on July 15, 1847, he proclaimed that the advent of Christ, which had occurred in 70 A.D. on the spiritual level, was now to be realized on Earth. He also published a book, *The Berean*, which was to become the "holy scripture" of the communities in Putney and Oneida, and in which he detailed his doctrine of communal life and the "complex" family.[14]

Noyes's influence was on the rise. His followers at Putney believed that the time would come to expand their activities. Close ties were formed with other perfectionist groups active in New England and New York. It was a period of religious unrest, the revivals of the 1830s, the Millerite movement, and the Fouriest activities in the 1840s.

The situation at home, however, was complicated. Until 1846 they had had correct relations with their Putney neighbors, since most members were from among the upper classes. But when rumors about their odd family relationships began to circulate, hostility soon followed. It quickly spread in the conservative puritan society of Vermont, who deeply resented Noyes's methods, to which he also added faith healing. He was accused of practicing sexual relations with some of his women patients as part of the treatment, and the township was up in arms. Some threatened to sue him and his companions for the immoral behavior in their community.

Groups of Putney citizens organized, intending to cleanse the "nest of inequity" and Noyes found himself accused of adultery and fornication, but was released on bail. Meanwhile the danger of a lynching threatened the whole community of followers, and they decided to disperse in several other states. In November 1847, Noyes found shelter in New York, and from there he continued to be in touch with the members of his community who remained in Putney and with those who had scattered all over the country.[15]

In September 1847, when the Putney community was persecuted, several groups of perfectionists met in Lairdsville, Oneida County, and decided to establish a community similar to the one in Putney. Among them was one Jonathan Burt, who offered his land on the Oneida Indian reserve to the planned community. Several families agreed to participate in this venture, and a few weeks later moved to Burt's house and there established a settlement. John Humphrey Noyes would argue later that it was a "heavenly intervention" that caused the establishment of this new settlement at a time when the Putney community was going into exile. Shortly after that he was invited to examine the possibility of joining the perfectionist community in Oneida.

The isolated site in the area, which was filled with perfectionist activity, seemed ideal for a model settlement of the kingdom of heaven, and also as a place from which to continue some missionary activities among their followers. A call went out to perfectionists who had been in touch with Noyes to join the new commune, and within a few months 50 members had assembled at Oneida. Among them were Jonathan Burt and the first settlers of Oneida together with survivors of the Putney community and a score of Vermont followers of Noyes. They were all young people, the oldest being forty years old. Most were Yankee farmers and mechanics, practical and diligent in all their efforts.[16]

The rapid growth caused problems of accommodation in the first winter in Oneida. All their efforts were geared to provide the needs of the society's communal way of life. The mansion house was only half finished and not ready for occupancy; a temporary plan was devised, and partitions of cotton cloth called "tents" were hung up on wires supported by wooden frames, thus serving as living quarters. The large interior space became a sitting room for the "tent" dwellers, and one large stove warmed the twelve rooms around it, effectively saving money.[17]

From the start they introduced a communal way of life. The children lived in separate quarters, supervised by members who had been elected to do the job. During the first year they had no constitution. Committees were in charge of all the aspects of their social, cultural, and economic life. A spiritual-ideological hierarchy, with John Humphrey Noyes at the top, was maintained. Some members assisted him, and modes of communal organization, inspired by their principles, were formed. Frequent general meetings promoted Noyes's special doctrine among the perfectionist newcomers who had decided to reject the American way of life and live according to their beliefs.[18]

At first everyone could join in if he was willing to learn and adopt the commune's doctrine and way of life, giving up his private property. The new candidate was asked to first pay all his debts and then transfer his possessions to the commune, to be returned without interest if he left. In spite of the hardships of the isolated and secluded settlement, many of those who joined were affluent followers from New England and New York who contributed their property. In 1857 Oneida had a capital of $108,000.

In 1849 there were 87 persons, 27 of them children under fifteen. In 1850 their number doubled and reached 172, and in 1851 they numbered 250. At that stage they began to curtail the acceptance of new members to avoid uncontrolled absorption, but mostly for economic reasons, namely, lack of land, capital, and means of production. At the same time many members dropped out because they could not stand the hardships and the unique demands put upon them by the commune's sexual practice. In 1855 their number dropped to about 150.[19]

Robert Fogarty, who wrote a doctoral dissertation on Oneida, studied the background of its members and their motives for joining the commune. He concluded that most had experienced revivals in the 1830s and 1840s and found it difficult to return to their former way of life. Noyes's doctrine and his group offered a unique combination of religion and a stable, secure, and later even prosperous existence. Most identified completely with Noyes's spiritual leadership that gave profound meaning to their lives. Out of 109 of the members who joined Oneida in the first two years, 89 were still there when it dissolved.[20]

A year after the establishment of Oneida in 1849, Noyes left for Brooklyn, New York, but he maintained his charismatic leadership of both the Oneida and the Brooklyn communes. His motives remain shrouded in mystery, yet it is clear that he wanted to promote his ideas and felt he had to be near the publishing houses of communal literature and periodicals. New York was where he met people from all over the world. He even went to the World's Fair in London in 1851, where he met Englishmen of all classes, adding a new dimension to the perfectionist's mission in the world. Noyes remained in Brooklyn until 1854, and Oneida was managed by his confidants, Erastus Hamilton and John Miller.[21]

The first six years at Oneida were a period of hardship. The tense relationship with the neighbors and the local establishments of the church and the state added to the suffering. Believing that he had the Lord's blessing, Noyes published his perfectionist doctrine as well as his ideas on marriage and sex; as in the past it caused a violent controversy. In 1850 a court of law undertook to investigate the most intimate practices of Oneida members, and both men and women had to testify. It was a severe trial. Several influential newspapers in New York joined the crusade against the commune. For a while it seemed as though the attack was successful in breaking the members' spirit to the extent that on March 7, 1852 they published a declaration in their newspaper, saying they were returning to the accepted family relations. But it was just a short retreat; in August of the same year they made it clear that their "complex family" was firmly rooted in their religious creed. They launched a counter-attack on their slanderers, and called upon their neighbors to testify on their behalf. Indeed most neighbors agreed to sign a declaration attesting to the fact that "members of Oneida were sober, substantial men and women of good behavior and solid position. Moreover their innovations were restricted to the family circle at Oneida. Society at large could have not justly complained that its taboos were violated." A new period thus began for the Oneida commune.[22]

The stability achieved in those years was mainly due to the clever leadership of John Miller, one of the Putney members, who was a gifted farmer and economist. From the beginning members of the commune had the realistic approach of Yankee businessmen. It found expression in their dual attitude of religious radicalism combined with conservative business acumen.

In order to exploit all possibilities at hand they established diversified farming. To begin with they cultivated the plot of 250 acres, which they gradually increased, until they owned 386 acres in 1859. They grew vegetables and fruit, but the land was poor and agriculture could not have remained their only income in spite of their diligence. Soon they searched for other industries that would utilize their mechanics, who constituted the majority of the members. They now manufactured chairs, brooms, shoes, bags, etc. One who had joined the commune in its first year, Sewel Newhouse, was the inventor of a special trap. He continued to manufacture it as a member of the commune, first in limited numbers, working alone, but as the fame and demand for his traps grew, it later turned into a major industry. Even so, the financial situation was not very bright, and in 1854, with the tragic death of John Miller, the economic condition deteriorated further. It was a period of crisis, and Noyes was recalled from Brooklyn and returned to reside in Oneida.[23]

John Humphrey Noyes's return after John Miller's death was also the end of his grandiose ambition for converting the world. He became more realistic, less visionary. His hopes for new communities were shattered when of all the existing ones, only Wallingford remained viable until 1880. Through Noyes's initiative the members of Oneida began to distribute their produce by themselves; they even became peddlers who, in addition to their agricultural produce, peddled some of their other manufactured ware. This was an exceptional trend among communes in general, as they all abstained from trading and commerce. In Oneida peddling became a respectable occupation, equal to others. However, during their wanderings they never lost their sense of uniqueness. Usually the peddlers were not absent for more than a week, but on their return these men and women were "cleansed of the worldly spirit by a thorough scrubbing and the criticism of their comrades." At first their industry developed on the basis of processing their agricultural produce. In time those were reduced and other industries soon became their major source of income.[24]

The year 1855 was a turning point in Oneida's economic development. Noyes induced Sewel Newhouse, who had so far guarded his professional secret, to accept additional workers at his trap workshop. The project gained momentum and rapidly developed subsidiaries, in which forged chains were produced among other things. When the reputation of Newhouse's traps spread, orders began to arrive from all over the United States and Canada. The workshops prospered and a large number of members were employed there. In 1857, a time of economic recession in the United States, Oneida finally became economically viable, because of their diversified economy that enabled them to balance profit and loss. The 1860s found Oneida a prosperous and dynamic community.

To their existing industries they added silk production, and this was to be one of their major businesses in years to come. During the Civil War, many orders of food, clothing, and the weaving industry were placed with the commune. These new circumstances caused their industry to expand above and beyond the work force at their disposal. At this stage they had to employ labor from the outside,[25] much against Noyes's conviction. He had always criticized the capitalistic "salaried bondage." The rapid expansion of the trap industry demanded additional hands, and even though all commune members made an effort, including the children, whose schooling was interrupted, they could not fill all the orders. At first twenty hands were hired, but in 1864 they already numbered forty at the trap factory. Soon the barrier broke and other branches hired help.

When Charles Nordhoff visited Oneida in 1874 he found not less than 200 hired workers, about the same number as commune members. They worked everywhere, on the farm and in the industry as well as in the kitchen and laundry. Nordhoff's critical eye immediately noticed the ill effect this had on the communal life: the monotonous and unpopular jobs were left to the hired employees while the members were the managers. Noyes's attitude to the situation was ambivalent. He consoled himself with the hope that it was not a permanent one, and that as soon as the world recognized the advantages of communal life, it would attract multitudes. However, he was aware of the harmful effects of hired labor and prosperity on the commune.[26]

The society stabilized and membership expanded. In 1868 Oneida numbered 210 members and Wallingford 52. This included several Yale students who were living in the nearby commune. University studies were one of the results of their economic prosperity.[27] Another result was their decision to better their living conditions. Until 1856 they had lived in the old wooden mansion house. Now they proposed to construct a solid red-brick community house. The building plans were discussed at public meetings because members of the commune regarded their accommodation as an organic part of their way of life. One of their members, Erastus Hamilton, who was a professional architect, was put in charge of the construction plans. He preferred to leave the primary planning to a committee that had been elected for that purpose. Deliberations lasted for about four years. A lot of attention was devoted to the environmental planning of the whole project, because years of communal life had taught them not to improvise. Finally, in 1861 the blue prints of a large red-brick building called "the second mansion" were ready.

The first wing was completed in 1862 and signified the beginning of their prosperity and the establishment of complex marriages. The second wing was the children's house, and it was completed in 1869 and signified the end of birth control and the formation of a children's society. Even though many members were involved in the mansion's construction, an architectural unity of style was maintained. When it was completed a decade later, an imposing solid building stood on an elevated part of the domain, commanding an extensive view of the surroundings.

The public rooms were on the ground floor and housed the kitchens, dining-hall, a commodious assembly hall with a stage and a balcony running around three walls and used for the community's entertainment and meetings, the large parlor for more intimate meetings, a library and a study room—all connected by a number of corridors so that members would meet several times during the day. The upper floors were devoted to sleeping apartments; each adult had his own room. This was the only U.S. commune which granted to each one of its members a private room. Several rooms shared a parlor, and the mansion's four wings formed a quadrangle in which everyone would gather on summer evenings.[28]

As on other communes, Oneida's high living standards found expression in its rich cultural activities. Since the 1850s special attention was given to the musical education. At first it was only an amateur effort in which small groups of members gathered to practice playing on wind instruments and recorders. Two years later this developed into a small orchestra which played with neither instruction nor a conductor. However, their collective enthusiasm bore fruit, and in 1857 they began to perform and gain recognition; one of their members was granted time off from work in order to study conducting and composition. In the spring of 1859 the orchestra had 25 musicians, had increased its repertoire, and performed in the neighborhood. One of the members was sent to spend several weeks in New York to improve his acquaintance with standard music and to study orchestral organizations. By coincidence, a Swiss music teacher came to the community in the same year. He and his family stayed for a year and he did much to raise the standard of vocal music and the concerts became an integral part of their cultural activities, to which neighbors were invited.

There were also negative aspects to the musical life on Oneida. In 1874 it became painfully apparent that some "evil spirit" compounded of jealousy, envy, and egotism was creeping into the music group. When this came to the attention of Noyes, he called the group together for a session of mutual criticism. In the course of this, some youngsters confessed to feelings of jealousy and frustration, that overtook them when the community fostered talented musicians who were given an opportunity to study outside the commune. Noyes diagnosed the musical malady as "primadonna fever" and pointed out the reasons which had brought it on: "Lately we have got our music altogether from the world and have gone to New York for musical education and we are suffering the consequences." He added that "the music has evidently become a selfish personal thing, they look on their talents, their reputations, ability and success in music as their own and are quarreling in their hearts about the matter, just as the world quarrels about money and other selfish rights." He concluded that they should separate music entirely from the idea of playing it to visitors.

The mutual criticism cleared the air, but contact with the worldly and spiritual-cultural environment continued.[29] There was an atmosphere of studies, and many members were showing an increasing interest in the cultural trends of the world. The attitude of Oneida toward the outside world was ambivalent. This was expressed during the Civil War, when the commune wholeheartedly supported the North but never did anything about it. Members did not enlist in the army (an administrative muddle helped them to avoid it). Although the commune contributed to the war effort by paying taxes—some would claim that they paid $10,000—they profited from the war when they produced supplies that were urgently needed. After the war Oneida was a very prosperous commune; this brought about a change in their religious and ideological attitudes, and they would never be the same again.[30] Henceforth the settlement was exposed to contradictions of another kind. There was an internal conflict between the steps taken to develop economically and the spiritual world and vision that had led them at the beginning. The rapid economic development, which established their independent existence in the American society, connected them with strong ties to the very society whose system they had hoped to change. It transpired that the effort they had put into survival had become an end in itself and caused profound changes in the fabric of their society and in their relationships with the outside world.[31]

Prosperity caused them to change their policy regarding birth control, and "stirpiculture" was introduced. This new method had two sources. The first was Noyes's doctrine, mentioned in his *Bible Communism* (published in 1848), in which he wrote:

> We are opposed to excessive and course oppressive procreation which is almost universal. We are opposed to random procreation, which is unavoidable in the marriage system.
>
> But we are in favor of intelligent, well-ordered procreation. . . . We believe the time will come when involuntary and random procreation will cease, and when scientific combination will be applied to human generation as freely and successfully as it is to that of other animals. . . . And at all events we believe that good sense and benevolence will very soon sanction and enforce the rule that women shall bear children only when they choose.

Darwin's theory of evolution published a few years later reinforced Noyes's concern and strengthened his resolve to introduce stirpiculture, i.e., planned procreation. Additional factors were the commune's economic prosperity combined with their wish to avoid stagnation, but most of all the younger men who had attended university and were already converts to Darwin's ideas and other scientific trends. They were ready to implement the doctrine of evolution and join the experiment that would be the scientific answer to social problems.

After a period of preparations and testing the practicality of the system among old and young members, they inaugurated in 1869 their daring venture in planned scientific procreation and named it *stirpiculture*. It was stipulated that it would be undertaken voluntarily and in total agreement of the participants. About 100 members of both sexes volunteered and signed their resolution "to offer themselves to be used in forming any combination that may seem desirable . . . to put aside all envy, childishness and selfseeking" and to "cheerfully resign all desire to become mothers if for any reason Mr. Noyes deemed them unfit material for propogation." During the first period the experiment was directed by Noyes and several of the founders. In January 1875 a stirpicultural committee was appointed by the community. It was composed of men and women, some from among the younger generation. Many women chose Noyes as their mate and during the next ten years at least nine of the 58 children born were sired by him.[32]

After stirpiculture was introduced and the number of children increased, the community became more concerned with education. There is not much information about these matters during the early years of Oneida. We know that the children were not sent to nearby schools but were taught locally by any member who was educated in a certain subject and had the right attitude. There was no permanent teaching staff and most were only part-time teachers. The few children in Oneida attended a one-room school, while the teenagers could choose their lessons after work. In 1855 evening classes for adults were started and many attended them. With the gradual decrease of work pressure and the advent of prosperity, adult schooling for all was introduced.

In 1862 a formal framework of education was adopted. The 6- to 12-year-olds were taught reading, writing, spelling, and arithmetic at the elementary school, which also instilled in them discipline and the communal way of life and its religion. The 12- to 20-year-olds attended a sort of "university" framework as they called it, in which their "professors" taught them as many subjects as were available on the commune. Some of the youngsters prepared themselves to become teachers after graduation. During 1863-64 there developed an atmosphere of learning and many of the adults attended classes on astronomy, geography, math, grammar, Latin, Greek, and even Hebrew.

In 1869 a school wing called the "seminary" was constructed. There were large airy rooms with the most up-to-date furniture and teaching aids available at the time. Children would learn during mornings and adults in the afternoon. Additional subjects were taught such as analytical geometry, trigonometry, and science classes of biology, chemistry, botanics, and physics. At this stage the influence of the youngsters was felt in the teaching staff. Five young members of the commune who were studying medicine, engineering, and law at Yale, came home during their summer vacation and introduced some other subjects into the curriculum. The whole commune was aspiring to get a sound education, and even wanted to turn baking and cooking into a science.[33] The library was well stacked with literature and all the periodicals of the time. The study room was a hive of activity.

Other changes were caused by stirpiculture. A new element had been introduced into communal life, and in spite of their pledges not to feel "envy and selfishness" there was a tension between members that had never been known before. The religious way of life which had characterized their earlier years was superceded by a new way, interwoven with scientific elements alien to their former spiritual world, which in time caused schism and discontent. Some researchers regard stirpiculture as the beginning of the end for Oneida.

This trend was also affected by the notoriety and by tensions with the outside world. When newspapers began to publish the "goings on," bad feelings that had been dormant among the church establishment and their puritanical neighbors were rekindled.[34]

Noyes had played a central part in the introduction of stirpiculture, but he was now losing his charismatic leadership. There were additional reasons connected with the internal development of the commune. After the Civil War Noyes was dissatisfied with the commune's single-minded concern with internal affairs and their aspirations to material prosperity. They were no longer motivated by their wish to reform society. Noyes began to search for new horizons, and discovered the world of other communes and socialist organization in the United States.

In 1870, when he published his book *The History of the American Socialism* about communal experiments in the past, he dealt with the causes for the failure of the communes which had dissolved. He pointed to the lack of homogenous religious ideology as one of the main reasons and called for a combination of socialism and religious revival as the only way to safeguard the commune in the existing society.

In the mid-1870s Noyes realized that his leadership was being undermined. The gap between him and the younger generation deepened. They became alienated and critical of the religious world he represented. Some of them, after a period of studies at Yale and being involved with secular and scientific ideas, were no longer willing to accept unquestionably the spiritual leadership of Noyes. They also revolted against the stirpiculture being directed by the older members who had the option to choose the young women for themselves. Their discontent rose to the surface. Being aware of it, Noyes began to prepare the transfer of leadership to his son Theodore, who had just returned to the commune with a doctor's certificate.

The first step in that direction was made when, in 1867, Noyes converted the *Circular* into the *American Socialist*, in collaboration with William A. Hinds. His aim was to open a window to the socialist world and to other communes in the United States and thus forge a mutual relationship. It gave him an opportunity to devote himself to general socialist and communal activities.[35]

The first issue made clear the aims of the *American Socialist*. A call went out to all the religious communes to unite. It was written by a member of the Wallingford Commune and directed toward the Shakers, New Harmony, Zoar, Beth-El, Aurora, Amana, and Oneida who together had about 5,200 members. After pointing out the unique aspects of each one, he nevertheless estimated that they had more in common than would meet the eye. They were all devoted to the establishment of the kingdom of heaven on earth, they all practiced communal life with the assumption that a sacred and pure Christian way of life could be realized only in a communitarian society. He concluded saying that their separateness would weaken their chances of survival, and that they should form an umbrella organization to influence others and transmit their convictions to each other and to the outside world. The second issue of the *American Socialist* included responses from two Shaker elders who were sympathetic to the suggestion of developing a dialogue among the communes but rejected the option of a union. They thought that the differences could not be bridged. The editor welcomed the Shakers' attitude and invited further reactions from other communes, explaining that even if it did not lead to a union, a dialogue would enhance mutual understanding. Thus the *American Socialist* served as a platform for all communes, those that still existed and those that had ceased to be, but whose doctrine and message were transmitted by the editors.[36]

Shortly after the publication of the first issue of the *American Socialist*, Noyes retired from the practical leadership of Oneida, which passed into the hands of his son Theodore. The transition was involved with many problems that intensified the tensions in the community. Noyes's leadership had not been established in the constitution and had been accepted because of his charisma during the early days of the perfectionists at Putney. He had been supported by a group of members who had gone with him all along. Theodore Noyes was not one of them, and his father had begun to promote him in the hierarchy of Oneida only in the 1860s. There were several obstacles to Theodore Noyes's being accepted: (1) He lacked his father's personality. (2) His ideology was not inspired by the revivalists' religious creeds but was based on a scientific-modern-Darwinist-positivist philosophy. Another obstacle was presented by his behavior. His involvement with one of the commune's ambitious young women far exceeded the established norms of communal life.

Theodore's disadvantages as a leader became evident as soon as he took on his new duties. He further antagonized his critics when he introduced bureaucratic methods that included strict supervision of all the committees' and members' activities. Everyone had to hand-in written reports, and this went against the grain of the spontaneous communal way of life. His position was completely undermined when he left Oneida with his companion and moved to the sister commune of Wallingford, and from there he tried to "manage" Oneida through written reports. Under these circumstances John Humphrey Noyes had no option but to return to active leadership of the commune, in which signs of disintegration were becoming evident. An opposition had crystallized and a period of uneasy relations within and without began.[37]

John Humphrey Noyes soon realized that he was not succeeding. It was 1878 and all the facets of life had changed. The commune was now affluent, its industry had expanded, and hired labor exceeded the number of members.

New candidates were being accepted, and there never was any shortage of those. Among them was a group from the Berlin Heights commune in Cleveland, Ohio, who practiced free love. Although members of Oneida were careful to avoid the stigma of free love, they trusted the newcomers and especially their leader, James William Towner.

Towner was a preacher turned lawyer who in the 1860s had assisted Oneida in a case against seceders. With the acceptance of the 12 members of Berlin Heights in April 1874, Oneida had 270 members; this was the largest group of new members to join the commune since its early days. The result was negative. Towner joined the opposition against Noyes which had crystallized among some of the young members who were joined by several of the older generation, among whom Hinds was the most prominent.[38] Oneida was beset by an atmosphere of discord it had never before experienced. People would gather in small circles and clans to struggle over positions of power within committees and at the public meetings.

In 1873 the situation deteriorated further when the Congregational Church of New York adopted resolutions denouncing the community as a "pernicious institution which rests substantially on a system of organized fanatism and lust." This resolution was initiated by the "Comstock Laws for the Suppression of Vice," and Comstock adherents found Oneidans an easy target for their arrows. The pretext was the Mormon's family laws. In New York State this was an opportunity to launch a campaign against Oneida. Into this crusade stepped Professor John W. Mears of Hamilton College, who was chosen by the Presbyterian synod in October 1874 to head a committee that would report on the moral practices at Oneida.[39] The Baptist Church also joined the denouncement. At first the Mears committee did not succeed in establishing any felony. Most of the local newspapers supported the commune and its members withstood the attacks valiantly.[40]

Further, 1873 through 1878 were years of economic recession and many Americans were unemployed. The commune exploited the situation and established several new industries; one of them, Oneida Silverware, would in time become the largest factory of its kind in the United States. Many workers were employed there, and they felt blessed to have an opportunity to work in excellent conditions and had no motive to undermine the stability of Oneida. Therefore Mears failed to raise opposition to the commune, but he never gave up, and in 1879 his chance came when representatives of several churches convened in Oneida County, and the commune was again accused of vice in the form of the complex marriage. Their sexual practices were compared to those of the widely detested Mormons, and the crusade against Oneida gained in momentum.

Oneidans tried to defend themselves by sending representatives to the convention, and again they were supported by the local papers; but their efforts were in vain. This convention also decided to appoint a committee that would investigate the "moral features" of Oneida, and rumor had it that the church was instigating federal and judiciary interference with the commune's practices. This time, the Oneidans did not face their adversaries united. Noyes was informed that several of the opposition within the commune were willing to cooperate with the persecution.[41]

It was a new situation which might have had disastrous results. Many members could be faced with imprisonment and Noyes himself might be accused of adultery as happened before in Putney in the early days of the commune. Then they had withstood their trial valiantly, but now there were different circumstances, and John Humphrey Noyes felt that he could no longer rely on all his comrades to stand united. He chose to listen to the advice of some of his closest friends, and on the night of June 20, 1879 Noyes secretly left Oneida and took the train to the Canadian border near Niagara Falls, outside the jurisdiction of New York State.[42]

His place of exile was kept secret even from Oneidans. His followers kept in touch through a go-between who delivered Noyes's instructions for the commune. The inner fabric of the commune was no longer intact. Tension mounted and Noyes reached the conclusion that there was no hope to protect the unique economic and family structure of Oneida, which could only prosper in an atmosphere of trust and unity, and he searched for a way of retreat and compromise. He was informed that although the sections within the commune were fighting with each other, they were far from wishing to dissolve the commune, which to them represented home and all things dear. But it was evident that the situation was desperate.

On August 26 the heads of the community received from its exiled leader a message advocating a peaceful retreat from its social policies: "I propose that we give up the practice of complex marriage not as renouncing belief in the principles and prospective finality of that institution, but in deference to the public sentiment which is evidently rising against it." He went on to advise his followers to adopt "Paul's Platform, which allows marriage but prefers celibacy." Noyes's advice came at a moment when it was urgent to release the pressure which could explode communal life.[43] As for continuing their communism, he proposed: "We shall hold our property and business in common, as now. . . . We shall live together in a common household and eat at a common table as now." Noyes hoped that "it will be a good and graceful thing to relieve them [Oneida's neighbors and well-wishers] at last from the burden of our unpopularity, and show the world that Christian communism has self control and flexibility enough to live and flourish without Complex marriage."

The commune accepted Noyes's proposal and quickly reverted to monogamous marriage practice. It suggests that most young members had all along hoped to return to the accepted norms. Abolishing complex marriages also showed Noyes to be an adroit tactician, and that his antagonists and the church had no cause to continue its crusade against Oneida. It also affected their periodical the *Socialist*, whose readership quickly diminished. There seemed to be no sense in continuing to invest in their propaganda efforts.[44]

The combination of retreat from complex marriage, the return to a monogamous family system, and at the same time maintaining the integrity of the community based on economic communalism, did not work. The internal cohesion that had been undermined and the acquisitive instincts that were acutely manifested among the newly established families prevented the functioning of the commune as envisioned by John Humphrey Noyes's proposals. Soon voices clamored to retreat from communism as well.[45]

Theodore Noyes raised the subject at a meeting of the commune's council. He claimed that members had lost their convictions which had served to forge them into one unity. A commune without this unifying doctrine was not viable, in fact it was harmful, because it curtailed the individual's freedom. The self-restraint without internal conviction might become a sort of coersion.[46] Most of the young people supported Theodore Noyes. There were two additional factions: one which clung to John Humphrey Noyes and included mainly the old members who wanted to continue as before, and the other, led by Towner and some of Hinds's followers, that insisted on the communal way and complex marriage without Noyes's charismatic leadership.

The commune soon became a hotbed of dissension which threatened the very existence of Oneida. The council was powerless and John Humphrey Noyes could not be reinstated.[47] His voice still carried conviction, and he was involved in all the developments, receiving information through members' letters and messengers who came frequently to hear his advice. His open letters were read out at public meetings and listened to attentively. In December 1879 John Humphrey Noyes advised Oneidans to strive to achieve an agreement on the future of the commune even if this signified a retreat from the communal way of life. His open-mindedness was greeted by the whole community with a feeling of relief. The danger of an immediate schism seemed to be over.[48]

During the winter, dissension again threatened the future of the commune. The Towner-Hinds camp was adamant not to alter any of the communal proceedings, whether in production or consumption. They threatened to secede if any principles were revised. On the other hand, the young members, led by Theodore Noyes, continued to demand changes in the economic structure, to abolish the commune, and to establish a holding company that would collectively maintain production and property. John Humphrey Noyes preached tolerance and searched for a solution that Towner's group would accept. His letters seemed to support the young people's attitude, which he believed were those of the majority. There was no way back and if the prevalent atmosphere was for change, this had to be adopted, and thus save the commune from complete disintegration.[49]

The oldtimers now supported Theodore Noyes and the Towner-Hinds camp found themselves isolated. A schism was imminent in the spring of 1880, when in addition to the ideological discussions, social discord threatened. This developed over collective education, which had been undermined when the complex marriage was abolished, and some of the new families chose to accommodate their children in their homes and return them to the children's house every morning.[50] The result was an undermining of the principle of communal education. The characteristic discipline of the children's houses suffered, and the member in charge of education, G. Kelly, one of John Humphrey Noyes's faithful followers, abdicated after accusing Towner bitterly. Some of his accusations were rooted in the near past, when Towner had attempted to undermine Noyes's leadership. This struggle, overshadowed by past controversies, deepened the rift between Towner's camp and the majority at Oneida. Tensions mounted and it again seemed that a schism was imminent, but another letter of Noyes, in which he clarified that he had no intention of taking over the leadership and cause the removal of the opposition, calmed the troubled waters, and the Towner group agreed to compromise. A search for an acceptable solution was started.

Hinds proposed a committee of six, two from each of the sections, whose task would be to find a solution that could save Oneida. He went so far as to say that he would accept any solution even if it meant giving up some communal aspects of their life.[51] His proposal was accepted, and the elected committee began its meetings in July 1880. In one of its first meetings the deterioration of the commune was outlined. They had already established that: (1) there was no longer any discipline; the fabric of communal life no longer held together; (2) about one-half of the population no longer believed in perfectionism or in Noyes's leadership; (3) the social ideological deterioration affected Oneida's economy, work hours were haphazard, their income had steadily diminished, and the earnings of the industrial plants had gone down drastically and debt was accumulating; and (4) the young generation was affected even more, as some had completely discarded communal practices and even privately bought riding horses, paying with the commune's cash.

It was evident that a way must promptly be found to halt the process of internal disintegration that was undermining the commune's foundations. The committee proposed several alternatives but could not agree on any. They decided to consult John Humphrey Noyes, and a mission was urgently sent to his retreat near Niagara Falls. The severe situation was set before him, and Noyes, who feared the dissolution of the commune if some of the members went to court with their demand to divide the property, came up with his own proposal. He suggested an independent intermediary who would decide which of the proposals were viable. The committee agreed, but it soon became evident that there was no need to apply to an independent intermediary. Theodore Noyes had come up with a detailed plan for a holding company which would maintain the community's unity and allow those circles who preferred it to continue as a commune. It was a compromise that answered the cardinal demands of all the groups. Its advantage was that there would be no need to rely on external intervention. When John Humphrey Noyes heard of his son's proposal he agreed to support it, relieved that no intermediary was required after all.[52]

In August 1881 the committee formulated a detailed plan based on Theodore Noyes's plan, taking into account the requirements of all the population of Oneida. Towner's attempt to doubt its legality failed. On August 31 the public meeting, which included all adults and children, was called upon to accept the proposal to divide the property and to reorganize. They all realized the fatefulness of the moment. After months of deliberations there was general agreement, only a few objected to the proposals. Immediately after the meeting a contract was drawn, signed by each and every member of Oneida.[53]

On September 1, 1880, 203 members agreed to organize and divide their property. Oneida was now The Oneida Holding Company, Ltd. Their new statutes specified that the property be divided according to seniority and the amount every member had invested when joining the commune. There were further bitter discussions, but at the end, under Noyes's influence, almost full consensus was achieved. Only Sewell Newhouse voted against the agreement, while several others, among them Towner, abstained.

The system agreed upon divided their assets into 24,000 shares, each valued at $25. Every adult received $60 in cash and shares valued at 50 percent of the amount he had invested on joining Oneida, and 4.25 shares for each year of membership from the age of sixteen. Every child received $100 for each year of his life and $200 on reaching sixteen, for further education. Members had other definite advantages: (1) the right to work in any of Oneida's industry; (2) the right to live in the company's houses at a low rent to cover expenses; (3) the right to buy at wholesale prices from their stores; and (4) the right to use the kitchens and other public conveniences, like the concert hall, reading room, library, gardens, etc. The society agreed to support the children, the old, and the sick through a pension scheme and a fund that would see to the children's education up to sixteen, and support those who wished to continue their studies.[54] The agreement specified a system of management which was to go into effect immediately after signature of all members.

Everyone attested to their feeling of enthusiasm and willingness to make the new economy work. For many, though, the use of money for the first time after thirty years of absence from a capitalist economy was an embarrassing experience. Oneida Company was now a unique holding company whose members were a closely knit community and whose management represented the whole congregation. In January 1881 members received the shares, the property was divided, and the new arrangement went into effect.[55]

John Humphrey Noyes did not return to Oneida even then. The aged man remained in his exile on the Canadian border. He contemplated his failure to establish a daring religious and social experiment. He comforted himself somewhat by saying that they had toured *terra incognita*, drawn its maps, and returned without loss of life.[56]

The establishment of the holding company brought relief from the tension that had troubled Oneida, but unity was not maintained long. In 1882 the Towner group seceded to California, where they established a community near Los Angeles. In the 1880s there were additional secessions, mainly from second generation Oneidans who left to make their way in the world.

During the whole troublesome period contact was maintained with their aged leader. The community regarded themselves responsible for his well-being, and several of the oldtimers joined him and lived with him, establishing a full communal partnership as in the past. In 1886 John Humphrey Noyes passed away at the age of seventy-six. He was buried in the Oneidan graveyard.[57]

In 1890 only about one-half of the members were left. Most of them lived in the mansion house which had been adapted to the new family set-up. Those who had no place there moved to a site that had formerly belonged to Oneida, and on it they established the Kenwood community.

When Noyes was no longer there to unite the Oneidans, the perfectionist belief also lost its power as a cohesive force. On the other hand, they were now united by their economic enterprises, and their affinity with the past traditions and their *esprit de corps* served them well. In the 1890s a new leader appeared, Pierpont Noyes, one of the founder's sons who had, together with a group of other young people, left Oneida after its dissolution and succeeded in the world of business. His keen attachment to his birthplace, family, and community made him return to Oneida after being absent for fifteen years. He immediately attempted to save Oneida from the severe economic difficulties that had been caused by mismanagement, and soon reached a position of leadership. In 1899 he was appointed general manager of the company enterprises, a position he would hold for many years.

Under his guidance the Oneidan enterprises moved into the industrial era, adapting to the pace of the rest of the country. From 1911 through 1915 the silk factories and the trap and canning industries closed down because they showed no profit. Instead Oneida Silverware steadily developed into a prosperous industry with a country-wide reputation. Pierpont Noyes also devoted himself to rehabilitating the community's social relationships, and especially tried to attract some of the second generation ex-members. In addition to material prosperity he promised them satisfying and valuable jobs and tried to revive their belief in the uniqueness of Oneida—the community with a utopian vision.

In those years Edward Bellamy's ideas on cooperation gained momentum and found an echo also in Oneida. But it soon transpired that there was no way back to a communal life of radical socialist religion. Affluence and middle-class ways and mores had replaced the ideals of an earlier era. Besides, many workers in the area were now dependent on Oneida's industries, and not one of the members considered the possibility of sharing their lives with the workers.

There were two separate communities which later developed into two separate local councils: Kenwood and Sherril. Pierpont Noyes introduced a system of social welfare for the workers who in addition to high salaries also received tuition for their children, adult education, etc. Still, they were isolated in their own separate community.[58] In Kenwood, some cultural activities developed. In 1911 they celebrated John Humphrey Noyes's centennial. The admiration and esteem for his personality and leadership were expressed both orally and in writing, but were entirely based on nostalgia and lacked any serious intention to reaffirm his doctrine.

A clear expression of Oneidans' affinity to the past was the undertaking by the industrial company, Oneida Ltd., to preserve the site as an historical monument. The mansion, its rooms, and library have been extremely well maintained, and so have most of the archives, although some of the diaries and private letters of commune members seem to have disappeared mysteriously. Perhaps Oneida's heirs were worried about disclosing too much of their controversial practices.

I chanced to visit the historic site in 1981 and was overcome by the impressive structure that was still intact and well maintained a hundred years after the dissolution of the commune. Wandering through corridors of the mansion, which could vie with any of the European palaces, brought to mind many chapters that had been beautifully described by members in their reminiscences. I met some of the descendants and was impressed by their spontaneous and open-hearted conversations. They did not have any inhibition to speak of their odd ancestry and their complex family tree. Some of them told me that they were collecting the letters and diaries of their forefathers with the aim to publish them.

Of special interest was my meeting with Mrs. Leslie Stone, John Humphrey Noyes's granddaughter, a dynamic and lively lady. In spite of her advanced age she guided me through all the mansion's wings and was glad to hear of my interest in the history of Oneida: "It is important that our generation learn about my grandfather,'' she said. ''He was far ahead of his times in recognizing the advantages of communal life, and in freeing the women, especially from the bondage of the monogamous family.'' Throughout my visit I was imbued with a spirit of reverence to Oneida's heritage, which was clearly manifested in the attitude of descendants toward their ancestors' controversial past and the maintenance of the impressive mansion house.

Notes

1. Alexander Kent, ''Cooperative Communities in the United States,'' *Bulletin of the Department of Labor* 35 (July 1901):598.
2. Robert Allerton Parker, *A Yankee Saint: John Humphrey Noyes and the Oneida Community* (New York: Putnam, 1935), p. 18; Louis J. Kern, *An Ordered Love! Sex Roles and Sexuality in Victorian Utopias—The Shakers, The Mormons, and the Oneida Community* (Chapel Hill: University of North Carolina Press, 1981), pp. 208-12; Spencer C. Olin, ''The Oneida Community and the Instability of Charismatic Authority,'' *Journal of American History* 67, no. 2 (September 1980):287; Robert D. Thomas, *The Man Who Would Be Perfect* (Philadelphia: University of Pennsylvania Press, 1977), pp. 14-17.
3. *Perfectionist* is the general term applied to Protestant groups that appeared in the United States in the first half of the twentieth century. These groups included followers who had formerly belonged to various denominations such as Methodists, liberal Calvinists, and Mysticists who believed in inner illuminations. They had seceded from the established churches and were called ''Free churches.'' All had one thing in common, namely the notion that man could overcome his inferior position caused by the Fall and Original Sin and reach personal perfection by faith and through ''inner illumination.'' The roots of perfectionism go back to early Christianity and the belief in the Kingdom of Heaven. This doctrine returned in several periods of Christianity. The impetus in nineteenth-century United States was given by the Methodists who acknowledged man's ability to improve his way of life and achieve a higher state of perfection through Christian love, which would enable him to reach perfection if only in the hereafter. In the early nineteenth century the revivals influenced circles and groups of people to believe in moral perfectibility to such an extent that it would free them from sin. Among them were, on the one hand, extremists who sanctioned every arbitrary and unrestrained behavior, and on the other, groups such as the Shakers who accepted all kinds of limitations and restrictions in order to be purified. Noyes definitely rejected those groups that sanctioned a life of sin. Thomas, pp. 22, 28, 39-40; Olin, pp. 288-90; Lawrence Foster, *Religion and Sexuality: Three American Communal Experiments of the Nineteenth Century* (New York: Oxford University Press, 1981), pp. 76-77.
4. Thomas, p. 47; Foster, p. 78.
5. Thomas, pp. 78-79; Parker, pp. 30-38; William Alfred Hinds, *American Communities and Cooperative Colonies* (1878. Reprinted and enl. Philadelphia: Porcupine, 1975), pp. 157-63; Maren Lockwood Carden, *Oneida: Utopian Community to Modern Corporation* (Baltimore: Johns Hopkins University Press, 1969), pp. 1-9; William Hepworth Dixon, *A New America* (London: Hurst & Blackett, 1867), p. 5; Constance Noyes Robertson, ed., *Oneida Community: An Autobiography, 1851-1876* (Syracuse: Syracuse University Press, 1971), pp. 1-6.

6. Parker, p. 44; Foster, pp. 79-81; Thomas, pp. 87-90; Kern, pp. 214, 239.
7. George Wallingford Noyes, ed., *John Humphrey Noyes, The Putney Community* (Oneida, New York: Oneida Press, 1931), pp. 3-8.
8. Parker, p. 60; Kern, p. 215; Foster, p. 82.
9. Parker, p. 64; Foster, p. 84; Thomas, pp. 91-96.
10. Foster, pp. 82-86; Thomas, pp. 96-98, 125-27; Robert S. Fogarty, "The Oneida Community, 1848-1880: A Study in Conservative Christian Utopianism" (Ph.D. dissertation, University of Denver, 1968), pp. 105-25.
11. George Wallingford Noyes, pp. 68-73; Parker, p. 96; Foster, p. 87; Hinds, pp. 168-69, 170-72; John McKelvie Whitworth, *God's Blueprints: A Sociological Study of Three Utopian Sects* (London: Routledge and Kegan Paul, 1975), pp. 108-9.
12. Foster, pp. 88-92; John Humphrey Noyes, *History of American Socialism* (1870), reprinted as *Strange Cults and Utopias of Nineteenth-Century America* (New York: Dover, 1966), pp. 626-27. Thomas, pp. 98, 106-11; Parker, pp. 65-68; Dixon, pp. 34-35; Kern, pp. 208, 217-18.
13. Foster, pp. 94-98; Thomas, p. 98; Parker, pp. 65-69, 119; Dixon, pp. 34-35; Robert H. Lauer and Jeanette C. Lauer, *The Spirit and the Flesh: Sex in Utopian Communities* (Metuchen, N.J.: Scarecrow Press, 1983), pp. 80-82, 133-41.
14. Parker, pp. 105-13; Foster, pp. 99-100; Robertson, *Autobiography*, pp. 10-11; Whitworth, pp. 106-8; Hinds, p. 177; Carden, pp. 17-22.
15. Robertson *Autobiography*, pp. 11-12; Whitworth, pp. 116-17; Hinds, pp. 176-80; Kern, pp. 207-08.
16. Carden, pp. 22-26; Fogarty, *Oneida Community*, pp. 204-06.
17. Dolores Hayden, *Seven American Utopias; The Architecture of Communitarian Socialism*, 1790-1795 (Cambridge, Mass.: 1976), pp. 206-07.
18. Whitworth, pp. 120, 142-49; Parker, pp. 161-73; Robertson, *Autobiography*, pp. 13-14.
19. Hinds, p. 183; Whitworth, pp. 148-49; Parker, p. 176; Foster, p. 103.
20. Fogarty, *Oneida Community*, pp. 206-12.
21. Parker, pp. 190-94; Carden, pp. 86-87.
22. Parker, pp. 178-89; Foster, pp. 111-15; Carden, pp. 80-84; Robertson, *Autobiography*, pp. 260-67.
23. Whitworth, pp. 148-51; Foster, p. 115.
24. Parker, p. 207; Carden, pp. 37-45.
25. Carden, pp. 77-80; Robertson, *Autobiography*, pp. 215, 226-29; Parker, pp. 212-13.
26. Robertson, *Autobiography*, pp. 215, 224, 226.
27. Ibid., p. 52; Whitworth, p. 151.
28. Hayden, pp. 188-219.
29. Parker, pp. 244-52.
30. Whitworth, pp. 138, 146-47, 154; Parker, pp. 210-11.
31. Whitworth, pp. 147-48, 154; Fogarty, *Oneida Community*, pp. 187-96, 200-201.
32. Parker, p. 257; Kern, pp. 233-34; Foster, pp. 118-20; Whitworth, pp. 127-30; Carden, pp. 61-65; Constance Noyes Robertson, *Oneida Community: The Breakup, 1876-1881* (Syracuse: Syracuse University Press, 1972), pp. 22-24.
33. Kern, p. 251; Robertson, *Autobiography*, pp. 173-76; Rosabeth Moss Kanter, *Communes: Creating and Managing the Collective Life* (New York: Harper & Row, 1973), p. 365; Pierepont Noyes, *My Father's House: An Oneida Boyhood* (London: John Murray, 1937), pp. 88-112.
34. Parker, pp. 253-64; Foster, p. 119; Kern, pp. 243, 250, 252-53; Robertson, *Autobiography*, pp. 335-50.

35. On the undermining of the status of John Humphrey Noyes because of physical weakness and loss of his voice see Whitworth, p. 15; Parker, pp. 260-64; Fogarty, *Oneida Community*, pp. 24, 44, 50; Robertson, *Autobiography*, pp. 24, 44, 50; Carden, pp. 89-91; Olin, pp. 292-93; Robertson, *Breakup*, pp. 15-21, 22-24.
36. *American Socialist* 1, no. 1 (March 1876).
37. Parker, pp. 274-75; Whitworth, pp. 140, 153, 160-61; Carden, pp. 92-96; 85-86; Robertson, *Breakup*, pp. 48-65.
38. Olin, pp. 293-96; Kern, p. 247; Carden, pp. 99; Pierepont Noyes, pp. 113-18.
39. Robertson, *Breakup*, pp. 94-95; Whitworth, pp. 148-49, 153-60; Parker, pp. 268-74; Carden, pp. 98-101.
40. Hinds, pp. 204-8.
41. Robertson, *Breakup*, pp. 76-110; Carden, p. 101; Whitworth, pp. 157-58; Hinds, pp. 204-8.
42. Pierepont Noyes, pp. 151-63; Robertson, *Breakup*, pp. 110-20; Olin, p. 296; Carden, pp. 102-3.
43. Olin, p. 296; Carden, pp. 102-103.
44. Whitworth, pp. 140-41, 160-62; Parker, pp. 285-88; Robertson, *Breakup*, pp. 123-56, 160-65, 186; Hinds, p. 210; Kern, p. 279; Pierepont Noyes, pp. 163-70.
45. In his book Pierepont Noyes states that the abolishment of complex marriage was a direct cause of the breakup of the community. See Pierepont Noyes, p. 170.
46. Robertson, *Breakup*, pp. 200-205.
47. Olin, p. 287.
48. Robertson, *Breakup*, pp. 207-11.
49. Ibid., pp. 220-24.
50. Pierepont Noyes, p. 164.
51. Olin, pp. 299-300; Robertson, *Breakup*, pp. 262-79.
52. Robertson, *Autobiography*, pp. 289, 291, 296.
53. Pierrepont Noyes, p. 175, Robertson, *Autobiography*, pp. 301-3; Carden, p. 104.
54. Pierrepont Noyes, p. 181; Whitworth, p. 162; Hinds, pp. 214-21.
55. Parker, pp. 288-301; Robertson, *Breakup*, pp. 217-301; Carden, p. 109; Pierrepont Noyes, pp. 166-84; Hinds, pp. 221-31.
56. Shalom Wurm, *Communal Societies and Their Way of Life* (Tel Aviv: Ayanoth, 1968), p. 257 (Hebrew).
57. Foster, p. 121.
58. Carden, pp. 188-212.

8

Icaria: The Socialist Immigrant Communes

During the 1840s new immigrant groups reached the shores of the United States with the intention of establishing communitarian units in the New World. These groups were different from the preceding ones; they did not emerge from persecuted religious sects but from socialist and communist organizations that had been involved in radical political activities in Europe. Their members were inspired by utopian theories designed to change the social reality through the establishment of model settlements. The most renowned of the European socialist circles reached the port of New Orleans early in 1848. They were disciples of the French utopian Etienne Cabet[1] and followed their leader's call to establish a communitarian society on the principles of his utopian novel, *Voyage en Icarie*.[2] Before arriving in the United States they had been politically active in France since 1840.

Etienne Cabet had aspired to legalize his political activities and to achieve the collaboration of various social circles and classes in France. He was also against the use of violence and opposed revolutionary activities. Nevertheless, under the prevailing circumstances in France after 1840 when social problems were acute, the authorities cracked down on his movement, which was suspect of being communist and radically revolutionary. Oppressions and persecutions were inflicted against them. Yet, Cabet abstained from violence and insisted on nonviolent propaganda. The most efficient and widespread among those was his utopian novel and its impact on the French public; it was published in five editions between 1842 and 1847.

An additional platform for his propaganda efforts was the weekly *Le Populaire*, which appealed to the masses and included short, simple articles filled with messages and slogans that were easily understood. It was widely read and in 1846, with 4,500 copies, was regarded as one of the most popular radical weeklies. It also attracted a readership that formed the core of Cabet's followers who were called Icarians. Icarian cells were to be found mostly in the industrial areas in France and included mechanics and established workers rather than members of the lower classes.[3] In 1844-45 their number grew steadily, and the Icarians outweighed the other radical opposition parties which at the time included Saint Simonists, Fourierists, Proudhonists, and the followers of Louis Blanc. An estimated number of 100,000 followers read the literature of Etienne Cabet at that time.[4]

During 1845-46 a tendency of secterianism was noticeable among the Icarians, prompted by a combination of internal and external factors. Their utopian ideology, which demanded radical social change, conflicted sharply with their nonviolent political convictions. Those did not provide effective methods of changing French society and politics. Moreover, the Icarians were more isolated than other radical parties, the liberals regarded them as too radical while socialists and other revolutionary parties ignored them because of their absolute rejection of violent reactionary activities to overthrow the ruling classes. Under these circumstances their internal cohesion was reinforced and a tradition of regular meetings, ideological discussions, and social cultural activities developed.

A sectional ethos came into being which was gradually invaded by religious, messianic elements. The affinity with early Christianity which had always been present in Cabet's doctrine, now increased. In 1846, a time of deep economic and social crisis in France, the Icarians were convinced that their message would bring salvation and that Cabet was the Messiah.[5] Still, maintaining a realistic approach they realized that the Old World was no place to establish a new society. They opted to search for an alternative in the New World, in which there were still wide-open spaces for settlement.

This was the background for the surprising manifesto which was published by Etienne Cabet in *Le Populaire* on May 9, 1847. Its headline was: "Workers Let Us Proceed to Icaria." In it he explained to his followers that because they had been persecuted as communists in France they had no alternative but to leave en masse the old and decaying Europe in order to be honorable citizens and human beings. He called on his followers to emigrate to the United States and establish settlements in the new territories. He estimated that about 20,000 would follow his call and establish a foundation for the model nation of Icaria, in which life would proceed according to his utopian principles—"each for all and all for each," and "from everyone according to his ability to everyone according to his needs." Cabet concluded his address, promising his followers to join them in this endeavor: "I will go with you, I will participate in your condition: I will be fed, clothed, lodged and treated as yourselves without any other privilege than that of being burdened with the greatest portion of care, watchfulness and responsibility."[6]

The reactions to the pamphlet were diverse. His socialist rivals regarded it as an expression of despair and a desertion from the political and social struggle in France. The newspapers were filled with vile criticism. Even his followers, especially the oldtimers, were critical, and some of them left the party as a result of its sudden altered directions. On the other hand many of his followers, especially the newcomers, accepted the challenge of emigration, and in the summer of 1847 *Le Populaire* was inundated by a flood of letters from followers who pleaded to be accepted as candidates.

Cabet's reaction to this ''massive demand'' was to work out a program of selection which he called ''social charter'' and which was in fact a contract to join the Icarian community. In it he formulated some of the principles of the new community, including the conditions for being accepted in the circle of ''the chosen'' on the basis of ''quality over quantity.'' He proposed to elect himself as ''gerant unique,'' the only manager for ten years, and to grant himself sole authority. This, he argued, was his due because of the deep trust his followers felt for him, and because he could devote himself utterly to serve the community without seeking personal gain. The paragraphs that dealt with membership stated explicitly that on joining the community all private property was to be handed over to the general purse. Those who left would not be recompensed but would receive a generous grant. Cabet was aware of the severity of these conditions but wanted to warn the new candidates to be certain of their decision. If in doubt they should reconsider and stay at home, because they were interested only in strong-willed people of conviction.[7]

In September 1847 Cabet went to London to seek the advice of Robert Owen, who had established a utopian settlement in the United States. There he contacted a large American real estate company (Peter's Company that was selling land in Texas, which had just joined the Union and was interested in attracting settlers). He understood that he had bought 1 million acres on condition that by July 1848 a settlement would have materialized.[8] From among the hundreds who had volunteered to settle in Texas Cabet chose sixty-nine. On February 3, 1848, three weeks before the revolution broke out in France, a pioneer group left Le Havre for New Orleans. They had all signed the treaty, promising to adhere to communism and to obey Cabet's instructions for the next ten years in which he would be their sole manager, even though he was not going out with them.[9]

On disembarking in New Orleans they heard about the revolution in France and five returned home right away. The others adhered to their original plan and proceeded up the Red River, close to where Dallas is situated today. After a trek full of hardships they finally arrived there in May, only to discover to their dismay that instead of 1 million acres they had acquired only 100,000 and even those were subdivided into 320 acre plots and not adjoining. This fact would abolish any attempt to establish a communal settlement as planned.[10]

In spite of their disappointment the pioneering group insisted on adhering to their mission. They began to build log huts, which according to their contract had to be constructed by July 1, and finished the first thirty on time. However, their travails were not over and in the same month an epidemic of malaria felled many of the pioneers, and four died. In addition their doctor went mad, and they realized their lack of experience with the farming conditions in the area. All this, together with their sense of isolation, prompted them to leave the settlement in September and to proceed to New Orleans to meet their families and to save them the disappointment and the travails of the road.[11] On the way they met a group of newcomers en route to Texas who informed them about the fate of their movement in France. The revolution had brought new hope for social change in France and there was no longer any strong urge to emigrate overseas to establish a community.

Etienne Cabet's movement hit low ebb, but after the June Massacre of 1848 they became newly motivated and Cabet, who had remained in France throughout, reorganized his followers to join the Texas commune. Even the news of the pioneers' hardships did not affect them, and by the end of the year there were hundreds who willingly joined their leader on his way to settle in the United States. Several days before Napoleon III was elected president of France, the 60-year-old Cabet led 480 followers to Texas. They arrived in New Orleans in January 1849 and were met by members of his group who had stayed there to greet the newcomers. The first days were hard. They too were overcome by fever, and when several died about 200 decided to return to France, taking about one-third of their capital with them. Cabet and 280 loyal followers decided to proceed with their plans to establish a communitarian settlement in the New World.

Icaria in Nauvoo, Illinois

After the failures in Texas and Louisiana, they searched throughout the United States[12] and soon discovered Nauvoo, Illinois, a Mormon ghost town with many houses and public places for the commune's institutions. They did not have enough money to buy more than 800 acres of farmland and some of the houses but in spite of these limitations Cabet believed he had found the right place, with pleasant neighbors and good physical conditions.[13] After all the hardships the Icarians had undergone during the past year, conditions in Nauvoo seemed ideal. They began right away to lay the economic foundation, instilled with optimism and hoping they had reached their haven.

The Icarians were especially keen to reconstruct the deserted Mormon temple and to turn it into a public building that would serve the new commune spiritually and materially. A great effort was invested during the first two years; yet in June 1850 a storm destroyed the walls of the huge construction, putting an end to their hopes of using the physical foundations left by the Mormons. Nevertheless, they were not discouraged and continued to believe in the future of their settlement. Many applications for membership arrived from France and the pressure to find swift accommodations prompted them to give up their attempt to reconstruct the Mormon stone houses and adopt cheaper and faster methods. The forested area and the sawmill they had acquired provided building material. The first to be constructed was a central public building 120-feet long, 40-feet wide. On the ground floor were the dining-room, kitchen, and an assembly hall, while the upper floor housed families and singles.[14]

The monogamous family was strictly maintained in Icaria, but Nauvoo children were collectively educated. Babies remained with their parents until they were weaned and then were transferred to the children's house, where they spent most of the day under the care of those who were in charge. School children lived in separate houses for boys and girls. Children spent Sundays with their parents but could also see them at leisure during the week. Cabet was very interested in education, which he regarded as the means for creating a new person. Under his direction people were allotted work as educators and teachers, and he himself was involved and met with the pupils at lectures on ideological matters. The school provided not only an ideological education; a variety of subjects such as grammar, mathematics, geometry, history, geography, drawing, and music were taught. Because their native language was French, much time was devoted to the teaching of English, to speed up their process of becoming U.S. citizens.

The children's day was divided between studies and work. Boys worked in the fields and workshops while girls helped in the kitchen and with housework. The educational institution expressed the broad cultural interest of the Icarians. Indeed, their cultural activities were varied. In the evenings they would meet in study groups and have ideological discussions or entertainment. The Icarians had brought many books from France, and a library of about 4,000—the largest in Illinois—served the community. Their orchestra of 50 musicians performed for the neighbors as well. These cultural activities accompanied and supported the social development of the prospering community.

New members kept arriving from France and Germany where a group of socialists, under the leadership of Whitling, had attempted to establish their own community; when they failed they decided to join Nauvoo in 1858.[15] In the population census of 1854 there were in Nauvoo 405 members, of whom 325 were French and 65 German. In 1855 their number increased to 500. Even so, there was a continuous stream of people coming and going; it is estimated that about 2,000 people had passed Nauvoo between 1849 and 1856.[16]

The economic conditions, which at the beginning had seemed to be so promising, were not sufficient to support the growing community. In those years new territories in the West were being opened up for settlement with governmental encouragement. Etienne Cabet decided to explore the possibilities and in 1853 sent a mission to tour the frontier areas of Kansas, Nebraska, and Iowa. In their report they suggested western Iowa, and in 1854 Cabet acquired 3,000 acres in Corning, Iowa. Soon the first group of about 20 pioneers set out West and began to clear the land for settlement.

Local conditions in Iowa were unsuitable for immediate occupation, and the Icarians continued their economic activities in Nauvoo. Means of production were limited. Farming was not profitable and was geared only to local consumption. The flour mill and distillery were not fully exploited because they lacked raw materials. Their forested countryside could have provided ample wood for the sawmill, but the Icarians, who had been laborers and artisans in French towns, found it difficult to get used to the hard labor of the wood cutter with his axe and hand-saw, under primitive conditions.

Their ideological convictions were of no help in overcoming hard conditions of labor in field and forest, and many faltered. The few who carried on could not make the ten economic branches in the settlement prosperous. In the carpentry shop, the shoemakers', the furniture factory, the men's clothing workshop, and in the printing press only men were employed. Only few places employed women—the laundry, a sewing shop, and flax weaving.[17] The Icarians were in debt and could only survive with the help of donations from France. The money was from a fund collected by Cabet's followers there and from membership fees advanced by new candidates. This way the community received thousands of francs which enabled them to proceed with their economic development, and after five years in Nauvoo it seemed that their collective effort was at last paying off.[18] While the material aspect seemed to be encouraging, their social and ideological well-being was not. To understand this process we have to look back at the early days in Nauvoo.

Quarrels and Schism

Etienne Cabet stayed in the settlement only a short while before he had to return to France in order to stand trial there. Some political adversaries had accused him of cheating his followers by falsely collecting money for a so-called settlement in the United States with which he absconded. Cabet returned to France equipped with proof from the state of Illinois and was acquitted. The victory over his political enemies raised his spirits and speeded up the rehabilitation of his movement. There were again prospects for growth and for additional settlements in the United States. His stay was prolonged in order to help his wife, who managed the central office in Paris. In 1852 Cabet returned from France encouraged by his legal victory, by the new prospects for his movement, and by the approval and sympathy he had encountered in the Owenist circles in London as well as from socialist ones in New York. He was greeted enthusiastically by his followers and spoke optimistically about the future of communism on both continents.[19]

Meanwhile the situation in Nauvoo had deteriorated. Factions had formed over ideological questions and over their attitude toward the commune. Not all members were equally committed to the principles of communal life. Many of the newcomers who had arrived in large groups in the early 1850s were ideologically and spiritually unprepared to withstand the pressures and the physical strain that communal life entailed. Furthermore, temptations from the prosperous neighborhood which had gradually developed around Nauvoo were too much for some, and the most industrious and talented members hoped to be successful outside the commune. Difficult questions on the limitations of communal rules on additional privacy and individualism were raised by some members. There were many cases of private property and unjustified absences from work. This was the situation when Cabet was urgently asked by some of his loyal followers to return to Nauvoo to put a halt to this deterioration.[20]

After his return Cabet was faced with tension and strife among the members and his leadership was undermined, threatening the whole venture. In France all Icarians had agreed to adhere to the principles of the commune and accept Etienne Cabet's absolute leadership. During the first years he had attempted to manage all Icarian affairs democratically, primarily in order to adapt to the Illinois constitution. However, when he discovered, on his return from France, that democracy had only served members to deviate from communal ways he decided to return to the authoritarian position he had held before. This tendency was violently opposed mainly by the young members who resented Cabet's interference in all matters. Tension mounted especially since the aged Cabet, concerned with the future of the commune, tended to become even more authoritarian and strict. Besides, he regarded an authoritarian leadership as vital for the success of the commune during the transition from capitalism to communism, and in his utopian novel the dictator-leader was named Icarus. From disagreements on their financial and economic affairs, matters deteriorated and encompassed disputes about clothing, their way of life, problems of work and personal affairs. But the most severe disagreement concerned freedom of speech.

There was an uprising against the oppression of free thought.[21] Cabet ignored the annually elected council which was supposed to balance his authoritarian leadership. Tension erupted in 1855 when he proposed changes in the constitution, namely to elect the leader and his second in command for a period of four years instead of one. He also proposed to grant the leader the power to demote any functionaries who were unacceptable to him. He explained the need for these amendments in the urgency to fight deviations in the commune within the framework of the constitution. Cabet estimated that not all members were mature enough for a communitarian democratic constitution and had exploited democracy to undermine its principles.[22]

His ideological campaign was fought with dictatorial means and enraged his opposition. He was completely in charge of the commune's media, the newspaper, the printing press and communication with the Paris office and could therefore impose his decisions without consulting even his closest friends. One decision concerned instructions to the Paris office to stop the immigration of new members until 1857, when he hoped to complete the reorganization. He also published defamatory notes against the internal opposition via the Paris office, causing public opinion in Nauvoo to rise against him. In May 1856 the public meeting discussed the activities of the office in Paris and decided to abolish it because of its one-sided partisanship. At the meeting it also transpired that most members opposed Cabet's policy and the deep schism concerning their leadership became evident.[23]

Instead of limiting the dispute to within the commune, Cabet, whose weakness became more pronounced with age, undertook to air it publicly and even proposed to split the commune. Furthermore, in an effort to divide the commune's property equally, he enlisted the help of the courts. Later, one of his loyal followers attempted to explain Cabet's dictatorial deterioration:

> Those who loved him and must find excuse for his actions thought the men who influenced him by their flatteries and tale-bearings were spies sent by the French Government to destroy Icaria. . . . However this may be, he began to be very arbitrary and soon asked to be made dictator for 10 years. This occasioned great dissension. Many stood by him simply through love and respect. Some few certainly had evil motives. The great majority opposed him but with regret, preferring to be true to the principles of independence he himself had taught them rather than to submit to dictation.[24]

A minor civil war ensued, and both sides used physical force. On August 3, 1856, Cabet's followers attempted to take over the printing press and dining-room by force. In the melle several were wounded and the police had to intervene.

It became evident that the schism between Cabet's followers and the majority of commune members was final. Proximity rather than healing the rift made it more acute. Many members who until then had not taken sides were so revolted by the internal violence that they left the commune. Emile Valet relates in his memoirs how the internal strife had undermined not only his trust in any of the two rival factions but also made him despair of the very ideal which had brought him to Icaria. He therefore decided to seek his luck elsewhere. He concluded bitterly: "We arrived at Nauvoo hoping to establish heaven on earth, instead we find that we have created hell."[25]

Cabet completely lost his head during the struggle over the commune. In his anger he misused his legal position and took over the books of the commune and its deeds for the new land acquired in Iowa. He also tried to undermine the economic viability of the majority. Life became unbearable, and it was mutually decided to split. The majority cast out the aged leader and founder of Icaria, and his followers, who were the minority, decided to leave with him and seek a new place where they could realize their ideals.

St. Louis, Missouri

On October 15, 1856 Cabet, along with 180 followers, left the Icarian community at Nauvoo.[26] It was a tragedy for all concerned, for the aged leader and his loyal followers as well as for those who stayed on and who regarded themselves as the realizers of the Icarian dream. Cabet and his followers set out to St. Louis, Missouri, and in the developing town they found work and accommodation. Soon after reaching St. Louis, on November 8, Cabet died of a heart attack. He was sixty-nine when, broken hearted, frustrated, lonely, and far away from his home and followers, the visionary and man of action succumbed to the hardships of the recent years and to the heart break and disillusionment of the schism and his commune.[27]

The small group who had followed Cabet were now orphaned and lost. They were faced with many difficulties. In St. Louis they could not find a suitable building for their communal life. Members had to disperse in different parts of the city. In spite of these limitations they insisted on maintaining their communitarian principles. They shared their income and after a while even established a communal kitchen and dining-room. The artisans among them worked at various jobs and made furniture for other members' apartments. Their inclination toward ideological propagandistic activities prompted them to publish a theoretical periodical, *Revue Icarien*. Attempting to stem the influence of the external society, they established an independent school for their children and ideological courses for adults. They were also successful economically, and in 1857, during a countrywide depression, their commune prospered.[28]

After a year and a half in the city they found a domain on the 28-acre farm of Cheltenham, six miles from St. Louis. Proximity to the city enabled some to continue working at their jobs there. At the same time they developed an independent farm and marketed their produce in the nearby city. In spite of this promising beginning, conditions were not auspicious for a communal settlement. The area was malaria infested and the high cost of land prevented them from enlarging their estate. However, they still had the financial and moral support of their friends in France. The Icarians there regarded the members of the Cheltenham community as Cabet's loyal heirs and were generous with their donations. This helped the commune to purchase a printing shop and renew the publication of ideological literature and propagandist material.

For several years the group maintained its stability and numbered about 150 members in 1858. Yet, the history of Icaria Nauvoo was repeated when, after several years of economic stability, a violent dispute erupted in the summer of 1859 over their decision to draw up a constitution. The minority demanded a democratic way of life while the majority, in keeping with their mentor's doctrine, demanded an authoritative leadership which, they believed, would prevent any deviation from the communal way of life. When the minority of 42 members realized that they were up against a zealous majority and that there was no chance to influence them, they seceded during the early stages of the dispute.

The majority stayed on at Cheltenham, existing as a commune. They were not strong enough to withstand the economic hardships that befell them. During the Civil War only 20 members remained there, and some of them preferred to enlist in the army of the North rather than stay on the disintegrating community. A further calamity was the closing of the Icarian office in Paris in 1860. Three years later Cabet's followers in France joined the Internationale, and the Icarian movement ceased to exist independently. Without the support from France the commune was dissolved on March 4, 1864. Those few who wished to remain in the area moved to St. Louis.[29]

Icaria-Corning, Iowa

The majority group of 250 members fared no better. They remained in Nauvoo for a short period after Cabet and his followers had left taking with them the account books and other legal documents of the commune as a "means of punishment." The economic situation deteriorated further, but contrary to expectations no ideological revision followed the unreasonable steps of the aged leader; in spite of the struggle and schism the Nauvoo commune members regarded themselves as loyal Icarians. They were led by two ideologists, Gerard and Marchand, who had both been among the founders of the Icarian movement in France.[30] The limitations of economic development in Nauvoo prompted the commune to speed up the transfer to their lands in Iowa, where a group of 18 members were clearing the land. They had to prove their ownership and, lacking the purchase deeds which Cabet had removed, they were faced with a prolonged lawsuit which they finally won. The land was theirs but the commune was heavily in debt. In 1857 the Nauvoo property was estimated at $60,000 while their debt was about $19,000. Yet they decided to move the commune from Nauvoo to Corning in Adams County as soon as possible, and in 1860 the whole community transferred to Iowa.

The pioneering group had managed to clear only 200 acres on which they erected log cabins to accommodate 30 families. They then began to farm the land and establish auxiliary branches, a flour mill, a steam-powered saw mill, and a printing shop. Conditions in the Midwest were harsh; there were no roads, and the agricultural settlement found it difficult to market their produce in the sparsely inhabited area. Some of the settlers gave up and left, and in 1863 there were only 35 left, including children. In spite of this crisis that was the year when matters improved.[31] In 1864 the Cheltenham commune had been dissolved and Icaria-Corning began to prosper.

Following the Civil War, farm produce was in great demand, and prices soared. This prosperity enabled the commune to invest in development; they bought large herds of sheep and cattle and with the income acquired additional land. They now owned 1,900 acres. The 1870s found Corning a variegated and prosperous farming community with improved living conditions. The sawmill was equipped with a modern steam engine that improved efficiency. They also established a large workshop for the repair of wagons.[32] As soon as they were affluent enough they decided to construct a central building which would include their dining-room and become the hub of the commune. Instead of the rickety log cabin they constructed a solid building. Below ground level they placed the kitchen and store rooms; on the ground floor they built the large and commodious dining-room with a special elevator to carry up the food and dishes. (The commune shared three daily meals and on several evenings and weekends the hall served for their cultural activities, entertainment, and public meetings.) The second floor accommodated the families, a sewing room, and a library.

Now that they had their cultural building they were not satisfied with the rough exterior of earlier times and were concerned with the aesthetic appearance of the settlement. A member artist decorated the dining-room walls with colorful murals, inspiring all with a feeling of well-being. Finally, the pioneers' log cabins were replaced with commodious wooden family houses, some of them semi-detached. The number of rooms was adapted to the size of each family. All houses formed a square around the central building. The commune improved its central laundry facilities, and the large brick building was provided with steam, as was the kitchen.

When in the 1870s the commune seemed to prosper they decided to embark on a propaganda drive to attract new members.[33] In a pamphlet prepared for that purpose they reported that the commune numbered 80 inhabitants who owned 2,100 acres, 700 of which were cultivated and the rest was wooded grazing land; they had a livestock of 600 sheep and a few hundred pigs; and they were the proud owners of a modern steam-powered flour mill. The report provided an address for those who wished to join the commune.[34] A great push forward was provided by the railroad, which opened up markets for their produce. Their income grew steadily, and the balance sheets of 1860-1878 (kept in the library of the University of Nebraska, Omaha), depict a significant improvement in their farming sales and an increase in their payment of income tax. The debts gradually decreased. In 1877 the population was 83, and about 50 new candidates applied for membership.

New candidates and members from other communes were frequent visitors, but only a handful stayed on. One of the reasons for their difficulty in absorbing new members was the language barrier, since most Icarians spoke French. Most of the new members were therefore immigrants from the French Icarian movement and some who had left Nauvoo and now returned "home."[35] The 1860s were the years in which their communal way of life crystallized. They meticulously adhered to the ideals of equality, cooperation, and democratic government. After the debacles of the earlier schism, they strove to establish a tradition of democratic management. The public meeting in which all men over 21 voted (women had no vote) was the sovereign institution. They strictly kept to the rules and "even the president could not sell a bushel of corn without being instituted by the public meeting."[36]

The state constitution did not recognize communal property, and the commune was required to register as a holding company in which each member owned shares valued at $400. Every new member had to hand over his entire property with which he would be credited if he decided to leave. The commune's constitution demanded of each member to contribute as much as he could and to execute all the orders of the commune's management.[37]

Simultaneously with the commune's economic and social prosperity cultural activities were developed. Their library had about 2,000 books, mostly in French. They established a drama circle and a choir which performed a real opera, inviting all their neighbors to attend. Their propaganda pamphlet was fairly successful, and in 1877 many people applied for membership.[38]

In spite of this optimistic description, the Icarian settlement in Iowa was fated to follow its sister communes, and while prospering economically, they began to deteriorate on the ideological and social level. This was the result of events in Europe, where the fall of the Paris Commune in 1871 caused some of its members who had managed to escape, to seek shelter with their socialist brothers in the far west, in Iowa. They brought with them a radical revolutionary spirit which instilled some of the young members with a new fervor.[39] The Icarians had maintained relations with French socialists, and French newspapers arrived regularly, but written reports were not as effective as the tales of war and fighting told by those who had escaped the Paris Commune.

Soon two camps emerged. On the one hand there were the oldtimers who, because of their age, were battle-weary and no longer sought political confrontations. They were immune to new influences and trends. On the other hand the young members aspired to instil Icaria with the new radical socialism. They demanded a real democracy in which women too would have the right to vote and wanted to add industry to the commune's enterprises. Modernization, they hoped, would attract many new candidates. The oldtimers regarded this demand of the younger members as a tactical move intended to undermine the oldtimers' majority and insisted on their traditional, limited absorption policy.

On hearing about the dispute, Icaria's friends from New York who had kept in close contact with the commune sent a commission to mediate between the two camps. Their efforts were in vain and the schism widened. In 1876 four French activists of the Socialist Internationale in New York applied for membership at Icaria. They hoped that as members they could help bridge the gap between the camps, and since both sides regarded them as potential reinforcements, they were accepted. Among them were Emile Peron and Arsene Sauva, who had gone to France to participate in the socialist activities there and had just returned to the United States. They immediately began to organize cultural and ideological activities, evening classes, and the Sunday school tradition was resumed its study of Cabet's writings. The social and cultural life on the commune, which had been dormant for some time, was revived.[40]

A year later both camps agreed to elect Arsene Sauva for president, hoping to improve the atmosphere. It soon transpired that there was no chance of success, because the young members were too determined to alter the face of Icaria, refused to listen to any proposals of compromise. At this stage they decided on a schism. Ironically, the renewal of ideological activities had brought about additional friction when the minority criticized the older generation for being apathetic and for having turned their backs on Cabet's doctrine. This attack relied in part on events from the past, and they even accused the oldtimers of being responsible for Cabet's secession from Nauvoo after they had renegaded on this ideology.

There was no way out of the conflict and the young members, who had taken the initiative, called for several public meetings to deal with the problem. The majority, out of consideration for the settlement, proposed that the minority leave, taking with them their share of the property. The minority demanded a different course, namely to split the community in two and to divide its property. Determined to get their way they organized separate committees and worked separately, and even had their own public meetings. They established two separate committees and economic entities, hoping that the majority would have to agree to a complete split up. As time passed things came to a head. Verbal violence developed into minor skirmishes and hostilities. Communitarian life further deteriorated, families stood divided, and old friends stopped talking to each other.[41]

The actual split came about through an incidental matter that had nothing to do with ideology. During the early days at Corning, when conditions had still been harsh, members were encouraged to tend their own private gardens near their homes. There they grew fruit, vegetables, and mostly vines. As soon as matters improved the commune decided to abolish the gardens, which had encouraged individuality and private enterprise and were adverse to communal way of life. The young members were upset when not everyone complied with the decision. The oldtimers were more tolerant and regarded the breaking of the rule as insignificant. The young claimed it to be a matter of principle and fought the private wine-owners with all their might. In 1877, when the wine harvest was being planned, the young members proposed to harvest the private lots first; the oldtimers objected. It was this decision that prompted the young members to secede and to divide the property.

As before, the period of separation was unpleasant in the extreme. Principles and customs were ignored. The young went so far as to enlist the help of the courts. On October 17, 1878 the verdict was given to divide the community in proportion to the number of members in each camp. The oldtimers, who were in the majority, were allowed to remain on the site, but for their own reasons they preferred to establish a new community on the eastern outskirts of Icaria.[42] The minority inherited the farm and all its buildings and called themselves *Young Icaria*.

Young Icaria

From its inception efforts were made to introduce in Young Icaria a way of life based on the radical principles which had caused the schism. The constitution formulated in 1879 was intended to maintain their communitarian doctrine and prevent any seceders' attempt to misuse it. In the introduction the commune's aim was clearly set out: to prove on the basis of their concrete daily experience that a communal way of life based on solidarity is feasible. The constitution specified explicitly all the principles which they had aspired to achieve in the past—the vote for women, abolishment of the presidency that might be the source of despotism, and a tighter relationship with the militant socialists movement. It also ensured that no single person or circle could take over the management of the settlement by a set of rules according to which committees were elected twice a year. The members insisted on complete communism, and all property was handed over to the commune.[43]

Until 1880 Young Icaria experienced a fairly difficult period. They had too few hands to cultivate their lands, the debts of this new-old settlement were heavy, and in order to repay them they searched for new sources of income and established a carpentry shop, a shoemaker, and a broom factory in the nearby town. Their efforts paid off and the prospects for the future seemed rosy. Their enterprises were profitable and the debts gradually diminished. The Icarians now had leisure for cultural activities such as the establishment of an orchestra. They also expanded their educational program and established a large, comprehensive school for Young Icarians together with the mother commune.[44]

Socially there was an improvement when new members were absorbed, and by the end of 1879 they numbered 80. Some of the newcomers were veteran socialists who had been among the periphery of Etienne Cabet's followers. Among them were Armande Dehay, the son-in-law of the renown socialist leader Jules Leroux, and Emile Peron, who had been among the oldtimers in Icaria and who was an autodidact and an outstanding teacher and educator at the school. Everything seemed to prosper, but it soon became clear that the pretensions of Icaria and their exaggerated expectations caused their downfall. Reality could not possibly reflect their dreams, and even though they aspired to be a large model commune they remained a small, isolated community, deeply involved in their own struggle to cultivate their land. As townsmen and active socialists none of them had ever grown used to the dreariness of a farmer's daily efforts, far away from the center of culture and political activity.

Soon secessions began and the first to go were some of the most prominent political members, among them Armande Dehay, who continued to search for a place in Texas or California in which he would establish a commune under more auspicious conditions and in a better climate.[45] These secessions caused the remaining Icarians to doubt their vision of a model settlement and disputes over matters big and small brought about a serious deterioration in the social framework of the community. Faults in the democratic management of the settlement prevented decision making, and the economy was paralyzed. Their ideal was tainted, and after a period of deliberations the Young Icarians decided to search for a new place of settlement with better climate and more favorable conditions to establish a prosperous community that would also fulfill their cultural aspirations.

In 1881 several missions set out to tour Tennessee, Louisiana, and California. At the same time a letter from their former comrades Dehay and the brothers Leroux arrived at Young Icaria. It said that they had acquired some land in Sonoma County in California and offered the Young Icarians to unite and form a community together. The letter was filled with enthusiastic descriptions of the landscape and the climate in California and they also mentioned the socialist perspective of a settlement close to San Francisco which at the time was the hub of socialist activities.[46]

In 1883, after the Young Icarians had realized that their chances in Iowa were slim, they gave in to the temptation to join their Californian comrades who had established the settlement of Icaria Speranza. Emile Peron was put in charge of selling the property in Iowa to raise funds to pay their debts as well as those of Speranza's.

When Icarians from Iowa arrived in California they found comfortable and promising conditions for settling in a fertile area close to San Francisco. They immediately started to develop their agriculture and planted fruit trees and a vineyard although they aspired to invest mainly in mining and industry. Again they paid special attention to their constitution and adhered to its rules. The name of their settlement expressed the union of Icaria and Speranza (after a book by Leroux).

The commune was organized as a joint stock company and not as a cooperation, which ensured the individual's liberty and prevented authoritarian management. General meetings were called only twice a year, and all adults, men and women over 21, participated in them. The commune was managed by five committees—work, consumption, education, trading, and accountancy committees. Property rules were more lenient than at Icaria. They could keep a limited amount of private property and personal effects and also receive presents from outside sources after giving an account about them. They did a yearly balancing of profits and losses and in case of a profit half of it was reinvested while the other half was divided among members as premium. They also introduced a different work system such as prizes for nonabsence from work. When they needed more hands they hired them.

Nevertheless, they were deep in debt and were eager to receive the money from their Iowa property. But Peron, who was supposed to remit the money, used the money to buy Normandy horses in France, intending to establish a stud farm in Speranza. He had done this without consulting anyone in Icaria-Speranza, and when it became known anger erupted. Close friends of the commune who had lent them some money and were expecting repayment were upset and sued the commune. In June 1886 the Corning court gave a verdict that the entire property of Icaria-Speranza was to be sold in order to pay their debts, and the rest was to be divided among the members. We have little information about the end of Icaria-Speranza. In July 1887 the *Altruist*, edited by A. Longly, carried an item about the dissolution of the commune.[47]

New Icaria

When Icaria split up in 1879 the majority moved to the northeastern end of their land and established New Icaria. They owned 1,100 acres of agricultural land, and in March they started to construct housing and service buildings. At the beginning conditions were harsh but the settlers were determined to overcome all difficulties, and in 1883 they had managed to repay most of their debts even though they lacked manpower. At the time they numbered 34, among them ten women and twelve children under age thirteen.

In 1884 Albert Shaw visited them and later wrote a comprehensive study about New Icaria. In it he enthusiastically described the cultural level he found on the commune: In the modest family house he found books and periodicals. The houses were situated in the middle of a tastefully planted park. Visitors were impressed by the educated members, who all knew English, but among themselves spoke fluent French.[48] The commune was managed by a democratically elected committee supervised by the public meeting. The president who headed the commune during the first period was E. Marchand, one of the Icarian oldtimers. He was a distinguished personality with a broad education and an impressive educational attitude toward the younger generation. Marchand was unique in that he had been for years the recognized leader of the commune who never aspired to rule.[49]

The New Icarians tried to achieve good relationships with the outside world. They did not isolate themselves and were even involved in national politics. At election time they usually supported the Republican party. Some of their members joined the army of the North during the Civil War. Their children were educated at the local school together with the Young Icarians. Most of the teachers were not commune members and came from outside. They had a large library of French books. Their periodical, *Revue Icarien*, was also in French.[50] The most serious difficulty of New Icaria was that its members were elderly, while most of the young people did not join the commune. Those who did aspired to the standard-of-living of the American farmers in their neighborhood. They lacked manpower even for the limited farm they ran, and they had to hire workers.

In spite of all the setbacks, the commune existed for sixteen years after the schism. But the aging community could not continue to be economically viable, and soon there was no one to take over the leading positions. Mary Marchand Ross, the former president's daughter wrote about the final years and dissolution of the commune in an article published in 1901 in the *Social Gospel*, the periodical of the Christian Community:

> In New Icaria there were not enough able bodied men to do all the farm work and they were obliged to hire strangers. This was not communism, besides there were not enough men to fill offices in the community. Mr. E. F. Bettannier had been elected president for 10 consecutive years after which my father was president for one year and he was followed again in office by Mr. Bettannier the last year of the existence of the colony. At the end of this administration Mr. Bettannier refused to serve any longer, and as my father was then over 80, he found the duties of office too laborious and refused. . . . As they could not elect an executive officer on February 3rd 1895 at the annual election, my father made a motion to dissolve the commune.[51]

His proposal was adopted. The oldtimers realized that they could not prevent dissolution, and the process was accomplished in a pleasant atmosphere. They all managed to make the transition to a private life satisfactorily. Most were well established in their new places and they were not embittered by their communal experience. Mary Marchand Ross kept in touch with many oldtimers from Icaria and wrote in her article that many of them had written to her that they missed their communal way of life of shared work and responsibility. They added that during those years they had never worried about the next day and had enjoyed the beauty of life without taking advantage of others. In her memoirs *Child of Icaria*, which was written many years later, she concluded her fond memories.

> We never thought that our failure was due to impractibility of its principles, but to the ignorance of the masses and the greed of the few who are able to rule the world for their interests alone, and our hopes still live for the advent of the Commonwealth of the World when all will have become enlightened and can say that no one can be happy unless all are as brothers living each for all and all for each.[52]

Notes

1. Etienne Cabet was born in 1788 in Dijon, France, to a family of artisans. He studied law, and after a short time of practicing as a lawyer he moved on to politics. During this period he was attracted to liberal opposition circles and the Carbonari who prepared the background and were involved in the 1830 revolution. In appreciation of his activities, the ''bourgois king'' Louis Philippe granted him the position of public prosecutor in Corsica. Cabet was dissatisfied with this job in the remote area and soon resumed his political activities in his home town. In 1831 he was elected representative to the National Assembly, where he was close to the radical Republicans. In 1833 he began to publish the weekly *Le Populaire*, which became the liberal Republican's platform for opposing the government. The sharp critical articles against Louis Philippe, who was accused of reneging on the principles which had made him king, brought the government's wrath on Cabet. In 1834 he was charged with subversive actions, arrested, and sentenced to an alternative of two years in prison or exile. He chose the latter and was exiled for five years in Britain. This period in London was the turning point in his life. His political and intellectual horizons expanded after he met liberals and socialists, among them Robert Owen, with whom he became friendly. At the same time it was his chance to study history and philosophy and thus got to read Thomas Moore's *Utopia*. Deeply influenced, he was inspired to write his own utopian novel, *Voyage en Icarie*, in which he expressed his newly formed political ideas. These were far removed from the liberal ones which had so far guided him. Cabet now adopted a doctrine that was a blend of utopian thought, communist ideas on government, and Jacobean attitudes toward political organization (rejecting the violent terrorist ways of secret organizations). Thus, on the eve of his return to France, Cabet's political doctrine crystallized into the foundation of a new political school of thought—the Jacobean utopian communism. In 1839 Cabet returned to France; shortly after his book *Voyage en Icarie* was published and well received. It had a wide circulation among workers, artisans, and the lower and middle classes. Cabet was encouraged by it and was filled with the belief that he had brought a new message to the political life in France. Influenced by the doctrine he had adopted in London, he drew up a plan centered around oral and written propaganda as the means for starting a mass movement with communist convictions. These masses were to be the voters who would democratically take over the government, and after that was accomplished, would elect a leader with absolute authority—in Cabet's own words ''a dictator''—who would lead society in the

period of transition to a communist regime. Christopher Johnson, *Utopian Communities in France: Cabet and Icarians, 1839-1851* (Ithaca: Cornell University Press, 1971), pp. 43-48, 59.

2. The structure and content of *Voyage to Icaria* is typical of most utopian novels: a journey to a remote place and an imaginary ideal social regime. In *Voyage to Icaria* the British Lord William Carisdall visits a far away and unique country, which since 1872 has had a communitarian government under the revolutionary Icarius, who dethroned the former rulers. After a 20-year transition period, he nationalizes all property and nature resources, introduces complete equality among the citizens, and establishes a communitarian democratic republic. The visitor Lord Carisdall goes on conducted tours, has long conversations with important people, falls in love with his host's daughter, and becomes a citizen of Icaria. He, however, returns to England to tell of his adventures and to preach the ideology of the new regime he has witnessed. Most of the book is devoted to realistic descriptions of the communitarian way of life in all its aspects, political structure, work, education, and family life. More's influence is evident and so are the communitarian principles of early Christianity. These are realized in Icaria through a strict regimentation; order and discipline are the foundations of the Icarian government. Glenn Negley and J. Max Patrick, eds., *The Quest for Utopia* (College Park, Md.: McGrath, 1971), pp. 555-78.
3. Ibid., pp. 82-83, 175-205; Etienne Cabet, *History and Constitution of the Icarian Community* (1917, Reprint. New York: AMS Press, 1975), pp. 219-20; Christopher H. Johnson, "Communism and the Working Class before Marx: The Icarian Experience," *American Historical Review* 76 (1971):650-60.
4. Johnson, pp. 99-108, 133-36, 145-58; Robert Sutton, "The Icarian Communities in America, 1848-1898," *Communities: Journal of Cooperation* 67 (Winter 1985):43-44.
5. Sutton, pp. 208-14, 233; Albert Shaw, *Icaria: A Chapter in the History of Communism* (1884. Reprint. New York: AMS Press, 1973), pp. 6-20; Emile Vallet, *An Icarian Communist in Nauvoo: Commentary by Emile Vallet* (Springfield, Ill.: Illinois State Historical Society, 1971), pp. 15-16.
6. "Community of Icarie," (London: F.I. Watson, 1847); *Cooperative Communities: Plans and Descriptions*. Eleven pamphlets, 1825-1847. (New York: Arno Press, 1972), pp. 1-3; Johnson, p. 238.
7. *Cooperative Communities*, pp. 7-9.
8. Cabet, pp. 220-21; Martha Browning Smith, "The Story of Icaria," *Annals of Iowa* 38, no. 1, 3d Series (Summer 1965):39; Odie B. Faulk, "The Icarian Colony in Texas," *Texana* 5 (1967):138-39.
9. Marie Marchand Ross, *Child of Icaria* (1938. Reprint. New York: Hyperion, 1976), pp.111-12.
10. Faulk, pp. 135-37; William Alfred Hinds, *American Communities and Cooperative Colonies* (1878. Reprinted and enl. Philadelphia: Porcupine, 1975), pp. 366-68; Morris Hillquit, *History of Socialism in the United States*, 5th ed. (New York: Dover, 1971), p. 135; Smith, p. 40; Vallet, pp. 16-17; Jane Dupree Begos, "Document: Henri Levi's 'The Perilous Voyage to Icaria' (1848)," *Communal Societies* 3 (1983):147-57.
11. *Icaria: Brief History of Icaria* (Icaria, Iowa: Icaria Press, 1880), p. 6.
12. Cabet, pp. 223-24; Smith, p. 40; Faulk, p. 137; Hillquit, p. 116.
13. Sherman B. Barnes, "An Icarian in Nauvoo" *Journal of Illinois State Historical Society* (1941):237; Shaw, pp. 48-49; Shalom Wurm, *Communal Societies and Their Way of Life* (Tel Aviv: Ayanoth, 1968), p. 163 (Hebrew).

14. Sutton, p. 45; Vallet, pp. 22-24.
15. The communitarian settlement Communia was established in northeastern Iowa by a group of German immigrants of socialist utopian (mainly Fourierist) convictions. After the first years of existing in economic and social difficulties they asked for help from the (German *Arbeiterbund*) Workingmen's League which had just been established in the United States. This is how in 1851 they formed relations with Wilhelm Weitling, the living spirit of the union. Through Weitling Communia received aid from the union funds which they invested in economic activities. Furthermore, the union papers opened a propaganda campaign in order to attract new members to the communal settlements. As a result of these relations Communia's social and economic life prospered and their numbers increased. But some of the newcomers were not ideologically motivated and soon friction and strife endangered the very existence of the commune. In the face of this threat, Wilhelm Weitling decided to quit his union activities and to move to Communia and take matters in hand. At first the members granted him complete administrative authority but after a while he realized that only a minority were prepared to accept this leadership. Matters deteriorated and internal strife increased, until in 1854 Weitling despaired and resigned from his post and left the commune. Others followed him and Communia gradually degenerated and was dissolved in 1859. Some of its members who had left in 1854 decided to continue their communal way of life and joined Icaria which was geographically and ideologically close. On the establishment of Communia and its history see Gary W. Armstrong, "Utopians in Clayton County, Iowa," *Annals of Iowa* 41 3d series (1971-73):924-36; George Schulz-Behrend, "Communia, Iowa—A Nineteenth-Century German-American Utopia," *Iowa Journal of History* 43, no. 1 (January 1950):27-54; Hillquit, pp. 144-50; Armstrong, pp. 928-30; Melvin J. Lasky, *Utopia and Revolution* (Chicago: University of Chicago Press, 1976), p. 110; Carl Wittke, *The Utopian Communist: A Biography of Wilhelm Weitling, Nineteenth-Century Reformer* (Louisiana: 1950), pp. 244-75.
16. Wayne Wheeler, Peter Hernon, and James H. Sweetlove, "Icarian Communism: A Preliminary Exploration in Historiography, Bibliography, and Social Theory," *Communes: Historical and Contemporary*, ed. Ruth S. Cavan and Man S. Das (New Delhi: Vikas Publishing House, 1979), p. 130; Shaw, p. 50; Smith, p. 41; Hinds, pp. 118-30; Barnes, pp. 237-38.
17. "Colonies Icarrienne," *Icariana*, (September 6, 1854), a collection of documents from the Library of the University of Nebraska at Omaha. Special Collections' Department (bounded in Israel: Library of Tabenkin Institute).
18. Vallet, pp. 25-29.
19. Shaw, p. 61; Hinds, p. 370.
20. Shaw, pp. 53-56; Barnes, p. 241; Vallet, pp. 33-34.
21. Wheeler, p. 131; Shaw, pp. 56-59; Vallet, p. 26; Cabet, pp. 233, 286; Sutton, p. 46; Everett Webber, *Escape to Utopia* (New York: Hastings House, 1959), p. 233.
22. Wheeler, p. 132; Shaw, p. 55.
23. Vallet, pp. 34-35.
24. Marie Marchand Ross, "Ventures in Idealism, II, Icaria," *The Social Gospel*, New Series 9, Whole No. 38 (April, 1901), p. 5.
25. Vallet, p. 36.
26. Etienne Cabet, "Farewell of Mr. Cabet and the True Icarians to the Inhabitants of Nauvoo," *The Center for Icarian Studies Newsletter* 6, no. 2 (Summer 1984):1-2;

Hillquit, p. 118; Smith, pp. 41-42; Shaw, pp. 59-61; Ruth A. Gallagher, "Icaria and the Icarians," *The Palimpsest* 2, no. 4 (April 1921):99-103.

27. Shaw, pp. 59-61; *Icaria, Brief History*, p. 7.
28. Shaw, pp. 67-70; Hinds, pp. 275-376.
29. Sutton, p. 46; H. Roger Grant, "Missouri's Utopian Communities," *Missouri Historical Review* 65 (October 1971):37.
30. Shaw, pp. 75-76; M.B. Smith, p. 42; *Icariana*, p. 8.
31. Vallet, pp. 37-38; Wheeler, p. 132; Shaw, p. 76; Hinds, p. 377; *Icariana*, pp. 6-7; Gallaher, pp. 103-5.
32. Charles Gray, "The Icarian Community," *Annals of Iowa* 6, 3d series (1903-1905):111; Lyma Tower Sargent, "The Icarians in Iowa," *Annals of Iowa* 41, 3d series (1971-1973), p. 960.
33. Ross, *Child of Icaria*, pp. 36-45.
34. Sutton, p. 47; "Situation of Icarian Community, 1877," *Icariana* (see note 17 above).
35. Sutton, p. 48; Wheeler, p. 133; Hinds, pp. 382-84; On the attempt of Alcander Longley to join Icaria see Hal D. Sears, "Alcander Longley, Missouri Communist: A History of Reunion Community and a Study of the Constitutions of Reunion and Friendship," *Bulletin of Missouri Historical Society* 25, no. 2 (January 1969):127; "The Icarian Community," *The Communist* 1, no. 1 (January 1868):7.
36. "The Icarian Community"; Ross, *Child of Icaria*, p. 86.
37. Sargent, p. 961; Roy W. Swanson, "Iowa of the Early Seventies as Seen by a Swedish Traveler," *Iowa Journal of History and Politics* 24, no. 4 (October 1925):573-81.
38. Sutton, p. 48; M.B. Smith, pp. 43, 52.
39. Wheeler, p. 133; Hillquit, p. 136; Gallagher, p. 107; *Icaria: Brief History*, pp. 10-11.
40. Shaw, pp. 98-100; M.B. Smith, pp. 53-54.
41. Ross, *Child of Icaria*, pp. 86-90; "Icaria," *American Socialist* 3, no. 7 (1878):52; "Icaria," *American Socialist* 3, no. 11 (1878):84; "Icarian Crisis," *American Socialist* 3, no. 37 (September 9, 1878).
42. Theodore Gorham, "Troubles in Icaria," *The Center for Icarian Studies Newsletter* 6, no. 2 (Summer 1984): 4-5; Shaw, pp. 100-108; Smith, p. 55; Gallagher, pp. 108-9; Ross, *Child of Icaria*, p. 99; Sargent, pp. 962-64; *Icariana*, p. 10-16; Wheeler, p. 134.
43. "Icarian Constitution," *Icaria: Brief History*, pp. 14-39; Shaw, pp. 129-30; Hinds, p. 387; Sargent, p. 965.
44. Smith, p. 58; *Icaria: Brief History*, pp. 12-13.
45. Robert V. Hine, *California's Utopian Colonies* (New Haven: Yale University Press, 1966), p. 64.
46. Hinds, pp. 388-90; Shaw, pp. 133-35; Hine, pp. 64-70.
47. Sargent, pp. 965-66; Hine, pp. 74-76.
48. Ross, *Child of Icaria*, p. 105; Sargent, pp. 964-65; Shaw, pp. 115-17; Herbert A. Wisbey, Jr., "Research Note: Rufus Rockwell Wilson's Tour of Five Utopian Communities in 1888," *Communal Societies* 3 (1983):145.

"There was not wanting something of a private home life in each of the humble cottages, in which one was sure to find books and papers. . . . The park upon which the cottages fronted had been laid out with some care and taste, and promised to be a charming place when the trees were grown. . . . The visitor could not fail to be impressed by the intelligence of every one, the pleasant and polite manners of the women, and the bright and pretty appearance of the children. . . . Most of the members can converse in English, but French is used exclusively in the community, and it is spoken with great accuracy and purity. The government is, of course, purely democratic.'' Shaw, pp. 115-16.

49. Ross, *Child of Icaria*, pp. 111.
50. Ibid., p. 129; Shaw, pp. 118-20.
51. Ross, *Child of Icaria*, pp. 113, 120, 125, 127; Ross, *Ventures*, p. 7; Smith, pp. 59-62; Gallaher, pp. 110-12; Barthinius L. Wick, ''Social and Economic Themes,'' *Midland Monthly* 3 (1895):375-76.
52. Ross, *Child of Icaria*, p. 142.

9

Victor Considerant and the Fourierists at La Reunion

In 1855, when the first schisms appeared among the followers of Etienne Cabet, another socialist group of immigrants arrived in the United States, hoping to establish a communitarian society there. The group was multinational and included French, Belgians, Germans, Swiss, and Swedes. They were all followers of the Fourierist school of thought who had assembled under the influence of Victor Considerant,[1] a disciple and spiritual heir of Fourier.

Victor Considerant landed in New York on December 14, 1852, and spent the first weeks after his arrival at the North American Phalanx in New Jersey. From there he set out to visit the Fourierists in New England and Boston and included a visit to Oneida. On his return he initiated a meeting with Albert Brisbane, and together they planned to renew Fourierist activities in the United States, starting with a propaganda campaign, reorganization, and then proceeding to the establishment of settlements. The most important result of this meeting was the proposal to establish a new Fourier settlement with European and American Fourierists which would serve as a model, to prove what could be achieved by correct planning and meticulous preparations.

In April 1853 the two set out to choose a site for the settlement. They opted for Texas because by then the eastern states were no longer open to new settlements, and land prices there were high. On the other hand, the Midwest, which was recently opened to settlements, suffered from a harsh climate and did not, according to them, have the optimal conditions for a model Fourier settlement.

Texas left a strong impression on Victor Considerant, and he was convinced that the potential to establish a center of Fourierist communities in the area was excellent. He hoped they would eventually influence other neighboring states. On his return to Europe in August 1853, Considerant summarized his impressions in two books; one was published in New York in English, *The Great West: A New Society and Industrial Life in Its Fertile Regions*, the other, *Au Texas*, was published in Paris in French.

He had aimed the language of the books at a readership among whom he hoped to find followers for his project. In the English book there are enthusiastic descriptions, such as:

> Nature has done all. All is prepared, all is arranged. We have only to raise those buildings which the eye is astonished at not finding; and nothing is appropriated nor separated by the selfish exclusiveness of civilized man; nothing is cramped. What fields of action! What a theatre of manoeuvres for a great colonization operating in the combined and collective mode! What reserves for the cradle of harmony, and how powerful and prompt would be its development. . . . A horizon of new ideas, new sentiments and hopes, suddenly opened before me, and I felt myself baptized in an American faith.[2]

In addition to an enthusiastic description of the Texas landscapes and the prospects there, Considerant's books also contained a detailed plan for the establishment of Fourierist phalanxes. He wrote in an optimistic spirit about the prospects of this southern state. Appealing to socialists to join the colonization enterprise in what he called the "Promised Land," he proclaimed:

> Friends, the Promised Land is a reality. . . . Believe me the land of realization, the Promised Land is yours. One strong resolution, one act of collective faith and this Country is conquered. I bring you the news of salvation, I show you the way and I propose the inauguration. Let us only unite in purpose . . . and the new social era will be founded.[3]

Considerant envisioned the settlement as a model community which would influence its environment. It was to his credit that in spite of his enthusiastic proclamation to set out to the "promised land," he refrained from enticing the prospective participants with vain hopes. He implored them to proceed cautiously, insisting on the need for large investments which would not bring any profits. He warned them of the hardships and the sacrifices and proposed a cautious and revolutionary plan for the development of the colony. First, a society would be established to purchase the land and prepare it for settlement.[4]

In September 1854, shortly after the publication of his books, Considerant founded the European Society for the Colonization of Texas, in order to establish a settlement according to the plan he had formulated in his books. The society undertook to purchase land and to provide transportation for all immigrants from the port of entry to the Texas location, and also to ensure the first stages of development. The joint stock company would be based upon a capital of $1,000,000, which would be raised from different circles. Considerant was not averse to accepting capitalists into his venture. He tempted them with promises of high profits and high dividends, claiming that this step was justified because (1) the settlement needed capital, and (2) he had devised a system of profit sharing based upon the input of capital and labor according to the Fourierist principles.

This attitude was expressed also in his social concept according to which the settlement was to include groups from variegated backgrounds. Members could be capitalist shareholders or investors of labor who had no means of their own. In addition to these two groups Considerant agreed to accept hired workers, nonmember residents, and pensioneers. Every resident could determine his own status within the general framework.[5] He even permitted a partnership between the settlement and private settlers in the area.

Victor Considerant was appointed as the society's agent in Texas. He was to purchase the land, deal with the authorities, and organize the whole venture. The immediate response encouraged the founders. Several hundreds of people applied to participate in the endeavor and in December 1854, Considerant and his wife departed for the United States with optimism.

His great expectations foundered on the disappointments that awaited him, his early optimism soon turned to defeatism. One of the first problems he had to face upon his arrival in the land of his dreams was the drastic change in the political attitude toward the colony. During his first visit in 1852 he had been received with open arms, his colonization plans were welcome in a state that was eager to attract new settlers and encouraged the selling of land. Not anymore. In 1854 he encountered a wave of supernationalism in the South and in Texas.

The Know-Nothing party, which was antiforeigners and opposed their influence in local politics, had gained a broad base of support since the elections. They proposed a number of legislations to hinder immigrants from being granted citizenship and bar all Catholics from public offices. No wonder then that when the group of French socialists arrived, the local press was hostile. The *Texas Gazette* and the *Texas Times*, both of Austin, led the opposition to the socialist community in Texas. They published articles and letters criticizing the settlers on the grounds that they were communists, abolitionists, atheists, foreigners, and posed a threat to the pure American way of life. The sharpest attack was aimed at Victor Considerant himself and his conviction as expressed in his books. Among the few newspapers that defended him was Horace Greeley's *New York Tribune*. But, being a socialist paper, it only served to stir up the conservative Texans and to fire their opposition.[6]

Considerant was surprised by the intensity of the prevalent hostility, yet he kept his faith in American democracy. Addressing the American people directly, he published a retort in the form of a pamphlet, in which he logically and systematically refuted every accusation which the newspapers had made against the experiment. His efforts fell on deaf ears, and even those few voices that pointed out the potentially great contribution of the new settlers were of no avail. The authorities reflected the general attitude of distrust, and when in December 1855 Considerant presented a petition to the legislature, appealing for grants of land in Texas, his request was consistently refused. On September 1, 1856, after much debate in the legislative institutions, the governor signed a bill to incorporate the American-European Colonization Society in Texas.[7]

Even worse than the external obstacles were the insurmountable internal problems the utopian settlement faced from the outset. When Considerant and his wife arrived at La Reunion, near Dallas, in June 1885, they found the place in a state of anarchy. Almost 200 colonists had made their way to the proposed location without preparation or planning. The first group had arrived in February 1855, and additional settlers kept coming from France, Belgium, and Switzerland. The first pioneer stage, according to Considerant, should have been carried out by a small group of Americans, used to the climate and conditions of the frontier area. These, however, were not attracted to his colonization plan, and the few who did join arrived later. His plan called for selecting among the candidates those with farming experience, workers, and mechanics who would form the pioneering group during the first phase of colonization. They were supposed to lay the foundations of a viable farming and industrial settlement. From the beginning this plan was far from being realized. Most of the first to arrive were Fourierist activists and the cultural elite of professionals, artists, musicians, lawyers, scientists, and philosophers from France, Belgium, and Switzerland. Unsuited to the hard life on the frontier, they were unable to perform the tasks required to establish a successful economic operation. Those few who had any experience at all were a great help in the early months.[8]

La Reunion was situated near Dallas (today the site is within the city). The advantages were clear: the settlement was near a developing urban center, yet in a hilly forested countryside. Only after the foundations had been laid did the disadvantages become apparent: lack of water, harsh climate, and poor soil, which not even once yielded a decent crop. La Reunion's proximity to the city also turned out to be a disadvantage. Land prices rose drastically, and when Considerant tried to acquire additional land to absorb the newcomers, he was cheated by speculators, and the society's funds were misspent. Neither Considerant nor any of the other leaders ever managed to establish an economic or political order out of the chaos and anarchy which the rapid absorption of hundreds of immigrants had caused.[9]

The Society of La Reunion was established as an economic and social organization whose task was to acquire land, develop farming and industry, and establish a council of representatives in charge of the economic and social aspects of the settlement. The society owned 430 unviable acres and 500 head of cattle. They had acquired some agricultural equipment, begun to dig wells and canals, constructed some living quarters and farm buildings, and planted a vegetable garden. However, the prevailing atmosphere prevented planned development. There was no attempt to rely on scientific farming, no economic efficiency, and no planning as Victor Considerant had originally envisioned, even though he himself was the general manager.

During the first year family houses were built but not a central phalanstery as had been planned. There followed an office building, a general store, and some workshops, a foundry, a candle and soap factory, and services such as a laundry and a central kitchen and dining-room.[10] From its first days there was an attempt to introduce communal consumption. Members paid the kitchen and dining-room to provide equal fare for all. After a while this proved to be unsatisfactory. Communitarian ways were not to the liking of the individualistic French Fourierists, and they decided to serve meals as in a restaurant, where everyone paid for his meals. Problems arose when some of the restaurant managers embezzled funds, and they decided to abolish the restaurant and divided it into 12 small kitchens and dining-rooms. This in turn affected their living quarters too, and after a while the settlement, which had never been rigidly communitarian, decided to return to private consumption. Only their property and work system remained communal. There are no detailed accounts of their work system. They seemed to have rotated according to the Fourierist principle of ''work through joy'' and changed jobs frequently. But they did not adopt the Fourierist ''series'' or general system of work, and the result was unprofessional and incompetent.

Each member had different jobs and therefore never reached a high level of proficiency in any. Considerant, who was supposed to lead and direct the settlers, lost heart when he realized the failure of his utopian experiment. A deep depression seized him and he was overcome by defeatism. This undermined his comrades' determination to continue, and soon after his arrival he decided that they had failed. Instead of handing over the leadership to someone more competent, he held on, concentrating mainly in representing the colony outside. He traveled all over, seeking support for the experiment. His prolonged absences prevented him from being involved in the daily problems of the colony, and he could no longer contribute or instruct as a leader.[11]

During that period his wife was a source of strength and a faithful ally to her husband. She encouraged and supported him spiritually and undertook to be actively involved in the commune. Her home became a cultural and social center. She performed at all the physical tasks to which she had been unaccustomed, encouraging other women to do the same and to be equally involved with the men in the commune's affairs.

For three years Considerant attempted to promote his colony without any success. His vision was too far removed from reality. He had hoped to establish a settlement of 1,200 people, but it never exceeded 350. Following the first waves which had brought the hurried, unprepared settlers, small groups kept arriving. In 1858 Considerant again attempted to recruit support in France. When Napoleon III relaxed the political restrictions, Considerant was allowed a short visit to France. He was disappointed to find a disintegrating movement that could offer no support. On his return to the United States he was even more disillusioned. Arriving in La Reunion in the winter of 1859, he found it in a process of dissolution. Under these circumstances he and his wife decided to abandon the struggle and they moved to San Antonio, Texas. It was the end of Victor Considerant's attempt to establish a Fourierist communitarian settlement.[12]

A year before the final failure, Considerant prophesied the dissolution in his book, *Du Texas, premier rapport à mes amis*, published in Paris in 1857. In it Considerant blamed himself entirely for the failure of La Reunion. Even if his personal ineffectiveness as a leader was one of the causes, it was not the only one. From the beginning the venture met with a number of setbacks that prevented it from becoming the utopian model settlement; these were:

1. The refusal of the state legislature to grant the society territory, the hostile atmosphere, and opposition to the French settlers, which pushed them into a corner after a prolonged struggle.
2. The hard climate and the poor soil conditions were a disappointment after the optimistic expectations which had guided Albert Brisbane and Victor Considerant when they chose Texas for their experiment.
3. The hoped-for collaboration between experienced American frontiersmen and European Fourierist immigrants was not realized. The settlement became a French island isolated from its environment. Many of the settlers could not even communicate with their neighbors because they did not speak English.
4. The social and professional background of the settlers prevented the successful establishment of a communitarian workers settlement. Most of the immigrants had a hard time getting used to the physical conditions, the climate, and the hard agricultural work. In addition, even though Fourierist ideals had motivated them all, there soon appeared schisms and tensions between groups from different countries, mainly between Belgium and French immigrants.
5. The absence of selection brought to the settlement people who were not idealistically motivated and who soon became the focus of corruption and embezzlement, thus clouding the atmosphere.
6. The leadership lacked crew spirit. Frequent and violent personal strifes undermined the efficient management of the colony's social and economic affairs.

Above and beyond these specific reasons, another cause was the prevailing conditions in Texas. Between 1855 and 1859 this was not the ideal place for a developing Fourierist phalanx that intended to combine farming and industry in an atmosphere of spiritual freedom. The economic, cultural, and political structure of the state was diametrically opposed to the utopian Fourierist vision. There was absolutely no chance that such an experiment would prosper in the Texas of those days.[13]

Notes

1. Victor Prosper Considerant was born in 1808 in Salina, France, to a lower-middle-class family. He graduated as an engineer from the École polytechnique, served as captain in the army but left his military career while still a young man. Considerant was troubled by the social problems of his time and while searching for solutions, encountered Fourier's doctrine and became one of the activists of the movement. After Fourier's death in 1837, Considerant was regarded as his spiritual heir and did much to promote Fourierism in Europe and in the New World. Between 1837 and 1849 he published about twenty books and scores of pamphlets and was involved in editing journals that contributed to the expansion of Fourierism. His influence penetrated many circles, those of people without means and those of the intellectual socialist elite. Personalities such as Wilhelm Weitling, Alexander Hertzen, Louis Blanc, and others encountered Fourierism through him. He initiated the establishment of Fourier societies in many cities throughout Europe and the United States. His influence in radical circles was profound, and his activitics contributed to ideological unrest in France on the eve of the 1848 revolution. When it erupted Considerant was at the hub of events and was elected to the Constitutional Assembly, to thc Luxembourg Commission, to the Labor Committee, and to the National Assembly. When Napoleon III became president, Considerant was among the most active oppositionists, and in 1851 he was arrested and exiled. He managed to escape to Belgium, where he lived until 1852 and then went on a tour of the United States to meet with the Fourierists there and see for himself what kind of settlement they had established. This changed his entire life and activities. During his political exile in Belgium his utopian ideas began to take shape, and following the success of the revolutionary zeal of 1848, he envisioned a settlement according to the Fourierist model as a way to change the existing social order. Earlier he had scoffed at Fourier's ideas, believing that the European society was not yet ripe for a social experiment such as the phalanstery. Rondel V. Davidson, "Victor Considerant and the Failure of La Reunion," *Southwestern Historical Quarterly* (January 1973):278-81; William J. Hammond and Margaret F. Hammond, *La Reunion: A French Settlement in Texas* (Dallas: Royal Publishing Co.), pp. 21-23, 35; George Lichtheim, *The Origins of Socialism* (London: Weidenfeld & Nicolson, 1969), pp. 71-74; William L. Langer, *Political and Social Upheavals 1832-1852* (New York: Harper & Row, 1969), p. 229.
2. Hammond and Hammond, p. 36; Victor Considerant, *The Great West: A New Social and Industrial Life in Its Fertile Regions* (New York: 1854), pp. 4-6.
3. Considerant, pp. 4-6, 27.
4. Hammond and Hammond, pp. 47-48.
5. Ibid., pp. 53-58; Davidson, p. 286.
6. Hammond and Hammond, pp. 63-69; Davidson, pp. 288-89.

7. Hammond and Hammond, pp. 71-84; Davidson, p. 290.
8. Hammond and Hammond, pp. 85, 91-92; Davidson, p. 287.
9. Hammond and Hammond, pp. 95-100.
10. Ibid., p. 101.
11. Ibid., p. 103-8.
12. Davidson, pp. 291-94.
13. Hammond and Hammond, pp. 110-14; Davidson, p. 294.

10

New Odessa: A Jewish Commune of the Am Olam Group

In January 1882 a group of 65 young Jewish people from Odessa arrived at New York harbor. It was one of several groups of the Am Olam (the eternal people), whose members had socialist convictions and who had come to the United States to establish model communitarian colonies.

Am Olam had sprung up in various parts of Russia, principally in Odessa, as a result of the pogroms that broke out in southern Russia in 1881. Its founders were intellectual Jewish youths, mainly gymnasium and university students, who were searching for answers to the Jewish predicament. They developed a firm belief that farming was the noblest occupation for people, and were prepared to exemplify these ideals in their own lives. Some left for Palestine and were known as the Bilu, the majority turned to the United States and formed a part of the huge wave of emigrants from tzarist Russia.

In the United States the Hebrew Emigrant and Aid Society was formed to assist the refugees, and one of its aims was to prevent the new arrivals from crowding in the large cities. The society therefore prepared plans for settlements in the frontier states, and after some investigations proposed to establish Jewish farming colonies in the newly opened territories of Minnesota and South Dakota. Their report insisted that, "No colony should be organized on a communistic and co-operative plan, and the refugees should not be disposed of collectively, but individually. Communist colonies have succeeded in this country but in very few instances. . . . Colonization must be conducted strictly on business principles and not on charity."[1] Most of the farming colonies established by Am Olam in the United States were such, and only a small number of the colonies introduced communitarian principles for a short period in their first years (e.g. Bethlehem Yehudah, in South Dakota). The only group to adopt communitarian principles from its inception was the Odessa group.

The Am Olam of Odessa was founded on the Shavuoth festival (Pentecost) of 1881, a short while after the May 3-5 pogrom. The group was made up of two parts—the first were young radical intellectuals, among whom was Paul Kaplan, who in time would become their leader in the United States; the others were small businessmen: shoemakers, tailors, and tradesmen. The process of integrating the two groups caused much tension. The young intellectuals had been assimilated in the Russian culture and were influenced by its radical literature and inspired by utopian socialism. They claimed that the move to farming should go together with a communitarian way of life. The others were mainly concerned with the national aspiration of adopting a productive way of life as farmers, a move which did not entail the abolishment of the old social order or giving up their private property and family farm.

During the process of crystallization the radical party was reinforced and their plan for a communitarian settlement was adopted. While still in Odessa they had shared expenses and in September 1881 began to search for ways to leave Russia. Several groups gathered in Brodi, waiting for a chance to emigrate, sending frequent messages to Jewish communities in the West asking for assistance in their endeavor to emigrate. During this waiting period on the border town they formulated the society's set of rules. Its thirty-seven paragraphs opened with a declaration of principles: collective ownership of the land and the means of production and independent colonization signifying that no hired labor was to be used (except for instances specified in the regulations). The internal strife between the radicals and those who favored private farming was solved by granting members the option of choosing between two separate units—"the family," which was completely communist and "the cooperative," which was made up of private farms. The regulations for both units were similar in order to maintain the founding principles mentioned above.

The declaration specified that each member should work according to his ability and receive according to his needs. However, members could spend their budget any way they pleased. The sovereign institution of the commune was the public meeting, which dealt with all matters of principle as well as with current affairs. Regulations stipulated its authority and the modes of decision making. Most of those were to be decided by a simple majority of two-thirds. New members had to pass a probation of one year. Men and women were to enjoy equal rights in both units. A special paragraph was devoted to the family unit and stipulated that the eighteenth birthday would be the earliest age to enter marriage. Marriages and divorces were declared at the public meeting of "the family."[2]

The Odessa group left Russia in several groups and gathered in New York between January and July of 1882. The New York Jewish community was not very helpful because of the group's socialist convictions, their radicalism, and atheistic attitudes. They did not receive aid even when they set out westward.[3] Most of them were young and without means, and the group was faced with a difficult financial situation, which prevented them from purchasing the land needed to realize their aspirations.

They managed to contact some of the outstanding men in the Relief Organization for Russian Jews and secured their cooperation. Among them were Jacob Schiff, the banker who contributed a large sum of money for the purchase of land in the West; Julius B. Goldberg, a lawyer, and Michael Heilprin, a liberal revolutionary who had been active in the 1848 revolution in the Habsburg empire. Heilprin became interested in their vision of a model communal settlement and enthusiastically set out "to collect means for this object at a time when everyday brought into our port vessels with refugees."[4] He managed to raise $2,000 which, in addition to Schiff's contribution, was enough for the purchase of the land in the West.

The colonists realized that preliminary farm training was essential. This would enable them also to raise additional funds through their work. Therefore, in mid-1882 they split into several groups; some worked on farms in Hartford, Connecticut, others in Indiana, and the majority remained on Long Island, where they worked on farms and other jobs. About 60 who had stayed in New York rented a house on Pell Street, where, together with other members of Am Olam, they formed an urban commune. Here they put their communal theorics into practice, pooled their earnings, and divided the household tasks. The urban commune existed only for a short while, until they had acquired land and could proceed with their plans.

During that period they formed ties with radical circles from among the Russian and Jewish immigrants, among them William Frey, a non-Jewish Russian nobleman and former professor of mathematics in the Military Academy at St. Petersburg, who preached positivism to the Russian immigrants in New York.[5] The charismatic personality of this man, who had sacrificed his social position and his career in order to preach his ideals, attracted the Am Olam groups, and they asked him to join in their venture. Hoping to influence them with his positivism Frey accepted, but not before warning them of the less pleasant aspects of his personality and doctrine, which might cause friction between himself and the young idealists.[6]

In July 1882 several parties set out to scout for land in Texas, Oregon, and Washington State. Frey was among those who set out for Oregon, and there they found land which seemed suitable. They recommended a parcel of 760 acres of land in Douglas County, Oregon, about 250 miles south of Portland. The group began to assemble first in Portland and later on their own land.[7]

One of the remaining testimonies on the Odessa group's life and the pioneers in Oregon was a personal letter written by a group member who at the time was living in St. Louis, Missouri. On November 1, 1881, he wrote that they had chosen Oregon on the shores of the Pacific Ocean and bordering with California, because among all the North American states this area was renown for its excellent climate and fertile land. He added that on July 30 the first group of 21 men and 5 women had set out by steamer to Oregon. They had arrived a month later with the sum of $4,000, one-fifth of which had gone toward expenses. He ended by saying that he was still in St. Louis, where he was working at the time, and hoped that in the spring he would join the others in Oregon.[8]

In the spring of 1883 about 50 members had assembled in Oregon. Their land was far from a populated area, but was rich and well watered, and the conditions were good for an agricultural settlement which was to serve as a model for their social ideals.[9] There was a small Jewish community in Portland that maintained good relations with the settlers.

Soon after their arrival a large two-story frame-building was put up. The upper story was used for sleeping quarters. On the lower floor were the kitchen, dining-room and assembly hall. At the same time they began to clear the land, and sow wheat, oats, and a variety of vegetables, mostly for home use. The river and the creek were full of fish and the prospects were good. During the first two years they cultivated 200 acres but even though no great technical knowledge was needed to make it productive, they did not concentrate only on farming. They set themselves to cutting wood from their forest and sold it to the nearby railroad company.[10] This was an important source of income and helped the commune to overcome their financial hardships of the first months. Some of the members worked outside the commune at various trades, and their wages were added to the common chest.

At the end of the first year their number had grown to 70, most of them between twenty and thirty. An atmosphere of optimism prevailed and found its expression in the letters they sent their friends in the East,[11] as in the following example: "As soon as we got together we began to work enthusiastically and were indeed successful, even though the food was poor, bread, potatoes, lentils and sometimes milk. . . . On the 15th we were paid and could now be certain to fulfill our commitment. Yet we have no illusions and know how much effort awaits us. During the 16 months of the contract, hard labor will be demanded but then we can pay our debts for the farm and even buy some necessary tools."[12]

During the first two years their economy developed gradually and social conditions improved. They formulated their constitution, which closely followed the first set of rules of the society, and were recognized officially by the Oregon State authorities as the Cooperative Society of New Odessa. Among other provisions the constitution included mutual aid to promote the physical, spiritual, and moral constitutions of each member. The society's property was not stock. Capital and work contributed by members would not be rewarded, and could not be returned upon leaving the commune. No colonist could have work outside the commune, or engage in any form of commerce. The work in the colony was to be distributed according to the individual's abilities. They insisted on equal rights for men and women at work and management. All the colony's affairs were decided by the public meeting; any member of the colony who attained his eighteenth birthday was eligible to vote. New members had to pass a probationary period of one year. In case of failure to pass probation, the member was required to leave the colony with his or her share in the crop. Full communitarian principles were introduced as to property and work; nevertheless members had a certain independence as to living quarters and consumption.[13]

In spite of this economic prosperity the colonists chose to live under a strict regime: "Rigid regulations were in force. Everybody worked. . . . There were fixed hours of labor and assigned tasks not only on the farm and in the forest, but also in the kitchen and about the house." Men and women shared all jobs. They kept a strict and simple diet, influenced by William Frey's theory of proper nourishment.

A detailed description of the colony, given below in part, can be found in the "History of the Commune Colony, New Odessa," published in the *Yalkut Ma'aravi* (New York, 1904 [in Hebrew]):

> The work in the colony was really hard. The workers, far from being idle, even took upon themselves additional jobs. Most of them had never worked before, and they were unaware that there is a time for work and a time for resting. The first year, therefore, found many of them ill with exhaustion. Even so that year they succeeded to clear more than 100 acres of forest, according to their contract to provide the railroad company with 150 cords of wood each month. In addition they built a large house to accommodate about 50 people comfortably, planted several acres of vegetable gardens as well as 12 acres of barley. They also built fences over one mile long, constructed a big powerful cart, manufactured all their logging tools except for their axes and saws, and sent two to four daily to help the women in the kitchen and laundry. They numbered only 35 men and women, and every day several of them were ill. In the years to come New Odessa became a model agricultural farm.[14]

The colony attracted many visitors, most of whom were impressed by the enthusiasm and idealism of the young intellectuals who had undertaken to establish a new way of life. Although they were insufficiently experienced, they compensated for it with their devotion to the cause. The intellectual character of the colony was manifested in the way they spent their evenings. After work they would assemble to discuss matters pertaining to the state of the world and their own communal life. One evening a week they devoted to self-criticism, to improve themselves and promote their collective harmony.

Although most members were poor they had brought their books with them and had collected a rich library, which played an important role in their life. Several evenings were devoted to music under the guidance of William Frey's wife, and to philosophy and mathematics under William Frey himself. They were both the hub of the colony and were involved in promoting their positive religion.[15]

A letter written on August 2, 1883, depicts the atmosphere there:

> A month has passed since the arrival of the Frey family. Their coming regulated our spiritual life. . . . On Mondays, Tuesdays, Thursdays and Fridays we have Mathematics and English and the Philosophy of Positivism with William Frey. . . . Every Sunday we get up at 6:00—right away a noisy discussion on women's problems is begun. Women demanded equal rights from the beginning and began to work in the forest. Men took turns in the kitchen and laundry. Soon however the women discovered that they were not strong enough for forestry work and things went back to normal. Now, however, they have changed their minds and are trying to prove that they are physically stronger.[16]

Thus, William Frey's social and cultural activities were appreciated at first. Soon, however, a group of followers tried to force the whole colony to accept his doctrine. His zealous adherence to matters of their vegetarian diet caused internal conflict. In the second half of 1884 Frey reformulated their constitution, which was now an "agreement" in which members undertook to share their assets, improve themselves, devote their lives to the principles of altruism and moral activities, which would be realized by all mankind. This agreement was formulated according to the principles of positivism which Frey tried to enforce in the colony. He believed that New Odessa was to become a model positivist colony and presented his convictions as those of the commune.[17]

Harmony reigned until the end of 1884, when schism appeared between the adherents of Frey, who became even more zealous, and an opposition group led by Paul Kaplan, one of the Odessa group founders. He had been active in administrative matters of the colony and was a radical believer in communism. From early on he distrusted Frey, and when he realized that Frey was going too far in enforcing his theories, he undertook to refute them publically. Kaplan succeeded in mustering most of the members around him, and when Frey realized that their viewpoints were irreconcilable, he and about fifteen of his followers left the colony. After an attempt to settle in the area, he gave up and returned to New York with his wife and followers.[18]

The departure of Frey's party hastened the disintegration of the colony. After the early days of enthusiasm, there followed grey days of petty disappointments that left their imprint on the young idealists. Their frustration was the result of private and public causes. The small group of 65, who were mostly singles, lacked any kind of privacy. They saw no chance of raising a family on the commune. Some of the women who had joined them through marriage were not motivated to the same degree, and the harmony of the colony suffered.[19]

After their initial enthusiasm had waned, they began to suffer from the isolation from their Jewish roots. Many members were eager to continue their education, but then the evening courses were stopped and their idealistic way of life was undermined by disputes and tensions. A short while after Frey's followers had left, the community building, which had housed their abundant library, went up in flames. They had lost their treasure, and 1885 saw many secessions; others gave up and left.[20]

The colony existed two more years, but the initial enthusiasm was gone. At work they put in a minimal effort, and visitors who arrived then told of a mounting dissatisfaction, idleness, and frustration. The public meetings and cultural activities suffered from sparse attendance. Their ideological motivation had disappeared, and life in the West became meaningless. In March 1887 the colony was dissolved by the regional court and the property handed over to a receiver.

Years later, when former members of the colony wrote their memoirs, they could find no satisfying answer as to the reason for the disintegration. Hertz Borgin, who dealt with the history of the Jewish workers movements in the United States, mentioned four factors as the cause of dissolution: the dispute between Frey's positivists and Kaplan's group; insufficient funds; the harsh conditions; and the waning idealistic commitment. A visitor during the last year of the colony described the members as being apathetic and spiritually stagnating. He wrote in the *San Francisco Oberland* that they had no religious principles, no political organization, and no moral code of behavior, except their aspiration to "be good."[21]

A different analysis was given by Abraham Kahan concerning the colonization experiment in New Odessa. He put the blame on the hard physical labor which was too much for the young people, the cultural desert in which the young intellectuals from Odessa found themselves, the social frictions caused by romantic affairs, and the destruction of all intimacy following their mutual criticism.

Kahan admitted that most members of New Odessa would disagree with his analysis. Paul Kaplan, for example, explained the failure of the commune as a set of coincidences which might have been prevented.[22] Only a few of the members remained in the area. Most returned to the cities. Some started a cooperative in San Francisco. A group led by Kaplan operated a cooperative laundry in New York for a while.

Two common elements can be observed among former members of New Odessa: (1) Only a few remained farmers. After their enthusiasm had waned, they returned to their studies and joined the liberal professions. Paul Kaplan became a doctor, Peter Firman a chemist. (2) Most of them continued to support ideals of social reform and were active in radical movements.[23]

This was the end of the only serious experiment to establish a model colony by Jewish intellectuals and socialists. Furthermore, New Odessa was the last commune to be established by socialist immigrants. Henceforth the initiative would come from American groups motivated by ideologies rooted in the American experience.

Notes

1. Leo Shpall, "Jewish Agricultural Colonies in the United States," *Agricultural History* (July 1950):127-32.
2. *The Russian Jew* ([yearly] 1882), pp. 524-26 (Russian).
3. Gabriel Davidson, *Our Jewish Farmers and the Story of the Jewish Agricultural Society* (New York: Fischer, 1943), pp. 226-27.
4. Davidson, p. 228; Shpall, p. 134; Uri D. Herscher, *Jewish Agricultural Utopias in America, 1880-1910* (Detroit: Wayne State University Press, 1981), pp. 37-39.
5. William Frey (1839-1888), whose real name was Vladimir Konstantinovich Geins, was born in Odessa to an aristocratic family, educated in a military academy, and served as an officer in the Imperial Guards. As a young man he was influenced by doctrines of Saint Simon, Fourier, and Cabet, left the army and joined the radical underground circles. After years of activity in Russia he despaired of achieving social change in the Old World. In 1868 he and his wife emigrated to the United States, intending to establish a model communitarian settlement there. On his arrival he adopted the name of William Frey and tried to join Oneida but was rejected. In the 1870s he joined some small groups that attempted to establish a commune in the Midwest, but this experiment did not survive long. In spite of the disappointments caused by their communal experience, he and his wife continued to search for an alternative society based on communitarianism. In the late 1870s they were caught up in positivism and began preaching their own version, filled with elements of mysticism, ascetism, and a strictly vegetarian diet. At this stage they met the people of Am Olam and joined them for a while in their colonization venture at New Odessa. On the biography of William Frey see Avrahm Yarmolinsky, *A Russian-American Dream: A Memoir on William Frey* (Kansas: The University of Kansas Press, 1965).
6. Ibid., pp. 96, 99-100; Herman Rosenthal and Adolf M. Radin, eds., "Chronicle of the Communist Colony Known as New Odessa," *Yalkut Ma'aravi: ma'asaf Shnati* 1 (1904-5), pp. 48-49 (Hebrew).
7. *Yalkut Ma'aravi*, p. 50; Davidson, pp. 229-90.
8. S. Drexler, supplement to M. Tugan-Baranovski, *Socialistic Colonies* (Ein-Harod, Israel: Hakibbutz Hame'uchad Press, 1946), pp. 191-92 (Hebrew).
9. Helen E. Blumenthal, "New Odessa 1882-1887: United We Stand, Divided We Fall" (M.A. thesis, Portland State University, 1975), p. 50.
10. Herscher, pp. 39-40.
11. Davidson, pp. 230-31; Shpall, p. 134.
12. Drexler, in Tugan-Baranovski, p. 192.
13. Blumenthal, p. 52; Shpall, pp. 134-35.
14. *Yalkut Ma'aravi*, p. 51.
15. Herscher, p. 46; Yarmolinsky, p. 102; Davidson, p. 232.
16. Drexler, in Tugan-Baranovski, pp. 193-94.
17. Yarmolinsky, pp. 103-4; Shpall, p. 135; Davidson, p. 233; Blumenthal, pp. 63-64.

18. Davidson, p. 233; Blumenthal, pp. 68-69.
19. Yarmolinsky, pp. 105-6.
20. Herscher, p. 48; Davidson, p. 233; Shpall, p. 135.
21. Herscher, pp. 47-48; Blumenthal, p. 71.
22. Drexler, in Tugan-Baranovski, pp. 195-96.
23. Yarmolinsky, p. 106; Blumenthal, pp. 76-78.

11

The Kaweah Cooperative Colony in California

In the giant Sequoia forests on the western slopes of the Sierra Nevada in central California a communal settlement was established in 1887. It was situated in majestic scenery at the foot of Kaweah Mountain. This commune was to become the forerunner of several attempts to establish indigenous American socialist colonies on the West Coast.

The founders of Kaweah were radicals, socialists, and union functionaries who were aware of the broad aspects of the social problems they had encountered during the struggles and failures of their unions in San Francisco in the 1880s. Burnett Haskell was the driving force of the group; he was a colorful character, a combination of prophet and adventurer not to be classified in ordinary categories. (Some regarded him as "the most intellectual labor leader in the West."[1])

An Alternative Social Unit

Burnett Haskell was born in 1857 in northern California. His family was among the first to settle in the area. He never persevered in anything he undertook to do; he studied at Oberlin College and at California and Illinois universities but did not graduate. Instead, he went to Chicago and found odd jobs as a laborer. Tiring of the hard work, he returned to California, where he finally graduated as a lawyer in 1879. For a time he practiced law, but then turned to journalism when his uncle bought the *Truth*, a newspaper in San Francisco, and offered him the editorship.[2] Thus a new chapter began for Haskell. His profession as a journalist introduced him to the social problems and the union struggles in San Francisco.

In 1882 he put the *Truth* at the disposal of the radical circles in the trade unions. The paper gave expression to the wide variety of socialist and anarchist ideas of his generation; articles by Henry George and Herbert Spencer appeared side by side with those of Karl Marx, Ferdinand Lasalle, Kropotkin, and Bakunin. It was this eclectic approach that later gave rise to the speculations that Haskell had tried to merge the various theories he published. Others regarded it as a further example of his unstable character. This claim was reinforced by Haskell's strange attempt to dynamite one of the government buildings in San Francisco, and to prepare a list of the people who were to be put to death as soon as the revolution began.[3]

Haskell became very active in the San Francisco trade unions. He was one of the main organizers of various union activities. The most outstanding was the struggle against cheap Chinese labor. The *Truth* was turned into a platform for a group that crystallized around this struggle in 1882. Their activities waned about a year later, but Haskell kept in touch with them and in 1883 they turned into a pseudo-underground radical cell known as the International Worker's Union. There too Haskell's typical eclectic approach prompted him to try and combine the elements of the two famous "Internationals," Marx's and Bakunin's.

With the expansion of union activities Haskell had aspirations to turn his paper into a daily. He was unsuccessful, but he became more involved in San Francisco union activities and his influence extended to all of California and the entire West Coast. After 1886 a downward trend began, mainly because he and his comrades realized the hopelessness of their struggle for reforms as a means to overthrow capitalism. They began to think of an alternative—a socialist utopian society. They studied both the European and European-American versions that had been published at the time. Lawrence Grönlund's book found favor in the wide circles of U.S. radicals who were frustrated and looked for an alternative utopian way of life.

When in November 1884 Haskell convened a meeting of his readers and followers in San Francisco, approximately 100 turned up. The social problem was discussed, and at the same meeting a plan was advanced for a collective settlement that would serve as an example for an alternative, noncompetitive society. An agreement was reached not to go ahead with any plans unless there were optimal conditions for success such as suitable land, natural resources, marketing outlets, and options for agricultural development. The first step was the setting up of a Land Purchasing Association. Funds were provided by the members themselves and the Land Purchasing Association started to examine the possibility of buying a tract of suitable land for the colony. In the autumn of 1885 they got a chance to purchase forest lands in Tulare County in California.[4]

This area had not been settled yet, and according to the Timberland Act of 1878 there was a chance to buy via a direct approach to the local land commission. There was a feeling of urgency because some capitalist entrepreneurs were planning to acquire the land. The association's members were called upon and within a few days, at the beginning of October 1885, fifty-five people handed in their applications at the Visalia land registrar. They asked for 160 adjoining acres of forest land in Kaweah County. Most of the applicants were from San Francisco or nearby. Out of the fifty-five, seven gave the same address on their applications. These were members of the sailors' union who were deeply influenced by Haskell and his circle. They were the first to hand in their members' applications, thus showing a strong group solidarity and conviction in the cause. Some of the members were without means and had to be aided by a collective fund established for that purpose. Most of them intended to settle there, but even those who hesitated promised to hand over their land to the colony in order to maintain land continuity. The small county land registry office was taken by surprise. The applicants were a mixed lot of urban radicals, union functionaries, and farmers who had one thing in common, their naive, idealistic belief in the model cooperative colony.

This was not how the registrar or the officials in Washington, D.C., saw it. They were suspicious of the collective application, of the seven who had registered the same address, and of talk about the construction of a railway to connect the forest area to the main line. Might not these applicants be undercover agents of the Southern Pacific Railway Company attempting to bypass the law in order to purchase land under favorable conditions? There was a precedence when in a similar way an attempt had been made to buy land in the Humboldt region. Fate would have it that Charles Keller, one of Haskell's people in charge of purchasing the Kaweah lands, was the very man who had uncovered the corruption in the Humboldt affair.

Although no proof could be found against the cooperative group, Washington decided to freeze the whole project. When the applicants came to pay their purchase fees sixty days later, they were told that there would be no sale but that they could instead lease the land until a full investigation was launched. Being confident of their innocence they opted to postpone the final purchase of the lands and lease them for the time being. This, they believed, was an advantage because they had difficulties raising the whole amount needed. Nobody could foresee the complications this would cause; in fact the whole future of the colony would be affected by these "roots bearing poisonous and bitter fruit" (Deuteronomy 29/18).[5]

The Road to the Mountain

The first obstacle that the group faced was to find a way up the forested mountain to their colony. The land, which was at a height of 6,000-8,000 feet, was considered inaccessible. This may have been why it had not been exploited by foresters or investment companies until then. When it became clear that a railway was out of the question, the group decided on a less ambitious plan, which was just as difficult, namely the construction of a mountain road. They decided to tackle the job by themselves, and it became the focal point of the group's existence while they were waiting for the finalization of the purchase of their lands.

The first settlers arrived in the area at the beginning of 1887. They set up tents and called this temporary camp *Arcadia*. It was to be the first of seven erected along the road under construction. Other camps were set up on the colony's land and were intended to serve as the site of the future settlements. The road construction work had begun a few months earlier, in October 1886, when ten to fifteen people started out on the job. It took four years to complete. In June 1890, after eighteen miles of tortuous mountain road had been completed, the height of 8,000 feet was reached.[6] Conditions were harsh. They had to cut through granite rocks without proper engineering equipment. When the work was completed it was the first accessible road from the south into the Sequoia forests. (A modern road would not be constructed until the 1930s.) When the area was declared as a national park, thousands of tourists still used the old road and the settlers proudly claimed that theirs was one of the most heroic and cheapest road construction feats.

Although there were many who doubted the group's ability to finish the task, they were instilled with a sense of urgency to prove that a collective effort could achieve wonders. In addition, they just could not do without access to their lands. Thus the road work became the focal point of the group's existence, geographically—since the camps were built alongside the road—but also economically and socially, because the physical and the engineering jobs were all done by members of the commune. The funds were raised from various sources, donations, loans, and membership fees. The road cost $50,000 in cash and $250,000 in work invested by the members of the collective.[7]

Kaweah social life was not smooth sailing. Several months after the roadwork began and most members were still in the cities, a dispute between two camps arose about the legal aspects of the colony. Kaweah until then was considered to be a voluntary association; now it would have to be declared a legal entity in order to manage land property problems as well as economic activities. Without submitting the question to the general meeting, the members of the managing committee took it upon themselves to establish the colony as a corporation, which legally would be a more centralized entity. Either because of its content or because of its undemocratic procedure this step upset many members. They knew that Burnett Haskell was of their opinion and called him back from Denver, where he was on union business.

When Haskell returned to San Francisco in October 1887 he became intensely involved in the dispute. Of the 135 members, 100 objected to the establishment of a corporation. Haskell joined their ranks and violently expressed his opinion, claiming that even though a corporation would legally be a more centralized form and easier to supervise, it would on the other hand enable everyone to buy a share and join the commune. This would leave the community without the option of selecting its members, one of the most important principles that would ensure the future viability of the colony.

The dispute continued for five months. In that period Haskell formulated a set of regulations, according to which the colony would be organized as a joint stock company which would enable it to screen all new applicants. In March 1888 the set of regulations was put to the vote and the majority supported Haskell's proposals. A minority of about fifty who did not accept the decision, left the colony, among them several veteran members on whose names parcels of land were registered. Some objected to the rights of the collective use of their lands and opened proceedings against the colony. Thus, a situation was created which undermined the collective while it was still in process of organizing itself. It also gave rise to suspicions of the group and its leaders and caused hostility in certain circles in San Francisco, thus curtailing the collective's chances to expand. Even worse were the seeds of an internal dispute that were sown and which would, in the coming hard times, undermine the collective from within.[8]

The Dynamics of Schism

In retrospect, the harmful schism of Kaweah in 1888 is puzzling. On examining Haskell's set of regulations, one soon realizes that there was hardly any difference between him and those who supported the corporation. Both sides had adopted the principles of organization from Grönlund's utopian book, which had inspired the founders of Kaweah from the outset. There was only one main difference: in Haskell's set of regulations the selection of new candidates was a matter of principle. He knew that the survival of Kaweah as a utopian model depended on its human element. As in many cases of a schism in a small community of strong ideological motivation, here too the dynamics of a split were in action. As soon as two zealous groups began to seek supremacy, enmity and suspicion resulted, especially since there was no authoritative personality to rise above and bridge the gulf between the rival groups.[9]

The internal struggle over matters of principle and legality influenced the overall ideology of Kaweah and served as a catalyst for crystallizing its doctrine. Burnett Haskell played a central role in formulating the set of regulations and publishing a series of articles in the *Commonwealth*, a periodical founded in 1888 as a platform for the movement behind Kaweah. In its issue of November 1, 1889 Haskell's article, "A Pen Picture of the Kaweah Cooperative Colony Company," gave a most concise and crystallized picture of Kaweah's ideology and economy as well as its plans for the future. In that article Kaweah was depicted as a "compromise between a communist society in which there is no room for any individualism and competitive capitalism where justice and solidarity are sacrificed on the altar of avarice.'' Further, Haskell regarded Kaweah as ''the means to ensure its members from want and the fear thereof, by providing them with housing and their daily needs, as well as with education and culture. Encouraged by a harmonious set up in which everyone would earn the full value of his work, every member would do his job for the benefit of all.''[10]

In Haskell's ideological formulations as well as in other publications Kaweah was depicted as an antithesis of competitive industrial capitalism, as a place of mutual aid and brotherhood. Early Christian principles which had been updated were the foundation of Kaweah; Grönlund and Bellamy, the American utopianists whose books had been published in 1884 and 1888 respectively, greatly influenced Haskell. In his plan for the organization and administration of Kaweah, Haskell named Grönlund as having inspired him. Although Grönlund dealt with a wider social frame rather than with the single social unit, Haskell adopted his principles of hierarchy and of division into sections. He also opted for Grönlund's method of electing functionaries and accepted their being responsible to that authority.

In Haskell's opinion, this concept of administrative hierarchy was not antidemocratic. He insisted that his aim was to establish the colonies' institutions on a real democratic foundation, namely, that each and every member would have equal opportunities. In a society where private property had been abolished and where there were no privileged members, the administration would be professional rather than authoritarian. Grönlund and Bellamy both insisted on a professional administration. They were suspicious of the rule of the masses. Their orientation on an intellectual middle class as the focal point in the society of the future had been noted by many of Grönlund's and Bellamy's critics. It was not by chance that the ideologists of Kaweah adopted the same attitude. They, too, had arrived at their ideology through the process of criticizing the competitive capitalist society on one hand, yet fearing the masses of the labor unions on the other. The idea of a collective settlement at Kaweah grew out of the frustration of those who were active in the labor unions and realized the hopelessness of their struggle against capitalist society.[11]

The Principles of Collective Property

The principles of property also were adopted from Grönlund's *The Cooperative Commonwealth*, which inspired Kaweah's ideologists. His principle of a time-check system was used to pay for work done. Kaweah built its economy on the time-check principle. The check was issued in denominations of 10-20,000 minutes. All work claimed equal value, the carpenter and the trustee both received 30¢ an hour. However they did not profit from any dividends. The property—including land, building, and equipment—was collectively owned. Personal belongings and houses were privately owned, but a unit could not exceed 150 square feet. Consumption was collective as well. A communal diningroom served members from the first days and a communal store, in which labor notes were the accepted currency, sold essentials. Work was allocated according to each member's preference and ability. In time, new branches were developed; except for road construction these included various agricultural branches, construction work, teaching, art, and service jobs.

The set of regulations also dealt with absorption of new applicants. Full membership was achieved after the purchase of a $500 share. An advance cash payment of $100 could be supplemented with pay slips earned while working on the site. Every progressive person could apply. In time, people were checked as to their socialist knowledge and whether they were acquainted with Bellamy's and Grönlund's writings.

In an article published in the *Commonwealth* in 1889, Burnett Haskell stressed the need for "progressively minded members with a high moral standard" who identify with the great movement toward a better way of life for humanity. "One of our aims is to prove that social problems can be peacefully solved through establishing an industrial cooperative."[12] Did the Kaweah colony justify these expectations? Did it pave a practical way to solve social problems through industrial cooperation? Until 1890 the perspective was rosy and things looked promising. Following the schism of 1888 the economy and society recuperated rapidly. There was a sense of achievement between 1888-1890. According to Haskell's above-mentioned article the farm was flourishing and the road construction proceeded as planned.

Even though road construction was the main activity (about 20 members worked at it daily), it was not the only occupation of those years. The farm was expanded as membership increased. In 1890 there were 300 members who lived in seven temporary camps scattered along the road under construction. Only a few wooden houses had been erected, and most of the people lived in tents. The moderate climate throughout most of the year made living under the stars comfortable for the young and singles. The atmosphere did not lack a romantic spirit of the pioneering days. The scenery was breathtaking, an abundance of mountain streams, waterfalls, and crystal-clear lakes among the massive forest trees turned the harsh living conditions into something people could enjoy.

Chance visitors mistakenly came away with the impression of a continuous picnic combined of fun and games and little work. One visitor ended his description in the *Nationalist* saying that in Kaweah "life is a daily picnic." In reality, between 1887 and 1890 the foundations of their farm were laid. Vineyards and orchards were planted along the road. Arable land was cleared and a watering system was started. In the temporary camps workshops were erected: a carpentry shop, a shoemaker's, a sawmill, and a leather workshop. The first tractor was bought, and Haskell's modern printing shop was transferred from San Francisco to Kaweah. Vegetable gardens provided the temporary camps with fresh produce and the rivers and lakes with fish when meat was scarce. A feeling of optimism prevailed. One of their dreams was to turn the area into a tourist site with a big hotel and convention halls that would attract sympathizers and new members.[13]

A Periphery of Sympathizers

In spite of the economic success, there was a vast gap between the dream and the reality. The settlement suffered from want because there were few profitable branches and most of the effort was spent on the road construction job, the colony's enterprise for which they themselves had to raise funds. Under these circumstances it was of paramount importance to promote outside connections. These helped in the loan and fund-raising and in organizing a peripheral movement of sympathizers and potential future members.

Haskell was at the center of this activity, publishing propaganda and explaining the colony's mission. Some time after the colony was established he opened an office in San Francisco in order to promote the communitarian ideas. In April 1888 he started to publish the weekly *Commonwealth*, aimed at radical circles. Many of its columns were devoted to the Kaweah experience and as a result sympathizers formed groups in San Francisco, Los Angeles, Chicago, Denver, and New York. They devoted themselves to fund-raising whether in the form of donations or loans or as membership fees.

Haskell actively courted the nationalist movement which prospered under the influence of Bellamy's book. We have already mentioned the ideological affinity between Kaweah and Grönlund and Bellamy which caused many to regard Kaweah as a Bellamist colony. The growing tide of nationalism, therefore, could benefit Kaweah and bring it supporters as well as donations. More important, it paved the way for new members who arrived from all over the United States and from as far away as England. One of the more interesting newcomers was Philip Winser, a farmer from Kent who sold his farm after reading Bellamy's *Looking Backward* and set out to join Kaweah colony, eager to prove that cooperation and nationalism offered practical keys to the salvation of society. However, he arrived in the West in February 1891, during the crisis that caused Kaweah to disintegrate one and a half years later.

If Bellamy's work drew many a member to Kaweah, so also did purely personal reasons. A cooperative Eden offered refuge from a cold, competitive world. Yet they were soon disappointed. The commune was far from providing a high standard-of-living, and those who were not ideologically motivated could not hope to survive the harsh pioneering conditions of the tent camps along the mountain road.[14] There are no detailed accounts about the social background of Kaweah members. Most of them seem to have had a professional middle-class background, a fertile background for idealism. Some were skilled laborers from trade unions, a few were artists, musicians, or literati.

Daily life within the colony was rich and variegated. After work there were a variety of activities, discussions, and study groups, concerts, sports, singing, recitals, a choir, and an orchestra. Whenever they managed to organize a concert this would attract settlers from the neighboring areas and turn into a cultural event. Among the members there were many artists. Besides talented musicians who had majored in conservatories there were also painters and photographers who immortalized the different aspects of Kaweah. In addition to all the above activities, they began on January 1, 1890 to publish the *Kaweah Commonwealth*, which turned into a source of activities and income and contributed to the widening of their horizons.

Educational and cultural activities were of vital importance in raising their standards. Adult education was undertaken by the school masters who taught the children during the day. The educational institutions encompassed a toddler's house, a kindergarten, and a school. The curriculum was aimed at forming a humane, liberal person who would be able to live a harmonious social life. The gap between intentions and reality was wide. Many interpreted these liberal principles to mean education without any order or discipline. This of course affected the children, many of whom complained about their teacher's "tyranny" and "injustice." When these complaints were discussed at the public meetings, some teachers were dismissed, and this further undermined the educational institutions, which became a source of bitterness rather than of moral inspiration.[15]

This was not the only area where their lofty ideals of harmonious personal relations gave way to the harsh reality of internal squabbles. Beneath the idyllic life in the breathtaking mountain panorama, the picnics, and the cultural activities there appeared tensions that caused endless quarrels and discussions on daily affairs. Some described Kaweans as devoted to lengthy disputes even during the work day. Haskell himself was one of the most virulent critics of this aspect of Kaweah. In an article written after the commune had disintegrated he said: "These little pinpricks . . . killed the noble purpose and enthusiasm of the enterprise and slowly drained its life away." Instead of the fraternal friendly feelings one found Kaweah divided into many fractions. "Discussions about what Brown had to eat and how Smith was pretending to be sick to escape work were met with interest, instead of an interest in literature and art. . . . It was a huge family and everybody seemed to have the business of everybody else nearest his heart."[16]

In the winter of 1889 another major disagreement erupted. It centered around the publication of a complete list of nonresident members and their addresses to which Haskell continuously opposed on the ground that open publication would unfairly expose individuals to the charge of socialism. Resident members, however, looked upon this reluctance as an attempt to conceal illicit activities by Haskell and some of the trustees. There seemed to be suspicion and criticism of Haskell's own personality. He was always absent and away at San Francisco, and his failure to be prompt with replies caused James Martin, general secretary and Haskell's long-time friend to label him "unfriendly, uncomradelike and unbusinesslike." By 1891 the personality conflict between these two pillars of the community had become an open rupture.[17]

The Fight against Legislation

When in June 1890 the eighteen mile mountain road was completed, new prospects opened up for the logging of the rich forests on the mountain. In order to speed up their efforts a nearby sawmill was hired, and the lumber was transported there. This enterprise was badly planned and inefficiently managed and therefore production was much lower than expected; but expectations were still high. Another occasion for optimism was in 1889 when the new federal government sent representatives to reexamine the land claims. As mentioned above, shortly after the Kaweah claims were filled, the area was withdrawn from registration and the existing petitions suspended for further investigation. Meantime, under the advice from the land office, the settlers "squatted" while the cooperative venture began. Now, when suspicions of collusion with the railroad colony were refuted and the road finished, there was a chance of a positive decision.[18] But instead a new catastrophe awaited which would completely undermine the colony.

On September 25, 1890, congress proposed a legislation to establish the Sequoia National Park. This would include only a small part of Kaweah lands and the Nature Protection people as well as colony members were content with the legislation. After all, they were aware of the uniqueness of their environment. The Association for the Protection of Nature had proposed to safeguard the rights of the "socialist settlement" to its lands, just as other national parks had safeguarded Indian rights. However, a week later, during the last session of congress in September, the legislators decided to set apart the adjacent lands, doubling the area of the National Sequoia Forest, which would now include the Kaweah settlement. The law was passed in October. When two weeks later the news reached Kaweah, members were dumbfounded and furious. These hasty procedures raised many questions. There was no way of determining who stood behind the legislation and why it had been rushed through. For many years the mystery remained unsolved.

Recently the Californian scholar Oscar Berland, in his painstaking historical research pointed out a ''behind the scene'' involvement of Daniel Zumvalt, a lawyer who represented the Southern Pacific Railway Company in Tulare County. According to evidence uncovered by Berland, Zumvalt was in Washington at the time of the hasty legislation. There are no clear-cut findings and none of those involved are still alive today; they took their secret to the grave. Nevertheless, there is no doubt today about the involvement of the Southern Pacific Railway Company. A detailed map of the Sequoia National Park with its amended boundaries was put into use on October 16, 1890, ten days after the legislation was passed and eleven days before the members of Kaweah even heard about it. Why would the Southern Pacific Railway Company be interested in it? After all, they usually were opposed to nature protection laws. Several possibilities come to mind: (1) tourism would expand the railroads; (2) fear of the colony which might break the company's monopoly of the logging and the lumber business in northern California; (3) the Southern Pacific Railroad owned a large sawmill in the area and feared Kaweah's competition.[19]

The Government versus Kaweah

The members of Kaweah strongly protested against the legislation, claiming ownership of the land. Only a trick of fate could have caused the monopolistic Southern Pacific Railway Company to benefit from a law of the protection of nature, while the socialist collective had to fight for private ownership of land that was to become public property. The county and the press stood firmly behind the colony. Years of neighborly contacts had convinced the people of the area that the eccentric socialists were a positive economic factor. The federal government, however, ignored the protest and ordered the colonists to stop their logging activities and to clear the land immediately.

The only option left was to seek a lawsuit. This occurred when Kaweah trustees were charged in the U.S. District Court at Los Angeles on January 2, 1891 with the unlawful cutting of trees growing on public land. Kaweah members hoped that they would have an opportunity to prove that the land was theirs. Haskell, who was a lawyer, went to court. While the local Tulare County newspapers stood behind the colonists, because they regarded the legislation as unfair to the settlers, the other news reporting was hostile. Editors in California took delight in printing black and ludicrous accounts of the colony based on accounts of former disgruntled members of Kaweah.

Moral aid came from the director of the law school of the University of California, William Carey Jones, who set out to defend the colony in an article published in the *Quarterly Journal of Economics*, in October 1891. After a lengthy review of the case between the colony and the federal government, he wrote: ''In the matter of the controversy with the government, I can come to no other conclusion than that a great injustice has been done to those persons who in good faith made filings for timber claims in October 1885. . . . The claim of the case is not clear to my mind. It is difficult to find consistency in the decision of the land office. . . . But even the law seems to me to incline in the favor of the timber land claimants.''[20]

Jones believed that the government should amend the legislation, which was unclear and obscure. Even if that were impossible, congress had a wide scope to deal fairly with the colonists whose adherence to their enterprise was admirable. As to the defense's claim that the giant trees should be protected, he was convinced that everybody, including the colonists, were in full agreement. The settlers clearly perceived that the giant trees would be worth a thousand times more standing as a tourist attraction than if they were cut into lumber. This was clearly stated in a pamphlet published by Kaweah in 1889 in which they presented logging as an act of vandalism.[21]

Support for the commune, however, was rare. Most of the press was hostile and published slanderous reports of the communal life at Kaweah. Even before the case was settled against them, they were adversely affected when their reputation suffered, causing a drastic drop in the financial support of their followers and affecting the colony economically. At the beginning of 1891 there was still hope that Haskell would succeed in his lawsuit and the expulsion order would be rescinded. When on April 16, 1891, the axe fell, it was a death blow to the colony which had already been eroded from within.[22]

As mentioned above, the social disintegration was caused by the squabbles between the two central figures of the colony, Burnett Haskell and James Martin. These two, who had been close friends, were now divided. Martin, who most of the time had been the colony's general secretary, objected to Haskell's absenteeism and a majority of Kaweah members sided with him.[23] Haskell indeed had neglected the land claims problem and allowed new members to believe that the land titles were not seriously endangered. But the psychological reason for the attack against him was the deep frustration of Kaweah members when they realized that their pioneering enterprise was doomed. Their impotent fury was turned against Haskell, who had been their spiritual leader throughout all these years yet lacked that integrity that a great leader of pioneers needs. His failure with the lawsuit undermined his authority. He remained at Kaweah throughout 1891, but his belief in the enterprise was doomed.

The process of disintegration began right after the crisis of October 1890, when a large number of members left the community. This trend grew with the split between the two leaders and reached alarming proportions when the press started its hostile attack. Toward the end of 1891 the financial crisis, caused by the drop of supporters' donations, brought bankruptcy. In January 1892 the settlement was legally dissolved. A few members attempted to stay on but in April they too gave up. Some members stayed in nearby settlements. James Martin tried unsuccessfully to reach some agreement of compensation for the colony members from the country and the government.

Isolated and disappointed, Haskell retired from his radical activities to write about the Kaweah experience. In a mood of personal and ideological disillusionment, he wrote his article in November 1891. Ten years later he rewrote and edited it for the periodical *Out West* (September 1902) and said: "Kaweah colony failed, but it struggled. . . . Lessons may be drawn from this tale of work and idleness, noble purpose and weakly practice, joy, faith, sorrow, and disaster." The article reviews the stages of growth and integration; it is a historical document of an observer biased but accurate because he was familiar with the facts. In spite of the melancholic vein of his conclusions Haskell inserted an element of optimism, saying: "Men are not yet civilized enough to do right for right's sake alone and to labor for the lore of production itself."[24] Only a few years elapsed and different people in other parts of the United States attempted to experience the communal way of life. Their motivation was socialist and their methods of organizing their settlement were like those of Kaweah.

Notes

1. Ira B. Cross, *A History of the Labor Movement in California* (Berkeley: University of California Press, 1935), p. 158.
2. Robert V. Hine, *California's Utopian Colonies* (New Haven: Yale University Press, 1966), p. 80.
3. Ibid., p. 79; Cross, p. 164; Dane Kennedy, "The Kaweah Colony" (honors thesis, University of California at Berkeley, 1973), pp. 6-8, 11.
4. Kennedy, pp. 9-13; *The Commonwealth* 3, no. 15 (May 24, 1899); Burnett G. Haskell, "Kaweah, How and Why the Colony Died," *Out West* 17 (September 1902):300-309; Ruth R. Lewis, "Kaweah: An Experiment in Cooperative Colonization," *The Pacific Historical Review* 17 (November 1948):429; Hine, p. 78; William Carey Jones, "The Kaweah Experiment in Cooperation," *The Quarterly Journal of Economics* 6 (October 1891):53.
5. Oscar Berland, "Giant Forest's Reservation: The Legend and the Mystery," *Sierra Club Bulletin* (December 1962), p. 71; Kennedy, pp. 13-16; Lewis, p. 430; Hine, pp. 78, 82; Jones, pp. 54, 64-65; "A Brief History of Kaweah," *The Commonwealth* 3, no. 15 (May 24, 1899):71-72.
6. Kennedy, pp. 16-19; Lewis, pp. 430-31; "A Colony Trip," *Kaweah Commonwealth* (July 19, 1890).
7. Hine, p. 90; Lewis, p. 431; Kennedy, p. 36; Haskell, p. 316.
8. Lewis, p. 434; Hine, p. 92; Kennedy, pp. 20-23; "Brief History of Kaweah," *The Commonwealth* 3, no. 17 (August 1, 1899):13-15.
9. Kennedy, pp. 23-25.
10. "A Pen Picture of the Kaweah Cooperative Colony Company," *The Commonwealth* 3, no. 20 (November 1, 1899):112-14.

11. Jones, pp. 55-58; Kennedy, pp. 30-34; Hine, pp. 81, 87; "A Pen Picture of the Kaweah Cooperative Colony Company," p. 118.
12. "Question Answered," *The Commonwealth* 3, no. 15 (May 24, 1899); "A Pen Picture of the Kaweah Cooperative Colony Company," p. 113.
13. Lewis, p. 432; Hine, p. 90; Haskell, pp. 317-18; Kennedy, p. 36; "A Pen Picture of the Kaweah Cooperative Colony Company," p. 119.
14. Lewis, p. 436; Hine, pp. 84-86.
15. Haskell, p. 318; Lewis, p. 435; Hine, pp. 89-91; Kennedy, pp. 42-45.
16. Haskell, pp. 318-19.
17. Kennedy, pp. 39-41; Jones, p. 63; Hine, pp. 92-93.
18. Berland, p. 72; Haskell, p. 321; Lewis, p. 436.
19. Berland, pp. 78-80.
20. Kennedy, pp. 50-51; Hine, pp. 94-97; "The Kaweah Colony Persecution," *Kaweah Commonwealth* 3, no. 3 (March-April 1892). (A protest from the supervisors of Tulare County.)
21. Hine, p. 96; "Kaweah Cooperative Colony," *Kaweah Commonwealth* (September 27, 1890).
22. Haskell, p. 321; Lewis, p. 437; Hine, pp. 97-98. "Our Country Speaks," *Kaweah Commonwealth* (May 2, 1891).
23. Hine, p. 93.
24. Kennedy, p. 52; Haskell, p. 322.

12

Ruskin: The Communitarian Settlement in Tennessee

In April 1893 a socialist weekly, *The Coming Nation*, began to appear in Greensburg, Indiana. Its editor was Julius A. Wayland,[1] who aimed at attracting working-class people to socialist ideas through popular journalism. The weekly was a success and gained a fairly wide readership. Within six months it had reached a circulation of 13,000 and could therefore exist without commercial advertisements. Early in 1894 Wayland came up with an idea that would raise his sales and expand his circulation and concomitantly would enable people to come into contact with socialist ideas, and perhaps even realize them. He published his plan in his weekly, under the title "A Co-operative Village."[2]

Wayland asked his readers for help, and the number of subscribers expanded to 100,000, having realized that this would raise the yearly profits of the journal to $23,000. According to his plan this amount would be invested in land purchased in order to establish a settlement that would be named the Cooperative Commonwealth. The clever editor promised that those readers who brought 200 or more new subscribers or contributed $100 would become the "founding members of the society." This unusual plan made waves; many applications from all over the United States reached the editor's table. Yet in Greensburg itself the paper and its ideology were extremely unpopular; Wayland and his assistants were boycotted.

Under the circumstances his wish to move and to establish a settlement where his journal would flourish was reinforced. Therefore in the summer of 1894, even before the target of 100,000 subscribers was achieved, Wayland announced in his editorial that the time had come to realize his plan. After a short period of searching, he and his assistants decided to purchase a 1,000 acres about 50 miles from Nashville, Tennessee. The area was sparsely populated and the land cheap. In time it became clear that this was caused by the poor quality of the soil. One of the reasons for choosing the site was its position near the road and railway. Wayland realized the importance of fast communication for economic, political, and social reasons. On July 21, 1894, Wayland declared that the next issue of his weekly would be published in the new settlement. He called on the founding members to join in establishment of the settlement. The August 2 issue of the weekly gave Tennessee City as the place; it had been the name of the place before the communal settlement was established there.[3]

Wayland and his assistants on the weekly were the first to arrive at the new settlement. They immediately set out to organize the printing of the journal. Meanwhile other settlers began to arrive from throughout the United States, and in the summer of 1894 there was 32 people—2 women and 20 men—all from the urban middle class. It was a group of intellectuals prompted to find an alternative way of life because of the depression of 1893 and motivated by the socialist ideals they had encountered in Wayland's weekly.

They had a variegated professional background which included a carpenter, a mechanic, a shoemaker, a baker, a barber, a blacksmith, five printers, three doctors, and several teachers and farmers. In the first few months they cleared the land and the forest and constructed the first building that was to house the printing shop and the editor's office. The weekly was meant to be their main source of income during the first period. Wayland suggested that they call their settlement Ruskin in honor of the aged English socialist whose ideas were greatly admired by the founders. At that time Ruskin was already at the end of his days and his contact with the settlement was loose.[4]

Ruskin was established as a mixture of a cooperative association, as provided by the state's constitution, and a communal settlement in matters concerning work, consumption, and the ownership of several branches. Wayland initiated the legalization of the settlement by means of a charter signed by 20 members in August 1894. The charter legalized the Cooperative Society of Ruskin in the constitution, which was anchored in capitalistic laws. According to the charter their joint capital was $17,050 owned by the shareholders; the value of a share was $500. Men and women could own shares, and they managed the settlement and elected its officers. Wayland was elected president at the first meeting. He continued to own the printing shop and thereby was granted more power and authority than the other members. At first, while busy establishing the settlement, they all accepted that Wayland had brought the weekly and the press to the settlement and these were his private property, but after some time this fact caused some controversy.

Until the end of 1894 life proceeded harmoniously. The two systems developed side by side. On the one hand there was the cooperative, anchored in the capitalistic constitution and recognizing the shareholders' ownership of the property, and on the other hand the communal framework was established. This included the work schedule and communal consumption, the elements that lent the settlement its communal framework. Members constructed the buildings jointly; different kinds of work were assessed equally; a communal kitchen and dining-hall supplied their meals; accommodation, food, medical treatment, and other basic necessities were provided without payment. Other items were supplied by the communal store in return for vouchers printed by the society. Work in the printshop was the main occupation until they began to develop farming on a small scale. They bought cows, planted fruit trees, and sowed the arid land. There were some attempts to develop industrial workshops.

When the first months of joyful creation had passed, problems cropped up. They were the result of the capitalist cooperative communal structure of the settlement.[5] A dispute between the "individualists" and the "cooperativists" disrupted the tranquility. Some of the settlers had abandoned their socialist ideals right from the beginning. They searched for ways to establish a system of private property and work for pay. In the October 13 editorial the internal disputes were decried. The editor warned that the petty quarrels and the internal strife might undermine the settlement. Moreover, a controversy between the various socialist streams surfaced. Yet the worst fight ranged over the personality of the commune's founder: many criticized that Wayland privately owned the printshop and the weekly.

Unwilling to alter the status quo, Wayland looked for ways to legitimize his position through compromise. He suggested that he would remain the supervisor and manager of the paper, which would be leased to the community under conditions specified by him. As president he imposed this arrangement on the community, but many members were dissatisfied. They claimed that the weekly was their main source of income and a situation in which it was not owned by the cooperative was unthinkable. The number of Wayland's critics increased, and they accused him of running the paper in a totally capitalistic manner. Gradually, a group of members demanded that the journal's property and management be transferred to the commune according to their prevailing principles.

The struggle between his followers and his critics continued throughout the year. In the spring of 1895, when without consulting the commune's officers, Wayland tried to enforce a decision to acquire a new and expensive printing shop, things came to a head, and he was forced to resign, against the wish of his followers. The atmosphere got even more hostile following a series of stormy meetings, and in July 1895 Wayland decided to leave Ruskin. In his last editorial of August 1895 he gave expression to his feelings of frustration. He did not give up his socialist activities and declared that he would carry on his publishing efforts. Leaving Ruskin, he received high compensations and moved to Kansas City, Mississippi, where he began to publish the socialist journal *Appeal to Reason*. Later, when Ruskin was dissolved, *The Coming Nation* was sold to none other but Wayland, who was eager to republish his cherished weekly; but this would be under completely different circumstances.[6]

Wayland's secession did not prevent the paper from being published regularly. A new editorial committee was established, and life in Ruskin went on undisturbed. New members kept arriving in Tennessee, and in 1895 the settlement numbered about 100 persons. The settlement had to be moved to another site nearby; the transfer of all the people, structures, and equipment to the new site began at the end of 1895 and testified to the vitality and adaptability of the commune. The decision to move was taken when it became clear that the soil was unfertile and unsuitable for farming. They acquired 800 acres of undivided land in an area with a better farming potential. A stream that flowed through the land and the green countryside presented a lovely environment. Two enormous and beautiful stalagtite caves found nearby were a rare addition which attracted many visitors. The caves also served as the commune's food stores and provided shelter from the heat. They were also used as accommodation and work places and sometimes even for their public meetings.[7]

The transfer to the new site opened up a period of intensive economic activity. The fertile soil produced good crops, and the weekly reported at length about their prospects and claimed that the reputation of Ruskin's produce promised them a good chance for export. Some of their produce appeared on the markets as early as 1897, among it flowers, seeds, herbs, and a medicinal herb called *Ruskin cure* and used for burns, stings, inflammations, and other skin diseases. Ruskin also marketed logs, work clothes, suspenders, books, and chewing gum. These were all widely advertised in their paper and successfully sold during the first couple of years of the settlement. Yet the members were amazed to realize that their economy was not balanced and not efficiently handled. For instance, even though they farmed 800 acres, they had to buy some of their basic supplies outside because of bad planning. The managers of the agricultural branches were mostly northerners who looked down on southern methods of farming and had ignored their neighbors's advice. Instead, they introduced methods which were unsuitable to local conditions. The fertile land was underexploited and their agriculture stunted. The main income still came from their printing shop, and the publication of the weekly and other socialist literature. The ever-growing readership of the paper raised their expectations for a higher income, but as a result of inefficient bookkeeping it is difficult to estimate their profits. Mismanagement and professional errors prevented the printing shop's development. The introduction of hired workers in production was one of the most severe blows to their socialist ideals.[8]

At the beginning of 1897 the new Ruskin was established. In the center of the settlement a three-story building housed the editor's office, the printing shop, and the communal dining-room. It provided accommodation for new candidates and visitors and housed the library and bookstore. On the third floor there was a hall that seated 700 and hosted their shows, concerts, and lectures. The main building was surrounded by about seventy-five houses for the 250 inhabitants who had gathered from thirty-two states and from six countries overseas.

The year 1897 was the apex of the social and economic development of Ruskin. They now owned 1,800 acres in both the old and the new sites, a widely distributed weekly, a printshop, a variegated farm, a sawmill, a cannery, and a mechanized and time-saving steam laundry operated by a small number of men and women. Members of Ruskin worked nine hours daily according to a communal work schedule. They were paid with vouchers, each unit representing one hour of work, and these were used locally. Members who could not work were allotted vouchers valued at twenty-five work hours every week and children got ten. In return for vouchers the general store provided necessities other than housing, food, education, and medical services which everyone received according to his needs. Most of the members took their meals at the communal dining-room. Food was prepared by about twenty-five members of both sexes who were on kitchen duty every day. Economists who visited Ruskin estimated that services were performed efficiently. Members worked in shifts and took turns on holidays. In spite of the advantage of communal eating, some members criticized the noise, the quality of the food, and the serving.[9]

The years 1896-97 were Ruskin's best years. Despite the difficulties, the prospects looked promising. Their enterprises prospered and the income was high. The financial basis of the commune was secure. Most of their debts had been paid, and even neighbors who had been suspicious in the beginning, now admired the uniqueness and advantages of Ruskin. In the 1896 presidential elections, most of the members voted, like their neighbors, for the popular democratic candidate William Jennings Bryan. The local school was recognized by the regional board of education. There were eight classes and the school year lasted for ten months. Half of the teachers' salaries were paid by the educational authorities of the county.

The Fourth of July celebrations contributed to enhance relations with their neighbors. Ruskin organized a public picnic in an area close to the caves, and about 2,000 people attended the free meal. It was to become a tradition until the commune was dissolved,[10] and convinced their neighbors that in spite of their radical social doctrine, Ruskin's members were a group of serious and honorable people, anxious to contribute to the advancement of the area.

A number of reasons, most of them internal, caused Ruskin's deterioration in 1897. Tension and hostility were growing between the founding members who were shareholders and the newcomers; the lack of communication between them required the intervention of the judiciary authorities of the state.

This gap was rooted in the constitution and in the profound differences in the background and mentality of the two groups. The constitution had established a hierarchical structure of management; a council of thirteen members and an executive committee of three were in charge of daily affairs. Shareholders had the right to supervise their institutions through monthly general meeting and caucuses. In time there changes were introduced in the constitution, shareholders' meetings were called only once in a while, and the managers' authority increased.

The managerial circle now enjoyed an administrative as well as ideological hegemony. They were actively involved in the weekly and their ideas, which were often expressed in writing, represented the image of the commune within and without. An ever-widening gap appeared between the managerial minority and the silent and working majority. This was reinforced by the differences of attitudes and background. Most of the founding members were of the urban middle classes, romantically and intellectually involved with socialism and believing in the principles of cooperative harmony. While they were against the competitive, achievement-oriented society, they also opposed violent class struggles. Those who joined them were people from rural areas and the lower classes who had a completely different educational background and also differed in their attitudes toward communal life. Their lack of active involvement in the commune's management and, being blue collar workers, they caused bitterness and resentment in the founding fathers' circle, who managed, guided, and did all the intellectual jobs on the commune. This was the background for all the discussions and disputes, whether big or small; it created an atmosphere of mistrust in which every dispute could erupt into a major battle, and those were not rare in those days.[11]

One of the most disputed topics was the severe criteria applied to new candidates, because the founders were uninterested in expanding the circle of shareholders. Nevertheless newcomers kept arriving and created a rather large group of residents who were not members. Wives of new members were also prevented from buying shares. The problems surfaced several times between 1898 and 1899 and was the final straw that caused the break up.

Before discussing it in detail, let us look at other reasons for the strife. The attitude toward the family and free love was in fact theoretical. In a settlement based on the family unit, relations were proper and the housing was provided for the family unit which in most cases included children. Visitors were impressed by the harmonious atmosphere within the families and their numerous children; they thought that this was the result of the communal way of life which freed the family from economic worries. During the settlement's existence several new families were formed in most cases through civil ceremonies. This was regarded by the people of the area as free love, and members of Ruskin were defamed. After relations with their neighbors had improved the attacks ceased, but this did not prevent internal strife on the subject. It came to a head when a group of anarchists, who believed in free love, joined Ruskin. They fought for their right to promote their ideas and the dispute erupted and gained momentum because of the extremist position both sides maintained and because of the prevalent tense atmosphere. The whole dispute was theoretical and had no practical impact.[12]

Their attitude toward religion was another source of conflict. During the early years, atheism and agnosticism prevailed in Ruskin, mainly influenced by Wayland's militant anticlericalism. The weekly served as a platform for his convictions and gave them extra weight. In those years members who kept their affinity with the church had to walk all the way to nearby villages. After Wayland had left this changed: more freedom was granted to members of the different religions, but a church was never constructed in Ruskin.

The weekly also underwent a change when the editorship was handed over to a religious preacher, Casson, who had left the Methodist church to found the Worker's Church in Lyn, Massachusetts, and in 1899 joined Ruskin and became editor. Under him the weekly was tinted with the spirit of ''socialist Christianity'' of Protestant circles. These changes caused tension and strife and added fuel to the quarrels, deepening the schism between those who were still religious and the large group of atheists who did not willingly accept the new trend.[13]

Matters of education also brought tension. During the first period of Ruskin, the problems of education were considered with all seriousness and much effort was invested in it. Educational institutions for all ages—a kindergarten, a school, and adult study groups and courses—were established. Members of the commune taught at the local school and searched for ways to integrate theoretical and vocational lessons with a socialist education. Some time later they even considered the establishment of a college in which socialist economic theories would be taught. The idea was presented to the readers of *The Coming Nation* early in 1897, and they were asked to enlist in the fund-raising and contribute their own money to the future college. The idea attracted many, and letters of supporters were published, among them those of Professor Frank Parsons and the socialist leader Henry Demerest Lloyd.

Contributions began to arrive, and on May 15, 1897, the weekly published the laying of the cornerstone of The College of the New Economy at Ruskin. But not everything went according to plan. Dark clouds threatened the commune. The inspiring vision of a college later became a source of tension between warring groups who blamed each other for the failure of the plan.[14] Nevertheless, all these disputes did not directly cause the schism of Ruskin; they were a fertile background that hastened the fatal *coup de grace*.

Until 1897 the weekly did not reflect the internal quarrels. Its readers got an impression of the harmonious communal life in Ruskin. In the second half of

1897 the controversy leaked out. The managers were severely criticized for mismanagement, waste, and despotism. The disputes over the family and free love, religion, anarchism, and socialism all found expression in the weekly. Readers now realized that the internal relations were undermined and nothing could reestablish harmony in Ruskin.

In June 1897 the internal struggles were left in charge of the courts and that was the beginning of the end which rapidly brought about the final disintegration of Ruskin. The first suit was brought by three seceders who demanded the value of their shares. Their plea was rejected, but this only opened the way to other frustrated seceders, and during 1898-99 nine additional cases were brought to court. This demanded time, energy, and money from the commune, but worse than that was the very fact of the judiciary intervention, which took matters out of the members' hands.

The legal battles were the straw that broke the camel's back and led to the disintegration of the commune. One such example was the demand of a new member who had come to Ruskin at the end of 1898 penniless, and who after being accepted as a member demanded a share for his wife as well. This had been the practice among the founding members but did not apply to newcomers. The claimant demanded that new shares should be issued in order to be divided among the wives of new members. He claimed that he had supporters from among many disgruntled members of Ruskin. A small group of founding members objected violently and appealed to the court to issue an injunction against a possible decision to issue shares to the wives. The battle encompassed the entire community, on one side the ''injunctionists'' who were the minority, and on the other the majority who opposed the injunction. When the founders realized that they were indeed a minority they opted for a fatal step: as shareholder they demanded to dissolve the commune in order to reorganize. The storm that broke out caused the community to split into splinter groups and this brought on the end of Ruskin.

In May 1899 an attempt was made to stop the deterioration and all members were called upon to participate in finding a way to bridge the gap, but to no avail. The schism had become too deep and the courts did nothing to mend it. During the discussions between the representatives of the various groups everyone agreed that under the circumstances there was no way out but to dissolve the settlement. Most of the 800 inhabitants of the commune were shocked.[15] Many were not aware of the struggles which had been going on within a small group of activists. Many newcomers had only just arrived there full of expectations, hoping to begin a new harmonious chapter in their lives. About 250 of them searched for a way to continue their communal way of life and organized in a new society called the Ruskin Commonwealth. They intended to use some of Ruskin's property in order to establish the new settlement.

According to the court's ruling a receiver was put in charge of selling Ruskin's assets to pay their debts and to compensate the 138 shareholders; The property, which had been estimated at $100,000, was sold at an auction on June 27, 1899, and the only ones to profit were the lawyers, who were paid generously for their services. It was a sad day for members of the commune to watch their property being sold and grabbed up by bargain hunters. After their debts and the lawyers had been paid, each shareholder received only $36, and even that after several years.[16]

The 250 members who had decided to go on with their communal way of life purchased the printing shop in order to continue publishing the weekly at their new site. During their search they came across another communal settlement which had only just been established in Georgia. The Ruskin founders were not strong enough to keep going, and the union of the two groups filled them with new optimism. The Ruskin people arrived in Georgia in October 1899, and in spite of their earlier disappointments they constructed their new settlement in the manner of the Tennessee commune. They took special care not to repeat the mistakes of the past and formulated a set of rules in which they specified the rights and the obligations of the members.

Compared with Tennessee, conditions here were harsh. At first they were optimistic; a journalist of the *Brooklyn Eagle* who visited them noticed the discrepancy between their material difficulties and the idealistic spirit that prevailed on the settlement. He enthusiastically described the ''suntanned people'' wearing tattered clothing who gather in the diningroom to discuss poetry, literature and matters of universal importance during their meals.[17]

It soon became evident that the good spirits could not endure. The settlement was doomed. The harsh climate, their inexperience in farming, the financial difficulties, and the waning of their idealism after their earlier disappointments all combined to undermine the commune. In 1900 a visitor found there only 140 of the 250 members who had started out, and even they said that they would not continue with their communal life much longer. We know that the Ruskin Commonwealth no longer existed in 1903 even though its name was still printed on the map.[18]

Notes

1. Julius A. Wayland, journalist, publisher, and a versatile man, was born in 1854 in Versailles, Indiana, of a poor family. He succeeded in climbing the ladder of local politics and got involved in the publication of the local newspaper. His ardent Republican convictions caused controversies with his readership in Missouri, where he had lived as a young man; he moved to Pueblo, Colorado, where he made a fortune in real estate. In the 1890s he switched from being a radical capitalist to become a militant socialist. Influenced by a local, English-born cobbler, he was active in socialist circles and avidly read socialist literature of all shades.

Adopting the most radical trends, he soon became an aggressive critic of capitalism, of which he was an integral part. His socialist activities revolved around the local populist circle whose paper he edited. Simultaneously he broadened his socialist horizons, read the American uptopians Bellamy and Grönlund, and got in touch with the English socialist John Ruskin. In 1893, when recession hit the United States and social hardships increased, he came to a turning point in his life, sold his property and began to publish *The Coming Nation*, a socialist journal that was to have a great impact on socialism and communal settlement in the United States. Robert Ewing Corlew, "A History of Dickson County, Tennessee," *The Tennessee Historical Commission* (The Dickson County Historical Society, 1956), pp. 137-38; John Egerton, *Visions of Utopia: Nashoba, Rugby, Ruskin, and the "New Communities" in Tennessee's Past* (Knoxville: University of Tennessee Press, with the Tennessee Historical Commission), pp. 63-68; Howard Quint, pp. 175-89.

2. "A Cooperative Village," *The Coming Nation*, no. 37 (January 13, 1894), p. 3.
3. Egerton, p. 67; Quint, pp. 189-92; William Alfred Hinds, *American Communities and Cooperative Colonies* (1878. Reprinted and enl. Philadelphia: Porcupine, 1975), pp. 488-89; Alexander Kent, "Cooperative Communities in the United States," *Bulletin of the Department of Labor*, no. 35 (July 1901):605.
4. Egerton, pp. 67-68; Corlew, p. 139.
5. "The Ruskin Colony," *The Coming Nation*, no. 103 (May 11, 1895), and no. 101, (April 27, 1895); Quint, p. 192; Kent, p. 605; Egerton, pp. 68-70; J.W. Braam, "The Ruskin Cooperative Colony," *American Journal of Sociology* 8 (July 1902-May 1903), p. 668.
6. Corlew, p. 146; Egerton, pp. 70-74; Quint, pp. 192-93; Kent, pp. 606-7.
7. *The Coming Nation*, no. 109 (June 22, 1895); Corlew, p. 140; Egerton, p. 74; Hinds, pp. 492-93.
8. Quint, p. 193; Egerton, p. 74; Corlew, pp. 140-41; Braam, pp. 670-71; Kent, p. 607.
9. Corlew, pp. 140-45; Braam, p. 673; Isaac Broome, *The Last Days of the Ruskin Cooperative Association* (Chicago, 1902), pp. 79-84.
10. Egerton, p. 78; Hinds, p. 494.
11. Braam, p. 678; Corlew, p. 142; Broome, pp. 37-59; Egerton, p. 75; Corlew, p. 145.
12. Kent, p. 608; Broome, pp. 105-28; Corlew, p. 147; Braam, p. 675; Egerton, p. 78; Frederick A. Bushee, "Communistic Societies in the United States," *Political Science Quarterly* 20, no. 4 (1905):633-35.
13. Braam, p. 676; Corlew, p. 143; Broome, pp. 89-104.
14. Ibid.
15. Egerton, p. 79; Broome, pp. 25-36, 155; Corlew, pp. 147-48.
16. Broome, p. 170; Corlew, pp. 148-49.
17. Kent, pp. 608-12.
18. Corlew, p. 152; Kent, p. 612; Hinds, pp. 497-99.

13

Communitarian Settlements and Socialist Parties in Washington State

At the end of the nineteenth century, a few years after Kaweah was dissolved and simultaneously with the establishment of Ruskin, Tennessee, a new center of communitarian activity crystallized in the northwestern part of Washington State. This area was just beginning to be settled and in a short period dozens of differently motivated communitarian settlements sprang up. Three of them were inspired by socialist ideas, one by anarchists and two by esoteric religious trends (Mormons and the Church of Progressive Brethern).

The first communitarian experiment in Washington State was called the Cooperative Colony in Puget Sound. It was established in 1887 in Port Angeles on the northern shore, and its founders came from the socialist circles and the unions in Seattle and Tacoma, and from the townships in northern Washington State. They aspired to establish a communitarian community that would pave new roads for workers and settlers in the state. The driving force was George Smith, a Kentucky-born lawyer who had been active in California and Oregon. The founding members were mostly intellectuals from the eastern United States, among them Harvard graduates, who were acquainted with European cooperative movements and socialist utopianism. In 1887 George Smith published a detailed plan for an integral cooperative; it called on members to buy shares, and the target was $150,000. His call was answered, and soon over 1,000 members had registered. The land purchased was the Strait of Juan de Fuca on Puget Sound.

We can deduce the speed of the colony's development from the fact that in June 1887 there were already 240 settlers, most of whom had come from Washington State. The hasty organization and their lack of clearly specified communitarian aims caused difficulties in defining their community. Controversies about problems of organization, ways of management, and principles of cooperation arose among the members and created tensions. The worst of those flared up between the "theorists" and the "practical" members and caused a large number of the founding members, who had been motivated by their utopian idealism, to leave. Among them was George Smith, who left in February 1888.

From the start the colony functioned as a productive cooperative. The communitarian framework included mainly industrial enterprises: The first was a large sawmill that began to operate in 1887. Then came a construction firm which built the settlement and also worked in the neighboring towns. A printing shop was established, and two years after the settlement was founded a steam ship began to ply Puget Sound as a means of public transportation. In the early stages the public buildings were constructed: a central building, an assembly hall, and a temporary common kitchen and dining-room, which never developed any further because the members preferred to have their private houses and plots for cultivation. During the first years the principle of equal pay was meticulously maintained, but it impaired their profits, and the members soon opted for an ordinary pay system. Consequently, the colony lost its cooperative features a few years after its inception, and the period between 1894 and 1900 passed in squabbles over the division of the property.

The cooperative colony at Puget Sound, which had started out with a vision of achieving a model society through integrated cooperation, did not proceed far in its endeavor. Instead, a nondescript western frontier town sprung up and most of the idealist founders returned to their radical activities in the city.[1]

About ten years after the colony at Puget Sound was dissolved two more serious attempts of communal life were made in the same area. The first—Equality—was established in 1897, the other—Burley—in 1898. Their members had been affected by the ideological turmoil within socialist and radical circles on the eastern coast in the 1890s.

The Settlement Policy of the Socialist Parties

During the decade preceding the establishment of the commune in Washington State, several significant events had taken place in the history of social reform in the United States. The background was the utopian literature of Edward Bellamy and Lawrence Grönlund who had both advocated the advantages of a communitarian society on a national and community level. They attracted many followers from a variety of social circles and influenced the ideological and political unrest that reached its apex during the William Jennings Bryan presidential election campaign in 1896.

The failure of the populist circles and their candidate caused frustration and despair. One of the outcomes of this mood was the strength of settlement trends of the national political organization, the Brotherhood of the Cooperative Commonwealth (BCC). This political movement, which attracted national following and the support of many radicals, had been established in 1895 in the East. The BCC had three central aims: (1) to foster the education of Americans according to socialist principles, (2) to unite all followers of socialism and cooperation within one national organization, and (3) their immediate aim was to find a western, sparsely populated state and settle it with people who aspired to live in socialist communities, a model cooperative commonwealth that would demonstrate the advantages of common production, distribution, and consumption. Gaining a territorial and political base would enable it to take over the state institutions and thus lay the foundation for a socialist government in one state; they could then convert the entire nation.

This ambitious yet naive plan appealed to many followers of the reform movement as a nonviolent alternative to conventional political methods, especially after their failure in the 1896 elections.[2] It began in the socialist reform circles of New England, Maine, and New Hampshire that planned to establish colonies along the East Coast. But after they realized the difficulties of achieving their idea in the densely populated East they opted for the West, especially California, which had only just been opened for settlement. Prominent in the circle were Norman Wallace Lermond and Ed Pelton, both former populist activists with close connections to socialist and reform circles in New England. They tried to attract other prominent personalities such as the socialist Henry Demarest Lloyd and the professor of economics at Boston University P. Parsons. Henry Demarest Lloyd was ready to join in but doubted the feasibility of their colonization plans. His reservations discouraged many of the other prominent followers; nevertheless, the organization expanded throughout the country, and in 1897 there were 125 active circles with about 2,000 registered members in various cities.[3]

The BCC's chances for achieving their goals increased when Eugene V. Debs was attracted to their colony plan. In 1897 he was actively involved in the formation of the United Social Democratic Party, in which he planned to include the American Railway Union (ARU), the BCC, dissidents from the Social Labor Party, and other groups. While building the union, Debs was ideologically attracted to the colonization plans of the BCC but from a different perspective. He did not believe in a model utopian settlement irradiating revolutionary influence on society, but he regarded the concentration of socialist colonies in one territory as assisting the workers in their struggles, either by absorbing those who were unemployed or by giving a haven to those who had been blacklisted. Prominent members of the Socialist Labor Party, who opposed the BCC's colonization plans and who favored a concentrated political effort in the cities and among the unions, tried in vain to stop Debs from supporting the BCC. At the founding convention of the SDA in June 1897, Debs gave a programatic address in which he supported the West Coast colonization plans. However, BCC leaders could clearly discern the different nuances in his attitude. Even though the colonization plan was included in the program, the propounders of political struggles took care to understate its significance within the general targets of the party.

The new party had no clearly defined program and in 1897, during its first year, there ensued a struggle between the different attitudes. Despite a façade of joint participation, the BCC proceeded separately. Lermond confirmed that there would be no merger with the SDA and hastened the practical preparations for their colonization plans.[4] Although there was no definite decision the convention proposed a committee of three "visionaries with practical instincts" who would examine the possibilities and come up with proposals at the convention in 1898. When Lloyd and Grönlund refused to undertake the mission, three others were elected—Borland, Willard, and Hanton—who immediately proceeded to carry out their mission but encountered many obstacles.[5] The first obstacle was financial. The national council of the SDA was not forthcoming and funds had to be raised in the party's branches. The three committee members were inexperienced and wasted many months in fruitless research for a suitable colonization area. By the spring of 1898 they had no practical proposition. Suddenly they were confronted by an idea far removed from the original one: During their visit in a Colorado mining town they were offered a gold mine of "great potential" according to its owners. The committee members, who were eager to achieve anything at all on the eve of the second convention, began to bargain for the mine, but the deal was not put through in time for the convention.[6]

The second SDA convention in June 1898 was to outline the ideological platform of the party and thus end the internal struggle between the "political activists" and the "colonists." In the period between conventions a bitter ideological controversy had emerged between the two trends, finding expression in socialist journals and public meetings. Both camps were planning their strategy for the coming convention and attempted to attract as many followers as possible.

The political activists came mostly from among Marxist circles within the Socialist Labor Party who had adopted the principles of class struggle and overtaking the government via political means as a way to realize socialism. On the other side were different shades of anti-Marxists, anarchists, populists, and Bellamists who were united only by their opposition to the ideology of class struggle and were searching for a nonviolent way to settle the socialist problems. They regarded the cooperative idea as an alternative to class struggle. As the date of the convention approached, the two camps became more militant.[7] The colonists attempted to have as many delegates as possible to pass a decision in favor of colonization simultaneously with political activities. The struggle centered around the elections of representatives of each faction in the various committees. It erupted after an argument over Cyrus Willard's recommendation to purchase the Colorado mining property without proposing how to finance the venture. The proposal was not rejected but only deferred to be reexamined.

The showdowns became inevitable when the platform committee offered two conflicting reports. A majority report called for political action while the minority recommended a combination of colonization and political activities. The debate was lively and lasted long into the night, and when several of the delegates had retired, the vote showed 52 delegates for the minority report of colonization and 37 against. Thus, in the early hours the colonists platform was adopted by the SDA. It was, however, a pyrrhic victory. The minority walked out to meet in a different hall and there created the Social Democratic Party (SDP). Debs had not participated in the floor debate and at first remained cautiously enigmatic. But it soon became clear that he was sympathetic to the political activists who showed an immediate organizational and political aptitude.[8]

After the secession of the "rebels," the colonists became the dominant faction within the SDA and started to organize according to their platform, namely political as well as colonization activities. They published their message in the *Social Democrat* and attempted to attract prominent people. Lawrence Grönlund regarded them for a while as the people who would realize his doctrine and supported them and their journal. Soon, however, he realized that all the leaders of the party had left the SDA and joined the SDP, who were showing organizational efficiency. The SDA learned that victory could be an illusion.

Shortly after this the party died. The journal ceased to appear four weeks after the convention and the branches closed one by one. Only the colonization circle remained, and they proceeded at once with their mission to try and save the party.[9] The national council of the SDA concentrated on raising funds and attracting members for the colonization project. Willard journeyed west, accompanied by J.S. Ingalls, a young Minnesota lawyer who had been active at the convention. They started their tour in a small mining town in Colorado, where unemployment had disillusioned the miners, among them supporters of the colonization at the recent SDA convention. They agreed to join a settlement but objected to Colorado. Willard and Ingalls proceeded westward to Seattle where circles of followers were active and where shortly prior to that Equality had been established by members of the BCC. Assisted by local functionaries they soon found suitable land south of Puget Sound, near the mouth of the Burley River. Willard was empowered by the national council of the SDA to purchase land, and he soon acquired 260 acres to which additional plots were added later, reaching 1,000 acres altogether.[10]

They started to clear the land and late in 1898, at a time when the SDA and the BCC were deteriorating on the political level, they established two colonies in the far West, on Puget Sound. The settlers took their first steps inspired by the belief that they were the pioneers of a huge camp who would follow in their footsteps. Nobody did, and the settlers were left to struggle on their own in the pioneering conditions of the forests of Washington State. Each of the settlements developed separately, and they each deserve special review.

Equality

Equality was named after Bellamy's second novel, published in 1897 following *Looking Backward*. Equality was established on the northern shore of Puget Sound near Edison, on a plot of 280 acres. Between October 1897 and June 1898 additional acres were acquired and Equality owned 600 acres. In November 1897 a group of 15 people began to clear the land and prepare the settlement for the coming of new members in the spring. Their main effort was invested in clearing the forest and building log huts for their accommodation. The first two-story log hut was finished in February 1898 and named Fort Bellamy. On the first floor were the kitchen and dining-room and the second accommodations. Four additional big log huts were constructed during the winter and some dormitories, to house the many families and singles who were expected to arrive in the spring. They were optimistic as to the future, and when the BCC under Lermond, who had remained in Maine, published a call to all socialists in the land to come and join the new colony Equality, many responded. People asked for information and it seemed possible that one-third of the 3,000 members of the BCC would join the colony, but time would prove them wrong. The hundreds did not arrive in the spring. Only after the leaders of the BCC led by Lermond moved to Washington State in March 1898 did scores of new settlers arrive. At this point the formative stage of Equality had ended.[11]

During the first year foundations for a communitarian settlement were laid. Their society's doctrine was the unifying factor of the community. It also shaped their social way of life and their economic set up. The support of the BCC who had not only published propaganda but also helped them financially, inspired the young colony with an optimistic belief in the future. In the summer of 1898 additional members kept arriving and in the autumn they numbered 300. There were two kinds of members in Equality, those who had paid their fees and moved to the settlement, and those who were registered in the BCC and were a tax-paying "reserve" who would join the settlement after having paid a $160 membership fee, among them prominent members of progressive circles in the United States such as G. Herron, the historian G. Commons, and the author and journalist William Dean Howells. Among the colonists were a few families from Maine and New Hampshire and the majority from the Midwest and from towns on the Pacific Coast. Even though they had all been members of the same movement, their motivation for joining the colony varied. Some were socialist idealists or utopians, others searched for a way of life that would provide security from their economic trials. The community was eager to absorb skilled members but those were not always successful, and many of the newcomers had no specific training at all.[12]

From the start Equality's social life was well organized. Their affairs were managed by democratically elected committees. Among the leadership group Ed Pelton was most prominent. He had been active in the BCC in New England and was among the founding members who organized the colony from its first days. Pelton was not a charismatic leader but very well liked. He was also a practical person and his word carried weight. When he was killed in a work accident in 1900, it left a tragic impact on the colony that had lost its popular leader.[13]

At first the conditions were typical of a frontier settlement. Yet their socialist ideology enhanced the colony with a unique quality of communal life. Hardships dictated mutual aid, which their ideology fostered. Their communal dining-room, kitchen, and stores were efficiently run even though not on a high standard. Epicures might have complained about the uncouth and crowded conditions, but during the first year there were only a few complaints. The prevailing mood was optimistic. The decision to move the headquarters of the BCC from Maine to Edison, a town near Equality, was significant for the future of the colony and the movement. The BCC activists were strengthened through their direct participation in the central effort of the movement: additional members registered and contributions increased. After transferring to Washington State the leaders of BCC bought a printing shop and established it in Equality in order to publish their new journal, *Industrial Freedom*. The press became a source of work and income and the task of writing and editing it was handed to Ault, a young journalist from Kentucky who had joined the colony in April 1898. Even though he was just 18-years-old he was one of the prominent members of Equality.[14]

It soon became evident that the transfer of the headquarters to Edison triggered off problematic relationships between the national organization and the colony. The functionaries of the BCC regarded themselves as responsible for the national movement and in charge of the colony which was its cardinal project. Equality was meant to be one of the many colonies spread out over Washington State, a cornerstone of the future socialist commonwealth. Members of Equality saw the situation in a different light. Having received massive support during their first year, they now thought that the most important concern of the BCC should be continuous assistance to Equality, which was at the center of the movement's colonization effort. When there was no influx of new members and Equality remained the one and only colony, its members thought that the BCC should first and foremost ensure its existence instead of undertaking more commitments for new colonization.

Furthermore, geographical proximity caused tensions when the pioneering colonists, who lived frugally, complained about the "affluence" of the BCC functionaries who lived nearby in Edison. They even accused them of spending the money that had been contributed for the colonization activities. Equality demanded that the BCC headquarters should be moved to the settlement. The ensuing struggle in April 1898 almost caused a schism, which was finally avoided through compromise. The colony would be autonomous as to the funds provided by the movement. Responsibilities were clearly defined, the land was registered under the name of the BCC, and all members of the movement could join the colony. Since Equality was the stronger and more organized of the two sides, the agreement would not be a lasting one and new problems would arise. Events in Equality would be affected by what was occurring in the SDA at the time. Events in June 1898 would be fateful for Equality and the whole colonization effort of the party.

At the time when the controversy between the political activists and the colonists raged in the SDA, the tension between the settlers of Equality and the functionaries in Edison increased. The compromise satisfied no one and schisms reappeared. It was triggered off when Lermond, the spiritual father of the BCC, decided in August 1898 to leave Washington State and return to Maine, from where he hoped to resume his activities on a national level. His leaving undermined the stability of the group who had come West with him, and some of them left as well. The center in Edison had lost its status and conditions were ripe for the settlers to win the local controversy. They passed a decision to transfer the BCC's headquarters to Equality. The settlers, who regarded Equality as the hub of all national activity, had gained a point in February 1899, but they had not foreseen the result. From the point of view of public support, they had cut off the branch on which they were sitting.

Equality was now an isolated settlement and all activities outside it were reduced to a minimum. Relations with other branches had been loose even before and now, when there was no headquarters to promote national activities, there was no hope to advance colonization. Membership dropped from about 3,500 to 250 which meant the loss of "reserves" for the colonization and drastic curtailment of financial assistance. In February 1899 Equality functioned without a national movement. The *Industrial Freedom* was still being published there and paid lip service to the ideal of colonization in Washington State. But the April 1899 issue admitted that conditions were not yet ripe for the "grand plan" and it would be better to develop Equality rather than "scatter our forces to the four winds in an attempt to establish several struggling communities simultaneously." These words expressed the process of alienation from the original ideals of the BCC and Equality but were of little assistance to the few new colonies that did appear in Washington. They sent out a call to socialists throughout the land to come, and join Equality and the general targets of the BCC were neglected. The colony was preoccupied with internal social and economic matters.[15]

From the point of view of economic development Equality seemed to be a success. From its first winter the colony had started to clear the land for farming. They leased land from neighbors in order to provide their own essentials. Within a year they had cleared fifty acres for crops and another fifty for pasture. They had planted 3,500 vines and other fruit trees. In the spring of 1898 agriculture was their principal branch. Their success in growing vegetables prompted them to expand their marketable products. They grew potatoes, vegetables, oats, and barley, and only the difficulties in marketing their produce in the nearby towns Seattle and Tacoma prevented their expanding further. They also laid foundations for animal husbandry and early in 1898 bought horses, cows, hogs, and chickens. In the summer of that year they built a large barn and a central building for their livestock which prospered and were the envy of their neighbors, who marveled at the success of these city people.

An important source of income was lumbering. In this forested area they had begun by using borrowed and leased equipment. Later they bought a large sawmill with funds from the BCC. Most of the men worked there and it continued to grow until 1902, when they had to lease it to outsiders.

Another branch which depended on local conditions was fishing. Puget Sound was rich in resources and they put in a big effort to develop a landing stage, bought a sloop and some smaller boats. However their inexperience could not be overcome by their diligence and industry and their fishing attempts never prospered. Several small industries such as shoemaking, tailoring, dressmaking, coppering, blacksmithing, wagon repairing, harness making, and furniture making developed from services provided initially to the colonists. Another unique activity was the production of cereal coffee, which they hoped to sell outside but with limited success. Equality never progressed beyond trying to meet their own needs and after the first good years, hard times arrived and their ambitions declined.[16]

Life on Equality was not concerned with economics alone. During the first year solid foundations for a communitarian life were laid, including accommodations, consumption, cultural activities and education. The communal kitchen and dining-room played an important role in their lives. Three times daily members would meet for leisurely meals and social events. Work was organized, and men and women were placed at all production and service jobs. Members received a weekly budget in tokens which were used locally for their necessities. After building the first two-story building described above, they discontinued the construction of large houses and each family had its separate house. The children lived with their parents and were taken care of by nurses and teachers during work hours.

Special attention was devoted to education. Early in 1898 a department of education and recreation was formed to plan schooling for the many children of all ages that had gathered in Equality. A local school was established for the younger ones and a few older children went to Edison for their schooling. The department was guided by a clear educational philosophy of socialist principles.[17] But the school was not a great success. It lacked suitable teachers, parents did not cooperate, and the school soon lost its uniqueness and taught usual subjects. Still, compared with other schools a high standard was maintained.

Recreational and ideological activities among the youth were more successful. Discussions on theoretical ideology and general topics were held. The youth circle was actively involved in the colony, assisting their elders at different tasks. Most Equality members who had come from the cities were experienced in political and union activities. They had an intellectual-cultural background and recreation was an important factor in the backwoods colony's leisure hours. They had debate circles, lectures on up-to-date topics, choral evenings, music, and a band which also played at the many dances. They owned an extensive library and its books were avidly read. Members performed at the frequent concerts, including the celebrations of Equality's birthday on November 1, the Fourth of July, and May 1, to which the neighborhood were also invited.

The first four years were years of tranquility. Socially Equality was the communal success story in the West. In spite of the hardships of a frontier settlement and of personal tensions which erupted from time to time, their communal life functioned well. Everything seemed to run smoothly, but even during those years things began to go wrong. It was the gradual undermining of the colony's ideas. One of the symptoms was the colonists' neglect of their settlement plans and of capturing Washington State for socialism. Instead they focused on Equality's well-being and this in the long run was the reason for the colony's failure. The first symptom was the steady decrease in membership. Reserves had dwindled and cessation started. The more prosperous the state became, the more talented and professionals who could earn their living outside the commune were tempted to leave. In 1900 their number was 120; in 1903 there were only 38 people left.

In 1902 the *Industrial Freedom* suspended publication and its editor was among the seceders. By then Equality had lost its utopian-idealistic motivation.[18] The early aspirations of being pioneers in the West were forgotten. The colony was a self-contained community whose members tried to make a living and gain a small profit. Their steady economic progress was not sufficient to prevent many from leaving, to better their living standard.

This gradual deterioration of a commune which had only recently been a success story, attracted many reformers who attempted to revive the colony according to their own ways. The first was Alonso Wardall, the Rochdale co-op organizer who visited Equality in 1903 and encouraged the colony to adopt the cooperative. He was turned down. Two years later a more serious and intensive attempt was undertaken by Alexander Horr, an ex-anarchist New Yorker who in the 1890s had been attracted by Theodore Hertzka's utopian ideas. The situation on Equality presented him with the opportunity to experiment with his theory. Horr was accepted as a member and after gaining the trust of some members he invited his followers to come to Equality and begin to organize life there according to the utopian principles of Hertzka.

There were two sides to Horr's activities. On the one hand he tried to revive the colony by injecting a new ideology, on the other hand this was a well-motivated attempt of a new group to take over the institutions and the property of the colony. It could not pass without repercussions; not all members of Equality agreed to adopt the new ideology. There ensued tensions within the new leadership such as the colony had never known previously.[19] Violence erupted and in 1905 accusations of assault and battery were brought in front of the court.

Henceforth the colony knew no peace. Instead of reviving the commune Horr's group had only precipitated the end. In 1906, while the court was hearing the dispute about property rights, a fire broke out in the barn and the flames shot across a path and destroyed the stables and cowshed, the pride and joy of Equality. The fire was the death coup of Equality. Each faction accused the other of arson but nothing was ever proven. Thereafter there was no longer a core of members who maintained Equality in its previous form. On June 1, 1907, ten years after the first idealists arrived in Washington State, the court ordered the colony to be dissolved and its assets to be sold.[20]

The Cooperative Brotherhood at Burley

In September 1898, the Cooperative Brotherhood at Burley was legally registered in Washington State. The society's aim was to establish a settlement that would rely on collective ownership of the land and communal production and consumption.[21] Its founders, Cyrus Willard and J.S. Ingalls, were optimistic as to the society's chances, hoping that the SDA would succeed in enlisting thousands of settlers within a short period.

The first colonists to arrive were unemployed miners from Colorado under their local leader J.C. DeArmond. They had been motivated by their socialist ideals and their wish to solve their acute unemployment problems, and the first group was made up of eleven men, four women, and a boy. The first months were typical of any pioneering settlement: harsh conditions of clearing the land and constructing houses but harmonious relations within the community and between their vision and reality. These miners, who had all gained experience in social struggles and were radicals who regarded the colony as a communitarian-equalitarian unit, were joined by a small group of middle-class intellectuals and idealists who had been influenced by the utopist visions of Bellamy and Grönlund. They were not as radical as the ex-miners, and the different attitudes soon caused tension between the two groups, but at first it was not expressed in hostility.[22]

Willard arrived at Burley soon after it was established and began to publish the local paper *The Cooperator* to promote propaganda and educational activities. This was shortly after the *Industrial Freedom* had been the SDA's platform, because the *Social Democrat*, the party's organ, had ceased to exist. Willard acquired the mailing list of the SDA and published his paper in a small, primitive printing shop on an old press he had purchased. He himself was the editor, and the reporters were members of the colony and party functionaries. The first issue appeared in December 1898 and had only eight pages, and in its editorial Willard specifies the journal's goal: to disseminate communitarianism throughout the world. He hoped to attract progressive people to their venture. In the central article there appeared the story of the establishment of the colony, its legal registration, and the election of is managing body—Willard, Barnes, DeArmond, and Ingalls of Washington. He went on to relate the purchase of 1,000 acres and enthusiastically described the beauty of the site and its prospects. Willard stated that one of the reasons for the hasty establishment of the journal was to attract as many newcomers as possible from throughout the country to Burley. Side by side with communal life each family was promised their own separate house in which to continue their former lifestyle. The only difference would be that they would work together in large groups instead of wasting their strength on individualistic efforts.[23]

The publication of *The Cooperator* was of vital importance for the colony. In addition to its propaganda effect and the work it provided, it also enhanced the colony with uniqueness and independence. From the start Burley was not dependent on the SDA, which at the time was in the throes of disintegration. The journal promised Burley a longer life span. It served to maintain contact with followers throughout the country and provided them with information about all the events on the colony. It also published news about the peripheral circles of the party. Willard was also involved in laying the foundations of the colony's institutions and organizing its work and cultural educational activities. He regarded himself as the founder of Burley and its spiritual leader. But as he was not very popular with the members, he was forced to leave after a short period.

When Willard reached old age in the 1930s he wrote his autobiography and devoted a whole chapter to the period of Burley. He gave an extensive description of the growing tension and the deepening schism between himself and the group, expressing his frustration with the communitarian ideal as realized at Burley.[24] Far from being objective or modest, Willard stressed his immense contribution to the establishment of the colony and called himself the "founder of Burley." He related his personal hardships during the first period and his willingness to make sacrifices for the group. According to him relations soured when his newlywed wife arrived at Burley. She came from an upper-class Chicago family and had never known want. The furniture and clothing she brought with her were above the prevailing standard and caused jealousy and envy, especially among other women. Consequently she was never accepted.[25] But Willard himself was responsible for some of the friction between the members of the colony because of his haughty behavior. Regarding himself as the founder, he also claimed that his talents would be wasted if he did ordinary work such as lumbering. The gap deepened when he accused other members of undermining his leadership and putting obstacles in his way.

In addition, there was an ideological discrepancy between Willard and most of the members of the Cooperative Brotherhood (the colony's official name, even though it was known as Burley). He had embraced socialism after having gone through a period of theosophical doctrine, which continued to influence him during his time at Burley. He tried to preach theosophy unsuccessfully, and renewing his ties with theosophy in the West, he went to Point Loma, near San Diego, to participate in their convention. Shortly after returning to Burley he and his wife decided to leave and join the theosophical community in Point Loma. In his autobiography he admitted that his decision to leave had been caused by his disappointment with the communitarian experiment of the socialist colony but mainly because he could not stand the ideological dictatorship of the majority which chokes all private initiative. He also pointed an accusing finger at the lack of culture and finesse in the personal relations on the colony. He saw around him uncouth and unrefined people who were trying to take over but were lacking the necessary skills. His short-lived experience on the socialist colony only convinced him that in order to succeed they needed some sort of religion as a binding factor. This he had found in theosophy and therefore decided to join the Point Loma community, where he thought that the ideological, personal, and climatic conditions were promising. In spite of the central place Willard had occupied at Burley, his and his wife's leaving caused no crisis. The colony continued to prosper.

Membership of the Cooperative Brotherhood included both residents and nonresidents, as mentioned above. The "reserves" (nonresident) numbers steadily increased and in June 1900 reached 1,000 registered members. Among those who applied for membership were people from all over the United States, from Britain, Germany, Australia, New Zealand, and even the Philippines.[26] It gradually became apparent that the rapid growth of the colony through absorption of members who were unprepared for pioneering life was undesirable. In the editorials of their journal there appeared notices that only pioneers were required. An editorial "Pioneer Material" stressed that: "In the present pioneer stage of our industries a peculiarly constituted individual, both physically and mentally, is required to successfully cope with conditions at Burley." The editorial went on to warn the newcomers not to expect immediately good conditions because, "for the pioneer work it needs individuals who are willing and able to make sacrifices with cheerfulness. Those who think more of the cause then they do of themselves . . . will make good pioneers."[27] In spite of these warnings, many arrived without being called for and their candidacy was discussed only after they had come; some were turned back. The average number of the population was 120.

The colony was managed democratically by an elected committee of trustees. The general meeting had the authority to decide all matters of principle pertaining to their communal life. One of the topics most discussed was how to keep autocratic tendencies in check and maintain democracy. Another topic was the scope and limits of communitarianism. At first the colony was established as a producing unit in which all profits were reinvested. In February 1901 a new set of rules limited the communal practices and increased the families' budget so that individual members could enjoy the profits of their work directly. In spite of criticism that this was a return to the "evil" system of salaries, the ruling was accepted.

A further topic under discussion was their colony policy—whether to invest in Burley or develop additional colonies. After the BCC had collapsed, the tendency at Burley was to concentrate on their own needs rather than establishing new settlements. In this respect they repeated the practice of Equality and with the same result. Meanwhile, the economic effort invested by the members brought prosperity. In February 1901 every economic department was granted autonomy. Department managers formed the board of economic management which met over a week and actively steered the settlement's development. At Burley also lumbering was the central enterprise and served the local building activities and later the neighborhood as well. During the first winter they had purchased a sawmill, but only after finding experts to guide them did they succeed in overcoming their inexperience, and in 1902 the sawmill prospered. Demand was so great that they even considered taking on hired hands, but their socialist convictions were so strong that they rejected the idea and decided to carry on by themselves.[28] As a result of their success they considered developing other industries, but only one—the manufacture of cigars—materialized and became more than a workshop. Their agriculture prospered as well—the land was fertile once it was cleared and irrigation canals constructed. The climate was moderate.

Their journal *The Cooperator* was important not only as a source of income but also as a means of keeping in touch with the world, and with their periphery. It also enhanced the colony's reputation and brought a regular stream of visitors and applicants for membership.[29] These visitors generally encountered a content population. In the days of the colony's fame, life was a moderate combination of the communal effort and extensive privacy for the family. Members said that they were partners only in ways that made life easier, namely work and production. Working together they advanced faster than if the same number of people had executed it separately. While they produced collectively they also built separate houses with plots attached for individual cultivation. Only singles were accommodated in the big central building called "the hotel."

Meals were taken together three times daily, and visitors praised the pleasant atmosphere in the communal dining-room.[30] After work members participated in cultural activities. Religious tolerance prevailed and just as Willard could practice his theosophical doctrines, so could other denominations. Several religious ministers joined the colony, and one of them became the editor of *The Cooperator* and left his impact in several editorials that dealt with Christian socialism.

Tolerance was also evident in matters of education. Even though their attitude was serious and they strove to instill their children with knowledge and values, they did not succeed in establishing their independent educational system. The children were sent to the regional school which after a time was established at Burley. But even then it was not distinct from any other school except for its higher level of education and the "manual training classes."

One thing that distinguished Burley from similar experiments was the quality of its people. The founding members were the Colorado miners who were later joined by middle-class intellectuals. They maintained a policy of selection and were known as "a collection of choice souls."[31] Most of the members had been active in the movement and continued to be involved, traveling to conventions and lectures. Some were active in unions, others were populists, nationalists, theosophists, and Christian socialists. The colony itself did not radiate any political or ideological doctrine. The people who lived in the neighboring settlement attended the entertainment and recreation offered by Burley but continued to be suspicious of "those dreadful socialists."

The same process which had undermined Equality took place at Burley. Members abandoned their colony's goals and concentrated on furthering their own settlement. Within a short period this weakened their will to maintain a unique community. They were involved in their own economic and social affairs and felt that they were stagnating. They stopped growing and some departments were unprofitable and had to be leased.[32] In 1903 Alonzo Wardall, promoter of cooperatives according to Rochdale, came up with a suggestion to organize the colony as a cooperative. He succeeded in convincing a group of members who were eager to transform Burley. They proposed to divide the property into shares. Buildings and institutions that could not be divided would be managed through a cooperative society. Wardall moved to Seattle, and conducted the transformation from there. In 1904 the reorganization was started in stages. The stores were turned into cooperatives, then some production departments were added, and finally the ownership of the land was transferred. There was an opposition that even reached the court, but this could not stop the process. The colony continued as a cooperative until 1912, when it was dissolved. In 1913 a receiver was appointed. Burley ceased to exist, without leaving any impact: of its ideals to turn Washington State into a socialist commonwealth no trace remained.[33]

Notes

1. Charles Pierre Le Warne, *Utopias on Puget Sound, 1885-1915* (Seattle: University of Washington Press, 1975), pp. 16-52; Frederick A. Bushee, "Communistic Societies in the United States," *Political Science Quarterly* 20, no. 4 (1905): 635.
2. Howard Quint, *The Forging of American Socialism: Origins of the Modern Movement* (South Carolina, 1953), pp. 282-85; Le Warne, pp. 55-56.
3. Quint, p. 285; Le Warne, p. 59.
4. Le Warne, pp. 60-61; Quint, pp. 285, 288, 291-95; Bushee, p. 635.
5. The three elected committee members were Richard Hanton, a London-born engineer who had emigrated to the United States as a young man; he became a radical journalist and active in reform movements and in the socialist Labor party. The second, Cyrus Willard, of an established Boston family, became involved with theosophy in the 1890s and was among the founders of The Nationals Club of Bellamy's followers. Later he was interested in workers' problems while serving as correspondent in Chicago. Willard had extensive knowledge in socialism and corresponded with renowned socialists such as Wilhelm Morris, Sidney Webb, and the aged anarchist Peter Kropotkin. The third member on the committee was Borland, a former railway stoker who had been injured in a work accident and since then had begun to be an active unionist and newspaper reporter. Le Warne, pp. 130-32; Quint, pp. 303-4.
6. Quint, pp. 305-6.
7. Ibid., pp. 309-10.
8. Ibid., pp. 310-14.
9. Ibid., pp. 316-18; Le Warne, pp. 134-36.
10. Cyrus Field Willard, "Autobiography" (ms in Houghton Library, Harvard University), pp. 11-13.
11. William Alfred Hinds, *American Communities and Cooperative Colonies* (1878. Reprinted and enl. Philadelphia: Porcupine, 1975), p. 531; Le Warne, pp. 63-64.
12. Le Warne, pp. 74-80; Hinds, p. 532; Ernest S. Wooster, *Communities of the Past and Present* (1924. Reprint. New York: AMS Press, 1974), pp. 47-49.
13. Le Warne, p. 73.
14. Ibid., p. 87.
15. Ibid., pp. 68-72.
16. Ibid., pp. 80-83.

17. Ibid., pp. 94-95.
18. Le Warne, pp. 102-3; Wooster, p. 47; Bushee, pp. 635-36.
19. Wooster, p. 48; Hinds, pp. 534-35.
20. Le Warne, pp. 90, 106; Wooster, pp. 47-49; Hinds, pp. 534-35.
21. Hinds, p. 536; Bushee, p. 637.
22. Willard, *Autobiography*, pp. 15-16, chap. 15.
23. Cyrus Field Willard, ''An Accomplished Fact,'' *The Cooperator* 1 (December 19, 1898); James S. Inglas, ''The Time Has Come,'' *The Cooperator* 1 (December 19, 1898); J.B. Fowler, ''Colony Notes,'' *The Cooperator* 1 (December 19, 1898).
24. Willard, ''Autobiography'', chap. 15.
25. Ibid., pp. 18-23.
26. Ibid., pp. 21-28, 33-34, 38; Hinds, pp. 536-37; Bushee, p. 637.
27. ''Pioneer Material,'' *The Cooperator* 2, no. 48 (November 10, 1900).
28. Le Warne, pp. 146-47, 150; Hinds, pp. 537-38.
29. Hinds, pp. 538-40; ''Local and Personal,'' *The Cooperator* 1, no. 48 (November 11, 1899); ''Knights of Brotherhood,'' *The Cooperator* 2, no. 9 (February 9, 1900); ''Home Items,'' *The Cooperator* 2, no. 13 (March 10, 1900).
30. Hinds, pp. 538-40; Colony Notes,'' *The Cooperator* 1 (December 19, 1898).
31. Le Warne, pp. 160-63; Hinds, p. 540; ''Colony Notes,'' *The Cooperator* 2, no. 25 (June 2, 1900).
32. Le Warne, p. 162; Bushee, pp. 637-38.
33. Le Warne, pp. 162-66; Bushee, p. 638; ''Why Some Cooperative Efforts Have Failed,'' *The Cooperator* 3, no. 29 (June 29, 1901).

14

The Christian Commonwealth in Georgia

A unique commune was established in Georgia in 1896. Its founders had come from among Christian Socialist circles and they intended to create an open, nonselective communitarian society. These circles had been formed within the radical sects of the social Christians in the last two decades of the nineteenth century.[1] Its most prominent personality was the Reverend George Herron of Indiana. He was a Congregationalist minister who had achieved fame in the 1880s through his passionatc prcaching against the foundations and values of capitalist society, and who tried to reach those socialists who were attracted to religion. Traveling widely, he gave lectures in working-class circles and they became his followers. During the 1890s he published eight books in which he expressed his Christian Socialist theories. He attacked capitalism as based on private property, avarice, greed, and exploitation.

His criticism was based on the socialist analysis of capitalist exploitation and he even accepted the Marxist doctrine that morality and values were preconditioned by the economic system, which had to be changed in order to bring about the reform of morals and values. According to Herron there was no possibility of a moral renewal within the capitalist regimes. The innovation of his approach was in the attempt to enhance Christian values with socialist significance. The concept of *atonement* was of a special social meaning, and he called on Christians to regard the cross as a symbol of the suffering and agony that any social change would demand. This was his version of the Christian message for the social ills of his generation. He demanded renunciation and sacrifice: renunciation of private property as a means toward social change.

The social equation was to prove that communism plus Christianity would be the way to man's and society's salvation. There was to be no individual salvation away from social salvation, namely by escaping from obligations to society. Herron stressed the relationship between Christianity and socialism and called for a fraternity of both doctrines. His ideas left an impact on workers and radical clergymen during the late nineteenth century. Some of his followers went a step further and began to realize Christianity and socialism in practice.

Their driving force was Ralph Albertson, a young pastor of the Congregational church in Springfield, Ohio. He had advanced socialist ideas and was influenced by the writings of Henry George, Bellamy, and Tolstoy. The plight of the workers greatly disturbed Albertson, and during a stay in Chicago in 1894 he formed ties with socialist and anarchist leaders and was influenced by them, but he rejected their revolutionary ways. The communitarian idea became an important part of his thinking and, intending to establish a harmonious life there, he resigned his pulpit and joined a small colony in North Carolina, the Willard Cooperative Colony.

During his stay there, Albertson contributed a series of articles to *The Kingdom*, a Christian Socialist journal in which he presented his ideas on a communitarian colony. Simultaneously there appeared articles on the same subject by John Chipman of Florida and G.H. Gibson of Nebraska, and a lively debate ensued in which the opposition rejected the isolationist trends of a communitarian colony in rural surroundings. As a result of these articles a small group of Christian Socialists decided to realize the idea and to found The Christian Commonwealth Colony.

A circular printed in 1896 stated that there were 25 families ready to settle in Florida or Georgia, in which land could be purchased cheaply. The circular read: "We have accepted the law of love, the standard of Christ, the teaching of the same Spirit that led Christ and his disciples to have all things in common." Admittance to the colony was open to all; "beggar and professor would be equal."[2]

In November 1896 they purchased a deserted cotton plantation of 1,000 acres east of Columbus, Georgia, and soon after the first contingent of colonists arrived. In January 1897 the official name was declared to be The Christian Commonwealth Colony, and there were about 100 settlers who had come from Ohio, Florida, Nebraska, Washington, Massachusetts, and California. They were joined by the communitarian group from North Carolina, to which Albertson belonged.

Members were asked, but not required, to sign the covenant in which their goals and principles were stated. These were well defined after a prolonged period of ideological discussions. The founders, who were all Christian Socialist followers of Herron, had despaired of the competitive capitalist regime and undertaken to establish a brotherhood of cooperation within capitalism, not by withdrawing from society but "by giving up private property and its pursuit, and making ourselves brothers to all men." They adopted the open door policy, and were driven to abolish the double standard of most established Christian churches and sects. Like all utopians they believed that through serving as an example they could prove that the kingdom of heaven on earth was feasible.[3] They regarded all obstacles and hardships as "a cross they had to bear" for the sake of society, as Herron had asked of them.

With other socialists they aspired to establish an egalitarian, classless society, but unlike Marxists they did not believe in class struggle or violent revolutionary activities. They hoped that their communal life would instill their members with a feeling of harmony and goodwill. The open door policy admitted everyone, even tramps, and would willy nilly provoke positive reactions and be the real proof of Christian love. But their most important principle was the collective ownership of all property. Only personal belongings were left in the individual's possession, which enabled each member to foster his unique tastes and preferences. They shared all property and all work. Abolishing the principle of salaried work, they even scorned "work notes" and any other form of inducement. Everyone received his food, clothing, and accommodation, and everyone was granted the right to vote. In this respect the Georgia colony was different from all other U.S. communes. It was another aspect of the open door policy, presented by members as vindicating the colony against criticism that it was separating themselves from the world and withdrawing from society.[4]

The Commune's Idiosyncrasy

Curiosity and interest in the commune was widespread. Its reputation increased after their monthly the *Social Gospel* began to appear in February 1898 for the following eighteen months. The decision to publish their own periodical was passed after a debate; some members claimed that it was a luxury and a waste of money and that they should better invest their efforts in improving the colony's economic conditions. Ralph Albertson undertook the responsibility of publishing the monthly and distributing it. He succeeded in making it a profitable business with 2,000 subscribers mainly from among those who were deprived of the Christian Socialist periodical *The Kingdom*, which had been closed down; the *Social Gospel* took its place. It was a serious journal, with five to six pages of information about the commune and 30 additional pages devoted to general theoretical issues such as the pacifist Christian Socialist point of view.[5]

The monthly was the platform for several prominent publicists from those circles, among them P. Crosby, a well-known jurist who had given up his legal and diplomatic careers to devote himself to Christian Socialist publicists. Crosby was influenced by Tolstoy, whom he had met during a tour of Russia and with whom he kept in touch. Tolstoy got to know of the commune through Crosby and corresponded with the editors of the *Social Gospel*. The British socialist leader, Keir Hardy, was also among those who shared interest in the commune and its monthly. Many others from a variety of social backgrounds sympathized with the commune. The Marchand family, ex-Icarians, who had moved nearby, were frequent visitors, as were professors from Yale, Harvard, and Columbia Universities.

During the first two years the colony developed steadily, fully adhering to the communitarian principles and their open door policy. Members were aware of the danger of unselectivity and the joining of antisocial, nondesirable elements whose only motive was to enjoy material security. The colony counted on their poverty to protect them from members who came for selfish reasons, and indeed about 25 percent of the scores who had come in the first year left because of the harsh physical and spiritual conditions. They could not get used to a system where the individual's contribution was never a basis for rewards.[6]

New members kept arriving from throughout the country as a result of the information about the colony published in *The Kingdom* and later in the *Social Gospel.* In 1898 their membership was about one hundred. It was the apex of the commune. Their development was described in a pamphlet published that year.[7] Most of the effort of the members was devoted to clearing the ground for cultivation, building cottages and workshops, and laying foundations for future development. The first edition of their local paper summed up their economic achievements: 14 cottages for families, a large bachelors' hall, dining-room, school, printing shop, and the monthly's editorial. They had also constructed barns, a sawmill, a blacksmithshop, and a flour mill. They had cleared 200 acres for cultivation and fenced 300 for pasture. An orchard of 35 acres was planted, and they planned to add an orchard of 10,000 Japanese plum and peach trees. They raised oats, rye, some wheat and barley, corn, sweet potatoes, and garden vegetables. Their farm stock was small, consisting of a few cows, horses, pigs, and a flock of poultry.[8]

Work was organized communally. Labor was allocated after daily consultations with department heads; deep commitment to their jobs was the only incentive for each member's contribution, as was their communal need and sense of responsibility. The *Social Gospel* dealt with this frequently: "Everybody . . . found in the common good the only reward they wanted and the displeasure of the community the greatest punishment possible." Another outstanding characteristic of the colony was their special membership, which included people of a high education level. An article about the various department heads pointed out academicians such as William Damon, who for nineteen years had taught as professor of theology at Napa County University, California, ministers of the church, engineers, and other professionals.[9]

In 1898 they began to plan an industrial enterprise, and calls for funds in the form of donations or investments were addressed to the friends of the colony.[10] The effort bore fruit and at the beginning of 1899 a cotton mill was opened for the manufacturing of towels. It was a new aspect of the commune's economy, because while other departments produced for their community's needs and only little of their harvest was marketed, the cotton mill's produce was intended to be sold on the competitive market. Thus the colonist could not escape the capitalist system which they had so violently criticized. In reports on the colony's economic affairs there was evidence that the mill took up much of their effort.[11] After a period of six months they realized that they had bought faulty equipment and that a further $250 were needed to replace the cheap and antiquated looms. Again they applied for help through their periodical and received double the amount they had asked for, mainly because of the generous donation of $250 from a friend in Paris. The same issue of the *Social Gospel* reported on the resumption of the mill's production and the many orders they had received.[12]

In spite of optimistic predictions, the colony began to deteriorate. To understand the reasons we have to study the social development and internal organization of the commune.

Progress and Heartbreak

During the first two years the colony progressed according to the principles of its founders, namely, full communitarian production, work, and consumption as well as social and cultural activities. The family unit was maintained, and if there were rumors in the neighborhood that the sex relations of the members were irregular, this was not an uncommon allegation where communes were concerned. Just as in the other cases, it expired that at no time was an unconventional attitude towards sex tolerated at the Christian Commonwealth Colonies, and the rumours were the result of an imagination which could not accept anything that was different.[13]

Children lived with their parents in cottages, and every family had a budget for clothing and other expenses. Their distinctively marked clothes were washed in the communal laundry, and they kept to a norm of attire to avoid inequality.[14] At first, before they had a communal dining-room families ate at home, but later most had their meals together, and only four preferred to continue having their meals separately. The food was wholesome and satisfying, but there was not much variety and no luxuries. The dining-room was pleasant and also served as a social meeting place.

The intellectual make up of most of the members made them devote special attention to educational and cultural activities. A school was started right away, and they also aspired to establish a university to enhance their youngsters' education and to satisfy the requirements of the Christian Socialist movement which were not met by the existing institutes of higher education.[15] These plans never materialized. The local school was taught by members and recognized by the regional school authorities. Some of the area's settlements sent their children to the commune's school whose curriculum did not differ greatly from that of other schools. The only subject taught in addition to the regular ones was the principles of communitarian life. Letters written by ex-pupils testify to the success of this side of their education.[16]

Educational activities were also extended to the adults, who attended every class—the most popular were discussions on literature, philosophy, and the sciences. There were also courses on general education that met three times a week and were tutored by members. They owned an extensive library of 1,400 books.[17] On Sundays there were intensive, mostly religious activities, with a Bible study group that met before the Sunday morning service. There was complete religious freedom and many different denominations were represented in the colony. Ralph Albertson was a Congregationalist, but other founders were Presbyterians, Episcopalians, and Quakers.[18]

The government of the colony was democratic and there was no authoritarian leader. Albertson, who had been the most influential member and a natural leader of the group, refused to be elected president. He chose to concentrate on oral and written educational and propagandist activities. From the first days of the colony they insisted that their community was a movement and not a single commune.[19] No wonder then that during their second year they began to plan a new colony in west Florida. They sent out a call to all their followers to join the new colony under John Chipman.

The optimistic enthusiasm which had characterized the colony began to receed in 1899 when a number of social, personal, and economic calamities struck. A severe drought in the summer of 1898 and heavy snow in the winter of 1899 demolished their crops. Their food supplies were rationed and their income significantly reduced.[20] Yet, the worst was still to come, and it would affect their open door policy. One of the members who had been on the commune for a certain time wrote a book in which he presented the commonwealth as a free love colony. His explicit purpose was to discredit the colony in the conservative South. After a lengthy ideological debate he was expelled, but returned some weeks later intending to undermine the commonwealth from within, with the aid other embittered and disgruntled members. Their aim was to cause the colony to be liquidated and its assets distributed. They hoped that because of the Commonwealth's pacifist principles there would be no use of force in handling the affair.

However, in a general meeting of all members it was decided to fight the issue in court and rid the colony of all undesirable elements with the help of the local sheriff. This was regarded by many as the final surrender of their principles and a discredit to their faith. Not all members supported the decision to resort to legal measures; among them was Albertson, who regarded this as the final ideological surrender. He consequently wrote a literary work in which he described the colony's deterioration.[21] In view of their leader's opposition the *Social Gospel* gave much space to discussing the issue and in general supported the decision to turn to the court, explaining it as a vital necessity.

The internal debate in fact had already began earlier, when the colony was incorporated in November 1899. This was looked upon as an important and the first concession to expediency, for it meant that the forces of the state were involved in protecting their property and their way of life from undesirable elements that exploited the colony. In the summer of 1899 an additional calamity struck in the form of a typhoid epidemic that hit scores of members. The physical weakness that followed also undermined their morale. One of the victims was Albertson, who was critically ill for many months and on recovering went to recuperate away from the colony. His absence affected the management of the commune. This coincided with a wave of abandonments that further diminished their work force and undermined their morale. Among those who left were several of the founding members.[22]

Albertson returned in order to try and save the colony from complete disintegration. A small group of members remained for another six months. They attempted to carry on the economic activities, stressing the importance of their continuing to be a model commune. With this in mind they got in touch with Ruskin and Burley, the two other socialist communes, and in April there was even talk of a union between the Christian Socialist Commune and Ruskin. This was supported by the *Social Gospel*, but it became clear that the Christian Socialist Commune would have to give up too many of their principles and that the spirit of the commonwealth could not be maintained, and the union never materialized.[23]

A handful of loyal members stayed on until the spring of 1899, when they realized that there was no hope of reviving the community's life. They decided to dissolve the colony and sell its assets. The list of members entitled to a share in the proceeds was given to the court and included all those who had been members of the colony within the past six months, although in leaving they had forfeited all legal claims. They received only $8.50 each, but the principle of equality was maintained.

Ralph Albertson, who lived on the colony from its first to its last day, later attempted to sum up the experiences of establishing the commonwealth. He estimated that the creativity and practical approach inherent in the commune could have ensured its unique existence without selectivity of members, with a lack of capital, in an arrid area, and on a cotton farm on which the soil had lost its fertility. Using an apologetic tone, he did not put the blame for failure on the open door policy, which was one of the important principles of the commune and its raison d'être. Instead he blamed the financial difficulties, poor soil, and the cruel typhoid epidemic for the deterioration of the colony in its early years, preventing it from developing its unique character and realizing its full potential. On the other hand, objective observers such as the Reverend Dr. Alexander Kent, and Professor Bushee attribute the dissolution of the colony to the open door policy and to the influx of low-grade colonists which this policy encouraged. They also claimed that the leaders of the colony "lacked business sense."[24]

Most of the colonists, on looking backwards across the years, regarded the experiment as one of the most important interludes in their lives. Professor Damon, one of the colony's founders, wrote several years later: "I have never regretted the efforts we made at that time. . . . I believe we are better and stronger men and women for the experience we gained."

Notes

1. Social Christianity ensued from Calvinist Protestantism. A novelty was their attitude toward social matters and the removal of religion from its theological, ritualistic confinement while integrating it with social activities. Calvinists reacted against the Lutheran and Catholic practice of separating matters concerning this world from the perfect hereafter. They also rose up against the isolationist concept of the *Chosen* that was a characteristic of the Pietist-Separatist sects. Social Christianity demanded involvement and activity in world affairs in order to improve and change them. The call went out for more social involvement but they were neither radical nor socialists. On the contrary, most adopted liberal conservative attitudes on social matters and only a minority went as far as to transfer their social commitment into actively striving toward changing the regime in the spirit of socialism. James Dombrowski, *The Early Days of Christian Socialism in America* (Ph.D dissertation, Columbia University, 1937; reprint. New York: Octagon, 1966), pp. 14-30, 180-90.
2. Dombrowski, pp. 132, 136; Alexander Kent, "Cooperative Communities in the United States," *Bulletin of the Department of Labor* 35 (July 1901):612-13; *Social Gospel* (February 1898).
3. Dombrowski, pp. 147, 193.
4. Ibid., pp. 140-44; "Colony Notes," *Social Gospel* (August 1898):26; "The Strain of Love," *Social Gospel* (February 1898):21; "Equality and Unlikeliness," *Social Gospel* (November 1898); "The Assistant Cook," *Social Gospel* (July 1898).
5. *Social Gospel* (February 1898; April 1898; August 1898). The *Social Gospel* followed the life of the community until its decline. The newspaper continued to appear in New York State for several years.
6. Kent, p. 613; Dombrowski, p. 146; "Colony Notes," *Social Gospel* (March 1898).
7. *Social Gospel* (April 1898); William Alfred Hinds, *American Communities and Cooperative Colonies* (1878. Reprinted and enl. Philadelphia: Porcupine, 1975), p. 522.
8. *Social Gospel* (February 1898); Dombrowski, pp. 148-49.
9. Kent, p. 613; Hinds, p. 524; *Social Gospel* (March 1898):23; "Colony Notes," *Social Gospel* (April 1898):22-23.

10. "Our Present Needs," *Social Gospel* (February 1898):25-28; *Social Gospel* (September 1898; October 1898).
11. *Social Gospel* (January 1899):23; (February 1899):23; (April 1899):23; (September 1899):25-26.
12. "The Cotton Mill," *Social Gospel* (November 1898):26-27.
13. Dombrowski, p. 152.
14. "Colony Notes," *Social Gospel* (April 1899):22; "Colony Notes" *Social Gospel* (August 1899).
15. *Social Gospel* (February 1899):28, (July 1898):24.
16. Kent, p. 614; Hinds, p. 523; *Social Gospel* (March 1898):21; (August 1899):21; (June 1899):24.
17. Dombrowski, p. 156; *Social Gospel* (February 1898); (December 1898):26.
18. "A Sunday Evening Talk," *Social Gospel* (June 1898):21-22; Dombrowski, pp. 154-55.
19. *Social Gospel* (May 1899):24-25; "Colony Notes," *Social Gospel* (April 1898); "A New Colony," *Social Gospel* (October 1898):20.
20. *Social Gospel* (March 1899):23-25; (June 1899):28.
21. Dombrowski, pp. 148, 164; *Social Gospel* (January 1899).
22. Dombrowski, pp. 148, 164-65; Kent, pp. 613-15; "A Law Suit," *Social Gospel* (July 1899); *Social Gospel* (January 1899):21; (July 1899):24, (August 1899):28; (September 1899):27; (October 1899):30-31.
23. *Social Gospel* (September 1899):27; (November 1899):28; "A Quiet Month," *Social Gospel* (April 1900):29; "The Assistant Cook," *Social Gospel* (June 1900):16.
24. Hinds, pp 528-29; Kent, p. 616; Frederick A. Bushee, "Communistic Societies in the United States," *Political Science Quarterly* 20, no. 4 (1905):625-26; Ralph Albertson, *A Survey of Mutualistic Communities in America* (1936. Reprint. New York: AMS Press, 1973), pp. 415-16.

15

Llano de Rio: A Socialist Commune in California and Louisiana

In 1914 five socialists from Los Angeles chose to celebrate May 1 in an original way: on that morning they set out to establish a model communitarian settlement. The site they had chosen was in the Mojave desert in southern California about 45 air miles north of Los Angeles but over 90 miles across the desert. Their equipment consisted of a covered wagon, two pairs of horses, one cow, nine pigs and a lot of faith. Under the circumstances of those times theirs was indeed a daring venture, and they needed much optimism to expect their small kernel to prosper in the arid desert conditions and the barrenness of the California Socialist Party. But after only several days the socialist colony in the desert was joined by a growing number of members. Within a year they numbered about 300 and owned an impressive inventory. Two years later the founders could celebrate May 1 at a festive rally attended by about 800 settlers. Thus, with momentum and rapid tempo Llano, the biggest socialist communitarian experiment of the twentieth century in the United States was established.

The initiative to establish the commune and the vision which fostered it during its early stages are linked with the personality of Job Harriman, a lawyer and one of the most outstanding figures within the American Socialist Party in the beginning of the twentieth century; Harriman had been the socialist candidate for mayor of Los Angeles in the 1911 elections and was defeated.[1] His failure, in addition to the other political setbacks of the Socialist Party he had experienced caused him to despair of achieving socialism via the political struggle. While pondering on his defeat he recalled utopian ideas with which he had been instilled in the past. Abandoning his political career, Harriman devoted himself to establish a model communitarian colony. Several years later the aged Harriman told about the change in his life to Ernest Wooster, who was preparing the history of Llano.[2]

In that interview Harriman claimed that the change in his convictions had occurred as early as 1900. It was when he realized that the Socialist Party should be involved in the trade unions. The defeat in the presidential elections had reinforced his conviction "that the movement must have an economic foundation." He began to turn his attention to the study of means by which he "could lay some such foundation, even though it be a small as well as an experimental one." With this in mind he began to establish a communitarian settlement. In the interview Harriman explained:

> Having been a socialist for 23 years and a believer in the theory of economic determinism and in Marx's philosophy of surplus value as determined by the social labor power necessary to produce products . . . I assumed that if a co-operative colony could be established in which an environment were created that would afford each individual an equal and social advantage that they would . . . react harmoniously to this environment and the extreme selfishness and greed as it appears in the capitalist . . . would be done away. . . . The purpose of all this was to show that a community could live together in harmony, could produce its own living, direct all of its members, maintain a higher standard of living than is usually maintained—and all with far less labor. . . . I thought that if this could be done we could use this community as an example by which other communities could be built. . . . It became apparent to me that people would never abandon their means of livelihood, good or bad, capitalistic or otherwise, until other methods were developed which would promise advantages at least as good as those by which they were living.[3]

A Socialist on the Road of Settlement

After these ideas had crystallized in Harriman's mind, he set out to realize them. The first step was to gather a group of socialist activists who, like him, were disappointed by the results of their political achievements. Together they sought to establish a model settlement. Touring the vicinity of Los Angeles, Harriman discovered a large tract of about 9,000 acres which was about to be sold cheaply. It was part of the Antelope Valley in the Mojave Desert, an arid area considered suitable for cultivation because of the abundant sources of water nearby. Several attempts of settling the area had previously been made. The land belonged to the Mescal Water and Land Company, which was interested in attracting settlers and had begun a project of digging a tunnel to bring irrigation water from the rich aquifers in the area. When this failed the company withdrew and decided to sell its shares cheaply. Harriman was quick to exploit the situation, and raised only a small amount of money among his business acquaintances in Los Angeles, but it sufficed to ensure the purchase of the company's shares.

After having acquired the shares, he set out on a campaign to raise more funds and attract candidates for a settlement. This was accompanied by a wide propaganda campaign for a model communitarian settlement, emphasizing the advantages it would have in developing the area. Simultaneously, Harriman and his friends bought the socialist journal the *Western Comrade* and turned it into the platform for the movement and its ideas. The paper published several articles that described the advantages of Antelope Valley as a "veritable Eden" and the future colony as "a gateway to freedom." The *Western Comrade* gave a detailed description of the valley, which lay at an altitude of about 3,500 feet and had a pleasant climate in spite of the desert area. The articles described the beautiful vistas of the mountains surrounding the colony, and depicted the land as having rich agricultural potential when irrigated. Several places being watered by creeks were described as especially attractive for tourist development.[4]

Their extensive propaganda was a success and many candidates were anxious to join the new colony. Most of them came from socialist circles even though the ideological aspect of their enterprise was not emphasized. Shares were sold according to the capitalistic procedures, but soon they were urged to adapt the stockholding company to the needs of the settlement enterprise and put their efforts into organizing new candidates rather than to raising funds. They therefore established the Llano del Rio Company in 1914, named after one of the two creeks on the proposed settlement's land.

The company was officially registered in California and eventually issued two million shares. To become a member in the colony a candidate was required to purchase 2,000 shares of stock, 500 paid immediately in cash and the rest during the stay on the settlement. Each settler was promised a daily wage of $4 but had to allot $1 of this to the purchase of his remaining shares. The remaining $3 wages would cover all living costs. The company agreed to provide all supplies at cost and to provide living quarters, education, and health services. Any surplus income was to be credited to the member at the end of each year. Nobody could acquire more than 2,000 shares, thus avoiding inequality and preventing the company from turning into a capitalist holding company. On joining, members were not asked to give up their private property, only to promise not to make any use of it. Membership was not automatically granted to those who bought shares. Each candidate had to hand in his application and was screened by the board of directors. This enabled them to supervise the absorption of new members.[5]

Llano

In the spring of 1914 there were already scores of potential members. The first steps were taken when the symbolic cornerstone was laid on May 1. Early in 1915 the company numbered 300, 150 of which were members in the new colony Llano.[6] During the next three years the population increased steadily, reaching an apex of 1,100 in May 1917. Most of the members came from socialist circles in California and states west of the Rockies. Others came from the East and New England and some even arrived from Europe. Some members had experienced communal life in Washington State and in Ruskin, Tennessee. Most were established workers or belonged to the middle classes, because the $500 purchase of shares prevented the joining of less affluent candidates. Many declared that they had experience in farming, others were tradesmen or industrial workers, constructors, miners, drivers, or printers. Within three years the colony had spread over 9,000 acres, one-third of which had been legally acquired and the other was leased at different conditions. There were 1,400 acres under cultivation and the rest was being cleared. The colonists were negotiating the purchase of additional plots nearby in order to turn them into recreation and tourist sites.[7]

The first months were devoted to construction work. The rapid expansion of both population and economic activities entailed intensive building efforts to keep in step with their needs. This dictated the use of temporary building materials for housing, and desert conditions allowed for accommodation in tents, wooden huts, and even some adobe brick houses.[8] There was hardly enough time for planning or aesthetic considerations, and the colony took on the aspect of impermanence. Even three years later there were few well-built houses. The central public building included a club, living quarters for singles, and a large dining-room and was constructed on local stone foundations and its walls and ceiling were manufactured from wooden logs, giving it a distinctively different architecture. All public, social, and cultural activities of the colony took place there. Within the first year the school building was constructed and so were a printing shop, several workshops, and agricultural buildings. Three years later a large settlement with scores of wood and adobe houses had spread out over a wide area of desert land, while here and there green fields broke up the arid monotony. It was an active and lively colony that regarded itself as the forerunner of a row of socialist settlements and Llano was to be its urban cooperative center. Its design and city plans were discussed at the general meetings; its maps were published in its periodical.[9]

Llano's development from its inception was characterized by a trend to establish a mixed economy. After three years there was a list of 66 industrial and service enterprises. To get an idea of their variety let us mention some of the more outstanding: Among the agricultural branches there were crops of corn, wheat, rye, alfalfa, cotton, peanuts, strawberries, sugarcane, a large vegetable garden which provided all the settlement's needs (in fact, the colony grew most of its provisions—75 percent in 1916 and 90 percent in 1917), orchards of pears, plums, vineyards of wine and table grapes. The livestock included 200 cattle, a pigsty, a chicken house, a rabbit hutch and fish hatchery (some fishpards were being planned), and a bee hive. Side by side with their farming their service and industrial branches included a cabinet shop, and a shoemaker's, a cannery, a lime kiln, sawmill, and a printing shop in which local and socialist magazines were printed. Their inventory included tractors for farming and land clearing. Enormous capital and manpower were invested in the development of irrigation systems on which their future in the desert depended. Three years after its inception there were high hopes for the economic prosperity of Llano.[10]

The colony showed impressive prospects in other areas as well. From their early days they had devoted a great deal of attention to the education of their 150 children. The Montessori School took in children from age two and a half to six. The older ones attended classes up to junior high school. The man who founded Llano's educational establishment was George Pickett, one of the first members of Llano. He was an outstanding person who also put his stamp on the colony's character throughout its existence. He had never enjoyed any formal education as a boy and was not an educator. Before joining Llano he had been an insurance agent, a salesman, a baseball coach, and a dance teacher. When asked to take charge of education in the colony, George Pickett and his wife, who were childless, devoted themselves heart and soul to turning it into the focus of the colony's social life.

Their educational enterprise was to be unique. Pickett was the initiator of a decision that 40 acres be set aside for classrooms and a library. He developed a children's farm that included horses, goats, rabbits, and chickens. The children worked on their own farm, tending their livestock and also participated in the work on the colony. There soon evolved an educational framework that integrated regular school subjects with practical work and vocational training on the colony's branches. The school and its farm were called "the children's colony." It formed a kind of conclave within the settlement, with independent study and social activities. The children participated in the general activities but also undertook special assignments under Pickett's guidance such as road repair work and helping on large construction projects. An organic integration evolved between the school and the colony. Members studied in adult classes and children joined the commune's cultural activities such as concerts and dances, whether organized by the children themselves or by their elders.[11]

"The Eyes of Socialists Everywhere are Upon Us"

Life on Llano included a variety of social and cultural activities. The founders were convinced that they were establishing a model society on their colony and were eager to enrich the social and ideological activities after work. Most visitors were impressed by the intellectual atmosphere that prevailed everywhere, whether in the social club, the dining-room, or in small circles at members' houses. World affairs, ideology, politics, and philosophy were frequent topics of conversation. Every Sunday afternoon they attended a forum on ideological matters in the members' club house. Adult classes were held in the school on weekday evenings. An extensive library was at the disposal of members and children. Hobbies were encouraged and an art studio was opened to members under the guidance of a well-known sculptor. A drama circle performed from time to time and a mandolin orchestra gave concerts. Musicians among the members gave recitals and even performed in the vicinity. There were also many sports activities—a swimming pool was dug in the first year, tennis courts and other ball games such as baseball, basketball and football were popular. Teams would compete outside the colony. Some of the most popular social occasions enjoyed by all were musical evenings, theater shows, and especially dances. These took place each Saturday night. Children had their own dances and also took classes in dancing. These parties attracted many outsiders from the area. The climax of the social activities occurred once a year on May 1, when the colony celebrated its birthday. It was a holiday on which all members enjoyed a picnic; speeches were held side by side with games and entertainment was provided by the members themselves. Many of their neighbors and socialists from Los Angeles also attended.[12]

Relations between Llano and the Socialist Party of California were complicated and ambivalent. Often a feeling of tensions and alienation prevailed. An active socialist cell of scores of members was the focus of the colony's ideological life. Many of the members attended its weekly meetings. George Harriman, the president of the board of directors and the spiritual leader of Llano, regarded the colony as a socialist experiment, a model community which would lead the way toward social change of the capitalist system. In a pragmatic article, "Llano—Community of Ideals,"[13] published in the colony periodical, he explained that "it was undertaken by a number of socialists, though it was in no way connected with the socialist party. . . . It is our belief that primarily this is an industrial process, secondarily it is political. Industrial action is vital initiatory, impelling and radical. Political action is essentially conservative. It will require more than votes to put socialism into operation. Voting is important but industrial action is imperative."

Harriman's ideas were considered utopian by members of his party. In spite of the personal relations he had with its functionaries and his standing in its institutions, his devotion to Llano caused many misunderstandings even though not a schism. Llano was regarded by the Socialist Party leaders as a hopeless utopian experiment that removed many party members from the cardinal political struggle. This was expressed in a letter written by the Los Angeles Socialist Party's secretary to the members of Llano:

> A mistaken notion has appeared in the minds of some of the colonists that I was opposed to the Colony, and that I was fighting it. This is the farthest from the truth. On the contrary I have been very solicitous for its success and would rejoice with you in seeing it realize its full purpose and object. . . . [However] the promoters of the Colony made a mistake in not clearly and definitely showing that there was no connection between the party and the colony. My reasons for

> stating this are that many people went into the colony with the idea that it was a socialist institution and having an exaggerated idea as to what the colony would accomplish, expecting the inauguration of the Co-operative Commonwealth.[14]

Further evidence of the ambivalent relations between the party and Llano may be found in the memoirs of Walter Milsap, one of the founders of Llano. In a 1969 interview he recalled that the colonists were never active in any of the election campaigns even though they were members of the Socialist Party, that they were busy making a living and building a roof over their heads, and that therefore the party withdrew its support. Many members of the colony did not even belong to the Socialist Party. Although they had to sign a declaration of principles that contained socialist elements, there was no specific paragraph that demanded a political socialist identity. The same was true concerning the founding principles of Llano. The *Western Comrade* specified elements of equality, cooperation, an identity of interests between the members, and that the community owned the means of production, a promise to provide work for the unemployed, the creation of a harmonious social environment (not one of competition), a fight against selfishness and greed, and without ever mentioning the theory of socialism. Members of Llano were careful not to identify too closely with the Socialist Party, in order to attract members from a broader periphery and also because their areas of interest differed from those of the urban party.[15]

An effort was made to attract many visitors who would spread Llano's reputation far and wide and bring new colonists. Most of the visitors were from socialist circles in California and other western states; some came from further away. One article even bragged that "the eyes of the socialist world are on Llano."[16] It is doubtful that this was the case in 1915, but the *Western Comrade* published many of the visitors' impressions, some of whom even joined the colony. Until 1917 the population increased steadily. Yet, sharp-eyed visitors could doubtlessly discern that not all was well; it was not just the overt poverty and the Spartan existence that could be explained by the pioneering conditions in the desert: Worse by far were the first schisms which had appeared in the colony's social fabric.

Internal Friction

The administration of Llano was frought with internal controversies from the outset. On the one hand it was a corporation which represented the stock holders and on the other it attempted to establish a democratically managed system that would represent all the members of the commune. During their first years in California the stockholding company, run by a board of directors, attempted to appoint a managing board and an executive board from among the members. The managing board appointed a farm manager who had authority over all the department managers. They met every evening to plan the next day's work. These regular meetings were actually the sole permanent economic institution. During the first year, members proposed that the general meeting would be the institute that directly represented public opinion. They succeeded, and the general assembly was open to everyone aged eighteen and over. Yet, its authority was never clearly defined and soon the general assembly degenerated into a chaotic platform on which everyone could air his theories. According to members of Llano it was "democracy rampant, beligerent unrestrained; an inquisition, a mental pilory, a madhouse of meddlesomeness and attempts at business, a jumble of passions and idealism and all in deadly earnest."

Most attacks were aimed at those in positions of authority, many of whom had to resign because of public opinion. Members involvement did not further the colony's interests. Some groups exploited the situation in order to advance their own causes; not all were idealists and there were even some who were after material gains. There was an attempt to revise the constitution by establishing more efficient institutions, but lacking an authoritative leadership, the experiment failed. Harriman was not a talented executive, and he was absent most of the time. The hardships of the early years were blamed on him, and the administration came under constant attack for mismanaging the commune.[17]

Life was objectively hard and frustrating in these early years, but there had also been unrealistic expectations, and more than anything the blame should be put on the inexperienced management. Most members had come to the commune expecting a heaven on earth. They were dissatisfied with the scarcity of homes, the lack of community services, the inefficient work procedures and the general mismanagement. Having hoped for a life of prosperity, they were provided with only the bare necessities. It was not surprising therefore that a group of dissidents organized an opposition called "the welfare league," to resist the politics of the administration. The leadership and Harriman reacted by strongly suppressing them and most were forced to leave the commune for the reason that an opposition was not to be permitted on a commune that aspired to achieve a harmonious life. The opposition members moved to Los Angeles, from where they directed a bitter tirade of propaganda against Llano.

The expulsion of the opposition did not remove all internal unrest. Others organized in underground groups but were given a choice of disbanding or leaving. Many of ex-Llano members who had gathered in Los Angeles continued to fight legal battles against the commune. They accused the management of mishandling funds and found support in a recent California legislation of the Blue Sky Law, which was aimed at protecting small investors from losing their money in the many unsound stock companies that were springing up all over the state. The law entailed supervision of financial company balance sheets by the California Commissioner of Corporations. To examine the accusations of the dissidents, an inspector was sent to examine the commune's finances. The Llano funds were found to be seriously mismanaged. Among other defects the supervisor found that members' share monies had been used to finance the daily necessities of food and fodder. As a result the commissioner stopped all Llano shares from being marketed in California.

Harriman, worried about these limitations which would curtail the colony's freedom of action, initiated a financial manipulation. He was assisted by Mr. Eglestone, who created a parallel company in nearby Nevada, making use of the prevailing practice to transfer shares to a fictitious company. The Llano del Rio Company of California thus became the Llano del Rio Company of Nevada.[18] These financial manipulations saved the Llano Company from state interference and provided it with the vital freedom of action to attract new members. These, in turn, brought much-needed funds to keep the colony going. The Harriman-Egleston manipulation only served to sweep the colony's financial problems under the carpet, without solving their basic economic problems. Llano's economy was rapidly expanding but did not make any profit. The desert conditions and members' inexperience contributed to the colony's lack of rentability. Even after the irrigation system had been completed, their high hopes never materialized.

All these problems did not succeed in undermining Llano's morale as much as the disappointment caused by their failure to exploit the water resources. The rapid growth of the colony, which in 1917 numbered 1,100 members, made them utterly dependent on exploiting all available water resource. Harriman, who had in the past consulted irrigation experts, estimated that their colonization effort in the desert would enjoy abundant water. Accordingly, the colony planned to dam reservoirs and dig wells for underground aquifers that would provide sufficient water to irrigate some 50,000 acres. During the colony's three years of existence, vast funds as well as an enormous physical effort had been invested in constructing dams and digging canals, a tunnel, and wells. In 1917 it became evident that all their efforts had been in vain because the hoped-for underground aquifer in the Antelope Valley had not materialized. A series of earthquakes had resulted in the water being diverted in a different direction.

In addition, 1917 was a drought year and neighboring farmers demanded their share in the little water that was available. Yet in May of that year an article published in the *Western Comrade* described a plan of irrigating 50,000 acres in an attempt to hide the truth. All those who considered joining the colony were promised abundant land and water; this did not help. During the summer matters came to a head and in the October 1917 issue of the *West-*

ern Comrade there were indications that Llano could not support its population because of irrigation problems. The writer went on to state that Harriman was on the lookout for an alternative site for the colony.[19] In fact, Harriman had started to search for additional areas of settlement as early as 1916 and checked possibilities in Oregon, Arizona, and other parts of California. There was also a suggestion to join another socialist group in Nevada. This was the very same colony that had cooperated with Harriman in his financial manipulations. For various reasons nothing came of it.

Early in 1917 Harriman heard of land that could be purchased from a large company in west Louisiana, The Gulf Lumber of St. Louis. They had finished clearing the land of the more profitable kinds of lumber and their main sawmill had just gone up in fire. They offered 16,000 acres of cleared land which included the company's camp and installations. The price was very tempting, but Harriman hesitated to bring the matter before Llano's board of directors before checking all the details. After months of collecting information he finally brought his suggestions to the board members and the general assembly. It was in August of 1917, during the arid and depressing period of disappointment, and the assembly enthusiastically embraced the new options and decided to send a mission to Louisiana. Harriman and his friends were careful not to present the search for a new site as a failure of the Llano experiment. This might have undermined the movement's efforts and prevented others from joining the colony. He presented the move as a step toward expansion because of increased membership. The move to the new area was presented as intended for only those members who craved adventure and new beginnings. The minority who were attracted to the beauty of the desert and its climate would stay on to cultivate a small intensive farm.

In September the mission returned and published an enthusiastic report in the *Western Comrade*. They stressed the advantages of the new site, and the style of their descriptions was similar to the propaganda that had appeared prior to their settling in California. They told of the large hilly area of cleared land in west Louisiana, where the climate was healthy and pleasant, which was important because Louisiana was infamous for its alligator-infested swamps and unbearable humidity. The report cited official government papers on health conditions, climate, and agricultural prospects for the area; it mentioned the proximity to several means of transportation by rail, road, and river. The abundant water resources were prominently stressed, but of paramount advantage was the abandoned camp and installations of the company whose assets were meticulously listed: 27 good buildings, an 18-room hotel, about 100 huts, a store, office building, and large sheds of 130-300 feet. No wonder, then, that in the desert conditions of California the report seemed to promise the beginnings of a new prosperity. Many were ready to move to Louisiana.[20] As soon as the assembly had voted on the move, Harriman set out to materialize the deal; he got a loan of $5,000 for the first down payment.

Toward New Llano

The transfer to the new colony began in October 1917, at the same time that the United States entered World War I. As most members of Llano were pacifists, it seemed to have left little impact on the colony. Their main concern was the complicated transfer of the population and equipment to a location 2,500 miles away. They were filled with great expectations—it was going to be an exciting experience, an adventure. Harriman and other functionaries were the first to set out. They were followed by a group of 30 men, who had an 18-day journey by car over the rough roads of the South. Most of the people and equipment were transported by rail. From among Llano's enterprises the printing shop, cannery, carpentry, and shoemaker were moved; some of the machinery took months to reach the new settlement. After the first enthusiasm, the monotony of preparation set in. Many recoiled from the idea of the hardships they would have to face and finally only 130 set out by rail. Altogether, from among the 1,000 Llano members only 200 moved to Louisiana.[21]

By January 1918 about 300 people had arrived at the new colony. In addition to those who had moved from California, there were 25 Texas families who had been persuaded by the land dealer to join the colony. These were people of a different mettle; they had no ideological background and some had little education. Their motives were materialistic and many believed that the colony was about to make a fortune. Stories about potential oil wells were spread and soon sharp differences caused friction between the Californians and the Texans.

At first, conditions seemed to be in accordance with the enthusiastic descriptions. The land was situated in wooded hills close to the Texan border, and rivers flowed everywhere. The climate was temperate and, the abandoned camp near the county town of Leesville, Louisiana, was just as described. Some minor jobs were needed to put the place in order, and it soon became known as New Llano.[22]

When in April 1918 the first installment was due to be paid to the Gulf Lumber Company, Harriman had to go to California to raise the money by selling some of their land there. To his amazement he discovered that during the short period since the emigration to Louisiana the colony had deteriorated significantly. The economic hardships and the lack of prospects for improvement had caused severe demoralization. Further, most of the central members had moved to New Llano, and many others had found outside jobs during the wartime boom. The few who had remained were entangled in a legal dispute which was to undermine the colony's existence completely. Harriman was extremely upset to discover that the man who had caused the commune's financial problems was the very person who at one time had been his confidence man and the treasurer of the finance company. He had turned renegade and by using financial manipulations had transferred some of the property to his own name. During the legal procedures Llano was found to have a debt of $85,000.

The California settlement was doomed. Harriman stayed on to lead the legal fight and to attempt to save some of the property to buy the land in Louisiana. After lengthy procedures he succeeded in lowering their debt, but for that he had to sacrifice his private property and health. Worse still was his enforced absence from the management of the new colony during its formative years. He therefore missed the chance to realize his life's ambition.[23]

New Llano was managed by a group of functionaries led by E. Wooster, the editor of the socialist journal printed in Llano. Wooster did not have the personality to lead or to manage the colony's economy. During his leadership New Llano deteriorated socially and economically and reached a low point never known previously. First there was the schism between the Californians and Texans. The latter lacked all communitarian motivation, and as soon as they discovered that they were not living on a gold mine (or an oil field) and that they were living a life of poverty, they stopped working. Violence erupted and the Leesville police had to intervene. The best way out of the crisis seemed to be a division of the inventory so that the Texans would leave.

In addition to the social crisis the colony suffered from severe economic hardships during 1918-19. The settlers who had been inexperienced farmers in California were even less successful in Louisiana. Moreover, these were drought years and the farm yielded hardly anything. They made a meager living selling firewood and the products of their baker and shoemaker. Their income did not even cover living expenses, not to mention payments for the land. In extreme need they asked their Californian followers and others for contributions which were not late in arriving. This success would become a curse: begging for funds was adopted as a way of life. Eventually members realized that charity could not replace their providing for themselves and began to despair. Many left to return to California and in the fall of 1919 there were only fifteen families left at New Llano. It was a period of low ebb for the colony, one which would not recur until its final year.[24]

At the beginning of 1920 matters gradually improved, largely thanks to George Pickett. In Louisiana he decided to use his previous experience as a salesman, and in the autumn of 1919 he set out on a long journey to raise funds and recruit new members. On his return in November he brought with him, in addition to contributions, two new members—Theodore Cuno and his wife, an elderly and well-to-do socialist couple. In spite of their advanced years their joining New Llano was a great boon. Besides the financial help which enabled the colony to pay the annual installment to the Gulf Lumber Company, they contributed much to the social and ideological life.

Theodore Cuno was born in Westphalen, Germany, where he had been active in socialist circles. He was a member of the first Internationale, collaborated with Marx and Engels, and was persecuted and arrested in Germany. After traversing a few European countries he settled in Italy, where he met his wife and together they established the local branch of the Italian Internationale. In 1873 the couple emigrated to the United States, where Cuno continued his socialist activities. Cuno became a prosperous publisher and his name as a reporter and socialist was well known in radical circles; on his arrival at New Llano he had already acquired a wide reputation. In spite of being 77-years-old he did not retire on his laurels but immediately became involved in the colony's affairs. He talked with the members, published articles in newspapers, and soon acquired the position of "elder." His socialist background and his vast experience as well as his natural intelligence contributed much to the society he had joined.[25]

Pickett's Leadership

In the elections for the board of managers in 1920, Wooster was demoted. He had mismanaged the colony's economy and became increasingly pessimistic about the future. George Pickett was elected vice-president, the top managerial post during Harriman's prolonged absence from New Llano. Pickett's dynamic leadership infused the colony with new order. His eloquence and gift of persuasion instilled those around him with new hope for a prosperous New Llano.[26]

He continued on his propaganda tour, intending to draw new members and contributions. It was of vital importance to pay the installments to the Gulf Lumber Company and ensure the ownership of the land. Their debts in 1920 added up to $600,000, and Pickett, besides directing a concerted campaign for contributions, began an industrial expansion program. That year a brick kiln and sawmill opened, both providing needed building materials which were also marketed. By 1921 a dairy farm was in operation, but the colonists abstained from drinking milk so that they could sell it in Leesville.

Their printing shop had been transferred and got a boost when in 1921 an able socialist editor, Carl Gleeser, joined the colony. He was ready to begin the weekly *Llano Colonist*, which had been suspended when the colony moved to Louisiana. The printing press was also used for the local parish newspaper and other socialist publications which spread the news of Llano and provided effective means of soliciting needed contributions and new members. This was of great importance during the 1920-21 depression that influenced many unemployed socialists to join New Llano. They were attracted by the community ideals and the hope for a secure future. As a result membership rose to 165 in the winter of 1921.

Life on the colony settled down, and the school, which had been closed during the years of recession, was again active when experienced teachers joined the colony. Their social life regained its California days' vitality. One of the first buildings they built was a large wooden-floored dance-hall in which their famous dances were again held. The only thing that never took off again was New Llano's farming. They cultivated only 300 acres without the use of modern implements. The sole agricultural enterprise which was properly cultivated was a 600-acre rice farm acquired in 1922 which was 70 miles south of New Llano. A group of members managed to run the farm successfully and for many years this was an important source of income.[27]

Late in 1922 Harriman returned to New Llano and tried to regain his authority as president and to reinstitute democratic management procedures. Friction developed between him and Pickett, who together with his followers had assumed complete authority and had abolished all pretence of democratic administration. They claimed that efficiency and profitability had precedence. In 1923 matters deteriorated even further. In February leading socialist journalists couple, Kate and Frank O'Hare, joined New Llano, intending to renew the publication of the *American Vanguard.* This journal had enjoyed a circulation of over 20,000 and was closed during the war years because of its pacifist opinions. They hoped that its publication would advance the propaganda campaign of New Llano considerably and also make a profit for the colony. The O'Hares asked for complete independence in editing the journal and were given a trial period of one year. Pickett was displeased with the arrangement.

Shortly after this, and influenced by the O'Hares, William E. Zeuch, an economist from the University of Illinois in Urbana, selected New Llano as a site for the special cooperative college he had long advocated. It was to grant college education to workers who would combine studies and work. They would earn their free room and board by working 24 hours a week on the commune. The Commonwealth College also asked for organizing and financial independence. Members of New Llano welcomed the idea of a college which would be integrated with the local educational institutions and provide higher education without removing the students from their environment and place of work. In September 1923 the college began to operate with only a few scores of students. Even so, its comparative independence raised objections from Pickett's followers, who claimed that both the *American Vanguard* and the college were exploiting the colony without contributing anything.

The friction between Pickett's and Harriman's followers led to a confrontation in the 1923 elections. Pickett was not reelected and was persuaded to take a leave of absence. He went to New Jersey, where he remained for some time, but kept in touch with his followers, who constantly undermined Harriman's authority. They began to raise funds for an alternative educational institution such as the Kid Colony, which had been Pickett's brain-child in California. They intended to replace Zeuch's Commonwealth College with an alternative educational system in the spirit of Llano.

In March of 1924 Pickett returned to Louisiana prepared to fight the rival groups and to take over control of the colony's management. In the 1924 elections Pickett's group gained a majority of 60 percent and according to their former agreement an organized opposition could not be permitted to remain on the colony. The schism was inevitable and caused the secession of an important part of the leadership: Zeuch and his group left for Mena. Arkansas, where he established his college as an independent settlement and was joined there by some of Harriman's followers.[28] The latter, aged, ill, and disappointed, returned to California, where he died in 1925.

Harriman's final years as president and spiritual leader of New Llano had been devoted to soul searching. He admitted making several mistakes which were the result of his optimistic attitude toward the communitarian experiment as a model community. His experience had made him adopt a more realistic attitude toward the chances of a lonely communal outpost in the middle of a capitalist environment. He also came to realize the limitations of socialist ideology in altering people's personalities. People just could not easily adjust to a selfless, harmonious way of life after having been used to competitive ways. Nevertheless, Harriman did not completely despair of his ideals. A communitarian way of life could be achieved by means of selecting members, educating them, and developing a set of moral and social values. His faith was not shaken, and he never repented his life's work.[29]

A new era began for New Llano in 1925: George Pickett resumed his authoritarian leadership. In the past he had succeeded in saving the commune from financial and social debacle and was the accepted leader of a kernel of active members. But after 1925 he became controversial. Some regarded him as a power-hungry dictator, others as a devoted idealist who shouldered all the colony's troubles. All agreed that his authoritarian leadership was caused by the fact that everybody else rejected all responsibility for the management of New Llano's economy and social life: "Let George get on with the job" was a favorite saying and resulted in his being reelected year after year. As one of the board of directors and farm manager he had wide authority and was surrounded by loyal "yes men" who executed his policy. In addition he was a gifted operator who had no difficulty in persuading his fellow members. During that period the general meeting gave way to weekly "psychological meetings" where vital matters were discussed but no decisions made. They were a kind of soul-searching meetings and Pickett's influence was limitless.[30]

Under Pickett's leadership changes were introduced. The communal element of New Llano was reinforced. The daily salary of $4, which in California had been paid to everyone, was abolished. Instead, a 48-hour work week was adopted. In return everybody was provided with the basics: food, health services, education, and postage. There were different ways of communal consumption. Food was prepared in the communal kitchen to which a dining-room was attached, but most families preferred to have their meals at home so that the dining-room catered more for the singles. As for housing, the trend was communitarian. In the early days of the colony members were accommodated in the old company huts but renovated them privately. In time this caused inequality, and to prevent members from becoming disgruntled, housing affairs were put in the hands of the building committee, which undertook all the construction work. Furniture remained private property, but acceptable norms were maintained throughout. Most members used private funds to purchase luxuries which the commune did not provide. Clothing and shoes were supplied, but some were privately bought.[31]

Social Awareness

Admirers and critics alike agree that Llano's greatest communitarian achievement was its highly satisfying social, cultural, and intellectual life. Throughout the years, ever since their days in California, the commune never neglected activities of a cultural nature: debating societies, study groups, art classes, recreational activities, community singing, a choir, an orchestra, and a drama circle provided a varied fare. They constructed a 300-seat theater hall with a movie projector, an innovation practically unknown at the communes. The library, which had been transferred from California, now contained about 5,000 volumes. Members of New Llano were proud of their library, which was considered to be the most outstanding in the western community. Yet their pride and joy were the dances which continued to attract people from the neighborhood. Pickett, a former dancing instructor, was personally involved in it. Week after week he taught old and young all the new dances they cared to learn.[32]

Educational activities also played an important role in the colony. After the above-mentioned crisis concerning the community college, Pickett devoted his attention to the reestablished Kid Colony and to the fostering of its unique ideas, as conceived by him. These aspired to good health, industrial proficiency, better human relations, cooperative habits, the acquisition of knowledge, and the ability to think for oneself. He ignored diplomas and grades and most teachers were members who had no formal training. The state of Louisiana approved of this unorthodox arrangement and even paid the salary of two teachers. In general, the elementary classes may be regarded as a vocational school into which the high school classes were integrated at a later date. All pupils from the first grade and above attended classes for half of the day and worked the rest of the time. Pre-school children were brought up in the nursery, which was a part of the Kid Colony that was made up of the first three grades. Each morning the bus would collect all the youngsters from their homes and return them to their parents after work. Pickett regarded the Kid

Colony as a means of communitarian education, one which would prepare them for life on a cooperative community. However, not everything went according to his plan and in the early 1930s Pickett had to face the fact that although the school had succeeded in providing knowledge and vocational training, it had failed to instill within the children a loyalty to their communal ideals. Ideological convictions were nonexistent and most left to live in different social environments, thus proving that their ideological indoctrination had not been intense enough to withstand the temptations of the external society.[33]

The failure of the second generation's ideological identification was not solely caused by the educational system. The blame must also be put on the ideological weakness of the adult society during the 1930s. There seems to have been an ongoing process of diminishing fervour ever since Llano moved to Louisiana. While in California the members still felt an affinity with socialism, this reached a low point in the 1930s during Pickett's leadership. There was no longer any homogeneity as to their party affiliation in those years. Pickett himself remained loyal to his socialist convictions but he devoted no time to political activities and belittled the importance of ideological collectivism. His main concern was the widening of the periphery of followers and he was active in many circles—from ardent Marxists on the one hand to Christian religious ones on the other. He even tried to influence liberals and many pacifists were attracted to Llano so that by 1928 they formed the most organized and the largest ideological unit within the colony. Their ideological pluralism could be seen in the election results. While in California everyone had voted socialist, in New Llano their votes were split and many opted for nonsocialist candidates.

In the 1936 presidential elections most votes were given to Roosevelt.[34] Pickett's abstention from political activity was not motivated by his preference to remain uninvolved in social problems. From the early days of his leadership he had hoped to turn Llano into a world center of cooperative units which would strive to establish an alternative to the existing regimes. Many leaders of the cooperative movement visited the colony and Llano was in touch with most of the communes in the United States (except for the Hutterites, whose religious ideology was a complete anathema to members of Llano). These ties extended all over the world and even reached Palestine, where in 1931 the kibbutz's periodical *Mebifnim* published a short article on Llano that included correspondence between the two movements and information about their economic and cultural activities. The article expressed the admiration felt by the kibbutz movement toward the model that Llano represented.[35]

The presumptions that Llano might be regarded as a model for an alternative society proved to be completely unfounded during the financial crash of the 1930s. The global recession which undermined the very foundations of capitalism raised hopes in unemployed and frustrated socialists that New Llano would point the way to an alternative system. They reached out for help and trusted New Llano to provide it. Like refugees they arrived at their imagined haven, and the population of the colony suddenly swelled from 180-200 in the 1920s to over 500 in 1930.

More than anything else this sudden increase was to have adverse results. The core of socialist members, which included 40 of the California oldtimers, found itself to be a minority among the many newcomers whose ideological motivation was negligent. Even before the recession many had joined the commune because of the economic advantages it offered. These were advertised in the recruiting propaganda in *The Colonist*; it read:

> Dear Friend, How would you like to live in a community where you have no House Rent to pay; No Board or Grocery Bills to meet each week or month, No Fuel or Light Bills presented to you every 30 days, No Water Bill harrassing you every quarter, No Doctor or Nurse Bill and indeed no Funeral Bill should this sad fate befall you or your dear ones. No charge for dancing to the music of a good orchestra on one of the finest floors in Louisiana, where every effort will be made to place you in the job or position that you like best or can function best in. . . . Where you are an equal owner of everything on these odd thousands of acres of Llano Colony.[36]

No wonder, then, that many of the newcomers were looking for economic advantages and these were lacking in the 1930s. New Llano's economy was deteriorating rapidly and not as the result of the general recession alone.

At the time of the economic recession in the 1930s most of the land was owned by the colony. Its debts had been paid and the colony could have established a sound agriculture, but this was not the case, their farm branches were limited. One of the cooperative movement's leaders, Henry Lassere, who visited the commune in 1926, reported his impressions of the colony's variegated agriculture.[37] Like in California, it included livestock—cows, chickens, pigs, goats, horses, and mules—a vegetable garden, various crops, and orchards. But these were all much smaller than the Californian ones.

Instead, their main effort was invested in developing crafts and industry. These too were the same ones that had occupied them in California—a printing shop, a cannery, a carpentry shop, etc. They added a factory that made baskets and crates for farm produce, marketed firewood, and established a hotel. In 1925 Pickett initiated their most important enterprise, a central ice plant which stored the farm produce of the area and provided the nearby town, Leesville, with ice. During the summer scores of workers were employed there. Altogether there were fifty branches which provided employment throughout the year and members enjoyed a variety of job possibilities. This advantage was emphasized during the recession years.

The article published in the kibbutz's periodical *Mebifnim* said that although there was disbelief in Llano's propaganda claim that it could provide jobs for one and all according to ability and choice, this was indeed the case. Any new member who was proficient at his job and contributed to the commune's income, was given the chance.[38] All these advantages could not save New Llano from the difficult financial problems with which it was beset ever since the California days. The old debts in addition to new ones weighed heavily and caused a permanent state of near bankrupcy. Pickett had managed to overcome this threat with the help of donations from followers. He explained the need for fund-raising by claiming that a pioneering effort such as Llano could not survive the hardships of its beginnings without external funding. Time and again this ''begging'' was to save the day, but Pickett was severely criticized from within and without for adhering to the system which in the long-run caused much harm.

A Strange Combination

The first critic was Henry Lassere, who had formed close ties with New Llano. Attempting to characterize the socialist experiment of the commune, he defined its method as being

> rather a queer combination of capitalism, communism and philanthropy. . . . Capitalism because any possible surplus production made by the colonists above what is consumed by them would result in an increase of value of the property which belongs to the stock company. . . . Communism because all colonists have (or rather are supposed to have) an equal share in whatever goods and privileges the colony is in the position to offer them. . . . Philanthropy—Llano often asked for financial help claiming that it was an educational and more or less charity institution. . . . What is worse is that the money they receive as gifts or contributions of any kind and for any purpose will ultimately benefit the shareholders of the stock company, as it has been explained above, rather than the colony itself.[39]

Henry Lassere, who was acquainted with the cooperative movements in the world including the Palestinian model, proposed that New Llano should adopt the public settlement funding ''similar to the National Jewish Fund. . . . The purpose of which would be to permanently secure use of land, buildings and means of production to the cooperative colony, that is to say to the very group of colonists who at any time are actually members of the colony.[40]

Pickett ignored the criticism as well as the constructive advice. He continued to manage Llano's economy in his own way. In the 1930s the profitability of all branches declined sharply, whether because of the global Depression or for internal reasons. One was a low work morale which had never been high and now deteriorated even further. This was mainly because of the influx of new members from among the unemployed who were just seeking a haven and whose idealist or socialist motivation was nil. There was also a relative increase in the number of elderly, even retired members, a fact which lowered the efficiency of the colony's work force. Under these circumstances the advantages of a communitarian economy became a liability. All of this and the frequent rotations of jobs caused a drastic decline in the branches' profitability and their debts mounted. As always, Pickett tried to raise funds, but to no avail; the Depression had severely curtailed this source of income. Reality had to be faced, their standard of living was drastically reduced, and it was felt in the cut of such basics as food, clothing, and services. In 1932 disgruntled members formed an opposition group and adopted the name that had been chosen back in California, The Welfare League.[41]

The local paper began to publish articles criticizing Pickett's financial policy. He was suspected of misusing funds, default on repayment of monies deposited by stockholders, and misrepresentation of conditions in the colony. Pickett tried to refute all these accusations but felt the ever-growing animosity.[42] Searching for ways to calm matters, he set out on another of his formerly successful fund-raising missions. He hoped to establish an unemployment fund and to finance the expansion of New Llano's economy. With this in mind he returned to his plan to search for oil on the colony's land. Once again he succeeded, and in 1932 he purchased land in south Louisiana and in New Mexico. They also began to drill for oil on Llano's land. Even so, the unrest did not abate, and while Pickett was busy promoting his new plans the opposition, led by Ernest Webb, a California journalist who had joined the colony in 1930, gained momentum. The Welfare League declared that it was striving to raise the members' standard-of-living and to halt Pickett's authoritarian administration. They intended to reintroduce democratic institutions in several steps. Their first decision was to form a trade union which would represent members' social rights. The second was to abolish all voluntary work on Saturdays, which had been introduced by Pickett to raise production.

Pickett realized the danger of the opposition and retaliated in the weekly psychological meetings organized by his loyal followers. In the summer of 1932 matters came to a head. During a psychological meeting in July, Pickett declared that there was no place on New Llano for an organized minority whose ideas differed from those of the management. In his address he expounded his theory of ideological collectivism as cardinal to a society such as Llano which had to struggle against the alien system that surrounded it.[43] War was declared on the dissidents and Pickett had the upper hand. The League members were expelled, but they did not give in. Some of them settled in nearby Leesville, from which they mounted a counter-attack on the commune, and even slandered New Llano among its followers. When in 1934 The League in Leesville was abolished, the hope for peace and tranquility did not materialize. Other controversies stirred up New Llano's social life and propelled it toward its final stage.

Between 1933 and 1935 Pickett devoted his time to a new idea that demanded his full attention. After F.D. Roosevelt had been elected and the New Deal introduced, Pickett tried to enlist the federal government in support of New Llano. He planned that the colony would serve as a model for rural settlements and as a means to solving unemployment problems. With the help of the senator from Texas he proposed legislation in 1933 in support of his plan, expecting that he himself would be put in charge of the program and thus turn New Llano into a country-wide movement. He had to stay in Washington months on end, lobbying among congressmen and promoting his ideas, and at the same time he also succeeded in raising funds to overcome the immediate financial problems of Llano.

Pickett's prolonged stay in Washington undermined his position within the Llano board of directors. He had relegated authority to his loyal supporters in the hope that through them he might continue his leadership. However, during his short visits he realized that waves of criticism had undermined his position and many of the members were frustrated. At one point Pickett was convinced that congress was about to pass the law and he would be appointed head of a national Llano movement, and he considered giving up his managerial functions on the colony, but his hopes never materialized. The committee appointed to discuss his project was slow to publish its findings, and when it finally did so, its whole character had been altered and Llano was relegated to a corner. Pickett never despaired and carried on his fight for another two years, when he realized that it was in vain and that the New Deal had in fact ignored Llano.[44]

In 1935 Pickett decided to resume his activities at home, but a surprise awaited him. During his lengthy absence profound changes had taken place in the social fabric of the colony. From the sporadic organization of disgruntled members, there had developed a widely based opposition led by Eugene Carl. This young, talented, and dynamic member who had joined Llano some time earlier rapidly gained the trust of its members. On the tide of the general criticism of the old leadership and especially of Pickett, he rose to lead the opposition. While Pickett was involved with his grandiose projects, life on the colony had rapidly deteriorated. Poverty was evident everywhere, members clothing and shoes were tattered, the roofs leaked, their food was meager, and their health undermined. Criticism spread like fire.

The Vision and Its Decline

On May 1, 1935, the signal for the "revolt" was given through the pamphlet "The Llano Declaration of Freedom." It called for the resignation of the present management, demanded the vote for every resident of 18 or older, and the election of a new board of managers. These demands were supported by everybody present and when three days later a general assembly convened, a new board of managers was elected, none of them a follower of Pickett, who was away in Washington and sent a message accepting the election's results and agreeing to the new management's decisions.[45] These called for a new economic policy, one which would put New Llano on its feet again and raise the standard of living of its poverty-stricken members. The new board stopped the purchase of new land units and concentrated on reconstructing the Llano economy in Louisiana by introducing more efficient work methods. They discontinued the fund-raising policy and tried to introduce more businesslike methods in order to cure New Llano's financial ills.

Their plan did not materialize. It was hampered by the many enemies from within and without. Pickett, who had only pretended to hand over his leadership, returned late in May and began to undermine the new administration's policy. Only a few of the members followed him, and when he was found out the majority attempted to apply his own principle calling on an adverse minority to leave. Pickett did not budge and continued his campaign, seeking assistance from the state's judiciary system. The situation deteriorated and reached a stage of violent confrontation between members. Pickett refused to leave and held on by any means. Both sides were entrenched and the battle raged for a whole year, until in April 1936 an external factor forced them to unite against the danger that threatened the very existence of the commune.

In April 1936 the district court placed New Llano in the hands of a receiver. This did not come as a surprise, because early in 1935 a suit had been brought against the colony by several ex-members who demanded compensation. They were represented by McDonald, a lawyer who had been an active member of New Llano between 1922 and 1925 and had left after directing severe criticism against Pickett and the board of managers. McDonald represented a group of six seceders, mostly elderly people who claimed the return of their share money as promised in the Llano's contract. Their claim went unanswered, because Pickett's measures to combat the financial difficulties of 1930 included the abolishment of repayments. McDonald regarded this as a breach of promise and an unfair step against individuals in the cause of public interest. He brought suit against the Llano board of managers for the sum of $4,262 in shares. The court decided in favor of the plaintiff and Pickett, who knew that no such money was available, feared the confiscation of all communal property. He immediately began to pawn most of their means of production. McDonald attempted to stop Pickett's maneuver and asked the court to appoint a receiver, which was granted early in 1935 but following the Louisiana law, a moratorium postponed the execution until April 1936. Meanwhile the new board of managers under Eugene Carl had been elected and agreed to cooperate with the receiver, hoping to cure the colony's financial ills and to repay their debts.[46]

New Llano's economic management, now in the hands of the receiver, introduced some radical changes. On the one hand the lengthy confrontation between the two rival groups ceased; both had too much to lose and began to cooperate to save the commune. On the other hand the commune's prestige had suffered severely, and it could no longer be regarded as a model economic enterprise. In 1936, while the economic situation in the United States was improving, the prospects of New Llano looked bleak. Many of those who had sought shelter there during the Depression were considering the return to their former way of life. Most of the young members who had led the revolt in 1935 left, and the population steadily grew older; many of the oldtimers were followers of Pickett and that enabled him to be reelected in 1937. He attempted to instill the commune with hope as he had done in 1920, but failed. Most of the members were simply too tired and frustrated after years of hunger and hardship.[47]

Pickett was faced with the task of fighting a "rearguard action" against dissolution. In an enormous effort he invested all his spiritual and physical powers as well as his private property in the attempt to save the colony's means of production from being liquidated; it was all in vain. In May 1936 they despaired of finding oil on New Llano land and most of the agricultural branches had failed and were leased to neighbors. Only the ice plant continued to function until the autumn of 1937. Pickett continued to publish the *Llano Colonist* and pleaded with their followers to save the commune, but for once there was no helping hand. In October 1937 the ice plant closed down. New Llano had come to a standstill.

The last issue of the *Llano Colonist* appeared in December. In his farewell editorial Pickett admitted the failure of his life's work, but there was no note of despair in his words. He still believed that the future of communitarianism depended on the human factor. He had no regrets. After many years of total devotion to the Llano movement he was convinced that nowhere else could he have found a way to contribute as much to society at large and at the same time experience the satisfaction he had earned through working with friends in the cooperative movement of Llano.[48]

Pickett was not the only one to sum up his thoughts in this manner. In 1948 his rival A. James McDonald published a book, *Llano and What It Taught Us*. He attempted to recall the experiences of the past objectively, helped by other people's evidence. In the chapter that dealt with the moral of the experiment he wrote:

> With a number of former Llanoists I am convinced that communal producer cooperation can be successful and as nearly permanent as other human institutions. It furnishes the most satisfying social life to be found anywhere. It affords, too, as high an ethical or moral standard as is attainable in human

association. . . . Colonists of those early years got glimpses of paradise in their daily life and associations. They can and many still do look back with longing to the beautiful social life.[49]

Llano's contribution to those who experienced it may be realized by the fact that many remained loyal to the commune's ideals years after having left it. In California former members formed a movement that continued to hold meetings and publish a journal till after World War II. Only when the last of its members had died did it cease to function.[50]

The fate of Pickett and those who remained at New Llano was bitter when the communal services collapsed after 1937. Most of those who stayed on were elderly and had to make do with their pensions. They paid a low rent for their huts and somehow cultivated small plots near their homes which often provided their only source of food. From 1938 till 1939 Pickett continued to fight the attempts to liquidate the property and to sell their land, but all he achieved was the postponement of the harsh edict until 1939, when it was sold at a ridiculously low price that hardly sufficed to repay the creditors and legal expenses. He went on living there in one of the huts near the Kid Colony he had fostered. Alone, destitute, and ill his life still revolved around Llano. He mustered enough strength to found the Llano movement of ex-members and followers and even attempted to revive a communitarian experiment of the oldtimers. In his last years Pickett lived through his memories. He died in 1962, "the last of the Mohicans" from a generation of socialist visionaries, practitioners of communal societies in the United States. His death occurred at a time when a new generation rekindled the flame of the communal vision. These young people, who had not been deterred by the failures of their predecessors, began to weave the fabric of alternative societies motivated by a variety of spiritual and social ideals.

Notes

1. Job Harriman was born in 1861 in Indiana and educated for the ministry at Butler University, Indianapolis. He left that vocation for the study of law at the University of Colorado and after graduating moved to California in 1886, where he practiced law. In 1890 he became a socialist and from then on was publicly involved with the various American socialist parties. At first he was attracted to utopian circles and influenced by Bellamy and became active in The Nationalist clubs. Later he was interested in the Altruria commune, which had been inspired by William Dean Howell's book, *A Traveller from Altruria*. His affinity with utopians did not prevent him from being active in party politics. For twenty years he was involved with the struggles of the factions of the American social parties. Evidence of his high standing is the fact that during the 1900 presidential election he was vice-presidential candidate on the socialist ticket headed by Eugene V.

Debs. After their defeat he retired from politics and practiced law in Los Angeles, where he became labor candidate for mayor in 1911. His chances were good because he enjoyed massive support of the unions, but his election was prevented by a drastic switch in public opinion, as a result of the McNamara brothers' affair, who had been accused of bombing the Los Angeles *Times'* building, a paper which had been hostile to the unions and had fought Harriman's candidacy. Labor lawyers headed by him defended the brothers; to their consternation the brothers confessed a few days before the elections and destroyed any chances of a socialist candidate being elected. Paul K. Conkin, *Two Paths to Utopia: The Hutterites and the Llano Colony* (Lincoln: University of Nebraska Press, 1964), p. 106; Robert V. Hine, *California's Utopian Colonies* (New Haven: Yale University Press, 1966), pp. 114-16.

2. Ernest S. Wooster, *Communities of the Past and Present* (1924. Reprint. New York: AMS Press, 1974), Introduction.
3. Ibid., pp. 118-20; Hine, p. 117.
4. *The Gateway to Freedom* (Llano, Calif.: Colony Press, 1915), pp. 4-13.
5. Ibid., pp. 25-27. A. James McDonald, *The Llano Cooperative Colony and What It Taught* (San Antonio, Tex.: Carleton Printing, 1950), pp. 15-16.
6. *The Western Comrade* 2, nos. 9-10 (January-February 1915); *Llano View Book* (Llano, Calif.: Llano Press); Conkin, p. 115.
7. Michael Dermody and Robert V. Hine, "California's Socialist Utopias," *Communities: Journal of Cooperation*, no. 68 (Winter 1985):56; *The Western Comrade* 5, no. 1 (May 1917).
8. *The Western Comrade* 2, no. 10 (February 1915); *Gateway to Freedom*, p. 23.
9. *Llano View Book.*
10. *The Western Comrade* 3 (August 1915; September 1915; October 1915); *The Western Comrade* 4 (June-July 1916); *The Western Comrade* 5 (May 1917).
11. *The Western Comrade* 2 (January-February 1915); *The Western Comrade* 4 (November 1916); *Gateway to Freedom*, pp. 17-18; Conkin, p. 130; Dermody and Hine, p. 57.
12. *The Western Comrade* 2 (January-February 1915); Conkin, pp. 150-51.
13. *The Western Comrade* 3 (August 1915); *The Western Comrade* 4 (March 1917).
14. *The Western Comrade* 4 (June-July 1916).
15. *The Western Comrade* 2 (May 1915); *The Western Comrade* 3 (April 1916); *The Western Comrade* 4 (June-July 1916).
16. *The Western Comrade* 3 (August 1915).
17. Wooster, pp. 122-23; Conkin, pp. 127-29; Hine, pp. 122-23.
18. Wilbur S. Shepperson, *Retreat to Nevada: A Socialist Colony of World War I* (Lincoln: University of Nevada Press, 1966), pp. 19-28; McDonald, p. 19; Hine, pp. 123-24.
19. *The Western Comrade* 1 (May 1917):9; *The Western Comrade* 5 (October 1917), Dermody and Hine, p. 56; Robert V. Hine, *California Utopian Colonies* (New Haven: Yale University Press, 1966).
20. *The Western Comrade* 5 (October 1917).
21. *The Western Comrade* 5 (November 1917); Conkin, p. 113.
22. Shepperson, p. 30; Conkin, p. 111; McDonald, p. 28.
23. McDonald, p. 21; Wooster, pp. 126-27; Shepperson, pp. 30-31.
24. Wooster, pp. 125, 127-29; Conkin pp. 115-16; McDonald, pp. 24-25.
25. Conkin, pp. 115-16, 164-65; McDonald, p. 25.

26. Conkin, p. 116; McDonald, pp. 26-27; Wooster, pp. 128-30.
27. Watson Thomson, *Pioneer in Community: Henri Lasere's Contribution to the Fully Cooperative Society* (Toronto: Ryerson Press, 1949), p. 28; Conkin, pp. 116-77, 168-69; McDonald, pp. 28, 45, 56.
28. Raymond and Charlotte Koch, *Educational Commune* (New York: Shocken, 1972), pp. 12-16.
29. Ibid., pp. 12-21; McDonald, pp. 29-36; Wooster, Introduction, pp. 127-31; Thomson, p. 28.
30. Conkin, pp. 134-36; McDonald, pp. 52, 73-76.
31. Henrik F. Infield, *Cooperative Communities at Work* (London: Kegan Paul, Trench, Trubner, 1947), pp. 32-34; McDonald, p. 48; Conkin, p. 119.
32. Infield, p. 34; Conkin, pp. 150-53; McDonald, pp. 45-49.
33. Conkin, pp. 156-57; McDonald, pp. 44-45, 48; Infield, pp. 35-36.
34. Dirmody and Hine, p. 57; Conkin, pp. 119-20, 153; Infield, pp. 27-28.
35. Thomson, p. 25; "The Commune Llano," *M'bifnim: Hakibbutz Hame'uchad Quarterly,* no. 50 (February 1931):20-21 (Hebrew).
36. Thomson, pp. 29-30; Conkin, pp. 123-24, 160.
37. Thomson, pp. 29-30.
38. M'bifnim, p. 21.
39. Thomson, pp. 29-30.
40. Shalom Wurm, *Communal Societies and Their Way of Life* (Tel Aviv: Ayanoth, 1968), pp. 282-83 (Hebrew); Thomson, pp. 34-35.
41. Infield, p. 33; Conkin, pp. 168-71.
42. The schism at New Llano and the expulsion of the minority in 1924 did not prevent the forming of a new opposition against Pickett's authoritarian rule. Between 1926 and 1928 a violent internal struggle erupted with an opposition group headed by W. Burton, who used to be Pickett's right-hand man and even had supported his authoritarian leadership in the belief that it would benefit New Llano. In time he realized the damage that had been caused, undermining internal freedom and reenforcing the lack of discipline. The dispute invaded areas of administration and finance, and at this stage the courts took over. After a lengthy trial the verdict, given in 1928, was in favor of the New Llano administration and against the opposition. However, it forbade the management to expel members of the opposition and ensured their freedom of speech. Thomson, pp. 32-33; McDonald, pp. 37-38; 52; Conkin, pp. 136-37; Wurm, pp. 280-81.
43. McDonald, pp. 41-43, 59-62; Conkin, pp. 140-41.
44. Conkin, pp. 142-43, 172-74.
45. Ibid., pp. 143-44, 177-78.
46. McDonald, pp. 63-66.
47. Infield, pp. 37-38.
48. *Llano Colonist* (December 1937).
49. McDonald, pp. 78-79.
50. Dermody and Hine, p. 58.

16

Sunrise and Anarchist Communities

Most Anarchists considered mutually linked communities of independent producers as the nuclei to their vision of a society without governments. In the United States, the large experimental field of social utopias, anarchist circles appeared simultaneously with the debut of socialism during the first half of the nineteenth century. However there were only a few attempts to realize their vision of a future society. During the nineteenth century only a handful of utopian communities were established by anarchists. Most survived for short periods only and none formed communal entities, because their founders and members were close to the individualistic trends of anarchism.

The pioneer founder of anarchist communities was Josiah Warren, who had started out as a follower of Robert Owen in New Harmony in 1825. The failure of Owen's utopia had led Warren onto the road of anarchism. At first he adopted Owen's idea of an equitable market of exchange based on the value of work. He tried to realize the idea in Cincinnati, Ohio, where he established an "equity or time store" in which producers could trade in their wares for the value of work invested in their production. The store was to be the core of a community of producers who would voluntarily gather around it. The experiment lasted for three years (1827-1830) and was abolished when the difficulties of an equitable commerce system in a big city increased. Warren did not give in and renewed his efforts in a rural area.

First Attempts

In 1831 Josiah Warren acquired a plot of land in Tuscarawas County, Ohio, where he established the anarchist community Equity (named after his time-labor system). It was the first of its kind in the world and had six families who voluntarily incorporated their independent, individual units within their communitarian means of production (a sawmill). The experiment was discontinued in 1835 because of the harsh climate in the area and an epidemic that felled the small community. This failure did not deter Warren and even instilled in him courage to try again. Economic conditions were unfavorable in 1837, when the United States was hit by a deep depression. This led to the rise of the Fourierists, who attracted many followers from circles aspiring to social reform and who could have been the natural periphery for Warren's ideology. He himself severely criticized the compulsive organizational framework inherent in Fourier's theories.

When Fourierism began to recede, Warren renewed his efforts to establish an anarchist community. He bought a plot of land near Clermont Phalanx in Ohio in 1847, and founded the colony Utopia. He was personally involved in the community's life during the first year of its existence. Warren renewed the integrated economic structure in which each family owned its own lot and house, but members cooperated in running their sawmill and a printing shop in which a newspaper and anarchist propaganda were published. Their communitarian activities were administered without any permanent institutions, set of rules, or constitution. Their public meetings were more of a social affair. Utopia was intended to be a community without institutions or leadership. Warren, whose natural leadership was reinforced by his initiatives, left the settlement in 1848, a year after it was established. Although the community existed until 1865, it gradually lost its original anarchist features.[1]

After Warren had left Utopia, he got in touch with intellectual circles of reformers in Boston and New York City. Among them was Stephen Pearl Andrews, a New York intellectual who had been involved with several reform movements in the 1840s. Together they set out to establish an anarchist community near New York City in 1851. Acquiring 750 acres, they set aside 90 acres for 40 family plots and called their settlement Modern Times. Having prominent intellectuals among its founders and the proximity to New York attracted additional settlers, and in 1853 the population reached 60. Here, too, they adhered to the principles of a noncoercive administration, no set of rules, or constitution.

Soon they realized that they would not succeed in establishing a cooperative economy or even provide services and sufficient food for local consumption since most of the settlers earned their living in New York City. Nevertheless, a few communal branches such as an orchard, a market, and vegetable garden were started. In 1854 they established a communal dining-room which was run as a cafeteria and served those who wished to eat there. They also published and printed several periodicals and anarchist literature. Modern Times began to attract a variety of anarchists, reformers, radicals, and the curious. Their reputation and proximity to the city accelerated the community's growth, which as a matter of principle proceeded without any kind of selection. Among those who joined Modern Times were all sorts of eccentrics, some intent on abolishing the monogamous family. The community acquired a reputation of being "a nest of sexual irregularities and free love."

Later, more ideologically motivated groups joined, causing internal stress and fractions.

One of these groups—the positivists—were actively trying to impose their ideology on other members. This resulted in strife and friction with the anarchist-individualistic founders. When in the middle of the century some ex-Brook Farmers joined Modern Times, its population rose to about 200. The 1860s and the stormy years of the Civil War undermined the social structure of the colony and some of its founding members, among them Josiah Warren, left in 1863. In the following years the community gradually lost its special features.

The years following the Civil War were unsuitable for experiments in anarchist settlement ventures. Warren never resumed his initiative in that direction, and in those years no one continued in his footsteps. New ways and other aims took precedence among the anarchists in the United States. On the one hand they expanded their literary and journalistic efforts and on the other they got more and more involved with the labor movement's struggles, especially after several of the European anarchists began to arrive, seeking shelter in the New World.[2]

Toward the end of the nineteenth century there was a renewed attempt to establish an anarchist community. It was the settlement Home, situated near a group of socialist communes in Puget Sound County in Washington State. Among its founders were several ex-members of socialist communes who had turned to anarchism. They did not object to social organizations per se but to the authoritarian administration of their former communes. Together they acquired land and founded a cooperative society, The Mutual Home Association, which owned the land and was a firm foundation for the colony's existence. Most of the land was communally owned and only a part was allotted for family plots. Just as other anarchist communities, they did not adopt a communal way of life and their collaboration was to be found in their operating credit and consumption cooperatives; they also operated a printing shop in which anarchist periodicals and literature were published.

Many of the anarchist periodicals—the *New Era*, *The Agitator* and *Discontent*—all with a wide circulation, were published at the Home printing shop. The community enjoyed an intensive intellectual life thanks to many anarchist personalities who visited them frequently such as Emma Goldman and Alexander Berkman. The colony became a "Mecca" for U.S. anarchists, but this fame in the end proved harmful. When President McKinley was assassinated in 1901 by an anarchist, a widespread hysteria swept the country. Home became the target of harassment and was constantly troubled by the police. Members were also subjected to their neighbors' wrath because of their living in a so-called nest of free love. The unselective absorption policy had brought to Home people from different circles and among them indeed believers in free love and even nudists. From 54 people in 1899 the community increased to 230 in 1910. This growth undermined their anarchist homogeneity.

Rival factions caused the community to be rift with strife, and it gradually lost its idealistic magic. The educational system, in which new anarchist teaching methods were used, collapsed, and members' hopes for the young generation were disappointed. Between 1910 and 1915, while the colony was undergoing a process of disintegration, its teachers and pupils took no active part in maintaining their idiosyncrasy. The colony continued to exist during the second decade of the twentieth century and even increased its membership, mainly from among anarchists, but it had lost the element of a model anarchist community.[3]

While Home was gradually fading away, a new anarchist community—Stelton—was established in New Jersey. It was founded mainly to provide the site for a modern school named after Francisco Ferrer. The school itself had been founded in 1911 in New York City by anarchist circles and had adopted unconventional libertarian methods of education. In its first years it included a number of prominent educators who were attracted by the school's modern methods. Their existence in New York was made difficult because of police harassment, and the founders decided to move the school to rural surroundings on which an anarchist colony would be established. That community would provide the core of students and also serve as an educational environment for the students and a social one for its educators. A tract of 140 acres was bought in Stelton, New Brunswick, of which 10 acres were allotted to the school. The rest was sold to settlers for their family plots. As at other anarchist communities, they established a combination of private family units and a collective economic enterprise, namely, their educational institution.

On May 16, 1915, a pioneer group of 32 students and six educators left New York for Stelton. The first period was difficult. They had no proper accommodations and both staff and pupils, who were all boarders, suffered from the cold in the winter and the heat and humidity in the summer. In spite of the hardships the colony took shape, acquiring a core of members and a periphery. In 1919 they numbered about 100 families that were connected with the settlement, 20 of which resided there permanently. They found occupation at the school, doing a variety of jobs as staff, caretakers, and teachers. All the other members maintained small auxiliary farms and continued to work in New York, New Brunswick, or Philadelphia.

The educational institution was the vision and venture that kept the colony alive. During the early years all members were involved in school activities and felt responsible for it. A special atmosphere prevailed as a result of the combination of work, study, and recreation within a mixed community of adults, youngsters, and children where nobody enjoyed special privileges.

Teachers undertook to do service and caretaker's jobs while the youngsters participated in policymaking. Later on the educator Harry Kelly boasted of Stelton's uniqueness: "We built a community around a school, something which had never been done before so far as we know. Communities always come first and schools after, but we reversed the order and today the school dominates the community instead of being an incidental part of it."[4]

But the lofty aspirations of the educational institution and the anarchist colony did not last. Except for the school, there was nothing else to evoke enthusiasm in Stelton. Conditions were hard, the climate uncomfortable, the place looked neglected and uncared for. The colony was beset with ideological strife during the 1920s. Several of the anarchists were influenced by the Russian Revolution and became communists, thus losing their regard for the unique educational institution. The school continued to function thanks to a number of devoted anarchist educators who insisted on carrying on, but theirs was a lost battle. The colony began to wane in the 1930s and the school with it. Like the other anarchist colonies mentioned above, Stelton underwent a long period of disintegration that followed the first years of anarchist-inspired cooperative tendencies. None of these colonies attempted to establish a communal way of life; there was only one such attempt during the 1930s.[5]

Sunrise: A Jewish Anarchist Commune

A group of Jewish anarchists established a communitarian settlement in 1933 in the United States. The influential man in their venture was Joseph Cohen, a Russian-born immigrant who ever since his arrival in the United States in 1903 had been active in anarchist circles. From 1915 to 1925 he lived in Stelton, where he was involved in the modern school dedicated to the system of free education. This experience prompted him to consider the establishment of an anarchist community based on communal principles. After leaving Stelton, Cohen devoted his time to the editing of a Yiddish paper, the *Freie Arbeiter Stimme*.

In the autumn of 1932 Cohen got involved with the establishment of a commune, and this almost happened by chance, according to his memoirs.[6] A group of anarchist activists had come to bid Cohen farewell on the eve of his departure on a lecture tour throughout the United States. Those were the days of the great Depression and most of their conversation dealt with the conditions of the working class in the country. When he was about to depart, he lightly added an afterthought: "Yoine, I'm going to organize a communist colony." The friend was surprised and reacted with disbelief, but the same Yoine soon adopted the idea and actively began to promote it.

In January 1933, on his way back from his lecture tour in the West, Cohen met Yoine in Chicago and was amazed to learn that his announcement had triggered off results. Yoine had begun to organize anarchist friends in Detroit who decided to establish a commune. After a number of programmatic discussions they formulated a plan for a communitarian settlement of about 150 families. The project was widely advertised in the *Freie Arbeiter Stimme* as "A Project for a Cooperative Collective Society," and Cohen took over the initiative. For years it had been his dream to establish a commune and this had been reinforced on his travels through the Depression-weary United States. He arrived at the conclusion that an alternative system to the existing one was an imperative.[7] Now, all of a sudden, he had comrades who were willing to go along with him. It was a turning point in his life and on his return to New York Cohen resigned from the editorship and prepared to join the Detroit group.

Some time later Yoine informed him of an opportunity to acquire a 10,000 acre farm in Michigan for a reasonable price. Both hurried to see the owners in Philadelphia and found out that they could purchase this active farm, including real estate and equipment, for a cash down payment and several installments. They got together a number of people who had expressed their readiness to join the venture, and a committee was delegated to inspect the farm, which was ninety-five miles away from Detroit. Most of them were townsmen and inexperienced in farming, but they were favorably impressed by what they saw and after having talked to the farm manager, decided to go ahead with the purchase; many were on the verge of losing everything in the Depression and were anxious to find a foothold of some kind.

Negotiations were difficult. The owners insisted on prompt payment and there was an urgent need to raise money for the first down payment. They initiated a campaign to attract new candidates, and as an incentive membership fee was reduced from $1,000 to $500. A meeting on May 1, 1933, was attended by hundreds of people and resulted in many applications to join the Cooperative Farm Community. The group organized during May and June. It included many members from eastern cities, from Detroit and Chicago. Negotiations with the owners had almost been settled, and the pioneer group was on its way; on June 25 they settled in one of the abandoned buildings and waited for the transaction to be finalized. A few days later the formal procedures had been completed, the first installment paid, and on June 27, 1933, the Jewish anarchist group became the owners of Prairie Farm, whose name was changed to *Sunrise*.[8]

The farm was spread out over a wide plain near populated areas and enjoyed easy contact with the ninety-mile distant Detroit. Some of the land was wooded, about 5,000 acres of it grazing land, and 3,500 acres suitable for cultivation, 2,000 of which were growing crops such as peppermint, soy beans, sugar beets, fodder, corn, and cereals. There were also some vegetable plots, a flock of sheep, some cows, and work horses. The inventory included five tractors, three trucks, and a variety of farm machinery.[9]

On the farm there were three separate settlements, each with its own name. They contained 3 good houses, 2 dormitories, 39 shanties, 15 barns and numerous smaller buildings. Of those, the workers' shanties were the most neglected as they had housed cheap labor and successive groups of migratory workers. In addition there was a well-built barn for sheep, some office buildings, smaller barns, and workshops.[10]

The group that had gathered there found both work and accommodation. The farm was handed over in active production, employing scores of hired hands. To ensure the smooth running of the farm they had to keep the hired workers for the time being, until enough members arrived to take over. They were faced with a double dilemma—an emotional one as well as one of principle: On the one hand anarchist, socially-minded members had to turn into employers who paid their migratory workers a pittance, and on the other hand they had to cope with the professional workers who tried to exploit the situation and demanded extra high pay and preferential conditions. They also faced the problem of raising cash for the twice-a-month pay checks.

The only source of income in those first months were the membership fees paid by new members, hence they were compelled to attract as many candidates as possible. During the early months conditions were good. The reaction to their first propaganda campaign was positive and many applied for membership, mainly from eastern cities, where a pedantic selection of members was maintained. Candidates aged forty-five and older and children-encumbered families were rejected. They also did not accept people whose convictions differed from their own such as conservatives, reactionaries, religious, or active communists. Nevertheless, the homogeneity which had characterized the anarchist founders was disrupted. Their urgent need to absorb as many new members as possible and their inherent liberalism, prompted them to accept also progressive socialists and union functionaries whose doctrine was far removed from that of the anarchists. This would, in time, lead to ideological factionism and cause a schism, the root of all evil.[11]

A week after the farm had been acquired, the people on Sunrise celebrated the Fourth of July among a throng of visitors. Many curious onlookers from the area had come in the wake of the wide publicity given to the purchase of the "million-dollar property" by a group of poor anarchist workers. Their reputation as "millionaire workers" had attracted not only the curious but also made Sunrise into a sort of Mecca for the radicals in the area. Some of them considered joining the colony, others volunteered to stay for periods of time and lend a hand. During the summer months there was plenty of work on the farm which had been sadly neglected by the previous owners. Weeds threatened the crops and every available pair of hands was put to weeding, even at the expense of other branches. In spite of the influx of volunteers who stayed for short periods, they did not manage to do the job and additional labor had to be hired to save the crops from being overrun with weeds.

This intensive effort was crowned with success and the first harvest in the autumn of 1933 was encouraging. These early days were a period of euphoria. Everybody willingly worked from 6:30 A.M. until 7:30 P.M.[12] Even the townsmen and professionals, who were unused to work in the field under a scorching sun, stood up to the physical strain thanks to the high morale of the romantic pioneering days and the sense of participating in a visionary enterprise of social magnitude.

Among their visitors that first summer was the well-known socialist Norman Thomas, who was deeply stirred by the sight of so many people working industriously without any overseers or material incentive: ''Here we have a living and inspiring example of the coming socialist order that will liberate mankind from its bondage,'' he enthusiastically said.[13] From its very first days Sunrise began to lay the economic and social foundations for their communal life, while also investing all their efforts in the running of the existing farm.

The Members of Poalei Zion

The steady influx of new members continued throughout the summer and was only halted in the fall for lack of accommodations. There were already 216 inhabitants (about eighty families) and most of them were Jews from various states in the East and Midwest. Many were former garment industry workers. The group of founders were mainly anarchists but others came from a heterogeneous ideological background. Some were socialists, others union activists, communists or, even members of Poalei Zion. During the first months this caused no problems; they were all united in their purpose.[14]

The first task was to establish the physical foundations for their commune and to construct proper housing for singles and families. Most of the existing dwellings were occupied by the hired workers, and until they left, some barns and sheds had to be partitioned to serve as accommodations. Flats were constructed for couples and dormitories for singles. From the start they introduced communal consumption and a kitchen and dining-room served the community. They used temporary structures and only later built special houses. They constructed shower booths and rudimentary sanitary requirements in the various dwellings. At the same time the commune was faced with the need to provide adequate educational facilities for their fifty-five children, thirty three of whom were between the ages of four and fourteen. These were accommodated in a special children's house under the care of educators.

An elementary school was established even though the local school board objected, mainly because of the communal character of the colony. According to a Michigan state law, members of the school board had to be tax payers and entered as such on the tax assessor's rolls. Sunrise members were not individual tax payers and therefore unqualified to run their own school. After many conferences and attempts to find a way out the problem was solved through the aid of the district school board, and the colony got its own school and even an annual subsidy of $800 to pay teachers' salaries. Most teachers were members, and when it became clear that fees for sending older children to the regional high school in town were too high, they decided to teach them at home. The teachers who had taught the lower grades undertook the additional task of teaching the higher grades as well.[15]

After the early euphoric months of intensive activities, autumn set in and with it problems and social friction. The first concerned the question of whether Yiddish or English should be spoken. A minority of zealous "Yiddishists" demanded that their language should be adopted, but they were opposed by the anarchists in the colony's leadership and by many members who claimed that Yiddish would cause national barriers and isolate the younger generation. The advocates of Yiddish, who had joined the colony hoping to continue the tradition of the Jewish unions and party cells, did not accept defeat. Their grievance caused them to form an opposition.[16] Soon this dispute would fall on fertile ground when social and administrative problems multiplied.

Sunrise was established without any formal constitution. During the preliminary discussions they had not gone beyond a rough and informal draft. Therefore thc first months were a period of trial and error and an ad hoc set of rules, which was in tune with the anarchist views of the founders, who objected to any kind of formal administration even on the level of their small community. The founding group had elected a temporary management, but after their membership increased and most of the newcomers did not belong to the anarchist movement, they felt the need for a set of bylaws and proposed to hold elections. A committee was put in charge of formulating a program, but as the anarchists showed little interest in these proceedings and did not care to serve on it, most of those elected were from among the socialists and the union activists. When a detailed set of rules was presented at several public meetings, most anarchists objected and it was not adopted. For the first time the internal friction between the two camps was evident. A split now divided the anarchists, who supported the temporary administration, from the Yiddishists, the socialists, and the former union activists.[17]

Members of Sunrise faced election in an atmosphere of mistrust and misunderstandings. Joseph Cohen, who had so far served as secretary of the temporary administration, decided to step down when he could not accept the election results. The community refused to accept his resignation and demanded that he remain at his post, for he was trusted by everyone. Cohen agreed, but to avoid being involved in the campaign, he left on a short vacation to New

York City. During his absence the opposition won the election and their organization proposals were adopted. They gained a majority on the new board of directors. In January 1934, while Cohen and other anarchist leaders were away, they took over and a dispute erupted. Cohen hurried back in order to try and settle matters, but the new administration had managed to dig in and would not compromise. Cohen and all his anarchist friends abdicated from their posts and this resulted in a management crisis; the opposition could not function properly and Cohen again assumed office. He called the entire commune to a general meeting, where it was decided to reject the opposition's proposals and to reappoint an anarchist administration under Cohen.[18]

This did not settle the matter. On the contrary, the defeated opposition went underground and began to cause renewed friction among the members. The crowded and shabby quarters under harsh winter conditions contributed to the general feeling of despondency. Most members had come from the East Coast and suffered during the long and cold Michigan winter nights. It was a hotbed of discontent, fully exploited by the opposition. They not only undermined the board of directors' position among Sunrise members, but went so far as to send a sharp derogatory article to the *Freie Arbeiter Stimme*, which had adopted a hesitant attitude toward the commune after Cohen resigned. The article was published in the name of "freedom of expression" and did much harm, because in addition to bitter criticism of Cohen, accusing him of undemocratic procedures, it also advised future candidates to postpone their coming to Sunrise.

Cohen's administration took several steps to defend themselves against the opposition. Promising to return 50 percent of membership fees to everyone who left the colony by April, they hoped to get rid of the disgruntled members. None of the opposition leaders swallowed the bait, but about twenty others took the generous offer, thus depleting the commune's cash reserves. Another step was more constructive. They decided to issue a local newspaper called the *Sunrise News*, in which they intended to publish all the administration's decisions, give everyone a chance to express his opinions, and provide their wide periphery with information concerning the colony. The paper began to appear in April 1934 and was continued until early in 1936.[19] Even though it was meant to relieve internal pressure, the *Sunrise News* was rejected by the opposition, who began to publish their own bulletin in Yiddish, but after two issues the administration put an end to it.

In the spring of 1934 farming activities, dormant during the winter months, were resumed. Ploughing, sowing new crops on additional flats of land, preparing their agricultural equipment, and learning how to use it kept members busy and filled them with a sense of creativity. All internal strife was relegated to the background. New members began to arrive again, at a slower pace than during the preceding summer; they soon filled the places of those who had left, but that did not significantly contribute to the population growth, and there was still a lack of manpower for the most urgent field work. Weeds were again one of the severest plagues and threatened their crops. The *Sunrise News* called on all members to devote their free time to weeding, and people were moved from less urgent jobs to field work. Once again the colony was compelled to employ a large number of hired workers. In the peppermint field alone 150 were engaged. Members were aware of the danger inherent in employing outsiders, as evident in the following editorial:

> We came here to do our own work and to live by our own effort, without exploiting anyone. . . . The hiring of labor on a farm like ours arouses resentment among many members. . . . While it is true that we are giving our hired help much more than we take for ourselves and are consequently not benefiting in any degree from their labor for the time being, we cannot deny at the same time that we are placing ourselves in the position of employers and try to get out of hired men as much as we can. . . . The second cause for resentment is a mercenary one: we simply cannot afford to spend the money on hired labor. Every dollar . . . is taken out of the badly needed money for the repair of our houses and other pressing needs. . . . There is one more element—a very unpleasant one—in the whole situation. Our people are not applying themselves to the work with the same degree of zeal and willingness. Some work themselves to death while others merely pass the time. There are even some who use work hours in the fields for discussion purposes to settle the problems of the universe in general and of our community in particular. This is very annoying and aggravating to those who do more than their share in the effort to keep things going.[20]

In spite of the tremendous effort invested, results were disappointing. A severe drought followed by floods destroyed their crops and complicated their financial problems.[21] Their annual income was about $50,000 and barely covered their expenses. Not enough money was left for improvements or expansion. When the 1934 crops failed, they had to find other sources of income and were finally forced to a step that was ideologically an anathema to every anarchist, namely to apply for government funds. It must be noted that they had been offered assistance by the Roosevelt administration, but had been reluctant to make use of it as a matter of principle. When there was no way out they gave in. The person in charge of the government's colonization funds was Dr. Zeuch, the ex-member of Llano; he was very understanding and after a visit to Sunrise recommended that the loan be given. In the spring of 1934 they received the money, which for a time helped them overcome their financial difficulties.[22]

One of the most complicated problems that the anarchist commune had to deal with was the organization of labor and the establishment of a proper work system. At first they tried to solve the problem of work discipline according to their principles. They met every evening to discuss the needs of the following day and each member was asked to choose his or her task. Soon the disadvantages became evident when only a few of the members chose to do the more strenuous jobs. It was also a waste of professional man power. They therefore adopted a different method. The workers were divided into three groups: (1) craftsmen, who were engaged in the repair work of the old shanties; (2) household workers, mostly women, who did the cooking, cleaning, and serving; and (3) field workers, which included most of the members. This third group suffered from the same drawbacks as the former method had. People would leave for work every morning and were allocated their jobs according to need. Soon they began to voice their dissatisfaction ''at being handled like coolies'' and shifted about the farm without even knowing what they were supposed to do. Adopting yet another method, they elected a committee that would make up a list of all workers and assign their jobs for the following day. This was the way they managed their work during the autumn and winter months, but dissatisfaction arose again because of the compulsion inherent in this system.[23]

A Serious Effort and Prolonged Hardships

In the spring of 1934 several events prompted the colony to search for ways to raise work morale without the use of compulsion. In the background was the general feeling of frustration and discontentment. There also was an urgent need to overcome the economic adversities through an intensive effort of work. After lengthy discussions they elected a committee which undertook to divide the colony into small productive units, assign them equal amounts of work, and place the responsibility on the units themselves. This would give them a chance to work as a group and at the same time take into consideration individual preferences.

The proposal was adopted at the general meeting on April 14, 1934, and according to it the entire work force was divided into small units of six to ten members. There were twelve field units (altogether seventy-seven members) and each was assigned several fields. The units arranged their own work schedule and were socially autonomous as well. All other members (102 altogether) were divided into specialized units of construction workers, tractor drivers, teamsters, dairy men, teachers, cooks, waiters, etc. Coordination was the responsibility of the work manager, who kept in touch with the unit heads. Work allocation, rotation, and work hours were discussed within the units which were also responsible for the results and for work morale. There was an attempt to maintain strict fairness in the amount of work assigned to each unit. The plan was to be realized early in June.[24] The idea of work units, which had been enthusiastically adopted by all members, was rejected by their agricultural advisers and by the hired professional workers who were still in charge of some branches. The work managers fell under their influence and soon doubt invaded others, especially when it was evident that some of the units were negligent in their work and more efficient units had to come to their assistance.

The commune's main economic problem—work morale—went unsolved. Worse still was the problem of absenteeism, which especially affected the former Detroit people who made a habit of going off periodically to the city and staying there longer than had been planned. Others envied them their "vacations" and followed suit, hence the problem became acute and threatened to undermine the whole system. It was evident that something had to be done even at the expense of the commune's principles. They decided to charge each unjustified absentee member with the cost of hiring a laborer. This form of coercion was anathema to their anarchists doctrine and showed the acuteness of the problem in the summer of 1934.[25]

Sunrise's first anniversary was celebrated enthusiastically in the last week of June 1934. Every member's attention became focused on the preparations and as a result morale was high. Many visitors arrived from the neighborhood, others from as far as the East Coast, so that for a few days the population was doubled. Commune members served the visitors and took them on guided tours, enjoying their guests' appreciation of their achievements. The celebration included speeches and performances by the members. The central address was delivered by Joseph Cohen, who pointed out the achievements as well as the setbacks:

> During the preceding year we have established a new community on the basis of voluntary cooperation and have proven to our own satisfaction that the thing can be done. . . . It is true, we did not suffer any privations and did not get a taste of real pioneering in an undeveloped country, the way the first settlers in this country and our brothers in Palestine and Argentina have lived. . . . We came here to live and learn, to experiment, change and improve as we go along. There is so far no reason for anyone to get discouraged. . . . Let me remind you . . . that we want to establish here a community of free and equal people, all living and working together like one big family, without bossism of any kind, without exploitation or oppression. . . . We have made but a small start in this direction. Many visitors were infected by the general enthusiasm and reported their favorable impressions of the colony's achievements in only one year.[26]

The festive days were over; the trials of daily life once again left their impact on the members of Sunrise. The atmosphere was one of bitterness, discontent and criticism. A series of articles in the July and August issues of *The Sunrise News* gave evidence of the situation. The author writes about undercurrents of criticism which were expressed in many disruptive ways. He believed that this was the result of the commune ignoring the small daily wishes of its members. As possible improvements he suggested that they vary their diet, enforce silence and civility in the dining room, improve working conditions (for example stop the habit of waking people with a gong "like soldiers in barracks"), and enable each member to identify with his chosen place of work.[27]

It seems that the author was naive in his belief that criticism could be halted. Within weeks the criticism turned into a flood which threatened to undermine the communes administration. The signal was given in an article in which the author attaches the faults of Sunrise's collectivist organization. "We should not be concerned about the merits . . . as about the demerits of our collective. That there are demerits, i.e. causes for pain, there is no particle of doubt . . . even the staunch upholders of our collective form of living feel discomfort and even pain at one time or another . . . it was definitely understood that it was only an experiment . . . now, after a patience trying trial of one round year—quite ample, one thinks— it was found . . . full of demerits. . . ." The author mentions a few: 1) loss of individuality 2) loss of the right to assert oneself 3) loss of the right to autonomy 4) loss of responsibility 5) loss of privacy and 6) loss of initiative. He continues on these lines and ends up suggesting that they "dissolve partnership with this system" and establish small private units which could form a cooperative if their owners chose to do so.[28]

The proposal was adopted by a few members and discussed at several meetings, while most members rejected it, because they feared that the division of the farm into private units would cause many immediate bankruptcies of those who lacked agricultural experience. Even among those who would survive, wide gaps would ensue between the talented and less talented. They feared that their model anarchist colony would become just another ordinary village. At this stage their idealistic doctrine was still strong enough to reject the proposal of abolishing the commune.[29]

The discussions concerning the work units left a strong impact on the colony's life, which surfaced during the autumn of 1934 elections. Cohen's dictatorial measures were again criticized and there was a proposal to replace him. Although he was eventually reelected, it was in fact a no confidence vote, considering that previously he always had been elected unanimously and this time he gained by a simple majority. The situation deteriorated further when rumor spread that the financial affairs of the commune had been mismanaged. Worse still were accusations of embezzlement, and a storm began to brew when malicious letters to the tax authorities were discovered. Matters calmed down only after a certified accountant had examined the books and found no irregularities.

In addition to the prevailing tension and scandals, the harsh winter conditions of the Midwest once again contributed to the low ebb of communal life. Many decided to leave, and in the spring of 1935 there were only seventy families left, some of whom were also considering a move. During the summer twenty additional families left, mainly as a result of the significant improvement in the country's economy. This was a period of a new prosperity that was also felt in nearby Detroit when the car industry was revived and with it other industries. Many of the unhappy members of Sunrise were among those who grabbed at the chance, but among those who left were also some contributing members who were sorely missed by the colony.[30]

The second anniversary of Sunrise was celebrated in the last week of June 1935. Among those who attended were representatives of labor unions and many visitors. Speakers were optimistic, and again Cohen addressed the assembly. Summing up the previous year he talked expansively about the local educational institutions and declared that during the third year they should devote themselves entirely to fostering the intellectual life of the colony. There was a wide gap between the achievements of their educational institutions and the cultural life of the adults.

Sunrise had invested immensely in the construction of their school. In the second year there were ninety pupils—fifty attended the elementary school and forty the high school. Eight members taught them and took care of their needs. About forty lived in a communal home, which was to be expanded so that all the children could be accommodated there. Many courses were taught at different levels and some took place in the evenings to enable adults also to profit from them,[31] but this was to no avail. The spiritual and cultural activities of the adult population were shallow; their level was much lower than might have been expected in a radical and highly motivated Jewish community. The exhausting physical work and the social problems caused members to neglect their reading habits. The library was neglected and only few exchanged books; even newspapers were not read by everyone.

During the few years of Sunrise's rural existence, its members rapidly isolated themselves from world affairs and limited themselves to local affairs, even though they were living close to urban centers.[32] This process worried the administration, and they proposed to establish an institute for the study and research of the history and the principles of the cooperative movement. When Cohen announced these plans during the anniversary celebrations, he explained that one of the institute's aims should be the fostering of an intellectual atmosphere of study among young and old to prevent the mental deterioration caused by their almost exclusive devotion to farm work. This plan did not materialize, for in the summer of 1935 the commune's economic problems were too severe to be ignored.[33]

Spring was a period of hope: more experience had been gained, and new farming implements were introduced. But nature appeared to be against them. They were beset one after the other by pests, drought, flood, and finally some of their fields went up in flames. The income from their farm was disappointing and the commune urgently needed loans. Among those who came to their aid were the federal relief funds of the New Deal and some private firms they worked with. A source of additional aid were the royalties paid by an oil company that had acquired the concession to drill on their fields. Although oil was not found, the money helped to relieve their financial straights and members' pocket money was raised to $10 a month.

Perhaps the most discouraging problem was their low work morale and lack of organization. The unit system had not brought the much-needed change, and at the end of 1935 it was decided to have a permanent and professional work management that would be assisted by elected members from each unit. Hoping to have a more stable work organization, they decided that every male member had to contribute 275 work days annually and women worked 225 days. They intended to share their profits accordingly, but this method never was put to a test, because shortly after this a radical change overtook Sunrise and the farm was put up for sale.[34]

Sunrise's Decline

The sale of the farm to the government was suggested in the spring of 1936, during negotiations for a loan with the representative of The Rural Resettlement Administration (RRA) who claimed that the office was unable to consider the application of Sunrise because of the size of the farm and its communitarian structure. In the middle of the negotiations one of the representatives came up with the idea to turn the whole farm over to the government. He explained that they would stand to lose nothing because: (1) the government would buy the land and the payment would take care of their investments and their debts; (2) members who wished to return to the city would receive compensation and be free to do so; and (3) those who wanted to remain would be given priority as new settlers under the government project. They would have to apply for land as individuals but there was no objection to their choosing holdings near each other or to their working the fields collectively.

When the proposal was made known to the members, they reacted favorably. By April, sixty families had left, causing serious manpower shortages. When the proposition was discussed at the general meeting of April 15, 1936, a majority voted in favor of the sale. A minority of ardent believers in communal principles objected, claiming that not enough time had elapsed in order to examine their communitarian way objectively. They still believed that a serious effort would put the colony on its feet. Cohen was not among the minority; he too had lost heart and abstained from voting. In later years Cohen admitted in his book *In Quest of Heaven* that he was inclined to believe that those few members of the minority had been right. He felt that the consequences of the majority's decision sealed the fate of Sunrise. Immediately after the vote the contract with the RRA was signed and the farm sold at $268,000. At first they were told not to grow any summer crops because the deal would go through within thirty days, but there was a delay and members proceeded to cultivate the fields and gather their crops. In December 1936 the deal went through and the commune received $277,629 which sufficed to cover all their debts and return members' investments, but hardly any cash left to divide among them.[35]

From April to December 1936—the period between the decision and its execution—several events took place on Sunrise which were to affect the future of the commune. The first was a law suit brought against the colony's administration by an opposition group who had left previously. As soon as they heard that the farm was to be sold, they started proceedings at the federal district court in order to dissolve the commune and asked that a receivership be set up. They charged the administration of the commune with conspiracy to defraud members, with dishonesty, tyranny, corruption, misuse of funds, refusal to give an account for the money handled and even with "subversive activity against the Government of the United States and the laws of the land." Their aim was to build a strong case against the commune, undermine its reputation, and have it declared bankrupt so that a receivership might be set up before the farm was sold.

Thus the seceders hoped to have their say in the division of the property. Their motives became clear when the opposition's attorney offered to settle the case out of court if the commune were willing to pay his clients a large sum in compensation. His offer was rejected out of hand. On August 4 the formal hearing was opened and continued for five days. All work on the farm stopped and most members attended the sessions, confronting the group of seceders. The hearings attracted wide interest in the area, and the courtroom was jammed with commune members and with seceders who had arrived from far away to serve as witnesses for the prosecution. They were joined by special correspondents who reported daily to the Detroit newspapers and by curious public.

The witnesses for the prosecution were not averse to throwing mud at the commune's administration and also included ideological accusations. They pointed out the anarchist background of most members and especially that of the secretary, who had been the editor of the anarchist Jewish journal. Their testimony was not supported by any proof, and in a long and detailed verdict the judge dismissed the case. He went so far as to praise the experiment of the urban Jewish settlers whose social vision had prompted them to establish an agricultural community. The Judge also dealt with the attempt to besmirch them politically, saying:

> They are charged with being Reds which means being disloyal to the government. I find absolutely nothing to justify that charge. The very fact that they

> tried to live together down there, and have lived together in this way, living in common, I guess you can call it communistic, but that is an economic term applied to their economic way of living and has nothing to do with their ideas of how the United States of America should be run at all. . . . This loyal band of people with that property, will continue and make a living and I hope a better one than they have been making. They are entitled to it for what they have done and gone through with. I would like to see the thing succeed as an example to mankind, of what a group of people could do that were willing to suffer and endure and work and strive for the mutual good of them all. . . . There has been no conspiracy. There has been a working together in the spirit of the law under which they are incorporated and in the spirit in which these men got together in the first instance. . . . It's the others, the very ones that are charging wrong doing, that have done the wrong.[36]

The verdict brought great joy and relief. Nevertheless, even the many words of praise of an objective observer such as the judge could not reverse the trend of internal disintegration. Since their decision to sell the farmstead, the process of internal disintegration began. Several members decided to leave as soon as the sale went through. Others continued working the farm, but the commune came to a halt. One after the other the communal institutions closed down. First was the children's house whose inhabitants were removed to the parents' homes, which after the many secessions were large enough. During the summer the kitchen and dining-room gradually began to cater only to the singles. Most members were happy with the new arrangement except for a group of zealous believers in the communal way who were unwilling to give it up. For them and for the singles the kitchen and dining-room continued to function. Members were allotted locally grown produce free of charge and could buy the rest for a weekly budget of $2. This temporary arrangement continued until the end of the year, when the farm was sold.

Early in 1937 Sunrise was faced with the question of future existence. According to the general meeting's decision of April 15, 1936, membership fees and compensation, in proportion to the working period on the colony, were to be paid to those who remained until the sale went through. Most of the members left once they had received the money. There were only 25 families who wanted to carry on, but they preferred not to stay in the cold climate of Michigan and therefore did not exploit their option of purchasing back their land. Instead they decided to seek land in the South. Their choice fell on Virginia.

In April 1937 a delegation of five members set out to find a new domain for the commune in Virginia. The report they sent was encouraging, and the Michigan group began to plan their move. Hoping to learn from their past mistakes they decided not to set out on their communal enterprise with capitalist notions of stockholders who might expect preferential treatment. Therefore they reduced membership fees to a minimum of $100 and hoped to raise the funds for their land purchase and construction plans by applying for loans which would be repaid as soon as their farm began production. Early in the summer of 1937 the delegation reported that they had found a 640-acre farm that would fill their requirements, and the group decided to go ahead with the purchase.

The farm was bought in July 1937, and when the time for moving arrived they discovered that of the 25 families that originally had opted for the communal life only 19 remained. Once again it was internal strife that continued to plague them. Only in December 1937 did they set out. The pioneer group that arrived in Virginia after the cold Michigan winter was filled with hope and the promise of a new beginning. Soon, however, they realized that their optimism had been premature. They were beset with internal friction on trivial as well as on important matters. The partial success of their first economic ventures did not improve the situation. In the summer of 1938 the small group suffered a significant setback and loss of members.

The chances for survival grew remote when Cohen, still the secretary and the living spirit of the colony, decided to leave in the autumn of 1938. He thought that the end was imminent and did not want to be the last to leave because that would only justify the rumors that he had caused the dissolution of the commune so that he and his followers would share the property.[37] When Cohen left in November 1938 there were 12 families left who survived together until the summer of 1939.

On September 1 the general meeting decided to put their property on the market and to dissolve the society. It caused no surprise; the small disunited and disappointed group did not stand a chance of becoming the core of a viable community. The circumstances in 1939 were entirely different from those of the Depression years that had been the main incentive for the commune's foundation.

Loyalty to Anarchism

Years later, when Josiah Cohen reflected on the five years of Sunrise, he came to the conclusion that its failure had been unavoidable. He blamed this on a number of mistakes and omissions that undermined Sunrise's chances of survival, some of which had accompanied them from the outset: the rush in which they had organized, bought the farm, and formed their community. As a result they gathered a heterogeneous group of individuals who had no farming experience. This unselective policy of accepting members resulted in the lack of a common ideological denominator in a community that aspired to realize their anarchist social vision. According to Cohen one of their cardinal problems was the inner contradiction between their anarchist ideology and the necessity to apply authority or to enforce regulations that the working of a farm demanded. This inconsistency caused friction, schisms, and endless discussions that led to a number of crises and no problem could ever be solved effectively. Their ideological differences threatened to topple the commune several times during its short existence.

Furthermore, the lack of a strong social leadership affected the farm management and resulted in sloppy work habits, unprofitable branches, waste and neglect of equipment and property. No wonder then that reality was completely different from their expectations. The commune had been established to provide security for the people who had hoped to escape the Depression, but they faced even worse economic hardships on the commune at a time when the outside economy was recovering from the Depression in the late 1930s. Cohen believed that this was one of the most serious problems of Sunrise. Too many had joined the commune for the promised economic security, material plenty, and social harmony. The ideal had been portrayed to attract new members, and it worked as a magnet on people who were suffering from the Depression. No warnings that they would have to face pioneering conditions, want, and toil could deter them at the time. ''They were carried away by the beautiful vision of the promised land and listened only to the words that pleased them. Reality, when it turned out to be nothing like the dream, irritated them to such an extent that they wished to kill the thing that had disappointed their expectations.''[38] In due course they turned against the commune's administration and those who had supposedly misled them.

The result was an embittered membership and secession. Most of the people were unwilling to face the harsh pioneering conditions, and when matters looked up all around them they were just as quick to leave as they had been to join it before. In spite of their disappointment and frustration with the commune, most members fondly recalled Sunrise in their memoirs, and many remained loyal to their ideals of anarchism and socialism.

Notes

1. James J. Martin, *Men against the State* (Colorado Springs: Ralph Myles, 1970), pp. 7-14, 22, 36-38, 57-63; Grace Adams and Edward Hutter, *The Mad Forties* (New York: Harper & Brothers), pp. 271-81; John Calvin Spurlock, ''Anarchy and Community at Modern Times, 1851-1863,'' *Communal Societies* 3 (1983): 32-35; Yehoshua Arieli, *Individualism and Nationalism in American Ideology* (Harvard University Press, 1964), pp. 283-84; 289-86.
2. Martin, pp. 65-87; John Humphrey Noyes, *History of American Socialisms* (1870), reprinted as *Strange Cults and Utopias of Nineteenth-Century America* (New York: Dover, 1966), pp. 97-101; Adams and Hutter, pp. 282-94; Spurlock, pp. 37-47.
3. Charles Pierre Le Warne, *Utopias on Puget Sound, 1885-1915* (Seattle: University of Washington Press, 1975), pp. 186-226; Stewart H. Holbrook, ''Brook Farm, Wild-West Style,'' *The American Mercury* 57 (July-August 1943): 216-23.
4. Paul Avrich, *The Modern School Movement* (Princeton: Princeton University Press, 1980), pp. 69-220, 221-22, 230-31.

5. Laurence Veysey, *The Communal Experience: Anarchist and Mystical Counter Cultures in America* (New York: Harper & Row, 1973), pp. 77-177; Avrich; pp. 219-22, 243-55, 319-49.
6. Joseph J. Cohen, *In Quest of Heaven: The Story of the Sunrise Cooperative Farm Community* (New York: Sunrise History Publications Committee, 1957), p. 24; Norman Spector, "The Sunrise Colony: A Case Study of the Economic Failure of a Utopian Socialist Community" (Ph.D. dissertation, Ohio State University, 1958).
7. Veysey, p. 117; Cohen, pp. 215-17.
8. Cohen, pp. 35-37.
9. Ibid., pp. 40-42; Spector, p. 36.
10. Henrik Infield, *Cooperative Communities at Work* (London: Kegan Paul, Trench, Trubner, 1947), pp. 41-42.
11. Cohen, pp. 42-43; Spector, pp. 38-39.
12. Infield, p. 45.
13. Cohen, p. 72.
14. Infield, pp. 42-43; Cohen, pp. 55, 62, 73.
15. *Sunrise News* (April 20, 1934); Infield, p. 46; Cohen, pp. 58-59.
16. Cohen, pp. 67-68.
17. Ibid., pp. 73-76, Appendix A; Spector, pp. 50-51.
18. Cohen, pp. 76-79; Spector, pp. 51-53.
19. *Sunrise News* (April 6, 1934; April 20, 1934; May 18, 1934); Cohen, pp. 83-84.
20. "Notes and Comments," *Sunrise News* (July 14, 1934).
21. *Sunrise News* (July 21, 1934; July 28, 1934; August 4, 1934).
22. Cohen, pp. 134-44; Spector, p. 63.
23. Cohen, pp. 91-93; Spector, pp. 43-46.
24. "The Units Basis of Organization for the Colony," *Sunrise News* (April 20, 1934); Spector, pp. 47-49, Appendix B.
25. *Sunrise News* (June 9, 1934); "Minor Difficulties," *Sunrise News* (July 28, 1934); Cohen, p. 95.
26. "Address of Welcome to the First Anniversary Celebration," *Sunrise News* (July 7, 1934); "Impressions of a Visitor," *Sunrise News* (July 28, 1934); "A Day in the Farm," *Sunrise News* (August 31, 1934).
27. "Minor Difficulties," *Sunrise News* (July 28, 1934); "Minor Problems," *Sunrise News* (August 18, 1934).
28. Ellis Grosmer, "Problems and Possibilities," *Sunrise News* (September 21, 1934).
29. *Sunrise News* (November 17, 1934).
30. Cohen, pp. 101-5, 112; Infield, pp. 44, 49; Spector, pp. 74-75.
31. *Sunrise News* (September 21, 1934).
32. Cohen, pp. 197-98.
33. Ibid., p. 121.
34. Spector, pp. 85-87.
35. Cohen, pp. 170-78.
36. Ibid., pp. 170-71, 231-50.
37. Ibid., p. 193.
38. Ibid., pp. 195-214.

17

The Hutterites: A Bridge between Past and Present

On July 5, 1874, the *Harmonia*, sailing from Hamburg, arrived at New York carrying immigrants from eastern and central Europe. Among them was a group of 300 sectarians who called themselves the Hutteran Brothers. They stood out in their extraordinary appearance and their uniform attire: the women's hair was covered with blue, polka-dotted kerchiefs, their wide, long dresses were of a dark material. All the men were bearded and wore black jackets, suspenders, and black, wide-brimmed hats. Even though they had come from southern Russia, their language was German. Unlike other immigrants who preferred to settle in the eastern United States, the Hutterites set out west to the new territories.

Their first station was Lincoln, Nebraska, where they decided to settle temporarily until a place for their permanent settlement was found. A number of members set out to tour the nearby areas for a site. They could have acquired private flats quite easily according to the Homestead Law, but they preferred to establish a communal colony and had to purchase the 2,500 acres of adjoining land in South Dakota with their own funds. Wishing to maintain their unique way of life they opted for communal settlements, just like other communal religious settlements that had preceded them. Their unique attribute was that they had existed as a commune even before coming to the United States; they belonged to a sect that had been living in communes for 350 years. Hence their character and religious communal traits were firmly established.

Historical Background: The Sixteenth Century

The Hutterites emerged as a movement early in the sixteenth century, during the Reformation. They belonged to one of the radical Anabaptist sects that rejected the authority of the Catholic and the Protestant Church. Their identity as a separate group among the Anabaptists was formed in 1528 in Nikolsburg, Moravia, where in 1526 the Duke Leonard von Liechtenstein had offered them shelter from the persecutions in neighboring principalities. Two years later their freedom was threatened when war broke out in that region. The pacifists among the Anabaptists preferred to leave the town to avoid bearing the sword, and about 200, led by their spiritual leader Jacob Wiedeman, left Nikolsburg.

According to the Hutterites' chronicle they decided to share their property, to identify with the Christian apostolic way of life and thus strengthen their community in exile. This decision forged them into a unique group among the Anabaptists and became a matter of principle as much as their pacifist outlook. They soon found shelter in nearby Austerlitz, ruled by Ulrich von Kaunitz and his brothers. Some time later another group of pacifists arrived, and they too adopted the *Gutergemeinschaft* (community of goods).[1] Late in 1529 a third group joined them; they came from south Tyrol and were led by Jacob Hutter, who was born of a poor ancestry in the hamlet of Moos and had been a hatter (hence his name). He was a born leader and soon extended his influence over all the other pacifist Anabaptists in and around Austerlitz. By 1531 there were about 14 different groups, and Hutter forged them into one unit. Those who did not agree to adopt a community of goods had to leave. Within three years of his active leadership Hutter succeeded in making the heterogeneous following into an integrated community with mandatory principles. By 1535 he was the acknowledged leader of all the Anabaptist circles who lived in communes around Austerlitz in south Moravia, but external circumstances cut short his leadership.

The years 1534-35 were a period of hardships for Anabaptists everywhere. In and around Münster, Westphalia, war raged between the militant Anabaptists and the Catholic and Protestant nobility. It ended in the Anabaptists' defeat and was followed by a wave of persecutions throughout Moravia. Alarmed by the Münster disaster, King Ferdinand of Austria demanded the expulsion and extermination of the Anabaptists. The Hutterites escaped into the fields, forests, and the mountains. Hutter himself attempted to flee to his homeland, Tyrol, where he was caught and imprisoned. In Innsbruck he was tortured to make him reveal the hiding places of his followers, but his spirit was not broken even when on February 25, 1536 he was burned at the stake. Hutter's martyrdom left a great impact on his followers. His heroic death and his former spiritual leadership turned him into a symbolic figure and a source of inspiration for the community that after his death called themselves the Hutterian Brethren.[2]

During the short period of Jacob Hutter's leadership of the Anabaptists in Austerlitz, their first tenets and the mode of their communal life were forged. The people had congregated from different places in Tyrol, Moravia, and south Germany. They differed from other Anabaptists in their pacifism and in their adherence to their paramount principle—*Gutergemeinschaft* or the community of goods. Hutter's charismatic leadership instilled the community with a soul-lifting belief in themselves with a feeling of being a "holy community" and "God's chosen." This gave them internal strength to withstand the many tribulations through which their tortuous road led them.

A short time later the persecutions stopped, and the Moravian nobility was again anxious to have them on their estates. Besides being religiously motivated, they hoped to profit from the Hutterites' diligence. Most of them had come from the working classes and almost all crafts were represented among them: artisans, apprentices, farmers, builders, and even pharmacists and doctors. The combination of their know-how with their religiously motivated industry spread their reputation. The Hutterites believed that they had to tend to their domain as "the garden of God" and they meticulously preserved order and cleanliness. They took care to do every job willingly and to achieve a high quality in every respect. The nobility was therefore well rewarded by the influx of a population such as this on their estates.[3]

Close ties developed between the Hutterites and the Moravian nobility which in time led to the community that could now build their own settlements, called *Bruderhof* (the brothers' farmyard). In return for rent and some feudal taxes they were allowed to construct all the buildings which their communal way of life entailed—accommodations, education, public utilities, and various workshops. On their land they could plant orchards and raise livestock, cattle, sheep, and horses. The nobles undertook to respect their religion, free them from state taxes, avoid conscripting them in times of war, and to protect them from enemies and persecutors.[4]

Jacob Hutter's Heritage

After Hutter's death the leadership of the sect was transferred to a *Vorsteher* (leader) who had the highest spiritual status. His authority extended over all the Hutterite settlements and all the missionary delegations that set out to make converts. The spiritual leader following Hutter was Peter Riedemann, who had joined the sect in 1530 and was outstanding among the brethren in his wide theological learning. In the years 1540-1542 he was imprisoned in Hessen for his Anabaptists preaching. During his imprisonment he formulated the Principles of the Hutterian Doctrine, and when he was elected *Vorsteher* in 1542 the sectarians adopted his tenets as the authoritative version of their religion. This resulted in Riedemann being the acknowledged spiritual heir of Hutter and his partner in founding the Hutterian brotherhood.

Riedemann's theological tract was published in *Rechenschaft*,[5] later translated as *Account of Our Religion, Doctrine, and Faith of the Brothers Whom*

Man Call Hutterians. The book was based on the Old and New Testaments and included besides the Hutterites' doctrine also a set of rules and proposals for their daily life. The communal aspect was also briefly dealt with, but only two paragraphs among the ninety that deal with their way of life specified their communal principles. The community of goods was presented as the result of their being a religious brotherhood living in separate communities: "Those who have fellowship, have all things in common together." Communal sharing of material goods was presented as the highest spiritual achievement: "he who becomes free from created things, can then grasp what is true and divine."[6]

Although the principles of material and spiritual sharing of Riedemann's theology were adopted from the Christian apostolic tradition, a unique element—the concept of *Gelassenheit*, peaceful submission to God and to the believing group—was stressed which would become one of the characteristics of the Hutterites' communitarianism. Under the theology of *Gelassenheit*, together with the forsaking of private property they practiced the communism of love in production and consumption.[7] The theological tract was requested by the Hutterites' elders and was to provide answers to religious problems of their sect, which had expanded during Peter Riedemann's time. A communitarian constitution was needed to unite the settlements now spread all over Moravia and Slovakia and could no longer rely merely on Hutter's charismatic heritage. It was also imperative to protect the settlements from the trends brought by new members that posed a threat to the Hutterite doctrine. It was a timely request that enabled the sect to preserve its unity after Riedemann's death in 1556; a new period began of rapid growth and expansion for the Hutterites.[8]

The Golden Period

The Hutterite chronicles speak of a "golden period' during 1565-1592, when the Hutterites in Europe prospered. The spiritual leaders who left an impact on the sect in those years were Leonard Dax and Peter Walpot—both fostered missionary activities; it was a turning point in the sect's attitude and was the result of their strong sense of being called to spread the gospel after having experienced communal living during a whole generation. Hutterite missionaries were sent to many areas in central Europe: Bavaria, Baden, Württemberg, Switzerland, the Rhineland, Silesia, Prussia, Poland, and even Denmark and Sweden. Hutterite missionaries were involved in theological disputes with Catholics, Lutherans, and Calvinists. In many countries where their preaching was forbidden, they went underground. Many were arrested and tortured to death, becoming martyrs of their faith. Martyrdom added a sense of sacred mission to their activities and enhanced their influence. From all over German-speaking Europe, converts came to join the Hutterite settlements whose reputation spread far and wide.

Leonard Dax attempted valiantly to formulate a theological tract to help the missionaries to refute Catholics, Lutherans, and followers of Zwingli, but to no avail. The schism between the Christian churches that accepted the secular governments and the radical Anabaptists such as the Hutterites was unbridgeable. Peter Walpot, on the other hand, concentrated his efforts mainly on those sects that were spiritually close to the Hutterites. Since the 1540s relations had developed between the Hutterites, the Polish Brethren, and the Swiss Brethren. They even established a communitarian settlement jointly with the Poles, but this proved to be a mistake. They had different religious convictions to which the Poles, mostly of an aristocratic background, added a strong intellectual attitude; they were "seekers of the truth" and could not adapt to the rigid Hutterite doctrines. Peter Walpot objected to religious pluralism in his sect and severed all contact with the Polish Brethren in 1570.

Relations with the Swiss Brethren, however, prospered. These had begun in the early years of the Anabaptist movement in 1540. Many of the Swiss Brethren adopted the Hutterite doctrine and moved to Moravia where they established Hutterite-like settlements. From their chronicles we learn that by 1570 there were about twenty Swiss Brethren communities in Moravia which existed side by side with about seventy Hutterite Bruderhof. Hundreds of Swiss joined the settlements in Moravia in those years.[9]

In addition to missionary activities, Peter Walpot's leadership brought prosperity in many other areas of their life. This period would forever be recalled as the golden era of the Hutterites in Moravia. Walpot established his residence in Neumühl in southern Moravia and it became the spiritual headquarters of the Hutterites. All the religious books, archives, documents, and epistles were collected there and missionaries received guidance and support. From the center at Neumühl, Peter Walpot sent epistles to guide the Bruderhof elders in religious matters and in all the aspects of their communal life. He invested a special effort in matters of education, perhaps because their missionary efforts had brought an influx of new members who arrived without any spiritual training. To maintain the sect's original convictions, a great effort had to be invested in educating them.

At a time when the majority of people never even attended school there was no illiteracy among the Hutterites. Everyone got an elementary education. On every Bruderhof there were two educational institutions, the "little school,[10]" in which children aged two to six were taken care of by a "school mother" who had been meticulously chosen for the task. The other was the "upper school," in which six to twelve year-olds were taught by male teachers. The school was not just a place for instruction. Children spent their entire day there, thereby enabling their parents and particularly mothers to work on the commune. Children slept in children's houses and the schoolmasters were entirely responsible for training the young in communal living. They had to teach them the sect's religious values, instill in them the fear of God, and foster them with the spirit of *Gelassenheit*. The schoolmaster had to prepare these children for the communal way of life of sharing, and at the same time good discipline was stressed. Children were taught reading and writing to enable them to read their religious literature. They also received vocational training, preparing them for life on the Bruderhof.

Secular education was frowned upon; the Hutterites firmly objected to any higher education they regarded as a form of "groping in the darkness of Egypt." This violent rejection may have been the result of their campaign against the churches who dominated all institutions of higher learning. However, taking into account their high standard of education, one can safely presume that they had their own teachers' seminaries. Evidence of this were Peter Walpot's frequent meetings with educators and the Hutterite elders which were devoted to discussions on matters of education. A written document giving the detailed account of Walpot's speech at one such convention in 1568 has been found. It is impressive in its explicit directives on the imperatives of education and its values.

Most of the speech was devoted to Hutterite school discipline. Walpot asked the school supervisors "to take care that no disunity, strife or boisterous speaking is heard by the children, but rather a peaceful, cheerful good-natured and sober life and quiet walk. They shall inspire the youth likewise to quiet and sober living and give them a good example." Walpot was aware that children had to be disciplined. He even admitted that punishment might be called for, but this would have to be undertaken by the schoolmaster and the youth should not be hastily disciplined: "The school masters and sisters shall admonish . . . yet not occupy the time of the children with lay preaching. . . . [They should] inspire the youth with ideals of piety." If punishment was called for, "the children shall be trained not to resist the rod, but willingly accept punishment." In addition to many details of daily behavior of schoolmasters and children, he also gave instructions to the night nurse: "if a boy or a girl has some particular unclean habits, such a one may be awakened in order to be cured of such unclean habits according to a good discipline. If it happens once or twice that someone wets the bed, possibly in a dream, it shall be overlooked with the hope of improvement." The entire speech was a testimony of the responsibility demanded of educators. The parents played a small role and could invite their children home only if the schoolmasters agreed. In conclusion, Walpot appealed "to all of you who have the youth in charge . . .

that you perform your duties faithfully with all diligence, as far as possible, by the grace of God. . . . Let each one deal with the children by day and by night as if they were his own."[11]

Conventions such as this were not an unusual event. There is evidence that others took place during the 1570s under Walpot. He summarized the discussion that took place in an educational codex, *Schulordnung*, in 1578. In it he detailed the theoretical aims of Hutterite education and the practical and daily rules of behavior, hygiene, and their curriculum. The codex served the sect even after Walpot's death, and when in 1590 it was reexamined during a convention on matters of education, it was found to have withstood time well. They decided not to introduce any innovations and the traditions of Walpot's time were maintained, and so was the reputation of the Hutterites' institutions of education, which gave the Hutterites the strength needed to face the adversities and hardships they were to encounter in the future.[12]

The Great Article Book and the Great Chronicle

Forty years after Hutter's death, the elders of the sect felt impelled to begin collecting and editing their religious literature for future generations. This had accumulated in the form of declarations of faith by missionaries, epistles distributed by the elders, and documents of defense against and disputes with their opponents. The danger that all of this would vanish without a trace was real. Meanwhile a new generation had emerged that did not know Jacob Hutter or the founding fathers and their literature. The good life during the golden period on their prosperous Bruderhof caused them to be insensitive to theological arguments. Peter Walpot, who had established the spiritual center in Neumühl, was motivated to collect and edit their religious literature. He initiated and participated in writing *The Great Article Book* in 1570, in which all the religious writings of the sect up to that time were compiled and synthetized. It was unique in its simple style, easy to follow for one and all. Its five chapters included the Hutterites' entire doctrine and one chapter was devoted to the "community of goods" and the principles of the commune.[13]

Simultaneously, and with the same purpose in mind, a history of the sect was compiled. The living spirit behind this enterprise was Kasper Braitmichel, one of the sect's elders who, having a clear handwriting and an aptitude for history, began to collect all the documents he could lay his hands on from the early days of the Anabaptists. In fine Gothic script he went on writing year after year until his death in 1573, when other chroniclers took over. The fruit of their labor was finished in 1665 and formed a tome of 612 pages, titled *Geschichte Buch*. It is a rich source of information about the sect in Moravia until the calamities of the Thirty Years' War early in the seventeenth century. The book includes chapters on the sect's missionary activities, its martyrdom, and vivid descriptions of the Hutterites' way of life in Moravia.[14]

One of the descriptions reads as follows:

> Christian community of goods was practiced according to the teachings of Christ and his practice with the disciples as well as the usage of the apostolic church. All shared alike in one common treasury, one common house, and one common table, there being of course special provisions for the sick and for the children. . . . Everyone was his fellowman's brother and all lived together in harmony as a peaceful people who did not give any assistance to the bloody business of war. . . . They were subject to the authorities and obedient in all good works that are not contrary to God, the faith and conscience. . . . They did not make themselves fashionable, immodest, proud and unsuitable clothes. . . . There was no singing of shameful songs . . . but Christian and spiritual songs. . . . The places of leadership were occupied by elders, men who taught the word of God . . . engaged in the ministery of reconciliation. Other talented men were in charge of management of temporal affairs, supervised finances, provided for supplies and did the buying and selling. . . . Still others were in charge to arrange the work which each man was to do so that each did what he was best able. There was no usury nor taking of interest, no buying or selling for gain. There was only that which had been obtained through honest labor, through daily work of various descriptions, including all kinds of agricultural and horticultural work. There were quite a few carpenters and masons who built many substantial dwellings . . . for noblemen citizenry and others especially in Moravia but also in Austria, Hungary and Bohemia. . . . Numerous mills were rented from the owners at their request and operated by brethern as millers. . . . In short, no one was idle; each did what was required of him and what he was able to do, whether he had been poor or rich, noble or commoner, before. . . . It was a perfect body, where each member served and was served by every other member.[15]

The facts speak for themselves. These authentic descriptions give evidence of a flourishing communal life in which industry, a sense of vocation, and profound religious beliefs were integrated. These descriptions might have been slanted; but they were reinforced by visitors—friends and foes alike. An abundance of such descriptions exist in the literature of Hutterites' rivals who intended to slander but, like Balaam, their words inadvertently turned to praise when they described achievements and success. One of the Polish Brethern wrote an essay in 1570 attacking the Hutterites: "They all lived communally and all worked. The men lived separately from the women, each individual had his work assigned and the people simply obeyed. No idlers were tolerated. The stronger men were sent out to fell trees and to thresh grain." Similar attacks were made by one of Tcheck Brethern, by a German professor from Tübingen, and by an Italian who chanced to visit a Hutterite Bruderhof and stayed there for a while.[16]

One of the most detailed descriptions of the Hutterites' way of life may be found in a book written in the sixteenth century by Christopher Andreas Fisher, a Catholic priest. The author was sent by the head of the Catholic Church in Moravia to spy on the Hutterites and to publish a defamation. In his "Fifty-Four Reasons for Intolerance of the Hutterites," he called the Bruderhof not a beehive, as they would prefer to be thought of, but "a colombarium [dovecote], where noise and pollution prevailed." Yet, as soon as he began to describe the Hutterite community he unintentionally listed many productive crafts. He complained about the Moravian nobleman who preferred the Hutterite craftsmen to "Christian" ones, and was most critical of the noble ladies who preferred to hire Hutterite nurses for their children. He was also upset by the Hutterite doctors who practiced among the nobility.[17]

This gives evidence that in the late sixteenth century the Hutterites in Moravia practiced an advanced medicine and hygiene. They also manufactured and sold cures and several of their doctors were quite famous, among them George Zobel, who in 1581 was called to the court of Rudolph II in Prague. He remained there for about six months, curing the emperor of a serious condition. A few years later he was called to the Habsburg Court to advise on fighting the plague in Bohemia. There is evidence about other doctors of high reputation, but as there were no institutions for higher education on the Hutterite settlements, one may assume that these doctors joined the sect after graduating from medical school. Their activities were not curtailed, but the Hutterites insisted on their adhering to the communitarian way of life in regard to their clothing and private property and also expected them to participate in the work performed on the Bruderhof.[18]

The picture that emerged from various sources depicted a variety of up to 40 professions which included most of the industries of the period, except for arms manufacture or luxury items. Finance and trade were forbidden on principle. The Hutterite produce was of excellent quality and in great demand. In the sixteenth century the Hutterites developed their ceramic industry, manufactured roof and wall tiles and decorative tableware in which a colorful design complemented the functional forms and shapes. Their ceramic products were unique and had never before been produced in Moravia and received the name *Hutterite ceramic*. Presumably the know-how had reached them via Italian and Majorcan artisans who had joined their bruderhof in the wake of Hutterite missionary activities. Ceramic was one of their most prosperous industries.[19]

All work places were located within the Bruderhof, and everybody preferred to live and work inside the boundaries of their community. Those who were called upon to serve the sect outside were soon overcome by homesickness and hurried back. In time, though, the number of people who worked away from the Bruderhof increased. Their reputation as craftsmen, constructors, farmers, and children's nurses caused the Hutterites to be in great demand on noblemen's estates. Their leaders did not object to this trend because of its economic advantages that increased their income and expanded the sect's influence. Salaries were handed over to the communal purse, and external workers received their needs as customary in their Bruderhof.[20]

Early in the seventeenth century the sect grew significantly and included 25,000-30,000 members in about 100 Bruderhofs.[21] This increase dictated the reformulation of rules; the first rules had been formulated during the "golden age" and had the *Shoemakers' Ordnung* of 1561. The rules or *Ordnungen* arranged the various professions and included patterns of work organization intending to stop deviances and to set norms. Late in the sixteenth century they included paragraphs forbidding overtime work for private income. Some of the paragraphs were testimony of a growing external influence due to their wide-ranging economic activities. Temptation increased and the spirit of *Gelassenheit* and adherence to communal principles decreased. This internal deterioration occurred at a time when wars brought persecution and limitations on the Hutterites in the Habsburgian Empire.[22]

Persecutions: The Seventeenth and Eighteenth Centuries

In 1593 a war between the Habsburgian and the Ottoman Empires broke out. It would continue until 1606 and was fought on Moravian land. The Hutterite Bruderhofs were hit hard and from the first day they knew no peace. Troops confiscated their food, looted and destroyed their centers. Many of the local nobility who had been tolerant of the Hutterites now changed their attitude and forced them to pay war taxes. When they refused, their property was confiscated. Their pacifist principles prevented them from fighting back and when persecution increased they hid in caves and caverns that had been dug beneath their settlements. The situation grew even worse when twelve years after the war had broken out, the Turks and Tartars invaded Moravia and sixteen Bruderhofs were destroyed completely. Many Hutterites were killed and 240 were taken prisoners.[23] Even when the war was over the Hutterites were not allowed to lick their wounds and to reconstruct their settlements. Twelve years later the most terrible of wars broke out in central Europe—the Thirty Years' War.

In 1618 Bohemian Protestants revolted against the Catholic rule of the Habsburg emperor Ferdinand II. In the first year Moravian Protestants joined the Bohemians and as a result Ferdinand II invaded Moravia. The Hutterites were immediately damaged. Their settlements stood out among the poverty-stricken villages of Moravia, attracting the invaders with their full barns. Because of their non-resistance philosophy, they were easy prey, and within a few months thirty Hutterite Bruderhofs had been destroyed. In 1620, after the Protestants had been defeated at the battle of The White Mountain, the Catholic armies looted, killed, and destroyed all Hutterite Bruderhofs in Moravia. What the sword had spared, hunger and disease finished off. Hutterite sources estimate that by 1621 one-third of the sect had perished. This was the background for a massive exodus of Hutterites who escaped over the border, hoping that the situation would improve. In the autumn of 1622 the governor of Moravia, Cardinal Franz von Dietrichstein, got an emperial permission to order the expulsion of all the Hutterites who refused to embrace Catholicism. He was notorious for his hostility to the Hutterites "renegades" and used force, deception, and temptation to break the spirit of their leaders and thus compel them to give up their religion. Dietrichstein failed: only a minority of 230 Hutterites embraced the Catholic faith and the others preferred exile to religious coercion. They were ordered out of their settlements within a month and had to leave their entire property behind. Pennyless they crossed the Moravian border, never to return to the country that had offered them peace, protection, and prosperity for over ninety years.[24]

In the winter of 1622 the remaining Hutterites left Moravia on a long trek into exile and wanderings. They went eastward into north Hungary (Slovakia today), Transylvania, Wallachia (Rumania today), and south Russia. They would go through 250 years of wanderings before they found a new haven in 1874, when they finally reached the United States. During the years of suffering and hardship the sect almost disintegrated several times, and many of their communal practices were undermined, even abolished, for periods of time.

At first the Hutterites from Moravia found refuge on estates of the north Hungarian nobility. Some Hutterite settlements had existed there during the golden era of the sixteenth century. The oldest was Sabatish, established in 1546 and during that year it absorbed about 3,000 refugees—but they did not find peace and quiet there because the area was too close to the war zone and again they suffered from looting, destruction, and killing. Even though the new colonies were not deserted, the hardships left their mark. Many were killed, the spirit of others was broken, and some deserted their faith and returned to Moravia and Catholicism. According to Hutterite sources, there were a mere 1,000 left in the north Hungarian colonies.[25] Those that remained true to their faith continued their communal way of life as before. Evidence for this is found in Hans Grimmelhausen's book *Der Abendteuerliche Simplicissmus*. The author was a Catholic who wrote about the Thirty Years' War and embroidered it with descriptions of the Hutterite colonies in Hungary. He was impressed with their perfect Christian way of life even though he regarded them as heretics. His descriptions of their communal life and their economic activities were remarkably similar to descriptions of the golden era:

"There was no anger, no jealousy, no vengeful spirit, no envy, no enmity, no concern about temporal things, no pride, no vanity, no gambling, no remorse. In a word, there was throughout and altogether a lovely harmony."

Unlike Grimmelhausen, who visited for short periods only, the Hutterites who lived there at the time attested that in reality relations were far from perfect. A process of deterioration had set in which would undermine the very foundations of the communes. The *Klein Geschichte Buch* (*Little History Book*) reviewed the period between the Thirty Years' War and until the early nineteenth century. According to its author, members' motivation to live a true and harmonious communal life was receding. Many were tempted to gain private property by means such as moonlighting or selling produce privately. The gap between those who labored for the common good and the "phony" Hutterites widened; these phonies were like parasites who enjoyed the economic security provided by the commune. Many complaints were voiced against those who worked outside the commune and did not maintain a modest life style. They were attracted by luxurious ways and kept some of their income in order to equal their standard of living to the one prevailing outside the communes.[26]

The Hutterite leadership and its communal traditionalists were aware of the deterioration and attempted to halt it with the help of *Ordnungen* which were intended to establish clear rules of behavior in all areas of life. This became more evident than ever during the leadership of Andreas Ehrenpreis, who was to become one of the most outstanding of the Hutterite leaders.

Ehrenpreis was the leader between 1639 and 1662 and during that period he collected all the *Ordnungen* that had been issued in the past. Adding his own rules, he hoped that it would serve as a kind of codification of the sect's daily procedures. This, then, was the *Little History Book*. Among other paragraphs was the *Gemeinde Ordnung* that dealt with community rules. Private money was forbidden because, "those who have money at their disposal tend to strive to increase it and in time are tempted to provide for themselves." The rules clearly specified the authority of functionaries and department managers: They should regard themselves as trustees who owed allegiance to the commune and had to report to it. Members were required not to be too choosey about their work and to avoid leaving the unpleasant jobs to others. A paragraph dealing with presents forbade members and their children to accept gifts in the form of money or goods. At the same time they were not allowed to give presents to their friends because they would thus be using community property.[27]

These specific provisions indicated that there were tendencies which had to be checked. Although Ehrenpreis's enterprise of collecting the *Ordnungen* was of great importance, it had no practical impact. Soon it was evident that even the most specific sets of rules could not ensure a stable communal life.

Individualism and the instinct to accumulate private property had gained the upper hand during the long period of the sect's deterioration and was not to be halted. The fiber of communal life had grown thin and lost its raison d'ětre even among the most zealous traditionalists. There were too many phony Hutterites who exploited the communitarian framework for their parasitic existence. Accumulation of private property was rampant. When in addition they were persecuted by the authorities and robbed by hostile neighbors who had an easy time looting their communally stored property, the Hutterite leadership decided to take a far-reaching step. They abolished the commune and introduced private farming in which every one would be responsible for his own property. One colony after the other followed suit between 1685 and 1686 and the curtain came down on the Hutterite communes in Hungary.[28]

After the communes had disintegrated, the Hutterites attempted to exist as a separate religious sect and to maintain some of their communitarian customs, but they failed. The church authorities enforced the baptism of their children, a practice they had always avoided. The Hutterites were also beset by missionaries who gradually succeeded in converting most of the sect to Catholicism. The final blow came during the reign of Maria Theresa of Hapsburg (1740-1780). She supported the Jesuite missionaries who had declared their intention to obliterate the "heretic" Hutterite sect. In a combined effort of missionary zeal, pressure, persecution, torture of body and soul, confiscation and destruction of the Hutterite religious literature the Jesuites succeeded in enforcing the conversion of everyone in the sect. In the 1770s there were no Hutterites left in Hungary, but not all was lost. In that terrible period in Hutterite history a miracle happened. While the Hungarian colonies were beset by war, hunger, and total destruction, a small Hutterite community was existing peacefully 500 miles away in Alvinz, Transylvania.

The settlement was established in 1621 under peculiar circumstances. Its founders were actually abducted by the prince of Transylvania, who wanted to import a Hutterite population to develop his estates. The sect's leaders turned down his plea even though he had promised them complete religious tolerance. They feared a trap in this far-removed location that was also near the Turkish battlefields. Even though the prince's agents abducted about 200 Hutterites and forcefully transported them to Transylvania, the latter were amazed to realize that they had indeed been granted complete religious freedom and could establish their communal settlement as promised.

Thus, while their Moravian and Hungarian brothers were persecuted, exiled, and destroyed during the war, the "abducted" Hutterites of Alvinz lived securely. They established a prosperous commune that in time could send financial support to their persecuted brethren in Hungary. When in 1685 the Hungarian Hutterites had decided to abolish the communes, the Alvinz colony maintained their communal way of life, but not for long. The same process which had occurred in Hungary now overtook the isolated colonies in Transylvania. In 1695 they too decided to give up their communal life. But, unlike their Hungarian brothers, they were not persecuted and could maintain their traditions and religion and keep the sect's books intact.[29]

A period of low ebb set in. Only a handful of Hutterites in Alvinz survived from the prosperous sect which one hundred years earlier had numbered about 3,000 members. That situation was to last for sixty years when, like the Phoenix, the sect rose out of the ashes. The catalyst to this revival was a chance meeting in 1755 between the Hutterite survivors from Alvinz and a group of Lutheran refugees who had been exiled from the Catholic duchy of Carinthia, in the heart of the Hapsburg Empire. Having been involved in revivalist upheavals, they were receptive to radical religions, and when they encountered the Hutterites in Alvinz, they enthusiastically embraced their traditions and ideology. The group numbered 220 and, settling in the district, they initiated a revival of Hutterite communitarianism.

Thus in 1761 the Kreuz settlement was established and included members from both Carinthia and Alvinz. They organized their life in the tradition of the Moravian Bruderhof during the golden era. The period of tranquility was soon over when the very same Jesuites who had persecuted the Hutterites in Moravia began to do the same in the principality of Transylvania. They intended to destroy them completely and exile the Hutterite leaders across the border into Walachia, which at the time was under Moslem-Ottoman rule. The Hutterites soon found out that the local Islamic rulers were tolerant and willing to grant them parcels of land for settlement. Encouraged, the leaders secretly returned to Transylvania and convinced their brethren to emigrate to Walachia.

In October 1767 the Hutterites took to the road and, leaving their settlements, crossed the lofty Carpathian Mountains into a land of new opportunities, religious freedom, and security. They settled near Bucharest, but again fate was against them. When in 1769 war erupted between the Ottomans and the Russian tzar, the Hutterites were caught between the fighting camps and once again subject to looting, plunder, and destruction. In 1770 the area was occupied by the Russians and, realizing that Walachia was not secure after all, the Hutterites set out east in search of a haven. As luck would have it, the Russian general Rumiantzev, who had been among the conquerors of Walachia, was eager to settle some Germans on his Ukrainian estate. This was in accordance with the settlement policy of the tzarina, Catharine the Great, and the meeting between the Hutterites and the Russian general was therefore of mutual advantage. He invited them to his estate in Vishenka, in the county of Kiev, and even helped transport them there.

In 1770 the Hutterite refugees crossed into the Russian Empire and onto their new domain. The lease contracted between the Hutterites and

Rumiantzev granted them optimal conditions: freedom of religion, permission and assistance to build houses suitable for their communal life, exemption from war taxes and army service, and they were also excused from appearing before the common courts. It was almost everything the Hutterites might have needed to establish their colonies in the mode of the Moravian Bruderhof.

Into Russia and the Nineteenth Century

In the following years a steady stream of German Protestants, encouraged by the authorities, arrived in Russia. Hutterite emissaries attempted to convince the survivors among their Hungarian and Transylvanian brethren to join this immigration but to no avail. They succeeded, though, in forming ties with the Mennonites, a fact that was to influence the Hutterites' future in Russia.[30] During the Vishenka period there were several attempts to steer the sect in new directions. It misfired and even caused damage by strengthening the traditionalists who adopted the attitude that nothing should be changed; they insisted that the way of life and the regulations stipulated in the holy books should be strictly adhered to. The tranquil period at Vishenka ended after the death of their benefactor, Rumiantzev, in 1796. His sons, who had been living away from the estate, tried to sever the special contract with the Hutterites and make them vassals. In their hour of need the leaders appealed to tzar Paul I, who supported their claim and decreed that the contract was indeed valid. To legalize their claim hc granted the Hutterites equal rights with the Mennonites, who at the time were arriving from Prussia to settle in the Ukraine and enabled them to cultivate state-owned land in the area.

In 1802 the Hutterites abandoned their settlement in Vishenka and the forty-four families (about 200 people) moved to Radichev, about twelve miles away. Here they were granted even better conditions, a larger area for cultivation (2,000 acres), and a more fertile land. Within a short while they established a colony similar to the Moravian Bruderhof. Spacious houses served their communal living, consumption, and educational functions. They again worked at all the crafts which had occupied them in the past. Their farming efforts in field, orchard, and animal husbandry prospered, as evident from reports of Mennonite visitors and Russian government officials. Noteworthy are some of the detailed reports of an inspector named Bunin who was sympathetic to the Hutterite communitarian way of life and their religion. He devoted several chapters to matters of education, and especially interesting are his description of the baby houses, where mothers used to reside from the day of giving birth and until the child was 18-months-old. We may assume that at this time the Hutterites still practiced communal education and the children slept in children's houses as had been their practice in Moravia.[31]

Despite the promising beginning and the optimal conditions, the Radichev community began to disintegrate several years later. The cause was internal friction that developed after the founding fathers, whose faith had been strengthened during their years of hardships and wanderings, passed on. The new generation, which had grown up in the tranquility of Russia, was less motivated and did not adhere to traditional values. Hoping to introduce innovations, they met with the opposition of their conservative leadership who had experienced the bitter results of change and deviations and were loath to introduce even the smallest modifications. The gap between the sides became unbridgeable. The innovators began to scoff at some sacred customs of communal life, introduced private property, and neglected the public's. They lacked a serious approach to duties and work, and their discipline grew slack. All this had a demoralizing effect on the society; neglect was evident everywhere and production rapidly decreased.

Under these circumstances the government inspector intervened. He suggested that those who opposed communitarianism move to a Mennonite colony. However, even after this was accomplished, the situation did not improve. Shortly after, a fire broke out and destroyed most of the houses in Radichev. When the Hutterites set out to rebuild their settlement they realized that even those who had so far adhered to their communal way were now opposed to renewing the old order. They therefore decided to establish a community of private farms and the commune was abolished in 1819. Consequently, the members who had joined the Mennonites returned to Radichev.[32]

Thus, again, the Hutterites experienced a period of noncommunal life, but the sect maintained its religious convictions. For a period of forty years (1819-1859) a spiritual vacuum inflicted their life and educational system. Radichev also had economic difficulties, mainly because they lacked land for their private farms. In 1834 the Hutterites asked to be transferred to state-owned land in another area. This was granted, and in 1842 they moved to an area inhabited by Mennonites in Molotchna, Crimea. The Mennonites were Anabaptists who established their colonies of private farms based on mutual aid and collective responsibility. The Hutterites were offered the same conditions and within a few years had established five separate settlements at some distance from one another. Influenced by the Mennonites, they agreed to divide their sect into several communities, a step they had feared because of the danger from assimilation. Now that their settlement had reached a certain size they would divide it, a practice that would characterize the Hutterites in the United States in later years.

Living near the Mennonites contributed much to the Hutterites, because the former were excellent farmers and willing to teach their neighbors farming methods on the plains and prairies. This too would later benefit the Hutterites in America. The most important result of their settling near the Mennonites was a speeding up of the return to their communitarian tradition. Those elements among the Hutterites that lacked the sect's traditional motivation soon assimilated among the Mennonites, but the conservatives were prompted to adhere to their Hutterite idiosyncrasy. Their preachers continued to read the holy books to the congregation and did not neglect the chapters that referred to *Gutergemeinschaft* (community of goods) which had been practiced in the past. They stressed the difference between this and the Mennonites who were only partially communitarians. An intense yearning for the golden period overcame the sect.[33]

The spiritual renaissance began in the middle of the nineteenth century, when the Hutterite preacher Michael Waldner had visions. During one of his trances an angel ordered him to save his congregation from the flames of Hell by gathering them in an "ark." This, according to Hutterite tradition, referred to the Bruderhof that was often depicted as Noah's Ark. Waldner undertook the sacred mission to renew the Hutterite Bruderhof and in 1859 established a communitarian community whose members called themselves *Schmiedleute*, in honor of Michael Waldner, who was a blacksmith. A year later another preacher, Darius Walter, gathered a group and founded a second communitarian community by the name of *Dariusleute*. Both communities developed under similar circumstances but never intermingled because of their separate leadership. They established the foundation for the revival of communitarian communities in Russia and existed side by side for fifteen years, until they were again forced to resume their wanderings. When the Hutterites set out they did so separately, even though they took the same road.[34]

The communitarian revival of the Hutterite communities in Russia coincided with political change in that country. A process of Russification had set in, demanding governmental supervision of public schools; the teaching of Russian was made mandatory and threatened to undermine the religious educational foundations of the Mennonites and the Hutterites. Worse still was the 1871 conscription law that endangered the very existence of these pacifist sects. Their leaders rushed to the capital, St. Petersburg, to reaffirm their contract. The answers they received from the officials there did not reassure them. Under these circumstances the only option seemed to be emigration. They therefore sent an expedition to the United States, which at the time was attracting immigrants from all over Europe.

In 1873 two Hutterites set out to the United States. Although they were not members of a commune, they represented the entire sect including the communitarians. Touring the country, they were deeply impressed by the vast options of settlement and the religious freedom. Yet their main concern was the mandatory military conscriptions. To clear the matter they were granted an interview with President Grant. After their meeting in Long Beach on July 27, 1873, the Hutterites had the impression that the president was sympathetic to their cause, even though nothing was promised. A short time later they received a letter from the president's office in which he stated that he could not promise them any exemption from army service, but he added that he could promise that "for the next fifty years the United States will not be entangled in another war in which military conscription will be necessary."

This sentence sufficed to make the decision early in 1874 to emigrate to the United States. The first two groups to leave were the Schmiedleut and Dariusleut who sold their property to the Mennonites and on June 7, 1874, set out on their way. The other Hutterites followed within the next few years.[35] Once again the whole sect took up their wanderings, leaving Russia, in which they had found a safe haven for 104 years. The only difference was that this time they went west, crossing the ocean to a place they considered to be the "promised land." They were filled with the hope of a new beginning, yet, carrying their history with them wherever they went, they merely revived their ancient traditions in a new place.

The New World: The Hutterites in America

In the five years between 1874 and 1879 the entire Hutterite sect of 1,200 emigrated from Russia to the United States. Most of them were not commune members, but all settled near the first Hutterite Bruderhof in the prairies of South Dakota. They established private farms there and in time, as their ties weakened, assimilated and were integrated with the Mennonites in the area. Among the immigrants who arrived in 1877 was a new group that had been established in Russia two years earlier by the teacher Jacob Wipf and was called *Lehrerleut*. They, too, maintained their separate entity on coming to the United States, just like the Schmiedleut and the Dariusleut.[36]

By 1880 the remainder of the sect immigrated, and according to the U.S. census there were 443 Hutterites living in communes. This was to be the nucleus of a Hutterite renaissance. After 350 years in Europe, most of which had been threatened by war and persecutions, there began a long period of peaceful existence in the wide-open spaces of South Dakota. In the 1870s the newly opened area was sparsely settled, thus enabling the Hutterites to establish their settlements in remote and secluded parts of the country.[37]

The first years were a time of physical hardship. The newcomers had to get accustomed to the conditions in the area, its climate, nature, and agricultural prospects. Their relationships with neighbors and the authorities were peaceful; They were undisturbed by their neighbors who showed no interest in their doings, and the authorities had granted them complete freedom, enabling them to adopt their communal way of life to the new circumstances. The similarity between the conditions on the Russian steppe and the South Dakotan prairie helped them to get rapidly used to the farming methods there. The transition from a mixed economy that had characterized the sect in Moravia to an agricultural one practiced in Russia was reinforced. The Hutterite communes in the United States were based on extensive farming and in this they completely differed from the European Bruderhof, where crafts and industry had been predominant.

The Hutterites settled in three separate communities in South Dakota. The Schmiedleute established Bon Homme in 1874, the Dariusleute established Silverlake in 1874-75, and the Lehrerleute established Old Elmspring in 1877. A few years later the growing population caused each of them to be divided. This was be their practice from then on, and when a colony reached the optimal population of 150 they would split up to establish a new one. In this respect, too, the American commune differed from the European ones, although there had been a precedence in Russia through Mennonite influence. The system called on every colony reaching a population of about one hundred to split into two social units. Families would remain intact and form modular units on which the new settlement would be based. Then the old commune would acquire additional land, and after that had been cleared and a population of 150 had been reached, the final division took place and a new settlement emerged. A lot was cast to decide who was to leave for the new colony.[38] Two significant consequences of this procedure were the maintaining of optimal economic and social units and on the other hand the abolishment of the communal children's houses; the latter began to sleep in their parents' houses. A settlement that split every ten to fifteen years and never reached a larger population than 150, could not keep communal children's houses. In that too the American settlements differed from those in Europe.

Relationships with Other Communes

The Hutterites were averse to maintaining relationships with their neighbors but sought contact with older communes in the United States right after they arrived in South Dakota. The first step was taken by Bon Homme when they ran out of capital after the purchase of their land. A year later the elders asked the affluent Harmony commune for a loan of $3,000 to finance the construction of a flour mill. Harmony representatives were invited to visit the young commune and were impressed by the Hutterite communitarian way of life. Granting them the loan, they also proposed to maintain contact, as both sides felt the affinity in their way of life and beliefs. However, they differed sharply on the subject of the family. The monastic followers of Rapp recoiled from the family-centered characteristic of the Hutterites. Still, their relationships and assistance continued for another ten years.

Parallel to the close contact with Harmony, the Hutterites developed relationships with inspirationalist Amana, which was closer geographically and also in their way of life. The Schmiedleute of Bon Homme were the most active among the Hutterites in maintaining relations with other communes. When in 1878 their population increased so that they had to split up, they encountered financial difficulties and asked Amana for assistance. Although this was granted, it did not suffice, and the Hutterites again approached Harmony. This commune had reached old age and in addition to financial help offered excellent conditions of absorbing the new colony on their land. The Hutterites accepted the generous offer and in 1884 the daughter commune of Bon Homme moved to Pennsylvania. The members of Harmony went so far as to regard the newcomers their material heirs, but nothing came of it because the Hutterites realized that they could not get acclimatized in the new area with its different economy and alien population. Two years later, in 1886, the Hutterites returned to South Dakota to establish their colony in Milltown, on the James River. The ties with Harmony were never renewed.[39]

There is also no information about further relations with Amana. The Hutterites resumed their isolated existence and in the second decade needed no further assistance. They had survived the difficult period of every beginning and were on their way to success and prosperity.

During the first two decades of settlement in South Dakota the Hutterite colonies developed without interference. From each of the parent communes of the various *Leute* there emerged at least two additional ones. In 1848, when the Spanish-American war broke out, the Hutterites' future clouded over. Fearing conscription or any other involvement in the war effort, they urgently sent a mission to Winnipeg, Manitoba, in Canada, to examine the possibility of settling there under special conditions. Representatives of the Canadian Ministry of Interior visited the Hutterites to inspect them; their impressions were extremely favorable and they advised their authorities to grant the Hutterites similar conditions to those enjoyed by the Mennonites. Meanwhile the war was over and the immediate threat with it; yet some Hutterites, especially the Dariusleute, continued negotiations with Canada. In 1899 the government of Manitoba granted them special terms, according to which Hutterite settlers were to be exempt from army service and allowed to live communally and maintain their independent educational system. The Canadians were eager to attract industrious settlers to the Manitoba prairies and hoped that the favorable conditions and privileges would tempt all the Hutterites to leave the United States. In fact, just a single Dariusleute commune moved to Canada and after six years, in 1905, they all returned to the United States.

In those years the legal status of the Hutterites in the United States underwent an important change. The different *Leute* had settled in separate areas keeping their own religious institutions. They now realized that they were in need of some regional organization that would give them legal standing and protection from external influences. In 1905 they therefore established the

Hutterite Bruder Gemeinde (Hutterite Society of Brethren). This religious-economic corporation was legalized by the state. Its main purpose was to ensure the rights of their communal property and protect the commune from legal jurisdictional demands of seceders. The management of the *Gemeinde* was entrusted to a committee that was elected for three years by a majority of all male members. This committee represented the Hutterites before that state and the local authorities. The *Gemeinde* contributed significantly to the legal position of the Hutterite settlements, but that did not alter the internal relations of the *Leute*. They still kept their separate identities within the *Gemeinde*.[40]

Difficulties in Times of Peace and Prosperity

Between 1874 and 1917 the Hutterites experienced a period of peace and prosperity unknown since the "golden period" in Moravia. They utilized it to advance their economic and social growth. Their aptitude for prairie agriculture resulted in prosperous farms, but the usually conservative Hutterites' adaptability to technological know-how contributed more than anything else to their prosperity. Rapidly and efficiently they adopted every novel idea in farming and economy. This dual trend was no chance event. The Hutterites' bitter history had taught them to foster their colonies' economic foundations. At every station of their long, lonely road they managed to adapt their production methods to the prevailing conditions.

They arrived in the United States at a time when immense technological change occurred on the farms. They realized that they would have to adapt gradually so that this modernization would not undermine their social fabric. As a result, within a few years one could observe the most advanced equipment both on their farms and in service branches. Still, modern technology was intended only to improve their methods of production and was never used to advance their standard of living or to provide any form of luxury. For instance, while modern tractors were cultivating their fields, the Hutterites used carts and surreys for their own transportation. Later, when trucks carried their produce to the markets, there was not even a single private car on any of their colonies. During the 1910s visitors reported enthusiastically about the Hutterites' modern mechanization methods. We read about steam and gasoline engines in their workshops and flour mills; large tractors and new fangled threshing machines cultivated their fields. They were the first in the area to introduce electric generators and use modern ice installations to freeze their produce and transport it to the markets.

The Hutterites' adaptability to change was also apparent in the planning of their new settlements: the houses were of modern design and architecture but the layout was strictly traditional and remained identical on all their settlements. In each colony there were four to five houses for accommodation that were set up in a quadrangle. The dining-room was in the center and at both its narrow ends were the service buildings, on one side the laundry and store-room and on the other the school and toddlers' houses. The colonies were usually established on remote locations such as at the foot of a hill or in a riverbed to ensure their seclusion. As far as possible the Hutterites tried to limit contact with their neighbors to economic affairs.[41]

In 1917 there were nineteen Hutterite settlements in the United States with a population of about 2,000. Relations with their South Dakota neighbors had so far been correct, but when the United States entered the war this changed drastically. The Midwest was overcome by patriotic chauvinism. The German-speaking pacifist Hutterites became an object of hostile incitement. Other German-speaking pacifists such as the Mennonites were less persecuted. Perhaps the Hutterites' absolute refusal to participate in the war effort, even in alternative forms of services or just by buying liberty bonds, provoked an intensive fury against them. Their leaders' pathetic appeal to President Wilson asking that their young men be exempt from army service was never answered.

On May 17, 1917 congress passed the Selective Service Act, which compelled every young man who was a conscientious objector to serve in a nonbelligerent unit. This legislation left no alternative for the young Hutterites, but the elders decided not to yield. Prompted by their elders, the conscripts presented themselves at the enlistment centers but refused to don uniforms or do any kind of work to help in the war effort. These young, bearded men in their odd clothing who hardly spoke English were complete strangers to any army procedure. They were subjected to torment, contempt, and terrible degradation by sadistic commanders. All attempts to clarify their moral standing and conscientious objection failed. The Hutterites expressed readiness to perform any kind of civil service instead of serving in uniform, but this was refused. The situation deteriorated in April 1918, when the war secretary ordered to court marshal anyone who did not submit to the Selective Service Act. Many were sentenced to long periods of internment, among them the Hutterites. A few months later public opinion demanded to separate the honest objectors from the "phony" ones. A committee had to establish the facts and reduce the sentences of the former.

Before these steps were taken scores of Hutterite youngsters had been interned and endured severe torment. The suffering of four of these internees was to become notorious. They were the three Hofer brothers and Jacob Wipf, all from the Rockport colony. Having refused to don uniform, they were sentenced to thirty-seven years in prison. This was reduced to twenty years and they were sent to the infamous Alcatraz Prison in San Francisco Bay. After four months in the dungeon, they were transferred to Fort Leavenworth,

Kansas, where two of the brothers, Jacob and Michael Hoffer, succumbed to the tortures that finally killed them in November 1918.[42]

Their ordeal shook the Hutterite sect and prompted them to decide on emigration to Canada. The first step had been taken back in 1917 when the Selective Service Act was passed. The elders, sensing the coming tribulations, checked with the Manitoba authorities whether they would still grant them the special condition of 1899. An affirmative answer reached them just as emigration became an urgent necessity. Hostility in the newspapers and among their neighbors was on the rise, and in the spring of 1918 violence against the colonies erupted. Their property was looted and their marketing efforts undermined. As a result the South Dakota Hutterites began to sell their property and buy land in Manitoba and Alberta in Canada. In the autumn of 1918, when the martyrdom of the Hofer brothers became known, they decided to hasten the economic procedures.

During 1919-20 most of the land in South Dakota was sold. Simultaneously they moved to Canada and established new colonies there. By 1922 the process had been completed and 15 colonies existed in Manitoba and Alberta. Only Bon Homme, the first Hutterite settlement in the United States, remained intact. Others whose land had not been sold left their settlements behind, a tragic evidence of the Hutterites' fate and an infamous reminder to their South Dakota neighbors.

The transition to Canada was accomplished separately by the three *Leute*, and as a result they established three centers—six Schmiedleute colonies in Manitoba, five Dariusleute and four Lehrerleute colonies in Alberta.[43] The transfer did not go smoothly. Much to their consternation, the Hutterites found out that even in Canada people were antipacifists and anti-German. The massive Hutterite immigration scared their neighbors and, pressured by public opinion, the Canadian Parliament limited Hutterite immigration and colonization. As soon as the war was over the limitations were lifted. The second decade of their settling in Canada was a period of tranquility and expansion for the Hutterites. The Dariusleute were most prolific and established five further settlements, while the Lehrerleute established two, and the Schmiedleute only one. They maintained their identities and remained conservative and socially secluded on the one hand but adopted technologically advanced methods of production and construction on the other.[44]

During the 1930s an important change occurred, prompting the Hutterites' return to the United States. It began during the great Depression and the initiative came from the South Dakotans who now realized the colonization assets of the Hutterites and their former contribution to agricultural development. They knew that Hutterite presence would set the economic wheels in motion again and asked them to come back. Hoping to return to their abandoned settlements the Hutterites accepted the invitation right away, especially when in 1935 a new South Dakota legislation granted them the same rights they had enjoyed in Canada and promised to renew the 1905 treaty which safeguarded their communitarian property. Following their tradition, they again kept to the separate areas of resettlement for each of the *Leute*. The Schmiedleut, who had stayed on in South Dakota, exploited the new opportunities and acquired the land of the others, establishing their new colonies in South Dakota. Most of the Dariusleute and the Lehrerleute remained in Canada, and only a minority returned to the United States to settle in Montana. World War II found the Hutterites distributed in fifty-one colonies—five in South Dakota, two in Montana, and the rest in Manitoba and Alberta in Canada.[45]

During World War II the Hutterites' persecutions did not recur. The experience of World War I had brought about special laws dealing with conscientious objectors and giving them the option of serving as farm workers instead of being conscripted. The Hutterites could now fulfill their civilian duties without any problems or compunctions. Their expansion continued even during the war, and their numbers increased from fifty-one settlements in 1940 to ninety-three in 1950, with a population of 8,542. In South Dakota the Schmiedleut had fifteen settlements; in Montana the Dariusleut had twenty-five and the Lehrerleut fifteen, and in Manitoba there were twenty Schmiedleute settlements.[46]

The Canadian Experience

While the Hutterites prospered in the United States during World War II, they were beset by severe difficulties in Canada. These were mostly the result of economic problems with their neighbors. The local population began to fear the Hutterites' monopolistic landownership in an area where the population was rapidly increasing. The Hutterites were ready to pay high prices for the land they needed for their daughter colonies and outbid competitors every time. Further, their economic viability and success caused jealousy and envy among the small holders in the area, while the retailers complained that the Hutterites did all their business with wholesalers and contributed nothing to local business and trade. This ''economic hostility'' was reinforced by hatred of all Germans and a general resentment of pacifists in times of war.

In 1942 parliament passed a law forbidding the sale of land to enemy aliens, including the Hutterites. This law was repealed as soon as the war was over, but another ruling of 1947, the Communal Property Act, forbade the Hutterites to expand their holdings above 6,400 acres. They were also forbidden to acquire land for new settlements in an area of forty kilometers adjacent to any existing colony. It was the most anti-Hutterite legislation in Canada and remained so until 1962, when another ruling again permitted the purchase of land for existing settlements. This hostile law did not cause any Hutterite colony to be uprooted, but it inadvertently pushed them to expand to two other provinces—Saskatchewan and British Columbia. It also reinforced their inclination to return to South Dakota and Montana.[47]

Hutterite expansion in the United States and especially in South Dakota also caused fears there. Ever since 1949 a relentless effort by the farmers' representatives in South Dakota had been invested to curtail land sales to the Hutterites. They succeeded in 1955, when the House of Representatives passed a law forbidding acquisition of additional land for existing Hutterite colonies. This caused an outcry in public opinion. Circles fighting for civilian rights supported the Hutterites who for once were not alone in their struggle. They succeeded not only thanks to public opinion but rather because of their survival capacity, which gained momentum. The legal harassment far from limiting them could not even stop their amazing demographic increase as a result of their ideal of large families, high standard of hygiene, and the economic security provided by the communal way of life.

From Modest Beginnings

In 1963 the Hutterite population in the United States and Canada was 14,000 with 142 settlements. Twenty years later, in 1983 they had reached a population of 33,000 in 300 settlements, about one-third of them in the United States. Hence, since their arrival in the West in 1874 the Hutterites had multiplied from about 400 to more than 30,000. In the year 2000 they may be expected to reach 60,000.[48] In spite of their "via dolorosa" in hostile and alien environments, this movement has not only survived but shown a unique viability.

The rapid growth of Hutterite population in the United States and the continuous branching out of their colonies did not impair their cohesiveness. The similarities between the three *Leute* were manifest in several areas such as family relations, supervision over religious discipline, regulations concerning their way of life, adaptation to change, and the territorial proximity of their new colonies. The distinction between the *Leute* was minute and one could easily draw a collective profile of the Hutterite colony as a communal settlement and a sectarian-religious community. Until recently, without exception, they continued to be unique in their appearance and special attire: the women wore calf-long skirts and covered their hair with a dotted scarf. Men wore black suits and suspenders, and all were bearded. They looked exactly as their ancestors did when they had laid the foundations for their first settlement in America in 1874. Their colonies had the same character as they had had in the nineteenth century.

The diversified economy that had characterized their Bruderhof in the golden era in Moravia has given way to extensive farming with only a few service branches. Adapting their economy to the prevailing conditions of the prairies in the United States and Canada, they have cultivated mainly cereals, maize, and fodder. Their animal husbandry includes sheep, pigs, and cattle for meat and milk production. They have poultry farms of chickens, turkeys, and geese. Besides all of these the colonies have maintained excellent services such as garages, smithies, carpentry shops, and shoemakers. A special branch, that of bookbinding, has developed out of their religious needs.

Each colony has owned 5,000-10,000 acres, depending on the area and its conditions. Only a small part of their produce has been for local consumption and the rest marketed, which entailed an extensive network of relationships with the external economy. They have had to face a dilemma caused by their wish for seclusion on the one hand and the objective necessity to promote relationships with the outside world, if on the economic level only, on the other.

Mechanization has continued to be at a high level and technical adaptability has characterized all their farming and service branches. In the words of their spiritual leaders: "Nothing is too modern if it contributes to production." They have supported every kind of sophisticated innovation as long as it does not affect their religious-social traditions. This attitude has been a part of the Hutterites since the beginning. Their horses and oxen have been replaced by steam, gasoline, and electric engines, and their primitive farming tools by air-conditioned tractors, combines, and hydraulic machinery. They have introduced modern and sophisticated methods in poultry and animal husbandry, air-conditioning and freezers in store rooms and kitchens. A fleet of trucks has transported containers to the markets. Their settlements have been connected to electricity and telephone lines to promote their means of production, but there still is a strict dividing line between production-required modernization of the kind that eases the work load or makes it more efficient and the other kind that provides comfort or a higher standard of living. Accordingly, the Hutterites have refused to introduce radio or television and have no use for private cars.[49]

The Hutterites are instructed in the maintenance of their modern equipment by representatives of the manufacturing companies and are guided by federal or regional experts in methods of agriculture. Many of their department heads are in touch with experimental farms. But it is their industry and diligence that primarily contribute to their success. Hutterite youngsters are used to working from the age of fifteen, under the guidance of their elders, and each learns at least two jobs. This contributes to the colony's prosperity and profitability, even though they have to support a population half of which are children under fifteen. They have even managed to amass substantial profits that enabled them to acquire additional land every decade.

The Hutterites, who had been pioneers of compulsory education as far back as their Moravian days, have an independent system even today. Their cardinal effort has been invested in maintaining their unique and autonomous methods in the face of state interference. They have had to fight a massive battle until they at last achieved legal recognition of their independent educational institutions. Accordingly they abstain from sending their children to local village schools and even their smallest settlement has its own elementary school in which children up to the age of fifteen are taught the state secular curriculum in English. Most of the teachers are hired, which enables the Hutterites to choose and supervise their teaching staff who usually live on the settlement. Although this may be a source of external influence, relations are usually correct and teachers avoid behavior offensive to the community (for instance, women teachers abstain from using makeup).

In order to instill in the children their religious and social values and prevent the external influences of the public school system, the Hutterites keep up a system of complementary education. For two hours daily they are taught the history of their sect, its literature, and songs in German. Thus the indoctrination of the young generation begins in the kindergarten and continues in the "German school." The teachers in charge of these classes enjoy a high regard and invest great efforts that are repaid by their success in limiting external influences. In spite of their proximity to cities and "civilization," for many years there had been no increase in the number of young Hutterites leaving the commune: During the seventy years from 1880 to 1950, a steady 2.5 percent or 258 men and 11 women left their settlements and about one-half of them eventually returned.

In recent years there has been a steady increase in the number of youngsters who go out into the world, which has gradually come closer.[50] Many of the Hutterite settlements are quite close to big urban centers such as Winnipeg, Manitoba, Lewistown, Montana, or Sioux Falls. Highways pass nearby and the number of visitors is on the increase. Under these circumstances, external influence has resulted in deviances among the young. Private property, luxury items, and fashionable attire are no longer an exception, but there seems to be no sign that these may endanger the sect or undermine the commune's existence.[51]

A Talent for Survival

The Hutterite talent for survival has puzzled many social researchers who, ever since the 1950s, have invaded the colonies to gather material for various disciplines such as the social sciences, anthropology, and psychology. Their study has made it possible to penetrate the exterior façade and disclose some signs of stress, anxiety, and even insanity (mainly of manic depression), but not beyond the accepted norms of the general society. Nevertheless, psychologists have come to the interesting conclusion that they are surprisingly nonviolent, have no competitive instincts, and hardly any feelings of envy.[52] Researchers have also discovered among the young adolescents "a private property instinct" that has prompted them to deviate from accepted norms. This led to a prophesy in the 1950s that within a few years a youth revolt might occur; yet still in the 1980s no such revolution has taken place. Most communes have succeeded in absorbing the deviances and carry on with their way of life. J.W. Eaton, the sociologist who has studied the phenomenon, defined it as *controlled acculturation*—a process in which a certain culture is infiltrated by another culture's customs and absorbs the new ways within its basic set of values. Controlled acculturation is acceptable only when the infiltrated society is well organized and has authoritarian origins as well as an internal viability that can withstand pressure and change.[53]

In the Hutterites' controlled acculturation, there is no retreat from basic values. Even when they adopted American methods they never identified with the American way of life and its culture. They have throughout adhered to their autonomous ways. Eaton assumes that there was no way to completely avoid assimilation, but so far there is no evidence to support his assumption. On the contrary, their impressive survivability has increased their numbers in recent years. A cardinal contributing factor is their biological vitality, and their natural increase is one of the highest in the world (41 per 1000), almost twice as high as that of their rural neighbors (22 per 1000). Hence the Hutterite family fulfills a valuable function.[54]

One of the most outstanding features that singles out the Hutterite communes in the United States today and distinguishes it from the Moravian Bruderhof is the position of the family within the community. The family unit had always been an organic part of the Hutterite commune; there were never any attempts to introduce monasticism or extended-family communities. While the family in the Hutterites' European past fulfilled only a limited and secondary function, it has gained in importance in the United States. This was one of the results of abolishing the communal children's house and placing the children with their parents overnight. It reinforced the family's responsibility as a socializing agent for the younger generation's education. Family affinity expanded and deepened. The Hutterites' tendency to spend their free time together found expression at the community level as well as within the family, which is usually large and had a wide age range. The average family has ten to twelve children, a function of their positive attitude toward birth and their economic security. Almost all adults are married; there are hardly any singles and no divorce at all. Most marriages take place within the sect, and outside partners are rare. As a result there are only sixteen surnames among the Hutterites—the same as they had on arrival in the United States.[55] Their high natural increase, large families, and the younger generation's stability are the source of the Hutterite growth.

Since their arrival in the United States the Hutterites have avoided missionary activities. They have been very reluctant to absorb new members and only rarely agreed to do so, after being convinced of the candidate's serious intentions. The period of candidacy lasts one year at least and only about one hundred new members have been accepted during their stay in the United States. Twice in the past fifty years the Hutterites agreed to attempt relations with other Christian groups.

In 1936, Julius Kubbasek, a Hungarian communist who had turned to religion after emigrating to Canada, got in touch with the Hutterites. While studying the Scriptures he had formulated a doctrine similar to the Hutterites' and gathered some followers. He asked that they be accepted in one of the settlements as an independent community, and the Hutterites, who were deeply impressed by him, agreed to do so. After a year's trial period they realized that the attempt to absorb Kubbasek and his group within an existing Hutterite settlement had failed. Kubbasek, his followers, and several Hutterites moved to Ontario, Canada, where they established an independent commune near Toronto. At first relations with the Hutterites in the West were maintained, but in time the Huttterites began to object to the Ontario communes' way of life and to Kubbasek's authoritarian leadership. In the 1950s relations ceased and the Kubbasek commune continued to exist independently.

More stable and intensive ties developed between the Hutterites and the Bruderhof in Germany. The founder of this movement was Dr. Eberhard Arnold, a theologist and activist in the German Christian Student's Union. He had established a commune called *Bruderhof* in the tradition of the Anabaptists. When in 1928 he heard about the Hutterites in the United States, he searched for a way to get in touch with them and join their community. In 1930 he traveled with his wife Emmy on a mission of the colony to Canada. The Hutterite leaders were profoundly impressed by Arnold's personality and his religious convictions. In a rare gesture they instated him as "servant of the Word," the Hutterite leader of his German community. Arnold died in 1935, and the Bruderhof had to leave Germany because of Nazi persecution. After an attempt (1939-1940) to settle in England in the middle of World War II, they moved on to Paraguay, the only country willing to grant them refuge.

Only after the war could relationships with the Hutterites be resumed. In 1950 Hutterite emissaries visited the Bruderhof in Paraguay. There, in the depth of the rain forest, on the Ibate commune, they held a conference to examine the correlation between religious values, only to discover many discrepancies in their way of life and doctrine. As a result the gap between the two groups' religious leaderships widened. Even so there was a group among the Hutterites at Forrest River, North Dakota, who searched for a way to forge relationships with their Paraguayan brothers. They invited them to join their settlement, much to the annoyance of the Hutterite leadership. This led to a split within Forrest River, and all those who were loyal to the Hutterite leadership left the commune. Meanwhile, the Bruderhof in Paraguay was dissolved and all the members moved to the United States, where they settled in Rifton in New York State in 1954. This, in turn, prompted the members of Forrest River to leave their remote North Dakota settlement and move closer to the Bruderhof in the East. They acquired land in Farmington, Pennsylvania, and established an additional Bruderhof called Oak Lake.

The Forrest River affair clouded relations between the Hutterites and the Bruderhof but did not sever them. Twenty years later the Brothers made a move to pacify the Hutterites. A conciliatory mission went to Canada and apologized for the Forrest River affair. This apology and the renewed contact succeeded in forging a stable relationship between the Hutterites and the Bruderhof. In 1974 they called themselves The Hutterian Society of Brothers. This step did not mean a complete and extensive union and both movements maintain their separate framework and uniqueness. They are also geographically remote from each other. The renewed contact between the Hutterites and the Bruderhof has caused some spiritual upheaval in both movements. It must be assumed that its effect will be felt in years to come.

The development of the Bruderhof with its three prosperous settlements at Rifton in New York, Deer Springs in Connecticut, and New Meadow Run in Pennsylvania is of the utmost interest. Their history is one of the most important chapters in the communal experience of our times, but this is beyond the historical scope of the present book.

A Personal Impression

I would like to end this chapter on a personal note. During my short visits to modern day communes in the United States, I got to know the Bruderhof of the Society of Brothers. My visit there was an exciting and most interesting experience. I formed personal relationships with several of the brothers, was interested in their way of life, and came to admire the unique combination of their zealous adherence to traditional religious values with a spiritual-cultural openness to the modern world. In my conversations with the brothers I sensed their great admiration for the Hutterites but also their differences.

Compared with the Hutterites, the brothers are more conversed in the modern world. This was confirmed when I had the opportunity to visit Bon Homme, one of the old Hutterite settlements in the United States. It was on a summer day in 1978. My stay was short, just a glimpse to gain some impressions. The visit was an emotional experience. Perhaps most significant was the lack of any surprises, everything was just as I had expected it to be. My impressions served to reinforce the picture I had formed of the Hutterites while reading the literature about them.

One distinctive episode is indelibly imprinted on my mind. It was during the evening hours in the elder's room where a group of Hutterites had gathered for a lively conversation about their way of life. I questioned them in detail about daily affairs and their answers were frank and expansive, usually ending with the sentence: "According to what is written in the Book." Suddenly the elder asked me: "Would you like to see it?" Before I could grasp his meaning, he went to the nearby room and I could hear the opening of a drawer. Soon he returned, holding a tome in his hand; on seeing that book I became speechless: Only in museums, locked behind glass vitrines, had I ever seen a volume such as this. It was in fact the *Great Chronicle*, which had been written in the sixteenth century and of which only four volumes still exist. Here, then, was one of them, kept in a drawer of a remote South Dakota community. "This is where everything is written," the elder explained. "This is where we find all the instructions for our daily life." But then he added with a twinkle in his eyes: "But we are not so foolish as to continue ploughing with a pair of oxen when modern equipment is available."

Just then the approaching sound of an engine infiltrated the room. The sight of the sixteenth-century *Great Chronicle* held in the elder's hands and the sound of the tractor on its way back from the fields combined perhaps more than anything else to make me realize the unique existence of the Hutterites which has no equal in any of the other communes in our time.

Notes

1. John A. Hostetler, *Hutterite Society* (Baltimore: The Johns Hopkins University Press, 1977), pp. 15-16; John Horsch, *The Hutterian Brethren, 1528-1931* (Cayley, Alberta, Canada: Macmillam, 1977), pp. 6-8.
2. Horsch, pp. 8-17; Hostetler, pp. 13-24; Leonard Gross, *The Golden Years of the Hutterites* (Scottdale, Pa.: Herald Press, 1980), pp. 27-29.
3. Horsch, pp. 13-15.
4. Hostetler, pp. 39-41; John W. Bennett, "Frames of Reference for the Study of Hutterian Society," in *Communes: Historical and Contemporary*, ed. Ruth Shonle Cavan and Man Singh Das (New Delhi: Vikas Publishing House, 1979), pp. 27-28.
5. Peter Rideman, *Account of Our Religion Doctrine and Faith of the Brothers Whom Men Call Hutterians* (London: Hodder & Stoughton, 1950).
6. "Those who have fellowship, have all things in common together." "He who becomes free from created things, can then grasp what is true and divine." Ibid., pp. 43, 90.
7. For the definition of *Gellasenheit* see the glossary in the appendix to Leonard Gross, *The Golden Years of the Hutterites* (note 1 above).
8. Hostetler, pp. 29-31.

9. Hostetler, p. 57; Horsch, pp. 27-29, 39-47; Gross, pp. 165-67.
10. Hostetler, p. 54. A sort of kindergarten was established 270 years before modern kindergartens came into being by Friedrich Froebel in Germany.
11. Ibid., pp. 321-28; Shalom Wurm, *Communal Societies and Their Way of Life* (Tel Aviv: Ayanoth, 1968), pp. 8-9 (Hebrew). A complete version of the Codex from 1578 can be found in John A. Hostetler, Leonard Gross, and Elizabeth Bender, eds., *Selected Hutterian Documents in Translation, 1524-1654* (Philadelphia: Communal Studies Center, Temple University Press, 1975), pp. 13-33.
12. Horsch, pp. 33-37; Hostetler, pp. 53-54; Gross, pp. 32-34.
13. Gross, pp. 200-04; "An Epistle Concerning Communal Life: A Hutterite Manifesto of 1650 and Its Modern Paraphrase," *Mennonite Quarterly Review* (October 1960):24.
14. Lee Emerson Deets, *The Hutterites: A Study in Social Cohesion* (Philadelphia: Porcupine, 1975), pp. 5-7.
15. Horsch, pp. 21-24; Gross, pp. 31-32.
16. Gross, pp. 36-41.
17. Hostetler, pp. 50, 56, 62.
18. Horsch, pp. 29-32, 38; Hostetler, pp. 37-38, 62.
19. Gross, p. 33; Hostetler, pp. 44-45.
20. Horsch, p. 71; Hostetler, pp. 42-44.
21. Hostetler, pp. 79-80; Wurm, pp. 12-13.
22. Gross, p. 35-210; Hostetler, p. 43.
23. Horsch, pp. 51-53; Hostetler, pp. 61-63.
24. Horsch, pp. 53-63; Hostetler, pp. 63-67, 80.
25. Horsch, pp. 63-68.
26. Ibid., p. 73.
27. For a Hutterian epistle from 1650 that extols the communal tradition denounces servitude to Mammon and points out the efforts taken during that period in the field of education see "An Epistle," *Mennonite Quarterly Review* (October 1960):19-28.
28. Hostetler, p. 68; Horsch, pp. 75-77.
29. Hostetler, pp. 68-74; Horsch, pp. 79-84; Victor Peters, *All Things Common: The Hutterian Way of Life* (Minneapolis: University of Minnesota, 1965), p. 26.
30. Peters, pp. 31-3.
31. Ibid., pp. 32-33; Hostetler, pp. 93-104.
32. Peters, pp. 33-34; Wurm, pp. 16-17.
33. Hostetler, pp. 104-7; Peters, pp. 35-37.
34. Hostetler, pp. 107-8.
35. Arnold M. Hoffer, ed., *History of the Hutterite Mennonites* (Freeman, South Dakota: Pine Hill Press, 1974), pp. 48-58.
36. Peters, p. 42.
37. Hostetler, pp. 115-20.
38. Gross, pp. 21-28; Hostetler, pp. 185-94; John W. Bennett, *Hutterian Brethren: The Agricultural Economy and Social Organization of a Communal People* (San Francisco: Stanford University Press, 1967), pp. 55-56, 181-83.
39. Paul K. Conkin, *Two Paths to Utopia: The Hutterites and the Llano Colony* (Lincoln: University of Nebraska Press, 1964), pp. 49-52; Hostetler, pp. 122-23. For an explanation of the ties with Harmony see Karl J.R. Arndt, *George Rapp's Successors and Material Heirs, 1847-1916* (New York: Associated University Press, 1971), pp. 129-39.

40. Conkin, pp. 52-54, 78; Hostetler, pp. 123-26. For relations among Hutterian settlements in Canada see Bennett, *Hutterian Brethren*, pp. 73-74.
41. Conkin, p. 544; Hostetler, pp. 124-26; Gross, p. 21; Bennett, *Hutterian Brethren*, pp. 266-72; Deets, pp. 9-11.
42. Hostetler, pp. 129-30.
43. Peters, p. 49.
44. Conkin, pp. 61-64.
45. Ibid., pp. 65-66; Hostetler, p. 132.
46. Conkin, pp. 66-67.
47. Ibid., pp. 67-70; Hostetler, pp. 134-35; Bennett, *Hutterian Brethren*, pp. 32-33.
48. This information was given to the author by the researcher L. Anderson; Conkin, p. 90; Deets, pp. 13-15.
49. Conkin, pp. 79-81; Hostetler, pp. 296-302; Peters, pp. 109-11; Bennett, *Hutterian Brethren*, pp. 79-88, 165-76.
50. On the introduction of modern technology see Conkin, pp. 85-87. John A. Baden and Mary Anna Hovey-Baden, "Education Employability and Role Taking among North American Hutterites, *Conference on Child Socialization*, John A. Hostetler, coordinator (Philadelphia: Temple University College of Liberal Arts, 1969), pp. 235-51; Russel E. Lewis, "Controlled Acculturation Revisited: An Examination of Differential Acculturation and Assimilation between the Hutterian Brethren and the Old Order Amish," *Communes: Historical and Contemporary*, ed. Ruth Shonle Cavan and Man Singh Das (New Delhi: Vikas Publishing House, 1979), p. 88.
51. Conkin, p. 92; Bennett, *Hutterian Brethren*, pp. 88-105, 253-54.
52. Bert Kaplan and Thomas F.A. Plant, *Personality in a Communal Society: An Analysis of the Mental Health of the Hutterites* (Lawrence: University of Kansas Publications, 1956), pp. 30-64, 78-101; Bennett, "Frames of Reference," pp. 34-35; Hostetler, pp. 224-23, 262-68; Conkin, p. 93; Bennett, *Hutterian Brethren*, pp. 249-50, 261-64. Their research, based on representative models of scores of Hutterite men and women, showed a normal distribution of feelings and attitudes toward aggression, fear, anxiety, care for health, enjoyment of sex, self-confidence, autonomy, and the tolerance of deviances. The one fact which was significantly unusual was the low value attributed to competitiveness and the relatively low materialistic instincts (these were mainly evident in the younger generation). Kaplan and Plant, pp. 30-64, 78-101.
53. Joseph W. Eaton, "The Hutterite Accommodation to Social Change," *Communes: Creating and Managing the Collective Life*, ed. Rosabeth Moss Kanter (New York: Harper & Row, 1973), pp. 509-22.
54. On the ability to Survive see Hostetler, pp. 285-302. Amendment to the theory of Eaton see Lewish, pp. 81-90; Bennett, *Hutterian Brethren*, pp. 135-40, 259-65, 277-78. On the problems of existence of the Hutterian settlements today see Deets, pp. 52-59.
55. On the interest of genetics' scholars in the phenomenon of the survival see Hostetler, pp. 266, 290-94; Bennett, *Hutterian Brethren*, pp. 114-27, 129-30.

Part II
A COLLECTIVE PROFILE IN A COMPARATIVE APPROACH

18

Ideological Principles

The communes described in this book existed as separate autonomous and exclusive settlements. They differed from the general society in their way of life, institutions, social setup, and their systems of production and consumption. Their separate existence and idiosyncrasy were a matter of choice. It was consciously made by the founders of each commune and its members, who opted to realize their beliefs and doctrine via the communal way of life. To this end communes were social units established through self-realization. Hence, any discussion of their social way of life has to be preceded by an examination of their founders' spiritual world. As any other attempt at generalization, this may pose a problem because the ideological and religious motivations that brought about the establishment of 270 communes encompass an enormous variety. Even so, a comparative study of those basic principles comprising their beliefs and doctrines reveals common denominators that may help us to draw a characteristic profile of the convictions and creeds that brought about the establishment of communes and ensured their existence.

A basic common element was their voluntarism. The founders of communes and their members undertook to establish and live in them from a free, voluntary, and conscious choice. There was no compulsion by any external factor such as political regime, church, or party. All those who joined a commune did so voluntarily, inspired by their religious or ideological convictions. While the founding generation had made an ideological choice, the next generations were naturally affected by family relations, affinity to their home, tradition, and also plain inertia. A historical study of communes that existed for several generations shows that young in each generation were free to choose their way of life on reaching adulthood. Thus the principle of voluntariness was maintained. Still, there were significant differences in the ideological level of members, even in those communes characterized by their strong convictions. There was usually a core of members whose attitude toward their way of life was ideologically motivated and who examined and organized their daily activities accordingly; these were surrounded by a periphery of members who, after having taken the first voluntary step, carried on with their daily routine.

All those who have studied the history of the communes agree that the presence of an ideologically motivated core of members who adhered to their doctrine or religion, as well as the predominence of their central principles, was an essential element that ensured the commune's existence and its survival.[1]

Charles Nordhoff, the American journalist who toured the communes in 1874, gave wide expression to this theory in his book, *The Communistic Societies of the United States.* Reviewing the history and the way of life of the large communes, he concluded that the common doctrine was the foundation on which communal life was established. Contrary to many observers of his time who thought that only religious belief could fit this need, Nordhoff claimed: "It seems to me that both these theories are wrong; but that it is true that for a commune to exist harmoniously, it must be composed of persons who are of one mind upon some questions which to them shall appear so important as to take the place of a religion, if it is not essentially religion, though it need not be fanatically held."[2] He was pointing to the example of Icaria that, even though not a religious commune, was inspired by a socialist doctrine to which its members adhered as to a religion.

From a historian's vantage point it is evident that those religious doctrines that were anchored in Protestant theology had priority in the motivation to establish the early communes. For 150 years through the early nineteenth century, the various Protestant denominations were the source that led to establishing communes in the New World. They germinated within the radical doctrines in Europe and absorbed some of their characteristics such as the separation from the church against whose "corrupt" political establishment they rose. Inspired by their belief they aspired to realize their own way of life and to create "a holy commonwealth."[3] This may be regarded as the prime motive to the formation of secluded "communities of believers" whose social background was among the lower classes. Such communities sprang up in the seventeenth and eighteenth century in an area rife with religious ferment in central Europe along the Rhine, in the Netherlands, and in England.[4]

The Religious Communes

Affinity with the Communitarian Tradition in Christianity

The sects owed their radical character to their rejection of church ritual, to their boycott of any establishment, and to their social background (farmers, artisans, and apprentices). They challenged both church and state and were involved in serious confrontations that led to their being persecuted. In the process of these persecutions close ties of cooperation were formed within the sects themselves. In time they deepened and received religious sanction through their affinity with the traditions of apostolic Christianity. Accordingly, they venerated the Apostles' way of life as described in the New Testament: "And all who believed were together and all had things in common and they sold their possessions and goods and distributed them to all as any had need" (Acts 2/4), and "Those who believed were of one heart and soul and no one said that any of the things which he possessed was his own but they had everything in common" (Acts 4/32).

These verses inspired many a radical and communitarian trend throughout the history of Christianity and were also adopted by the religious sects that established communes. Their communal way of life and the practice of mutual aid resulted in their secluded existence and were anchored in ancient Christianity, thus receiving religious sanctions. The sects' communitarian ties were reinforced when persecutions forced them to emigrate to the New World. The hardships they suffered during the crossing, the difficulties of adapting to a new land, and their decision to establish separate settlements for their sect were steps toward a profound process of communitarianism. It was the path chosen by the pietists and the separatists on their arrival from Europe, and was also the Shakers' way until they became a movement of American communes.[5]

Seclusion

Gathering in separate religious sects to realize their unique doctrines before establishing a commune did not characterize immigrant communes only; a similar process also was evident in indigenous American communes. Oneida was established as a communal settlement after a long period of crystallizing their perfectionist theories under the leadership of John Humphrey Noyes. The same was the case with other religious communes in the second half of the nineteenth century. It may, therefore, be assumed that religious communes were not created to materialize an a priori utopian dream but were rather the result of a process in which the communal theory was formulated gradually. The theory was not uniform. The different religious doctrines of the sects resulted in a variety of communes and in a diversity of their spiritual concepts.

The similarity in the process and the common apostolic Christian sources that nourished them point to several characteristics that enable us to complete the profile of the religious communal world. Elmer T. Clark devotes a chapter to the subject in his comprehensive book, *The Small Sects in America,* pointing out basic doctrines as the background for their spiritual world. According to Clark, the sects' isolation, accompanied by the church establishment's ostracism, was first and foremost the result of their own need for seclusion and isolation. It was one of the tenets of their religions among which the millenary doctrine was cardinal.

Millenary Expectations

Inspired by their millenary doctrine the sects felt compelled to practice their unique way of life away from society and thus prepare themselves for the kingdom of heaven. They had to be isolated from the existing world, which they believed was doomed.[6] A review of the religious communes in America does show that most adopted millenary doctrines. Most members believed that the heavenly kingdom was imminent and expected great cosmic change. They regarded their secluded settlements as chosen communities that would find salvation. They differed in their intensity of expectations and the exact date of the Messiah's advent. Several communes whose doctrine was "premillenary" spent their lives in constant expectation for the kingdom of heaven to materialize. Others whose doctrine was "intermillenary" regarded their settlements as existing within the kingdom of heaven. The Shakers, for instance, believed that this was the case and acted accordingly on their communes. The perfectionist doctrine of Oneida specified that the kingdom of heaven was being realized in their community. Millenary expectations were a central element in the doctrine of the pietist and the separatist sects that were founded in the eighteenth and the beginning of the nineteenth century. It was also cardinal for the adventists, who established communes in the second half of the nineteenth century. (Amana was an exception because it lacked the millenary element.)[7]

Perfectability

Clark pointed out another aspect of the religious communal sects, namely, their belief in man's ability to achieve moral perfection. This was contrary to the Christian concept of man's inferiority as a result of the Fall and Original Sin. Naturally, perfectability was strongly disclaimed by the church establishment. The sects' belief in perfectability was integrated with their millenary expectations—they were about to realize a perfect way of life that would ensure their salvation and an eternal life in the kingdom of heaven. All religious communes aspired to create ideal conditions so that their members might achieve the desired state of perfectability. Oneida was an example of this. Perfectability was the foundation of their doctrine and they were convinced that communal life would morally cleanse them. The commune created a society in which man's baser instincts, the materialistic and the selfish ones, were replaced by altruistic values. Accordingly, the religious commune was not only a pragmatic means to ensure the existence of isolated religious sects, a secluded haven for "the chosen," to shield them from a world of sin while anticipating the kingdom of heaven on earth, it was also a social environment that meant to advance the process of cleansing and purification of the world of sin. This was at the core of the theory of the Hutterites who, unlike other sects, accepted the theory of the Fall. They believed that man was conceived in sin and achieved the salvation of rebirth only through a spiritual baptism on entering the commune as a full member. Only communal life could release man from the condition in which he found himself after the Fall.[8]

The belief in the commune's purifying power and in the moral elevation inherent in its way of life encouraged elements of utopism to take over in those communes that regarded their settlements as model communities. They believed that their society had a beneficial influence on the outside world and would inspire secular social reformers as well.

Model Communities

The idea that communes were model communities surfaced at several stages in Shaker history, especially during Frederick Evans's leadership in the late nineteenth century, and in Oneida during the 1870s. In those cases the commune appeared ex post facto as a model society. It became such without premeditation. There were several examples of clear-cut utopian tendencies: Brook Farm was established by religious people who intended to realize their doctrine and to influence the external society through their way of life and the educational institution they founded. The Christian Commonwealth, established by Christian socialist circles, was a religious commune intended to be a model way of life, thus influencing the external society and at the same time be actively involved in the struggle against private property and competition.[9] The few communes who believed in this integrated their sectional religious creeds with socialist theories concerning the problems of society, thus forming a bridge between the religious communes and the socialist ones.

The Socialist Communes

Experiments in Socialist Utopia

Beginning in 1820 the scope of communes in the United States expanded to embrace a growing number of secular, socialist ones. Just as in the religious communes, among them too were different but finite ideological motivations. Not all believers in socialism participated in the communal experiment in the United States. It was a venture undertaken only by those who regarded communitarian settlements as a means for solving social problems or for serving as a model society; in other words, it was undertaken by those with socialist-utopian ideologies. Accordingly, their communes acquired characteristics of utopian communities as defined by R.W. Hine: "A group of people who are attempting to establish a new social pattern based upon a vision of the ideal society and who have withdrawn themselves from the community at large to embody that vision in experimental form."[10]

The spiritual world that fostered socialist communes and the ways that led to their inception differed from that of the religious communes. As mentioned above, most religious communes had started out as separate communities of believers. Their communitarian ways had been formed gradually until they led to communes. Most socialist communes on the other hand established theirs without a preceding period of preparation. Only Icaria was somewhat of an exception, because its members arrived in the United States as a group who shared their beliefs. However, they had had no opportunity to practice communal life prior to the establishment of their commune. An additional and significant difference was the role played by the communitarian ideologies. Unlike the religious communes, in the case of the socialist communes their utopian communal theory came first and was the guiding force in their life. Even before their colony was established, they drew detailed blueprints of the way they envisioned the model communitarian society of the future. Most of them were experiments of universal socialist theories. Their communitarian ideology and the vision of a future society attracted people to the settlements.

A detailed examination of the characteristics within the socialist communes reveals in addition to the above-mentioned differences a wide range of significant similarities in both their ways of achieving their aims and in the tenets of their belief. First and foremost among these similarities is the voluntary element of their communal life. The socialist communes, just like the religious ones, were motivated by their trenchant criticism of the existing regime and its institutions.

Criticizing the Existing Order

As was the case of the religious communes, the socialist ones also expected radical changes within the existing systems and chose to isolate themselves from society in order to establish their units of a future society in secluded spots. They, too, were founded by people who adhered to their doctrine that man could better himself as a human being and at the same time improve society as a whole and create a perfect system.

The perfectability of the religious communes was adopted by all socialist utopians who regarded the communal way of life, the abolishment of private property, the fostering of a harmonious work relationship, and communitarian consumption as the highest moral norms. They believed that their high morality in itself would be enough to influence society, that their social units would through their very existence become the focus of change. The commune as a model society was the cornerstone of the utopian theory.

The similarity between the religious and the socialist communes was evident not only in their way of life but also in some tenets of their ideologies. From the very beginning the socialist communes felt an affinity with the religious ones. They were interested in all that went on in religious communes, aspired to an interrelationship, paid them visits, and showed them a high regard. In time they established a bridge of understanding and mutual aid in spite of the vast differences in their spiritual worlds.

Even though the socialist communes were established by atheists, they never tried to enforce their atheistic convictions on others and a religious tolerance prevailed. Socialist commune members could practice their religion freely just as they had done before joining. Even a militant atheist such as Robert Owen never proposed that atheism be an obligatory norm at New Harmony.

Affinity between Religious and Socialist Communes

Religious and socialist communes existed side by side in collaboration. The socialist communes regarded the religious ones as their "older sisters," acknowledged their seniority, and admired their survivability. The religious communes were happy to assist them in any way, be it advice or material aid. In practice, there were wide areas of mutual fertilization.

In his comprehensive study *The History of Socialism in the United States,* Noyes discusses the correlation between the appearance of religious and socialist communes and points out the connection between the religious revivals and the social unrest that were both followed by the establishment of communes. Noyes also formulated a theory according to which the future success of the communal experiment in the United States depended on the integration of religious beliefs and socialist doctrines.[11]

Noyes himself was a case in point, for he set out as the founder and leader of a religious commune and later turned to socialist journalism when he published the *American Socialist.* Another example of transition from religious communality to socialist activity were the Unitarian transcendentalists of Brook Farm who became active in the Fourierist movement. And vice versa, there were members of socialist communes who joined religious ones: Frederick Evans, for example, arrived from England with the intention to join one of the Owenist experiments, but in the process of his search he found himself in a Shaker settlement, where he eventually became the spiritual leader. During the second half of the nineteenth century, when many despaired of the survival of the socialist communes, quite a few socialists applied for membership in religious communes whose stability and communitarian way of life had impressed them. The best example for the integration of religious communitarianism and socialist ideology may be found in the Christian Commonwealth, but since it existed for only a short tiime it never succeeded in opening a way for others to follow.[12]

In conclusion, the spiritual world of commune members was inspired by many and variegated sources. Religious beliefs, philosophical concepts, and socialist-utopian ideologies were all involved, simultaneously and in parallel lines, in molding the communal way of life. As we have seen, a review of the communes shows their many doctrines, each commune with its unique world. Even so, an analytical examination, one that would uncover the differences, could arrive at the common denominator. In addition to the above-mentioned total of common beliefs there is another element shared by all communes, namely the existence of a belief (or an ideology) as an activating and establishing principle on which the entire communal system is based. This, I believe, is the first and last of communal life and all the rest ensues from it.

Notes

1. Rosabeth Moss Kanter, *Commitment and Community: Communes and Utopias in Sociological Perspective* (Cambridge: Mass.: Harvard University Press, 1972), pp. 114-15, 122-23; Frederick A. Bushee, ''Communistic Societies in the United States,'' *Political Science Quarterly* 20, no. 4 (1905): 653; Ralph Albertson, *A Survey of Mutualistic Communities in America* (New York: AMS Press, 1973; 1st ed. 1936), pp. 422-23; John V. Chamberlain, ''The Spiritual Impetus to Community,'' in *Utopias: The American Experience,* ed., Gairdner R. Moment and Otto F. Kraushaar (Metuchen, N.J.: Scarecrow Press, 1980), pp. 126-39.
2. Charles Nordhoff, *The Communistic Societies of the United States* (New York: Shocken, 1965), p. 387.
3. On the nature of the Protestant sect and its reference to the communal, separate way of life see Ernst Troeltsch, *The Social Teachings of the Christian Churches,* vol 1, trans. Olive Wyon (New York: Harper & Brothers, 1960), pp. 331-43. On the Anabaptist sects, seclusion and communal way of life, see Max Webber, *The Protestant Ethic and the Spirit of Capitalism* (Tel Aviv: Am Oved, 1984), pp. 70-74 (Hebrew).
4. Arthur Bestor, *Backwoods Utopias: The Sectarian Origins and the Owenite Phase of Communitarian Socialism in America, 1663-1829,* 2d ed. (Philadelphia: University of Pennsylvania Press, 1978), pp. 20, 23; Albertson, p. 422.
5. Alice Felt Tyler, *Freedom's Ferment* (New York: Harper & Row, 1962), pp. 108-9; William Alfred Hinds, *American Communities and Cooperative Colonies* (1878. Reprinted and enl. Philadelphia: Porcupine, 1975), p. 152; Bertha M.H. Shambaugh, *Amana That Was and Amana That Is* (Iowa City: Iowa State Historical Society, 1932), pp. 47, 53; Donald Egbert and Stow Persons, eds., *Socialism and American Life,* 2 vols. (Princeton: Princeton University Press, 1952), pp. 143-45; Maren Lockwood Carden, *Oneida: Utopian Community to Modern Corporation* (Baltimore: Johns Hopkins University Press, 1969), p. 22; Robert Allerton Parker, *A Yankee Saint: John Humphrey Noyes and the Oneida Community* (New York: Putnam, 1935), p. 89; Robert D. Thomas, *The Man Who Would*

Be Perfect: J.H. Noyes and the Utopian Impulse (Philadelphia: University of Pennsylvania Press, 1977), pp. 96-97; Karl J.R. Arndt, *George Rapp's Harmony Society, 1785-1847*, rev. ed. (New York: Associated University Presses, 1972), pp. 35-40, 56, 70-75; Bestor, *Backwoods*, pp. 4-7, 20-22; Nordhoff, pp. 69-70; Charles J. Erasmus, *In Search of the Common Good: Utopian Experiments Past and Future* (New York: Free Press, 1977), pp. 135-36; E.O. Randall, *History of the Zoar Society: A Sociological Study in Communism* (1904. Reprint. New York: AMS Press, 1971), pp. 6-7, 19.

6. Elmer T. Clark, *The Small Sects in America* (New York: Abingdon-Cokesbury, 1949), pp. 163-64; "American Communities," *American Socialist* (August 30, 1877):273-74.
7. Delburn Carpenter, *The Radical Pietists: Celibate Communal Societies Established in the United States before 1820* (New York: AMS Press, 1975), pp. 226-27; W.R. Perkins and B.L. Wick, *History of the Amana Society*, Historical Monograph no. 1 (Iowa City: State University of Iowa Publications, 1891), pp. 64-67; Hinds, p. 152; Carden, pp. 11-17; Egbert and Persons, pp. 133, 192.
8. John A. Hostetler, *Hutterite Society* (Baltimore: Johns Hopkins University Press, 1977), pp. 140-52; Lee Emerson Deets, *The Hutterites: A Study in Social Cohesion* (Philadelphia: Porcupine, 1975), pp. 19-28; "An Epistle Concerning Communal Life: Hutterite Manifesto of 1650 and Its Modern Paraphase," *Mennonite Quarterly Review* (October 1960):27-28; Carden, pp. 11-17; Parker, pp. 24, 160.
9. Marguerite Fellows Melcher, *The Adventure* (New York: The Shaker Museum, 1975), p. 9; Katherine Burton, *Paradise Planters: The Story of Brook Farm* (1939. Reprint. New York: AMS Press, 1973), pp. 14-16; Nathaniel Hawthorne, *Blithedale Romance* (New York: W.W. Norton, 1953), pp. 17-18; Arndt, *Harmony Society*, pp. 104-20, 236; Parker, p. 240; Egbert and Persons, p. 135; Hinds, pp. 252-56, 522.
10. Robert V. Hine, *California's Utopian Colonies* (New Haven: Yale University Press, 1966), p. 5; Bestor, *Backwoods*, pp. 12-16, 256.
11. Kenneth M. Roemer, *The Obsolete Necessity: America in Utopian Writings, 1888-1900* (Kent, OH.: Kent State University Press, 1976), p. 52; John Humphrey Noyes, *History of American Socialism* (1870). Reprinted as *Strange Cults and Utopias of Nineteenth-Century America* (New York: Dover, 1966), pp. 25-28, 46, 51, 187, 191-97; Charles Pierre Le Warne, *Utopias on Puget Sound, 1885-1915* (Seattle: University of Washington Press, 1975), pp. 4-14; Egbert and Persons, pp. 190-97, 155, 175, 201, 204; Bestor, *Backwoods*, pp. 10, 12, 47-49.
12. Fredrick William Evans, *Autobiography of a Shaker and Revaluation of the Apocalypse* (1888. Reprint. New York: AMS Press, 1973), pp. 1-25; John Fletcher Clews Harrison, *Quest for the New Moral World: Robert Owen and the Owenites in Britain and America* (New York: Scribner's, 1969), pp. 94-95, 100-102, 106-8, 134-38; Albertson, pp. 415-16; W.A. Hinds, "Pleasant Hill Shakers," *American Socialist* 1, no. 31 (October 26, 1876): 245; Bestor, *Backwoods*, pp. 38-39, 47-48, 50-56; Egbert and Persons, pp. 155, 160, 190-91, 195; John Humphrey Noyes, pp. 23-28, 103.

19

Social Activity and Management

An examination of the administrative procedures in communal settlements points to conspicuous elements of authoritarian leadership. In most commmunes there were no democratically-elected institutions as was the case in most American communities of a similar size. Alexander Kent, who visited the communes in 1901 as representative of the Federal Department of Labor, remarked in his conclusions that "democracy in a cooperative community has so far proven a source of weakness rather than of strength.[1]"

A historical review shows that most communes set out under a charismatic leader. This phenomenon was prevalent in all religious communes and was organically interrelated in the process of their establishment. They regarded their charismatic leader as a visionary, a revelation, a man of God—the instrument through which they would be inspired with the Holy Spirit. This leadership was created in a variety of ways in the religious sects, and was evident at least during the formative years of the communes and usually throughout their existence. The charismatic leader provided a sense of security and stability during the critical period of the commune's early days. The leader gathered the members, molded them into a social unit, instilled in them belief, raised their hopes and expectations, and guided them on to the path of their communal way of life. All of this created from the very beginning a paternalistic authoritanian leadership and administration that became the norm.

Members of religious communes drew spiritual strength from their charismatic leader and therefore became dependent on him. The more stability and power these relations provided in the first period of the commune's existence, the bigger the danger that would threaten them in the future, especially after the leader's death. Still, most found a way to overcome the crisis and there were only a few cases of religious communes that disintegrated as a result of their charismatic leader's death. Two "classic" ones are Bethel and Aurora. Most others empowered their administrative institutions with their former leader's charisma. It would be passed on to a single heir or to a small circle who would carry on according to the established authoritarian norms that had crystallized in their former leader's time. One of the most outstanding examples of this is found in the Shaker history. They began to organize as communes a short time after the death of their spiritual leader, Ann Lee. The authoritarian management of Shaker communes was the legacy of the charismatic founder of the sect. The administrative system of each community was theocratic. This was also the case at the federative level of the Shaker movement as a whole. At the top of the hierarchy there were two—a man and a woman—who reigned over all aspects of life, the spiritual, religious, economic, and social ones.

In other stable communes evolved the same process of selection of management and authority, after the death of their spiritual leaders, from among the generation of the founding fathers. For instance, in Amana after the death of the *Werkzevge* a council of trustees took over the management on the federative level, while a committee of elders managed the settlements. This was the case in Harmony after Rapp's death, and also in Zoar after Baumeler's.[2]

The hierarchic structure in the religious commune was not always centralized. A number of daily social and economic demands arose with which the spiritual leadership could not or would not cope. This was the background for a separation of authorities. Most of communes with separate authorities granted preference and superior power to the spiritual one. The Shakers developed a complicated hierarchic structure in which the economic functions were relegated to deacons who were supervised by the elders. George Rapp in Harmony did likewise when he left the economic and financial management as well as all foreign relationships to his adopted son, Frederic Rapp. The same was the case in Oneida, where the authority was clearly divided when John Humphrey Noyes, its charismatic leader, relegated authority to a small circle of close friends from among the oldtimers. They became an elite whose authority was inspired by Noyes, but they were independent and managed most of the social and economical daily affairs.[3]

The Hutterites are unique among religious communes in that they have a hierarchic management but no charismatic leadership in their colonies. The communes of this religious movement have existed for about 450 years. Here is an example of a religious commune's survival on the strength of its religious principles without any direct sanction of the charismatic leader. In their early years they were led for a short time by the charismatic Jacob Hutter. In spite of his absence, there is still an authoritarian element in their institutions. It is an interesting and unique combination of authority and democratic elements, general elections but also a "casting of the die," which somehow signifies the "finger of God" and divine interference. Researchers of the Hutterites claim that they are conditioned to discipline after generations of being used to an authoritarian leadership in their settlements.[4]

In the socialist communes authoritarian leadership was unusual, mainly because spiritual authority of a charismatic leader did not go together with the values of utopian socialism, in which equality was both the aim and the means. Nevertheless, socialist doctrine could accept the leadership of a great personality who would devote himself to political or economic initiatives in order to advance the establishment of a model society during its formative stages. Furthermore, in the first stages of socialist communes the conditions were such as to require the leadership of a personality whose ideological authority would unify the founding group in the transition from the old ways to establishing cells of the society of the future.

In those communes where the founder and utopian theoretician joined the new settlement, he soon stood out because of his special position within the group. Objectively and subjectively he believed himself to be the first among equals because, after all, the commune had been his vision. This was not a matter of superiority but rather of responsibility toward the members of the group who, being less aware of their ideals than he was, had to be guided. Such a leader regarded himself as the architect of the masterplan who had to supervise every detail of the evolving model society to ensure its success. In some cases perhaps, purely personal motives may have been at play; these would inevitably widen the gap between the utopian theoretician and his flock who had expected to be equal members of their enterprise. A case in point is the early days of Icaria, where a struggle between Etienne Cabet and his followers ended with the ousting of the elderly Cabet from the settlement he had inspired.[5]

A history of the socialist communes that existed for any length of time (e.g. the North American Phalanx, Icaria, Kaweah, Equality, Burley, Ruskin) shows that generally there was no regular charismatic leader nor authoritarian administration. Nevertheless, those communes did not succeed in establishing stable and democratic procedures even though their constitutions were based on democratic foundations. After a period of direct democracy with endless debates to the point of prohibiting efficient management because decisions could not be made, the pendulum would swing to a period in which a power-hungry dynamic personality took over. He would have unlimited authority in all social or economic areas, as George Pickett had in Llano.

In most cases the members of the commune welcomed this centralized authority because they were fed up with the discussions and strife and were anxious to have an efficient manager. At the root of this was the nonauthoritarian syndrome which originated in the form of ideology in socialist communes. Unexpected as it may be, most lacked an all-encompassing ideology that would sanction and enforce the community's decisions. Because there was no undisputed theoretical authority, the democratic general meeting would be drawn into endless trivial debates that only an efficient authoritarian leadership could prevent. This could only continue for a limited time or for as long as the leader could prove his efficiency and his powers of persuasion. The commune's members had the option to leave even though some of them had burned their bridges. If their leader failed to persuade them to accept his authority and to stay on, there was no way of stopping them.[6]

In the history of the religious and socialist communes reviewed here there were not many examples of a tyrannical leader or group who misused and exploited the commune for personal gratification or other external purposes. In the few exceptions uncovered, much heresay and gossip are interwoven with actual facts.[7] There are instances where leaders were given extra status and honor and sometimes significant material advantages in housing as well as the freedom of movement outside of the commune; yet this did not lead to tyranny and exploitation because the very atmosphere of the commune did not contribute to such a system. The leaders lived within the community. They were an integral part of it and personally involved with its members. In most cases they did the same jobs as others, whether in production or the services. Therefore it was impossible to erect a barrier of superiority behind which a tyrannical regime might flourish. Collective means of production made the amassing of private property an impossibility. But most of all, the element of equality within a voluntary society was a sufficient barrier against the totalitarian authority of a single person. The communes remained open, voluntary societies whose members had the option to leave and to return to the outside world. A tyrannical system would survive only when the communal structure had been eroded from within. This never happened in any of the communes under review.

In this connection we have to mention the functional division between the spiritual authoritarian leadership and the daily management which was usually decentralized and involved many members intensively. This was the case in most religious communes even though it was not done democratically. In Oneida the charismatic leadership, far from oppressing members' activities, supported the intensive involvement of all in the daily management such as only a few others achieved. Social life on Oneida was intensive and it could boast of twenty committees with about 250 members actively involved in economic, spiritual, cultural, and educational affairs. Every evening the whole community would meet to discuss various matters, most of them dealing with social activities, some with personal affairs in ("mutual criticism") but also with theoretical and ideological topics (Noyes's "home talks"). Journals, dailies, and weeklies served as platforms for members who felt the urge to express their thoughts and moods and were also a source of information on current affairs. Only a few communities could boast of such varied activities in which every member was directly and actively involved. In Oneida public opinion was of great importance and Noyes was aware of it, even if it finally was one of the reasons for him losing his leadership and leaving the commune.[8]

Oneida was not the only commune in which authoritative leadership in spiritual matters was combined with a decentralized management of daily affairs. This was also the case in various degrees on other religious communes. In Amana, for instance, general elections took place once a year, an annual report was published, and a representative of each family had voting rights. In Aurora, Beth-El, and Zoar all institutions and social councils were democratically elected. The Hutterites had an extensive system of "guided democracy" which after hundreds of years of experience became an efficient instrument for measuring public opinion. This decentralized system was not just a pragmatic means of managing the settlements but also helped the commune's leadership to be aware of public opinion and sensitive to its changing moods.[9]

Wherever the democratic representation of public opinion was missing, the communes developed alternative ways for members to have their say. One of these was the system of mutual criticism. In these general meetings all members were subjected to the opinions and criticism of their peers, and the feedback was immediate. The meetings were suppose to enhance harmonious relationships within the community and guard against the vicious gossip that is the bane of many small communities. These meetings were not abused and had a strong impact; they achieved their aims but they also served as a means for the spiritual leadership to strengthen its supervision and control. Oneida perfected the system and mutual criticism was one of the main functions of their nightly meetings. Other communes (Amana, Harmony) conducted such meetings less frequently. Most of the other communes found ways of their own for members to express their feelings. In the early celibate communes (Ephrata, Moravian, Shakers) the system of confessions was adopted, in others (Harmony) people would meet in small, intimate groups for a free discussion of their feelings.[10] Even some of the socialist communes adopted these soul-searchings methods as part of their democratic institutions when those deteriorated into sterile debating societies. An example for that was the socialist Llano where Pickett introduced the weekly psychological meetings.[11]

Communal life demanded a strong personal involvement of its members. This, in return, required an outlet for their feelings. The most authoritative leadership realized that blind obedience, repressed thoughts, and obtuseness would not contribute to the establishment of a community. They therefore had to find a way for their members to express themselves. In most communes a kind of symbiosis developed between the authoritarian spiritual leadership and elected institutions responsible for the economic and social spheres. Wherever this symbiosis or "participatory democracy" functioned, it promised harmony within the commune.

One of the main aspirations of all communes was to achieve an inner harmony, one that would ensue from their shared belief and doctrine. The religious communes were more successful than the socialist, because every member had to adopt the tenets of their religion as a condition for joining the commune, and this served as a strong framework. Further, authority was acceptable to their way of life and norms of behavior. The leadership oppressed any attempt of opposition from the outset, including political ones. In the religious communes there was no place for political pluralism.[12]

In spite of this, unity was often violated, as for example in Economy, where the Count De Leon influenced the dissatisfied and disgruntled members, thus causing the schism of the commune. This also happened when Towner's opposition to Noyes of Oneida undermined his leadership. In both cases, internal factional organization damaged the harmony of the commune and endangered it.

If this was rare in religious communes, it was a frequent occurrence in the secular ones. Their history is frought with strife and schism caused by factional organizations. This was one of the outstanding differences between religious and socialist communes, and it stemmed from the heterogeneous background of the latter and the lack of a deep commitment to their ideology, especially an authoritarian one. But most of all they lacked a period of preparation and social cohesiveness prior to setting out on their communitarian venture. Socialist ideologies were not authoritatively sanctioned even though their intellectual profundity and vision attracted ardent followers. After the first days, which were in a sense an ideological honeymoon, violent disagreements on daily affairs and on matters of principle would emerge. In most cases the controversies were not settled satisfactorily and led to the establishment of rival factions, causing internal tension and ripping apart the social fabric. New Harmony was a typical example of this process and it disintegrated after three years of continuous disagreements. Even relatively long-lasting social communes (Icaria, Llano) did not escape factionality and schism caused by ideological controversy.[13]

Hoping to achieve harmony by means of a homogeneous membership, which would promise a consensus of opinions and a close personal relationship, most communes limited the number of their members; only a few had more than 1,000 (New Harmony, Beth-El, and Llano in the California period) and only for a short while. The large, stable communes had 600-800 members (Mt. Lebanon, Shakers, Harmony) in their early years. Most communes numbered 200-300 people. The limiting of membership was motivated by the urge to live a harmonious life that would be possible only if members knew each other intimately. This also ensured their ideological collectivism and made supervision by the leadership feasible. An outstanding example was the Hutterite settlements which limited themselves to a population of 180 and when they exceeded this number they would split their settlement into two equal parts.

In the same spirit the Shakers organized in communal units ("families") of approximately eighty people and in settlements that did not exceed a population of 600, no doubt because this was the optional number of an agricultural production unit in the early nineteenth century. Still, the commune restricted its membership even after they changed to industrial economy. Amana, for instance, developed an industrial-based economy yet chose to establish seven separate settlements instead of a single one of 1,700 people. Throughout their history not one stable commune exceeded 600-700 souls.[14]

Most communes were closed and selective communities. Only a few had an open door policy. One of these was the Owenist New Harmony where approximately 800 members were unselectively absorbed in the first months of the settlement. The other, the Christian Commonwealth, accepted members unselectively out of principle.[15] Both these communes did not survive for any length of time, and it would be hard to draw any conclusions about the effect of their policy on the enrichment of their social and spiritual life. All other communes had a policy of selection to some extent. Religious communes regarded themselves as the ''chosen,'' and selective absorption was inherent in their outlook and way of life. A subjective factor of selection was the prerequisite to accept the tenets of faith. In socialist communes, too, ideological conditions of acceptance prevailed. All future members had to agree to socialist principles. In Kaweah, for example, all prospective members had to fill out a questionnaire in which they gave information about their socialist education, outlook, and religious convictions.[16]

The socialist communes advocated religious pluralism; most had members of various denominations. Freedom of religion and of opinion prevailed much more than on religious communes, erroneously creating the impression that in most socialist communes there was no selectivity; yet, a policy of selection was a matter of principle on most, and all of them insisted on a period of candidacy. Its character, length, and conditions differed in each commune. Members were examined as to their behavior, manners of adaptation to socialism and its ways, and acceptance of the commune's discipline, doctrines, and beliefs. The more unique and crystallized a commune's faith was, the longer the period of candidacy, and the harsher its conditions. Most large and stable communes set out with a wide periphery of followers and potential members. Of the religious communes established by sects, not all candidates joined the settlement right away. At first the sect existed side by side with the commune and provided its reserves. This was the case on the European sects Harmony, Zoar, and Amana and the American religious ones—Oneida and the various Adventist sects, and the Shakers in its early days.

The Shakers attempted to form a pattern by establishing three ''orders''—the novitiate order, the junior order, and the church order (also called ''senior order''). The first two served believers as periods of transition into the commune. In all communes the periphery gradually shrank while the settlement absorbed followers from among them. The focal point of the sect's activities were transferred to the effort of constructing the settlement and removing it from external matters. During that time the missionary activities receded, though eventually there would again be periods of missionary efforts.[17]

In most socialist communes there was no period of organization as a separate group prior to the establishment of the settlement. Yet they all had a periphery of followers. Socialist communes grew in periods of social and ideological agitation in which the periphery crystallized. Among these were the Owenists in the cities on the East Coast in the 1820s, the Fourierists in the 1840s, the Brotherhood of Cooperative Commonwealth, the members of the Social Democratic Party in the 1890s, and the Californian socialists in the 1920s.

Icaria was the only socialist commune that was similar to the religious ones in that its founders had organized in separate ideological groups before the establishment of their commune in the United States. The periphery had a parallel existence in France for a long time and was the only source of new immigrants who joined the commune. Icaria kept its ethnic and ideological homogeneity and was aided financially by its French periphery during the first two decades of its existence. These connections were so important that they were the focus of the struggle between the hostile sections. When the periphery diminished, the contact with the commune was discontinued, and this caused significant change within the communes in the United States. The emphasis was transformed toward the construction of settlements and their unique way of life. On the other hand, since newcomers were few stagnation ensued and the beginning of disintegration trends were evident. Examples may be found in all the communes that had a wide periphery at the outset. The Shakers, Harmony, Amana, and the Hutterites are an exception in that they could expand and develop through their own efforts and their large natural increase.[18]

After having lost contact with their periphery most communes in America did not consider the members of other communes with similar doctrines as a logical substitute. This was a common characteristic of all American communes—they were all autonomous, separatist, and isolationist. There was no successful attempt to establish unions or federations. The few attempts at establishing ties between communes never lasted long. On the other hand there was substantive contacts between them in the form of mutual visits, economic ties, mutual aid, and an exchange of information, as evident in the history of Harmony, Zoar, Amana, Oneida, and the Shakers. Inspired by Noyes, who put his newspaper the *American Socialist* at its disposal, Oneida more than others supported close ties between communes.

All this had no significant results; in all cases where communication began, concrete plans foundered because of the communes' wish for isolation or their ideological or religious exclusiveness. The lack of a general social motivation prevented them from overcoming their isolationism. The religious communes had no such motivation and the socialist ones that did were so short lived that there could be no thought of a nationwide federative framework. American communes that established a federation were the Shakers, the Hutterites, and Amana—all branches of the same creeds and the same sects. Here the federation served to disperse its members because there were too many for one large community. Thus the inspirationalists divided into seven Amana settlements and the Hutterites divided into two when they reached the membership of 180. The Shakers differ somewhat in that their communities were founded by members from different backgrounds, but as soon as they entered the church order they were united and all their settlements had the same form and an identical faith. As a rule, throughout their history American communes remained isolated, small, separatist, and autonomous communities, each struggling with its own problems. There was hardly any attempt to combine efforts and to strengthen their foundations and even less to widen their influence.[19]

The small communities with their close personal relationships carried elements of intimate, family-oriented communities (*Gemeinschaft*) but after a period of crystallization they became a sort of structural social organization (*Gesellschaft*).[20] Patterns of organized and ordered relationships were molded in the early days of even the smallest commune, and sets of rules were formulated in order to create an established way of life and an administration in accordance with their principles.

There was a significant difference in the degree to which the various communes adopted regulations and constitutions. All socialist ones had started out as social organizations with a well-defined constitution and set of rules; their common denominator was the immediate acceptance of a constitution. In some, their constitution preceded the establishment of the commune (Llano), in others it was formulated during the first days (Kaweah) or soon thereafter (Icaria).

The religious communes, on the other hand, started out with a covenant and all members agreed to adhere to its tenets.[21] The detailed set of rules that ordered their daily lives and norms of behavior were created during the first years and only at a later stage, after a period of testing, all the elements of their faith and norms of behavior would be molded into a constitution. Yet not all communes had such a code. Oneida, for instance, had none and the meeting of mutual criticism served as their guiding lines. In time most constitutions were adapted to the internal needs of the community and modified according to relationships with the state authorities. Usually external pressure, such as economic ties, political, and judicial relations with state institutions, was the cause and in many cases the result of ex-member's demands for compensation. Most constitutions were in accord with state laws, thus giving civil legitimacy to the commune.[22]

A study of the constitutions that included a codex reveals no separate clauses on law enforcement or punishment of misdemeanors. This had to be seen in the light of the voluntary and ideological aspect of the commune. Nevertheless, we must not deduce that there were no problems of deviance or of lawbreaking. As a rule the communes could not compromise on this integral part of reality which required a punitive set of rules. All of them, religious and socialist, used different social sanctions, the most extreme of which was ejection. Lawbreakers were tried by the public or by elected committees, and sometimes (Harmony, Beth-El) by the spiritual leader. In the absence of any form of compulsion, public opinion was of utmost importance in cases of deviation from the norm. There were different methods of sanctions, the most lenient would be the publishing of the misdemeanor, next came castigation, then, in severe cases, the member's rights were withheld and his social status degraded. In the most extreme cases the member would be ejected. In general, the socialist communes took similar steps.[23] Only seldom were the punitive institutions of the state called in. This was more prevalent in the socialist commune, especially in times of internal strife and disintegration (Icaria, Ruskin, Llano) when communes turned into battlefields.

Although throughout the history of the communes they consistently battled deviance and lawbreakings, these did not occur often or continuously. In general, the communal colonies stood out as islands of internal harmony and peace. Visitors came away with this impression, including Alexander Kent, whose impressions were summed up in the following words: "Another feature common to all communities, whether successful or unsuccessful, is their freedom from all dissipation and crime. They need no jails or prisons. The men and women who compose them are with few exceptions high minded and honorable, however visionary and cranky. Most of them have high ideals and are disposed to live decently and soberly. There are individual exceptions of course, but this is the rule."[24]

Notes

1. Alexander Kent, "Cooperative Communities in the United States," *Bulletin of the Department of Labor,* no. 35 (July 1901):642; A. Khoshkish, "Decision-Making within a Communal Setting: A Case Study of Hutterite Colonies," in *Communes, Historical and Contemporary,* ed. Ruth S. Cavan and Man Singh Das (New Delhi: Vikas Publishing House, 1979), pp. 57-58; Max Weber, *The Theory of Social Organization* (London: Free Press of Glencoe, Collier-Macmillan, 1964), pp. 358-63.
2. Anna White and Leila S. Taylor, *Shakerism: Its Meaning and Message* (Columbus, Oh.: Heer, 1904. New York: AMS Press, 1971), pp. 77-80; Henri Desroche, *The American Shakers: From Neo-Christianity to Pre-Socialism,* ed. and trans. John K. Savacoal (Boston: University of Massachusetts Press, 1971),

pp. 211-19; Ralph Albertson, *A Survey of Mutualistic Communities in America* (New York: AMS Press, 1973; 1st ed. 1936), pp. 426-27; Donald Egbert and Stow Persons, eds., *Socialism and American Life,* 2 vols. (Princeton: Princeton University Press, 1952), p. 137; Bertha M.H. Shambaugh, *Amana That Was and Amana That Is* (Iowa City: Iowa State Historical Society, 1932), pp. 94-104; Theodore Caplow, "Goals and Their Achievement in Four Utopian Communities," in *Communes: Creating and Managing the Collective Life,* ed. Rosabeth Moss Kanter (New York, Harper & Row, 1973), pp. 116-17; Kanter, ed., *Communes,* pp. 143-48; Alice Felt Tyler, *Freedom's Ferment* (New York: Harper & Row, 1962), pp. 148-49; "American Communities," *American Socialist* 2, no. 39 (September 27, 1877):305.

3. Maren Lockwood Carden, *Oneida: Utopian Community to Modern Corporation* (Baltimore: Johns Hopkins University Press, 1969), pp. 85-88; Egbert and Persons, pp. 146-47; *Handbook of the Oneida Community 1867 and 1871 Bound with Mutual Criticism* (1867. Reprint. New York, AMS Press, 1976), pp. 11-13.
4. John A. Hostetler, *Hutterite Society* (Baltimore: Johns Hopkins University Press, 1977), p. 162; Lee Emerson Deets, *The Hutterites: A Study in Social Cohesion* (Philadelphia: Porcupine, 1975), pp. 29-34; John W. Bennet, *Hutterian Brethren: The Agricultural Economy and Social Organization of a Communal People* (San Francisco: Stanford University Press, 1967), pp. 147-55, 255-59; Kanter, ed., *Communes,* pp. 198-201; Khoshkish, pp. 50-58.
5. Albet Shaw, *Icaria: A Chapter in the History of Communism* (1884. Reprint. New York: AMS Press, 1973), pp. 53-67.
6. Paul K. Conkin, *Two Paths to Utopia: The Hutterites and the Llano Colony* (Lincoln: University of Nebraska Press, 1964), pp. 126-46; Carl Wittke, *The Utopian Communist: A Biography of Wilhelm Weitting, Nineteenth-Century Reformer* (Baton Rouge: Louisiana State University Press, 1950), pp. 250-64; John Egerton, *Visions of Utopia: Nashoba, Rugby, Ruskin, and the New Communities in Tennessee's Past* (Knoxville: University of Tennessee Press with The Tennessee Historical Commission), pp. 72-73; Robert V. Hine, *California's Utopian Colonies* (New Haven: Yale University Press, 1966), pp. 78-80; Rondel V. Davidson, "Victor Considerant and the Failure of La Réunion," *Southwestern Historical Quarterly* (January 1973): 291; Egbert and Persons, pp. 203-4; Mathé Allain, ed., *France and North America: Utopias and Utopians* (Proceedings of the Third Symposium of French-American Studies, March 4-8, 1974), pp. 45-46.
7. Herbert A. Wisbey, Jr., *Pioneer Prophetess: Jemima Wilkinson, The Publick Universal Friend* (Ithaca, NY: Cornell University Press, 1964), p. 155; E.O. Randall, *History of the Zoar Society: A Sociological Study in Communism* (1904. Reprint. New York: AMS Press, 1971), p. 34; Robert Allerton Parker, *A Yankee Saint: John Humphrey Noyes and the Oneida Community* (New York: Putnam, 1953), p. 193.
8. Parker, pp. 215-19; Carden, pp. 25-30, 85-88, 70-74; Kanter, *Communes,* p. 116.
9. "American Communities," *American Socialist* 2, no. 39 (September 27, 1877): 306; Shambaugh, pp. 94-104; Bennet, *Hutterian Brethren,* pp. 150-55; Deets, pp. 34-37.
10. Kanter, *Communes,* pp. 106-8; Parker, pp. 213-15; Delburn Carpenter, *The Radical Pietists: Celibate Communal Societies Established in the United States Before 1820* (New York: AMS Press, 1975), p. 217; Constance Noyes Robertson, ed.,

Oneida Community: An Autobiography, 1851-1876 (Syracuse: Syracuse University Press, 1971), pp. 128-49; Robert H. Lauer and Jeanette C. Lauer, *The Spirit and the Flesh: Sex in Utopian Communities* (Metuchen, N.J.: Scarecrow Press, 1983), pp. 157-60; Karl J.R. Arndt, *George Rapp's Harmony Society, 1785-1847*, rev. ed. (New York: Associated University Presses, 1972), pp. 97-98; William G. Bek, "A German Communistic Society in Missouri," *Missouri Historical Review* (October 1908): 61.

11. Paul K. Conkin, *Two Paths to Utopia: The Hutterites and the Llano Colony* (Lincoln: University of Nebraska Press, 1964), pp. 135-36.
12. Arndt, *Harmony Society,* p. 410. On collective, political voting see Carol Weisbrod, *The Boundaries of Utopia* (New York: Pantheon, 1980), pp. 41-42.
13. John Fletcher Clews Harrison, *Quest for the New Moral World: Robert Owen and the Owenites in Britain and America* (New York: Scribner's, 1969), p. 188; Charles Pierre Le Warne, *Utopias on Puget Sound, 1885-1915* (Seattle: University of Washington Press, 1975), pp. 67-68, 142-43; Isaac Broome, *The Last Days of the Ruskin Cooperative Association* (Chicago, 1902), pp. 33-68, 107; William Alfred Hinds, *American Communities and Cooperative Colonies* (1878. Reprinted and enl. Philadelphia: Porcupine, 1975), p. 496; Burnette G. Haskell, "Kaweah—How and Why the Colony Died," *Out West* 17 (September 1902): 317; Egerton, pp. 72-75; Shaw, p. 93; Wittke, p. 260.
14. Conkin, pp. 136-42.
15. Bestor, *Backwoods,* pp. 121-22, 186-87; Hinds, p. 527.
16. Yáacov Oved, "Kaweah: Socialist Commune in California," *Zmanim,* no. 15 (Summer 1984) (Hebrew); Hine, pp. 84-85.
17. John McKelvie Whitworth, *God's Blueprints: a Sociological Study of Three Utopian Sects* (London: Routledge & Kegan Paul, 1975), pp. 17-23, 40-50, 79-88.
18. John Humphrey Noyes, *History of American Socialism* (1870). Reprinted as *Strange Cults and Utopias of Nineteenth-Century America* (New York: Dover, 1966), pp. 211-18; Arthur Bestor, *Backwoods Utopias: The Sectarian Origins and the Owenite Phase of Communitarian Socialism in America,* 1663-1829, 2d ed. (Philadelphia: University of Pennsylvania Press, 1978), pp. 202-29; Hine, pp. 82-88; Hinds, pp. 369, 375-76; Egerton, pp. 66-68, 75; Conkin, pp. 121-23; Le Warne, pp. 129-39; Shaw, pp. 55-56; Egbert and Persons, pp. 14-15, 132-38; Hostetler, pp. 290-96.
19. Charles Nordhoff, *The Communistic Societies of the United States* (New York: Shocken, 1965), p. 417; Edward D. Andrews, *The People Called Shakers: A Search for Perfect Society* (New York: Dover, 1963), p. 221; *American Socialist* 1, no. 1; Bestor, *Backwoods,* pp. 47-48; Arndt, *Harmony Society,* pp. 539-40; Carpenter, p. 245; Hostetler, pp. 122-23, 188, 278-83; Shambaugh, p. 108; John W. Bennett, "Frames of Reference for the Study of Hutterian Society," *Communes Historical and Contemporary,* ed. Ruth S. Cavan and Man Singh Das (New Delhi: Vikas Publishing House, 1979), pp. 37-38; Otohiko Okugawa, "Intercommunal Relationships among Nineteenth-Century Communal Societies in America," *Communal Societies* (1983):68-82.
20. On *Gemeinschaft* and *Gesselschaft* in communes see Rosabeth Moss Kanter, *Commitment and Community: Communes and Utopias in Sociological Perspective* (Cambridge, Mass.: Harvard University, 1972), pp. 148-50; Stenley Meron *Zionism between Assimilation and Revival* (Tel Aviv: Am Oved, 1983), pp. 28-49.

21. Carol Weisbrod, *The Boundaries of Utopia* (New York: Pantheon, 1980), p. 69.
22. Ibid., pp. 45-58; J.W.T. "Community Contracts," *American Socialist* 3 (December 25, 1879):410-11; Jerold S. Auerbach, *Justice without Law* (New York: Oxford University Press, 1983), pp. 51-53, 65.
23. Lauer and Lauer, pp. 170-74. See also *Constitution of Icaria,* art. 169, sec. 5; *Iowa Journal of History and Politics* (1917):267-68; Dects, pp. 45-47; Khoshkish, pp. 56-58.
24. Kent, p. 646.

20

Education, Culture, and Rituals

Methods of Education

From the first days in their settlements, the communes paid special attention to education. Most established their own independent institutions to take care of their young. More than places of learning, their schools served as a socializing agent. It was imperative to instill the values of their special way of life in the young generation. The small number of communes that lasted longer than one generation points, among other things, to the problems of instilling these values. In spite of the difficulties in realizing their communal way of life, there was not a single commune that avoided the effort involved in establishing an independent educational system simultaneously with the first economic and social institutions.

In the religious communes there was the additional motivation of providing a religious education in the spirit of the sect. In some (Harmony, Zoar, Amana), schools even preceded the establishment of the settlements. They were one of the sect's main reasons to isolate themselves. In the secular socialist communes in which there was no authoritative ideological focus, the school was the main socializing agent, and in time also the center of educational and ideological activities. At a time when schooling was only sporadic in the frontier areas, the communes stood out as ''islands of education and culture'' that provided both boys and girls with an elementary education.[1]

All communes had one thing in common—they shared the responsibility of educating their children in the communal spirit and ideology. In communes where the monogamous family unit was maintained and children lived at home, the family took upon itself the main effort of educating the young. At a later stage they were concerned with supporting them emotionally. Even so, the commune, its institutions, and its teachers carried most of the burden of instruction and education at day centers. In all socialist communes (except for a short period in Icaria and New Harmony) and in most religious ones, this was the case. It is continued to this very day on the Hutterite communes.[2] In communes that abolished the monogamous family unit, whether because of principles of celibacy (the Shakers, Harmony, and for a short period Zoar) or as in Oneida where members lived in "extended family units," the youngsters lived in children's houses apart from their parents. In the Shaker communes the separation was complete whereas in Oneida children were allowed visits to their parents once or twice a week. Diaries of members who grew up in communes are fascinating documents. They admit us into the inner world of children who were raised communally, separated from their parents. Of special interest are memories of Shaker-educated children who described the unique atmosphere of strict discipline that instilled in them rules of behavior, and at the same time they recalled warm personal attention by members of the "family" who were not their biological parents.[3]

Pierrepont Noyes, son of Oneida's founder, devoted many chapters of his fascinating memoirs to his youth in the children's community. He was extremely critical of the cruel practice in which children were prevented from forming emotional relationships with their mothers. He recalled that his own weekly visits to his mother in her quarters were a privilege that could be taken away at any time. Nevertheless, his book is full of esteem for the achievement of communal education in forming his communal outlook.[4]

In Zoar, where celibacy replaced the monogamous family for a time (1822-1830), children were installed in children's houses mainly so that mothers could devote their whole time to work on the farm and at service jobs. But the conditions in the children's houses were such that after a few years they were abolished and the children returned to sleep at their parent's homes.[5] In the socialist commune sleeping in children's houses was only temporary if at all. As a rule, the socialist commune maintained the family unit and their children slept in their family's quarters.[6] Different and opposing approaches characterized the attitude toward communal sleeping arrangements. There was a great deal of experimentation, some of it daring and for the period, extremely progressive. In every commune one could find a nursery school and an elementary school. Few of the children had to go to school elsewhere.

The Hutterites were pioneers in establishing a tradition of education when in the sixteenth century in Moravia they started a *Klein Schul* (nursery school) and a *Gross Schul*. They continued this tradition when they emigrated to America. (They seem to have been the first to establish nursery schools in Europe too.)[7] It was crucial to have an educational system for toddlers as well to enable all commune members, men and women, to integrate fully in work on the farm and at service jobs. In communes where the children slept in their parents quarters, they spent most of the day at school. In some cases the school operated throughout the year; in Amana they had school for fifty-two weeks a year.[8]

High schools were rare in the religious communes. On the other hand in the socialist communes Ruskin and Llano there were short-lived attempts to establish colleges for higher education and ideological reinforcement. They failed. As far as we know, there were only two cases—Brook Farm and Oneida—where higher education was integrated into the communal life. Educational activity was of vital importance in Brook Farm's life. All its members taught, studied, or worked simultaneously. High-school education and coaching students for Harvard was an important source of income. The perfectionist doctrine of Oneida members prompted them to broaden their knowledge continuously to improve themselves and their potential. Education meant *improvement* and so did knowledge. Their scope of studies included theology, the sciences, and the classics. At one stage they tried to implement university studies on the commune, but proving unsuccessful, they sent instead five of their students to Yale.[9]

Whereas primary schooling was firmly embedded in all communes as a result of their communitarian existence, high-school education was rare. It existed only in those communes whose spiritual and ideological values had prepared them to be open to external culture and science. The teaching staff were usually commune members. Only seldom did teachers come from the outside, and then only in cases where they taught vocational subjects. Teachers were selected meticulously. They had to have proper qualifications and have didactic and ideological fervor.[10] Most of them were inexperienced, some autodidactic, and all of them continued their own specific self-education while working on the commune. Teaching, therefore, was another feature of mutual aid and organically embedded in the communal way of life. Those rich in knowledge shared it with their peers and instilled it in their younger generation.

In time, teaching became a profession which had to be studied. Communal teachers' seminars were nonexistent and candidates were sent to regular ones outside the commune.[11] Most communes tried to adapt their curriculum to that of the state they lived in. When, in the second half of the nineteenth century, various states passed their education laws, the problem arose of how to adapt communal education to the general one. Some of the obligatory subjects entailed bringing in teachers from the outside. The Hutterites, who had fought for their own school system, compromised by hiring teachers who taught general subjects. In most cases confrontation was avoided and the commune accepted the growing involvement of the state in educational affairs by compromising and teaching general subjects. They continued to teach religious and specific communal-ideological subjects side by side with the general education demanded by the state. Even the conservative and isolated Shakers found a way to adapt to state education by adding general subjects like geography, history, astronomy, geometry, and algebra. State supervisors were most impressed by the level of education on commune schools and spread their fame as institutions for character-building and religious education.[12]

Other religious communes—Amana, Zoar, and Harmony—adapted to the new laws and taught general subjects simultaneously with religion. Socialist communes had less of a problem because there were hardly any elements of specific subjects in their schools. These were integrated into the general system and subsidized by the state. In many instances they even became regional schools open to their neighbors. In fact they were communal schools with a small body of outside students.[13]

Communal schools had a reputation of being excellent institutes of education with a high level of proficiency. They attracted students from different circles, from affluent families who sought boarding schools for their offspring and also underprivileged children and "social cases" who found shelter in the communal schools. Even in the eighteenth century children of the well-to-do from Baltimore and Philadelphia were attracted to Ephrata, which excelled in the classics. Brook Farm was established as an educational community whose aim was to teach and educate boarders, and it attracted students from the neighborhood as well as from outside the state.[14]

The Shakers, too, exploited the reputation of their schools to attract students and prepare them for joining their sect. When the revival era was over and the stream of religious enthusiasm had dried up, the only source of growth for the Shakers was to absorb children in their schools. They accepted many orphans and children from broken homes, promising them an elementary and vocational education and giving them an option to join the commune when they were twenty-one. On the other hand they specified in their contracts with the children's guardians that they could expel those who showed signs of being rebels and who did not accept the Shaker's discipline.[15] In Oneida there was, at some time, a plan to open a school for the children of hired workers, but nothing came of it.

In socialist Llano an independent Kid Colony was established with the intention of absorbing children from the outside; this too, was unsuccessful. Consequently, most communal schools, except for Shakers' and Brook Farms', were involved in educating their own children only and did not attempt to use their school to instill in others their ideals or as a factor in absorbing new members. In spite of external influences and interference of the state by subsidizing the schools and teachers, or by dictating the curriculum, the communal schools and kindergartens managed to maintain their original function. They were the main socializing agent of the commune, teaching their special subjects in a unique atmosphere and through unique methods.

Schools differed from commune to commune. There was no similarity between a Shaker school and that at Brook Farm or at Oneida. There was no comparison between the atmosphere in the children's community in Llano and those of Harmony and Amana. Each commune had its own special educational institutions with their unique set of values and ideals. Yet, in spite of these differences, there was a common characteristic of all communal schools—the integration of work and study. This element distinguished them from the general school system and was inherent in the communal way of life. If we regard the school as the socializing factor for commune children, then integration of work and study expressed that continual socialization.[16]

From their youth commune children were taught to follow the work habits and proficiency of the adults. They were thus gradually absorbed into the life of the adult community. This happened on all communes but at a different level. In Brook Farm, established by a group of intellectuals, the integration of work and study took on the aspect of an ideal. Children of the well-to-do who studied there and who had never done a day's work prior to their arrival on the commune devoted several hours a day to hard physical labor in the fields, mucking manure or washing dishes in the dining-hall. Their tutors, besides preaching the lofty ideal of work, set them a personal example when they, as all other commune members, divided their time between teaching and agricultural work. Integration of study and practical life experience were combined in all possible ways.[17]

Oneida, like Brook Farm, was also established by intellectuals who devoted a great deal of their leisure time to self-improvement and a general education. There, too, children were expected to devote several hours a day after school to work at production and service jobs, thus integrating intellectual and physical work. Their tutors tried to give them the sense that they were truly participating and contributing to the commune's production. Both on Oneida and Brook Farm there was no separation between school life and the community's.[18]

In Shaker communes the children were an integral part of "the family." Their schedule was divided between work and study, according to the seasons. Boys would study in winter and the beginning of spring when agricultural work was dormant while the girls studied in the summer months and in the autumn.[19] Another characteristic of the Shaker communes was the private tutor who would coach each child at school and provide him with a profession.

In the communes established by German immigrants—Harmony, Zoar, and Amana—most members came from a working-class background where the apprenticing of children was a family tradition. The Hutterites also had a long tradition of regarding work and production as the focal point of their lives.[20] In those communes where work at a young age was a family tradition, school was interwoven in the commune's daily life. Even though the emphasis differed, the integration of physical work and spiritual activities was a matter of principle. The same was the case on the socialist communes where the ideological principle of physical and mental work was the foundation of education. The social background of their members dictated different attitudes, but all integrated children and youth in the commune's work schedule, whether in industry, building, service jobs or in any other project.[21]

Commune schools usually had a curriculum adapted to their way of life and spiritual world, even though they were under state supervision. Most had included in their curriculum communal values which were also reflected in their teaching methods. However, not all commune schools differed from the regular ones; this was usually the case on the short-lived communes which naturally lacked stability. Such a case was the religious commune Zoar, where the school gradually lost its uniqueness and the teachers became the core of opposition on the commune.[22] Beth-El, too, had no unique school system, nor did the socialist commune Burley.

Most religious and socialist communes were deeply concerned with matters of education. They adopted unique methods to ensure the indoctrination of the younger generation with ideological or religious principles. In that respect religious communes did not differ from any other religious education. The only difference was that their religious education was integrated with communal values. Lessons included a history of the commune and the sect, its theology and rituals. Individual education was accomplished through personal conversations about matters of doctrine, social values, and the communal way of life. Topics such as the abolishment of private property, the evil of selfishness, and of hostile attitudes were a part of the education for communitarian values. Discipline was also instilled together with the fear of God and the ethics of crime and punishment. They demanded respect of the elders and a voluntary obedience. The Shakers, for example, realized their educational philosophy in the children's houses, at work, and at school, and in demanding total commitment from the children to their way of life.[23]

In Amana, where the children were under parental supervision part of the time, the school demanded strict discipline which filled the children with respect for the elders. Children were guided by a specific set of rules on all matters. The Hutterites, too, have been guarding their old and unique educational institutions zealously to this day. Under pressure to adopt to modern ways, they have conformed to a certain extent, but they still adhere to the roots and traditions of their distant past. They insist on keeping their schools within the boundaries of the community, teach German (their holy tongue) daily, but more than anything they maintain their educational values of discipline, obedience, and *Gelassenheit*—an ego-abolishing modesty that enables the individual to identify with the community.[24]

Of special interest is the integration of religion and communal education in Oneida which was open to external scientific and cultural influences. In this commune the meetings of mutual criticism served to imprint on the younger generation their religious and communal doctrine. As customary in the adult population, children too had the meetings of indoctrination every afternoon. As to the effect of these meetings in instilling in the children religious values, fear of God, love of the Bible, and belief in the commune, we can read in Pierrepont Noyes's memoirs.[25]

The first socialist communes in the United States were involved in far-reaching experiments in education. New Harmony under Robert Owen attracted a large number of educators and scientists from among the intellectual elite of Philadelphia. A group under the leadership of the scientist and educator William McClure established a renown educational institution for 300 pupils. It gained widespread reputation for its modern methods which were a mixture of Pestalozzi's, Fallenberg's, and Owen's ideas. It was through the latter's influence that punishment was completely abolished. Teachers had to work hard in order to create a voluntary discipline in a school of over 300 pupils (including a nursery school). This attitude was radically different from any of the other religious communes which advocated a harsh discipline. Yet this was not the only difference. Education in New Harmony was vocational and science oriented while religious lessons and the classics were neglected. Robert Owen, who had a moralistic attitude, insisted on preaching values and on a special course in character-forming intended for those who would live communally. He had planned a number of general meetings of the adults and separate ones for the children, three times a week. There he intended to preach ideology and communal values, but the short life span of New Harmony prevents us from drawing any conclusions as to the success of his methods of character-building.[26]

Other socialist communes continued in the direction taken by New Harmony. In the second generation of socialist communes Brook Farm was the one to carry on educational reform. In addition to being receptive to the sciences, a variety of subjects, and a high standard of teaching, they also adopted an awareness of social problems and fostered a nondoctrinary education of values until they were taken over by Fourierist ideas. After Brook Farm was integrated into the Fourierist movement a further educational element was added, when many lessons were devoted to the study of Fourier's doctrine. Many of its members took part in regional meetings of Fourierists in Boston and New York. Its functionaries traveled widely and the colony became the movement's center for two years, which influenced the educational system and reinforced its ideological elements.

Later socialist communes lacked the educational fervor typical of New Harmony and Brook Farm. Even though most of their schools were unimaginative and unoriginal, they all struggled with the need for a separate school system to ensure the indoctrination of the next generations.[27] During the first years of Icaria, while Etienne Cabet was their leader, the school played a predominant part in the ideological education of the second generation. The children lived apart from their parents, in boarding school conditions, tutored by trained pedagogues. Cabet and several of the teachers gave special lessons on the ideology of Icaria. When internal dissension and economic hardships caused the schism in Icaria, collective education was abolished. The school suffered a serious set back. With the move to Iowa, in the 1870s, a regional school for the two Icaria colonies was established and children from the neighborhood were also accepted.[28]

In American socialist communes of the end of the nineteenth century, an effort was made to establish an independent system of education that would promote socialist values. But none of the settlements had a teaching staff dedicated and zealous enough to make this feasible for longer periods. In Kaweah's early days, while its members were still working on the road-construction job, there was an attempt to set up a modern school with liberal methods of education. It is not clear whether this was a success. Memories of the period include many tales about the lack of discipline. Children took advantage of the prevailing liberal atmosphere; they even complained to their parents whenever a teacher tried to enforce obedience. Such a complaint might have been taken up by the general meeting, and the liberal methods of education caused strife among members and expulsion of talented members from the teaching staff.[29]

Llano was the only socialist commune in which a serious attempt was made to establish a unique educational institution, first in California and later in Louisiana. George Pickett was the living force behind the experiment. He devoted himself to the founding of the Kid Colony, in which local teachers would guide their pupils to live a collective, socialist life. They were taught a profession through a practical creative attitude. Pickett strongly objected to an achievement-oriented education and was against granting degrees and certificates as a matter of principle. This was reflected in his method of education.

The Kid Colony existed for a long period, almost as long as Llano itself. Many students passed through it and if we were to assess the school's success by testimonials of pupils and their love for the school we might be convinced of its success. But if the criterion should be the number of students who joined the commune, Llano's educational system would be considered a failure. Graduates of the Kid Colony were no stabilizing factor in the commune; they left the commune as soon as they found a job outside.[30]

This failure of the Llano's childrens' community to imprint on the second generation the love of communal way of life was not an isolated case. On examining commune schools from this aspect we realize that in most communes graduates did not become a stabilizing factor. They either left or did not succeed in reversing trends of deterioration, whether social or economical. On the contrary, in many cases the schools were hot beds of opposition and criticism that undermined the communal establishment. This was the case in Oneida where the scientific-oriented education at the local school and university did not contribute to any sense of loyalty to the religious creed or to the leadership of Noyes. The same also happened in Zoar. Teachers of the local school, themselves second- and third-generation members, were the core of militants who fought to dissolve the commune and to divide its assets. Even Shaker institutions of education, which were a vital source of growth for their settlements and advocated intensive ideological indoctrination, did not in the long run succeed in the rearing of Shaker communes. In the early twentieth century most of the children educated in their schools left as soon as they had reached adulthood.[31]

On examining this failure we have to take into account the immensity of the task and the limited means as well as the prevailing conditions of the communes' place and time. In a society rent by strife there was a limit to the power of education in preventing deterioration unless they maintained a relative independence and a teaching staff with extraordinary educational capacities. These conditions did not exist. From the experience of the communes in this study we may assume that as soon as they were lost, their internal cohesion, social life, and schools lost all ideological convictions and vision and their deterioration was irrevocable. Utopian belief in the unlimited power of education, its ability to bring social change, to create a new man, and to overcome the heritage of an individualistic order[32] has not stood up to the test of the historical experiment of communes in the United States.

To all of the above we have to add an objective difficulty—the generation gap in communes that lasted for more than one generation. While every educational system has to tackle this problem, it was even more complicated in the voluntary communal societies that attempted to instill in the younger generation a set of ideals radically opposed to that prevailing in the general society. The educators had to face the challenge of imparting to the younger generation the values and motivation of the founders of the commune inspite of great changes all around them. The history of the long-living communes was full of conflict caused by the generation gap. We have mentioned the opposition and heresy in Oneida and Zoar; let us add the materialism and the craving for luxury in the technological society of Amana. But there were also reverse trends. In Icaria, for instance, young members fought against their elders' ideological and political indifference and against inequality. As a rule, the second and third generations grew up in a different environment from that of their fathers. Most lacked that emotional experience that had led them to join a sect or a commune and had built their ideological world. Only an intensive, systematic, and sophisticated socializing factor could bridge this gap; it never materialized in communal schools.[33]

The Hutterites were an exception in that they succeeded in overcoming the generation gap. Ever since immigrating to the United States they have managed to minimize the secession of their sons. This movement, with its communal history of 450 years, has succeeded in integrating into its educational system all the socializing factors inherent in it. Their methods are not sophisticated. Conservative, pedantic, and severe, they lack any pedagogical inspirations. Yet they have been successful because their education has been fully and systematically integrated in the Hutterite experience. Their nursery schools and primary schools have been a continuation of the family education and a bridge to the adult world. The children have been supervised by educators aware of a distinctive set of values and act accordingly. Their ancient tradition affects them wherever they may be. The children spend their entire day in an atmosphere of social togetherness; they share everything with their peers, work as well as pleasure. They live within a totally secluded and isolated world that succeeds in teaching such an emotional loyalty and patriotism that even when opportunity calls, the young members are not tempted to try their luck in the wide world.[34]

The Hutterite's success in maintaining their continuity proves that education is not enough. It is dependent on a total of factors that have little to do with education per se. Their experience and that of other communes of longevity is proof that wherever there are optimal conditions such as creed, ideology, a stable social life, and proper economic conditions, the educational institutions play an integral part as socializing agents and are also an impressive cultural and educational environment.

Ralph Albertson, a member of The Christian Commonwealth who intimately knew the communitarian settlements of the early twentieth century, summed it up in his comprehensive book: "In respect to their effect on character, the communist and cooperative colonies must have a word of praise. Both in children and in adults there was a socialization of outlook and a refinement of character which cannot be gainsaid. A number of people who were interviewed testified to the goodness of their brief life of economic fellowship."[35]

Culture and Rituals

Socialization on the communes was not only the result of educational activities or of religious and ideological indoctrination. An important additional factor was the daily cultural activities and the social rituals in which members of all ages participated together. These rituals were one of the cardinal expressions of the communal experience and an inspiring aspect of spiritual elation and togetherness. In religious communes, group rituals took the form of prayer meetings and services, while the socialist ones reaffirmed their unity in cultural activities and celebrations. Just as a unique system of education was an imperative to the commune's survival so was their cultural life and unique rituals. In addition to being of value in themselves, they enhanced communion, affirmed the community members' commitment, and forged their group loyalty. Rituals were an enriching and emotional experience of togetherness.[36]

In the religious communes, rituals, prayer meetings, communion of young members and new ones, and special festivals reaffirmed the member's feeling of commitment. They were a source of spiritual elation and of a jointly held religion which was interwoven with the communal ethos of their daily life. Rituals thus contributed to the commune's social cohesiveness. The level of cultural and artistic activities integrated within religious rituals differed from commune to commune. Those with a Protestant-pietist background (Harmony, Zoar, Amana, Ephrata) and also the Shakers and the Anabaptist Hutterites, adhered to the severe traditions of their sects and accepted their rigorous existence of nonindulgence. In these communes we find a complete abstention from any decorative art such as painting, sculpture, instrumental music, or elaborate architecture. Their egalitarian outlook prompted them to adopt an all-encompassing simplicity. They avoided all luxury. Oneida was different because its members had a perfectionist background and believed in man's ability to achieve perfection. They were lacking the puritan-pietist limitations and meekness and therefore their life throbbed with every kind of cultural and artistic creativity. Individual talent was encouraged and every member was expected to exercise his creative potential to the utmost. Nevertheless, here too there were limitations as a result of the collective ethos that aspired to achieve an all-encompassing harmony. Excellence was frowned upon and any kind of individualistic isolationism was criticized and checked.[37]

In the secular communes, cultural activities fulfilled the functions of rituals on the religious communes. Endeavoring to enrich the communal experience, they had a larger variety to choose from than their religious "sisters" who abstained from any form of entertainment. Many communes enjoyed dances, parties, picnics, drama circles, theater shows, operas, concerts, painting, and sculpture. In some modern ones photography, films, and sports activities were a part of their daily routine. These activities were a means of individual expression on the one hand and of mutual enrichment within the communal experience on the other.[38]

A special characteristic of all communes was their endeavor to foster an independent culture and if at all possible to avoid any paid for cultural activities. This is why most communes were the cultural center of their neighborhood. People from all over attended their festivals and shows. Their choirs and dramatic or musical circles appeared in nearby communities and contributed to a higher standard of cultural activities in the vicinity. Even communes that had no objection to external culture cherished their own lively and independent cultural activities. Members of Brook Farm, for instance, regularly attended concerts in Boston and generally attempted to keep in touch with intellectual developments, but they also fostered their own divergent and unique theatrical and musical performances.[39]

The focus of artistic and cultural activities were the holidays and festivals celebrated in every commune. Heights of collective ecstasy and emotion were reached at the celebration of the commune's anniversary or its spiritual leader's birthday. Religious communes had special days to celebrate their unique holidays in addition to the general ones. On some, the "Sabbath" was not on a Sunday but also on Saturday as in Ephrata, while Oneida abolished their Sabbath altogether. The Shakers had a day for inner communion as well as the open communion and public prayers and rituals on Sunday. The Hutterites, Amana, and pietist communes celebrated the special days of baptism of new members.[40] Socialist communes, too, had special days on which they celebrated events relevant to the history of their commune. They also observed some national or international dates such as the Fourth of July or May One. On those days they would invite guests from the vicinity and from the commune's periphery in the cities to participate in a festive convention. It was an opportunity to give expression to their artistic talent. The commune's choir, orchestra, and dramatic circle would perform but the stage would also be a set of propaganda. The whole event usually turned into an emotional experience that transcended their hum-drum everyday life.[41]

The most widespread cultural activity all communes shared was music. On the religious ones it was an integral part of the collective's ritual, whether during prayer meetings or any other collective gathering. The kind of music practiced differed between the various communes, but they all had community singing. On the religious communes they sang mostly hymns. All members would participate, giving expression to their collective feelings. This was a suitable way for everyone to express their personal feelings and simultaneously it also served as an indoctrination. The lyrics of the hymns included tenets of faith and the sect's history and tradition. As a result of their perpetual repetition, hymns served to internalize the religious message. In the experience of the religious communes, in which all the aspects of community life had a transcendental significance, hymnody was the language which transmitted melodic and oral symbols and commentary on the principles of their beliefs and was absorbed by each individual. Giving expression to their faith, the hymns therefore also enhanced their daily experience and became a part of the community's ethos. There was an additional aspect to the singing. Commune members did not just absorb the hymns' message but also composed their own. This was a means to a nonverbal flow of understanding and a reaffirmation of their faith on a daily basis. Composers of hymns had a special standing, and it is no wonder that in many communes composing was the privilege of the leaders; their musical talent was regarded as a gift from Heaven and contributed to their charismatic leadership.[42]

On the socialist communes music played a similar role to that in the religious ones. Here, too, it was an emotional experience on the individual and collective levels. However, while music in the religious communes was usually limited to liturgical litanies with an indoctrinary-educational element, music on socialist communes was varied and many sided. All had choirs and practiced communal singing; their repertoire was secular and adapted to holidays, festivals, and dances as well as to work and outdoor activities. Musical education played a cardinal role in the life of several communities and funds were allotted to foster it; an example for this is Brook Farm. Simultaneously to vocal music, socialist communes fostered instrumental performances and many had bands and orchestras that would play on festive occasions and give concerts in the area.

Most religious communes avoided instrumental music because of their religious principles. The Hutterites still do, fearing the incursion of profane music into the sacred. The Shakers abstained from accompanying their singing with instruments until the end of the nineteenth century, when their objection was lifted and pianos and organs were introduced.[43] In several religious communes (Oneida, Harmony, Beth-El), where musical education reached a high standard, there were excellent orchestras too. Dancing, which was an integral part of the socialist communes' cultural relaxation, was not tolerated in religious communes except at the Shakers. There, dancing was a characteristic element of their ritual. It had developed from the ecstatic beginnings of the sect. In time it turned into a stylized and refined ritual as mentioned above.[44]

Most communes maintained a higher standard of culture than their neighbors. Since all members could read and write, the establishment of libraries was imperative. These were usually the richest and most extensive in the entire frontier states. Many communes published their own journals. Printing shops were not only a source of income but a deep cultural necessity. In addition to internal publications some communes published periodicals and books that were then distributed throughout the United States. Even though they were often poor, most socialist communes spared no effort in publishing and distributing periodicals and other literary works printed in their shops.[45] The activity surrounding their journal was an important aspect of the commune's cultural and social life. There were significant differences between the various religious communes. Oneida, the Shakers, and Ephrata were extremely diligent in their religious and secular publications, but Zoar, Bishop Hill, and the Hutterites were not avid readers and hardly excelled in their publications.

Cultural activities on the communes gave personal talent a wide range of expression, yet it was limited to the immediate needs of the commune. Creative artistic talent was not fostered as such. Even Oneida, which promoted personal perfection, curtailed any outstanding attempts to excel. A survey of intellectuals and artists in communes shows a wide range of writers and just a few musicians. Only a handful achieved national fame, and those had acquired their art before joining the commune. It may be safely stated that the communes were not fertile soil for artists to grow. Their intellectual and cultural life was nurtured by the collective communal experience to which individual excellence was adverse. Nevertheless, the commune contributed enormously to the cultural life of its members. While reading the memoirs of ex-members, one repeatedly comes across their fond recollections of the rich cultural experiences, the likes of which they never found anywhere else after they had wandered off to the prosperous urban centers of civilization.

Notes

1. Donald E. Pitzer, *Proceedings of the International Conference on Kibbutz and Communes* (Yad Tabenking, 1986); Donald E. Pitzer and Josephine M. Elliott, "New Harmony's First Utopians," special ed. Reprinted from *Indiana Magazine of History* 75 (September 1979):244-46; Karl J.R. Arndt, *George Rapp's Harmony Society, 1785-1847*, rev. ed. (New York: Associated University Presses, 1972), pp. 38, 254; Bertha M.H. Shambaugh, *Amana That Was and Amana That Is* (Iowa City: Iowa State Historical Society, 1932), pp. 168-69; Donald Egbert and Stow Persons, eds., *Socialism and American Life*, 2 Vols. (Princeton: Princeton University Press, 1952), p. 201; Morris Hillquit, *History of Socialism in the United States*, 5th ed. (New York: Dover, 1971), p. 131; Gideon G. Freudenberg, *Robert Owen: Educator of the People* (Tel Aviv: Dvir, 1970), p. 142 (Hebrew).
2. On the Hutterites see John A. Hostetler, *Hutterite Society* (Baltimore: Johns Hopkins University Press, 1977), pp. 201-20. On socialist communes—Brook Farm—see John Thomas Codman, *Brook Farm: Historic and Personal Memoirs* (New York: AMS Press, 1971, 1st ed. 1894), p. 135.
3. Hervey Elkins, *Fifteen Years in the Order of Shakers: A Narration of Facts Concerning That Singular People* (Hanover: Dartmouth University Press, 1853. New York: AMS Press, 1973), pp. 22-23, 30, 37, 40, 42, 60. On the Shakers see Sylvia Minott Spencer, "My Memories of the Shakers," in *Communes: Creating and Managing the Collective Life*, ed. Rosabeth Moss Kanter (New York: Harper & Row, 1973), pp. 375-80.
4. Oneidans regarded their method as the most advanced in their generation. They insisted that taking the children's education out of the hands of their biological parents and putting trained personnel in charge was the most efficient method of education. It served the individual progress of each child and reinforced their communitarian values as well. Oneidans were very proud of their achievements when talking to outsiders. Maren Lockwood Carden, *Oneida: Utopian Community to Mordern Corporation* (Baltimore: Johns Hopkins University Press, 1969), pp. 50, 63-64, 69; Robert Allerton Parker, *A Yankee Saint: John Humphrey Noyes and the Oneida Community* (New York: Putman, 1935), pp. 219, 260; William Alfred Hinds, *American Communities and Cooperative Colonies* (1878. Reprinted and enl. Philadelphia: Porcupine, 1975), p. 193; Pierrepont Noyes, *My*

Father's House: An Oneida Boyhood (London: J. Murray, 1937), pp. 34-40, 47, 65-73, 125-27, 130-32.

5. "Zoar: An Ohio Experiment in Communalism," *The Ohio Historical Society* (1972):42-43; E.O. Randall, *History of the Zoar Society: A Sociological Study in Communism* (New York: AMS Press, 1971; 1st ed. 1904), pp. 44-46.
6. At New Harmony there was an attempt to establish a boarding school for members' children as an integral part of the educational institution. A similar experiment was underway at Icaria in its early years, at Nauvoo, and in the "kid colony" of New Llano. In all these cases it was a short, insignificant experiment. Freudenberg, pp. 42-43; Raymond Lee Muncy, *Sex and Marriage in Utopian Communities, Nineteenth-Century America* (Bloomington, Ind.: Indiana University Press, 1973), pp. 61-62.
7. Hostetler, p. 210; Katherine Burton, *Paradise Planters: The Story of Brook Farm* (New York: AMS Press, 1973; 1st ed. 1939), p. 149.
8. Shambaugh, p. 175.
9. Georgiana Bruce Kirby, *Years of Experience* (New York: AMS Press, 1971; 1st ed. 1887), pp. 95-100; Raymond Koch and Charlotte Koch, *Educational Commune: The Story of Commonwealth College* (New York: Schocken, 1972), pp. 12-16; Paul K. Conkin, *Two Paths to Utopia: The Hutterites and the Llano Colony* (Lincoln: University of Nebraska Press, 1964), p. 157; Constance Noyes Robertson, ed., *Oneida Community: An Autobiography, 1851-1876* (Syracuse: Syracuse University Press, 1971), pp. 173-77; Pierrepont Noyes, p. 68; Carden, p. 69.
10. Pierrepont Noyes, p. 41; Robertson, *Oneida Community*, p. 173; Elkins, pp. 76-80; Burton, p. 151; Conkin, p. 157; John S. Duss, *The Harmonists: A Personal History* (Philadelphia: Porcupine, 1972), p. 175.
11. Charles Pierre Le Warne, *Utopias on Puget Sound, 1885-1915* (Seattle: University of Washington Press, 1975), pp. 94-95, 160; Randall, p. 44; Elmer R. Pearson and Julia Neal, *The Shaker Image* (Hancock, Mass.: New York Graphic Society and the Shaker Community, 1974), p. 54.
12. The change came in the second half of the nineteenth century and government supervisors reported about Shakers with admiration. This spread their name as good institutions for the forming of good character and for religious education. Elkins, p. 76; Hillquit, p. 131; Charles Nordhoff, *The Communistic Societies of the United States* (New York: Shocken, 1965), p. 399; Edward D. Andrews, *The People Called Shakers: A Search for Perfect Society* (New York: Dover, 1963), pp. 188-89; Julius Friedrich Sachse, *The German Sectarians of Pennsylvania, 1742-1800: A Critical and Legendary History of the Ephrata Cloister and the Dunkers* (Philadelphia: By the author, 1899; New York, AMS Press, 1971), pp. 299-302.
13. Albert Shaw, *Icaria: A Chapter in the History of Communism* (1884. Reprint. New York: AMS Press, 1973), p. 119; Le Warne, pp. 94-96, 160; Marie Merchand Ross, *Child of Icaria* (New York: Hyperion, 1976; 1st ed. 1938), pp. 31, 103.
14. Sachse, pp. 297-308; Burton, pp. 55-56, 85-88; Freudenberg, p. 141.
15. It should be noted that in the contract signed with the children's legal guardians, the Shakers emphasized that they were not obligated to educate children that showed signs of rebelliousness or unwillingness to accept discipline. Such children were immediately removed from the framework. Pearson and Neal, p. 53;

Marguerite Fellows Melcher, *The Shaker Adventure* (New York: The Shaker Museum, 1975), pp. 151-60; Carden, p. 84; Elkins, p. 57.

16. Irvin L. Child, "Socialization," in *Handbook of Social Psychology*, Vol. 2, ed. Gardne Lindzey (Addison-Wesley), p. 677.
17. Nathaniel Hawthorne, *Blithedale Romance* (New York: W.W. Norton, 1953), pp. 16-18, 69-71; Burton, pp. 66, 149-50; Kirby, pp. 148-51; Hawthorne, pp. 16-18, 69-71; Growe, pp. 155-56.
18. Pierrepont Noyes, pp. 101, 120; Robertson, *Oneida Community*, pp. 311-13.
19. Elkins, pp. 49, 78.
20. Arndt, *Harmony Society*, p. 119; Shambaugh, pp. 176-78; Alexander Kent, "Cooperative Communities in the United States," *Bulletin of the Department of Labor*, no. 35 (July 1901):581-82; John W. Bennet, *Hutterian Brethren: The Agricultural Economy and Social Organization of a Communal People* (San Francisco: Stanford University Press, 1967), pp. 201-3.
21. Arthur Bestor, *Backwoods Utopias: The Sectarian Origins and the Owenite Phase of Communitarian Socialism in America, 1663-1829*, 2d ed. (Philadelphia: University of Pennsylvania Press, 1978), p. 183; Ross, p. 27. Freudenberg, pp. 41-42; Conkin, pp. 130-56, 159.
22. William G. Bek. "A German Communistic Society in Missouri," *Missouri Historical Review* (October 1908):101; Randall, p. 44; Hinds, p. 111; Le Warne, pp. 158-60.
23. Andrews, *The People*, pp. 186-94.
24. Shambaugh, pp. 178-86; Hostetler, pp. 52-54, 206-8; Bennet, *Hutterian Brethren*, pp. 247-48; Lee Emerson Deets, *The Hutterites: A Study in Social Cohesion* (Philadelphia: Porcupine, 1975), pp. 38-45.
25. Pierrepont Noyes, pp. 41-48, 82-84, 104-5.
26. Donald E. Pitzer, "Patterns of Education in American Communal Societies," *Proceedings of the International Conference, Kibbutz and Communes* (Efal, Israel: Efal Press, 1985); Paul Brown, *Twelve Months in New Harmony* (Philadelphia: Porcupine, 1972), pp. 36-37, 40-42, 75, 89; Freudenberg, pp. 40, 142; Bestor, *Backwoods*, p. 193.
27. Freudenberg, pp. 140-42; Brown, pp. 36-37; Harold F. Wilson, "The North American Phalanx," *Proceedings of the New Jersey Historical Society* 70, no. 3 (July 1952):199.
28. Robert P. Sutton, "The Icarian Communities in America, 1848-1898," *Communities: Journal of Cooperation*, no. 68 (Winter 1985):45; Emile Vallet, *An Icarian Communist in Nauvoo: Commentary by Emile Vallet* (Springfield: Illinois State Historical Society, 1971), pp. 30-31; Laurence Grönlund, *The Cooperative Commonwealth*, ed. Stow Person (Cambridge, Mass.: Belknap Press of Harvard University Press, 1965), pp. 196-208.
29. On Ruskin see also Isaac Broome, *The Last Days of The Ruskin Cooperative Association* (Chicago, 1902), pp. 89-92; Burnette G. Haskell, "Kaweah—How and Why the Colony Died," *Out West* 17 (September 1902):318.
30. Conkin, p. 159.
31. Robertson, ed. *Oneida Community*, pp. 22-39, 91-93; Hinds, pp. 57, 119-26; Randall, pp. 57-72; Robert Allerton Parker, *A Yankee Saint: John Humphrey Noyes and the Oneida Community* (New York: Putnam, 1935), pp. 261-62.
32. Freudenberg, pp. 283-86; Grönlund, pp. 196-97.

33. Kanter, *Communes*, pp. 493-94; Pitzer, *"Proceedings"*; David Cnaani, *Batei Midot* (Tel Aviv: Sifriant Hapoalim, 1960), pp. 80-83 (Hebrew); Rosabeth Moss Kanter, *Commitment and Community: Communes and Utopias in Sociological Perspective* (Cambridge, Mass.: Harvard College, 1972), p. 146; Elmer T. Clark, *The Small Sects in America* (New York: Abington-Lokesburg, 1965), p. 17.
34. Hostetler, pp. 52-54, 201-20, 287-88; Bennet, *Hutterian Brethren*, pp. 247-48, 253-54; Deets, pp. 16-17; A. Khoshkish, "Decision-Making within a Communal Setting: A Case Study of Hutterite Colonies," *Communes, Historical and Contemporary*, ed. Ruth S. Cavan and Man S. Das (New Delhi: Vikas Publishing House, 1979), pp. 53-56.
35. Parker, p. 243; Ralph Albertson, *A Survey of Mutualistic Communities in America* (New York: AMS Press, 1973; 1st ed. 1936), pp. 434-35.
36. Rosabeth Moss Kanter, pp. 47-48, 99-100.
37. Robert H. Lauer and Jeanette C. Lauer, *The Spirit and the Flesh: Sex in Utopian Communities* (Metuchen, N.J.: Scarecrow Press, 1983), pp. 155-56; Egbert and Persons, eds., pp. 626-630.
38. Shaw, pp. 69, 118; John Fletcher Clews Harrison, *Quest for the New Moral World: Robert Owen and the Owenites in Britain and America* (New York: Scribner's, 1969), p. 190; Conkin, p. 74; Egbert and Persons, pp. 631-36.
39. Kirby, pp. 102-5, 118-20; John Sullivan Dwight, quoted in Henry W. Sams, ed., *Autobiography of Brook Farm* (Englewood Cliffs, N.J.: Prentice-Hall, 1959), pp. 219-20; Sutton, p. 46; Charles Pierre Le Warne, p. 162; Bek, pp. 71-72; Katherine Burton, pp. 81, 224; Michael E. Dermody and Robert V. Hine, "California's Socialist Utopias," *Communities: Journal of Cooperation*, no. 68 (Winter 1985): p. 67; John Sullivan Dwight, "Music as a Means of Culture," *Atlantic Monthly* 26 (July-December 1870):321-31, quoted in Sams, ed., pp. 219-20.
40. Shalom Wurm, *Communal Societies and Their Way of Life* (Tel Aviv: Ayanoth, 1968), p. 334 (Hebrew); Marianne Dwight, *Letters From Brook Farm, 1844-1847* (New York: AMS Press, 1974; 1st ed. 1928), p. 88; Hostetler, pp. 166-73, 249; Delburn Carpenter, *The Radical Pietists: Celibate Communal Societies Established in the United States before 1820* (New York: AMS Press, 1975), pp. 217-18; Kanter, p. 100.
41. Ross, pp. 34, 40. For the special dress of the women (Bloomers) see "American Communes," *American Socialist* 2 no. 37 (September 13, 1877); Codman, p. 134; Le Warne, p. 162.
42. Stephen A. Marini, "Hymnody in the Religious Communal Societies of Early America," *Communal Societies* 2 (Autumn 1982):2-21; Daniel W. Patterson, "Shaker Music," *Communal Studies* 2 (Autumn 1982):54-63; Anna White and Leila S. Taylor, *Shakerism: Its Meaning and Message* (Columbus, Oh.: Heer, 1904. New York: AMS Press, 1971), pp. 329-40; Pitzer and Elliott, pp. 290-91; Sachse, pp. 128-65; Parker, pp. 244-52; Egbert and Persons, pp. 196, 625-36; Hostetler, *Hutterite Society*, pp. 169-72; Lauer and Lauer, p. 162.
43. Julia Neal, *By Their Fruits: The Story of Shakerism in South Union, Kentucky* (New York: North Carolina Press, 1947), pp. 256-57; Karl J.R. Arndt, pp. 250-60; Donald Macdonald, *The Diaries of, 1824-1826* (Clifton: Kelley, 1973; 1st ed. 1942), p. 250; John Sullivan Dwight, pp. 321-31, quoted in Sams, ed., pp. 219-20; Parker, pp. 241-53; White and Taylor, p. 340; "American

Communities,'' *American Socialist* 2, no. 38 (September 20, 1877):297. On the orchestra at Aurora see *Oregon Historical Quarterly* (Fall 1978):233-69.

44. Melcher, pp. 218-23; White and Taylor, pp. 329, 340; Neal, pp. 67-68.
45. Dane Kennedy, ''The Kaweah Colony'' (Honors thesis, University of California at Berkeley, 1973; located in Bancroft Library), p. 37; Codman, pp. 105-6; ''American Communities,'' *American Socialist* 2, no. 38 (September 9, 1877), p. 297; Ralph Waldo Emerson, ''Historic Notes of Life and Letters in New England'' (in part). First published in the *Atlantic Monthly*, October 1883; here reprinted from the Complete Works of Ralph Waldo Emerson, ed. R.L. Rusk (Boston: Houghton Mifflin, 1904), vol. 10, pp. 359-69, quoted in Sams, ed., pp. 225-26.

21

The Family and Women's Status in the Communes

The Family and the Commune: Adverse or Congruous Entities?

In 1870, John Humphrey Noyes wrote a comprehensive book, *History of American Socialism*, the first history of the communes in the United States. The author stated affirmatively that one of the most important factors that contributed to the commune's stability and to its longevity was the abolishment of the monogamous family and the subordination of the relationships between the sexes to communal principles. He reinforced his argument by naming a number of long-living communes which had practiced celibacy and by relating the case of Oneida, where the "complex marriage" had substituted the monogamous system. Noyes claimed that any communal experiment that maintained the family unit was doomed because of the inherent dichotomy that divides these social nuclei: "The highest ideal of a successful community requires that it should be a complete nursery of human beings, doing for them all that the old family-home has done, and a great deal more."[1]

Four years later Charles Nordhoff wrote a book on the same subject, *The Communistic Societies of the United States*. In it he summed up his impressions after a visit to fifteen of the then existing communes. In his conclusions he delicately refuted Noyes's assumptions on the status of the family in the communes, saying:

> It is also commonly said that all the communistic societies in this country oppose the family life, and that in general they advocate some abnormal relations of the sexes, which they make a fundamental part of their communistic plan. This, too, is an error. Of all the communes I am now considering only the Perfectionists of Oneida and Wallingford have established what can be fairly called unnatural sexual relations. At Icaria, Amana, Aurora, Bethel, and Zoar the family relation is held in honor and each family has its own separate household. . . . It seems to me a fair deduction from the facts, that neither religious fanaticism nor an unnatural sexual relation . . . is necessary to the successful prosecution of a communistic experiment.[2]

When writing this he did not know that at the same time the first group of Hutterites was setting foot on the shores of the United States. This was the beginning of the largest, most stable and prosperous of all the communal movements in the United States. It would prove him right in his claim that the abolishment of the family unit was not necessarily a guarantee of longivity. Later researchers and writers who wrote on the communes in the New World did not repeat Noyes's allegations. Even William Hinds, who had been a member of Oneida and one of its functionaries, claimed in the last chapter of his book that "successful Communism is not dependent on any single theory of the sexual relation, monogamous communities having been as prosperous as the celibate ones, and those favoring complex marriage as prosperous as those holding to monogamy."[3]

The deliberations on the position of the family in the commune are not arbitrary or groundless. Researchers from different schools of thought have come to the conclusion that the family and the commune are a contradiction in terms (mutually contradictory). The family, as an emotional focus anchored in biological relationships, is a centrifugal force which fosters selfishness and undermines the commune.[4]

Noyes's opinions on the polarity between family and commune are rooted in ancient thought. Plato dealt with the problem while discussing the communal system planned for the guardians in *The Republic*. He claimed that the monogamous family strengthened the concept of private property and was unsuitable for those who identified with the common interest. In one of the dialogues (*The Republic*, book V) Socrates proposes the community of wives and children as the source of the greater good for the state and claims that the community of families will make the guardians more true to their task of caring for the common good.

Later philosophers, too, came close to adopting Plato's ideas. Among the classical utopians Thomaso Campagnella's *Civita Solis* was the most extreme in this attitude toward the family. Modern utopians such as Robert Owen and Charles Fourier dealt with the question of the family, and each in his own way proposed measures to curtail monogamy. They hoped to enhance family relationships with a new significance within the harmonious society of the future they had envisioned.[5] Some reinforcement to those theories that point out the unbridgeable polarity between the family and the commune may be found in communal experiments throughout history—beginning with the Essenes, who lived a celibate life on the shore of the Dead Sea, continuing with groups of hermits in the Orient and orders of monks in the Middle Ages, and finally the extreme heretical movements like the Adamites, until the first celibate communes in the United States.

Karl Kautsky in his book, *Communism in Central Europe in the Time of*

Reformation, deals with communism in the cloisters and heretic sects and makes a distinction between "Communism in the means of production" which is "compatible with separate family life" and "common property in the articles of consumption," stating that "Communism in articles of consumption . . . leads to a certain hostility to separate family life, and necessarily also to a certain dislike to individual marriage." With the same approach Kautsky treats communism in the heretical sects, pointing out that "the economic basis of heretical communism is the same as the monastery, viz. a community of the household," thus giving place to similarities, one of which "is their aversion to marriage."[6]

A contemporary sociologist Rosabeth Moss Kanter deals with the unbridgeable polarity between family and commune. She regards the family as a set of emotional interrelationships that compete with communal affiliations and prevent their crystallization. As a result of the data compiled in her studies, Kanter arrives at the conclusion that successful communes, those which survived longer than one generation, had weakened family loyalties.[7] She thus reinforces Noyes's theory on the causes for commune survival.

Generations come and go but the controversy on the nature of the relationship between family and commune remains. No "liberating formula" has been discovered to abolish their polarity or make them complementary. But even if no generalization has been achieved, many concrete and diverse answers have been given to solve the concrete problems which the communes encountered along their way. Some of these were solutions to problems on both ends of the dichotomy—the family and the commune. But most of the solutions were a compromise between ideology and vision—a sort of modus vivendi on the one hand and reality as dictated by life on the other, which may exclude persistent theorizing but enable the communes to cope with it.

The history of the communes in the United States points to a diversity of arrangements regarding the status of the family within them. Only a minority abolished the family unit, whether by adopting celibacy and monasticism or as in the case of Oneida by complex marriages. In most communes the monogamous family was maintained under the supervision, to some extent, of the commune's institutions. There is no justification for identifying one kind with success and the other with failure. In contrast to the longevity of the celibate communes such as Harmony or the Shakers, we may point to the longevity of the Hutterites who have maintained the monogamous family unit all along. The short-lived socialist communes can be compared with the transient esoteric, religious communes that soon disappeared without leaving a trace. The diversified historical experience of the American communes shows that there is no undisputable basis for Noyes's theory that to ensure the survival and longevity of a commune it is imperative to abolish the monogamous family. On the other hand, all the communes that maintained the nuclear family were compelled to seek ways to adapt the traditional family structure to the social and economic structure of the commune.

These theoretical deliberations about the feasibility of a symbiosis between family and commune raise the question whether the abolishment of the nuclear family would not be more consistent with the substantial needs of the communes. Should we regard the existence of the family as a compromise impelled by reality? The history of communes that abolished the family indicates that most of them had a common denominator, namely, their being religious. Moreover, a thorough examination of the motivations for the abolishment of the family in the communes points to a direct linkage between their religious outlook and the appearance of this tendency.

A study of the process that led the first communes to abolish the nuclear family by adopting celibacy and a monastic way of life shows that in all of them (Ephrata, the Shakers, Harmony, Zoar) their organizing as communes was preceded by a period in which celibacy was extolled as the highest level of Christian purity. This doctrine was deeply anchored in Christian theology and was inspired by chapters in the New Testament that dealt with the superiority of spirit over flesh, sexual ascetism, and the inferior status of marriage.[8] They advocated the exalted state of life according to Jesus Christ in which all family ties had been severed: "And everyone who has left houses or brothers or sisters or father or mother or children or lands, for my name's sake, will receive a hundred-fold and inherit eternal life" (Matthew, 19/29). In those communes it was not the communal experience that caused the abolishment of the family, but rather their religious convictions.

These prompted Oneida to adopt the complex marriage system, which was founded on the New Testament's attitudes toward the family and marriage, especially in regard to the kingdom of heaven where, "Those who are accounted worthy to attain to that age and to the resurrection from the dead neither mourning nor are given in marriage" (Luke, 20/35). Noyes, the religious leader of Oneida, interpreted this not as a ban on sexual relations but as a negation of the monogamous marriage. Instead of a celibate community, they established one based on love and sexual relations free from the one-sided, selfish ties, that also flowed impartially between all the members of what they considered as a "holy community."[9] Oneidans believed that they were living in the kingdom of heaven on earth, that when they had renounced all selfish sexual relations they had been assured of salvation and cleansed of sin through their perfectionist doctrine. Religion was a cornerstone on which their way of life was based and an imperative for all who wanted to join Oneida. When religion of the young generation had been undermined, the first schism appeared in the complex family system and the process of returning to the monogamous family was excelerated.

In addition to religious motives there are psychological, sociological, and economic ones. The phenomenon of joining a commune in which there were no monogamous families must be seen on the background of the prevailing atmosphere of the American society in the eighteenth and nineteenth centuries. The communes were a haven for quite a few people, but mainly women, who had not been absorbed by the antagonistic, competitive society which was centered around the fortress of family unit.[10] However, even those who regarded the commune as a haven for their personal problems discovered the way via their religious experience and motivation.

Among the different motivations that kept people in "unfamilistic" communes, those directly concerned with the existence of the commune are negligible. Only a few cases are known in which the transition to celibacy, or to the abolishment of the monogamous family, were caused by economic or social imperatives of the commune.[11] In most communes reviewed here, the rational and emotional motivation that prompted people to join an unfamilistic commune was their religious belief, especially their concept of the superiority of spirit over flesh and celibacy over marriage. This doctrine was accompanied by religious sanctions that may have given those communes an inner strength that enabled them to survive in spite of their ineptitude to human needs. Presumably, this religiously inspired strength was the secret of their longevity rather than the suitability to the communal imperatives.

The potency of the religious doctrine in abolishing the nuclear family may be realized when compared with the socialist communes, in which criticism of the family institution and the monogamous family was also rife. Robert Owen, in his description of the private property system, was outspoken in his criticism of the monogamous family as being rooted in the laws of private property and sanctioned by the church. In his vision of the future society he outlined various ways to liberate family relations from the bondage of private property and religious sanctions. He hoped to reestablish the family within a free system of interpersonal relationship in a communitarian community. Reality in New Harmony, however, was significantly different. Those who joined the commune in Indiana were ready to change the system of production and property but objected to any far-reaching changes in their family relationships. When slanderous gossip accused them of sexual excesses, the leaders of New Harmony published denials in the *New Harmony Gazette* and praised the stability of the family institution on the commune.[12]

Charles Fourier undermined the sanctity of the monogamous family in his theories and claimed that the family in *civilization* (his term for the capitalist system) was adverse to man's nature and his social destiny. He accused it of having a harmful, alienating impact and even though he never proposed the total abolition of the institute of marriage he estimated that it would fade away within the harmonious society of the phalanxes. Fourier's followers in the

United States criticized the family as fostering antagonism, but blunted the extremist elements of this criticism because they realized these might cause opposition within the American society. Reality in the many Fourierist phalanxes echoed only to some extent even the moderate criticism of the family relations pronounced by American followers. Nothing different occurred in the family setup on the phalanxes which could express a divergent approach in the spirit of Fourierist criticism. While the Owenist and Fourierist communes raised the theoretical problem of the family, all other socialist communes avoided even wondering about it. The monogamous nucleur-family unit was adopted without qualm. In Icaria the stability of family life was a principle and as such it was incorporated within the community's constitution from the beginning.[13]

The same objections to marriage and the monogamous family were voiced in the 1870s when adherents of free love joined Oneida and several other socialist communes. One group joined Ruskin and caused disputes that raised a storm but never managed to alter the family institution on the commune. Altogether, the advocates of free love did not manage to gain a foothold in American communes. In spite of their negligible influence, they evoked gossip and slander that accused most communes, socialist and religious, of practicing free love and sexual excesses. Even some of the very conservative communes were not spared.[14] This hearsay was partly prompted by hostility toward the communal idea, but also by neighbors who did not grasp the meaning of communal existence. In their wild imagination they connected communal property with the sharing of partners and sexual promiscuity. This attitude was one aspect of the alienation between the communes and their environment.

Most of the religious communes established after the 1840s had a normal family life (except for Oneida). Amana, which had the same background as Harmony and other communes in the eighteenth century, was motivated by a theology that supported the moral superiority of celibacy. However, the realistic approach of its founders prompted them to maintain the family and thereby ensure their growth and survival. The result was ambivalent, on the one hand they preferred celibacy and the single state, on the other most of them did get married, even though they realized that they were lowering their moral standards. In Beth-El, Aurora, and the Christian Commonwealth there were no deliberations on the family institution. The Hutterites regarded the monogamous patriarchal family as an integral element of the commune rooted in the historic past of the sect's theology.[15]

So far we have pointed out the variegated arrangements in regard to the family-commune relationships. Beyond this variety there was another element common to communes—the objective necessity to adapt the functions of the nuclear family to the communal society. This adaptation took place in both kinds of communes, in those that abolished the nuclear family and in those that maintained it.[16] The communes that abolished the family took over most of their functions (except bearing of children in the celibate communes). Most used a family-based terminology to define their communal relationships. The Shakers called their units *family* and their members *brothers* and *sisters*, their spiritual leader Ann Lee was *Mother Ann*. The members of Harmony were the *large family*, and in Oneida family terms were adopted in all areas—the economic, intimate, emotional, consumer, educational, while fostering the *feeling of home* among all members.[17] In communes that maintained the nuclear family, the functions were divided according to their characteristics, ideology, and level of communitarianism.

The division of educational functions between the family and commune was dealt with in the previous chapter. We now concern ourselves with further aspects that are also the outcome of the family-commune relationships as, for example, the planning of the settlement.

The communal societies had to be constructed from scratch, and much thought was invested in the planning. Commune members had no ancestors they could consult with, and it was impossible to copy blueprints and methods from the outside world without harming the communal characteristics. Nevertheless, there did not exhibit much originality. In most cases they adopted a unique combination of the commonly-used housing plans of their area or their former homeland (the Shakers used New England houses and the typical German village houses prevailed in Harmony, Zoar, and Amana). These were combined with construction methods that the commune's ideology and necessity demanded.[18]

Many problems faced the planners of communes; the cardinal one was how much space to devote to the public institutions and how much to the accommodation of families and singles. Every commune needed a series of public buildings, the religious ones for their ceremonies, and the others for meetings and social gatherings. They also needed kitchens, dining-rooms, laundries, stores, etc. These buildings had to be carefully planned to be functional and efficient for their communal purposes. They had to combine the advantages of public buildings with the comfort and needs of the individual. It was a complicated undertaking that entailed experience and wisdom.

The Shakers constructed large and spacious buildings that provided their growing numbers with accommodation as well as dining-room and public meeting places. The living quarters as well as the public rooms and workshops were meticulously clean and functional. This did in no way harm their aestheticity, according to the Shakers' concept of "beauty in simplicity." Every aspect of private or public life was carefully thought out and planned with comfort and efficiency in mind. Shaker planning was a successful combination of public and private needs.[19]

Oneida established its community within a single impressive mansion. Its construction continued throughout the years of the commune's existence and much effort was invested in it. There was no unity in the large building with its magnificent exterior. It was a kind of architectural record of their development. Every wing represented a stage in Oneida's social, cultural, and economic development. The mansion combined all the communities' functions—halls for public meetings, a theater with stalls, and a spacious dining-hall. Small living rooms were surrounded by members' accommodations in accordance with their system of the complex family. The children's quarters were in a separate wing and their life was divided between all the other wings of the mansion. Long corridors connected the rooms and the various wings and were additional places where members would meet. The wings formed a patio that served the open air gatherings. The architectural concept of the Oneidan mansion differed completely from the simplicity of the Shakers', but both served the same purpose: to provide a family home for a commune in which there were no nuclear families.[20]

The family communes had to tackle similar problems when they planned their settlement. They had to adapt their houses to the needs of nuclear families and to those of the communal services and each came up with different solutions. This variety originated in the conditions of each settlement, its population, and unique ideological convictions. The Fourierist settlement started out in small provisional houses but those which survived (Brook Farm, The North American Phalanx, and the Wisconsin Phalanx) constructed a large central building on the principle of the phalanxes, which combined accommodation as well as dining- and social meeting halls.[21]

The socialist commune Icaria, after settling in Iowa, built modest, standard wooden family houses and a central dining-hall for all. Most of the socialist communes established in the late nineteenth and early twentieth centuries did the same. They all constructed a central dining-room that served the whole community and after they prospered they constructed public and social meeting halls to accommodate their cultural activities (e.g. Llano had a dance hall). Adjacent to the small family houses most communes built larger ones for singles, temporary residents, and for families whose houses had not yet been constructed.[22]

On the religious family communes there was a larger variety of constructions for individuals and the public. The Hutterites introduced a standard plan for their settlements. The communal dining-hall was surrounded by five to six semi-attached or terraced family houses. In the seven Amana settlements large family houses were built that could also accommodate two to three smaller families under one roof. Several families shared one dining-room and kitchen. There were about fifteen such kitchens and dining-rooms on every Amana settlement. In Zoar, Beth-El, and Aurora only the singles, widows, widowers, and temporary residents shared a communal dining-room. Families lived in separate houses and ate at home. Provisions were distributed from a central communal store.[23]

The architectural planning of a communal settlement entailed different solutions to the typical problems of the commune, namely, that of integrating the private space within the public-communitarian one. Communes that had abolished the family adopted centralized accommodations that also combined public and service institutions under one roof. On the family communes housing was decentralized and much thought had to be invested in creating a connection between the public and private sectors. The proportion of the investments in public buildings versus private housing reflected the spirit of internal social relations, whereas emphasis on public buildings contributed to the social morale (for example, the collective efforts invested in the construction of the phalanstery in the Fourierist settlements). The various communal settlements contributed to the planning of settlements with utopian aspirations in architecture as well as in the problems they revealed.

Integral communal consumption prevailed in all the communes that had abolished the family. Oneida, the Shakers, Harmony, and Ephrata all had adopted the principle that clothing and furniture were communal property meant for the use of the individual. In the celibate communes, where total equality prevailed, this principle was meticulously carried out. On Oneida, however, there was great openness to the individual's needs and tastes. Committees were elected to deal with problems of consumption. They prepared an annual budget and took care to divide everything equally, according to workers' needs and the commune's economic possibilities.[24]

The variety of housing methods adopted by the family communes was also apparent in the variety of consumer systems that reflected the private versus the public needs. There were different attitudes toward the character of the kitchen and dining-room, hence the scope of communal services differed. This also included the norms of private property as regarding clothes and furniture. In the socialist communes it was customary for families to retain their belonging throughout their stay on the commune. There was no strict rule as to the handing over of private property. Wherever family houses were built, private vegetable and fruit gardening was agreed upon. (The private vineyards in Icaria caused disputes between the young members who supported total equality and the older ones who were more tolerant).[25]

In the religious commune all private property was handed over to the commune. In some of them the families could keep their personal belongings. In all family communes there was a budget for the purchase of private items that belonged to the family. These were passed on to the next generation in long-living communes. The Hutterites' arrangement was typical for this kind of commune. The family constituted a consumer's unit with regard to clothing or family furniture. However, their modest and single way of life prevented a significant accumulation of family property. In all family communes there was a tendency to expand public services such as the collective purchase of clothing, a central sewing shop for repairs, and a laundry to free women from chores so that they could be available for the general work roster.[26]

Women's Status on the Communes

When the functions of the family were partially taken over by the commune it brought about a significant change in women's status. On most communes they were relieved of their household chores and child care. Many of them now had the option to join communal production side by side with the men. Simultaneously, tasks such as preparing food and serving it, house work and cleaning jobs, and making and laundrying clothes were regarded as service jobs and were performed by men and women. There was less differentiation between men's and women's jobs compared with the outside world, and flexibility of work allocation allowed for vocational mobility. This was usually also anchored in the commune's religious and secular outlook, which elevated women's status compared with the attitudes in the external society. This approach was shared by all socialistic communes and by most of the religious ones.[27] Those communes that had abolished the monogamous family devoted much thought to the problem of the equal status of women. On the communes which had adopted celibacy (Ephrata, the Shakers, Harmony, and others) men and women enjoyed equal status in the communal daily life. The most outstanding example were the Shakers, for whom women's equal status was a basic principle of their theology—Ann Lee was the woman Messiah and the female incarnation of the Messiah. Her heritage granted women equality in religious matters, and this naturally dictated equality in all areas of life. One man and one woman were put in charge of all the commune's affairs, whether religious, economic, or social. This outlook of equal status did not necessarily mean an equal identity of the sexes. The Shakers, who rejected any kind of sexuality and femininity, tried to disguise them by all means of clothing and appearance. Having been liberated from private household chores and from child care, Shaker women were free to devote as much time as men to spiritual and religious affairs. They were equal partners in the religious and spiritual experiences of the community. (During the "spiritualist" period of the Shakers women were more involved than men.[28])

In Oneida, where the complex marriage system had been adopted, there occurred the most radical change in women's status. They were given the biggest chance to be equally involved in various activities. From the early years women worked at all jobs. They worked on construction jobs, on the farm, and even in industry. Oneida maintained strict rotation and there was no differentiation between men's and women's work. While women performed "male jobs," men took over household chores, cooking, dishwashing, laundry, and cleaning. To make work easier they installed a steam engine in the laundry and boilers in the kitchen. One of the members even "invented" what was equivalent to a dishwashing machine. Men and women were fully integrated not only at work but also in all social activities such as participating and voting at public meetings. Women were well educated and actively involved in cultural activities and in publishing. They also took part in sports.

The living spirit behind this equality, which enriched Oneida, was its spiritual leader John Humphrey Noyes. He regarded the complete integration of both sexes in every aspect of the communal experience as a spiritual objective and social vision.[29] Noyes believed that this interrelationship would be realized if men and women not only worked together but approached each other while minimizing their different characteristics. Their mutual criticism contributed much to their closeness, to which women in Oneida gave expression via their clothing. They wore short dresses and "bloomers" that enabled them to move and work freely. Their short haircut also lessened their conventional feminine appearance.

Sexual and family relations on Oneida, as well as the status of women, aroused curiosity and gossip outside. Visitors would question the women and they would answer that they were content with their special status and rights and felt equal partners to men. However, there were also some who admitted that they doubted the feasibility of full equality. In fact, the Achilles' heel of Oneida was the paradox between the wide options and equality that were granted to women socially and at work, and their leader's Pauline-Christian outlook concerning the spiritual superiority of man and the inferiority of woman. In the spirit of this doctrine there existed in Oneida a hierarchical leadership with a man—Noyes himself—at the top. At the same time, on the lower level men and women were chosen regardless of sex and according to merit. There were some women whose spirituality was regarded as being higher than any man's. Still, the social system in Oneida was generally stamped with male superiority. This was uniquely expressed in their method of sexual relations, the core of which was "male continence." Perusing Oneida's literature, one may infer that women did not openly resent their relative inferiority. They enjoyed many advantages, whether at work and their spiritual development or their equality in choosing a partner for sex. Compared with the status of women outside the commune this was expedient. The general impression was that women were content. But in time, especially during its final years, there appeared hints in several journals testifying to a "women's underground" and their discontent with the existing system. They aspired to return to the traditional family ways and the force of this trend may be inferred from the enthusiasm with which they returned to the monogamous family in 1879.[30]

On the socialist communes the principle of equal rights for women was embraced by all. We have pointed out the utopian socialists' criticism of the monogamous family. This went together with stressing the need to raise the status of women to that of men. The strength of their conviction differed. While Fourier was radical and the first to use the concept of *feminism*,[31] Cabet was more conservative as to the family and woman's status in society, and the American Grönlund, compromised. He proposed to maintain the monogamous family but to abolish the element of economic dependence. He also supported the differentiation of work, claiming that there were significant physiological and mental distinctions between the sexes.[32] In realizing their vision, all socialist communes seriously attempted to grant equal status to women, whether at work or in society. Variations existed in the ways that this aspiration was materialized.

Icaria was the most conservative regarding the family and women's status. For many years women did not have the right to vote: this was achieved only in the 1870s, after a prolonged fight by the young radicals. On the other hand, the Fourierist communes—Brook Farm, the North American Phalanx—granted women full equality and they actively participated in most farm and industrial work. In all the other socialist communes, women had equal rights on their being accepted as members and could vote. There were, however, different local practices regarding their integration into work. In Kaweah, for example, the harsh pioneering conditions during their period in the work camps, while constructing the mountain road, offered the women a chance to participate in every kind of work. They even surpassed men in their devotion to fill the daily quota.[33]

In contrast to the ideological commitment to grant equal rights to women on the socialist communes, there were distinctions on the religious ones. All religious family communes were somewhat ambivalent. They had adopted the Pauline doctrine that women were spiritually inferior, and in most of them women could not vote. But they were considered equals in all other matters and were full partners with their men. An example is the inspirationalists of Amana, who believed that the Holy Ghost could also dwell in a woman. For many years Barbara Heinemann was served as the most authoritarian *Werkzeug* of the community. In general women could not be in charge of daily affairs whether on the local or the federative level. They were not granted the vote in public meetings and sat separately. At work they maintained a professional differentiation. Women did the service jobs—in the kitchen, children's houses, and household—and only seldom participated in easy manufacturing jobs. This was also the case on the Hutterite communes, where the large families were of a patriarchal nature. Women participated in meetings but did not have the right to vote, nor were they candidates for central roles. However, the Hutterian women were very active in local affairs, creating public opinion, criticisms, and raising complaints. Their indirect influence on all discussions and decisions was great.[34]

Beyond these different approaches to the principle of women's equality on religious and social communes, there was in all communes an objective reality that made it possible for women to be integrated in the community's life more than women in the outside society. Nevertheless, women were not equally involved even in those socialist communes that had granted them equal rights. Recent studies on the status of women in the historic communes clearly show that in everyday life women did not have equality in choosing their occupations. These studies mainly dealt with the allocation of duties and jobs on those communes considered most equalitarian—Oneida, Brook Farm, the North American Phalanx, and the socialist communes of the late nineteenth century.

It is evident from these studies that most of the workers in the service jobs—cooking, clothing, and cleaning and child care—were women. At the same time men constituted a vast majority in farming and industrial jobs, and even if women worked in those branches they did secondary and easier jobs. This differentiation also prevailed in managerial jobs. No women were to be found in executive jobs of administration and production, or as representatives of their commune. A few held managerial positions in educational, cultural, and social jobs. Furthermore, a bigger effort was invested in transferring women to manufacturing "male jobs" than getting men to do "women's work." This was mainly achieved through women's initiatives and justified those who claimed that male hegemony was the prevailing trend and women were supposed to adapt to men rather than vice versa. Job equality was not a mutual aspiration.[35]

In spite of these drawbacks, we can still say that the status of women on communes was higher than the average in most American communities of that time. It was no coincidence that the women who were actively involved with the movement for women's rights—Francis Wright and Margaret Fuller—were involved with the communes. It was characteristic that none of them actively joined a commune because they felt hampered by the limited scope of the communes. These were too narrow for their aspiration to change society as a whole.

The contribution of the communes to the equality of women and change in the status of the monogamous family was not in its direct influence on the general society but rather in the internal modifications that took place there. The communes served as a kind of live laboratory. A certain importance should also be ascribed to the example they set for an alternative life style and for exposing the options for different family relations.

Notes

1. John Humphrey Noyes, *History of American Socialism* (1870). Reprinted as *Strange Cults and Utopias of Nineteenth-Century America* (New York: Dover Publications, 1966), pp. 139-49; Charles Nordhoff, *The Communistic Societies of the United States* (New York: Shocken, 1965), pp. 388-89.
2. Ibid., pp. 388-89.
3. William Alfred Hinds, *American Communities and Cooperative Colonies* 1878. (Reprinted and enl. Philadelphia: Porcupine, 1975), p. 592; Ralph Albertson, *A Survey of Mutualistic Communities in America* (New York: AMS Press, 1973; 1st ed. 1936), p. 428.
4. David Cnaani, *Batei Medot: Essays on Communal Life* (Tel Aviv: Sifriat Hapoalim, 1960), p. 55 (Hebrew); Yonina Talmon-Gerber, *Individual and Society in the Kibbutz* (Jerusalem: Hebrew University Press, 1970), pp. 15, 19-20 (Hebrew).
5. Yanina Mailer, *La Doctrine de Charles Fourier* (Tel Aviv: Sifriat Hapoalim, with Tel Aviv University Press, 1974), pp. 62-65 (Hebrew); Plato, *The Republic*, Book V; Tommaso Campanella, "The City of the Sun," in *The Quest for Utopia*, ed. Glenn Megley and J. Max Patrick (College Park, Md.: MaGrath, 1971), pp. 329-34; Gideon Freudenberg, *Robert Owen: Educator of the People* (Tel Aviv: Dvir, 1970), pp. 145, 147, 202-3. (Hebrew); John Fletcher Clews Harrison, *Quest for the New Moral World: Robert Owen and the Owenites in Britain and America* (New York: Scribner's, 1969), pp. 59-62, 145, 202-3.
6. Carl Kautsky, *Communism in Central Europe in the Time of Reformation* (Tel Aviv: Russel & Russel, 1959), pp. 13-16.
7. Robert H. Lauer and Jeanette C. Lauer, *The Spirit and the Flesh: Sex in Utopian Communities* (Metuchen, N.J.: Scarecrow Press, 1983), p. 132; Rosabeth Moss Kanter, *Commitment and Community: Communes and Utopias in Sociological Perspective* (Cambridge, Mass.: Harvard University Press, 1972), pp. 89-91; Lewis A. Coser, *Greedy Institutions: Patterns of Undivided Commitment* (New York: Free Press, 1974), pp. 136-49.
8. Delburn Carpenter, *The Radical Pietists: Celibate Communal Societies Established in the United States before 1820* (New York: AMS Press, 1975), pp. 72, 81, 241-42; Henri Desroche, *The American Shakers: From Neo-Christianity to Pre-Socialism*, ed. and trans. John K. Savacoal (Boston: University of Massachusetts Press, 1971), pp. 139, 157-68; Karl J.R. Arndt, *George Rapp's Harmony Society, 1785-1847*, rev. ed. (New York: Associated University Presses, 1972), pp. 97-98, 417-20; Raymond Lee Muncy, *Sex and Marriage in Utopian Communities: Nineteenth-Century America* (Bloomington: Indiana University Press, 1973), p. 17; Cnaani, p. 59; Rom. 1:4-8; 1 Cor. 7:4-32, 29; Luke 20:27-40; Mark 12:25.
9. Constance Noyes Robertson, ed., *Oneida Community: An Autobiography, 1851-1876* (Syracuse: Syracuse University Press, 1971), pp. 265-68; Robert Allerton Parker, *A Yankee Saint: John Humphrey Noyes and the Oneida Community* (New York: Putnam, 1935), pp. 44, 56. Lawrence Foster, *Religion and Sexuality: Three American Communal Experiments of the Nineteenth Century* (New York: Oxford University Press, 1981), pp. 16, 81; Muncy, p. 165.
10. Louis J. Kern, *An Ordered Love: Sex Roles and Sexuality in Victorian Utopias—The Shakers, The Mormons, and the Oneida Community* (Chapel Hill: University

of North Carolina Press, 1981), pp. 292-95, 311-13; John Humphrey Noyes, pp. 624-33; Parker, pp. 115-17, 177-78, 280; Foster, p. 120; *Handbook of the Oneida Community 1867 & 1971*. Bound with *Mutual Criticism* (New York: AMS Press, 1976. Reprinted from 1867 edition. Wallingford, Conn.), pp. 49-58 Muncy, pp. 10-11.

11. *Zoar: An Ohio Experiment in Communalism* (Columbus, Oh.: The Ohio Historical Society, 1972); Muncy, p. 28.
12. Carol A. Kolmerten, "Unconscious Sexual Stereotyping in Utopia," in *Utopias: The American Experience*, ed. Gairdner Moment and Otto F. Kraushaar (Metuchen, N.J.: Scarecrow Press, 1980), pp. 72-76; Muncy, pp. 13, 54-57, 60-63; Freudenberg, pp. 145-147.
13. Lauer and Lauer, pp. 76-77, 123, 127-30; Muncy, pp. 68-70, 72-73, 86-88, 110-12, 118-20; Mailer, pp. 62-65.
14. John Egerton, *Visions of Utopia: Nashoba, Rugby, Ruskin, and the New Communities in Tennessee's Past* (Knoxville: University of Tennessee Press, with the Tennessee Historical Commission), pp. 77-78; Isaac Broome, *The Last Days of the Ruskin Cooperative Association* (Chicago: 1902), p. 123; Lauer and Lauer, p. 188; Muncy, pp. 119, 197-214.
15. Bertha M.H. Shambaugh, *Amana That Was and Amana That Is* (Iowa City: Iowa State Historical Society, 1932), pp. 117-25; John A. Hostetler, *Hutterite Society* (Baltimore: Johns Hopkins University Press, 1977), pp. 145, 201-6; Jonathan G. Andelson, "Living the Mean: The Ethos, Practice, and Genius of Amana," *Communities: Journal of Cooperation*, no. 68 (Winter 1985):37; Muncy, pp. 97-101.
16. Rosabeth Moss Kanter, *Communes: Creating and Managing the Collective Life* (New York: Harper & Row, 1973), pp. 279-300.
17. Marguerite Fellows Melcher, *The Shaker Adventure* (New York: The Shaker Museum, 1975), p. 147; Donald Egbert and Stow Persons, eds., *Socialism and American Life*, 2 vols. (Princeton: Princeton University Press, 1952), pp. 144-46; Pierrepont Noyes, *My Father's House: An Oneida Boyhood* (London: J. Murray, 1937), pp. 8-9; Lauer and Lauer, p. 218; Desroche, pp. 174-78; Foster, pp. 107-10.
18. Dolores Hayden, *Seven American Utopias: The Architecture of Communitarian Socialism, 1790-1975* (Cambridge, Mass.: MIT Press, 1976), pp. 34-35.
19. Edward D. Andrews, *The People Called Shakers: A Search for Perfect Society* (New York: Dover, 1963), p. 127; Hayden, pp. 76-92, 100-101.
20. Hayden, pp. 202-19.
21. Ibid., pp. 164-74; Muncy, p. 75.
22. Muncy, pp. 118-21; Hayden, pp. 289-310; *Cooperator* (December 19, 1898); Robert V. Hine, *California's Utopian Colonies* (New Haven: Yale University Press, 1966), p. 70.
23. Lee Emerson Deets, *The Hutterites: A Study in Social Cohesion* (Philadelphia: Porcupine, 1975), pp. 11-12; Shambaugh, pp. 135-36; Hayden, pp. 242-51; Muncy, pp. 100, 106-7; Cnaani, pp. 64-66.
24. Anna White and Leila S. Taylor, *Shakerism: Its Meaning and Message* (Columbus, Oh.: Heer, 1904. New York AMS Press, 1971), p. 305; Kanter, *Commitment*, pp. 94-95.
25. Charles Pierre Le Warne, *Utopias on Puget Sound, 1885-1915* (Seattle: University of Washington Press, 1975), pp. 92-94, 153; Paul K. Conkin, *Two Paths to*

Utopia: The Hutterites and the Llano Colony (Lincoln: University of Nebraska Press, 1964), pp. 152-54; Hine, pp. 69-70; John Humphrey Noyes, p. 431; Broome, pp. 79-84; Egerton, p. 68.

26. W.R. Perkins and B.L. Wick, *History of the Amana Society*, Historical Monograph, no. 1 (Iowa City: State University of Iowa Publications, 1891), p. 70; Emilius O. Randall, *History of the Zoar Society: A Sociological Study in Communism* (New York: AMS Press, 1971; 1st ed. 1904), p. 32; William G. Bek, "A German Communistic Society in Missouri," *Missouri Historical Review* (October 1908): 68, 104; "American Communities," *American Socialist* 2, no. 39 (September 27, 1877):306; Cnaani, pp. 64-66, 68; Nordhoff, p. 38; Hinds, pp. 116-17, 322, 338; Shambaugh, pp. 105-6, 353; Hostetler, pp. 190-94; Albertson, pp. 430-31.
27. Donald E. Pitzer and Josephine M. Elliott, "New Harmony's First Utopians," *Indiana Magazine of History* 75, no. 3 special ed. (September 1979):248-49; Kanter, *Communes* pp. 300-302; Muncy, pp. 214-16. Nordhoff, p. 391.
28. Carpenter, p. 222; Andrews, p. 60; Muncy, p. 216; Kern, pp. 120-34, 302; Foster, p. 229; Jean Harvey Baker, "Women in Utopia: The Nineteenth-Century Experience," in *Utopias: The American Experience*, ed. Gairdner Moment and Otto F. Kraushaar (Metuchen, N.J.: Scarecrow Press, 1980), pp. 61-62; Desroche, p. 177.
29. Robertson, ed., *Oneida Community*, pp. 83-84; Kern, pp. 259-260; John Humprhey Noyes, p. 636; Foster, pp. 104-5.
30. Lauer and Lauer, pp. 140-41; Hinds, pp. 186-87; Kern, pp. 269-79, 307; Robertson, *Oneida Community* pp. 294-97; Foster, pp. 105-6.
31. Nicholas V. Riasanovsky, *The Teaching of Charles Fourier* (Berkeley and Los Angeles: University of California Press, 1969), p. 208; Mailer, *La Doctrine de Charles Fourier* (Tel Aviv: Sifriat Hapoalim with Tel Aviv University Press, 1974), pp. 95-97 (Hebrew).
32. Laurence Grönlund, *The Cooperative Commonwealth*, ed. Stow Person (Cambridge, Mass.: Belknap Press of Harvard University Press, 1965), chap. 10.
33. Albert Shaw, *Icaria: A Chapter in the History of Communism* (New York: AMS Press, 1973; 1st ed. 1884), pp. 93, 145; Marie Marchand Ross, *Child of Icaria* (New York: Hypernion, 1976; 1st ed. 1938), p. 86; Muncy, pp. 220-22; John Thomas Codman, *Brook Farm: Historic and Personal Memoirs* (New York: AMS Press, 1971; 1st ed. 1894), p. 133; Katherine Burton, *Paradise Planters: The Story of Brook Farm* (1939. Reprint. New York: AMS Press, 1973), p. 238; Burnette G. Haskell, "Kaweah—How and Why the Colony Died," *Out West* 17 (September 1902): 318-19; "American Communities," *American Socialist* 2, no. 39 (September 27, 1877):305; Emilius O. Randall, *History of the Zoar Society: A Sociological Study in Communism* (New York: AMS Press, 1971; 1st ed. 1904), p. 47; Muncy, p. 217.
34. Kathleen M. Fernandez, "The Separatist Society of Zoar," *Communities: Journal of Cooperation*, no. 68 (Winter 1985): p. 29; Hostetler, pp. 145-46, 165; Deets, pp. 36-37; John W. Bennet, *Hutterian Brethren: The Agricultural Economy and Social Organization of a Communal People* (San Francisco: Stanford University Press, 1967), pp. 111-14, 145, 151.
35. Foster, pp. 104-5; Hayden, pp. 360-61; Muncy, p. 14; V.F. Calverton, *Where Angels Dared to Tread.* (New York: Bobbs-Merrill, 1941), p. 191; Kolmerten, pp. 76-83. Jon Wagner, ed., *Sex Roles in Contemporary American Communes* (Bloomington, Ind.: Indiana University Press, 1982), pp. 31-33.

22

Economic Assets and Liabilities

> All the communistic colonies in America after ten or fifteen years became so enormously rich that they have more of all desirable things they can consume, and there is scarcely any occasion for conflict. . . . [Those communes] had demonstrated that communism, the social life and work based on the common possession of goods is not only possible but has actually been realized . . . and with the best result.

This quote was written by the young Friedrich Engels and appeared in the *Deutsches Burgerbuch of 1845*. Engels, who in those years was close to Robert Owen's journal *New Moral World*, was influenced by the information he read in it about the American communes. To him they seemed to be a model of the communist way of life,[1] and this impression was common in the European socialist circles since the 1820s travelogues, telling about the American religious communes, had been published. Among the authors were famous politicians and economists such as the Duke of Saxe-Weimar and the economist Friedrich List. Even though there were different opinions about the beliefs and the way of life on the commune, everyone agreed as to their impressive economic achievements. Socialist reformers were most impressed, regarding this as a proof to the feasibility of their social vision. The information about the Shakers' success had decisive influence on Robert Owen's utopian vision and his decision to come to the United States.

It had similar influence on Etienne Cabet's utopian outlook and on the German Willhelm Whitling and the French Fourierist Victor Considerant.[2] The experience of the communes fertilized European socialist thought and was in turn enriched by the followers of European socialism—the Owenists and Fourierists who established scores of communes in the 1820s and 1840s. This extensive movement so impressed Engels that he went out of his way to prophesy about the communes' future saying:

> The Americans and especially the poor workers in the big cities, New York, Philadelphia, Boston, and so on have taken the matter to heart and have founded many societies for the establishment of similar colonies. The Americans are

> tired of remaining the servants of a few rich men who live on the people's labour and through the great activity and perseverance of this nation, it is evident that the community of goods will soon be introduced in a significant part of their land.[3]

As we know this prophecy never materialized. The Fourierist wave receded after several years and the high expectations for social change in the direction of socialism in the United States never came true. Engels himself turned his back on his earlier naive beliefs as expressed in *The Communist Manifesto* (1848). He openly sneered at utopian experiments. The religious communes he had admired, however, continued to prosper and so did some of the socialist ones, and everyone who visited them was enthusiastic about their economic achievement.[4] But there were others who criticized and pointed out the drawbacks of communitarian economy and its negative influence on the productive motivation of its members. Most of these critics were to be found in periodicals that dealt with the subject from an opposite or hostile attitude. The most critical of all were members who had left or who published economic evaluation at a time when their commune was disintegrating.[5]

Thomas Pears, one of the Owenites who enthusiastically joined New Harmony, wrote a year later to his friend in New York letters filled with disappointment of the chances to realize such a noble ideal. Burnett Haskel, founder and leader of Kaweah, in an article that summed up the commune's experience, expressed extreme pessimism as to the economic and social achievements and claimed that his generation had not been prepared to establish an egalitarian and communal economy. Levi Bimeler, grandson of the spiritual leader of Zoar, Joseph Bimler, led in 1895 the group that demanded to dissolve the commune. He claimed that communism killed man's ambition and will to progress; that it rewarded the lazy and the indolent.[6]

Amana, which existed prosperously for fifty years, suffered in the 1930s from the economic recession. One of the reasons was the lack of work motivation of its members and this went so far that the elders decided that the only way to survive was to abolish the communal economy, which they did.[7] The socialist commune Llano claimed to have an alternative to capitalism, but throughout their many years of attempting to establish an efficient and prosperous economy, they never succeeded to make ends meet. During its last years, Llano's members lived in a degrading state of poverty.[8]

It seems that there is no clear-cut lesson to be learned from the economic experience of the communes. Examples of a prosperous economy can be found in the abundance, especially among the long-lasting communes, but there is no difficulty in finding opposite examples even in stable communes, not to mention in the short-lived ones.

Focusing on economic success or failure may be misleading. After all, the main purpose of the communes was not the establishment of prosperous economic enterprises. Their economic undertakings were only a means to an end: to establish an independent existence and to realize their moral life and aims within an alien world. Further, on examining the history of the communes, one comes across an interesting paradox. Of all the communes, those that were established to realize a religious or social doctrine, and which had no specific economic motivation, discovered inherent forces that enabled them to become economically prosperous. The outstanding examples were the Shakers, Harmony, Amana, Oneida, and Icaria. Each of them was spiritually motivated by religion or socialism, and this was their raison d'ětre,[9] while those communes that were economically motivated, and many of their members had made clear that this was their reason for joining, did not achieve economic prosperity. Many collapsed because they were not economically viable.

Let us start with the problematic period of inception, the most critical time on all communes. Most were established without any external financial help, economic planning, and without available land equipment and mechanization. Each commune struggled during the early stage with a variety of specific difficulties. These were not identical, because there were vast differences between the various qualities of the communes. Yet, they all had one difficulty in common—the pioneering effort of establishing a new settlement that was not just a geographical entity but also a social innovation; an alternative way of life. This special endeavor had an impact on the economic problems as well, first of all on the raising of funds.

In this respect most of the religious communes had an advantage because they led a more communal way of life. Their capital was collected by sharing of all the property, the assets, and the chattels of every single member of the commune.[10] The communes had different approaches to the implementation of this process. The Shakers introduced a gradual membership based on different stages of handing over their private property, but as soon as a member was accepted into the "senior order" he had to hand over all his possessions. In other communes such as Harmony, members shared all their belongings from the day they emigrated to the New World. There were religious communes such as Zoar and Amana where the principle of communal property was executed only some time after having settled on their land.

Beyond the different approaches to communatarianism and the variations in the legal status, there was one principle common to all communes—membership was realized only by handing over all private property, regardless of the amount. Among those who joined the commune, some owned nothing and others were affluent. In the early days the Shakers were joined by farmers who handed their plots over to the family (the commune) and these formed the core of the parcel of land on which the commune settled. The new members would sign an agreement according to which they and their descendants gave up all claims to the property they had handed over to the commune. In some, this act was legalized and the society was incorporated or recognized as a "religious charity society." Thus the communal property was protected against claims of seceders and others. There was not always sufficient property at the members' disposal to ensure the commune's existence. In many cases contributions and assistance of the periphery of followers helped. These donations would sometimes arrive from distant sympathizers, as was the case of Zoar, whose members were assisted in their emigration to the United States by English Quakers.[11] However, those contributions were usually only a fragment of the commune's basic capital.

Most communes were financially independent. The principle of a community of goods was deeply rooted in their religion and was the strongest concrete expression of their affinity to early Christianity. The oldest and most stable of the religious communal movements—the Hutterites—is a case in point. Their history began in 1528 with the act of a "community of goods." In time, this was incorporated into their religious communal doctrine as one of their basic principles. Furthermore, according to the early Christian tradition of community of goods, the concealment of private property was regarded as a heavy sin. The first sinners were Anannias and his wife, whose punishment was death (see Acts, ch. 5, 1-12).

The sociologist Rosabeth Moss Kanter examined the nature of commitment in the long-lasting communes. In the handing over of the member's property to the commune she perceived an act of "sacrifice" and "investment" which deepened the individual's commitment and severed his affinity to the external world. In her study she pointed out the significant fact that it was an act that characterized all the stable communes.[12]

The situation differed in the socialist communes. Only a few (such as Icaria) insisted that the entire property be handed over to the commune. Most raised their capital through issuing shares. The principle of equal shares that would not be too high ($500-$1,000) enabled every member to acquire one by saving his salary for a while. Thus even members who had no private means could join the commune. The researcher Henrik Infield was right when he defined the social communes as cooperatives from the financial point of view and communes in the areas of work and consumption.[13]

Most socialist communes could not finance their establishment by the capital raised from shares. In the early period of economic development they needed money to purchase land and means of production besides building their homes and farmhouses. They raised funds by asking the periphery of followers, through their journals, to contribute to their pioneering enterprise. The Fourierist settlement had a unique way of fund-raising. According to their doctrine they could involve capitalists in the compound of their phalanstery. Some of the Fourierist communes established holding companies owned by followers who were absentee members. In addition there were communes fully financed by utopian philanthropists such as New Harmony by Owen and Silkville by the Fourierist Boissiere.[14] One has to realize that the socialist commune acted under the force of circumstances. They had to acquire land as soon as possible to gather their members, who were usually of limited means, on their domain. In the nineteenth century there were no public funds (such as the Zionist ones in our generation) that would undertake to establish communal settlements. In the prevailing conditions in the United States there was no prospect of any financial backing by the state.[15]

The communes raised funds in a variety of ways similar to the fund-raising of any fledging enterprise. The only difference was that the finances helped to establish a communal economy which, in its internal relations, abolished all private property. On the religious communes property arrangements were more homogeneous and consistent. In the socialist ones, on the other hand, these were heterogeneous and less consistent in their dispositions. Sometimes those developed into compromises between cooperations, shareholding companies and even philanthropic fund-raising. No doubt this interfered with the socialist communes' economic and communal development.

The problem of financing was only one aspect of the hardships at the early stage. Another was connected with purchasing and clearing the land. Lack of capital and the wish to seek secluded places far from the crowded cities drove the communes to virgin lands in the mountains and forests where the soil was poor. Most of those who joined a commune were completely inexperienced in farming and land-clearing, and this added to their toil and trouble. A further difficulty, especially in the early years, arose from the demand on a heterogeneous group to coordinate their actions harmoneously. This problem, social in origin, had economic implications mainly during the first years, when people from different social backgrounds had to cooperate in constructing the economic foundation of their independent settlement. They succeeded only when they were religiously or ideologically motivated and united, and when they had undergone a period of training for their communal life. On the other hand, if a heterogeneous group had gathered haphazardly and without the necessary preparations, it would cause difficulties and often led to failure. Such an example was New Harmony, which was blessed with capital, fertile land, and means of production but suffered from disharmony and lack of coordination among its heterogeneous membership. This caused troubles that radiated directly into their economy and hindered all activities.[16]

As we have seen the communes had to face many and variegated problems that hindered their early economic development. Those that did not manage to overcome the initial obstacles were powerless to proceed and move on into a period of economic prosperity. Most of them failed in their first years. The lack of means to provide their members with a decent standard of living, the physical hardships, and poverty deterred those who had joined the commune in search of a rapid solution to their economic distress. Hence, the stronger the economic motivation of the members the quicker they became impatient and the sooner disintegration overtook the commune.[17]

On the other hand, when members were motivated by spiritual-religious values or by socialist ideals, they were better prepared to face the years of trials and tread the path of penury and pioneering which would lead them to good times. Evidently, the commune's experience established a direct affinity between the level of ideological, spiritual-religious motivation and the ability to cope with the primary economic problems. This affinity was also maintained through later stages, but its relations became more complex.

All the communes we have dealt with in the present study began by establishing an agricultural economy. Their reason was either because they had started out as farmers' communities, or because they aspired to achieve independence of the external economy. However, only a few remained purely agricultural and most eventually integrated workshops and after a while, in a more advanced stage, incorporated industrial branches in their economy.[18]

Let us now look at the commune's unique agricultural basis. The first distinctive characteristic which stands out when comparing the communal farms to others of the same size is that they all adopted mixed farming, and there was not even a single commune which practiced monoculture. All communes had vegetable gardens, orchards, livestock, and crops. There were several reasons for this:

1. Most communes adopted autarchy at the beginning as a matter of principle.
2. The size of the community entailed the division of work-power into different departments.
3. A mixed economy provided work throughout the seasons.
4. Supplying the community's needs.
5. The available means of production, namely land and manpower.

Those communes whose membership was composed of ex-farmers and farm workers had an advantage in the early stages of laying their foundations, for their agricultural economy, for example, the Shaker communes, whose members came from among the rural counties of New England and later Ohio and Kentucky.[19] The dexterous and hard-working immigrants who established Harmony, Zoar, and Amana, and who had been either farmers or artisans in their homeland, soon discovered local agricultural aptitudes. Their model farms were greatly admired by all who visited them.

To these we have to add the influence of religion on agricultural work. Most of the religious communes regarded their settlements as part of the kingdom of heaven, as God's garden on earth. They developed their farms and tended their environment with a feeling of spiritual-religious commitment.[20]

From among the socialist communes—the stable Fourierist phalanxes—Brook Farm, the North American Phalanx, and the Wisconsin Phalanx preferred agriculture, because turning their settlement into an attractive blooming garden was an integral part of their doctrine. Icaria, whose ideology had a different source, also established a flourishing farming community in Iowa.[21]

Until the second half of the nineteenth century the communal farming settlement enjoyed another advantage, namely, the size of their farms. Most of the small family farms of their neighbors could not compete economically with the large mixed farms of the communes. There were of course also disadvantages and limitations to the communal farms, mainly in those whose members had come from an urban background without any period of preparation for living in frontier conditions and doing agricultural work. This was especially prevalent in the socialist communes. Another frequent disadvantage was the hasty purchase of cheap land without testing the quality of the soil. In many cases it turned out that the land they had purchased was unsuitable for agriculture. However, the most serious drawback was the lack of farming experience of the members. This, more than any other factor, prevented the economic stability of the communes in their early years. Later this would also undermine their economic foundations. John Humphrey Noyes regarded the rush to settle in frontier areas as one of the reasons for the Fourierist movement's failure.[22]

Not a single commune kept its autarchy, and not one remained a farming community. All of them underwent the characteristic process that began as an autarchy intended to provide the commune's needs, went on to foster the various branches that developed rapidly, soon to produce a surplus which was then marketed. After the dimensions continued to grow, the commune would give up the less profitable branches and concentrate on the more profitable ones. The Shakers, having started to market their produce, added a contribution to society by producing medical herbs that they had improved in their gardens. Harmony was an example of a commune that in a few years progressed from agriculture that supplied only the community's needs, to being the most important marketing factor of agricultural produce in large areas in the Midwest. The only exception was Ephrata, whose spiritual leader, Konrad Beisel, intentionally halted the economic development, fearing that materialism and the worship of mammon would undermine the commune's foundations.[23]

All communes, whether the ones that developed market farming or those who limited their production to local consumption, established workshops. They were intended to serve the home farm but gradually developed into manufacturing for the market too, and included flour mills, sawmills, blacksmiths, sewing shops, coblers, carpentry shops, and printing presses. The latter was a typical aspect of the communes which had undertaken to disseminate their ideology among the public but also used the printing shop to foster the education of members. It was begun in the early history of Amana. In Ephrata, the printing press was the central source of income. It was an important factor on most religious communes as on most of the more stable socialist ones.[24]

The process of stabilization brought with it a variegated economy that developed from mixed farming to a combination of agriculture and industry. Vineyards were the foundation of the wineries in Harmony. Sheep flocks provided the wool for the looms in Amana and Harmony. Mulberry trees were used for the silk industry in Oneida and Harmony. This process was of a great advantage and enabled the communes to be independent of external factors in providing their raw material, to the ire of their competitors and their ideological rivals. The communes were even labelled *monopolists* who benefited from advantages their diversified economy provided.[25]

The transition from agriculture to industry did not include all communes. The two largest and most stable of the communal movements took a different course. The Shakers returned to farming in the 1920s, at a time when their communes were deteriorating, and the Hutterites, who had excelled in the ceramics industry in Moravia, gave it up on their wanderings in Europe. They have been farmers since their arrival in the United States in 1874 and until the present day, growing crops and livestock.

The transition to industrial activities usually began after several stages in the development of the communal farming, and after the business acumen of members and leaders had grown. There were several factors that prompted the communes to develop industrial branches. A major reason was to provide artisans and craftsmen, who had joined the commune and had been occupied at service jobs, with a way to express their creativity and talents. The Shakers especially excelled in developing enterprises that manufactured goods fashioned and designed by expert artisans. They earned their produce such a reputation that they could have competed with large industrial plants; of renown was the Shaker furniture—their tables, chairs, chests of drawers, and stoves. Another factor for developing their industry was the communes' growing number of members who had to be provided with work after they became redundant in agriculture.

Thus standard industries with mass production were established and even though quality control was meticulously maintained, their produce had to compete on the open market. This entailed the introduction of the usual procedures such as employing agents and soon the industrial enterprises of the communes were infected with the dynamics of the external society, its rules, demands, and influences. Most communes tried to keep the balance between agriculture and industry. This was drastically upset in Harmony, when its decreasing and aging membership turned their assets into financial investment companies owned by the commune. A similar process occurred in Oneida, where the transition from farming to industry followed the outstanding success of their trap making in the late 1850s. The advantage of the industrial plants on Oneida was proven because it provided work for a large number of members without the extreme undulating of the agricultural work year. In time, more industries were added and Oneida's agriculture was limited. In Amana, Zoar and Beth-El the promotion of industries proceeded simultaneously with the development of agriculture.[26]

On the socialist communes industry was also introduced, but on a more limited scope, because most of them were short-lived. The Fourierist communes did not promote industry for ideological reasons. Fourier objected to large-scale industry and mass production which, according to him, prevented enjoyable and variegated work. The socialist communes of the late nineteenth and the early twentieth centuries aspired to establish industries. There were a number of attempts, including one in the oil industry, but none succeeded on the scope of the industries which Amana, Harmony, and Oneida had established.[27] Industry had far-reaching effects on the communal way of life, on the work relations and the economic structure. Industry strongly involved the communes with the capitalist economy. Manufacture and marketing created a relationship which far exceeded the acceptable norm of the religious communes' secluded way of life.[28] The dynamics of industrial development forced the communes to modernize their plants and to introduce mechanization. Members were sent to gain expertise at external institutions and factories. They returned with new ideas, rational ways of thought, and practical methods which could not, in the long run, exist harmoniously with the religious communes' values.

The most negative and far-reaching effect was doubtlessly the introduction of hired labor on a large and permanent scale into the communal economy. Hired labor had always been regarded as alien to the communal existence. Even so it invaded most communes. Only a small number escaped, among which the Hutterites are conspicuous.[29] The introduction of hired labor resulted in a strong feeling of displeasure. Members feared that they were deviating from the basic principles of the communal way of life. On the religious communes the hired workers were alien elements, nonbelievers who were staying among the "holy community" and within the kingdom of heaven on earth.

The socialist communes feared the appearance of contradicting relationships between employer and employee on their own settlements.[30] Wherever a group of hired workers lived permanently near the commune or even if they were just employed during seasonal work, an ambivalent relationship developed. The communal members demanded an efficient and dexterous execution of work from their hired workers. To calm their conscience they paid them a higher-than-average salary and put the cheaper communal clothing and food stores at their disposal. All of this did not prevent the hired workers from regarding the commune members as employers, nor did it attract them to the commune's model way of life.[31] They often even scoffed at the "oddity" of these ascetic capitalists.

There is no evidence that a relationship of mutual understanding and integration existed between hired workers and members of a commune. Apparently, this reality bothered many members and some of them considered it as a kind of permanent reminder of a state of sin. They attempted to rectify the situation by raising the cultural level of the hired workers. Oneida tried to open a school for its workers' children, but this never materialized. The animosity between workers and members and their children was described in Pierrepont Noyes's memoirs, in which he related his childhood experiences of tension with the hired workers.[32] The introduction of hired labor was a necessary evil that accompanied the commune's economic development. It usually occurred after the commune had started to market its products and when its leaders became more aware of the business factor in the economic management of the commune.

The specific situation that entailed the introduction of hired labor was connected to the widening gap between the means of production and availability of work power. This happened whenever the means of production increased more rapidly than membership, for instance the land expansion on the Shaker communes, the rapid growth of Amana's industries, a drastic decrease in membership such as an epidemic of cholera in Zoar in 1834, or a combination of factors such as the decision not to absorb additional members and to stop marriages and child bearing in Harmony. In those communes that did not have any natural increase—Ephrata, Harmony, and The Shakers—hired labor took root after the members were too old to carry on with any work beyond farm jobs and the household chores.[33]

Hired labor prevailed in all the communes which had established large industrial enterprises, but usually it had been introduced even earlier. In Amana and Oneida they hired hands for seasonal work. They employed workers in agriculture after the establishment of industry. At a certain stage members of Amana hoped that industry might rid them of the necessity to employ hired help because there would no longer be seasonal work.[34] However, reality, as they soon discovered, was different. The dynamics of the industrial enterprises dictated a rate of expansion according to market demands and competition. Thus hired workers became a vital factor and, even though there was an attempt to cut down their numbers in industry, they steadily increased. Within a few years the hired workers were one-third or even one-half of the entire industrial workforce.

Still, the problem of quantity was not the worst. In all places in which hired labor was employed—in agriculture, industry, or the services—they had to do the nonprofessional, unpleasant, and difficult jobs. Communal members did not share the effort and most of them were either overseers, managers, or worked at the easier and more satisfying jobs.[35] This division of work existed on all the communes that employed hired labor. It called for some soul-searching and there were indeed apologetic articles in many of the communes' journals, yet no remedy was forthcoming. On the religious communes hired workers were regarded as *aliens* and *nonbelievers*, while members were *the chosen* and *the sacred*. This elitist feeling prevented any change in work hierarchy. Aliens could not be made managers or even accepted on equal footing at the plant. Beyond these economic factors, there were also objective ones which stemmed from the different mental make up of both groups.

Things were no different on the socialist communes. Most of them did not exist long enough to develop large industries that would demand hired labor. Hands were employed in growing numbers for seasonal work in agriculture, on the North American Phalanx and in Icaria. Their numbers increased when membership decreased (as in New Icaria).[36] Their ideological perplexity was expressed with biting words by the anarchist members of Sunrise in describing the dead-end reached by a socialist commune which employed labor. Even though hired labor was an established fact on all stable communes (except the Hutterites), the negative attitude toward it did not alter. There were hardly any cases in communal literature where hired labor was legitimized. When William Hinds visited Zoar, most members openly admitted that the harm done by employing hired workers was great and that this caused "bad habits" to take root.[37] Nevertheless, members got used to having them around and could no longer manage without them, mainly because they did not want to lower their standard of living nor to increase their easy rate of work. Although there were several attempts to reduce the number of hired workers through dismissals, these were insignificant.

Hired labor was an established fact in all stable industrial communes. This produced a double standard: on the one hand the commune was regarded as "a community of the chosen" or a society in which social equality prevailed and which is diametrically opposed to hired labor and on the other, there existed a deeply rooted reality of uncleanliness, and of a society which exploited others. This double standard had a profound impact, undermining the moral fiber of the community and sowing the seeds of cynicism mainly among the younger generation. Perhaps the worst damage was done to the commune's work morale. Members who got used to leaving all the difficult, unprofessional, and unpleasant jobs to hired workers could no longer regard physical work as a sacred value without deceiving themselves; it had a negative impact on work motivation and damaged the inner-core of the communal economic system.

If there were a true indicator to a commune's achievement, it would not be measured in economic or financial terms but rather in the prevailing work morale. Work was not just a means to an end but had a moral, spiritual, and ideological value ensued from the communal life and from the religious or social doctrines of the commune members. It had spiritual and religious significance. The Shakers' slogan was "give your hand in work and your heart to God," and they, just as many other religious communes, regarded their settlements as the manifestation of the kingdom of heaven on earth.[38] The socialist communes regarded themselves as pioneers of a new social order which would, among other things, release workers from their claims of salaried slavery. The Fourierists added another sociopsychological dimension when they declared work should be liberating, attractive, and variegated. Work as an ideological element was the power behind the communes' economic system.

The ideological significance attached to work varied in the different communes and was expressed by the different systems of reward. Most communes that regarded work as a spiritual-ideological-communal value did not pay its members according to the work they had invested. On the other hand, those communes that did not attach any ideological significance to work paid for work invested with tokens, communal money, or other methods of individual accountancy. This system was adopted by most socialist communes which had been hurriedly established and whose members had no proper ideological preparation for the transition from the capitalist to the socialist system. On the Fourierist communes the differential pay system was a part of the general set-up on the phalanstery.[39] Icaria, with its high socialist ideology, adopted the communist way and everybody was entitled to receive all he needed without taking into account his contribution.

Most religious communes meticulously adhered to communal principles and there was no connection between work or professional effort invested and the amount of material reward. Here and there, especially at times of deterioration, there were deviations. Amana used to reward overtime or a special effort with special pay or gifts.[40] Zoar and Beth-El deviated in the final years of their existence from the communal principles of reward. On communes that adhered to the principle of complete separation between work and reward members invested much effort in work and achieved a high output without material compensation. This we infer from the Shakers and the Hutterites. The deeper work values were internalized, the higher their achievements in quality, efficiency, improvisation, and even creativity. A case in point was the Shakers' attitude toward work; its members got no material reward for their many inventions or improvements. But they were not the only ones. In other communes—Oneida, Harmony, Amana, the Hutterites, Icaria—we may find many examples of intense commitment to work growing out of a deep regard to its creative aspect and its contribution to the general public. The Christian Commonwealth, for example, elevated the principle of work for the public good to the level of a sacred and cardinal ideal.[41]

This special regard for work was manifest by the care devoted to creating suitable conditions. This was done by constructing comfortable workshops, by providing the tools, and organizing work hours to fit members' convenience. Every visitor came away impressed by the pleasant atmosphere, the silence, and the comfort prevailing in the communal workshops in contrast to the tension, the bustle, and the killing tempo on plants elsewhere.[42] The absence of work under compulsion went side by side with pleasant and variated workdays divided by short periods of rest. These were devoted to religious meetings, discussions on topical and social matters, and even to learning.

Fourierist settlements adopted the system of "series" together with the principle of attractive work. This meant that members could switch their place of work several times a day according to the Fourier doctrine. It is difficult to judge the success of the system and its efficiency because the Fourierist phalanxes were all short-lived. The same principle prevailed on most communes, and had three complementary elements:

1. *The imperative of rotation* was ingrained in the communal experience and was meant to make the equal and just division of difficult and unpleasant service jobs feasible. Furthermore, this enabled members to develop a many-sided affinity with the various branches and also prevented the forming of exclusive and elitist groups and professions.
2. *Integration of physical and spiritual work.* The usual division of workers versus management was an anathema, and most communes tried to avoid it. On the large industrial communes it was difficult to prevent job differentiation altogether. They took care to make it less stable and severe by rotating members from managerial posts to the work bench. There were many examples, the most outstanding being that of the Shaker elders, who were many-sided professionals and divided their time between "public affairs" and work. This was also the practice on Amana, Oneida, and others. The renowned leaders Bimeler and Noyes would also work on the commune but only on a limited scale. They were the exception to the rule. Communes which had no charismatic leaders, e.g. the Hutterites, had no such exceptions, and everyone did physical work. A teacher was also the janitor, and the preacher would lend a hand whenever he had time. All socialist communes adhered to the principle of the integration of physical and spiritual work. Brook Farm adopted it as a cardinal ideal. At New Harmony, with its many intellectuals, it was an impressive phenomenon. Cabet, Icaria's spiritual leader, was involved in all that went on, and participated in work on the farm. The idealist intellectuals who joined the later socialist communes were naturally expected to participate in the general work effort. At the same time, the communes maintained their moti-

vation of spiritual and intellectual activities and found ways to integrate both.[43]

3. *Working side by side*. To overcome the problem of seasonal work or urgent pressure in one department or the other the communes adopted the tradition of "a massive pitching-in" which had been the custom of New England even before communes were established in the United States. They had assembled all the farmers in the area to help each other finish seasonal jobs, in the manner of a beehive. The commune was even better equipped to rotate members according to the season. It was also an opportunity for members of different departments to meet in a communal effort.

All these three elements contributed to work equality and formed a broad foundation for economic democracy. During the periods in which communal life proceeded in an orderly fashion and these elements were adhered to, motivation was also high. This made visitors come away with the impression that "there were no lazy or idle members." This was an exaggeration; there were lazy members even on communes, as may be realized from the communal journals which dealt with problems of carelessness and the struggle against the scourge of laziness.[44] Nevertheless, the communal experience included a negligible and insignificant amount of inertia and indifference as long as the communal way of life proceeded according to the religious or socialist principles. But as soon as those principles were neglected in favor of business and economic criteria, schisms in the harmonious life of the communal members appeared and motivation dropped drastically.

New elements were introduced which could not be integrated into the system and even eroded the vital fabric that had earlier motivated the system. A case in point was the introduction of an alien element in the form of hired workers. The aim of these workers was to get paid, and they regarded their work as a means of existence rather than a value in itself. They aspired to material rewards and the quality of their work was of minor importance, intended only to serve their main purpose—a higher salary. All the characteristics of alienation apparent in their work left no room for individual creativity. They were continuously threatened with dismissal, because of the many unemployed who were eager to take their place; this and the members' demand for a higher output caused their work to be competitive and tense.

Job differentiation among the hired workers was severe, and they spent most of their years on the lower levels of their profession. Consequently, the prevailing atmosphere of work was completely different from that which characterized the communal experience as a whole. It was impossible to avoid the negative impact that eroded work relationships on the communes. Hired labor was introduced simultaneously with a rise of "business motivation" in the communes' economic activities, and with a lowering of their ideological-religious commitment. It may be difficult to distinguish between the impact of each separately, but the entire phenomenon may be described as a coexistence of the communal system on its ideological values and a business-like economy. This unbalanced coexistence could not survive, and soon unbridgeable adversities were created within the system. In Harmony this caused the surviving commune to be transformed into a capitalist holding company. In 1932 Amana was faced by the dilemma of returning to their fathers' communal ways or to integrate fully with the capitalist economy and dissolve the commune altogether. There were many more examples among the more stable and affluent communes—Oneida, Zoar, Beth-El, and the socialist Llano—from which we can deduce the extent of the phenomenon and its negative impact.[45]

Let us now return to the criteria for testing the economic success of communes. It was shown above that economic success in itself was no indication for the stability of the commune as a community with a unique set of values. History has taught us that in certain cases economic prosperity, far from ensuring the commune's existence, even carried within it the seeds of disintegration. As long as the communes' economic development was controlled by the spiritual or ideological leadership, which limited it in proportion to the commune's growth and expansion, that economic development was a positive and progressive contribution. The best illustration were the Hutterites, who utilized the riches and property they had accumulated to good effect, investing most of it in the purchase of land to finance new settlements for their members.[46] However, when the dynamics of economic development did not balance, the dynamics of social development—affluence—became an obstacle and even harmed the communes deeply.

Riches affected the communal existence on the personal level by raising members' expectations in comparison to the past. It also affected the communes on an economic level by binding them to dynamics anchored in the outside world of business.[47] In these cases where the communal property—land and factories—became a vested interest, they succeeded in maintaining the community's framework, but not the communal values. This happened in Amana and Oneida where the industrial enterprises survived the communes. The single commune that attempted to halt the trend of affluence and to keep its original aspect was Ephrata, but only such an extremely monastic-ascetic commune could take such steps. All the other long-living communes grew away from their ascetic beginnings. The trend they followed was one of economic development, affluence, extension of their means of production, and gradual improvement in their standard of living. The stable commune's assets accumulated through the years and enabled the members to receive a significant amount of property when they dissolved.[48]

Consequently, even when economic success smiled on the long-living communes, it did not ensure their communal principles. Yet we must not assume that economic failure would. It suffices is to look at the scores of short-lived communes that failed because they were unable to establish an independent economy and got entangled in financial difficulties from their inception. It is easy to prove that economic failure did not lead them to triumph. Members lived on a subsistence level and their penury defeated their aspirations to serve as a model for an alternative way of life. These communes did not attract any newcomers, and their founders soon despaired and gave up. The economist Charles Gide dealt with this problem in his book, *Communist and Cooperative Settlements*, observing that:

> Another peril, and perhaps the gravest of all, lies in the fact that these [communal] colonies are threatened as much by success as by failure. For if they do not succeed it means misery, ruin, dispersal, and a general rush for safety. If, on the other hand, they attain prosperity they attract a crowd of members who lack the enthusiasm and faith of the earlier ones and are attracted only by self-interest. Then there is a conflict between the older element and the new, and ultimately a demand is made for a sharing out, and each member goes his own way. We should not be surprised that these societies die young.[49]

Still, historical experience shows that not all of them dissolved at the outset; many survived for years but not because of their economic prosperity. In conclusion, we may say that the historical experience of the communes shows that whenever there were suitable conditions for communal life, there also developed stable and prosperous economics. This prosperity originated from the economic potential inherent in communal life wherein an ideologically motivated group of people combine their efforts. It could materialize only as long as the communal life functioned continuously over a long period. On the other hand, when these conditions were lacking the economic activities faltered, even if the commune had at its disposal ample financing and sufficient manpower. Hence, there is no way to examine economic success separately because the economic system is not independent of the communal life. It is integrated within the social and ideological systems; these are all interrelated and influence each other.

Notes

1. *Hedim*, no. 67 (January 1961):158 (Hebrew). Lewis S. Feuer, *The Western Political Quarterly* 19 (1966): 456-65.
2. Edward D. Andrews, *The People Called Shakers: A Search for Perfect Society* (New York: Dover, 1963), pp. 94-95, 131-34; idem, *The Community Industries of the Shakers* (Philadelphia: Porcupine, 1972), pp. 213, 224-26; Henri Desroche, *The American Shakers: From Neo-Christianity to Pre-Socialism*, ed. and trans. John K. Savacoal, (Boston: University of Massachusettes Press, 1971), pp. 294-95; Karl J.R. Arndt, *George Rapp's Harmony Society, 1785-1847*, rev. ed. (New York: Associated University Presses, 1972), pp. 210, 212, 268-86, 321-24, 339-47; Albert Shaw, *Icaria: A Chapter in the History of Communism* (New York: AMS Press, 1973; 1st ed. 1884), pp. 21-22; Carl Wittke, *The Utopian*

Communist: A Biography of Wilhelm Weitling, Nineteenth-Century Reformer (Baton Rouge: Louisiana State University Press, 1950), p. 238.

3. *Hedim*, p. 158; Lewis S. Feuer, "The Influence of the American Communist Colonies on Engels and Marx," *The Western Political Quarterly* 19 (1966):464-65.
4. Richard T. Ely, *The Labor Movement in America* (New York: Arno & New York Times, 1969), pp. 7-33; Charles Nordhoff, *The Communistic Societies of the United States* (New York: Shocken, 1965), pp. 386, 390; William Alfred Hinds, *American Communities and Cooperative Colonies* (1878. Reprinted and enl. Philadelphia: Porcupine, 1975), pp. 591-97; Shaw, pp. 84-85; Morris Hillquit, *History of Socialism in the United States*, 5th ed. (New York: Dover, 1971), pp. 128-30; Ralph Albertson, *A Survey of Mutualistic Communities in America* (New York: AMS Press, 1973: 1st ed. 1936), pp. 437-40; Alexander Kent, "Cooperative Communities in the United States," *Bulletin of the Department of Labor*, no. 35 (July 1901): 645-46; Andrews, *The People*, p. 119.
5. Henry Ammon James, *Communism in America* (New York: Holt, 1879), pp. 12-14, 19-20, P.B. Taylor, *Encyclopedia of Religion and Ethics*, Vol. 3, p. 780; Thomas Pears and Sarah Pears, *New Harmony: An Adventure in Happiness. Papers of Thomas and Sarah Pears*, ed. Thomas C. Pears, Jr. (Clifton: Kelley, 1973), pp. 75-79; Arthur Bestor, *Backwoods Utopias: The Sectarian Origins and the Owenite Phase of Communitarian Socialism in America, 1663-1829*, 2d ed. (Philadelphia: University of Pennsylvania Press, 1971), pp. 164-65; Emilius O. Randall, *History of the Zoar Society: A Sociological Study in Communism* (New York: AMS Press, 1971); 1st ed. 1904), pp. 49-50.
6. Randall, pp. 53-54, 67-68; Frederick A. Bushee, "Communistic Societies in the United States," *Political Science Quarterly* 20, no. 4 (1905):645.
7. Bertha M.H. Shambaugh, *Amana That Was and Amana That Is* (Iowa City: Iowa State Historical Society, 1932), pp. 364-71; Barbara S. Yambura, *A Change and a Parting: My Story of Amana* (Iowa City: Iowa State University Press, 1974), pp. 275-78, 280-83.
8. Paul K. Conkin, *Two Paths to Utopia: The Hutterites and the Llano Colony* (Lincoln: University of Nebraska Press, 1964), pp. 167-71; Isaac Broome, *The Last Days of the Ruskin Cooperative Association* (Chicago, 1902), pp. 68-88.
9. Bushee, pp. 650-55; Shambaugh, p. 154; John W. Bennet, *Hutterian Brethren: The Agricultural Economy and Social Organization of a Communal People* (San Francisco: Stanford University Press, 1967), pp. 156-60.
10. Randall, pp. 5-7; Arndt, *Harmony Society*, pp. 72-75, 260; Hinds, pp. 91-92; Shambaugh, pp. 105-6.
11. Donald Egbert and Stow Persons, eds., *Socialism and American Life*, 2 vols. (Princeton: Princeton University Press, 1952), p. 137; Desroche, p. 196; Marguerite Fellows Melcher, *The Shaker Adventure* (New York: The Shaker Museum, 1975), pp. 53, 90; Andrews, *The Industries*, pp. 29-30; Julia Neal, *By Their Fruits: The Story of Shakerism in South Union, Kentucky* (New York: North Carolina Press, 1947), p. 3; Robert Allerton Parker, *A Yankee Saint: John Humphrey Noyes and the Oneida Community* (New York: Putnam, 1935), pp. 167-69; Randall, p. 5; William G. Bek, "A German Communistic Society in Missouri," *Missouri Historical Review* (October 1908):62.
12. John A. Hostetler, *Hutterite Society* (Baltimore: Johns Hopkins University Press, 1977), p. 31; Rosabeth Moss Kanter, *Commitment and Community: Communes and Utopias in Sociological Perspective* (Cambridge, Mass.: Harvard University Press, 1972), pp. 80-82; Acts V: 1-12.
13. Henrik Infield, *Cooperative Communities at Work* (London: Kegan Paul, Trench,

Trubner, 1947), p. 18; Hinds, p. 536; Charles Pierre Le Warne, *Utopias on Puget Sound, 1885-1915* (Seattle: University of Washington Press, 1975), p. 39.

14. John Egerton, *Visions of Utopia: Nashoba, Rugby, Ruskin, and the "New Communities" in Tennessee's Past* (University of Tennessee Press with the Tennessee Historical Commission), pp. 68-69, 72-74, 76; Hinds, pp. 257, 488-89; John Fletcher Clews Harrison, *Quest for the New Moral World: Robert Owen and the Owenites in Britain and America* (New York: Scribners, 1969), pp. 180-81; Shaw, pp. 41-44; Egbert and Persons, p. 177; John Humphrey Noyes, *History of American Socialism* (1870). Dover, 1966. Reprinted as *Strange Cults and Utopias of Nineteenth-Century America* (New York: Dover, 1966), pp. 102-118, 404, 460-61; Katherine Burton, *Paradise Planters: The Story of Brook Farm* (1939. Reprint. New York: AMS Press, 1973), pp. 40, 197-98; Garrett R. Carpenter, "Silkville: A Kansas Attempt in the History of Fourierist Utopias, 1869-1892," *The Emporia State Research Studies*, 3, no. 2 (December 1954): 14-16.
15. Conkin, pp. 172-75; Joseph J. Cohen, *In Quest of Heaven: The Story of the Sunrise Cooperative Farm Community* (New York: Sunrise History Publishing Committee, 1957), p. 140; William J. Hammond and Margaret F. Hammond, *La Rèunion: A French Settlement in Texas* (Dallas, Tex.: Royal Publishing Co.), p. 114.
16. Bestor, *Backwoods*, pp. 160-67.
17. Cohen, pp. 209-14.
18. Ralph Albertson, *A Survey of Mutualistic Communities in America* (New York: AMS Press, 1973; 1st ed. 1936), p. 429; Shambaugh, p. 156.
19. Andrews, *The People*, pp. 116-25; Melchers, pp. 120-35; Andrews, *The Industries*, pp. 27, 48-53, 58, 219-24; Frederick William Evans, *Autobiography of a Shaker and Revelation of the Apocalypse* (New York: AMS Press, 1973; 1st ed. 1888), pp. 225-30; Neal, p. 159.
20. Arndt, *Harmony Society*, pp. 110-20; Bek, pp. 73, 101; Robert J. Hendricsk, *Bethel and Aurora: An Experiment in Communism as Practical Christianity* (New York: Press of Pioneers, 1933), pp. 109-11; Hostetler, pp. 35-43, 118-36; Shambaugh, pp. 150-56.
21. John Humphrey Noyes, pp. 404-47, 463; Hinds, pp. 267, 270-71; Hillquit, pp. 121-22; Shaw, pp. 67, 82-87, 117.
22. John Humphrey Noyes, pp. 233-37, 241-47, 510; Bushee, p. 653; Arndt, *Harmony Society*, pp. 283, 290-91; John S. Duss, *The Harmonists: A Personal History* (Philadelphia: Porcupine, 1972), p. 48.
23. Julius Friedrich Sachse, *The German Pietists of Provincial Pennsylvania* (New York: AMS Press, 1970; 1st ed. 1895), pp. 114-27. On Hutterite austerity see Bennet, *Hutterian Brethren*, pp. 167-76.
24. Maren Lockwood Carden, *Oneida: Utopian Community to Modern Corporation* (Baltimore: Johns Hopkins University Press, 1969), p. 40; Julius Friedrich Sachse, *The German Sectarians of Pennsylvania, 1742-1800: A Critical and Legendary History of the Ephrata Cloister and the Dunkers*, vol. 2 (Philadelphia: published by the author, 1899. New York: AMS Press, 1971), p. 118.
25. Hinds, pp. 301-2; Arndt, *Harmony Society*, pp. 404-8, 579-86; Shambaugh, p. 157; Neal, pp. 101-7; Duss, p. 72; Andrews, *The Industries*, pp. 248-54; Bennet, *Hutterian Brethren*, pp. 161-62, 176-80.
26. Andrews, *The People*, pp. 120-35; idem, *The Industries*, pp. 58-59; Melchers, p. 132; Nordhoff, pp. 389-90; Shambaugh, pp. 157-67; Randall, pp. 36, 51; Charles J. Erasmus, *In Search of the Common Good: Utopian Experiments Past and Fu-*

ture (New York: Free Press, 1977), pp. 152-53; Arndt, *Harmony Society*, pp. 210-11, 341-45, 579-86; Duss, pp. 46-48; Karl J.R. Arndt, *George Rapp's Successors and Material Heirs, 1847-1916* (New York: Associated University Press, 1971), pp. 61-84; Constance Noyes Robertson, ed., *Oneida Community: An Autobiography, 1851-1876* (Syracuse: Syracuse University Press, 1971), pp. 48, 212-64; Parker, pp. 205-10.

27. Conkin, pp. 170, 175-79; Le Warne, pp. 83-87, 150-52; Egerton, p. 68; Hinds, p. 490; Delburn Carpenter, *The Radical Pietists: Celibate Communal Societies Established in the United States before 1820* (New York: AMS Press, 1975), pp. 17-18; John Thomas Codman, *Brook Farm: Historic and Personal Memoirs* (New York: AMS Press, 1971; 1st ed. 1894), chap. 4.
28. Erasmus, pp. 150-51, 157; Andrews, *The People*, pp. 115, 152-56.
29. Hostetler, pp. 182-84.
30. Neal, pp. 222-23; Cohen, pp. 40-42.
31. Cohen, p. 47; Carden, pp. 69, 85; Robertson, ed., *Oneida Society* pp. 89-90, 215.
32. Pierrepont Noyes, *My Father's House: An Oneida Boyhood* (London: J. Murray, 1937), pp. 113-18.
33. Hinds, p. 107; Randall, pp. 35-37, 51; Desroche, p. 229; Melchers, pp. 237, 254-55, 302; Arndt, *Harmony Society*, pp. 341; Duss, pp. 116, 227; Aaron Williams, *The Harmony Society at Economy: Pennsylvania, Founded by George Rapp* (New York: AMS Press, 1971; 1st ed. Pittsburgh, 1866), pp. 40-41.
34. Shambaugh, pp. 151, 156, 158, 162, 175-200; Parker, pp. 208-12; Robertson, ed. *Oneida Society*, pp. 73, 224-26, 244, 249, 254-59; Hinds, p. 187.
35. Nordhoff, pp. 40, 393; Melchers, p. 237; Hinds, p. 316; *Handbook of the Oneida Community 1867 and 1871: Bound with Mutual Criticism* (New York: AMS Press, 1976; 1st ed. 1867), pp. 20-21; Shambaugh, pp. 137, 156, 158, 407; Yambura, p. 94.
36. John Humphrey Noyes, pp. 484, 493; Marie Marchand Ross, *Child of Icaria* (New York: Hypernion, 1976; 1st ed. 1938), pp. 113, 120, 126; Conkin, p. 171; Cohen, p. 47.
37. Hinds, pp. 106-7; Erasmus, pp. 154-57; Bushee, p. 645; Robertson, *Oneida Society*, p. 215; "American Communities," *American Socialist* 2, no. 37 (September 13, 1877).
38. Nordhoff, p. 129.
39. Albertson, p. 433; Robert V. Hine, *California's Utopian Colonies* (New Haven: Yale University Press, 1966), pp. 174-75; Le Warne, pp. 144, 180; Codman, pp. 87-91.
40. Shambaugh, p. 160; Bennet, *Hutterian Brethren*, pp. 199-201.
41. Andrews, *The People*, pp. 103-13; idem, *The Industries*, pp. 30-35; Arndt, *Harmony Society*, pp. 240-42; Shambaugh, p. 162; Robertson, *Oneida Society*, pp. 47, 212; Kanter, *Commitment and Community*, pp. 95-97; Rosabeth Moss Kanter, *Communes: Creating and Managing the Collective Life* (New York: Harper & Row, 1973), pp. 223-29; *The Social Gospel*, March, 1898, Published monthly by the Christian Commonwealth, Commonwealth, GA.
42. Shambaugh, pp. 160, 167; Nordhoff, pp. 400-401; David French and Elena French, *Working Communally: Patterns and Possibilities* (New York: Russell Sage Foundation, 1975), pp. 72-73; William M. Kephart, *Extraordinary Groups* (New York: St. Martin's, 1976), pp. 76-77.
43. Desroche, p. 224; Arndt, *Harmony Society*, pp. 242-47; Robert J. Hendrics, *Bethel and Aurora: An Experiment in Communism as Practical Christianity* (New

York: Press of Pioneers, 1933), pp. 39, 42; Bek, pp. 63-65; Shambaugh, p. 176; Codman, pp. 92-94; Hinds, p. 258; Hostetler, pp. 158, 270; Burton, pp. 29, 40, 130; Kanter, *Commitment and Community*, p. 95.

44. Nordhoff, p. 395.
45. Erasmus, pp. 158-60; Egbert and Persons, p. 150.
46. Hostetler, pp. 195-96, 181-82, 186, 268-69; Ivan A. Vallier, "Production Imperatives in Communal Systems" (Ph.D. dissertation, Harvard University, April 1959), pp. 349-77.
47. Bushee, p. 645; Erasmus, pp. 158-59; Shambaugh, pp. 224-27; Randall, pp. 49—50; John Humphrey Noyes, pp. 510-11.
48. Albertson, p. 440; Kanter, *Commitment and Community*, pp. 158-60; Infield, pp. 6-7.
49. Charles Gide, *Communist and Cooperative Colonies* (1930. Reprint. New York: AMS Press, 1974), p. 12.

23

Dualistic Relationships with the Outside World

Relationships between the communal settlements and the society around them were of a very special nature; it is doubtful whether their like existed in systems of interrelationships developed between small communities, unique in nature, and the society around them. There was not between them mutual interaction based on an exchange of services, nor were they relationships arising from tests of strength in power struggles or competition for influence.[1] The communes existed as small islands within the American society, viewed by their members as an "outside society," alien and opposed to their society, culture, norms, and values. Relationships between the communes and the external society, which had been stamped with the mark of *strange* and *foreign*, sometimes deteriorated into a sharp opposition, although they never really reached a point of polarized confrontation, except for isolated incidents. In general, we can say that the communes sought continued survival within a regime and a society highly contrasted in its nature to their own. They strove for a modus vivendi that would give them physical existence yet allow them to continue to maintain their socio-ideological uniqueness.[2] The relationships that developed moved between two diametrically opposed extremes: seclusion and isolation at one end, and active involvement at the other. The hesitations as to which of these two extremes to choose assumed considerable importance in the communal experience.

In the literature about the history of the communes in the United States, the prevailing opinion was that most of them strove to cut themselves off from society ("the outside world"), to go into seclusion and isolation in order to practice their faith and way of life undisturbed. These opinions were expressed in the first books published on the subject and were also adopted by historians and later scholars, but with certain reservations and clear distinction between religious communes and secular ones. All were in agreement that the religious communes desired to seclude and isolate themselves from the world around them.[3] This opinion was bolstered by the conclusions of scholars studying the Protestant sects. The opinion prevailing among these scholars was that the desire to cut oneself off from the world to realize the unique principles of one's faith is inherent in certain types of Protestant sects (mainly Anabaptists and Pietists), and is anchored in their religious views and their Christian origins.

Neil Smelser, in his *Theory of Collective Behavior*, discusses groups with well-crystallized orientation of values in a pluralistic society. He draws attention to the processes of withdrawal and seclusion in the American religious sects and points to the religious communes as a perfect example of such processes. Smelser adopts the view of T.E. Clark, who regards the religious-communist sects as "groups which withdraw from the world into settlements whose characteristic feature is the communal ownership of property."[4] Rosabeth Moss Kanter, in *Commitment and Community*, takes a similar view, claiming that severing ties with the outside world was one of the important ways of bringing about processes of commitment. For the communes, the outside world constituted a constant potential threat to their existence; hence most of the longer-lived communes ("the successful ones," as she calls them) developed a system of "insulating borders" that reduced to a minimum their contact with the outside world, either by settling in distant frontier regions or by imposing internal restrictions. Psychological, cultural, and intellectual fences erected between the two sides were so high as to become real barriers, expressed in the members' complete lack of interest in what went on beyond them in the world.[5]

Moss Kanter developed her conclusions into a theory claiming that seclusion served as a means of strengthening members' sense of commitment to the building of "successful" communes. Generalized opinions regarding the centrality of the element of withdrawal in the common experience of the successful communes could lead to the conclusion that there was a direct correlation between the degree of withdrawal and the ability to exist or the measure of survival of the communes. In other words, the more closed the commune was, the more perfectly it met the requirements essential to ensuring its continued existence. A conclusion of this nature could have far-reaching consequences regarding the understanding of what a commune is. It would be valuable, therefore, to examine empirically the ways in which withdrawal was achieved and its place in the communal experience, as viewed from a historical standpoint.

According to those studying the subject, withdrawal and seclusion in the religious communes were a typical phenomenon. The question therefore arises whether their segregation stemmed from their outlook and faith or had been forced upon them objectively because of the uniqueness of their small world that was unable to make a place for itself in a society so strange and alien to it. Study of their beliefs and creeds indicates a clear-cut desire on the part of all the members to separate themselves from society. We shall demonstrate this with examples taken from the principles of the stable communes.

Ephrata, the oldest of them all, existed as a tightly closed monastery. For the American-born Shakers, withdrawal from a "sin-steeped" outside world constituted one of the basic principles of their belief. The Shakers cultivated a sense of being special, being the chosen ones, subjects of the kingdom of heaven. In order to avoid as much as possible "contaminating" contact with the world, they set up a system of dependence that limited the contacts between their own people and the outside world; contact was restricted to a small number of trustees. These people conducted their business according to a rigid and detailed set of rules that reduced any contact between the two sides to the absolute minimum.[6] A similar approach was revealed by the perfectionists of Oneida. In the world view developed by John Humphrey Noyes the community was presented as a cell of the kingdom of heaven on earth and the outside world as "territory conquered by Satan." An elitist feeling of superiority toward the world around them was instilled in all members, and even penetrated the consciousness of their children. Although this commune maintained a wider network of contacts with the outside than did the Shakers, those who performed work outside the commune felt a need for "purification" on their return.[7]

The principles of a faith encouraging isolationism were also prevalent in all the immigrant communes, in addition to any objectively enforced segregation stemming from ethnic barriers of language, culture, or way of life. It was said of Harmony that an invisible wall separated the settlement from the outside world, while the separatists, founders of Zoar, intentionally chose a name that symbolized their desire for segregation from a "sinful world," and established an island of chosen ones who would be redeemed on the day of the Last Judgement. Among the inspirationalists, founders of Amana, the principles of seclusion became crystallized while they were still in Germany and continued to guide them in their choice of locations for settlement in the United States, constituting clear boundaries between them and the outside.[8]

Isolationism was a fundamental part of the way of life of the Hutterites over the 450 years of their existence in Europe and the United States. The Hutterites likened themselves to Noah's Ark, floating on the waters of a "flood of sin" in the life of this world. They viewed life on earth as temporary, and their commune as the only possible form of a pure Christian life, for the salvation of their souls and as a gate to life in the next world. Throughout their existence they had never sought ways to communicate with their surrounding world, claiming: "We are always on foreign soil." They zealously sought to accentuate their strangeness in various ways and especially through their special attire. This strangeness and alien ways, intentionally cultivated, created an air of constant conflict with the population around them. In the distant past such conflicts led to massacres (for instance, during the Thirty

Years' War in Moravia). With time, they learned to live with their differences and avoided extremist confrontations by migration and emigration to places where they could live according to their own ways.[9]

The desire for segregation as a matter of principle, which can be found in all the religious communes, was supported in the history of some of them by a feeling of siege forced upon them by the surrounding society. Moreover, most of the religious communes had experienced persecution by the church establishment during the earlier stages of their formation. Such maltreatment led most of them into a reaction similar to that of the Hutterites: they emigrated in order to avoid conflict. The communes persecuted in Europe moved to the United States, and the ones being molested in America pulled up stakes and moved to somewhere else on the continent (the perfectionists from Putney to Oneida, and the Hutterites from the United States to Canada). The persecutions, mainly during the early stages of commune history, strengthened the internal cohesion of the groups, making them all the more prone to withdraw and segregate themselves from the alien and hostile world around them.[10] These examples should suffice to give basis to the view that the desire for segregation was indeed characteristic of the religious communes, and was expressed in the principles of their faith. Let us turn now from the subjective principle plane to the ramified system of objective ties so that we may examine how this widespread network gave manifestation to the desire for segregation.

The first field to be examined is that of the ties of the communes with their neighbors. Did their desire for withdrawal close them off hermetically from all contact and intercourse with the inhabitants of their vicinity? The German communes, whose ties with their neighbors could be expected to be problematic because of their ethnic differences and the barriers of strangeness, proved to be otherwise. The Harmony group, which came to Pennsylvania from Wurtemburg in 1804 as a unified and well-consolidated religious sect, received advice, guidance, and financial aid from the more veteran local inhabitants from their very beginning. Moreover, during the early years, there was an outflow of people from the sect to the surrounding settlements. A considerable number of followers of George Rapp, the leader of the commune, were unable to adapt to the conditions of the new settlement, and left, to be absorbed by their surroundings. Ties developed with the local inhabitants (especially with those of German origin), which later led them to join the commune. Good-neighborly relationships were also established by other immigrant communes—Zoar, Amana, Beth-El, Bishop Hill.[11] These settlements contributed much to the development of regional services such as snow clearing in winter, fire fighting in summer, bridge repair and aid rendering in times of distress. Most instructive was the historical experience of the Hutterites who, for all their desire to cut themselves off, did not refrain from allowing ties of mutual aid to develop with the farmers nearby. They developed in their settlements service enterprises that supplied all the inhabitants in the region. Thus they cultivated a network of amicable relations with the outside.[12]

The idiosyncrasy of the communes attracted the attention of their neighbors. There was a constant stream of visitors coming to look and gain an impression, and in some cases to form a bond of friendship. The communes were always hospitable. Some even built hostels to receive their guests, sometimes seeing them turn into a place of refuge for the unfortunate and the oppressed of the district, especially during the winter months. The Shaker's communes and Oneida, established by native Americans, had no language barriers separating them from their neighbors, and if relations did sometimes become strained, it was because of tension brought on by opposition to their rejection of family ties and monogamy and their adoption of pacifism as a principle. Aside from these, warm and friendly relationships were the rule with the surrounding neighborhood circles. In Oneida, matters reached a point where, when certain churches began their persecution of commune members, a significant number of farmers in the area was found to have signed petitions in their defense.[13] The uniqueness of the communal settlement was an object of curiosity. Oneida turned the stream of visitors to economic advantage. Tourists from all over the country came to observe, and in the course of their stay were even given an opportunity to meet and talk with the members of the commune. Special booklets were printed in Oneida and circulated country wide, explaining the idea behind the commune, its principles and history, and stressing the contribution of these settlements to the development of the surrounding region. The Shaker settlements, as mentioned, from their very beginning had attracted many visitors whose admiration for the well-kept colony was sufficient to establish the reputation of the communes in the country. A constant stream of visitors descended on the Shaker settlements—even their neighbors came to participate in their prayer sessions, observe their dances, listen to their songs, and enjoy the hospitality which was one of the Shakers' strong points.[14]

Their openness toward people and the curiosity that brought a constant stream of visitors created a new reality which ran counter to the communes' desire for isolationism, but no effort was made to change the situation. The various religious communes took no drastic steps to close their gates and sever relations with their neighbors. On the contrary, over the years, the ties strengthened between the communes and their near surroundings and even expanded into other fields.

The communes' desire to close themselves off from the outside world included economic activities. We have pointed out above, that most of the communes at the outset tended toward autarchy—a desire to produce everything needed to supply their own requirements. Despite this desire, they were all forced by circumstances dictated by the nature of economic activity to maintain relations with the world around them, thus being integrated into the market in a manner and scope contrary to their original intentions. The transition from agriculture and services to specialized manufacturing of products destined for extracommunal markets was only one segment of a broader problem.

Another area connected with the problematics of external relations was the task of distributing the products and the routine of commerce. In all the communes except Oneida—where Noyes legitimized the trade of peddling—strong attempts were made to keep the members out of commerce, permitting them to engage in it only because it was a necessary evil they were compelled to practice. Here too, however, no serious effort was made to forbid it. Commercial relations with the outside world continued to expand and intensify despite self-imposed limitations and reservations. The main problem the communes faced was the human factor in this sort of activity. Cultivation of commercial ties made it necessary for the agents and merchants to remain outside the commune for extended periods of time, conducting negotiations with outsiders.

Even in Oneida the marketing jobs were regarded as defiling and required a period of purification after completion. Most communes made efforts to limit the number of members engaged in these occupations and assigned them only to a small number of carefully chosen trustees. Wherever possible, they left the sale of their products in the hands of outside salesmen and agencies, dealing with them in accordance with the accepted practices of a capitalist market.[15] Even the Hutterites, who had succeeded in preserving their seclusion, did not refrain from maintaining commercial relations with the outside world, adapting themselves, albeit with a measure of control, to the ways they were developing therein. This trend became quite pronounced during the period of their settlement in the United States. Their agricultural activities were outstanding in the manner and speed they integrated the developments of the American technology into their economy. They even put their advanced heavy agricultural implements—seeders, harvesters, and combines—at the disposal of their neighbor farmers who were behind in their work, and the contribution of the communes to the advancement of the private farms in the region was considerable.[16]

All the stable communes, in establishing themselves economically, had extensive economic ties with the world around them. Such relationships were being maintained concomitantly with the isolation of the religious, cultural, and social aspects of their life, and they continued to develop as the economic success of the communes increased. The latter enabled the communes to consolidate their standing and put them into positions of power and influence in their respective districts when they reached their peak. These usually were not exploited to hurt their economic competitors. On the contrary, in many instances the communes used their wealth to found enterprises that benefitted all the inhabitants of the region.[17] But despite all their altruistic deeds they were not able to dispel the atmosphere of envy that developed everywhere, widening the rift between the small farmers near them in straitened conditions and themselves, with their rapidly flourishing communal estates as a result of the advantages inherent in a mixed economy.

It was not surprising to find intentionally exaggerated descriptions in the press of the richness of the Shakers, Harmony, and Oneida, with hints at the deviousness of their methods (tax evasion, monopolies) as the basis for their wealth.[18] Similar cases of jealousy, rooted in the wide discrepancy between the economic achievements of the communes and the penury of the small farmers in their vicinity, were also evident between the Hutterites and their neighbors. Here too, it was possible to find occasional instances of defamation—that they paid no taxes, they discouraged commerce with the local retailers, preferring to buy in large lots from distant wholesalers. They were accused of attempting to take control of large contiguous pieces of territory, and to prevent this laws were passed, restricting the Hutterites with respect to land acquisition.[19] These tensions however, never developed into open conflicts because the communes did everything in their power to refute the accusations and reach understandings and a modus vivendi with their neighbors. These efforts to find a way to live together established the lines of permanent ties with the world around them.

The formation of religious communes as voluntary communities was based on elements of a religious bond common to all and serving as the basis for a covenant outlining their internal social relationships. Only some of them felt the need for legal backing by establishing their covenant in the laws of the country. As time passed and tensions between the communes and the outside world intensified—mainly because those who had left and their descendants disputed the rights to communal ownership of property—most of the communes took steps to give their intramural practices a legal foundation. Their intention was to use state law to formally legalize their own status in accord with their own beliefs and the established categories of the outside society.[20] Legalization of the commune's regulations created a permanent, formal system of interrelationships with the state institutions in legal categories essentially foreign to the world of the communes. This process already became manifest at the early stages of their development.

Most of the communes founded by German immigrants established themselves at the very outset as legally constituted societies so that the state authorities would recognize them. One year after the establishment of Harmony, its members signed the articles of the Harmony Society's constitution. These articles did not deal with the principles of their belief; their main purpose was to give the organization legal status vis-à-vis the authorities and to protect it from the dangers of possible liquidation due to external pressure. The members of Zoar acted similarly, establishing a formal constitution immediately after setting themselves up as a commune. Some years later they broadened its scope and adapted it to conform with the corporate laws of Ohio. The founders of Amana were so anxious to suit their laws to those of the state that on moving to Iowa—which was at that time still in its formative process—they held up the writing of their own constitution until the state's had been ratified in congress.[21]

The transition from a condition of "a law unto themselves" to one of adaptation to the laws of the state took place in the Shakers' communes when a number of legal suits were filed against them. These forced them to seek the services of the courts at an early stage in their history. The first suit was brought in 1799, when one of the members who had left sued Mount Lebanon for return of accumulated wages for work done and services rendered while he was a member of the settlement. The court rejected his claim, upholding the Shakers' position that the man had, on leaving, received compensation according to the internal laws of the commune of which he was a member. This precedent did not stop other suits from being brought, testing other exceptional principles adopted by the Shakers—separation of families, education of children separated from their biological parents, nonpayment of war taxes. The Shakers succeeded in turning aside all the claims, but the legal processes were heavy and drawn-out, necessitating the hiring of lawyers from outside to help them base their own constitutions on state law and American legal principles.[22]

Oneida, too, found itself in a similar position, having to defend itself in a court of law with the aid of hired attorneys. Later on one of these attorneys, R. Towner, joined the commune and guided the group from within in its involvement with legal processes.[23] The German communes, also wishing to give their constitution formal backing by state law, were not spared legal problems; they found themselves confronted with a series of law suits, some of which turned into long, drawn-out battles, even reaching the federal court. The communes usually won their cases.[24] The U.S. legal institutions were unwilling to compel them to act in a manner contrary to their principles, with respect to ownership of property and in other areas such as family, education, and pacifism. Against the sanctity of private ownership stood the principles of religious liberty and freedom of association. The American legal system recognized the right of commune members to organize in order to maintain their beliefs, thus enabling the communes to give their separateness a legal basis.

The religious communes maintained a measure of reserve or even denial toward a political regime. Their beliefs were either pacifist or antiestablishment and refused in principle to recognize the government as an institution. These beliefs notwithstanding, they saw no reason to enter into conflict with its various bodies. Most of them sought some sort of modus vivendi that would allow them to continue to exist within a state as separate, autonomous social cells. Particularly noteworthy were the communes that had originated in Germany, whose Lutheran origins made them acknowledge the state and their obligations to it.

Harmony maintained contacts with the state bodies throughout its entire history. Its spiritual leader, George Rapp, who became an American citizen upon arrival on its shores, applied to the president with a request to help settle the members of his sect on government lands, and to this end even undertook negotiations with the authorities in Washington.[25] Frederick Rapp, who later became the representative of the commune, carried on extensive political activity in the state of Indiana during the period of their settlement in New Harmony, and participated in some of the decisions that were important to the future of the state such as the selection of the site and planning of the capital city, Indianapolis. The involvement of Harmony people in local and federal politics also continued in later years and included participation in presidential elections and taking stands on political and economic questions.

Similar attitudes were taken by other German communes—Zoar, Amana, and Beth-El. All acknowledged the importance of political institutions in preserving social and economic stability and order. They therefore refrained from any moves that could bring them into conflict with the state. This was not an easy thing to do, since they consistently refused to cooperate with any activity that could be construed as supporting the army or war. No wonder, then, that during the Civil War they ran afoul of the authorities. They voiced support for the Northern Union, but avoided any direct involvement or participation in the war. Similar problems regarding the Civil War were faced by communes founded by native Americans who, while identifying with the war aims of the North but being extreme pacifists, avoided any kind of involvement.

The Shakers, too, suffered for their pacifism as far back as the Revolutionary War. Throughout their history they were in constant search of legal ways to make their pacifism a viable tenet. During the Civil War they approached the president, requesting him to grant them formal exemption from any military obligation and payment of war tax, promising to give financial support to society and contribute to civilian welfare and service projects.[26] A similar though slightly modified stand was adopted by the people of Oneida, who were prepared to compromise by payment of high taxes as an indemnity fee for the release of their members from military service. Unlike the German communes, the Shakers and Oneida refrained from any involvement in political life, neither participating in elections nor taking stands on questions arising from political struggle. Their attitude toward the political institutions was one of estrangement but not of hostility. On the contrary, there are in the Shakers' and Oneida's publications many expressions of appreciation for the principles of religious tolerance in the American political system, permitting them and their like a decent existence.

During this process of development a rapprochement took place between the communes and the state near the end of the nineteenth century, when Frederick Evans made his mark on the Shakers. At that time the trend toward identification with the political regime of the United States intensified. In the 1870s, when Noyes began publication of his newspaper, the *American Socialist*, a sympathetic approach to contemporary political problems became much more evident, especially toward the socialist groups that began to organize in the country.[27]

The Hutterites—to this day living by the principle of "the people shall dwell alone" (Numbers, 20:9)—in the United States and Canada also did not shy away from links with state institutions. These were initiated even before their immigration to the United States, when they requested and received assurances from President Grant that their pacifist singularity would be preserved. They maintained these links throughout their settlement in the frontier territories of South Dakota, then undergoing a process of political organization. During World War I the Hutterites engaged in a bitter and tragic conflict with the American authorities. On questions of enlistment in the army and taking part in the war effort they reacted in a characteristic manner, by emigrating to Canada, where they were able to receive suitable official assurances. Later, when the way was once again clear for return to the United States, close relationships with the local authorities were resumed. However, these continued to be fraught with tensions and contradictions, especially in anything connected with arrangements that would enable them to circumvent the laws of the country and maintain a separate educational system. On this subject, as with the other controversial ones that developed throughout the entire history of the Hutterites in the United States, their differences with the government were always resolved by working out a modus vivendi based on compromise and a measure of adaptation to the framework of the state laws.

The experience of the Hutterites, then, also supports the conclusion that all the communes, despite their attitude of reservation and estrangement toward state institutions and politics, found a way to exist legally within the American system.[28]

Until now we have been surveying areas in which the religious communes maintained extensive connections with the outside world. Although we have not encompassed all the possible fields, we have sufficiently shown that the withdrawal of the religious communes never went too far, and their isolationism was never hermetic. Moreover, we have also indicated the gap between principle and reality which forced upon the communes a network of contacts with the outside world. The communes themselves were also aware of this discrepancy. Anyone studying the literature of the communes will soon discover the inner struggle between their desire for isolationism on the one hand and the need to maintain communication and contact on the other.

Edward Andrews, one of the first contemporaries to study the Shakers, closely examined their vacillation between the desire to isolate themselves and the need to work in the outside world, which was already evident in their publications at the beginning of the nineteenth century. Andrews saw it as a typical phenomenon. According to him it was the very uniqueness of the Shakers that led them to maintain relations—albeit conflicting ones—with the outside while desiring to preserve their ways and bring converts to their camp.[29] J.M. Whitworth also dwelt on this inherent dilemma, in his socio-historical comparison between the Shakers on the one hand and Oneida and the modern Bruderhof on the other. He defined them as utopian-religious communes whose aim was to bring God's blueprint to realization on earth. Whitworth discerned in all of them an inner struggle between their tendency to isolate and close themselves off from a world steeped in sin and the need to work within it, to bring converts to their faith. Their struggle expressed itself in their being able to lead lives with a measure of viable detachment, but which did not cut them off entirely from the outside world and allowed them controlled communication with it.[30]

Whitworth's research made an important contribution to the understanding of the inner ambivalence of the religious communes in their attitude toward the outside world. Its weakness, however, was in limiting its treatment to a certain type of communes—those he defined as utopian. But this theory can and should be applied to all the religious communes. The generality of this outlook can be deduced from a similar theory put forward by Professor Ruth Shonle Cavan in relation to the closed religious groups, including the Hutterites. These groups, which cannot be included in Whitworth's category of "utopian" were indeed intentionally seeking to create a barrier between themselves and the world around them, but had never succeeded in leading lives that could be considered absolutely independent of the outside world. Thus, for them, too, a reality was created which, although characterized by a striving for seclusion, at the same time did not seek to avoid contact with the external society.[31]

On the basis of what has been said up to now, and with the support of the theories mentioned, it is possible to ascribe validity to the claim that all religious communes, even while cultivating their desire for seclusion, were forced to maintain a broad network of contacts with the outside world, a situation that grew out of their objective requirements for existence and despite their isolationist outlook.

The relations between the socialist communes and the surrounding society should have been without problems of the kind described above, since these communes, which had arisen to try to influence society in general, bore within themselves elements of integral involvement in that society. However—and this must be made clear—inspired by a utopian dream, the socialist communes intended to influence society in a special way: not by violent revolution, which they rejected outright, nor by a series of legislative reforms, which was foreign to their radical experience, but by the establishment of exemplary societies, bringing their influence to bear on their surroundings. This path imminently bore the seeds of the problems inherent in their complex relationship with the world around them: desiring to become exemplary societies, they could only achieve it by cutting themselves off from the society outside and nullifying its negative effects. So once again, the element of isolationism appears, but with different motives from those of the religious communes.

The complex relationships with the external world stood out clearly in the succinct definition given to one of the utopian communes by the Californian scholar Robert V. Hine: ''A Utopian commune . . . consists of a group of people who are attempting to establish a new social pattern based upon a vision of the ideal society and who have withdrawn themselves from the community at large to embody that vision in experimental form. The purpose is usually to create a model which other colonies and eventually mankind in general will follow.''[32] Further on in his argument Hine explained that the element of withdrawal had played an important role in the existence of the communes attempting to change society from within. He explained that the socialist communes, like the religious ones, had a negative attitude toward the nature of the existing society. They sharply criticized the competitive capitalist system, presenting the example of their own way of life as an alternative.

These utopian communes, wishing by power of example to establish here and now the society of the future, bore imminent elements of isolationism and seclusion expressed in a number of prominent aspects of their life style. The first of these related to their social makeup: by their very nature these communes were populated by elite groups that were not typical of the variety of groups usually found in society. For the most part they practiced strict selection in their choice of members. Candidates were required to declare their identification with socialist and cooperative principles and had to undergo a period of candidacy then finally be approved by the commune for full membership. The experience with nonselective acceptance of members was negative. Any community where it had been tried, even for a short time, soon switched to the system of selection. Even in those communes such as New Harmony and the Christian Commonwealth where selection was not formally practiced, people arriving there were for the most part motivated by social and moral forces. As a result of such a selection, a large number of active members with high potential would be concentrated in a single settlement. Assemblages of elite groups aroused criticism and disagreement in friendly circles, who felt this meant a certain amount of waste and that to influence society it would better distribute people of this calibre—the ''leavening material''—among a number of settlements rather than keep them all in one commune.[33]

Other objective processes of isolation and seclusion developed on a territorial plane among the socialist communes. In their search for suitable locations to set up their exemplary settlements they wandered into areas distanced from the centers of population. By doing so they brought upon themselves geographic isolation and were cut off from the centers of the very society which they desired to correct. John Humphrey Noyes, who noted this trend in the Fourierists, pointed this out in the 1840s, as one of the grave errors that brought about a weakening of their influence in American society.[34]

There were communes that wandered to the wilderness of the western frontier regions, thinking that there they could wield greater influence in shaping the institutions of the outside society in their own image, or at least in their own spirit. They very soon learned that the people inhabiting the frontier were not exactly the kind who were interested in adopting their social experiments. And so their geographic isolation was intensified by social isolation.[35] Alcander Longley, one of the enthusiastic founders of the communes in the Midwest, spoke of these difficulties, but consoled himself that they were only temporary. He hoped that when people finally understood the message of the communes—delivered by intensive education and propaganda—the word would quickly spread to bring about territorially continuous "spaces of fulfillment," and from there it would extend at one jump to society at large. Longley adhered to his belief and spent the rest of his life in communes. These were small ones, coming into being and then breaking up soon after, with the dream of "territorial continuity" remaining nothing more than a pipe dream.[36]

The socialist communes, except for Brook Farm, existed as small settlements, isolated, and far away from the centers of population and focal points of social and political activity. And so it happened that these socialist communes, which had arisen with the aim of being the forerunners of a movement which would change the face of society, found themselves existing in tiny backwater groups, in not-so-splendid isolation.

The geographic isolation had internal social consequences that intensified the process of seclusion. The barrenness of their existence in far-off places with no decent means of communication was a hardship that quickly became unbearable for the intellectually aware commune members who had come to live in these places from urban centers replete with a wide variety of spiritual and cultural possibilities. Add to this the hard physical life, the harsh climate, the primitive conditions, and back-breaking farm labor such as they had never experienced before, and it is clear that life became one long, exhausting battle for existence. The reserves of spiritual energy they had brought with them to help build their new society were all spent on desperate efforts to overcome the primitive conditions of everyday life. Those of them who had come fully charged with idealism found themselves wasting it on dozens of dull, everyday tasks, with no opportunity to free themselves for the spiritually uplifting activities for the benefit of society, as they had previously expected they would be doing. Others who had come from more deprived backgrounds, hoping to improve their lives, found themselves floundering in a dunghill of poverty and deprivation in some tiny, miserable hamlet. Both groups soon realized to their chagrin that the yawning chasm separating their expectations from the harsh realities of their actual lives was unbridgeable. In circumstances such as these, it was not long before their frustration and disappointment surfaced and exodus began. Only those hewn from real pioneer-idealist stock held on. They put all they had into the fight for existence, which grew more and more difficult. The prospects for becoming involved in outside activity and having greater influence on society grew dimmer. The overall aims that had originally brought them there gradually ceased to have any real significance.[37]

The wide gap between the socialist communes and capitalist society did not arise solely from reasons rooted in the communes themselves. The capitalists' attitude toward them was also a contributing factor. The relationships developed between society at large and the communes were unbalanced and in a state of constant fluctuation. Those whose system of values was based on private enterprise, individualism, and competition found it difficult to understand the phenomenon of groups of people living together and basing their lives on the principle of community of goods and the rejection of private enterprise. They also had misunderstandings with some of their own supporters. True, during the early stages of the communes—fraught with internal social crises and ideological upheavals—it was common to heap on them praise and admiration. Commune members were depicted as perfect idealists, taking upon themselves the burden of turning the vision of an ideal society into reality. Thus it was with Owenism and Fourierism in the United States, when a large number of the social and intellectual elite, charmed by the magic tidings heralding a new social order, built up exaggerated expectations far beyond the communes' ability to realize them.[38] Disappointment quickly followed suit, replacing the overoptimistic admiration with skepticism, contempt, and cynicism which, while not developing into open enmity, paved the way for the formation of a critical and negative attitude toward the communes in the outside world. Moreover, there were always groups of people who were unable to understand the idealistic motivation behind those turning to communal life and hence attributed to them all sorts of hidden negative motives. In those circles rumors were rife, talking of free love and "wild" sex in the communes. Suspicions also grew regarding secret plans for economic monopolistic take-overs of certain branches of manufacturing, marketing, or lands in the region.

Thus, despite the communes' desire to exert their influence by example, the actual reality around them was such that not only did the torch of their own special way of life fail to light the way for society at large, it did not even illuminate the near surroundings.[39] Even the socialist communes—which had arisen maintaining links with political movements whose intention it was to serve as a base for vigorous socialist activity—did not achieve any great degree of understanding or cooperation from outside people. Perhaps this can be better understood if we remember that the first communes of this type were made up of European socialist groups that had immigrated to the United States such as Icaria, Communia, Reunion, and New Odessa. These communities, isolated because of their ethnic background, made no effort to develop ties with their American milieu. The Icaria group, standard bearers of a revolutionary socialist vision, were unable to win over to their cause more than a handful of converts who were not French-speaking. The result was that the surrounding people regarded them as a band of socialist eccentrics, upholders of an un-American ideology, and therefore made no attempt to mix with them.[40] But even the other communes, founded from the 1880s onward by native Americans whose language and cultural background were the same as that of their neighbors, failed to develop two-way ties and cooperation with their surroundings.

Le Warne, writing on the communes of the northwestern United States, described the socialist communes' attempts to develop normal relations with their neighbors by organizing various regional cultural projects and nevertheless failing to break down the barriers of estrangement. The neighbors took advantage of all the opportunities offered them by the communes, but this did not in the end prevent them from heaping slander upon them and falsely laying on "those terrible socialists" all kinds of calumnies.[41] This atmosphere of alienation and estrangement also prevailed in other groups as well as in neighbors who felt distant from the spiritual world of the communes. Even among the groups closest to them—the political parties from whence they had sprung in the cities—one could find similar attitudes.

Interesting evidence on this subject was given by Walter Millsap, one of the veterans of the socialist commune Llano in California, in a personal interview to a historian who was compiling an oral documentation many years after the break-up of the commune:

> One of the strangest things that nobody seemed able to understand, was that our greatest opposition during the whole life of Llano Colony came not from capitalists at all. It came first from the labor union and second from the Socialist Party. . . . The Colony had been sympathetic with labor . . . but because the colony policy differed from the schemes laid down by the labor unions, that was bad. The labor unions could not support the colony. Some of the people in the colony were Socialist but we didn't get out and work for political candidates. . . . Our problem was getting food and shelter out of the land . . . so the Socialist Party washed their hands of us . . . and that was one of the peculiar phenomena that nobody could ever understand about Llano.[42]

This personal testimony is corroborated by information from a number of other sources describing the tense relationships between the communes and the Socialist Party.

As has been shown, there was in the relationships of all the communes with the outside world an inherent dualism that was manifest in an isolation/involvement syndrome on the part of the communes. This dualism was an objective feature characterizing all the communes and was derived from their experience as unique social cells existing in a milieu alien to them, and whose values were opposed to that milieu. We have shown that the communes constantly vacillated between two polarities—isolationism on the one hand and involvement with the outside world on the other. At the same time, considerable differences were observed among the various communes as to the extent of the leanings of the various relationships toward one pole or the other. The differences were always derived from the different world views the communes had adopted and the relative weight of principles stemming from their identification with one pole or the other. It is therefore appropriate to say that the degree of isolationism or involvement practiced was unique to each individual commune, while the element of dualism—the isolationism/involvement syndrome—was common to all the communes and had an objective and general nature inherent in the process of establishing a small society based on values entirely different from those of the larger society.

Notes

1. Peter M. Blau, *Exchange and Power in Social Life* (New York: Wiley, 1967), pp. 21-23, 93, 118-25, 314-21.
2. Ruth Shonle Cavan, "Patterns of Exchange between Closed Religious Subsocieties and the Core Society," in *The Small City and Regional Community*, Proceedings of the First Conference on the Small City and Regional Community, (Madison: University of Wisconsin. March 30-31, 1978), pp. 332, 333.
3. William Alfred Hinds, *American Communities and Cooperative Colonies* (1878. Reprinted and enl. Philadelphia: Porcupine, 1975), p. 24; Morris Hillquit, *History of Socialism in the United States*, 5th ed. (New York: Dover, 1971), p. 27; Ralph Albertson, *A Survey of Mutualistic Communities in America* (New York: AMS Press, 1973; 1st ed. 1936), pp. 434, 436. Donald Egbert and Stow Persons, eds., *Socialism and American Life*, 2 vols. (Princeton: Princeton University Press, 1952), pp. 127-28, 627; Arthur Bestor, *Backwood Utopias: The Sectarian Origins and the Owenite Phase of Communitarian Socialism in America, 1663-1829*, 2d ed. (Philadelphia: University of Pennsylvania Press, 1971), pp. 5-6, 255; Alice Felt Tyler, *Freedom's Ferment* (New York: Harper & Row, 1962), pp. 108, 127-28; David Cnaani, *Batey Medot: Essays on Communal Life* (Merchavia: Sifriat Hapoalim, 1960), pp. 41-44, 48 (Hebrew).
4. Neil J. Smelser, *Theory of Collective Behavior* (New York: Free Press, 1962), pp. 314, 335-37; Robert E. Park, *On Social Control and Collective Behavior* (Chicago: University of Chicago Press, 1967), pp. 241, 245; Clark, pp. 133-35.
5. Rosabeth Moss Kanter, *Commitment and Community: Communes and Utopias in*

Sociological Perspective (Cambridge, Mass.: Harvard University Press, 1972), pp. 63, 83-86; Julius Friedrich Sachse, *The German Sectarians of Pennsylvania, 1742-1800: A Critical and Legendary History of the Ephrata Cloister and the Dunkers* (Philadelphia: published by the author, 1899. New York: AMS Press, 1971), vol. 2, p. 196.

6. Edward D. Andrews, *The People Called Shakers: A Search for Perfect Society* (New York: Dover, 1963), pp. 204-23; idem, *The Community Industries of the Shakers* (Philadelphia: Porcupine, 1972), pp. 32-35, 54-55.
7. Pierrepont Noyes, *My Father's House: An Oneida Boyhood* (London: J. Murray, 1937), pp. 3, 115-18; Maren Lockwood Carden, *Oneida: Utopian Community to Modern Corporation* (Baltimore: Johns Hopkins University Press, 1969), p. 74; Allan Estlake, *The Oneida Community* (1900. Reprint. New York: AMS Press, 1973), pp. 60-61; John McKelvie Whitworth, *God's Blueprints: A Sociological Study of Three Utopian Sects* (London: Routledge & Kegan Paul, 1975), pp. 113, 121, 152-53, 163; Egbert and Persons, pp. 146-47, 175; Karl J.R. Arndt, *George Rapp's Harmony Society, 1785-1847*, rev. ed. (New York: Associated University Presses, 1972), p. 121; John S. Duss, *The Harmonists: A Personal History* (Philadelphia: Porcupine, 1972), pp. 44-54; Emilius O. Randall, *History of the Zoar Society: A Sociological Study in Communism* (New York: AMS Press, 1971; 1st ed. 1904), p. 6.
8. Bertha M.H. Shambaugh, *Amana That Was and Amana That Is* (Iowa City: Iowa State Historical Society, 1932), p. 362; Charles Nordhoff, *The Communistic Societies of the United States* (New York: Shocken, 1965), p. 44; Hinds, pp. 23-24; William G. Bek, "A German Communistic Society in Missouri," *Missouri Historical Review* (October 1908):65, 105.
9. John A. Hostetler, *Hutterite Society* (Baltimore: Johns Hopkins University Press, 1977), pp. 20, 82, 130-33, 146, 155, 173, 287; Ruth Shonle Cavan, "The Future of a Historic Commune: Amana," in *Communes: Historical and Contemporary*, ed. Ruth S. Cavan and Man S. Das (New Delhi: Vikas Publishing House, 1979), p. 332.
10. Whitworth, p. 81; Hinds, p. 51; John Patterson MacLean, *Shakers of Ohio* (Philadelphia: Porcupine, 1974), p. 362; Adelman, pp. 20-22.
11. Arndt, *Harmony Society*, pp. 67-68, 78-80, 102; Duss, pp. 21-23; Bek, pp. 71-72.
12. Hostetler, pp. 122-25.
13. Shambaugh, p. 90; Robert J. Hendricks, *Bethel and Aurora: An Experiment in Communism as Practical Christianity* (New York: Press of Pioneers, 1933), pp. 27-28, 110; Hinds, p. 87; Randall, p. 40; Mark Holloway, *Heaven on Earth: Utopian Communities in America, 1680-1880* (New York: Dover, 1966), p. 224; Arndt, *Harmony Society*, p. 205; Nordhoff, p. 43; *American Socialist*, 3, no. 38 (September 20, 1877):298; Robert Allerton Parker, *A Yankee Saint: John Humphrey Noyes and the Oneida Community* (New York: Putnam, 1935), p. 268; Carden, pp. 80-84; Constance Noyes Robertson, ed., *Oneida Community: An Autobiography, 1851-1876* (Syracuse: Syracuse University Press, 1971), pp. 17-24; *Handbook of the Oneida Community 1867 and 1871: Bound with Mutual Criticism* (New York: AMS Press, 1976; 1st ed. 1867), pp. 28-36.
14. Flo Morse, *The Shakers and the World's People* (New York: 1980), pp. 152-72; Carden, pp. 37-42.
15. Pierrepont Noyes, p. 15; Arndt, *Harmony Society*, pp. 205, 207, 210-11; Hendricks, p. 107; Bek, pp. 73, 100-101; Randall, p. 36; Shambaugh, p. 98.
16. Hostetler, pp. 125, 179, 195-96, 257-60; Paul K. Conkin, *Two Paths to Utopia:*

The Hutterites and the Llano Colony (Lincoln: University of Nebraska Press, 1964), pp. 55, 59, 68.

17. Arndt, *Harmony Society*, p. 71; Andrews, *The Industries*, p. 24; idem, *The People*, p. 217; Hendricks, p. 124.
18. Marguerite Fellows Melcher, *The Shaker Adventure* (New York: The Shaker Museum, 1975), p. 143; Duss, pp. 51, 71-73; Arndt, *Harmony Society*, pp. 260-65; Andrews, *The Industries*, pp. 53-54; idem, *The People*, pp. 217-18; Pierrepont Noyes, pp. 113-18.
19. Hostetler, pp. 131, 195-98, 257-60, 268; David Barkin and John W. Bennett, "Kibbutz and Colony: Collective Economies and the Outside World," *Comparative Studies in Society and History* 14, no. 4 (September 1972):472-73.
20. Carol Weisbrod, *The Boundaries of Utopia* (New York: Pantheon, 1980), pp. 62-74.
21. Arndt, *Harmony Society*, pp. 70-79; Nordhoff, p. 81; Randall, pp. 7-11, 41, 79; W.R. Perkins and B.L. Wick, *History of the Amana Society*, Historical Monograph no. 1 (Iowa City: State University of Iowa Publications, 1891), pp. 52-59, 82-89; Shambaugh, p. 95.
22. Weisbrod, pp. 45-50, 118-21; Andrews, *The People*, pp. 205-10.
23. Carden, p. 81.
24. Weisbrod, pp. 123-61, Arndt, *Harmony Society*, pp. 372-77. On lawsuits against the Hutterites see Hostetler, pp. 276-78; Randall, pp. 23-31.
25. Arndt, *Harmony Society*, pp. 62-65, 83-84, 105-80, 379-413, 517; Duss, pp. 24-25.
26. Shambaugh, pp. 95, 146-47; Hinds, pp. 113-14; Nordhoff, p. 104; Julia Neal, *By Their Fruits: The Story of Shakerism in South Union, Kentucky* (New York: North Carolina Press, 1947), pp. 186-214; Andrews, *The People*, pp. 80-81, 212-14; Anna White and Leila S. Taylor, *Shakerism: Its Meaning and Message* (Columbus, Oh.: Heer, 1904. New York: AMS Press, 1971), pp. 181-203.
27. Egbert and Persons, pp. 139, 147, 149; Melchers, pp. 175-85; Weisbord, pp. 77-78; Henri Desroche, *The American Shakers: From Neo-Christianity to Pre-Socialism*, ed. and trans. John K. Savacoal (Boston: University of Massachusettes Press, 1971), pp. 229-43; Andrews, *The People*, pp. 213-14, 219-20; Carden, p. 84; Whitworth, pp. 154-55.
28. Hostetler, pp. 113-14, 128-35, 256, 258, 260, 276-78; John W. Bennet, *Hutterian Brethren: The Agricultural Economy and Social Organization of a Communal People* (San Francisco: Stanford University Press, 1967), pp. 98-105; Weisbrod, p. 208.
29. Andrews, *The People*, pp. 204-8, 214-21; Egbert and Persons, p. 139.
30. Whitworth, pp. 210-35.
31. Cavan, "The Future," pp. 329-33; Hillquit, p. 129.
32. Robert V. Hine, *California's Utopian Colonies* (New Haven: Yale University Press, 1966), p. 5; Bestor, p. 256.
33. Hine, pp. 84-85; John Humphrey Noyes, *History of American Socialism* (1870). Reprinted as *Strange Cults and Utopias of Nineteenth-Century America* (New York: Dover, 1966), p. 653; John Egerton, *Visions of Utopia: Nashoba, Rugby, Ruskin, and the "New Communities" in Tennessee's Past* (University of Tennessee Press in cooperation with the Tennessee Historical Commission), p. 75. R.W. Emerson, W.H. Channing, and J.F. Clarke, *Memoirs of Margaret Fuller Ossoli*, 3 vols. (London: Richard Bentley, 1852), vol. 2, pp. 268-75, quoted in Henry W. Sams, ed. *Autobiography of Brook Farm* (Englewood Cliffs, N.J.: Prentice-Hall,

1959) pp. 216-17; William E. Wilson, *The Angel and the Serpent: The Story of New Harmony* (Bloomington, Ind.: Indiana University Press, 1975), p. 193.

34. John Humphrey Noyes, pp. 1, 510.
35. Bestor, pp. 233-36.
36. Kenneth M. Roemer, *The Obsolete Necessity: America in Utopian Writings, 1888-1900* (Kent, Oh.: Kent State University Press, 1976), pp. 53-54.
37. Joseph J. Cohen, *In Quest of Heaven: The Story of the Sunrise Cooperative Farm Community* (New York: Sunrise History Publishing Committee, 1957), pp. 197-98, 210-13; Avrahm Yarmolinsky, *A Russian's American Dream: A Memoir on William Frey* (University of Kansas Press, 1965), pp. 77-78; Charles Pierre Le Warne, *Utopias on Puget Sound, 1885-1915* (Seattle: University of Washington Press, 1975), pp. 770-72; John Humphrey Noyes, pp. 246, 265, 351-53; *The Coming Nation*, no. 103; *Cooperator*, no. 48.
38. Elisabeth P. Peabody, ''Plan of the West Roxbury Community,'' *The Dial* 2 (January 1842):361-72, quoted in Sams, ed., pp. 67-68.
39. Hinds, p. 254; Katherine Burton, *Paradise Planters: The Story of Brook Farm* (1939. Reprint. New York: AMS Press, 1973), pp. 104-5; Bestor, pp. 222-24; Robert V. Hine, *California's Utopian Colonies* (New Haven: Yale University Press, 1966), pp. 93, 98, 176. Joseph Cohen, p. 170; Conkin, p. 186.
40. Hine, p. 76; Albert Shaw. *Icaria: A Chapter in the History of Communism* (New York: AMS Press 1973. Originally published 1884), pp. 118-123.
41. Le Warne, pp. 72, 162; Cohen, *In Quest of Heaven*, p. 170; Hinds, pp. 531-34.
42. Walter Millsap, ''Llano Cooperative Colony,'' interview conducted by Abe Hoffman, completed under the auspices of the Oral History Program (University of California at Berkeley, 1969; located in the Bancroft Library), pp. 84-85.

24

Dissolution of the Communes: Options or Inevitability?

A shadow hangs over the history of the communes in the United States—that of scores of communes which broke up while still in their early stage. Only a few survived for more than ten years, and the number that lasted for a generation is minute. The exceptions to this are the Hutterian communes that have existed continuously from 1530 until the present. Except for these, the story of the U.S. communes is a collection of pathetic and sad case histories whose heroes were idealists and visionaries going forth to build God's kingdom on earth or create a new social order. Since their vision did not materialize and their expectations remained unfulfilled they abandoned their attempt, frustrated and disillusioned at seeing their vision smashed on the rocks of disappointing reality. In view of these episodes it might appear that there is substance in the claims of those critical of the communal idea—that the prospects for communes lasting for any length of time are nil, because they are based on principles that go against human nature and therefore contain elements that would inevitably destroy them. This generalization should be examined in detail in view of the historical facts presented in this book.

It should be stated at the outset that a comprehensive and comparative survey of the breakup of communes does not point to the existence of one single course that repeats itself in all the communes as a regular and predictable process. Disbandment was, as we have said, an occurrence common to most of the communes but affected each in its own specific way, depending on actual conditions—the makeup of its membership, the reasons for its establishment, and the difficulties encountered. The wide variety of disbandment processes make any attempt at generalization extremely difficult. A comparative study overcomes this difficulty by dividing the communes into groups with a common denominator, making it possible to pinpoint typical features. From the present study we can discern a clear difference in the processes of breakup between the short-lived communes and those which functioned as stable entities for several decades. In the more stable communes we can differentiate between the breakup processes they share with the noncommunal American communities and those that were exclusively characteristic of communes.

Short-Lived Communes

Most of the communes of this type broke up at their outset—in the initial stages of their existence—and some of them even before the end of their first year.[1] In many instances the reasons for the collapse were errors made during the process of formation, namely, lack of components essential for effective functioning. Sometimes random factors were involved, mishaps and calamities that had a fatal impact since these short-lived communes had not had time to become robust enough to cope with the disasters besetting them.

The large majority of these communes had been formed in haste, with no suitable ideological preparation, and without proper training in communal living given to their members who had come from diverse backgrounds and different geographical regions. Most had been attracted to the communes while searching for a panacea that would guarantee instant salvation for the troubles of society. There were also those who sought a personal sanctuary or a solution to their own personal problems. Thus, a motley band came together in these communes—idealists, religious, or social visionaries—and with them escapists whose personal problems led them to choose the commune. This heterogeneous society was also not free of riffraff and other unsavory types who seized the opportunity to get free board and lodgings without too much effort. In the absence of a firmly integrated social framework with clear regulations, and under the influence of a radical ideology putting faith—naive as it was—in every man as a person, the absorption of members was completely unselective. The social structure became amorphous and unmanageable. The varied social structure, a leadership without authority, and the lack of a clear and firm ideology were fertile ground for the ongoing differences of opinion, the formation of opposing cliques and warring factions, and the power struggles—all stifling any attempts to harness the various social elements for the advancement of clear social goals. Consequently, because of the special nature of communal conditions, the economic objectives were also not achieved.[2] In the economic as in the social sphere the feature characterizing these communes was the hastiness and a lack of minimal requirements for the establishment of an effective socio-economic body. For the most part they settled in difficult agricultural areas, on poor land, without agricultural training and without skilled teams with knowledge of working conditions. In most cases they even lacked the necessary financial resources for building the requisite infrastructure.

Most of the short-lived communes existed in dire material conditions except for New Harmony and some of the Fourierist communes who managed to obtain substantial funding during their formative period. Such conditions were typical during the early days of all pioneering frontier settlements. However, while as for settlements showing an ability to survive this period was only a stage in their transition to economic security and well-being; for the short-lived communes continual material deprivation became a way of life. Since some of those reaching the communes had gone there aiming to improve their living standards, their disappointment was quick in coming. But these were not the only ones to lose their enthusiasm. The gap between their expectations and the grim reality affected everyone. The feeling of helplessness slackened motivation, which in turn increased the deprivation and created a vicious circle rapidly leading to precipitate decline and collapse. What had been presented as the basis for a new society, rich in possibilities, turned out to have feet of clay. The smallest shock, external or internal, could bring about collapse. Many communes ceased to exist because of such common mishaps as fires, drought and other natural disasters, quarrels among members—even before they managed to utilize their human and economic potential.

Moreover, communes whose members had only recently formed a group were not easily able to break away from the world they had elected to leave. In such circumstances, the communal members were unable to cut themselves off from the outside world. Their mentality remained unchanged. The bridges to their past remained intact. Many of them retained private property and did not hand it over to the communes. Despite the change in location and social framework the members were unable to shake off the influences of the world in which they had so recently lived. These influences played a distinctive role in the rapidly increasing doubts about their new beliefs. Such people, so noted for their impatience and expectations that soon there would be a significant improvement in their lives, wanted this here and now and not in some unforeseeable future. Maximalist as they were in their expectations, their commitment to the communal group and the effort they themselves invested in it remained minimal. The results were quick to follow.[3]

In addition to the above, the short-lived communes lacked other elementary ingredients for consolidation and progress, and under these circumstances their breakup was indeed inevitable. The rapid collapse of social organizations due to lack of basic elements essential to their existence (quality of the human material, expectations, correct programs, economic conditions, etc.) is not confined to communes alone. Various socio-economic organizations (settlements, economic institutions) suffer from the same trouble. Thus, in spite of the large number of short-lived communes that broke up at an early stage, conclusions of substance should not be drawn concerning their communal nature, since their problems of existence and survival were not truly tested in this respect.

Long-Lived Communes

Dozens of communes managed to survive the critical early stages and to function for long periods. During their existence they overcame obstacles such as those described above and many others as well. But in the end they too succumbed. Here again one should try to pinpoint inherent factors operating as ongoing processes, not sporadic phenomena. Rosabeth Moss Kanter contributed greatly to the consideration of this subject in her book *Commitment and Community*. She indicated three main areas where the dynamics of the disbandment process operated in the communes: (1) the effect of the external environment which was in a state of constant change; (2) aging and the gradual undermining in the status of the founding generation; their death and a dearth of suitable replacements, both from among the second generation and by new recruits; and (3) the dichotomy in the communes between their desire to exist on the one hand as an innovative society with a scale of unique and alternative values, and on the other their need to survive as a socio-economic cell within an alien environment.[4] These areas constituted a comprehensive analytical framework for examining the dynamics of disbandment which brought about the liquidation of the long-lived communes.

In the history of the long-lived communes a substantial gap developed between the rapid rate of change in the surrounding environment and the slow, controlled changes that took place in the small, closed communal cells. The communes had two options open to them: to adapt to change, thus risking exposure to new ideas that might destroy "the old way" and erode the basis of the communes' beliefs, or to increase and intensify their seclusion, ignoring events taking place in the world, and in this case risking stagnation and increasing tension between themselves and the world around them. The communes chose various ways, veering between these two conflicting extremes. For instance, Amana and Zoar tried to seclude themselves, but without success. As the openness increased, external behavioral norms were introduced gradually in a controlled manner. Outside influences particularly affected the younger generation who later became an active factor in the process of dissolution of the communes. In Oneida, one of the most intellectually open communes, whose members kept up with world developments and innovations in science and culture, the changes taking place in the external society made themselves felt. The intellectual world of the young Oneidans of the late 1870s was very different from the spiritual one of the veteran members, and this was one more factor in the decision to disband the commune. Even in the closed society of the Shakers an argument developed among the leadership between those who supported isolation and those who favored increased involvement with the external society.[5]

The long-lived communes were unable to find an effective way to put a barrier between them and the alien environment. They failed to create a mechanism for integrating change into the communal system. In the historical experience there is proof that whenever these prochange influences penetrated, there was an intensification of the elements leading to a turning away from the old ways and undermining the communal way of life. The Hutterites have been an exception in that they have adopted a method of controlled seclusion and been able to survive for 450 years in a changing world without having to make significant changes in their own beliefs or way of life.

Another element contributing to the process of breakup in the long-lived communes was aging—the extinction of the founding generation with no suitable replacement to lend continuity. The process was especially severe in places with a charismatic leader or leadership. The most striking examples of this type of decline were in communes practicing celibacy and thus having no children—Ephrata, the Shakers, and Harmony. In Ephrata and Harmony the prohibition against child-bearing was accompanied by stringent restrictions regarding the acceptance of new members. The result was a decline of the communes as their founders aged, and their extinction when they died. The Shakers attempted to circumvent this process by taking in children from outside and training them to become members of their settlements upon reaching adulthood. The absorption of children enabled them to replenish their membership and keep their settlements going for several generations, particularly during periods when revivalist and evangelical religions were in vogue. As religious trends in the United States changed, their sources dried up. In the twentieth century the Shakers declined and eventually disappeared as a movement. There are only a few remnants surviving today. The Shakers' experience manifest the two factors combining to contribute to the breakup: aging and external changes.[6]

Aging and the declining influence of the founding fathers also affected those communes benefitting from biological renewal—Amana, Zoar, Icaria, Oneida and all the long-lived communes that failed to pass on to the younger generation the values and beliefs that had guided them in the early days. Attempts to absorb new members to replace the thinning ranks of the founding members were not successful. In Harmony the absorption of Count de Leon's group ended in a split; in Oneida, the absorption of Towner and his group led to the formation of internal factions and increased tension.

The aforementioned areas of breakup are not unique to the social dynamics operating in communes. Examination of the internal social structure of certain types of American communities based on a religious covenant reveals considerable similarity between them and the communes. In a study of the role of the American township in the formation of the nation, Page Smith points to this similarity and includes the communal communities as a subspecies of the "covenanted towns."[7] In the chapters dealing with the process of erosion that affected the covenanted communities, Smith mentions the elements described above which stem from the destructive effect of the rapid rate of change in American society and the disappearance of the influence of the communities' founding fathers.[8] Thus, the breakup of communities under conditions similar to those affecting the veteran communes was not exceptional in nineteenth-century American society. Hundreds of townships in the East, particularly in New England, established as covenanted towns striving to build ideal communities—a "city upon the hill"—eventually either lost their uniqueness and became townships like any other or were abandoned, their fate paralleling that of the communes. Moreover, the breakup of communities was a common phenomenon in the frontier West. Thousands of hastily established communities, lacking elementary conditions for survival, broke up and were abandoned.[9] Many of them exist today as ghost towns crouched alongside deserted roads—silent memorials to the fate of the waves of settlers who streamed westward, full of dreams, hopes, and desires for a new life. In view of this one may consider the breakup of the communes within the broader context of social patterns existing in American communities. Consequently, we can limit our analysis of the breakup of the communes to those factors connected directly with the communes themselves.

We can fix the factors for disbandment specific to the communes in the problematics arising from their ambivalence in their desire to create a unique, alternative value system while at the same time operating as a special cell within an alien environment. This problem finds no significant parallel in other types of communities. The breakup processes that developed arose mainly from the disturbance of the delicate balance between the two opposing poles—isolation and involvement. History shows that in every case where there was a move toward only one of these opposing approaches, it led to a serious erosion of communal life and its eventual destruction. Complete isolation led to a severing of ties with the outside world and to stagnation, while full adaptation to the conditions of existence and the rules of the outside world led to assimilation and loss of uniqueness. In both cases the communes ceased to function as a system characterized by duality, which itself was so essential to their existence.

The factor maintaining this balance and the mainstay of the communal system was the social or religious ideology that provided meaning and purpose to this special way of life. The ideological element was extremely important in strengthening the commune's general will to exist, both in the mobilization of forces and resources for the dissemination of their message and in the diligent building of a settlement which could set an example to others. Wherever it occurred, a weakening or disappearance of ideological motivation led to a disturbance of the commune's special balance between isolation and involvement, and to acceleration of the breakup process. We shall present a few examples to illustrate this assumption: at a certain point in their histories, when the members of Ephrata, Harmony, and the Shakers lost their faith in their ability to "spread the word" and in the coming of the kingdom of God during their lifetime, they became apathetic, isolationist, and stagnant. On the other hand, loss of faith and their sense of mission led Zoar, Amana, Beth-El, Icaria, and Oneida to overexposure to the surrounding society. This process eroded the barriers guarding the characteristics of communal life. The isolation which had previously given these communes a sense of superiority and pride in being "the chosen ones" or redeemed, gave way either to an exposure causing them to feel inferior to the surrounding society, or to an isolation resulting in petrification within it.[10]

These processes had implications for many social areas, of which the most striking were a weakening of the communes' educational process, abandonment of the old ways by young people, a growing generation gap, and the undermining of internal harmony. As ideological-religious motivation waned, pragmatism became more predominant and with it came renunciation of the communes' guiding principles and a desire for a revised lifestyle.[11] The dominance of pragmatic motivations devoid of ideological foundations had economic implications, including the most destructive elements of the legitimization of hired work as a permanent feature of the communal farms and the introduction of a capitalist work ethic in the form of competition, hierarchy, and reward. These and other elements stemming from integration into the capitalist system and inspired by the pragmatic approach put "Trojan horses" into the communes. Wherever they penetrated, the process of disintegration began to accelerate, hastening the end of the communes as unique, alternative economic cells.[12] In these cases, coexistence between the communal way of life and an economy based on capitalist values did not survive for long. Sooner or later the internal contradiction inherent in this coexistence flared up in every one of the communes. These destructive elements, essential and exclusive to the communes, exposed hidden internal conflicts, thus leading to a process of collapse from within.

Another factor in the disintegration process was rooted in the attitude of the external society toward the communes. Their isolation and different system of values aroused suspicion and hostility in the surrounding community, and this in turn brought pressures. In a pluralistic spiritual-cultural regime such as that of the United States, most of the pressures were applied by local bodies and church institutions rather than by central national agencies. These indeed were effective and caused the acceleration of the breakup or disbandment, especially when they were augmented by undermining processes from within. The most typical example was Oneida in its last years as a commune. So long as the communes preserved their internal balance, outside pressures did not by themselves succeed in undermining their existence. The many intrigues by neighbors and local authorities against the Shakers did not weaken their communities and sometimes even had the opposite effect, making them internally stronger and more robust. The same was true of the pressures brought to bear on the Hutterites during World War I.[13]

One of the great sources of weakness in the communes described in this book was their existence as isolated, independent communities with no overall federative framework such as religious sect or political movement. This fact did not in itself bring about the disintegrations, but it did make them critical when such processes took place; under such circumstances the communes were denied the resources of control and support which a federative framework could have provided when the breakup processes developed. Moreover, such a framework could have served as a protective environment, isolating the individual communes from the surrounding world and giving them greater ability to survive. In the history of the communal experience, wherever a federative system developed and the individual commune was connected to a group, its ability to survive increased. The Shakers, Amana, and the Hutterites were witnesses of this. A federative framework permitted reduction of direct contact between the individual commune and the outside world. Through it an interactive system was created for population movement, trade, training, guidance, and consultation. That the majority of communes in the United States did not belong to any federative framework and were not organized into a regional or national body, intensified the destructive influence of the disintegration processes, especially in the early stages when advice, guidance, aid, and additional manpower could have saved the commune and increased its longevity.[14]

In conclusion, a study of the disbandment processes—those characteristic of the communes and the ones they share with other small communities in the United States—shows that breakup of settlements was a common but not universal phenomenon. In the limited historical framework chosen for our survey (1735-1935), we have found dozens of Hutterite communes that stand as exceptions and demonstrate the ability to survive with very few cases of breakups and abandonment of settlements.

The Hutterites were able to survive thanks to a combination of factors: strong, uncompromising religious faith, a long-standing tradition of a communal way of life; strict rules of behavior for the older population and pressure-relieving receptivity to new ideas by the younger generation; all-encompassing education and socialization anchored in and combined with community and family traditions; biological vitality; strict reliance on their own labor; gradual adaptation to economic developments; controlled use of funds and property; maintenance of optimal size for communal frameworks together with planned social dispersion; and a continuous process of new settlement.[15] The Hutterites' ability to survive is therefore the fruit of a very special and unparalleled combination of religious and communal elements. Yet, if these were the only cases of the ability to survive in the history of the communes, it would cast doubt on the possibility of drawing general conclusions from this specific phenomenon. A broader view shows that the Hutterites were not unique in the history of communal survival.

To broaden our approach to the problem of survival we would have to go beyond the scope of this historical study to examine contemporary communes that have existed for over half a century with their vitality not only undiminished but rather are on the upswing. These communes, like other stable contemporary ones to be found in various parts of the world—the United States, Canada, Europe, Israel, and Japan—which have survived for more than a generation, indicate very strong powers of survival.[16] It is they that are able to make conclusive the argument that a preordained sentence of the fateful inevitability of breakup is not at all inherent in the history of communes.[16] The danger of extinction does not threaten communes more strongly than it does any other unique social formation attempting to maintain itself as a separate cell in an alien society, being unable to maintain a free system of interaction with the outside world. In many cases the processes of breakup or survival were really a question of free choice, particularly in those communes that had overcome their temporary status and attained optimal living conditions. Moreover, we assume that just as one could find internal forces of destruction in the history of past communes, it is also possible to pinpoint vital internal forces for survival in contemporary communes.

An important contribution to the study of this question can be found in Amitai Niv's research which examines the survival theory of the commune.[17] Niv's work is the first in this field and opens avenues for further research that may broaden and complement the scope of the theoretical tools locating survival mechanisms in the communes and deepen our understanding of the essentials of communal life. The development of this line of enquiry may well provide theoretical tools to support the approach we have indicated regarding open options, for survival or breakup, in a set of changing conditions. Returning to our historical perspective, we are still faced with the fact that the majority of the communes—except for the Hutterites—failed, broke up, and disappeared. This legitimately raises the question—Should we conclude that these phenomena in the history of communes are proof of failure? The answer depends upon the criterion by which we judge the phenomena. If the criterion is transformation of the general society, that is, the fulfillment of the vision of a new society in its messianic or socialist versions, then the conclusion that they were failures is inescapable. After all, in none of the communes with which we have dealt did the founders reach the full or even partial attainment of their vision.

However, evaluation of the communes by this criterion shifts the analysis from an approach to the communes' internal powers of survival to that of the nature of the ideals and visions they hoped to attain by their way of life. This context raises questions beyond the scope of our inquiry, such as—Can millenary beliefs be viewed as a viable blueprint for life on earth? Is it possible for a small minority to bring about a change in society merely by its exemplary way of life? Was there any chance for social change, given the conditions under which the American nation was formed? This criterion for examination of the communal way is not relevant to many of them, since only the socialist communes, and a small number of the religious ones, dreamed of bringing about changes in society at large. Most of the religious communes and some of the secular ones intentionally distanced themselves from activity in the outside community and had no aspirations to change the general society. Thus, this evaluation of failure can only be made in reference to the sector with pretensions of wielding influence. But if we adopt more relative criteria and examine the communes while making an inclusive balance sheet of their contribution to their members and society at large, then we can take into account the communes' indirect influence on the American society. If, in addition, we consider the attitude of their members to the period spent in the commune, we might then realize that by using solely the criterion of survival we are unable to make any clear-cut judgment regarding the failure or success of the communes.

We have described the contribution of the early communes to formation of the theories of communal living by the first European utopian socialists. To that we add their contribution to the socialist-communal consciousness in the United States as well as the encouragement derived from the example of their own lives by the reform movements in American society in the spheres of education, equal rights for women, cooperative agriculture, pacifism, and in religious life, where the communes exerted a multifaceted influence on the surrounding population. There were communes whose doors were always open for temporary absorption of the needy and destitute living on the fringes of American society. At a time when no formal welfare system existed, such communes played a positive role in their area. Their influence was also passed on to society at large by members who left. Many of those who went to live in the external society after a period of communal living, still retained the consciousness and values of the commune. It is not surprising that a large number of those of a high personal calibre went on to assume leading roles in the activities of the various reform movements, especially the ones whose religious and social values were close to those of the communes from which they had come. Some left the communes but not the communal life style, either because they joined other communes or through general activities in support of the communal ideal.[18]

Using a subjective criterion and examining the influence of the communes according to what their members said about their lives there, it becomes evident that along with defamation by renegades or others who had left because of averseness to the communal ideal, there was also high praise for the positive contribution this phase had made to their lives. Many of them described the communal period as the most meaningful of their lives, continuing to cherish their memories and regretting that they had been unable to continue on this way.[19]

Examining the phenomenon of the communes from the angle of experiments in social innovation and alternative life styles makes it clear that the effort was not in vain. Even when the communes failed and disappeared, they left their stamp on both their own generation and later ones. Their historical experience contained lessons that were passed on to other societies formed under different circumstances. After all, since the eighteenth century communes have been established in the United States in each generation, and in spite of many failures, the communal tradition continues even to the present time.

We opened this chapter with a reference to the dark shadow hanging over the history of the communes by the widespread phenomenon of disintegration. It is time to get out from under this somber sky and guide the study into the open space of the multifaceted historical approach that will enable us to see the interplay of light and shade forming the pattern of the communes' history, and put things in their correct perspective, that of the new beginnings that have been taking place continuously over hundreds of years. This phenomenon could be viewed as evidence of the vitality of the ideal that have been renewed endlessly in spite of the failures of its implementations. We find support for this evaluation in the comments of the economist Charles Gide who, in referring to the waxing and waning of communes in human history, said:

> The real proof of vitality lies not in continuance, but in rebirth, and this characteristic is possessed in the highest degree by the communities of which we are speaking: they are continually being born again from their ruins, and not a year passed but sees the birth of new communistic societies. The thing to be wondered at is that they can be established at all, considering how unfavorable are the circumstances.[20]

In the present book we have dealt with the history of the communes established under unfavorable circumstances as isolated islands in a strange and alien, though pluralistic, regime. These communes existed without contacts with broader social movements, with little connection with the processes taking place within the surrounding society, and usually without the ability to influence or change it. Under these conditions objective limitations restricted their ability to develop and prevented them from fulfilling their inherent potential as innovative and alternative societal forms. It is fair to say that the achievements of those communes that survived and developed were gained by utilization of inherent strengths and in spite of external limitations. Thus, one should see this historical chapter for what it is—an experience from which many lessons can be learned. It points out the various impulses that led people from different social backgrounds to choose communal living. It teaches us that the communal way of life is strong enough to exist and survive for decades, and more important, to make possible the formation of social cells that uplift and give meaning to the lives of their members.

Historical experience shows that life in the communes was viable, though it cannot be considered as the real test of the survival ability of this social form. Such a test can only be made in circumstances in which optimal conditions exist for the communes, and in which the communes are an integral part of a society that identifies with them and their scale of values, or when the society is in the process of development toward such values. In the history of the communes in the United States, no such circumstances existed. Had we wished to discuss this subject within this approach, we should have had to shift from the real to the ideal, thus exceeding the boundaries of this study and entering the world of utopia.

Notes

1. Rosabeth Moss Kanter, *Commitment and Community: Communes and Utopias in Sociological Perspective* (Cambridge, Mass.: Harvard University Press, 1972), p. 63; Julia Elizabeth Williams, "An Analytical Tabulation of the North American Utopian Communities, by Type, Longevity, and Location" (Ph.D. dissertation, Department of Sociology in the Graduate School, University of South Dakota, 1939).
2. Robert V. Hine, *California's Utopian Colonies* (New Haven: Yale University Press, 1966), p. 167-70; John Humphrey Noyes, *History of American Socialism* (1870). Reprinted as *Strange Cults and Utopias of Nineteenth-Century America* (New York: Dover, 1966), pp. 654, 650, 646. Joseph J. Cohen, *In Quest of Heaven: The Story of the Sunrise Cooperative Farm Community* (New York: Sunrise History Publishing Committee, 1957), pp. 195-206; Frederick A. Bushee, "Communistic Societies in the United States," *Political Science Quarterly* 20, no. 4 (1905): 651; Kanter, *Communes*, pp. 445-48.
3. Carl Guarneri, "The Fourierist Movement in America," *Communities: Journal of Cooperation*, no. 68 (Winter):51; Ralph Albertson, *A Survey of Mutualistic Communities in America* (New York: AMS Press, 1973; 1st ed. 1936), pp. 436-37; Morris Hillquit, *History of Socialism in the United States*, 5th ed. (New York: Dover, 1971), p. 136; Charles Pierre Le Warne, *Utopias on Puget Sound,*

1885-1915 (Seattle: University of Washington Press, 1975), pp. 164, 651; Arthur Bestor, *Backwoods Utopias: The Sectarian Origins and the Owenite Phase of Communitarian Socialism in America*, 2d ed. *1663-1829* (Philadelphia: University of Pennsylvania Press, 1971), pp. 160, 201; V.F. Calverton, *Where Angels Dared to Tread* (New York: Bobbs-Merrill, 1941), p. 349; Rosabeth Moss Kanter, *Communes: Creating and Managing the Collective Life* (New York: Harper & Row, 1973), pp. 450-54; David Cnaani, *Batey Medot: Essays on Communal Life* (Merchavia: Sifriat Hapoalim, 1960), p. 86 (Hebrew); John Humphrey Noyes, p. 560; Cohen, *In Quest of Heaven*, pp. 207-14; Kanter, *Commitment and Community*, pp. 139-41; Bushee, p. 629; Hine, pp. 171-76.

4. Kanter, *Commitment and Community*, pp. 142-46.
5. John McKelvie Whitworth, *God's Blueprints: A Sociological Study of Three Utopian Sects* (London: Routledge & Kegan Paul, 1975), pp. 81-86; Maren Lockwood Carden, *Oneida: Utopian Community to Modern Corporation* (Baltimore: Johns Hopkins University Press, 1969), pp. 89-95; Emilius O. Randall, *History of the Zoar Society: A Sociological Study in Communism* (New York: AMS Press, 1971; 1st ed. 1904), pp. 53-67; Bertha M.H. Shambaugh, *Amana That Was and Amana That Is* (Iowa City: Iowa State Historical Society, 1932), pp. 369-70.
6. Delburn Carpenter, *The Radical Pietists* (New York: AMS Press, 1975), p. 190.
7. Page Smith, *As a City Upon a Hill: The Town in American History* (Cambridge, Mass.: MIT Press, 1973), pp. 20-26.
8. Examining the dynamics of social disintegration, George C. Homans gives as an example of small New England town called Hilltown. He maintains that changes in the surrounding environment as well as demographic change within the town served as an accelerating factor in the process of disintegration. George C. Homans, *The Human Group* (London: Routledge & Kegan Paul, 1962).
9. David Russo, *Families and Communities: A New View of American History* (Nashville, Tennessee: The American Association for State and Local History, 1977), pp. 44-45, 49; Smith, pp. 33-36.
10. Anna White and Leila S. Taylor, *Shakerism: Its Meaning and Message* (Columbus, Oh.: Heer, 1904. New York: AMS Press, 1971), p. 205; Marguerite Fellows Melcher, *The Shaker Adventure* (New York: The Shaker Museum, 1975), pp. 245-46; Karl J.R. Arndt, *George Rapp's Harmony Society, 1785-1847*, rev. ed. (New York: Associated University Presses, 1972), p. 588; Donald Egbert and Stow Persons, eds., *Socialism and American Life*, 2 vols. (Princeton: Princeton University Press, 1952), pp. 119-22; Cnaani, pp. 85-86; Carden, pp. 81-111; Shambaugh, pp. 343-46; Whitworth, pp. 87-88.
11. William Alfred Hinds, *American Communities and Cooperative Colonies* (1878. Reprinted and enl. Philadelphia: Porcupine, 1975), p. 392; Marie Marchand Ross, *Child of Icaria* (1938. Reprint. New York: Hypernion, 1976), pp. 125-36; Whitworth, pp. 165-66; Calverton, pp. 348-49.
12. Shambaugh, pp. 364-65, 353; Carpenter, pp. 143-44, 190, 193, 210; Charles J. Erasmus, *In Search of the Common Good: Utopian Experiments Past and Future* (New York: Free Press, 1977), pp. 150-58, 160-61.
13. Raymond Lee Muncy, *Sex and Marriage in Utopian Communities, Nineteenth-Century America* (Bloomington, Ind.: Indiana University Press, 1973), pp. 228-29; John A. Hostetler, *Hutterite Society* (Baltimore: Johns Hopkins University Press, 1977), pp. 126-33; Whitworth, pp. 156-62; Carden, pp. 99-104; Kanter, *Communes*, p. 447.

14. On the federation of the Hutterian communities see John W. Bennett, ''Frames of Reference for the Study of Hutterian Society,'' *Communes: Historical and Contemporary*, ed. Ruth Shonle Cavan and Man Singh Das (New Delhi: Vikas Publishing House, 1979), pp. 36-37.
15. John W. Bennet, *Hutterian Brethren: The Agricultural Economy and Social Organization of a Communal People* (San Francisco: Stanford University Press, 1967), pp. 245-54; Erasmus, pp. 162-65; Hostetler, pp. 285-302.
16. Charles Nordhoff, *The Communistic Societies of the United States* (New York: Shocken, 1965), pp. 385-418.
17. In his study, Amitai Niv mentioned two ''ideal types'' of communal existence, the ''model'' type and the ''pioneer'' type. Both are representatives of a purely rational process that leads the communes toward disintegration. In the case of the model type, this was the logical result of their complete seclusion from the external world in order to protect their unique characteristics. In the case of the pioneer type, assimilation was the logical result of the communes' close ties and active involvement with the outside world. During his research, Niv examined two stable communes. The first—an American Hutterite *Burderhof*, which came close to the model type; the other—an Israeli Kibbutz, typical of the pioneer type. In his study he established specific processes that pointed to a survival mechanism that in the long run ensured the communes existence and prosperity. It is a process which on the one hand ensures that the commune does not deviate from its model type, but on the other hand prevents the destructive result of a rational development. His findings enabled him to draw a ''map'' of communal survivability—a yardstick according to which the process of improving chances of survival could be measured. Amitai Niv, ''Organizational Disintegration: Roots, Processes and Types,'' in *The Organizational Life Cycle* ed. G.R. Kimberly and R.H. Miles (San Francisco: Jossey Bass, 1980), pp. 375-94; Amitai Niv, ''A Search for a Theory about the Survival of Communes'' (Ph.D. Dissertation, Harvard University, School of Business Administration, 1976).
18. Georgiana Bruce Kirby, *Years of Experience* (1887. Reprint. New York: AMS Press, 1971), pp. 190, 226; Guarneri, pp. 53-55; Albertson, pp. 435-39; Hine, p. 177.
19. Robert H. Lauer and Jeanette C. Lauer, *The Spirit and the Flesh: Sex in Utopian Communities* (Metuchen, N.J.: Scarecrow Press, 1983), pp. 206, 214-17; Marianne Dwight, *Letters from Brook Farm, 1848-1847* (New York: AMS Press, 1974; 1st ed. 1928), p. 178; Katherine Burton, *Paradise Planters: The Story of Brook Farm* (1939. Reprint. New York: AMS Press, 1973), p. 312; John Thomas Codman, *Brook Farm: Historic and Personal Memoirs* (New York: AMS Press, 1971; 1st ed. 1948), p. 150; George B. Lockwood, *The New Harmony Movement* (New York: Dover, 1971; 1st ed. 1905), p. 87; Bushee, p. 654; Albertson, pp. 435, 438; John Humphrey Noyes, pp. 499-501; Hine, p. 177; Kirby, p. 185; Hinds, pp. 121, 395.
20. Charles Gide, *Communist and Cooperative Colonies* (New York: AMS Press, 1974; 1st ed. 1930), pp. 10-11.

25

Epilogue

The historical surveys in this book deal with communes appearing in the United States up to the 1930s, but their history did not end there. Old, established settlements such as those of the Hutterites have continued to exist, and alongside them arose a small number of new communes in the following three decades.

In 1965, a tidal wave of protest movements and student uprisings swept the nation, and the history of the communes in the United States took a sharp turn. These waves, made up of tens of thousands of "flower children," swamped American society, casting up hundreds of new communes of an entirely different kind. The differences were apparent in their social origins, their spiritual content, their members' motivations, the manner of their organization and behavior. They were young people gathered together for group living, with no bond of common commitment, no ideology, and no goals relating to society as a whole. The majority of the members of these communes tended toward anarchy, refusing to assume the burden of norms and binding frameworks. Without these, their communal lives were short-lived. The main feature of these communes of the 1960s was their transience. Most of them broke up shortly after their establishment, and only a few managed to survive for any length of time. The waves of protest and revolt which had sustained them subsided too, and the thousands of flower children fell back into the mainstream of society to be reabsorbed without a ripple.

It was not more than a few years later, in the 1970s, that renewed unrest plagued the ranks of American society—it was again the young people, turning away from the materialism and individualistic antagonism so rampant in their contemporary society, while seeking to give direction and meaning to their lives. In the course of their quest the vision of the communal society, based on interpersonal harmony, was revealed to them. Inspired by this, they set about founding communes as the nuclei of an alternative society. The ones they set up were small in terms of members, but their stability was relatively great and their involvement in social issues deep. In contrast, the revolutionary fervor so typical of the generation of the 1960s cooled, and their methods of struggle became more moderate. The goals were now more modest and realistic, focusing on the constructive task of building up viable communes. Such activity was also meant to serve as a means of spreading the message of living in interpersonal harmony through the example of their own life and the establishment of educational institutions for character-building. Changed, too, were the ideological motivations of that generation: gone was the culture of protest for protest's sake, together with the apocalyptic fantasies of "the age of aquarius." Greater weight was given to the more constructive approaches of building the cells of the alternative society, with inspiration drawn from a broad range of outlooks. The latter covered a wide spectrum—from radical-political and ecological doctrines through faith in fundamentalistic or deistic Christian religious sects to cosmic-planetary outlooks and the mysticism of the religions of the Orient. The forms of cooperation became more varied: along with the rural communes on their own self-contained economies, many urban ones sprang up, wherein the measure of cooperation practiced varied from a creche and communal meals to an integral commune.

In the 1980s there has been an increase in the geographical areas where communes have arisen. The United States still continues to be the leader, both in scope and intensity. But it is also possible to find communes in most of the countries of the West, the most prominent being Canada, England, Denmark, Holland, Germany, France, India, Japan, Australia, and New Zealand, and the kibbutz movement in Israel, which writes a special chapter in the history of communes in the world. The communes in the other Western countries are similar in their background and manifestations to those in the United States, and like them, came into being against a background of modern social deprivations, although the particular circumstances leading to their founding, established the special characteristics that made each one unique.

Out of all the communes existing in this generation, two large movements stand out in particular, demonstrating an ability to survive over more than one generation. One is the veteran Hutterite movement, with its history of 450 years of communal living, together with its offspring movement, The Hutterian Society of Brothers (the Bruderhof), whose communes date from 1920. The other is the kibbutz movement in Israel, which has been in existence, and continues to develop, since 1909. These movements, leading separate existences thousands of miles apart, are quite different in their ideological backgrounds, their spiritual worlds, and their ties with the society in whose midst they exist. In both movements there is a wealth of human resources and socio-economic potential, stabilizing and constantly expanding them. This constant growth enables them to survive and meet the challenges of living and working alongside noncommunal societies, each one separately and in its own special way.

A comprehensive view of the known communes extant in the world of the 1980s demonstrates that not only have they shown an ability to survive, but that they are also stable and growing in number. An estimate of the voluntary communes scattered throughout the world and the average length of their existence indicates a significant growth in relation to what we had known in the past. Yet, the failure of the historical communes to survive, and the short lives of the communes of the 1960s have not deterred new groups from attempting to reestablish cells of communal living through interpersonal harmony. But in the 1980s, even as in the past, these attempts can only be regarded as small and isolated islands in the vast sea of an acquisitive and individualistic society. Despite the significant growth in numbers and the geographical distribution of these modern communes, the relative size of their populations has not risen to a level of demographic significance in any of the Western countries. Today as in the past, those attracted to them are small groups of idealists, people of sensitive social conscience, dreamers and doers, and with them, too, a conglomeration of escapists seeking an easy solution to their own particular problem, with no broad social commitment on the individual's part. Now as in the past, it becomes apparent to those experiencing the creation of a new society that there is no easy road to a world that is all good. They were many who were unable to withstand the difficulties and frustrations with which their path was strewn. These fell by the wayside, to be replaced by others.

And thus, in a never-ending chain of failures and a new beginning, the march towards utopia continues; on this journey, the vision of the commune is there before them, like the North Star, steady in the heavens and guiding, revealing from time to time its vitality and constancy despite the ravages of time and circumstance.

Appendix

TABLE 1
American Communes 1663-1984

1.	Plockhoy Community	1663-1664	Delaware	R
*2.	Labadists (Bohemia Manor)	1683-1696	Maryland	R
*3.	Woman in the Wilderness	1694-1708	Pennsylvania	R
*4.	Irenia	1695-1697	Pennsylvania	R
*5.	Ephrata	1732-1813	Pennsylvania	R
6.	Bethlehem	1744-1762	Pennsylvania	R
*7.	Mount Lebanon	1787-1947	New York	SH
*8.	Watervliet	1788-1938	New York	SH
*9.	Jerusalem	1788-1820	New York	R
*10.	Hancock	1790-1960	Massachusetts	SH
*11.	Enfield	1790-1917	Connecticut	SH
*12.	Harvard	1791-1919	Massachusetts	SH
*13.	Tyringham	1792-1875	Massachusetts	SH
*14.	Canterbury	1792-1984	New Hampshire**	SH
*15.	Shirley	1793-1908	Massachusetts	SH
*16.	Enfield	1793-1923	New Hampshire	SH
*17.	Alfred	1793-1932	Maine	SH
*18.	Sabathday Lake	1794-1984	Maine**	SH
*19.	Gorham	1794-1819	Maine	SH
20.	Dorrilites	1798-1799	Vermont	M
*21.	Snow Hill	1798-1870	Pennsylvania	R
22.	The Union	1804-1810	New York	M
*23.	Harmony Society	1805-1814	Pennsylvania	R
*24.	Union Village	1805-1912	Ohio	SH
*25.	Watervliet	1806-1910	Ohio	SH
*26.	South Union	1809-1922	Kentucky	SH
*27.	Pleasant Hill	1806-1910	Kentucky	SH
*28.	West Union (Burso)	1810-1827	Indiana	SH
*29.	Harmony (New Harmony)	1814-1824	Indiana	R
30.	Savoy	1817-1825	Massachusetts	SH
*31.	Zoar	1817-1898	Ohio	R
32.	Pilgrims	1817-1818	Vermont	R
*33.	North Union	1822-1889	Ohio	SH
*34.	Economy	1825-1905	Pennsylvania	R
35.	Whitewater	1825-1907	Ohio	SH
*36.	New Harmony	1825-1827	Indiana	O
*37.	Yellow Springs	1825-1826	Ohio	O
*38.	Coal Creek	1825-1832	Indiana	R

TABLE 1
American Communes 1663-1984 *(Con't)*

39.	Goshen	1825-1826 Indiana	O
40.	Franklin	1826-1826 New York	O
41.	Forestville	1826-1827 New York	O
42.	Kendal	1826-1829 Ohio	O
43.	Valley Forge	1826-1826 Pennsylvania	O
44.	Blue Springs	1826-1827 Indiana	O
45.	Sodus Bay	1826-1836 New York	SH
*46.	Nashoba	1826-1829 Tennessee	O
47.	Teutonia	1827-1831 Ohio	R
48.	Kirtland	1830-1838 Ohio	R
49.	United Order of Enoch	1831-1834 Missouri	R
50.	New Philadelphia	1832-1833 Pennsylvania	R
51.	Oberlin Colony	1833-1841 Ohio	R
*52.	Equity	1833-1835 Ohio	M
53.	Grand Ecore	1834-1836 Louisiana	R
54.	Germantown	1836-1871 Louisiana	R
55.	Soneya (Groveland)	1836-1895 New York	SH
56.	Berea	1836-1837 Ohio	R
*57.	Brook Farm	1841-1847 Massachusetts	F
58.	Marlborough Association	1841-1845 Ohio	M
59.	Social Reform Unity	1842-1843 Pennsylvania	F
60.	Hopedale	1842-1867 Massachusetts	R-F
61.	Northampton Association	1842-1846 Massachusetts	M
62.	Teutonia	1842-1844 Pennsylvania	R
63.	Society of One Mentian	1843-1844 Pennsylvania	O
64.	Goose Pond	1843-1844 Pennsylvania	O
65.	Hunt's Colony	1843-1846 Wisconsin	O
66.	Jefferson County	1843-1844 New York	F
*67.	Sylvania Association	1843-1845 Pennsylvania	F
68.	Morehouse Union	1843-1844 New York	F
69.	Bureau County Phalanx	1843-1844 Illinois	F
*70.	North American Phalanx	1843-1856 New Jersey	F
71.	Peace Union	1843-1845 Pennsylvania	R
*72.	Ebenezer (Amana)	1843-1855 New York	R
*73.	Putney	1843-1848 Vermont	R
74.	Fruitlands	1843-1848 Massachusetts	M
75.	Skaneateles	1843-1846 New York	S
76.	Abram Brook's Experiment	1843-1845 Ohio	R
77.	Prairie Home	1844-1844 Ohio	F (S)
78.	Highland Home	1844-1844 Ohio	F
79.	La Grange Phalanx	1844-1846 Indiana	F
*80.	Sodus Bay Phalanx	1844-1846 New York	F
81.	Bloomfield Union Association	1844-1846 New York	F
82.	Leraysville Phalanx	1844-1844 Pennsylvania	F
83.	Ohio Phalanx	1844-1845 Ohio	F
84.	Alphadelphia Phalanx	1844-1848 Michigan	F
85.	Clarkson Association	1844-1845 New York	F
86.	Mixville Association	1844-1845 New York	F

TABLE 1
American Communes 1663-1984 (*Con't*)

87.	Ontario Union	1844-1845 New York	F
88.	Clermont Phalanx	1844-1846 Ohio	F
89.	Trumball Phalanx	1844-1848 Ohio	F
*90.	Wisconsin Phalanx	1844-1850 Wisconsin	F
91.	Iowa Pioneer Phalanx	1844-1845 Iowa	F
92.	Union Home	1844-1846 Indiana	S
*93.	Bethel	1844-1880 Missouri	R
94.	Voree (Mormons)	1844-1849 Wisconsin	R
95.	Philadelphia Industrial Association	1845-1847 Indiana	F
96.	Integral Phalanx	1845-1846 Illinois	F
97.	Canton Phalanx	1845-1845 Illinois	F
98.	Columbian Phalanx	1845-1845 Ohio	F
99.	Fruit Hills	1845-1852 Ohio	F
100.	Grand Prairie	1845-1847 Indiana	F
101.	Kristeen Community	1845-1846 Indiana	F
102.	Utilitarian Association	1845-1848 Wisconsin	O
103.	Spring Farm Phalanx	1846-1848 Wisconsin	F
104.	Pigeon River	1846-1847 Wisconsin	F
*105.	Bishop Hill	1846-1862 Illinois	F
106.	The Brotherhood	1846-1847 Ohio	M
*107.	Utopia	1847-1858 Ohio	F AN
108.	Bettina	1847-1848 Texas	S
109.	Zodiac	1847-1853 Texas	R
*110.	Communia	1847-1856 Iowa	S
*111.	Oneida	1848-1881 New York	R
112.	Kingdom of St. James	1848-1856 Michigan	R
*113.	Icaria	1848-1848 Texas	S
*114.	Icaria-Nauvoo	1849-1859 Illinois	S
115.	Nineveh	1849-1878 Missouri	R
116.	Ephraim	1849-1853 Wisconsin	R
117.	Jasper	1851-1853 Iowa	R
*118.	Wallingford	1851-1881 Connecticut	R
*119.	Modern Times	1851-1863 New York	AN
120.	Mountain Cove	1851-1853 Virginia	R
121.	Harmonia (Domain)	1851-1863 New York	RM
*122.	Raritan Bay Union	1853-1858 New Jersey	F
123.	Rising Star Association	1853-1857 Ohio	M
124.	Preparation	1853-1858 Iowa	R
125.	Grand Prairie Harmonial Institute	1853-1854 Indiana	F
126.	Ephraim	1853-1864 Wisconsin	R
127.	St. Nazianz	1854-1874 Wisconsin	R
128.	Berlin Heights	1854-1858 Ohio	M
*129.	Reunion	1855-1859 Texas	F
*130.	Amana	1855-1932 Iowa	R
*131.	West Amana	1855-1932 Iowa	R
*132.	South Amana	1855-1932 Iowa	R
*133.	High Amana	1855-1932 Iowa	R
*134.	East Amana	1855-1932 Iowa	R

TABLE 1
American Communes 1663-1984 (*Con't*)

*135.	Middle Amana	1855-1932 Iowa	R
*136.	Homestead	1855-1932 Iowa	R
137.	Memnonia	1856-1857 Ohio	M
138.	Union Grove	1856-1858 Minnesota	R
*139.	Aurora	1856-1881 Oregon	R
140.	Germania Company	1856-1879 Wisconsin	R
*141.	Icaria (Cheltenham)	1856-1864 Missiouri	S
142.	Harmonial Vegetarian Society	1860-1864 Arkansas	M
143.	Point Hope	1860-1861 Ohio	M
*144.	Icaria (Corning)	1860-1870 Iowa	S
145.	Adonai Shomo	1861-1897 Massachusetts	R
146.	Ora Labora	1862-1868 Michigan	R
147.	Celesta	1863-1864 Pennsylvania	R
148.	Amenia (T.L. Harris)	1863-1867 New York	R
149.	Christian Republic (Berlin)	1865-1866 Ohio	M
150.	Brocton (Salem on Erie)	1867-1881 Ohio	R
151.	Walla Walla (Mormons)	1867-1881 Washington	R
152.	Reunion (A. Longley)	1868-1870 Missouri	S
153.	Union Colony	1869-1872 Colorado	M
154.	German Colonization Company	1870-1871 Colorado	M
155.	Silkville	1870-1884 Kansas	F
156.	Progressive Community (V. Frey)	1871-1878 Colorado	S
157.	Chicago Colorado Colony	1871-1873 Colorado	S
158.	Western Colony	1871-1873 Colorado	R
159.	Friendship Community (A. Longley)	1872-1877 Missouri	S
160.	Bennett Coop. Colony	1873-1877 Missouri	S
161.	Social Freedom Community	1874-1880 Virginia	M
162.	Bon Homme (Hutterites)	1874-1984 Dakota**	R
163.	Silver Lake	1874-1875 S. Dakota	
164.	Women's Commonwealth	1874-1906 Texas, Wash. D.C.	R
165.	Dawn Valcour	1874-1875 New York	M
166.	Orderville (Mormons)	1874-1884 Utah	R
167.	Wolf Creek (Hutterites)	1875-1930 S. Dakota	R
168.	Investigating Community	1875-1876 Kansas	S
169.	Cedarvale	1875-1877 Kansas	S
170.	Fountain Grove (T.L. Harris)	1876-1900 California	R
171.	Modjeska Colony	1877-1878 California	M
172.	Esperanza	1877-1878 Kansas	R
174.	Elmspring (Hutterites)	1878-1929 S. Dakota	R
*175.	Icaria (Jeune Icaria)	1879-1887 Iowa	S
*176.	Icaria (New Icaria)	1879-1884 Iowa	S
*177.	Tripp Colony (Hutterites)	1879-1884 S. Dakota	R
178.	Rugby (T. Hughes)	1880-1881 Tennessee	M
179.	Thompson Colony	1880-1887 Kansas	S
180.	Sicily Island Colony	1881-1882 Louisiana	M
*181.	Icaria—Speranza	1881-1886 California	S
182.	Alliance Vineland	1882-1906 New Jersey	S
183.	Bethlehem Yehuda	1882-1885 S. Dakota	M
*184.	New Odessa	1883-1887 Oregon	S

TABLE 1
American Communes 1663-1984 (*Con't*)

185.	Mutual Aid Community	1883-1887	Missouri	S
186.	Tidioute Colony (Hutterites)	1884-1886	S. Dakota	R
187.	Shalam	1884-1891	New Mexico	R
*188.	Kaweah	1885-1892	California	S
189.	Nehalem Valley Coop.	1886-1892	Oregon	
190.	Jamesville (Hutterites)	1886-1918	S. Dakota	R
191.	Miltown (Hutterites)	1886-1907	Washington	S
*192.	Puget Sound Cooperative Colony	1887-1900	Washington	S
193.	Koreshan Unity	1888-1903	Illinois	R
194.	Rockport	1888-1934	S. Dakota	
195.	Lord's Farm (Woodcliff)	1889-1907	New Jersey	S
196.	Koreshan Unity	1890-1891	California	R
197.	Kutter Colony (Hutterites)	1890-1918	S. Dakota	R
198.	Rockport (Hutterites)	1891-1934	S. Dakota	R
199.	Union Mill Co.	1891-1897	Oregon	S
200.	Cooperative Brotherhood Winter Island	1893-1898	California	S
201.	Hiawatha Village Association	1893-1896	Michigan	S
202.	Narcoossee (Shakers)	1894-1912	Florida	SH
203.	Altruria	1894-1895	California	
*204.	Ruskin	1894-1899	Tennessee	S
205.	Colorado Cooperative	1894-1910	Colorado	S
206.	Koreshan Unity-Estero	1894-1980	Florida	R
207.	Home Employment Cooperative	1894-1906	Missouri	S
208.	Glennis	1894-1896	Washington	S
209.	New House of Israel	1895-1920	Texas	R
210.	Willard Cooperative Colony	1895-1896	N. Carolina	S
211.	Fairhope	1895-1908	Alabama	S
212.	Christian Corporation	1896-1897	Nebraska	R
213.	Christian	1896-1900	Georgia	R
214.	Freedom Colony	1897-1905	Kansas	S
*215.	Equality	1897-1907	Washington	S
216.	American Settlers (Duke)	1898-1899	Georgia	S
*217.	Burley Colony	1898-1908	Washington	S
218.	Point Loma	1898-1942	California	M
219.	White Oak (Shakers)	1898-1902	Georgia	R SH
*220.	Home Colony	1898-1921	Washington	S AN
*221.	Ruskin Commonwealth	1898-1901	Georgia	S
222.	Straight Edge	1899-1918	New York	R
223.	Friedheim	1899-1900	Virginia	R
224.	Lystra	1899-1902	Virginia	R
225.	Commonwealth of Israel	1899-1902	Texas	R
226.	Christian Social Association	1899-1904	Wisconsin	R
227.	Spirit Fruit	1899-1908	Ohio	R
228.	Niksur Coop. Association	1899-1900	Minnesota	S
229.	Kinder Lou	1900-1901	Georgia	S
230.	New Elmspring	1900-1918	S. Dakota	
231.	Freeland	1903-1906	Washington	S
232.	Arden	1900-1984	Delaware**	M
233.	Apalachicella	1900-1904	Florida	M

TABLE 1
American Communes 1663-1984 (*Con't*)

234.	Roycrofters	1900-1915 New York	SH. M
235.	Maxwell (Hutterites)	1900-1918 S.Dakota	R
236.	Zion City	1901-1906 Illinois	R
237.	Rosedale (Hutterites)	1901-1918 S. Dakota	R
238.	House of David	1903-1928 Michigan	R
239.	Temple Home (Theosophists)	1903-1913 California	M
240.	Spink Colony (Hutterites)	1905-1918 S. Dakota	R
241.	Beadle Colony (Hutterites)	1905-1918 S. Dakota	R
242.	Huron Colony (Hutterites)	1906-1918 S. Dakota	R
243.	Richards Colony (Hutterites)	1906-1918 S. Dakota	R
244.	Helican Hall	1906-1907 New Jersey	S
245.	Buffalo Colony (Hutterites)	1907-1913 S. Dakota	R
246.	Fellowship Farm (Westwood)	1907-1918 Massachusetts	R
247.	Little Lands Colony	1909-1916 California	M
248.	Tahanto	1909-1934 Massachusetts	M
249.	Millford (Hutterites)	1910-1918 S. Dakota	R
250.	Order of Theocracy	1910-1931 Florida	R
251.	Free Acres Association	1910-1950 New Jersey	M
252.	Fruit Crest	1911-1912 Missouri	S
253.	Helidon	1911-1938 Maine	M
254.	Lopez	1912-1920 Washington	M
255.	Spring Creek (Hutterites)	1912-1920 Montana	R
256.	Krotona	1912-1924 California	M
257.	Warren Range (Hutterites)	1913-1918 Montana	R
258.	James Valley (Hutterites)	1913-1918 S. Dakota	R
259.	The Burning Bush	1913-1919 Texas	R
260.	Bohemian Cooperative Farming	1913-1916 Tennessee	M
*261.	Llano del Rio	1914-1918 California	S
262.	Pisgah Grande	1914-1921 California	R
263.	Army of Industry	1914-1918 California	S
*264.	Ferrer Colony (Stelton)	1915-1955 New Jersey	S
265.	Nevada City	1916-1918 Nevada	S
*266.	New Llano	1917-1938 Louisiana	S
267.	Holy City	1919-1958 California	SH.
268.	Heaven City	1923-1927 Illinois	R
269.	Mohegan Colony	1923-1950 New York	M
270.	Commonwealth College	1923-1940 Arkansas	
271.	United Cooperative	1926-1939 California	S
272.	Wayne Produce Association	1921-1939 Georgia	S
*273.	Sunrise Cooperative Farm	1933-1937 Michigan	S
274.	Rockport	1934-1984 S. Dakota**	
275.	New Elmspring	1936-1984 S. Dakota**	
276.	King Ranch	1935-1984 Montana	
*277.	Sunrise Cooperative Farm	1937-1939 Virginia	

*Communes mentioned in the historical chapters.
**Existing communes.

Key:
R = Religious　O = Owenites　S = Socialists　M = Miscellaneous
SH = Shakers　F = Fourierists　AN = Anarchists

TABLE 2
Communes' Density, by Period and Geographical Location

	1663-1730	1730	1780	1790	1800	1810	1820	1830	1840	1850	1860	1870	1880	1890	1900	1910	1920	Date
1. MAINE				*												*		2
2. NEW HAMPSHIRE				****														4
3. MASSACHUSETTS				****		*			****		*				**			12
4. CONNECTICUT				*						*								2
5. VERMONT				*			*		*									3
6. NEW YORK			***		*	*	***	*	**** **** **	**	**	*		*	*		*	27
7. PENNSYLVANIA	**	**		*	*		**	*	**** ***		*		*					18
8. NEW JERSEY									*	*			**		**	*		7
9. MARYLAND	*	*																2
10. DELAWARE	*														*			2
11. OHIO					**	*	**** *	****	**** **** ***	***	**			*				29
12. INDIANA						**	****		**** *	*								12
13. KENTUCKY					**													2

Number of Communes

TABLE 2
Communes' Density, by Period and Geographical Location (*Con't*)

Number of Communes

	1663- 1730	1730	1780	1790	1800	1810	1820	1830	1840	1850	1860	1870	1880	1890	1900	1910	1920	Date
14. ILLINOIS									**** *				*		*			7
15. MICHIGAN									**		**		*	*				6
16. WISCONSIN									**** **	****				*				11
17. IOWA									**	**** **** *	*	**						14
18. MINNESOTA										*				*				2
19. KANSAS												**** *	*	*				7
20. TENNESSEE							*						*	*		*		4
21. MISSOURI								*	***	*	*	**	*	*	*			11
22. OREGON										*			**	*				4
23. WASHINGTON											*		*	****	*	*		8
24. CALIFORNIA												**	***	***	**	**** *		15
25. TEXAS									***	*		*		**		*		8

	1663-1730	1730	1780	1790	1800	1810	1820	1830	1840	1850	1860	1870	1880	1890	1900	1910	1920	
2ó. SOUTH DAKOTA												****	**** *		**** ****	*		18
27. MONTANA																**		2
28. COLORADO											*	***		*				5
29. VIRGINIA										*		*		**				4
30. WASHINGTON DC													*					1
31. ARKANSAS											*							1
32. LOUISIANA								**					*			*		4
33. GEORGIA														**** *	*			6
34. FLORIDA														**	**			4
35. NEVADA																*		1
36. NEBRASKA														*				1
37. ALABAMA														*				1
38. NORTH CAROLINA														*				1
39. NEW MEXICO													*					1
40. UTAH												*						1
	4	3	3	12	6	5	16	9	60	26	13	22	21	31	23	15	1	270

Index of Names

Index of Communes